COVENANT THEOLOGY IN REFORMED PERSPECTIVE

Collected essays and book reviews in historical, biblical, and systematic theology

Mark W. Karlberg

Wipf and Stock Publishers
150 West Broadway • Eugene OR 97401

Covenant Theology in Reformed Perspective
By Karlberg, Mark W.

ISBN: 1-57910-315-4

Printed by *Wipf & Stock Publishers, 2000.*

Library of Congress Cataloging-in-Publication Data

Karlberg, Mark W.

Covenant theology in Reformed perspective: collected essays and book reviews in historical, biblical, and systematic theology / Mark W. Karlberg

p. cm.

Includes bibliographical references and indexes.

ISBN 1-57910-315-4

1. Calvinism – History – Theology – Reformation to modern Age. 2. Covenant theology. 3. Reformed biblical theology.

BT155.K343 2000

Dedicated to my parents, Leo and Florence Karlberg,
and to my aunt, Dorothy Bloser,
For their spiritual discernment in the things of the Lord
And their sacifice for the faith in our generation

Soli Deo gloria

Permission to republish material was granted by:
Calvin Theological Journal
The Evangelical Quarterly
Foundations
Journal of the Evangelical Theological Society
Trinity Journal
The Westminster Theological Journal

and by

John Muether and Howard Griffith, editors, *Creator, Redeemer, and Consummator: Essays in Biblical Theology Presented to Meredith G. Kline*

Collection of Articles

CHAPTER ONE: "Reformed Interpretation of the Mosaic Covenant," *The Westminster Theological Journal* 43 (1980) 1-57.

CHAPTER TWO: "Reformation Politics: The Relevance of OT Ethics in Calvinist Political Theory," *Journal of the Evangelical Theological Society* 29 (1986) 179-91.

CHAPTER THREE: "Moses and Christ: The Place of Law in Seventeenth-Century Puritanism," *Trinity Journal* 10 NS (1989) 11-32.

CHAPTER FOUR: "The Original State of Adam: Tensions in Reformed Theology,"*The Evangelical Quarterly* 59 (1987) 291-309.

CHAPTER FIVE: "Covenant Theology and the Westminster Tradition," *WTJ* 54 (1992) 135-52.

CHAPTER SIX: "Justification in Redemptive History," *WTJ* 43 (1981) 213-46.

CHAPTER SEVEN: "Israel's History Personified: Romans 7:7-13 in Relation to Paul's Teaching on the 'Old Man'," *TrinJ* 7 NS (1986) 65-74.

CHAPTER EIGHT: "The Significance of Israel in Biblical Typology," *JETS* 31 (1988) 257-69.

CHAPTER NINE: "The Search for an Evangelical Consensus on Paul and the Law," *JETS* 40 (1997) 563-79.

CHAPTER TEN: "Paul's Letter to the Romans in the *New International Commentary on the New Testament* and in Contemporary Reformed Thought," *EvQ* 71 (1999) 3-24.

CHAPTER ELEVEN: "Paul, the Old Testament, and Judaism," *Foundations: A Journal of Evangelical Theology* 43 (1999) 36-44.

CHAPTER TWELVE: "Legitimate Discontinuities Between the Testaments," *JETS* 28 (1985) 9-20.

CHAPTER THIRTEEN: "Israel as Light to the Nations," *JETS* 28 (1985) 205-11.

CHAPTER FOURTEEN: "Covenant and Common Grace," *WTJ* 50 (1988) 323-37.

CHAPTER FIFTEEN: "Israel and the Eschaton," *WTJ* 52 (1990) 117-30.

CHAPTER SIXTEEN: "Doctrinal Development in Scripture and Tradition: A Reformed Assessment of the Church's Theological Task," *Calvin Theological Journal* 30 (1995) 401-18.

CHAPTER SEVENTEEN: "Reformed Theology as the Theology of the Covenants: The Contribution of Meredith G. Kline to Reformed Systematics," in *Creator, Redeemer, and Consummator: Essays in Biblical Theology Presented to Meredith G. Kline*, eds. J. Muether and H. Griffith (Greenville, SC: Reformed Academic Press, forthcoming).

Collection of Book Reviews

John von Rohr's *The Covenant of Grace in Puritan Thought,* in *TrinJ* 8 NS (1987) 84-7.
Richard A. Muller's *Christ and the Decree: Christology and Predestination in Reformed Theology from Calvin to Perkins,* in *WTJ* 49 (1987) 442-46.
Charles S. McCoy and J. Wayne Baker's *Fountainhead of Federalism: Heinrich Bullinger and the Covenantal Tradition,* in *WTJ* 54 (1992) 396-400.
I. John Hesselink's *Calvin's Concept of the Law,* in *WTJ 55* (1993) 168-71.
A. T. B. McGowen's *The Federal Theology of Thomas Boston,* in *JETS* 42 (1999) 544-546.
G. Michael Thomas' *The Extent of the Atonement: A Dilemma for Reformed Theology from Calvin to the Consensus,* in *TrinJ* 20 NS (1999) 116-19.
John Coffey's *Politics, Religion and the British Revolutions: The Mind of Samuel Rutherford,* in *JETS* 42 (1999) 543-544.
Leonhard Goppelt's *Typos: The Typological Interpretation of the Old Testament in the New,* in *JETS* 26 (1983) 490-93.

Don B. Garlington's *Faith, Obedience and Perseverance: Aspects of Paul's Letter to the Romans,* in *TrinJ* 18 NS (1997) 254-58.
Paul K. Jewett's *Election and Predestination,* in *WTJ* 48 (1986) 388-91.
Anthony A. Hoekema's *Created in God's Image,* in *WTJ* 49 (1987) 437-42.
[General editor) Wayne G. Strickland's *The Law, the Gospel, and the Modern Christian: Five Views,* in *JETS* 37 (1994) 447-50.
Sinclair B. Ferguson, *The Holy Spirit,* in *JETS* 42 (1999) 529-531.

NOTE: Some grammatical and spelling changes have been made in the quotations from the early Reformation writings. Other minor changes in the literature cited, including uniformity in the scriptural citations and the capitalization of the terminology "Covenant of Works" and "Covenant of Grace," have also been made in preparing these essays and reviews for republication in a single volume. Hebrew and Greek words have been transliterated. For abbreviations, see the *Journal of Biblical Literature* 107 (1988) 579-96.

TABLE OF CONTENTS

PROLOGUE

Preoccupation with the biblical teaching on the covenants has long been a distinguishing trait of Reformed theology. Yet in recent years, the covenant doctrine has increasingly become a topic of interest in evangelicalism, in large part because of the growing rapprochement between the dispensational and nondispensational schools of interpretation. It is the contention of these collected writings, however, that only (historic) Reformed theology provides the system of doctrine necessary for an exposition of the divine covenants which is faithful to the teaching of Scripture. The relationship between God and humanity is, in a word, covenantal. God does not deal with his creation apart from covenant. In the history of Christian theology a variety of definitions have been offered for the term. Essentially, "covenant" is a bond or relationship between two parties. In the covenants between God and humanity, the Lord God sovereignly imposes the terms of these arrangements in accordance with his own will and good pleasure. With respect to the history of Christian doctrine it is the unique contribution of Reformed theology to have developed and systematized the biblical doctrine of the covenants.

Biblical history is structured in terms of a series of distinct covenants. Following the traditional Reformed schematization, the divine covenants reflect the decretal purpose(s) of God in creation and redemption. Standing behind the creation of the world is the eternal plan or counsel of God. One particular feature of that plan is the "Covenant of Redemption" (to use of older terminology) made in eternity between the Father and the Son respecting the salvation of God's elect, those chosen in Christ by God the Father and effectually called to true faith and repentance in history by means of the regenerating and convicting power of the Spirit of God. Election to salvation is the *proper purpose* of redemptive covenant (the "Covenant of Grace" which spans the epoch from the Fall of Adam to the Consummation of history at the return of Christ). The first historical covenant is the "Covenant of Works," also called the "Covenant of Nature" or "Covenant of Creation." The former terminology of the "Covenant of Works," the one most commonly employed by Reformed writers, stresses the filial duty and obligation of the sons of God to render full and perfect obedience to their Creator. Wherever a covenant of works arrangement is found in Scripture (*e.g.*, at creation with Adam, at Sinai with the Israelite theocracy, and at the incarnation of the Son of God ["born of a woman, born under the law," Gal 4:4]), there is a corresponding time of probation, which is the God-ordained way to the attainment of the blessings promised in the first covenant.

While maintaining the twofold covenants, the initial Covenant of Works and the subsequent Covenant of Grace, Reformed theology has emphasized at the same time the singleness of God's purpose and plan. On the one hand, it recognizes the unity and continuity of the Old and New Covenants (or Testaments), while maintaining the difference and discontinuity between them. On the other hand, it affirms the ultimate unity of the many and varied covenants in the mind of God. Just as the manifold decrees of God encompass all things that come to pass in history, so also the singular decree of God unites them. Thus we may speak of the decree(s) of God as the ultimate cause, the predestinating purpose of God whereby all things are foreordained by God in his eternal counsel. Controversies in seventeenth-century Reformed scholasticism led to the division between infra- and supralapsarians. In the final analysis these debates highlight the *paradoxical* nature of biblical truth, truth that is *beyond finite human comprehension.* That which appears contradictory is ultimately resolved in the exhaustively rational mind of God. That is what is meant, in part, by the Creator/creature distinction, an important philosophico-theological element in Calvinist thought.

As already indicated, covenant theology in the history of Christian doctrine is a peculiarly Reformed dogma (as opposed to Lutheran or evangelical). It is what distinguishes "Calvinism" from other varieties of Protestant theology. Explicitly or implicitly, the doctrine of the covenants provides the organizational structure for the entire Reformed theological system. With reference to the *Westminster Confession of Faith,* written at the close of the Reformation period and standing as the epitome of confessional Reformed theology in that period of church history, B. B. Warfield rightly speaks of the covenant doctrine as the confession's "architechtonic principle." All branches of Reformed theology – British, continental European, and North American – give expression to this distinctive teaching. Although international travel and correspondence helped further the spread of covenant theology, the doctrine of the covenants was largely indigenous to British and continental soils (from there it was transplanted to America). Significantly, the great Reformed creeds and catechisms of the Reformation age continue to exercise a formative influence in dogmatic exposition down to the present day.[1]

With respect to the history of Reformed doctrine the origin of the specific theological discipline known as "biblical theology" (in distinction from "systematic theology") is to be found in the Reformed tradition, notably in its formulations on the doctrine of the covenants. Biblical theology gives special attention to the progressive unfolding of redemptive revelation in Scripture. Systematics, on the other hand, is concerned with the logical ordering of biblical teaching. Confessional theology (also called "Christian dogmatics") arises out of the church's need to restate biblical truth, oftentimes in the context of intense polemical debate and controversy. The early church faced questions relating to the triune personality of the Godhead and the person and natures of Jesus Christ as the God-man. By the time of the Protestant Reformation in England the Reformed church was able to adopt a comprehensive creedal statement, *viz.,* the *Westminster Confession of Faith,* a document which has withstood the passage of time.[2] *By this stage in the history of Christian theology the two-covenant doctrine had become a staple in Reformed thought.* It was not until the twentieth century that this vital dogma has been challenged.

The purpose of these essays is to defend, correct (where necessary), and elucidate yet further the teachings of Reformed covenant theology, and to do so in dialogue with its most ardent critics and supporters. The leading assaults against traditional teaching have come from two very different sources. The first comes from within Reformed orthodoxy itself, in the teaching of the late John Murray, longtime professor of systematic theology at Westminster Seminary in Philadelphia. The second source of criticism appears pervasively in contemporary NT research, notably in studies on Paul and the Mosaic law. Both of these theological developments will be thoroughly explored and critiqued in this collection of writings. Today the critical exegetical-theological debate centers upon the interpretation of Lev 18:5 ("do this and live"), in which biblical text the apostle Paul identifies the principle of *inheritance by works*, as opposed to *inheritance by faith.* These two principles, works and faith ("Law" and "Gospel"), are antithetical to one another. Historical theologians debate the question whether or not later Calvinism (including what is known as Reformed scholastic federalism, *i.e.*, seventeenth-century covenant theology) amounts to a departure from the teachings of John Calvin. Critical scholarship, in my judgment, has unfairly driven a sharp wedge between Calvin and the Calvinists. The chief doctrines under attack by these critics are (double) predestination, (legal) justification, and the Covenant of Works. Other aspects of Reformed doctrine currently disputed include the place of divine law in the modern-day state (questions relating to theonomic polity), the nature and significance of biblical typology (especially the relationship between the ancient Israelite theocracy and the NT church), and, lastly, the nature and extent of the atonement (*i.e.*, the particularism of the gospel of salvation in Jesus Christ, the only savior of sinners who by nature are objects of God's wrath and condemnation).

The special focus of this volume is the Calvinistic teaching concerning the Mosaic Covenant as anticipatory of the New Covenant established through the shed blood of Jesus Christ. For the most part, the essays and book reviews are arranged in their appropriate sections chronologically (by date of writing). To one degree or another they are summary explications of and elaborations upon my studies at Westminster Theological Seminary in Philadelphia.[3] (Twenty years of additional study and reflection have yielded some revisions in my own thinking – *e.g.*, the theological term "grace," the divine remedy for human sin and *demerit,* is applicable only to the redemptive era, not the preredemptive. The Protestant tradition has erred in defining/applying the term otherwise.) The essay entitled "Covenant Theology and the Westminster Tradition" marked the close of the first decade after the completion of my dissertation; the present publication marks the close of the second decade, and coincides with the beginning of a new millennium of theological expositon and polemics in the Christian church. These studies, then, comprise a restatement of the biblical doctrine of the covenants, along with refinements and modifications of some elements within the system of Reformed covenant theology. Study in the history of Christian doctrine is a study in the history of *doctrinal development,* the church's gradual and maturing apprehension of the Word of God over an extended period of time (leading all the way up to the return of Christ), a period also marked by seasons of doctrinal error, misapprehension, and even departure from the truth (*i.e.*, apostasy).

The story of the origins, development, and later critical assessment (in some instances radical reconstruction) of Reformed federalism is comprehensive of the entire theological enterprise – historical, exegetical, and confessional-dogmatic. The opening section of this book considers the historical-theological context of covenant theology in its early and later years of development; the second addresses the concerns of biblical theology and exegesis; the final section considers several matters of interest in systematics, including biblical hermeneutics, apologetics, theonomy (also known as Christian Reconstructionism), and eschatology. The book reviews direct students of covenant theology to some of the best works in these various and related theological disciplines and serve as an occasion to evaluate my own critique and defense of traditional Reformed teaching in terms of analyses of other specialists in these fields of study. Additionally, this exchange of ideas sheds further light on the many disputed points in contemporary biblical, systematic, and historical-theological interpretation. The Epilogue introduces the reader to the important subject of the historical development of Christian doctrine (pointing out both the similarities and the differences between doctrinal development in the Bible and in church history) and concludes with an assessment of the works of one of the leading, yet often neglected, Reformed interpreters of our day, Meredith G. Kline. His biblical-theological exposition, firmly rooted in classic Reformed covenant theology, has much to offer in the contemporary debates among both evangelicals and modernists.

NOTES

[1]See the recent work by Robert L. Reymond, *A New Systematic Theology of the Christian Faith* (Nashville: Thomas Nelson, 1998) and my critique of it in "A (New) Systematic Theology for Our Times: A Review Article," *Foundations: A Journal of Evangelical Theology* (Spring 2001). For the older dogmatic tradition compare also my review of Richard A. Muller's *Post-Reformation Reformed Dogmatics* (vol.1, Prolegomena to Theology; Grand Rapids: Baker, 1987) in *WTJ* 50 (1988) 364-370.

[2]"The place of the *Confession* in the history of Christian doctrine is such that a grasp of its significance is crucial for an understanding of the contemporary theological situation" (John H. Leith, *Assembly at Westminster: Reformed Theology in the Making* [Atlanta: John Knox, 1973] 12). This statement of faith is also "an illustration of outstanding theological achievement and technical competence. It holds together with remarkable logical clarity and is true to all the theological angles and nuances. The *Confession* is amazingly complete and comprehensive. It combines doctrine and practice. No theology today achieves this high level of technical competence" (*ibid.* 13-14).

[3]My doctoral dissertation interacts with the many and various strands of theological discussion and debate that has ensued in the course of church history from the time of the Reformation to the present. This study, entitled "The Mosaic Covenant and the Concept of Works in Reformed Hermeneutics: A Historical-Critical Analysis With Particular Attention to Early Covenant Eschatology" (Westminster Theological Seminary, 1980), is available through University Microfilms International (Ann Arbor, Michigan; London, England: 1981, #802493.

SECTION ONE – Historical Theology

SUMMARY ARGUMENT. The opening essay, the longest in the collection, lays the foundation for all that follows. In it we explore the Reformed understanding of the Mosaic Covenant as a particular administration of the single Covenant of Grace spanning the entire redemptive epoch from the Fall to the Consummation, yet one having the traits of a Covenant of Works. The resolution of the two antithetical elements – law and grace (works and faith) – within the Mosaic economy of redemption has been one of the greatest challenges facing Reformed interpreters of the Bible. Although the subject is exceedingly complex and difficult, the basic structure underlying the various and diverse covenants made between God and his people is, nevertheless, readily understandable and easy to grasp. Not until recent times – notably, the late twentieth century – has the orthodox biblical teaching on law and gospel been vigorously challenged. We begin our overview of federalism with the sixteenth and early seventeenth centuries (up to the time of the assembly of Westminster divines) and conclude with the late nineteenth and twentieth centuries.

Continental Reformed and Anglo-Puritan theologians made significantly different applications of the natural law doctrine that was commonplace within Protestantism. Most notably, it was the Puritans who attempted to establish godly societies ruled by the Word of God (*i.e.*, Christian commonwealths or theocracies). What dominated social and political thinking throughout the age of the Reformation was the medieval notion of the *corpus christianum* ("Christendom"). Abandonment of this notion had finally to await the establishment of religious freedom in the modern age. Central to discussions on natural law and the law of Moses, especially the civil laws in the Mosaic code, was an understanding of the biblical principle of "general equity." Debates on these issues led to the adoption of two distinct covenantal engagements, one ecclesiastical, the other political.

Alongside the dominant consensus found within mainstream Reformed thought, Puritanism in Old and New England manifested a number of other peculiarities, notably what has come to be called the "misinterpretation view of the Mosaic law." The third essay in this section, written at the request of Douglas Moo, NT scholar and editor of *Trinity Journal,* delves into the complex subject of Paul and the law from the standpoint of English covenant theology. According to the interpretation espoused by some of the Puritans, the principle of law enunciated in Lev 18:5 was construed as the principle of faith, *i.e.*, (saving) grace, not the principle of works (law). Crucial in these discussions were interpretations of the writings of the apostle Paul. Theological and moral treatises on the Christian life (including the threefold uses of the law of God – the civil, the elenctic or pedagogical, and the normative) abound in the Puritan literature. Particular emphasis was given to the "third use of the law," the so-called "regulative" or "normative." Preoccupation with the subject of the moral law led to the rise of Puritan casuistry; in some instances English moral theology resulted in moralism. Problematic also was Puritan teaching on the law as *preparatory to grace* and teaching on the Christian sabbath, viewed as the "badge" of Christian society.

The fourth essay addresses the weakest point in the Reformed federal system of doctrine, the reintroduction of the medieval, scholastic distinction between nature and grace – more specifically, the faulty distinction between a natural bond and a covenantal bond between Creator and creature. This chapter begins by exploring the background of late medieval thought, what is essential for understanding the theology of the Protestant reformers both in its early and later years of development. After comparing various opinions held among the federalists, a critical evaluation of contemporary Reformed thought is offered.

Section One closes with a review article evaluating David Weir's influential work, *The Origins of the Federal Theology in Sixteenth-Century Reformation Thought*. Pivotal to the current debate is the matter of the relationship between the prelapsarian covenant, the covenant between God and Adam at creation, and predestination. The majority of critics of Reformed scholastic orthodoxy (*i.e.*, federalism) have been influenced to one degree or another by the teachings of Karl Barth on covenant and election. Also, in place of the classic Protestant-Reformed antithesis between law and gospel is the Barthian notion of "law in grace." This dispute between the bi-covenantalists (orthodox federalists who espouse the twofold doctrine of the covenants, the Covenant of Works and the Covenant of Grace) and the mono-covenantalists (modern-day revisionists who teach only a single "Covenant of Grace" extending from creation to the consummation of world history) is, in the judgment of Colin Brown, "the conflict between orthodoxy and Barthianism." Surprisingly, the traditional Reformed doctrine has undergone thoroughgoing revision in the (new) Westminster School, what amounts to a repudiation of Old Princeton theology.

CHAPTER ONE

REFORMED INTERPRETATION OF THE MOSAIC COVENANT

Throughout the history of Christian doctrine the problem of the relation between the Old and New Testaments has been central to the interpretive task of the church. Indeed, this basic issue is one of the leading concerns of the NT writings themselves. The fundamental, biblical idea in both the OT and the New is the covenant of God. The OT writings explicate the Mosaic administration of the Covenant of Grace. The Gospels and Acts are concerned with the inauguration and establishment of the New Covenant through the coming of the Messiah, the Servant of the Lord, and the outpouring of the Spirit of Christ upon the church at Pentecost. The Epistles and Revelation develop more fully the theology of the covenant and its implications for New Covenant ministry in life and worship.

The doctrine of the covenant of God, including the relation between Old and New Testaments, finds its first articulate spokesman after the apostles in Irenaeus, who defended Christian theology against the false teachings of Marcion, specifically the latter's denial of the unity of the two Testaments.[1] The chapters on the covenant of God in the history of doctrine, beginning with Irenaeus' contribution, cover the entire history of the Christian church. But it is not until the time of the Reformation, considered in its widest range from the second decade of the sixteenth century to the writing of the Westminster Standards (1648), that the doctrine of the covenant comes fully into its own. Consequently, when we speak of federalism, the synonym for covenant theology, we are thinking of that variety of theology in the period of the Reformation which is characteristic of the Reformed tradition.

In fact, the genius of the Reformed theological tradition is evident most explicitly (and implicitly) in its development of federalism. The concept of the covenant is determinative for both its exegetical and theological reflection. And the distinctiveness of federalism is its biblical-theological method, what Ludwig Diestel calls the "organic-historical method."[2] This remains true of Reformed theology today. Adherence to the traditional interpretation of the covenant doctrine serves to distinguish orthodox Reformed theology from neoorthodox theology. One of the most important aspects of the traditional Calvinist teaching on the covenant is the use of the law-gospel distinction. The antithesis between law and gospel denotes two opposing principles of inheritance, appropriate to the Pauline teaching on the two Adams in Romans 5. The forensic contrast between the order of law (creation) and the order of grace (redemption) is one of opposition. Regrettably, much of recent Reformed theology has openly denied the importance of the law-gospel distinction, substituting in its place the Barthian notion of "law *in* grace." The neoorthodox school of interpretation maintains only one order or covenant, the Covenant of Grace, comprehending both creation and redemption. Otherwise, contend these neoorthodox critics, the speculative and dualistic notion of law and grace (comparable to the scholastic nature-grace dichotomy) results in a faulty conception of God as Creator and as Redeemer.[3] Others within the Reformed tradition have been less open in their rejection of the law-gospel contrast, but nevertheless are sympathetic to Barth's viewpoint. Repudiation of the law-gospel antithesis, however, immediately registers itself in other critical and related areas of Reformed exposition, particularly that of justification by faith and the atonement of Christ. The result is a *radical* reinterpretation of Reformation theology.

The central issue in this present debate in Reformed theology, both within and without confessional orthodoxy, as it turns out, is the interpretation of the Mosaic Covenant. It is our contention that within the historic Reformed tradition the hermeneutical key to this issue is the proper biblical assessment of the symbolic-typical aspect of OT revelation, and the recognition of the dual principles of law and grace operative in the Mosaic covenant administration. The Mosaic Covenant is to be viewed *in some sense* as a covenant of works. This has been the conviction of the vast majority of Reformed theologians in the early history of federalism (up to 1648).[4]

Before we begin our historical survey of Reformed interpretation of the Mosaic Covenant, it is essential that we acquaint ourselves with certain aspects and particulars of the leading critical assessments of federalism, especially of covenant theology's employment of the traditional contrast between law and grace, works and faith. Critics of continental Reformed theology generally distinguish two types or varieties of federalism, one speculative and one biblical.[5] The former is associated invariably with the rise of scholasticism in the period of Reformed Orthodoxy. The latter is more compatible with the method of salvation history (the *heilsgeschichtliche* method). According to these critics, the speculative variety of federalism employs such terminology as the "Covenant of Nature," the "law of nature" (otherwise called "natural law"), and the "Covenant of Works." The Covenant of Nature and the law of nature conceptualizations, so the critics argue, rest upon the medieval, scholastic dualism between nature and grace.

Thomas Aquinas was the foremost expounder of the dichotomy between a state of nature and a state of grace. This dualism was applicable to both the period of creation and the period of redemption.[6] The majority of medieval theologians taught as Thomas had that man by nature (at the time of creation) was endowed with certain inalienable rights. By nature man possessed intrinsic worth and dignity. As long as man exercised his gifts with wisdom and charity and was obedient to the law of God, he was worthy of blessing from God. Thus, *in strict justice* God was indebted to man. However, man by nature was in an unstable position. Although man by nature had the desire to do good (he was so constituted that his good inclinations might overrule his evil inclinations, which are not sinful *per se),* nevertheless his spirit warred against his flesh. God was pleased to bestow upon man the additional supernatural gift of grace in order for man to attain unto the final state of glorification, the beatific vision of God. The fall of Adam into sin made supernatural grace all the more necessary.[7]

The "Covenant of Nature" and "natural law" terminology simply perpetuated the speculative dichotomy between nature and grace. The Covenant of Nature suggested the idea that man possessed an intrinsic worth to which God was indebted to reward in the way of the covenant. Similarly, the "Covenant of Works" concept was perceived by these critics to be speculative in origin. The forensic distinction between law and grace had no basis in the Scriptures. According to H. E. Weber, by the use of this legal contrast, the covenant idea became couched in juridical-rational terms. The covenant was viewed as a mercantile contract between God and man.[8] Because of the widespread adoption of the Covenant of Works conception, federalism thus served primarily as a conveyer of rationalism.[9] Gradually, the notion of the Covenant of Works (Law) was associated with the Mosaic Covenant. Federalism continued to distort the biblical concept of the divine covenant of sovereign grace, especially with regard to the relation between the Old and the New Testaments.[10]

On the other hand, in sharp distinction from the scholastic, speculative type of continental federalism (which is by far the dominant variety in the period of Reformed Orthodoxy) there is the biblical variety as discerned by the critics. Heinrich Heppe, one of the leading advocates in the nineteenth century for this supposition, identifies the German Reformed school as the chief center for biblical federalism. Whereas the scholastic method treats scriptural truth objectively as an object of speculation, biblical federalism places its theological reflection in the context of faith, and thereby is marked by its acutely practical and personal concerns for the life of the church. That is to say, biblical federalism gives expression to a practical, versus a theoretical, "science of faith." Above all, biblical federalism avoids concentration upon the doctrine of double predestination.[11]

Critics of English federalism likewise discern two varieties of theology. Leonard Trinterud argues that the one is represented by the followers of Calvin, emphasizing the sovereignty and grace of God.[12] The other view is the Rhineland-Puritan conception with its accent upon the mutual character of the covenant relationship and its stress upon ethical requirements (the conditionality of the Covenant of Grace). With marked enthusiasm and a sense of relief, Holmes Rolston affirms the opinion that the *Confession of 1967* of the United Presbyterian Church in the United States of America signals the end of Reformed theology's long tie to federalism. He writes: "Indeed, it has seldom been realised by those reared in the Reformed tradition that the two-covenant concept which dominates the organisational substructure of all later Reformed dogmatics is totally absent from Calvin. More seriously, its fundamental incompatibility with Calvin's thought has gone all but unnoticed."[13]

To what extent are the critics of English and continental federalism conveying an accurate picture of the theology of the early reformers? How valid is the distinction between two types of federalism, one speculative and moralistic and one biblical and genuinely Calvinistic? To answer these questions we turn our attention now to the writings of some of the leading federalists in the sixteenth and early seventeenth centuries.[14]

1. Sixteenth-Century Covenant Theology

The sixteenth-century federalists were responsible for establishing the redemptive-historical structure of biblical revelation, and the covenant structure was the distinguishing mark of Reformed theological interpretation. Beginning as a term descriptive of the era of redemption, the covenant concept was broadened, in the interests of further systematic and historical reflection, to include the preredemptive period of biblical history. The entire development of the covenant idea was controlled and elicited by the Reformers' understanding of justification by faith, in its fundamentally forensic sense, and the coordinate law-gospel distinction.

Huldreich Zwingli and Heinrich Bullinger

Huldreich Zwingli (1484-1531), the father of the Reformed church, was a man of remarkable talent and ability for both teaching and preaching. Unlike Luther, Zwingli had a keen, perceptive and constructive mind suited for the task of systematizing theology. One of the underlying motifs of his theology was the Pauline doctrine of the representative headship of Adam based upon the teaching of Romans 5. This was highly significant, for it was indicative of a basic organic, historical point of view. Zwingli teaches that in Adam all stand guilty. But what is lost in the First Adam by his transgression is restored in the Second Adam, Jesus Christ, by way of his full and perfect obedience to the law of God. It is this obedience, *viz.*, the righteousness of Christ, which is imputed to the believer as the ground of his justification.[15]

This same organic-historical viewpoint governed Zwingli's defense of infant baptism. The burning issue in the growing controversy between Zwingli and the Anabaptists had been the question of the relationship of the OT to the New. Generally, the Anabaptists made use of the Old occasionally to illustrate the message of the NT, what they spoke of as the "simple gospel." Like Irenaeus, Zwingli insisted upon the crucial unity of the two Testaments. Since the infant Israelites were heirs of the covenant promises, even more so were the infants of NT believers.[16] The promises of the New Covenant were just as valid and trustworthy as in the days of Abraham. Zwingli perceived the unity of the Testaments precisely in terms of the unity of the Covenant of Grace.

While there is an element of truth to the suggestion that Zwingli begins his defense of infant baptism by simply referring to the practice of circumcision as the analogue of baptism, this is not to he interpreted finally as arguing from something less than the covenant itself. Understandably, he would begin by considering the sign of the covenant before proceeding to reflect more deeply, as he does, upon the nature and design of the establishment of the Covenant of Grace.[17] Zwingli's major contribution in federal theology is his emphasis upon the unity of the two Testaments, perceived explicitly in terms of the single Covenant of Grace.

In Heinrich Bullinger (1504-1575) we find a much fuller exposition of the theology of the covenant. Bullinger exercised an extremely influential role in the subsequent development of Reformed federalism.[18] With an even greater ability to systematize the truths of biblical religion, he was an ideal successor to Zwingli. Bullinger's theology was much more than an expansion and popularizing of Zwingli's. His originality was especially evident in the further development of the federal idea. Charles S. McCoy maintains:

> The roots of the covenant theology in the Reformed churches are to be found especially in Zurich with Ulrich Zwingli and to a limited extent in Geneva with John Calvin, and use of the covenant notion is widespread in the Reformed tradition from the earliest years of the Reformation. The real beginning of federalism, however, is found in Heinrich Bullinger, successor to Zwingli at Zurich.[19]

Bullinger teaches that man as created in the image of God was perfect and good. God inscribed his holy law upon man's heart, and man had the power and knowledge to perform that which was good and righteous. Bullinger gives expression here to the common Protestant interpretation of natural law. The function of the law of nature is to teach men what they are obligated to render to their Creator, as the apostle Paul affirms in Rom 2:14-16.[20] The law of nature reveals, among other things, that fellowship between the Creator and the creature requires perfect compliance with the law of God on the part of the creature. At this point, the term "works" appropriately describes this legal demand which, by sovereign disposition, qualifies the relationship between God and man.[21] Furthermore, Bullinger teaches that there is a fundamental continuity between the law of nature in creation and the law of nature as expressed in the Mosaic law. We need only mention here that this continuity resides in man's natural obligation – his duty – to render obedience to his Creator. The fact that after the Fall man as sinner is unable to please God does not eliminate his creaturely obligation.[22] (From this teaching comes the idea of the hypothetical law principle which states that *if* man as sinner can render perfect obedience to God, thus satisfying the ethical and legal demand of creation in the image of God, then he is justified before God.)

Bullinger's explicit use of the law/gospel distinction is usually associated with expositions of the doctrine of justification by faith and the doctrine of the Mosaic Covenant. Our primary concern is with the latter. Bullinger indicates quite clearly that the principle of law or works (antithetical to grace) functions in a characteristic and determinative way in the Sinaitic administration of the Covenant of Grace. The law of Moses is in some sense a repetition of the life-principle in the order of creation, sometimes spoken of as the law of nature, originally given by God to Adam prior to the Fall. Consequently, the exposition of the law feature of the Mosaic Covenant provides Bullinger with the opportunity to describe the similarities and differences between the Old and New Testaments.

Following the traditional pattern, Bullinger begins by emphasizing vigorously the essential unity of the Testaments. The substance of the Covenant of Grace pertains to the realization of the salvation of God's people through the person and work of Jesus Christ. Bullinger affirms, "In the very substance, truly, you can find no diversity: the difference which is between them consists in the manner of administration, in a few accidents, and certain circumstances."[23] This common formulation of the *essential* nature of the Covenant of Grace is imbedded within the Reformed tradition. The employment of scholastic terminology is clearly evident, *viz.*, the terms "substance" and "accidents." In substance there is unity; in accidents (the historical administrations of the single Covenant of Grace) there is diversity.

In his treatise *De Testamento seu Foedere Dei Unico et Aeterno,* the first extended exposition of the doctrine of the Covenant of Grace, Bullinger proceeds to a discussion of Genesis 17, the covenant made with the seed of Abraham.[24] Like the covenant made previously with Adam after the Fall and with Noah, the spiritual blessings are bestowed solely on the basis of God's saving grace, not on the basis of man's obedience to the law of God ("merit").[25] The spiritual seed of Abraham is restricted to the elect; they are the beneficiaries of the one and eternal Covenant of Grace. The elect of God comprises believing Jews and Gentiles, and this singular seed pertains to the "substance" of the Covenant of Grace. The salvation of the elect is the *proper purpose* of the Covenant of Grace.

While recognizing the proper purpose of the Mosaic Covenant as a distinct, historical administration of the one and eternal Covenant of Grace, Bullinger makes use of the traditional threefold use of the law (the civil, the pedagogical, and the regulative) to define the characteristic feature of the Mosaic Covenant. Of the three uses, explains Bullinger, "the chief and proper office of the law is to convince all men to be guilty of sin, and by their own fault to be the children of death." In this manner, he observes, "the law of God sets forth to us the holy will of God; and, in setting forth thereof, requires of us a most perfect and absolute kind of righteousness."[26] He concludes: "Therefore the proper office of Moses, and the principal use and effect of the law, is to show to man his sin and imperfection."[27] This is the pedagogical use of the law. The normative or regulative use of the law applies to those who have been justified and reconciled to God through Christ. The knowledge of Christ's fulfillment and abrogation of the law for justification is essential for understanding the nature of God's saving grace. The ultimate purpose of the Mosaic Covenant is to stimulate and encourage faith and obedience to Christ; the administrative works-principle is subordinate. Based on the interpretation of Gal 4:24, Bullinger concludes: "Therefore the law did gender the holy fathers and the prophets unto bondage, not that they should abide bondslaves for ever, but that it might keep them under discipline; yea, that it might lead them unto Christ, the full perfection of the law."[28] The Mosaic Covenant is not established exclusively on the principle of works. More importantly, there is the operation of sovereign grace and election. In preaching law and gospel, Moses leads God's people to salvation in Christ. Whereas the Old Covenant is characteristically one of bondage and servitude in which the believer is restricted under the tutelage of the law, the newness of the New Covenant includes an exceedingly greater and fuller experience by believers of the saving benefits of union with Christ, a greater freedom and liberty as sons of God and covenant heirs.

John Calvin

The most popular and influential theological treatise to come out of the Reformation is the *Institutes of the Christian Religion* of John Calvin (1509-1564). But as important as the *Institutes* are, they require the supplemental investigation and research of his other numerous writings, particularly his commentaries, in order to attain a fuller knowledge of and appreciation for his theological and exegetical ability. He is especially gifted in systematizing biblical theology. And the notable feature of Calvin's theology is its pervasively biblical-theological orientation.

While upholding the goodness, integrity and perfection of man's creation in the image of God, Calvin realizes that the original state is not the highest stage of man's blessedness. Calvin discerns more clearly than Bullinger the importance of biblical eschatology for the doctrine of creation. There is a specific goal and purpose for God's creative work, especially the creation of man in his own image. That goal is the glorification of the name and works of God. Although Calvin does not apply the term "covenant" to the original creation arrangement, nevertheless his doctrine is fully compatible with the later development of the Covenant of Works conception.

Unhesitatingly, Calvin perceives that the principle of works informs the order of creation. In commenting on Gen 2:16, Calvin cites 1 Tim 1:9 ("the law was not made for the righteous"), but indicates that this statement is not applicable to the pre-Fall state of Adam in innocence and uprightness. According to Calvin, the principle of works-inheritance governs the original state of integrity. The reward for faithfulness, based upon man's obedience, is eternal life.[29] In his interpretation of Hos 6:7, Calvin dismisses without further comment the suggestion that *adam* (Heb.) be translated "Adam." In his own conceptualization, Calvin restricts the term "covenant" to redemptive provisions. It appears that in this Hosea citation Calvin simply construes "covenant" as a reference to the *Mosaic* administration, thus explaining his rapid dismissal of the earlier suggestion that Adam was in view.[30] Undoubtedly, his interpretation of Hosea does not imply that he would oppose speaking of the creation order in covenantal terms. There is also a close correlation in Calvin's thought between the place of law in the first state of man and the idea of natural law.[31] The manifold revelation and experience of the graciousness of God in creation heightens man's culpability. "So much the greater, then, is the wickedness of man, whom neither that kind commemoration of the gifts of God, nor the dread of punishment, was able to retain in his duty."[32]

The ministration of law under the Mosaic Covenant serves to increase transgression in the economy of God's dealings with his Old Covenant people. The law is Israel's pedagogue until the coming of Christ. Like Bullinger, Calvin views the Mosaic administration in its characteristically pedagogical function. He is eager to maintain, at the same time, the substantial unity of the Covenant of Grace against the erroneous teachings of Servetus and the Anabaptists. The law is given by God through Moses

> . . . in order to humble men, having convinced them of their own condemnation. But because this is the true and only preparation for

> seeking Christ, all his variously expressed teachings [referring to the apostle Paul] well agree. He was disputing with perverse teachers who pretended that we merit righteousness by the works of the law. Consequently, to refute their error he was sometimes compelled to take the bare law in a narrow sense, even though it was otherwise graced with the covenant of free adoption.[33]

Calvin speaks of the abrogation of the law in the sense that it no longer condemns those who are united with Christ by grace through faith. Yet the proper and necessary distinction between law and grace under Moses does not obscure the more important operation of saving grace in the Old Covenant. Calvin closely weaves together the pedagogical use of the law with the typological system of the OT, so that "the gospel points out with the finger what the law foreshadowed under types."[34] Calvin reasons: "From this we infer that, where the whole law is concerned, the gospel differs from it only in clarity of manifestation."[35] As a result, Calvin distinguishes the *whole* law from the *narrow* law, Moses in his *universal* office from Moses in his *particular* office. In his exegesis of Rom 10:5-10, Calvin expounds:

> Paul now compares the righteousness of faith and the righteousness of works in order to make it clear how greatly they are at variance. The difference which exists between opposites is seen more clearly by a comparison between them. He is not referring to the writings of the prophets, but to the testimony of Moses, and for this reason alone, that the Jews might understand that the law had not been given by Moses in order to maintain their confidence in their works, but rather to lead them to Christ.
>
> The universal office which Moses had was the instruction of the people in the true rule of godliness. If this is true, it was his duty to preach repentance and faith. But faith is not taught without offering the promises, the free promises, of the divine mercy. The promises of the Gospel, however, are found only here and there in the writings of Moses, and these are somewhat obscure, while the precepts and rewards, appointed for those who observe the law, frequently occur. The function, therefore, of teaching the character of true righteousness of works is, with justification, properly and peculiarly attributed to Moses, as is also that function of showing the nature of the remuneration which awaits those who observe it, and what punishment awaits those who transgress it. For this reason Moses himself is contrasted with Christ by John, when he says, "The law was given by Moses; grace and truth came by Jesus Christ" (Jn 1:17). Whenever the word *law* is used in this restricted sense, Moses is implicitly contrasted with Christ. We are then to see what the law contains in itself when separated from the Gospel. I must, therefore, refer what I say here of the righteousness of the law not to the whole office of Moses, but to that part of it which was peculiarly entrusted to him.[36]

The principles of law and grace operated in various and distinct ways in the Old Covenant administration. The peculiarity of the Mosaic Covenant was seen in the emphasis on earthly and temporal benefits which served to direct the Israelites to the heavenly and eternal realities. This accounted for the status of childhood for the Old Covenant church. The people of God were restricted under the tutelage of the law of Moses.[37] Physical blessings and punishments were related to the principle of works-inheritance, appropriate to the typical sphere of the Mosaic administration. The typical punishments were "proofs of his [the Lord's] coming judgment against the wicked."[38] The OT types and figures pertained only to the "accidental properties of the covenant."[39] That is to say, the symbolic-typical system of the Old Covenant, coordinate with the principle of works-inheritance, was not to be construed to teach justification, *i.e.*, salvation, by the works of the law. If that were the case, the difference between the Old and New Covenants would be substantial, not merely accidental. The legal aspect of the Mosaic law itself was spoken of as a "covenant," because it was the characteristic means of Old Covenant administration. Although this conception was not fully worked out in Calvin's thought, the Mosaic covenant of law *(foedus legale)* was not equivalent to the idea of the Covenant of Works as that applied to the pre-Fall creation arrangement. The classic formulation of the unity of the Covenant of Grace, although not original with Calvin, is found in the *Institutes.* "The covenant made with all the patriarchs is so much like ours in substance and reality that the two are actually one and the same. Yet they differ in mode of administration."[40] The unifying substance of the Covenant of Grace was a way of speaking of the exclusive way of salvation through grace, of justification by faith, not human works. Our redemption was secured by the *meritorious* work of Christ, whose obedience and righteousness is imputed to us as the ground of justification.[41]

The biblical doctrine of sin depends upon the validity and integrity of the original Covenant of Works. According to Calvin, who on this point is representative of all the Reformed theologians, sin is, in the first place, transgression of the law of God.[42] The reason for the primary definition of sin in terms of law is to be seen in light of the importance of the *forensic* aspect of justification. There can be no fellowship and enjoyment of communion and life with God when there is the transgression of God's holy and righteous law. Only under the provisions of redemption, *i.e.*, the order of grace, is there forgiveness and reconciliation.

Zachary Ursinus and Casper Olevianus

These two German Reformed theologians are widely recognized as the most prominent of the sixteenth-century federalists, noted particularly for their writing of the popular and widely received *Heidelberg Catechism.* They were both students of Calvin at Geneva and Peter Martyr Vermigli at Zurich.

In his commentary on the *Heidelberg Catechism*, Zachary Ursinus (1534-1583) sets forth his views on the covenant of God, which like Calvin he restricts in application to the period of redemption. He conceives of the divine covenant with its two-party arrangement as an anthropological concept. It is not uncommon to speak of covenant as a mutual agreement between God and man comparable to those made between men. However, this mutuality is *never* construed in terms of equality of persons, as might be the case in certain human covenants.

Within the single Covenant of Grace, Ursinus perceives two aspects, depending upon the general or principle conditions of the covenant on the one hand, and the less general conditions on the other.[43] The accidental aspect of the Covenant of Grace pertains to the less general conditions, "in order that the faithful, by their help, may obtain those which are general." That is to say, the mode of administration is temporary and changeable according to God's saving design, and is thus subordinate to his eternal and unchanging purpose for the redemption of his people. The general conditions refer to the essence of the covenant, which is its proper purpose. The less general conditions of the covenant determine its particular historical-covenantal administration. Ursinus provides us here with a vital contribution in the development of the biblical interpretation of the covenant. With respect to the definition of covenant, Ursinus insists upon the importance of recognizing the substantial unity of the Covenant of Grace, but attempts at the same time to do fuller justice to the varying administrations of the divine covenant. He does so by speaking of the twofold *conditions*, one general and the other less general. He is pointing to the valid and crucial hermeneutical distinction between the two spheres of "conditionality" within the Mosaic Covenant arrangement. The law of God has multiple applications within the Covenant of Grace.

The promise of the law is conditioned on perfect obedience. Hence after the Fall, the law works wrath, being a ministration of death and condemnation.[44] Ursinus clarifies more precisely the sense in which the law of God is abrogated, and the sense in which it continues to be binding upon the people of God. The moral law has a distinct application appropriate to man's fourfold state: (1) nature uncorrupted by sin (man's state in creation); (2) nature corrupted (the civil and pedagogical uses of the law); (3) nature restored in Christ (the regulative use of the law); and (4) nature glorified (the eternal state).[45]

In his *Summa Theologiae* (1584), Ursinus makes his first application of the covenant idea to the original creation order.[46] After the Fall, God entered into the covenant with man a second time. The Covenant of Grace was made with the elect. In this catechism, Ursinus brings together the concept of the dual covenants and the traditional law-gospel distinction. The law pertains to the Covenant of Nature, *i.e.*, the Covenant of Creation, with its dual sanctions of blessing for obedience and curse for disobedience, based upon man's conformity to the law of God.[47] Earlier in his *Catechesis minor* (1562), which preceded the writing of the *Heidelberg Catechism,* Ursinus made no use of the covenant terminology, except with respect to the subject of infant baptism and the Lord's Supper.

In *An Exposition of the Symbole of the Apostles,* Casper Olevianus (1536-1587) expounds at length upon the theme of the kingdom of Christ with explicit application of the covenant idea. He weaves together the concepts of covenant and kingdom derived in large measure from Calvin's thought.[48] The foundation of the Covenant of Grace is the meritorious work of Christ, who satisfied the righteous demands of his Father as the Second Adam, and thus delivered us from the curse of the law. In Christ there is forgiveness of sin and renewal in sanctification. In the opening pages of his extensive treatment of the kingdom of God, Olevianus emphasizes man's culpability and guiltiness before the all-holy and righteous

God. Christ, in his office of priest and king, reconciles man and God and establishes his kingdom with those whom the Father has given him. This kingdom is manifested in the way of the covenant, the sum of which is contained in the articles of faith. The Covenant of Grace and reconciliation is unlike the covenant made with our fathers when God brought them out of the land of Egypt. This latter covenant was made void by their disobedience, whereas the Covenant of Grace cannot be made void. God's saving purposes for man's redemption in Christ are certain and efficacious. The Covenant of Grace rests exclusively upon the merits of Christ imputed to the elect through faith, such that "this whole covenant consists in faith alone."[49]

Perhaps the most important and influential treatise on the covenant to appear in the sixteenth century is Olevianus' *De Substantia Foederis Gratuiti inter Deum et Electos.* At the very beginning, Olevianus contrasts the New Covenant with the Old, *i.e.,* the Mosaic Covenant. Once again he stresses that the New Covenant is unlike the Old which was voided by the disobedient Israelites. The Covenant of Grace, the proper purpose being election in Christ, includes both remission of sins and renewal in the image of God. Olevianus tries to clarify further the distinctions needed to explain the twofold aspect of the one and eternal covenant with the elect. First, there is the substance of the covenant pertaining to the elect alone, and second, the administration of the visible church. While Olevianus does not want to separate or abstract these two aspects of the one covenant, yet he desires to take full account of all the biblical material. Genesis 17 does not restrict the administration of the covenant to the elect. Yet the administration of the visible church is not to be interpreted so as to be a means of accommodating the non-elect within the covenant. There are simply the two inseparable, though distinct, aspects of the one Covenant of Grace, the substance and the outward administration.[50]

In addition to the contrast between the Old and New Covenants, Olevianus speaks of that "first covenant" between God and man made in the image of God.[51] There is a fundamental similarity between the works-feature of the Mosaic Covenant and the works-arrangement in the order of creation. The covenant made with Israel rested "in part in their own strength."[52] Olevianus proceeds to speak of this legal aspect as a "covenant of law" *(foedus leqale),* in which man is obligated to perform perfect obedience in his own strength. The law of God is the eternal norm for justification and approbation, reflecting the dual sanctions of blessing for obedience and curse for disobedience, the promise of eternal life and the threat of malediction. All reasonable creatures are required to be conformed to divine law by virtue of their natural debt to the Creator. The Mosaic *foedus legale* employs similarly the dual sanctions of the divine law covenant. The more usual manner in which Olevianus expresses this idea of the works-principle is in terms of the "law of creation," rather than in explicitly covenantal phraseology. In the Mosaic Covenant, the law of creation is reestablished under Moses by way of the covenant (*ex pacto*).[53]

William Tyndale and Robert Rollock

M. M. Knappen contends that English Puritanism begins with William Tyndale (1484-1536). Tudor Puritanism "was not an indigenous English movement, but the Anglo-Saxon branch of a Continental one, dependent on foreign theologians both for its theory and for its direction in practical matters."[54] The covenant idea finds its earliest English expression in the writings of Tyndale. It may well be the case that Tyndale appropriated the concept when he was on the Continent. But that he applied it with some originality in his interpretation of the Scriptures is undeniable. In many respects, his formulation is closer to that of Ursinus than any other Continental federalist, although Tyndale and Ursinus developed their ideas independently from one another.

Tyndale was desirous not only to provide the Scriptures in the vernacular, but also to aid Christians in their own study of the Bible. Along with his translations, he provided various prologues to the books of the Bible. The most prominent feature of these introductions was the attention given to the matter of the relation between the Old and New Testaments. The OT stressed the temporal promises which were offered to the Israelites on the basis of their keeping of the law of Moses. Lev 18:5 stated the governing principle of inheritance by works, which principle was characteristic of the Old Covenant. The purpose of the law was to drive the Israelites to Christ and his redemptive benefits.[55]

From the outset, however, there was the tendency in Tyndale, symptomatic of the later English divines, to emphasize unduly the law-function of the Mosaic Covenant in terms of the individual's personal experience of conversion, rather than to discern the more basic redemptive-historical nature of Old Covenant administration. Perhaps the early beginnings of the later English federalist interpretation of the Mosaic Covenant (to be discussed below) can be traced back here to Tyndale. The principle of law under the Mosaic Covenant was defined in terms of the Jewish misapplication of the legal demand as the means of justification. Tyndale and the later English federalists taught that the Mosaic Covenant *became* a ministration of death and condemnation for the individual who misconstrued the place of the law of God in justification. (The predisposition to detail the conversion experience was exploited in the subsequent rise of casuistry in William Perkins and William Ames.)

What dominates Tyndale's exposition of the difference between the two Testaments is the law-gospel antithesis.[56] The period of the OT (law) is the time of infancy and childhood of all believers who were before Christ. Tyndale's interpretation of the uniqueness of the OT includes an appreciation for the rich typological significance of its ceremonies and institutions. In this context, Tyndale warns against false allegorical interpretation of the Scriptures.[57] The right use of types, insists Tyndale, must always reveal a legitimate christological focus.

German Reformed federalism was conveyed to Scotland through Robert Howie, a close friend of Robert Rollock (1555?-1599) and student of Olevianus at Herborn.[58] The leading Scottish federalist, however, in the sixteenth century was Rollock. In his *Treatise of our Effectual Calling* Rollock taught that the Word of God was to be understood explicitly in terms of the divine covenant. He made extensive use of the idea of the twofold covenant of God, the Covenant of Works and the Covenant of Grace. The former of these he identified as the legal or natural covenant, whose principle was summed up in Lev 18:5.[59] The promise of the Covenant of Works was not righteousness, for this Adam possessed by virtue of his creation in the image of God, but eternal life.

The works of man required in the Covenant of Works proceed from his own nature, and are not grounded upon the works of another. This is the heart, the forensic fulcrum, of life in the covenant. In the Covenant of Works, life is grounded upon the obedience and righteousness of man (human righteousness), whereas in the Covenant of Grace life is grounded upon the righteousness of Christ imputed to the believer through the instrumentality of faith (God-righteousness). Christ is the meritorious cause of justification; faith is the instrumental cause.[60]

The repetition of the Covenant of Works in the subsequent period of redemptive history serves a peculiarly pedagogical purpose. The giving of the law of Moses is preparatory in nature.[61] In fact, argues Rollock, "the greatest part of the OT is spent propounding, repeating, and expounding the Covenant of Works."[62] But in all of this, the law administration does not alter the substance of the Mosaic Covenant, whose proper purpose is consistent with the one and unchanging Covenant of Grace, of which the Mosaic Covenant is a particular, historical manifestation.

2. Early Seventeenth-Century English Federalism

By the seventeenth century the doctrine of the two covenants, the Covenant of Works and the Covenant of Grace, was unanimously adopted by the Reformed dogmaticians. The law-gospel distinction was vital to their theological interpretation of the history of creation and redemption. As a corollary to their fundamental biblical-theological conception of the history of revelation, the majority of Reformed theologians maintained that the characteristic feature of the Mosaic Covenant, with respect to its accidents, not substance, was to be understood in terms of a covenant of works arrangement consistent with the progressive manifestation and realization of the Covenant of Grace made with Adam after the Fall. The Reformed tradition emphasized the substantial unity and continuity of the one, eternal and unchanging Covenant of Grace in the era of redemption. The sixteenth-century federalists were unable to arrive, however, at a precise and detailed understanding of the way in which the Mosaic Covenant could be viewed as a Covenant of Works and a Covenant of Grace at the same time. All the essential and necessary ingredients for such an exposition, it should be noted, were *already* present in their thought. It required a further period of systematic and biblical-theological reflection before a more satisfying formulation of a complex issue would be reached. By and large, the Reformed theologians of the early part of the seventeenth century failed to progress beyond those formulations of the previous century. There were a few, notably among the English federalists, who contributed to a more consistent presentation of the Mosaic Covenant utilizing the traditional law-gospel contrast.[63]

During the period of the seventeenth century in England, the traditional Reformed interpretation of the Mosaic Covenant was applied to the political, socio-religious situation in new and startling ways. It is our contention that one must distinguish carefully between the theological conception of the Mosaic Covenant and biblical law on the one hand, and the *application* of the law of Moses, expressive of natural law, to the national institution on the other. The fact that the historical theologian must make such a sharp distinction between theological interpretation and application is indicative of a faulty and inconsistent perception of the essentially spiritual and ecclesiastical nature of the Covenant of Grace as the ministration of life, righteousness and blessing (2 Corinthians 3).

The English federalists taught that the Mosaic Covenant was one in substance with the New Covenant of Grace, but that the peculiar law-principle operated in a restricted sense within the Mosaic administration. The primary purpose of the law was to reveal sin and to lead Israel to salvation in Christ. This law aspect terminated with the New Covenant. On the contemporary political level, the Puritans applied the civil laws of the Israelite nation to their own situation on the basis of natural law. From the perspective of the divine establishment of natural law, they discerned a basic continuity between Israel and England, the "New Israel." The apparent confusion was bound to present problems for church-state relations. Greater theological consistency would come about in the long, protracted and agonizing period of tension and conflict during the seventeenth, eighteenth, and well into the nineteenth and twentieth centuries.

Among the leading English federalists in the beginning of the seventeenth century were James Ussher (1581-1656), William Perkins (1558-1602) and his most illustrious student, William Ames (1576-1633). The growing importance of the doctrine of the two covenants became evident by its inclusion in the *Irish Articles of 1615*, drawn up by Ussher. This confession of faith was the first to use explicitly the Covenant of Works terminology. In preparing the way for the writing of the *Westminster Confession of Faith*, the *Irish Articles* gave notable place not only to the federal idea, but also provided the basic order and structure for that of the *Westminster Confession*.[64]

It was in the context of the three major theological controversies in the early seventeenth century onwards, *viz.*, Amyraldianism, Arminianism and Antinomianism, that further reflection was given to the law of Moses. Central to the debates of Arminianism and Antinomianism was the place of law in the Christian life. One's understanding of the law of God in turn determined his conception of the doctrine of the covenants and of justification.[65] It was within this theological context that one must appreciate the Puritan emphasis upon the ethical requirements in the Covenant of Grace and upon the inseparability of justification and sanctification. Those who held Arminian tenets stood outside the Puritan (Calvinistic) tradition, while many of those who were labeled erroneously "Antinomian" by their opponents were nevertheless genuinely committed to the Puritan theology.

It is particularly this mislabeled group of Puritan "Antinomians" that we need to reevaluate in the interests of the Reformed hermeneutics of the Mosaic Covenant. The controversy between these two groups of Puritans, the majority of English divines and the so-called "Antinomians," is analogous to the Lutheran controversy between those who stressed Luther's second use of the law exclusively and those who maintained a third use of the law consistent with Luther's theology. In part, then, these debates were semantic.

E. F. Kevan reduces the entire controversy between the Puritans and the mislabeled Antinomians to the failure of the latter to perceive the gracious character of the Mosaic Covenant. He contends that these Antinomians made a "wide separation" between the two Testaments.[66] Nothing is further from the actual case of the matter. Although Kevan is correct in concluding that there was no substantial difference or fundamental incompatibility between both groups, the precise nature of the debate did not involve any denial of the Mosaic Covenant as a Covenant of Grace. It is certainly true that many of the opponents of the Antinomians did accuse them of this very thing. But in the heated debates the opponents failed to acknowledge and recognize their full teaching. The most important of those mistakenly labeled "Antinomian" was Tobias Crisp. We begin our survey of early seventeenth-century English federalism with a consideration of his thought.

Tobias Crisp

Tobias Crisp (1600-1643), more than most in his time, strove to develop in greater fullness and clarity the precise sense in which the Mosaic Covenant had to be considered as a Covenant of Works. He began by relating the obedience of Christ to the first Covenant of Works in creation by reference to the "covenant of Christ." But the two chief types of covenant in Scripture are the Covenant of Works and the Covenant of Grace. The foundation of the latter was the "delight of Christ with the sons of men."[67]

Without jeopardizing the substantial unity of the single Covenant of Grace, Crisp urged us to take sufficient account of the difference between the two Testaments. "Though Christ is the subject matter, in general, of both, and remission of sins the fruit of both yet, such a vast difference is between them, that he makes them two several covenants."[68] The Decalogue was a summary of the Covenant of Works in terms of the *characteristic* feature of the Mosaic Covenant. According to Crisp, Hebrews 7-10 contrasted the two covenants of grace, the Mosaic and the New. He interpreted this contrast to mean that "though Christ is the subject-matter of the Covenant of Grace, whether Old or New, and though there is remission of sins in both . . . yet, I say, there is such a difference between these two, that they are two distinct covenants one from the other."[69]

What is outstanding in the Mosaic Covenant, Crisp contends, is the typical-sacrificial aspect of its law administration to which Christ is the proper subject. Although Crisp's editor, John Gill, defends him against the false charge of antinomianism, Gill does not fully grasp the point that Crisp makes in distinguishing the two covenants of grace. The two covenants are not, as Gill indicates, two *essentially* different covenants. Rather, Crisp correctly desires to do justice to the principle of works in the *symbolico-typical sphere* of the Mosaic covenant administration.[70] In view of this consideration one must speak of a distinct Mosaic covenant of grace in relation to the New. As the writer to the Hebrews declares (7:11-12), the sacrifices of the Old Covenant, which were performed according to the principle of works operating in the symbolic-typical sphere, could not make atonement for sin. Atonement is accomplished only through the shed blood of

Jesus Christ, whose blood was typified in the Old Covenant sacrifices.[71] From the standpoint of the spiritual reality, *i.e.*, the core meaning (the substance or essence of the Mosaic Covenant) of the Old Covenant sacrifices, types and figures, these sacrifices are efficacious for the elect through the working of the Holy Spirit.

Similar to the Continental theologian Johannes Cloppenburg (1592-1652), although no doubt independently conceived, Crisp distinguishes between the experience of forgiveness of sins in the Old and in the New Covenants.[72] The strictness of the peculiar Covenant of Works under Moses is made appropriate to the fallen situation by sovereign, divine disposition. In this regard the Mosaic covenant of works is most unlike the original Covenant of Works at creation. The Old Covenant sacrificial system is not thorough with respect to each and every sin. Those sins left behind, notes Crisp, are removed (typically) by the yearly sacrifice on the day of atonement. The very establishment of the Mosaic Covenant is rooted in and nourished by the unbounded mercy and grace of God in Christ. The distinctive "covenant of works" aspect of the Mosaic Covenant is thus identical with the original Covenant of Works with Adam *in terms of the principle of inheritance.* In the former under Moses the reward of the covenant is earthly and temporal, whereas in the latter the reward is spiritual and eternal. The way of blessing and reward, the confirmation of life and communion with God and the consummation of man's creation in the image of God as the eschatological goal of creation is that of works. It is of law, not grace (soterically defined).

The chastening of God's people in the Old Covenant (typical punishment) is measured out in terms of the curse sanction of the Mosaic law. This is a crucial aspect of the operation of the law as a schoolmaster to Christ. With the coming of Christ at his incarnation, the full manifestation of God's redeeming grace to sinners terminates the need for the pedagogical use of the law in the history of redemption. There is no longer any need, according to divine wisdom, for temporal, physical blessings and punishments meted out by way of law administration under the Mosaic economy.

Federal theology makes significant strides in light of Crisp's theological formulation of the Covenant of Works conception and its application to the Mosaic Covenant. Crisp's insistence upon the two distinct covenants of grace, unfortunately, was all too easily misconstrued even by the majority of divines who shared his belief that the Mosaic Covenant was in some limited sense a Covenant of Works. Although Crisp has made definite progress in theological formulation, he still falls prey to ambiguity and confusion at important points in his exposition. In the argument he presents, Crisp maintains that the old Covenant of Grace must be annulled before the new can be established. But is not the one and eternal Covenant of Grace that which cannot be made void? Elsewhere Crisp has answered this question in the affirmative. Federal theology yet awaits further development before it can attain to a mature and consistent position regarding the nature of the Mosaic Covenant.

David Dickson and Samuel Bolton

David Dickson (1583?-1663) is among the first, if not the first, of the English federalists to give full expression to the so-called misinterpretation view of the Mosaic Covenant. Once the Covenant of Works established at creation is broken by disobedience, it is no longer possible for man as sinner to obtain justification by the works of the law. It is impossible to reestablish the same Covenant of Works in a fallen situation.

Regarding the Mosaic Covenant, Dickson argues in favor of the Jewish misinterpretation of the law of Moses to explain the law/gospel antithesis in the Pauline epistles. According to Dickson, the carnal Israelites perverted the law by turning it into a means of works-salvation. The reason for the repetition of the Covenant of Works under Moses is the disobedience and unbelief of the Israelites who continued to misinterpret the divine purpose for the law of God. As a punishment, God promulgated the law on Mount Sinai as a repetition of the original Covenant of Works, though hypothetical in nature ("*if* you can do this, you shall live"). For the same reason, Jesus repeated the legal demand of the Covenant of Works in his discourse with the rich young ruler.[73]

According to the traditional Reformed viewpoint, the giving of the Mosaic law is consistent with God's ultimate purpose of redemption. The works-principle is *subordinate* to that of redemptive grace, and consequently, is never covenantally instituted as a means of justification, not even hypothetically as a punishment for unbelief.[74] Dickson fails to realize that the judaistic error is the misapplication of the works-principle of inheritance in the typical, pedagogical sphere (where it *does* apply as an aspect of a divinely instituted administration) to the antitypical, spiritual sphere. Although it is evident that Dickson desires to recognize the works-feature of the Mosaic Covenant without obscuring the provisions of grace, he is left speaking of some vague formal works characteristic. Dickson's interpretation of the Mosaic Covenant shows something of the great variety of expression within the Reformed tradition. The extent of his influence upon the subsequent theologians is difficult to ascertain.

Samuel Bolton (1606-1654) was numbered among the conveners of the Westminster Assembly. His treatise, *The True Bounds of Christian Freedom*, was directed primarily against the Antinomians. Concerning the nature and extent of Christian freedom, Bolton maintained that the believer was freed from the moral law as a covenant "as that from which life might be expected on the condition that due obedience was rendered."[75] Through the vicarious, sacrificial work of Christ's reconciliation and atonement, in which Christ as covenant head and representative rendered full and perfect obedience to the righteous law of God, he terminated the law as a curse, so that man is no longer under a Covenant of Works. In his exegesis of Col 2:14 Bolton maintained that the whole law, including the moral law, was abolished with respect to the curse (justification). The law no longer condemned one who was united to Christ in his death and resurrection. According to Gal 3:17, the Mosaic law was given to Israel not as a Covenant of Works, but as a rule 430 years after the promise to Abraham. The law was not given as a means of justification, otherwise the law would make void the promise of God and prove God unfaithful to his word. "Our proposition is that there was no end or use for which the law was given which was incompatible with grace and which was not serviceable to the advancement of the Covenant of Grace."[76]

Bolton presents the various interpretations of the Mosaic Covenant and then offers his own analysis of the biblical material. The main interpretations of the Mosaic Covenant are three in number: (1) as a Covenant of Works, (2) as a subservient covenant preparing for the advancement of the Covenant of Grace with the coming of Christ, and (3) as a Covenant of Grace more legally dispensed.[77] Bolton contends, however, that there are only two distinct covenants in Scripture, not three. He expresses dissatisfaction with the idea of a third, subservient covenant *(foedus subserviens),* despite the appearance of the Mosaic Covenant as a repetition of the Covenant of Works. There are numerous reasons why it cannot be a legal covenant. On the basis of Jer 31-33, we learn that God is Israel's husband, and that the covenant is established for the manifestation and realization of God's purpose of salvation. There is no mercy in a Covenant of Works, and such a covenant would void God's promise to Abraham. A covenant of works under Moses would indicate mutability in the will of God, or else contradiction in his acts. God does not offer life and justification by means of the law, otherwise the Israelites would have been saved under different circumstances and conditions than in the New Covenant (Gal 3:18ff.). Thus, even the suggestion of a hypothetical covenant of works is wholly unacceptable (Gal 3:21). Because of the sinner's depravity, it would be contrary to the nature of a covenant to enter into such a solemn vow whereby one of the parties could not fulfill his part of the engagement.[78] The true nature of a covenant is that it is between friends. Finally, the Covenant of Works is not capable of renewal once it is broken, whereas the covenant between God and Israel is renewed time and again. The idea of the subservient Covenant of Works separate from the ongoing revelation of the single Covenant of Grace does not satisfy these objections.

Positively, Bolton distinguishes within the Covenant of Grace the *typical,* subservient covenant under Moses. That is to say, the law-feature of the Mosaic Covenant has relevance only to the unique *typical covenant* which is of temporary duration. Bolton's conception of the subservient, typical covenant is unlike the idea of a subservient Covenant of Works (hypothetical), which fails to understand the proper manner in which the administrative principle of works-inheritance operates in the Mosaic economy. The law principle, according to Bolton, has respect to Canaan and other physical and temporal blessings which are granted when and as Israel is faithful and obedient to the law of Moses (the principle of works). Bolton recognizes that his viewpoint is in the minority. He concedes that the majority of divines adopt the view of the two covenants, the original Covenant of Works and the subsequent Covenant of Grace, with the Mosaic Covenant considered to be more legally dispensed. The law-feature, in the majority view, is a bare *principle,* rather than an actual *covenant* administration. Bolton regards the subservient, typical covenant as an integral aspect of the Mosaic administration of the Covenant of Grace. (There is no inner connection in his thought, however, between the subservient aspect as typical and the grace aspect as antitypical.)

Bolton interprets the (normative) role of the law in the Mosaic Covenant as consistent with the Covenant of Grace, not the subservient covenant (works). Therefore, Lev 18:5 does not mean that we "shall live by them," but rather we "shall live in them." Bolton remarks: "We live in obedience, but we do not live by obedience. There is much difference between the two statements."[79] Primarily, Bolton refutes the opinion that Lev 18:5 as interpreted by Paul teaches a conditional works-*salvation*, hypothetical or not, under the Mosaic Covenant. As a result, Bolton's exposition combines elements of both the traditional view and the so-called misinterpretation view of the Mosaic Covenant, though his overall position lies closer to the former.

Edward Fisher and John Ball

Edward Fisher (1627-1655) and John Ball (1585-1640) authored two separate, but highly important treatises published in London in the same year, 1645, two years prior to the convening of the Westminster Assembly. Neither were members, however, of that august body. (Ball died several years previous.) Most interestingly, they were representative of two distinct Reformed interpretations of the Mosaic Covenant.

Although Fisher's *The Marrow of Modern Divinity* did not attract much attention when it first appeared, it was particularly important in the Marrow controversy in Scotland in the latter half of the seventeenth century. The heart of this controversy was not the nature of the Mosaic law *per se*, but rather the place and use of the law in preaching, *i.e.*, the second or elenctic use of the law in convicting the sinner of his guiltiness before God and his need for the grace of Christ. The immediate context for this controversy was the understanding of the doctrine of justification by faith alone. John Macleod describes here the rise of a reactionary Catholicizing movement which

> . . . sought to make the faith that justifies a kind of *fides formata*, a thing so elastic as to find within its ambit room for repentance and the good works of the penitent. Then this extended faith was made out to be not the mere instrument of effecting union with Christ, but a strict condition, the fulfillment of which is called for that one may win acceptance before God by obedience to the law of faith set forth in the Gospel as a new law. Thus the righteousness of God which is by faith in Christ was set aside as the ground of our acceptance; and our new life as believers and penitents was looked upon as so much of the ground on which our acceptance is built.[80]

Although the members of this movement often guarded themselves against the charge of making good works meritorious or the ground of justification by pointing to the righteousness of Christ, they denied or obscured the distinctive role of faith in the article of justification. Fisher's treatise served as an eloquent defense of the Reformed orthodox position.

The concept of works is critical to a biblical understanding of justification by faith and of the function of the Mosaic law instructing God's people in the way of justification by faith. The first part of the work is a thorough and comprehensive treatment of the two covenants, works and grace, and the second part is an exposition of the Ten Commandments. Included among the extended list of names of theologians to whom Fisher is indebted are Ball, Bolton, Bullinger, Calvin, Luther, Perkins, Rollock, Tyndale and Ursinus.

Fisher carefully distinguishes between the principle of works in the Mosaic law and the nature of the covenant more broadly conceived. The law can be considered in its normative use or in its formal, covenantal establishment.[81] Though the Covenant of Works once broken cannot be renewed, it is still binding upon all men, and for this reason all men are under the curse of the law.

The Ten Commandments delivered to Israel through Moses summarizes the Covenant of Works. Yet, as Fisher stresses, the giving of the law did not consist in a repetition of the *original* Covenant of Works.[82] The law is not a substitute for the way of grace, although according to Gal 3:19, it was *added* because of transgressions. "It was not set up as a solid rule of righteousness, as it was given to Adam in paradise, but was added or put to; it was not set up as a thing in gross by itself."[83] The Covenant of Works under Moses is not added by way of "ingrediency" as part of the Covenant of Grace "for then the same covenant should have consisted of contradictory materials," but rather "by way of *subserviency* and *attendance,* the better to advance and make effectual the Covenant of Grace."[84]

From this perspective of the subserviency of the Mosaic Covenant, believers and unbelievers are under the Covenant of Works, under the dual sanctions of blessing and curse which are brought to bear on the basis of their obedience to the law of God, rather than on the basis of the substitutionary work of Christ (grace). So it is, for example, that Moses and Aaron are not permitted entrance into the land of Canaan, the promised inheritance, because of their unbelief and disobedience. Both the blessings of this life and the calamities come upon God's people on the grounds of their obedience or disobedience respectively.[85]

The Pharisees sought to attain the spiritual, antitypical blessings by means of their own works, and reduced the internal, heart aspect of obedience to mere external, mechanical observance of the law. With respect to the former, the Pharisees did not consider that "the imperfection of the typical law, which, as the apostle says, made nothing perfect, would have led them to find perfection in Christ, Heb 7:19." According to Rom 9:31, 10:3, Ex 34:30 and 2 Cor 3:7ff., the Judaizers did not use the law "as a pedagogy to Christ, but terminated their eye in the letter and shadow, and did not see through them to the spiritual substance, which is Jesus Christ."[86]

The fullest treatment of English covenant theology appears in John Ball's *A Treatise of the Covenant of Grace*, which Holmes Rolston speaks of as a "variant form" of covenant theology. The reason for and the accuracy of this description will become clear in the course of our discussion. The law of God serves as the same rule for life in both the Covenant of Works (creation) and the Covenant of Grace (redemption), although it differs in the *manner or way of inheritance* (law or grace). While both divine covenants are freely established by God in his goodness and grace (nonsoteric), yet the supreme manifestation of his (soteric) grace and mercy toward sinners is unique to the redemptive arrangement, the so-called Covenant of Grace. When Ball addresses himself to the way of entrance into the Covenant of Grace, he reaffirms the traditional teaching on "justification by faith alone," a metonymy for justification by the sole merit of Jesus Christ. The righteousness of Christ, the meritorious ground of justification, is apprehended by faith, and thus in this respect, faith is the alone instrumental cause of justification. The efficacy of the Covenant of Grace is restricted to the elect, whereas the administration of the covenant is of wider scope.[87]

The difference between the Old and the New Covenants is primarily one of promise and fulfillment. The substance of the Covenant of Grace, pertaining to the elect, remains the same. There is one church throughout both Testaments. The meaning of Israel under tutors and governors is to be understood in the sense of preparation, rather than bondage under a law administration as such. According to Ball, the difference is more one of degree or intensity. His view stands in opposition to the interpretation of the Mosaic Covenant entertained by the majority of Reformed federalists, in which the pedagogical, tutelary function of the law as a principle of works-inheritance is related in some way to the symbolic-typical sphere of Old Covenant administration.[88] Rather, in Ball's view, the temporal blessings which accompanied the spiritual benefits under the Covenant of Grace are merely greater in proportion to the spiritual, whereas the reverse is the case in the New Covenant.[89]

The purpose of the covenant with Moses is to manifest the superabounding grace and mercy of God to his elect people, Israel. By means of the law of Moses, the people of Israel are covenantally instituted as a nation. It marks the inauguration of the "state Covenant," also called the Old Covenant because it was to pass away.[90] In his exegesis of 2 Corinthians 3 and Galatians 3, Ball restricts the letter-law aspect to the moral law appropriate to the Covenant of Nature (the law of nature) "as it has necessarily affixed eternal life to the punctual performance, or eternal curse to the disobeyers in the least title."[91] The apostle's use of "law," consequently, refers to the law of nature (a bare principle), specifically the principle of works which is *separate* from a covenant order. In Ball's understanding, to speak of this bare "law" as a covenant would mean that the Mosaic Covenant taught justification by works. He does insist, however, upon recognizing the law element in the Mosaic Covenant.[92] The Old Covenant ministration of death and condemnation is interpreted by Ball not in terms of the typical punishments for Israel's disobedience, but in terms of the Judaizers' misapplication of the law.

According to Ball, the words of Lev 18:5, "do this and live," when *abstracted* from the covenant context denote the biblical idea of law as the principle of works. However, he contends that in its proper covenantal setting, what he believes to be the correct intent of Leviticus 18, the law is consistent with grace, not antithetical.[93] The doers of the law are justified (Rom 2:13), though he explains that faith alone justifies for "good works are opposed to faith in the matter of justification."[94] The Mosaic Covenant is wholly devoid of any administrative element of works-merit.[95] Later, however, Ball concedes to the idea of a conditional element in the Old Covenant, *e.g.*, when God judges the house of David because of disobedience. The conditional element indicates blessing or judgment on the ground of man's own obedience, contrasting with the surety of grace in Christ. "Nevertheless, the promise of God was firm and sure to all the seed, in respect of the things absolutely promised, for the infidelity of man cannot make the faith of God of none effect."[96]

Quite clearly, Reformed theology is in need of clarification here. With good reason Daniel Fuller has remarked: "It is extremely difficult to grasp covenant theology's explanations of how a line of thought, which has the structure of the Covenant of Works, nevertheless functions as part of the Covenant of Grace."[97]

The Westminster Standards

The most definitive creedal statement to come out of the period of the Reformation is the *Westminster Confession of Faith,* along with the *Larger* and *Shorter Catechisms.* Since this *Confession* is unsurpassed both in its definition and comprehensiveness, and continues to be the creedal standard for a great many within the Reformed orthodox church today, it serves as an appropriate point of termination for our present historical survey. In light of the diversity of expression with respect to Reformed interpretations of the Mosaic Covenant and the concept of the Covenant of Works, what consensus were the Westminster divines able to attain? Do the Standards attempt to define a narrow position or permit diversity of thought within the limits of the Reformed system of doctrine?

The federal structure of the *Confession* is by no means idiosyncratic, but rather is reflective of Reformed catholic doctrine in its deepest and most characteristic insight into biblical truth. Indeed, it is the architectonic principle of the *Westminster Confession.*[98]

After the chapters on the decrees of God, creation, providence and man's fall into sin, the *Confession* defines the concept of covenant:

> The distance between God and the creature is so great, that although reasonable creatures do owe obedience unto him as their Creator, yet they could never have any fruition of him as their blessedness and reward, but by some voluntary condescension on God's part, which he hath been pleased to express by way of covenant (7.1).

The natural relationship between God and man is one of law: "reasonable creatures do owe obedience unto him as their Creator."[99] Repeatedly, the *Confession* ties together the first covenant and the principle of works-inheritance (6.6; 7.2; 8.4,5; 11.3; 19.1,6; *cf.*, especially the *Larger Catechism*, Q. A. 20, 38, 70, 71, and 93). The original covenant between God and man is the Covenant of Works, whose principle of inheritance is antithetical to that in the Covenant of Grace.[100] This fundamental doctrine in the Standards is vital to the exposition of justification by faith and the atonement of Christ. Peter DeJong remarks:

> There is by no means an antithesis between the covenant and the forensic representations of man's relationship to God. It is true that in Zurich, where the covenant idea first came up, the legal aspect of Christ's work was not as clearly seen and concisely formulated as in the more strictly Calvinistic confessions. However, the covenant idea easily embraced the forensic representation and was thus itself enriched. It did precisely this in the Westminster symbols, which have been quite

> generally regarded as the most complete and mature development of Reformed theology in creedal form.[101]

The Westminster Standards reaffirm its commitment to the traditional Reformed understanding of the similarities and differences between the Old (Mosaic) Covenant and the New Covenant. The *Confession* concludes with the statement: "There are not therefore two covenants of grace, differing in substance, but one and the same, under various dispensations" (7.6: *cf.*, *Larger Catechism* Q. A. 33-35). The Confession stresses that the purpose of the law of Moses is as a rule of life and righteousness (19.2). It has been commonplace in Reformed theology from the beginning to speak of the law as a "rule" for life both in creation and redemption. This is different from the use of the law with respect to the principle of inheritance in which there is an antithesis between law and grace and an abrogation of the law with respect to soteric justification. But the law of Moses also contained "several typical ordinances," as part of the ceremonial laws which have all been terminated by Christ (19.3). The civil or judicial laws have likewise expired, except as they can be applied now to civil legislation according to the principle of "general equity" (19.4). The civil laws no longer carry any typological meaning as they did in the Old Covenant. With respect to the typological picture, these civil laws of Moses signify the eternal, antitypical state of consummation glory. The *Westminster Confession* has left the door open to a diverse range of interpretation in giving detailed expression to the law-character of the Mosaic Covenant of Grace. Kevan correctly observes: "All the Puritans were agreed, that, into whatever category the Mosaic law had to be put, it was not given by God as a means of justification."[102]

3. Recent Covenant Hermeneutics

In this third part we direct our attention to the leading biblical and systematic theologies of those in the orthodox Reformed tradition of the nineteenth and twentieth centuries who contend for the historical trustworthiness of the Book of Genesis, essential to the very integrity of federalism. We highlight the more influential American Presbyterian and American-Dutch Reformed theologians. It is mainly to the credit of the Dutch Reformed theologians that federalism has continued to survive as a dynamic and vital expression of the Reformed faith. Our purpose is to explore the recent understanding of the concept of the Covenant of Works and its relation to the Mosaic Covenant as a further development in the history of federalism. By way of conclusion, we offer a brief biblical-theological exposition of the Mosaic Covenant.

Robert Dabney

Robert Dabney (1820-1898) adopts the popular misinterpretation view in his exegesis of the relevant NT passages which cite the law-principle in Lev 18:5. The Jews misapply the law of Moses by attempting to obtain justification by the works of the law, and, consequently, the Mosaic Covenant of Grace becomes a ministration of condemnation and death. "In dealing with this subject theologians perpetually forget how necessarily the apostles had to use the *argumentum ad hominem* against the Jews."[103] Dabney opposes the idea that the Mosaic Covenant is a species of the Covenant of Works, because such a recession counters the progressive nature of biblical revelation and redemption.

The problem is that Dabney can only conceive of the Covenant of Works functioning as a complete entity, *i.e.*, both in the typical *and* the antitypical spheres at the same time. From such a conception of the Mosaic Covenant, Dabney rightly detects a serious misunderstanding of redemptive revelation. According to Dabney, this is the similar opinion of Cameron and Amyraut back in the seventeenth century. This conviction led the Amyraldians to conclude that the Mosaic Covenant as a Covenant of Works had to apply, therefore, to the temporal, earthly sphere exclusively. In this manner, they avoided the erroneous conception of a hypothetical covenant of works-salvation. Dabney speaks of the Amyraldian's "ingenious modification of the legal theory of Moses' covenant." He comments:

> This is true, so far as a visible church-standing turned on a ritual obedience. But to the Hebrew, that temporal life in happy Canaan was a type of heaven, which was not promised to an exact moral obedience, but to faith. Were this theory modified, so as to represent this dependence of the Hebrew's church-standing on his ritual obedience, as a mere type and emblem of the law's spiritual work as a 'schoolmaster to lead us to Christ,' it might stand.[104]

Dabney's own view of the Mosaic Covenant, however, cannot consistently accommodate the legal element, which, in fact, he is willing to grant in the above citation. He concedes further:

> The legal conditions of outward good-standing were made more burdensome and exacting than they had been before. This last feature was not a novelty (see Gen 17:14), but it was made more stringent. . . . For this stringency was designed to be, to the Israelite, a perpetual reminder of the law which was to Adam the condition of life, now broken, and its wrath already incurred, thus to hedge up the awakened conscience to Christ.[105]

According to Dabney, however, all of this legal typology rests upon the misinterpretation of the law of Moses. To the spiritual Hebrew the temporal life in Canaan is promised to faith, not works. By name Dabney opposes the teachings of Calvin, Turretin and the Cocceian school regarding "the bondage, terror, literalness, and intolerable weight of the institutions under which OT saints lived," noting that such "will strike the attentive reader as incorrect."[106] Dabney stresses that the key is recognizing the use of the *argumentum ad hominem*: that is to say, the apostles "are speaking of the Mosaic institutions under the Jewish view of them."[107] The mistake of Dabney is that he is confused on the nature of the visible church in the Old Covenant, isolating it from the core, spiritual house of Israel, the invisible church. The necessary avoidance of defining the invisible aspect of the church in the New Covenant in abstraction from the visible aspect applies equally to the definition of the church in the Old Covenant as well. Dabney erroneously criticizes Calvin for distorting the sense of Galatians 4 when he refers the time of bondage to the Mosaic dispensation.

> As to the visible church collectively, and its outward or ecclesiastical privilege, this was true; but not as to individual believers in the church. . . . The time of tutelage was, to each soul, the time of his self-righteous, unbelieving, convicted, but unhumbled struggles. The time of the liberty is when he has flown to Christ. This, whether he was Israelite or Christian.[108]

Dabney's interpretation of the Mosaic Covenant as a pure Covenant of Grace is exegetically and theologically inadequate. He is driven to interpret the law-feature of the Mosaic Covenant psychologically, rather than redemptive-historically.

Charles and A. A. Hodge

Charles Hodge (1797-1878) teaches that the Mosaic Covenant is evangelical (that is to say, a Covenant of Grace), yet with the addition of the legal element, making it at the same time a legal covenant (a Covenant of Works). This law-feature is evident in the promise of national security and prosperity for Israel in the land of Canaan, and in the renewed proclamation of the works-principle (hypothetical), as found in the New Covenant as well (*e.g.*, Rom 2:6 and Lk 10:25ff.).[109]

Charles' son, Alexander Hodge (1823-1886), discusses the covenant idea at greater length and reveals a deep insight into and penetration of the role of the Covenant of Works in the history of creation and redemption. He maintains that the Covenant of Works is consistent with man's natural state. The covenant of creation is legal, conditioned upon man's "perfect conformity to the law of absolute moral perfection."[110] Its demands devolve upon man's own being and acting.

The period between the Fall and the Consummation manifests the progressive, ongoing administration of the one and eternal Covenant of Grace. By regeneration and renewal in sanctification, the Spirit of Christ brings to realization the spiritual kingdom of Christ, a kingdom of priests and kings forever. The Mosaic Covenant serves a peculiar and pedagogical role in the administration of the Covenant of Grace. The "legal element" was added because of transgressions. The reference of the symbolic-typical element of the Mosaic Covenant is to Christ. Although the mode of administration differs, the substance of the covenant remains the same. The principle of works-inheritance, which functions according to divine intent and purpose in the typical sphere under Moses' covenantal mediation, is the basis for all national blessings proffered to the Israelites. At the same time Hodge says of the Mosaic signs and symbols: "in the symbolical and typical significance of all the Mosaic institutions, they were a clearer and fuller revelation of the provisions of the Covenant of Grace than had ever before been made."[111]

Abraham Kuyper and Herman Bavinck

According to Abraham Kuyper (1837-1920), the Mosaic Covenant is unique and distinct from the original Covenant of Works. The law of Sinai belongs to the Covenant of Grace, although it is given in the *form* of the Covenant of Works, whereby the law affirms that the doer of these things shall live in them. The peculiar feature of the law under the Mosaic economy lies in its double purpose. On the one hand, it operates uniquely with regard to the dramatic-symbolic life of Israel. This is the meaning of the OT typological system. Canaan typifies the heavenly inheritance, Jordan the entrance into that eternal rest. On the other hand, the law functions in a wholly different, antithetical manner in terms of the enjoyment of the spiritual, antitypical blessings of redemption in Christ, which belongs to the elect of God.[112]

The reward of eternal life is not a matter of works-obedience, but rather of the saving grace and mercy of God towards sinners.[113] The biblical concept of merit is opposed to the idea of intrinsic worth (*cf.* the Thomistic nature-grace dualism). After the Fall, the Covenant of Works (merit) is not abolished, but rather it is modified. Because of the consequences of sin, man is incapable of keeping the law of God. Yet, the law forever remains the rule or norm for life. The righteousness of Christ is the ground of salvation.

Principally in light of 1 Cor 15:45-49 and Rom 5:12-21, Herman Bavinck (1854-1921) highlights the integral connection between the covenant established with Adam in creation and the eschatological goal of creation.[114] The meaning of Adam as type of Christ is to be understood in terms of this eschatological perspective. The type refers explicitly to the reality of the covenant representation of the two Adams. This type differs from the pattern of typology associated with the Mosaic Covenant, although the two are related in certain respects. In point of fact, the system of typology under the OT is valid *only* because of the prior pattern and parallel between the First and Second Adams. The meaning of the OT typology cannot be understood apart from the operation of the works principle, particularly as that comes to expression in the Mosaic Covenant. To deny the legitimate and necessary operation of the principle of works in the Mosaic economy, by conceiving of it as a pure administration of grace and promise is to destroy in principle the system of OT typology. The genius of the Reformed theological system finds fullest expression in the awareness of the essentially eschatological nature of God's creative work.

The "positive purpose" in the giving of the law under Moses is to point to another righteousness, *viz.*, the righteousness of Christ. Referring to the works-principle in the symbolic-typical sphere of the Mosaic Covenant, Bavinck exclaims: "When we take this vantage point of the apostle Paul, we get a delightfully illuminating view of the revelation of God in the OT, of the religion of Israel, of the significance of the law, of history and prophecy, of the psalms and the wisdom books."[115] Sound biblical hermeneutics requires the recognition of and proper use of the law-gospel distinction in handling the relation between Old and New Testaments exegetically and theologically.

Louis Berkhof, Geerhardus Vos and Meredith G. Kline

Louis Berkhof (1873-19S7) and Geerhardus Vos (1862-1949) were important links between Dutch and American Calvinism. Berkhof upholds the dominant Reformed view of the Mosaic Covenant, which sees it as a Covenant of Works in some restricted sense.

> The Sinaitic covenant included a service that contained a positive reminder of the strict demands of the Covenant of Works. The law was placed very much in the foreground, giving prominence once more to the earlier legal element. But the covenant of Sinai was not a renewal of the Covenant of Works; in it the law was made subservient to the Covenant of Grace. . . . It is true that at Sinai a conditional element was added to the covenant, but it was not the salvation of the Israelite but his theocratic standing in the nation, and the enjoyment of external blessings that was made dependent on the keeping of the law, Deut 28:1-14.[116]

Vos recognizes this same legal element as operative in the symbolic-typical sphere of Israel's covenant life.[117] This idea remains in large measure undeveloped in Vos' thought. Essentially this legal feature is construed as a bare principle, rather than as a covenant arrangement.

In the present day, no one has addressed himself more to this issue of the operation of the principles of law and grace under the Mosaic Covenant than Meredith Kline (born 1922). His chief works which take up this matter are *Treaty of the Great King* and *By Oath Consigned,* the former a commentary on Deuteronomy and the latter a theological study on the signs and seals of the Covenant of Grace.[118] Both of these works reveal Kline's exegetical and theological acumen. Commenting on the typical system of the Mosaic economy, Kline remarks:

> Israel's continued enjoyment of a habitation in God's land, like Adam's continued enjoyment of the original paradise, depended on continued fidelity to the Lord. Certain important distinctions are necessary in making such a comparison. Flawless obedience was the condition of Adam's continuance in the Garden; but Israel's tenure in Canaan was contingent on the maintenance of a measure of religious loyalty which needed not to be comprehensive of all Israel nor to he perfect even in those who were the true Israel. There was a freedom in God's exercise or restraint of judgment, a freedom originating in the underlying principle of sovereign grace in his rule over Israel. Nevertheless, God did so dispense his judgment that the interests of the typical-symbolical message of Israel's history were preserved.[119]

John Murray

In a concise, encyclopedic article John Murray (1898-1975) surveys the historical development of covenant theology and indicates his reservations concerning the notion of "works" in connection with the exposition not only of the

Mosaic Covenant, but of the covenant concept itself. He objects to the notion of a "Covenant of Works," since the combination of "covenant" and "works" involves, from his point of view, a contradiction in terms. His purpose in this article is to convince us of the need for a revised definition of the covenant idea. But it is his article entitled "The Adamic Administration" in his *Collected Writings,* which provides us with a more detailed exposition of his revision of the biblical concept of the covenant. Murray describes the first state of man created in the image of God as one of "perfect legal reciprocity," a state which is by nature contingent and lacking the full-orbed communion with God. As a creature, man's duty is to obey God; this comprises his natural relationship to the Creator. The second stage of God's providential ordering of the life of man is properly called the Adamic administration. Although Murray's preference is to restrict the term "covenant" to the provisions of redemption, he is not wholly adverse to speak of the second stage, the Adamic administration, as a covenant.[120] However, Murray insists, it is most objectionable to call it a Covenant of Works. The concept of works in this arrangement does not do justice to the "elements of grace entering into the administration."[121]

A second reason for Murray's reservation in speaking of an original covenant arrangement with Adam is that Scripture does not identify this creation order as a covenant. Thus, it is preferable to employ the covenant terminology in relation to the provisions of redemption. The gracious character of the creation covenant, or rather the Adamic administration, is nonsoteric. Consequently, "Whether or not the administration is designated covenant, the uniqueness and singularity must be recognized."[122] It applies only to the state of innocence, and to Adam alone as representative head. At this point in his exposition Murray avoids the parallel with the Second Adam. In fact, nowhere in Murray's writings does he consider the work of Christ explicitly in terms of the original covenant. Apparently for the first time in Reformed theology, the kingdom of Christ is divorced from the covenant concept in the federal system. Murray will speak of Christ redeeming us from the law in the sense of the law of works, the principle of strict justice.[123] But he does not relate Christ's atonement to a works-covenant arrangement, simply because in his view there is no such thing as a Covenant of Works in Scripture. The blessing of confirmation which Adam hoped for and believers now experience in principle is incompatible with a Covenant of Works arrangement.

For Murray, "covenant" and "works" are *antithetical* concepts, a novel proposal in the history of federalism. Murray writes:

> The view that in the Mosaic covenant there was a repetition of the so-called Covenant of Works, current among covenant theologians, is a grave misconception and involves an erroneous construction of the Mosaic Covenant, as well as fails to assess the uniqueness of the Adamic administration. The Mosaic Covenant was distinctly redemptive in character and was continuous with and extensive of the Abrahamic Covenants.[124]

Murray fails to note that on the point pertaining to the Mosaic Covenant as "distinctly redemptive in character" and "continuous with and extensive of the

Abrahamic Covenants" *all* of the Reformed federalists were agreed: the substance of the Covenant of Grace (which includes the Mosaic Covenant) remained the same. Differences arise, however, in their explanation of the peculiar law-function in the Mosaic economy.

The condition of the special Adamic administration is obedience. The tree of the knowledge of good and evil points to the dual sanctions of the covenant, the blessing for obedience and the curse for disobedience. Murray is concerned to stress the gracious nature of the Adamic Covenant, in order to guard against the idea that the reward of blessing and confirmation is bestowed on the ground of man's obedience, while agreeing that perfect and complete obedience is essential. Whereas the principle of works, "perfect legal reciprocity," comes to bear in the order of creation, the first state of man as made in the image of God, the principle of (nonsoteric) grace informs the entire, subsequent covenant arrangement in such a decisive manner that the concept of works is wholly irrelevant and misleading as a description of the covenant order. Although the principle of works is always binding by virtue of man's creaturely status, the concept of the covenant cannot be considered in legal terms. If the creation covenant is devoid of the works-element, how much more so then are the redemptive covenants, particularly the Mosaic, devoid of any works-element.[125] In his commentary on Rom 10:5-8, Murray remarks:

> The difficulty with the first [Lev 18:5] is that in the original setting it does not appear to have any reference to legal righteousness as opposed to that of grace. Suffice it to say now that the formal statement Paul appropriates as one suited to express the principle of law-righteousness. It cannot he doubted but the proposition, "The man that doeth the righteousness of the law shall live thereby," is, of itself, an adequate and watertight definition of the principle of legalism.[126]

Consequently, the apostle Paul *abstracts* the principle enunciated in Lev 18:5 out of the context of grace. Murray does not address the ensuing problem that in the event that the apostle is not representing the proper intent of the law-principle in his OT citation, what does this say about the Reformation hermeneutic of the analogy of Scripture, that Scripture interprets Scripture?

Although Murray does not reject the law-gospel distinction entirely, such a distinction has no relevance to the history of covenant administration, covering the periods of creation and redemption. This recognition that the law-principle does characterize the state of nature, man's natural relationship with God (however unfortunate though this dualistic conception is), safeguards his formulation of the doctrine of justification by faith and the doctrine of the atonement of Christ. Whereas Murray attempts to avoid the concept of works in the conception of the Covenant of Creation, he insists that it be recognized in the natural state. As a result, Murray's theological system is essentially compatible with the Westminster Standards, even though his repudiation of the works-principle in the Covenant of Creation sets off his thought from that of all previous federal theologians. Nevertheless, his theology is seriously deficient with respect to the operation of the principles of law and grace under the Mosaic Covenant, and the fundamental contrast between the order of creation (law) and the order of redemption (grace). His conception of the covenant *per se* is thoroughly noneschatological. Failure to relate the works-principle to the First and Second Adams in their *covenantal* capacities as representative heads obscures the meritorious nature of Christ's saving work in realizing the kingdom of God in the present semi-eschatological age of the Spirit.[127]

In order to develop consistently his idea of the uniqueness of the Adamic administration, Murray maintains the peculiar nature of Christ's obedience to the law of God. "The obedience Christ rendered fulfilled the obedience in which Adam failed. It would not he correct to say, however, that Christ's obedience was the same in content or demand. Christ was called on to obey *in radically different conditions,* and required to fulfill *radically different demands.*"[128] Apparently, Murray allows this partial truth to obscure the covenantal parallel between Adam and Christ. The radically different conditions and demands are discerned in the distinctly *redemptive* mission of Christ to save his people from their sins through his death upon the cross. Where the First Adam failed as a covenant breaker, the Second Adam succeeded in perfectly fulfilling the demands of the covenant by his active and passive obedience. The penal aspect of Christ's atonement is meaningless apart from the curse sanction of the creation covenant. The representative principle is crucial.

It is now clear what Murray had in mind by way of a revision of the biblical concept of the covenant.[129] While there is a marked degree of consistency in his systematic reflection on covenant and justification, it is most fortunate that his commitment to the theology of the Westminster Standards as expressive of Reformed orthodoxy restrained him from reinterpreting the vital doctrine of Christ's atonement and justification by faith. Yet those who adopt Murray's conception of the original covenant with Adam as a Covenant of Grace and at the same time deny the validity of the law-gospel distinction inevitably must radically redefine the Reformation doctrine of saving grace in the interest of systematic and biblical theology, as urged by such men as Holmes Rolston and Daniel Fuller.[130]

4. Conclusion: The Mosaic Covenant and the Concept of Works

The traditional distinction between law and gospel plays a crucial role in the Reformed exposition of justification by faith and the characteristic differences between the Old and New Covenants. The purpose of the giving of the law of Moses is to instruct Israel in the way of justification by faith. The majority of covenant theologians have attempted to do greater justice to the biblical teaching on the works-feature of the Mosaic Covenant. The popular misinterpretation view of the Mosaic law covenant finds its first full exposition in English federalism. The Westminster Standards sought to accommodate both viewpoints. Our study, however, has pointed out several problems with respect to this misinterpretation view which indicate failure to interpret adequately all of the relevant biblical texts and to present a consistent biblical-systematic theology of the covenant.

The critical supposition that there are essentially two different types of covenant theology in both Continental and English federalism is unfounded. The common root of all their criticisms, despite differences in argument and presupposition, is the rejection of the law-gospel contrast, which these critics regard as speculative, rather than biblical, in origin. The central focus in these discussions is the interpretation of the Mosaic Covenant.

Once we recognize and appreciate the full integrity of the biblical doctrine of the Covenant of Works as that which characterizes the first relationship between the Creator and the creature, we are prepared to consider the teaching of Scripture on the Mosaic Covenant as manifesting in some sense the features of the first Covenant of Works. Since the Fall and the establishment of the Covenant of Redemption (Grace) with Adam, the original Covenant of Creation is made of no effect, in that Christ is the exclusive meritorious ground of justification and life. Outside of Christ, all stand guilty before God on account of original sin and inherited depravity. They are all covenant-breakers. The covenant whose principle of life-inheritance is that of works can never be reinstituted. The operation of the works-principle, then, in the Mosaic Covenant cannot be interpreted so as to constitute the covenant under Moses as a Covenant of Works. Otherwise, the law which came four hundred and thirty years after Abraham would annul the promise of grace (Galatians 3). There is essential unity in the ongoing revelation of the Covenant of Redemption. The principle of works-inheritance as an administrative element in the Mosaic Covenant is limited to the sphere of the symbolic-typical. Since the spiritual benefits of redemption in the Mosaic Covenant are purely a matter of sovereign, saving grace, the pedagogical function of the law of Moses is typical. The earthly, physical blessings point to the antitypical reality. The operation of the works-law-principle, antithetical to the faith-grace-principle, in the Mosaic Covenant applies to a restricted, though characteristic, pedagogical sphere of covenant life. At all times this works-principle plays a subservient role in God's ultimate purposes of salvation for his people Israel.

The operation of this principle of works does not militate against the Reformed teaching that good works and faith are inseparable realities for the elect of God. As all of the theologians within the Reformed tradition maintain, saving faith is a working faith (James 2). Nevertheless, under the Mosaic Covenant works are judged in the sphere of typology (typical inheritance) apart from the substitutionary work of Christ (the principle of grace). The guaranteed, antitypical blessings for the elect rest exclusively upon the meritorious work of Christ. The exile of the people of God to Babylon (having *typical* significance) is possible only on the basis of the covenant lawsuit of Yahweh against his people, not on the basis of the grace of God in Christ in whom the covenanted inheritance is secure and indefectible. The Old Covenant prophets' call to repentance and obedience is not a call to Pharisaical self-righteousness, but rather to covenant faithfulness.[131] In terms of the substance of the Mosaic Covenant, the calling out of God's elect nation under the mediator, Moses, bespeaks grace and blessing of the highest order. The way of the covenant is the way of obedience, regardless of the fact that such obedience, in specific instances appropriate to the symbolic-typical picture in the old economy, is the ground of temporal judgment (blessing or curse). The pedagogical function of the law of Moses is directly associated with the principle of works-inheritance.

The error of the Judaizers was that they reduced the Mosaic Covenant to a religion of works-righteousness. They applied the works-merit principle in the pedagogical-typical sphere, where it did apply, to the spiritual-antitypical sphere, where it did not apply (Rom 9:32). That is to say, this legal principle which was operative in the Mosaic Covenant did not function in isolation from its broader redemptive context. Rather than reducing the Mosaic Covenant to a religion of works-righteousness, which was the fatal mistake of the Judaizers, who knew not the grace of God, we must recognize instead the restricted operation of the works-principle within the total covenant administration which Moses mediated, as enunciated in Lev 18:5 and affirmed by the apostle Paul.

In accordance with sound biblical exegesis, we must not reduce the Mosaic Covenant to a covenant of "pure grace," with no element of works in its administration. The two opposing principles of law and grace, therefore, were administratively compatible (Galatians 3 and Romans 10). The law-principle was the more distinctive and characteristic, although certainly not more important, feature of the Mosaic Covenant. The law was *not* offered as a means of justification, but served rather to convict Israel of sin and to point her to Christ (Gal 3:21-4:5).

The description of the Mosaic Covenant as one of bondage, death and condemnation (2 Corinthians 3) is appropriate to the symbolic-typical aspect of the OT economy, and is not to be explained away in terms of the popular misinterpretation view, which defines the legal characteristic in terms of the Judaistic perversion of the law. While elements of grace and promise are evident *at every point* in the historical revelation and encounter of God with his people Israel, one must do justice to the typical, pedagogical function of the works-inheritance principle. OT typology viewed from the perspective of the Mosaic economy serves to instruct Israel in the way of redemptive grace and truth. This is the tutelary function of the law of God. The ministration of bondage and condemnation is pedagogical, convicting Israel of sin and leading her to Christ. Just as the ceremonial laws of Moses typify the work of Christ, so does the reward of temporal blessing for Israel's obedience typify Christ's ultimate fulfillment of the Covenant of Works broken by Adam. The Messiah to come is the true Servant of the Lord, the Son of the living God. From this perspective, we can better understand the meaning of Israel, servant of the Lord, son of God (see, *e.g.*, Jdg 11:29-40; Pss 7, 11, 18 and 24 in light of this understanding of the works-principle in the typical sphere). The work of Christ, in conjunction with the law-principle of inheritance, is depicted in the typological system of OT revelation. At the same time, the law-principle has served as Israel's pedagogue pointing her to Christ and training her in the way of faith-righteousness, which is unto eternal life (antitypical).

The law-gospel distinction, when properly perceived and applied, is far from being obscurantist. Only one who is committed to a modern, critical viewpoint could make such a conclusion. The biblical-theological exposition of the OT, in order to be authentically christocentric, must do justice to the operation of the works-law-principle in the Mosaic Covenant. Only in this way can one arrive at a proper conception of OT typology. Failure to recognize this feature of OT christology will eventually militate against the NT doctrine of the atonement. The life of the Old Covenant people of God in the symbolic-typical sphere will be misconstrued and misapplied to the community of the New Covenant people. And a repudiation of the biblical concept of works (the law-gospel distinction) destroys the doctrine of the atonement of Christ and justification by faith.

ENDNOTES

[1]Irenaeus, *Against Heresies*, in *The Ante-Nicene Fathers*, ed. A. Roberts and J. Donaldson, revised by A. C. Coxe (I; Grand Rapids: Eerdmans, 1885), Book IV.
[2]Ludwig Diestel, "Studien Zur Föderaltheologie," *Jahrbücher für deutsche Theologie* 10 (1865) 210.
[3]G. C. Berkouwer (in *Sin*, trans. P. C. Holtrop, [Studies in Dogmatics; Grand Rapids: Eerdmans, 1971], 187-231) defends the usefulness of Karl Barth's idea of the "Law *in* the Gospel." From this perspective, there is no priority or discontinuity between the principles of law and grace, but rather an equal ultimacy that cancels out any suggestion of antithesis. Precisely in this connection, Berkouwer commends De Graff's rejection of the concept of the Covenant of Works and the related contrast between "merit" and grace. According to Berkouwer, it is not clear how those who adopt the idea of the Covenant of Works can offer decisive criticism against Rome's teaching on the meritorious character of works. This indicates a total misunderstanding of the Reformation teaching, especially the doctrine of justification by faith. Berkouwer is forced to reinterpret Reformation theology, which is exactly what he does in his book *Faith and Justification*, trans. Lewis B. Smedes, (Studies in Dogmatics; Grand Rapids: Eerdmans, 1971).
[4]This article is an abbreviation of my dissertation, "The Mosaic Covenant and the Concept of Works in Reformed Hermeneutics: A Historical-Critical Analysis with Particular Attention to Early Covenant Eschatology" (Th.D. dissertation, Westminster Theological Seminary, 1980). It includes a discussion of such critical matters as the relation between natural law and the law of Moses (in light of the rising interest in theonomic politics), the medieval, scholastic nature-grace dualism and biblical eschatology, and theological method and the rise of Reformed scholasticism.

The terminology of the works-inheritance principle, which is used throughout this article, must be clearly understood. It refers to the way in which God has established his original covenant with man. The confirmation of man in the way of glory, *i.e.*, in the state of consummation, is grounded upon man's faithful obedience to the Covenant of Creation (Works). The principle, then, which informs this arrangement is that of works. It stands in opposition to the principle of soteric grace in the Covenant of Redemption (Grace).
[5]*E.g.*, Otto Ritschl, *Dogmengeschichte des* Protestantismus, (III; Göttingen: Vandenhoeck & Ruprecht, 1926); Gottlob Schrenk, *Gottesreich und Bund im Aelteren Protestantismus Vornehmlich bei Johannes Cocceius* (Darmstadt: Wissenschaftliche Buchgesellschaft, 1967); and Ernst Bizer, "Historische Einleitung des Herausgebers," in *Die Dogmatik der evangelisch reformierten Kirche* by Heinrich Heppe, ed. E. Bizer (Neukirchen: Kreis Moers, 1958) xvii-xcvi.
[6]Thomas Aquinas, *Summa Theologiae*, ed. Thomas Gilby (16; New York: McGraw-Hill, n.d.) 131. For a discussion of the historical context for the development of the nature-grace dualism and other similar philosophical dualisms from a theological and scientific point of view, see Thomas F. Torrance, *The Ground and Grammar of Theology* (Charlottesville: University Press of Virginia, 1980).
[7]See *e.g.*, Heiko A. Oberman, "*Facientibus Quod in se est Deus non Denegat Gratiam:* Robert Holcot 0. P. and the Beginnings of Luther's Theology," in *The Reformation in Medieval Perspective*, ed. S. E. Ozment (Chicago: Quadrangle Books, 1971), and his *The Harvest of Medieval Theology: Gabriel Biel and Late Medieval Nominalism* (revised edition; Grand Rapids: Eerdmans, 1967).

Torrance, "Covenant or Contract? A Study of the Theological Background of Worship in Seventeenth-Century Scotland," *SJT* 23 (1970) 51-76; and Francis Lyall, "Of Metaphors and Analogies: Legal Language and Covenant Theology," *SJT* 32 (1979) 1-18.

[9]Weber, *Ibid.*

[10]A growing number of university theologians are equating the Protestant law-gospel contrast with the subsequent rise of anti-Semitism, notably the Holocaust in Lutheran Germany. See *e.g.*, Leonard Swidler, "History, Sociology and Dialogue: Elements in Contemporary Theological Method," *JES* 17 (1980) 60-1. This fallacious conjecture regarding an important doctrine in the history of theology might readily be ignored were it not for the seriousness of their point of view, motivated as it is by their passion for ecumenical dialogue and reassessment of religious particularism. *Cf.*, Paul Van Buren, *Discerning the Way: A Theology of the Jewish Christian Reality* (New York: Seabury, 1980); and John A. T. Robinson, *Truth is Two-Eyed* (Philadelphia: Westminster, 1980).

[11]Heinrich Heppe, *Dogmatik des deutschen Protestantismus im sechzehnten Jahrhundert* (Gotha, 1857) 1.152f.

[12]Leonard I. Trinterud, "The Origins of Puritanism," *CH* 20 (1951) 37-57.

[13]Holmes Rolston, III, "Responsible Man in Reformed Theology: Calvin Versus the *Westminster Confession*," *SJT* 23 (1970) 129.

[14]For the early beginnings of the covenant idea in ancient and medieval theology, see chapter two of my dissertation, "The Mosaic Covenant and the Concept of Works."

[15]Huldreich Zwingli, *The Latin Works and the Correspondence of Huldreich Zwingli,* ed. S. M. Jackson (Philadelphia, 1922) 2.41.

[16]*Ibid.* 48-9.

[17]*Cf.*, Jack Warren Cottrell, "Covenant and Baptism in the Theology of H. Zwingli" (Th.D. dissertation, Princeton Theological Seminary, 1971).

[18]See Joachim Staedtke, *Die Theologie des jungen Bullinger,* (Studien zur Dogmengeschichte und systematischen Theologie 16; Zurich: Zwingli Verlag, 1962).

[19]Charles S. McCoy, "The Covenant Theology of Johannes Cocceius," (Ph.D. dissertation, Yale University, 1957) 60-1.

[20]Henry Bullinger, *The Decades,* ed. T. Harding for the Parker Society, trans. H. I. (Cambridge: University Press, 1849), 1.195.

[21]For a critical discussion of the idea of natural law as a speculative theological concept, see the article of August Lang, "The Reformation and Natural Law," in *Calvin and the Reformation: Four Studies,* ed. W. P. Armstrong (New York: Revell, 1909) 56-98. See my dissertation for a defense of the natural law idea, "The Mosaic Covenant and the Concept of Works."

[22]Some Reformed theologians adopted the notion of a perpetual hypothetical principle of law-inheritance, which was *independent* of any actual covenantal engagement in the era of redemption. It was so construed because of their adherence to the doctrine of the one and eternal Covenant of Grace.

[23]Bullinger, *Ibid.* 3.293. *Cf.*, his *De Testamento seu Foedere Dei Unico et Aeterno, Commentarii H. Bullingeri in omnes Apostolicas epistolas* (Basel, 1537) 162.

[24]Bullinger, *De Testamento seu Foedere* 156ff.

[25]There is a proper and necessary use of the term "merit" in theological formulation. Rightly used, it applies to the forensic aspect of the covenant relationship. Adam's "merit," the fundamental demand for perfect righteousness in order to enjoy fellowship with God, was a divine endowment, a vital aspect of man's creation in the image of God. Since God cannot look upon sin, anything less than perfect righteousness nullifies man's communion with God. With the entrance of sin into the race, the ground or merit of

justification shifts from the perfect righteousness of Adam (a human righteousness), which has now been lost, to the perfect righteousness of Christ, the imputed God-righteousness. Life, *i.e.*, communion with God along with the assurance of eternal life, is restored in Christ. The inseparability of the works-concept and the covenant underscores the inseparability of holiness and life with God.

[26]Bullinger, *The Decades,* 3.237.

[27]*Ibid.* 239.

[28]*Ibid.* 296.

[29]John Calvin, *Institutes of the Christian Religion,* ed. J. T. McNeill, trans. F. L. Battles, Library of Christian Classics 20-21 (Philadelphia: Westminster, 1960) 1.15.8.

[30]*Cf.*, Anthony A. Hoekema, "Covenant of Grace in Calvin's Teaching," *CTJ* 2 (1967) 133-61.

[31]Calvin, *Institutes* 2.8.1, and 2.2.22.

[32]John Calvin, *Commentaries on the Old Testament,* reprint of the Edinburgh edition (Grand Rapids: Eerdmans, n.d.), *Genesis* 2:16.

[33]Calvin, *Institutes* 2.7.2.

[34]*Ibid.* 11.9.4.

[35]*Ibid.*

[36]John Calvin, *Calvin's New Testament Commentaries,* ed. D. W. Torrance and T. F. Torrance (Grand Rapids: Eerdmans, 1972), *Romans* 10:5-10.

[37]Calvin, *Institutes* 2.11.9.

[38]*Ibid.* 2.11.3.

[39]*Ibid.* 2.11.4.

[40]*Ibid.* 2.10.2.

[41]*Ibid.* 2.17.16.

[42]*Ibid.* 2.1.4.

[43]Zacharias Ursinus, *The Commentary of Dr. Zacharias Ursinus on the Heidelberg Catechism,* tran. G. W. Williard (Grand Rapids: Eerdmans, 1954) 98.

[44]*Ibid.* 104f.

[45]*Ibid.* 612ff.

[46]Question and Answer 10, in August Lang, *Der Heidelberger Katechismus und Vier Verwandte Katechismen,* (Quellenschriften zur Geschichte des Protestantismus 3; Leipzig: A. Deichert, 1907).

[47]On Ursinus' use of the covenant idea, Lang suggests, "the most important motive why Ursinus had made the covenant the central idea of the *Summa* was the emphasis of the law as the unchanging, divine life-norm even for the converted" (*ibid.* lxiv).

[48]This was much more fully developed and explored in the thought of Cocceius. See especially the study of Schrenk, *Gottesreich und Bund im Aelteren Protestantismus.*

[49]Gasper Olevianus, *An Exposition of the Symbole of the Apostles,* trans. J. Fielde (London, 1581) 122.

[50]While it is certainly true that covenant theology sought to counter any bare speculation on the decrees, as was more common in the Lutheran tradition (many Lutherans were driven to Melanchthonian synergism in reaction), it is simply false to suggest that federal theology attempted to deny or minimize in any way or to any degree decretal theology. In fact, just the opposite is the truth of the matter. Covenant theology, with its doctrine of the two covenants, desired to work out more fully the meaning and importance of the doctrine of double-predestination.

[51]Gaspar Olevianus, *De Substantia Foederis Gratuiti inter Deum et Electos* (Geneva: Eustathium Vignon, 1585) 9f.

[52]*Ibid.* 12
[53]*Ibid.* 13.
[54]M. M. Knappen, *Tudor Puritanism: A Chapter in the History of Idealism* (Chicago: University of Chicago Press, 1939) 4-5.
[55]*The Works of the English Reformers: William Tyndale and John Frith,* ed. T. Russell (London, 1831) 1.21-2.
[56]*Ibid.* 1.23, and 2.492.
[57]*Ibid.* 1.57.
[58]G. D. Henderson, "The Idea of the Covenant in Scotland," *EvQ* 27 (1955) 8.
[59]Robert Rollock, *A Treatise of Our Effectual Calling,* in *Select Works,* ed. W. M. Gunn (Edinburgh: Woodrow Society, 1849) 1.34-5.
[60]The scholastic term "instrument" is employed universally by the Reformers to specify the peculiar role of faith in soteric justification. Faith alone, apart from the ensuing fruit of good works, appropriates the righteousness of Christ. The term "instrument" is used in the interests of satisfying the need to distinguish the place of law and grace in the doctrine of justification. The sole instrumentality of faith in laying hold of Christ in justification does not obscure the necessity of good works as the fruit and evidence of saving faith. In terms of the logical priority of scholastic definition, good works consistent with grace follow, and are the evidence of, faith.

Those who reject the traditional law-gospel distinction also reject the scholastic definition of "imputed righteousness," faith as "instrument," "meritorious ground," among many other terms, as no longer meaningful. Consequently, there is no difference in creation and redemption with respect to the principle of inheritance.
[61]Rollock, *Effectual Calling* 43.
[62]*Ibid.* 46.
[63]Prominent Continental federalists include such representatives as Raphael Eglinus (1559-1622), Ludwig Crocius (1586-1659), Johannes Wollebius (1586-1629), Francis Gomarus (1563-1641), and Johannes Cloppenburg (1592-1652), among others.
[64]A. F. Mitchell, *The Westminster Assembly: Its History and Standards* (London: James Nisbet, 1883) 117.
[65]While it is the case that there are different emphases in the two English federalist lines (one stressing the sovereignty of God and the other the ethical requirements), it is wrong to conclude that there are two opposing theologies. Both viewpoints insist upon the importance of the doctrine of justification by faith as the governing principle which defines the peculiar character of the Covenant of Grace. That is to say, both stress the importance of the forensic aspect of justification and covenant. They are also concerned to recognize the necessary role of good works in the covenant way of life.

Although the difference between the dipleuric and the monopleuric conception of the Covenant of Grace is merely a matter of emphasis, it is an important one in the development of English Puritanism. The stress upon the conditionality of the Covenant of Grace resulted in the excessive concern for the preaching of law in order to quicken the guilty conscience and thus prepare one for grace. Puritan interest in the science of casuistry promoted the rise of preparationism, particularly in the latter part of the seventeenth century into the eighteenth. The Marrow controversy in Scotland was a response to this regrettable development in Calvinism.
[66]Ernest F. Kevan, *The Grace of Law: A Study in Puritan Theology* (Twin Brook Series; Grand Rapids: Baker, 1976) 23.
[67]Tobias Crisp, *Christ Alone Exalted,* in *Complete Works of Tobias Crisp,* ed. J. Gill (seventh edition; London: John Beinett, 1832) 2.85.

[68]*Ibid.* 246.
[69]*Ibid.* 250.
[70]*Ibid.* 251, the editor's note; also 253.
[71]*Ibid.* 257.
[72]*Ibid.* 259.
[73]David Dickson, *Therapeutic Sacra* (second edition; Edinburgh, 1697) 120ff.
[74]See note 22 above. The hypothetical works-principle is entirely different from the notion of a hypothetical Covenant of Works under Moses. The latter undermines the continuity of the single Covenant of Grace throughout the period of redemption.
[75]Samuel Bolton, *The True Bounds of Christian Freedom* (based on the 1645 edition; London: The Banner of Truth Trust, 1964) 28.
[76]*Ibid.* 77.
[77]*Ibid.* 88ff.
[78]*Ibid.* 90ff.
[79]*Ibid.* 102.
[80]John Macleod, *Scottish Theology in Relation to Church History Since the Reformation* (second edition; Carlisle: The Banner *of* Truth Trust, 1942) 133-4.
[81]Edward Fisher, *The Marrow of Modern Divinity,* with notes by Thomas Boston (Philadelphia: Presbyterian Board of Pub., n.d.) 29.
[82]*Ibid.* 62.
[83]*Ibid.* 63.
[84]*Ibid.* 63-4.
[85]*Ibid.* 78.
[86]*Ibid.* 82.
[87]John Ball, *A Treatise of the Covenant of Grace* (London: G. Miller, 1645) 24.
[88]*Ibid.* 34-5.
[89]In failing to do full justice to the context of typology in the OT, Ball is not accurate in his conception of temporal blessings in relation to the New Covenant. The temporal, earthly blessings are now bestowed by the Lord upon the just and the unjust (common grace). The typical blessings upon God's Old Covenant people were peculiar to that special, theocratic arrangement with its principle of works-inheritance coming to bear in that restricted sphere of covenant administration.
[90]Ball, *A Treatise of the Covenant of Grace,* 92-3. Ball cites Heb 8:13 at this point.
[91]*Ibid.* 100.
[92]*Ibid.* 113.
[93]*Ibid.* 136-7.
[94]*Ibid.* 137.
[95]*Ibid.* 142.
[96]*Ibid.* 154; see also 152ff.
[97]Daniel P. Fuller, *Gospel and Law: Contrast or Continuum? The Hermeneutics of Dispensationalism and Covenant Theology* (Grand Rapids: Eerdmans, 1980) 51. Fuller is correct in making this assertion, but this difficulty in Reformed interpretation does not warrant his proposed rejection of the law/gospel contrast. Indeed, Reformed theology is in need of greater clarity of expression. Further, Fuller gravely misunderstands the Reformation hermeneutic of the analogy of faith. This hermeneutic maintains that Scripture interprets Scripture, not that the clearer teaching of Scripture is used to ignore the "literal" meaning of the more obscure or difficult text of Scripture, as Fuller contends (*ibid.* 62). This is especially true with regard to the NT use of the principle of law stated in Lev 18:5. Fuller is guilty of the same mistake which he levels at those with whom he differs in the

exegesis of such passages as Rom 10:5ff. and Gal 3:12. In terms of his own argument, he is unable to maintain with consistency his own variety of "literal" interpretation (*cf.*, *e.g.* his interpretation of Phil 3:9 and Rom 10:5ff.).

Dispensationalism and "biblical theology" (as Fuller labels his own position in distinction from covenant theology [*ibid.* 204]) are two extreme hermeneutical schools of thought. In reaction to the traditional doctrine of covenant theology with respect to law and gospel, dispensationalism reduces the Mosaic Covenant to a conditional Covenant of Works with a principle of grace and Fuller's "biblical theology" reduces the Mosaic Covenant to a *conditional* Covenant of Grace (!) entirely devoid of a works-merit principle, which principle he repudiates. The position of John Murray is in many ways analogous to that of Fuller (see the section on Murray above, pp. 43-46).

[98]B. B. Warfield, *The Westminster Assembly and Its Work* (New York: Oxford University Press, 1931) 56-7.

[99]See my dissertation for a discussion of the Confession's use of the scholastic nature-grace dichotomy, "The Mosaic Covenant and the Concept of Works" 185ff.

[100]John H. Leith, *Assembly at Westminster: Reformed Theology in the Making* (Richmond: John Knox Press, 1973) 20. Leith contends that this confessional novelty is a part of seventeenth-century Reformed scholasticism. So also, Thomas F. Torrance, *The School of Faith: The Catechisms of the Reformed Church,* trans. and ed. with an introduction by T. F. Torrance (New York: Harper, 1959) xlixff.

[101]Peter *Y.* DeJong, *The Covenant Idea in New England Theology: 1620-1847* (Grand Rapids: Eerdmans, 1945) 49.

[102]Kevan, *The Grace of Law* 118.

[103]Robert L. Dabney, *Lectures in Systematic Theology* (Grand Rapids: Zondervan, 1972) 444. *Cf.*, however, 454f.

[104]*Ibid.* 453.

[105]*Ibid.* 453-4.

[106]*Ibid.* 457.

[107]*Ibid.* 458.

[108]*Ibid.* 460. This individualistic orientation accounts for the traditional interpretation of Rom 7:7-13. For a reorientation to this crucial Pauline passage, see my "Law in Pauline Eschatology: The Historical Qualification of Justification by Faith" (Th.M. thesis, Westminster Theological Seminary, 1977).

[109]Charles Hodge, *Systematic Theology* (Grand Rapids: Eerdmans, 1973) 2.117.

[110]A. A. Hodge, *Outlines of Theology* (edition of 1879; Grand Rapids: Zondervan, 1972) 310-311.

[111]*Ibid.* 376-7.

[112]Abrahan Kuyper, Sr., *Dictaten,* Locus de Providentia, *Peccato en Foedere* (tweede druk; Grand Rapids: J. B. Hulit, 1910) 4.149.

[113]*Ibid.* 109-10.

[114]Herman Bavinck, *Gereformeerde Dogmatiek* (Kampen; J. H. Kok, 1928) 2.525.

[115]Herman Bavinck, *Our Reasonable Faith,* trans. Henry Zylstra (Twin Brook Series; Grand Rapids: Baker, 1956) 81.

[116]Louis Berkhof, *Systematic Theology* (fourth edition; Grand Rapid: Eerdmans, 1941) 298.

[117]Geerhardus Vos, *Biblical Theology: Old and New Testaments* (Grand Rapids: Eerdmans, 1948) 143.

[118]Meredith G. Kline, *Treaty of the Great King: The Covenant Structure of Deuteronomy, Studies and Commentary* (Grand Rapids: Eerdmans, 1963); and his *By Oath Consigned: A*

Reinterpretation of the Covenant Signs of Circumcision and Baptism (Grand Rapids: Eerdmans, 1968).

I am personally indebted to Professor Kline for his willingness to interact with my ideas on the covenant, especially in working toward a clearer understanding of the principle of works-inheritance in the typical sphere of the Mosaic Covenant administration.

[119]Kline, *Treaty of the Great King* 65; *cf.*, 124ff.

[120]John Murray, "The Theology of the Westminster Confession of Faith," in *Scripture and Confession: A Book About Confessions Old and New,* ed. J. H. Skilton (Nutley: Presbyterian and Reformed, 1973) 146. See his "Covenant Theology," in *The Encyclopedia of Christianity* (Marshallton: National Foundation for Christian Education, 1972) 199-216.

[121]John Murray, *Collected Writings* (Carlisle: The Banner of Truth Trust, 1977) 2.49. Murray's distinction between the state of "perfect legal reciprocity" and the Adamic administration is equivalent to the scholastic nature-grace dichotomy.

[122]*Ibid.* 50.

[123]*E.g.*, John Murray, *Redemption: Accomplished and Applied* (Grand Rapids: Eerdmans, 1955) 45.

[124]Murray, *Collected Writings* 2.50.

[125]*Ibid.* 55-6.

[126]John Murray, *The Epistle to the Romans* (The New International Commentary on the New Testament; Grand Rapids: Eerdmans, 1965) 51.

[127]Murray, *Collected Writings,* 2.58. The great difference between Murray's view of covenant theology and Vos' is apparent in the latter's pervasively eschatological perspective. See especially Vos' analysis of covenant theology in his "The Doctrine of the Covenant in Reformed Theology," in *Redemptive History and Biblical Interpretation: The Short Writings of Geerhardus Vos,* ed. R. B. Gaffin, Jr. (Phillipsburg: Presbyterian and Reformed Publishing Co., 1980) 234-67.

[128]Murray, *Collected Writings* 2.58. Murray's unique viewpoint is applied to the doctrine of justification. In the original state of creation, as long as righteousness and justification were maintained by means of man's obedience this state was of perpetual duration. There could be no lessening of this mutable, noneschatological condition. By the grace and condescension of God, he was pleased to enter into covenant with man, whereby be could be elevated to the state of glory and confirmation. This reward could never be granted on the basis of man's works (merit). Such works could only merit in strict justice momentary justification and life. Repeatedly, Murray insists that "even perfect inwrought righteousness cannot ground the reward of eternal life" (*ibid.* 211-12). *Cf.,* his *Redemption: Accomplished and Applied* 127; and *The Epistle to the Romans* 1.353ff. What is demanded is a God-righteousness, as opposed to a human righteousness. The gift of eternal life is granted to Adam on the basis of the faithfulness of God, a God-righteousness. This is an unfortunate confusion of the orders of creation and redemption. Certainly there is a qualitative difference between the human righteousness and the imputed righteousness of Christ, a God-righteousness, since, as Murray also asserts, "it is divine and therefore *perfectly correspondent with the inherent justice of God it always elicits the divine approbation* whenever it comes into operation" (*Collected Writings* 2.213). The work of Christ is intrinsically meritorious. The proper biblical conception of the role of human works in the Covenant of Creation, forensically conceived, is entirely exclusive of any intrinsic merit. Murray's use of the expression "God-righteousness" as descriptive of the graciousness of the Adamic (covenant) administration is highly problematic. The failure to restrict the term to the soteric and forensic category raises serious questions which remain unresolved in Murray's theology.

[129]Murray ("Covenant Theology" 201) reacts against what he sees as a continued controversy in contemporary Reformed theology regarding the nature of the Covenant of Grace, whether it is conditional or unconditional. According to Murray, the root of the problem is the concept of "law" as antithetical to grace. This first surfaced in Scotland during the days of the Marrow Controversy (see note 65 above). In private conversation with James Torrance, I learned that in the view of Professors Torrance and Murray this problem continues to afflict the Scottish Reformed Church today. Consequently, both have redefined the concept of the covenant largely in response to this situation in Scotland.

[130]See Holmes Rolston, III, *John Calvin Versus the Westminster Confession* (Richmond: John Knox, 1972), and Daniel Fuller, "Paul and 'The Works of the Law,'" *WTJ* 38 (1976) 28-42, in addition to their previously cited works. Contrast the article of Andrew J. Bandstra, "Law and Gospel in Calvin and in Paul," in *Exploring the Heritage of John Calvin*, ed. D. E. Holwerda (Grand Rapids: Baker, 1976) 11-39.

Fuller maintains that Reformed theology has always had difficulty with its antithesis between law and gospel. He approvingly cites John Murray in his similar objection to this dualistic interpretation of the Mosaic Covenant. Both Fuller and Murray argue that the Mosaic Covenant is no less gracious than the Abrahamic. "If Paul was not using *nomos* in the revelatory sense in Gal 3:12, then some substantial changes would have to be made in the theology which stresses *sola scriptura* along with *sola* fide" ("Paul and 'The Works of the Law'" 42). Charles H. Cosgrove supports Fuller's exegesis which "challenges the very foundation of the traditional Protestant law-gospel distinction" ("The Mosaic Law Preaches Faith: A Study in Galatians 3," *WTJ* 41 [1978] 146). Cosgrove concludes: "No wonder Daniel Fuller closes his article with the suggestion that some substantial changes are necessary in the theology which stresses *sola scriptura* along with *solo fide*. In Galatians 3 the traditional law-gospel distinction vanishes" (p. 164).

[131]This covenant faithfulness is not synonymous with faith-righteousness. The latter denotes the forensic nature of life in the Covenant of Grace. The former expression is general in meaning, and is equivalent to that faith spoken of, for example, in Heb 3:18-19 and chap. 11. *Cf.*, Fuller's interpretation of Hebrews 11 in his study, *Gospel and Law*.

CHAPTER TWO

REFORMATION POLITICS: THE RELEVANCE OF OT ETHICS IN CALVINIST POLITICAL THEORY

In recent years renewed interest in the subject of OT ethics has been generated among evangelicals. As part of the church's scriptures, the OT has an important bearing on Christian living. Since the time of the Reformation there has been a Reformed consensus that there is an interconnection between OT laws, personal Christian life, and national public policy. But the relationship has not always been clearly defined, which accounts in part for the current intense debate on the role of OT laws in the formation of public policy in America's pluralistic society.

In the present article an analysis is undertaken of the teaching of the Reformed tradition, Continental and Puritan, concerning the nature and limitations of civil legislation. Issues and questions like the following will come to our attention: How does the NT church determine which OT laws are normative for Christian life today? How valid is the traditional threefold classification of the law of God? (Protestants have commonly spoken of three kinds of law in the Mosaic legislation: civil, ceremonial and moral. Additionally they have taught a threefold use of the law in the sense of the total Mosaic economy: civil, pedagogical and normative.) What are the grounds for the contention that the civil and ceremonial laws have been terminated by the coming of Christ (these laws having been fulfilled by Christ), only the moral laws being perpetually binding?

The Chalcedon school,[1] an offshoot of the Calvinistic tradition, has advanced a particular interpretation of God's law, known as "theonomy," which maintains the normative character of the civil laws of Moses in general. The theonomists contend that their teaching regarding the place and function of the Mosaic law in society at large sets forth the position held by the seventeenth-century Puritans. But what was early Reformed theology's view of the nature of OT ethics? In particular, how did Reformed theologians understand and apply the civil laws of Moses? What precisely did the Westminster divines mean when they asserted concerning the civil laws given to Israel: "To them also, as a body politic, he gave sundry judicial laws, which expired together with the State of that people; not obliging any other now, further than the general equity thereof may require" (*Westminster Confession of Faith* 19.4)?

1. Historical Setting of Natural-Law Doctrine

It will be helpful to recall certain aspects of the historical setting of the Reformation as we seek a proper reading of sixteenth- and seventeenth-century Calvinist political theory. The Protestant reformers inherited from the medieval period the erroneous notion of society as a single comprehensive entity known as the *corpus christianum.*[2] Christendom, defined as the earthly kingdom or domain of God, was an attempt, ultimately unsuccessful, to combine the realms of church and state into one body or organization. This cooperative enterprise sought to bring about the golden age of peace and prosperity under the banner of God's name. Millennial expectations played a prominent role in giving shape to this historical and cultural development.

Well into the age of the Reformation the responsibilities and legislative powers of civil and ecclesiastical leaders were not clearly differentiated. Hence rather than complementing one another the rule of magistrates and clergy overlapped. For example, during the period of the Reformation, members of the Reformed community were convinced that civil magistrates were responsible for both the establishment and the protection of the true faith.[3] It was only a matter of time, however, before the Reformation principles demanded a new conception of the role of the civil magistrate with respect to ecclesiastical and spiritual matters.

One of the most complex issues in the history of sixteenth- and seventeenth-century society is the role of the covenant idea in political philosophy. Although political covenants formed the basis of civil order in numerous centers of the Reformed faith, it is difficult to determine the precise relationship between covenant as a theological idea and covenant as a political theory. Charles McCoy observes: "There is, beyond the possibility of doubt, a crucial relationship between the covenant theology and the rise of federalism in political philosophy. This relationship is, however, elusive in both political and theological literature."[4]

In the opening years of the Reformation movement the Reformed doctrine of the covenant had arisen in the context of discussions relating to ecclesiology, including debates over the doctrine of the sacraments of infant baptism and the Lord's supper and, more broadly, over the continuity and discontinuity between Israel (the Old Covenant people of God) and the church (the New Covenant people of God).[5] Federalism as a political theory among the Calvinists was a somewhat later development. Franklin Littell notes that

> it was not until the time of the federal theologian and social reformer Johann the Elder (younger brother of William of Orange), of Herborn, that a quite different separation of covenants becomes normative - to be completed in the social and political philosophies of Althusius and Cocceius. With them, we can perceive the beginnings of an utterly voluntary church discipline on the one hand, and a political covenant pointed toward popular sovereignty and "secular" government on the other.[6]

The covenant or federal idea in political philosophy is clearly different from the covenant idea in Reformed ecclesiology, at least until the latter half of the seventeenth century. The medieval doctrine of natural law had served as the theological bridge connecting the ecclesiastical covenant with the political covenant under one socio-religious order.

According to both medieval and Reformation theology, natural law reveals man's creaturely debt of obedience to God. This moral debt is required of every man by virtue of his creation in the image of God.[7] Natural law as a divinely-given principle or rule of moral accountability is a constituent factor of the first covenant between God and Adam and the later covenant between God and Israel at Mount Sinai. The principle of natural law and the principle of works-inheritance operative in the original creation covenant and in the typical sphere of the later covenant with Moses commonly enunciate man's fundamental duty to obey God as his faithful and loving bondservant. With respect to the Mosaic Covenant, which was regulative of the Israelite theocracy, three features are to be distinguished. (1) The Sinaitic Covenant is compatible with God's ongoing program of redemption as that is progressively revealed in successive historical epochs from the Fall to the Consummation. Under the Covenant of Redemption (or the "Covenant of Grace" as it is traditionally termed) salvation is always and only by grace through faith in Jesus Christ.[8] (2) The law of Moses, properly speaking, serves a subservient, probationary function in the history of redemption. As indicated by the principle of works-inheritance regulative of life in the earthly kingdom, the reward of temporal blessing is granted to Israel on the basis of her compliance with the law of Moses, whereas the curse of God is meted out to her on the basis of covenant-breaking. (3) Most importantly for our present study, the Mosaic Covenant is a revelation and corroboration of the eternal law of nature.

2. Continental Reformed Theology

Huldreich Zwingli taught that all people were by nature bound to obey the law of God (natural law) and that the civil law was but an instrument of God designed to promote civil righteousness and peace among men (one of the benefits of common grace in the world). Spiritual righteousness, on the other hand, could only be realized by the regenerating work of the Holy Spirit producing faith and love in the hearts of those effectually called into the kingdom of Christ.[9] (The Church's preaching of the Word of God is directed toward this end.) The primary aim of external righteousness is the exercise of civil justice and equity in men's dealings with one another. In this way, government enhances the well-being of society. Civil righteousness is good only in a limited and qualified sense. It is of no profit in achieving one's justification before God. The particular "goodness" of civil righteousness itself, moreover, is realized only through the operation of God's common grace in the providential ordering and governing of the affairs of individuals within society. The outworking of natural law in the socio-political realm is expressive of God's sovereign will. According to Zwingli and later Reformed theology, God's decretive purposes lay behind all things that transpire in human history. Nothing falls outside of God's decree. This is the heart of the Reformed philosophy of history.[10] The civil institution, ordained and upheld by the providence of God, is not a sphere of human autonomy or self-determination, as suggested by the later Enlightenment doctrine of natural law.[11]

Heinrich Bullinger, Zwingli's successor in Zurich, taught that the writing of the law of God upon the hearts of all mankind at creation was one aspect of our creation in the image of God. With reference to Rom 2:14-16 Bullinger wrote:

> By these words of the apostle we understand, that the law of nature is set against the written law of God; and that therefore it is called the law of nature, because it seems to be, as it were, placed or grafted in nature. We understand, that the law of nature, not the written law, but that which is grafted in man, has the same office that the written has; I mean, to direct men, and to teach them, and also to discern between good and evil, and to be able to judge of sin. We understand, that the beginning of this law is not of the corrupt disposition of mankind, but of God himself, who with his finger writes in our hearts, fastens in our nature, and plants in us a rule to know justice, equity, and goodness.[12]

The writing of the law of God upon man's heart at creation by "his finger" indicated the sovereign efficacy and will of God in human affairs, not a deistic notion of a God who creates man and leaves him to labor in the strength of his own inherent power and moral virtue. Rather, the work of God in creation and providence was understood by Bullinger and the Protestant reformers to be dynamic, revealing his infinite wisdom and goodness.

Corresponding to the two tables of the law of Moses, so Bullinger taught, there were two divisions of the law of nature: (1) worship of the true God, which all people ought to render as creatures of God; and (2) love of one's neighbor. Representative of Reformed thought in general, Bullinger held the opinion that man's worship of God could be legislated by civil authorities.[13] At this crucial point the Protestant reformers, like their Roman Catholic contemporaries, misconceived (from our point of view) the legitimate limits of civil legislation. To a partial degree the Reformers' teaching on this matter was reflective of the long-standing medieval social outlook.

Acknowledging the common-grace operation of natural law in the world, the reformers could exemplify natural law by reference to civil legislation of great nations throughout history, notably Roman jurisprudence. Bullinger remarks:

> Therefore every country has free liberty to use such laws as are best and most requisite for the estate and necessity of every place, and of every time and person: so yet that the substance of God's laws are not rejected, trodden down, and utterly neglected. For the things which are agreeable to the law of nature and the Ten Commandments, and whatsoever else God has commanded to be punished, must not in any case be either clean forgotten, or lightly regarded. Now the peace and public tranquillity be firmly maintained, and judgments and justice be rightly executed.[14]

Although the normative status of the Mosaic civil code has changed, "the substance of God's judicial laws is not taken away or abolished, but the ordering and limitation of them is placed in the will and arbitration of good Christian princes," who must ensure the due submission of ruler and citizens alike to the law of God (natural law).

John Calvin had learned a great deal from Martin Bucer during his sojourn in the city of Strassburg. Following Bucer's lead Calvin continued to work out a clearer understanding of the relationship between civil and ecclesiastical authority.[15] Despite certain characterizations of Calvin's Geneva, the Genevan "theocracy" was substantially different from the ancient Israelite theocracy. The government of Geneva was theocratic only in the sense that the clergy sought to enforce civil morality, which was the proper responsibility of the magistrates. As in Zurich and Strassburg, the Genevan council, by recommendation of the consistory, enforced civil discipline.[16]

Through the efforts of Calvin, however, the duties of the Genevan council and the consistory come to be defined more carefully. In seeking to uphold the biblical distinction between two spheres of authority under God – *viz.*, church and state – Calvin opposed the desire of the civil magistrates to pronounce excommunication, an exclusively ecclesiastical form of discipline. Due to insurmountable pressure from the council Calvin found himself accommodating to its demands. Consequently, where ecclesiastical discipline overlapped with prescribed civil penalties, the consistory referred cases to the council. Although Calvin had learned from Bucer that religious discipline was to be exercised only by the church, neither Calvin in Geneva nor Bucer in Strassburg was able to realize fully his objectives.[17]

In the *Institutes of the Christian Religion* Calvin maintains that man is subject to the authority of God in the realm of civil government. He discusses the nature and purpose of government in the closing chapter. Civil government is a "divinely established order" that pertains "only to the establishment of civil justice and outward morality."[18] The distinction between spiritual and civil government, insists Calvin, ought to be obvious to all.

> Whoever knows how to distinguish between body and soul, between this present fleeting life and that future eternal life, will without difficulty know that Christ's spiritual kingdom and the civil jurisdiction are things completely distinct. Since, then, it is a Jewish vanity to seek and enclose Christ's kingdom within the elements of this world, let us rather ponder that which Scripture clearly teaches is a spiritual fruit, which we gather from Christ's grace; and let us remember to keep within its own limits all that freedom which is promised and offered to us in him.[19]

Calvin summarizes the function of civil government in the following words: "In short, it provides that a public manifestation of religion may exist among Christians, and that humanity be maintained among men." Calvin, then, makes an important point:

> Let no man be disturbed that I now commit to civil government the duty of rightly establishing religion, which I seem above to have put outside of human decision. For, when I approve of a civil administration that aims to prevent the true religion which is contained in God's law from

> being openly and with public sacrilege violated and defiled with impunity, I do not here, any more than before, allow men to make laws according to their own decision concerning religion and the worship of God.[20]

Unfortunately, Calvin does not go far enough in distinguishing the proper relation between protection of true religion and establishment of such by the civil magistracy, nor does he adequately define the legitimate sphere of civil legislation. On the government's responsibility to uphold the two tables of the law of Moses, Calvin remarks:

> If Scripture did not teach that it extends to both Tables of the Law, we could learn this from secular writers: for no one has discussed the office of magistrates, the making of laws, and public welfare, without beginning at religion and divine worship. And thus all have confessed that no government can be happily established unless piety is the first concern; and that those laws are preposterous which neglect God's right and provide only for men. Since, therefore, among all philosophers religion takes first place, and since this fact has always been observed by universal consent of all nations, let Christian princes and magistrates be ashamed of their negligence if they do not apply themselves to this concern.[21]

The Mosaic Covenant, observes Calvin, is an excellent example of the divinely established law of nature. Calvin illustrates the twofold duty of government – *i.e.*, the responsibility to ensure the true worship of God and the responsibility to promote social justice and peace – by reference to the Mosaic legislation insofar as it testifies to natural law.[22] According to the hermeneutics of the NT as Calvin understands it, the Israelite civil obligations of the Mosaic law are morally binding upon nations today only on the basis of natural law, the unchanging principle of equity and human welfare, not on the basis of the unique theocratic administration under Moses regulating the total life of God's elect nation. Calvin states his position in some detail:

> What I have said will become plain if in all laws we examine, as we should, these two things: the constitution of the law, and the equity on which its constitution is itself founded and rests. Equity, because it is natural, cannot but be the same for all, and therefore, this same purpose ought to apply to all laws, whatever their object. Constitutions have certain circumstances upon which they in part depend. It therefore does not matter that they are different, provided all equally press toward the same goal of equity.
>
> It is a fact that the law of God which we call the moral law is nothing else than a testimony of natural law and of that conscience which God has engraved upon the minds of men. Consequently, the entire scheme of this equity of which we are now speaking has been prescribed in it.

> Hence, this equity alone must be the goal and rule and limit of all laws.
>
> . . . . God's law forbids stealing. The penalties meted out to thieves in the Jewish state are to be seen in Exodus (Ex 22:1-4). The very ancient laws of other nations punished theft with double restitution; the laws which followed these distinguished between theft, manifest and not manifest. Some proceeded to banishment, others to flogging, others finally to capital punishment. False testimony was punished by damages similar and equal to injury among the Jews (Deut 19:18-21); elsewhere, only by deep disgrace; in some nations, by hanging; in others, by the cross. All codes equally avenge murder with blood, but with different kinds of death. Against adulterers some nations levy severer, other, lighter punishments. Yet we see how, with such diversity, all laws tend to the same end. For, together with one voice, they pronounce punishment against those crimes which God's eternal law has condemned, namely murder, theft, adultery, and false witness. But they do not agree on the manner of punishment. Nor is this necessary nor expedient. . . .
>
> For the statement of some, that the law of God given through Moses is dishonored when it is abrogated and new laws preferred to it, is utterly vain. For others are not preferred to it when they are more approved, not by simple comparison, but with regard to the condition of times, place and nation; or when that law is abrogated which was never enacted for us. For the Lord through the hand of Moses did not give that law to be proclaimed among all nations and to be in force everywhere; but when he had taken the Jewish nation into his safekeeping, defense, and protection, he also willed to be a lawgiver especially to it; and – as became a wise lawgiver – he had special concern for it in making its laws.[23]

The principle of natural law is eternal and unchanging. The civil laws of Moses are applicable to all nations only to the extent that they promote justice and equity. Whereas the typical-pedagogical aspect of the Mosaic law is terminated, the "substance" of these laws – what is identified as the law of nature – remains in effect. Consequently the civil laws of Moses are considered by Calvin to be a guide, not a standard or norm, for national public policy in any given period and culture.

In early Continental Reformed theology the category of "civil laws" in distinction from moral and ceremonial laws (according to the traditional threefold classification of God's law) is open to ambiguity and imprecision. To the extent that civil laws obligate society to uphold principles of natural law they are morally binding and therefore not arbitrary or dispensable. Nevertheless it is legitimate to speak of the termination of the specific covenantal administration of the Mosaic law (as a total, unified order or arrangement) in the course of the establishment of the New Covenant. The particular, historical civil code enunciated by Moses is no longer binding as a legal standard.[24]

3. Puritanism: Old and New England

Prompted by unique political and religious circumstances, English (and Scottish) theologians applied in a rather unorthodox manner the special theocratic administration of law of the ancient Israelite nation directly to God's present dealings with the English people. Just as the Mosaic Covenant set before the nation of Israel the dual sanctions of blessing for obedience and curse for disobedience, so did God now call England in similar fashion to faith and repentance in order to secure national prosperity. The English reformers were convinced that God was entering into a controversy with England, the "elect nation," the "new Israel."[25] (Later, in their preaching and writing the English and American Puritans frequently employed the language of the Old Covenant prophets as ministers of God's lawsuit against an unfaithful and rebellious people.[26])

By the middle of the seventeenth century, English reformers favored viewing the Mosaic civil laws as a standard or norm, rather than as a guide, for present-day legislation. This new development within English federalism appeared about the time of the Westminster Assembly (1642-48). No doubt influenced by the Scottish national covenants, which attempted to combine civil and religious purposes into one common agenda for the nation, Puritans made direct appeal to the Mosaic civil code. The relation between the civil and ecclesiastical authorities in the English national church was, to varying degrees, theocratic in its outworking. Magistrates assumed responsibility for church matters that in most instances were not their official concern. In the chapter on the civil magistrate, the *Westminster Confession of Faith* properly defines the role of the magistrates as "the defense and encouragement of them that are good, and for the punishment of evil doers" (23.1). But beyond this legitimate exercise of authority the *Confession* states:

> The civil magistrate may not assume to himself the administration of the Word and sacraments, or the power of the keys of the kingdom of heaven: yet he hath authority, and it is his duty, to take order that unity and peace be preserved in the church, that the truth of God be kept pure and entire, that all blasphemies and heresies be suppressed, all corruptions and abuses in worship and discipline prevented or reformed, and all the ordinances of God duly settled, administered, and observed. For the better effecting whereof, he hath power to call synods, to be present at them, and to provide that whatsoever is transacted in them be according to the mind of God (23.3).

This understanding of the role of the civil magistrate was not altogether new, but the theocratic rule of the magistrate was enlarged considerably during the seventeenth century, notably in the New England colonies. The Puritan ideal failed to find fruition in Old England, according to the emigrants, because "ungodly and unChristian magistrates" hindered the true reformation of the church.

Several years prior to the convening of the Westminster Assembly, Thomas Cartwright made an attempt in England to revive the Mosaic civil laws in defense of the permanent and binding authority of the old code, though not without arousing intense debate and opposition. John Whitgift countered Cartwright by arguing for the cessation of the Mosaic law, claiming the support of such theologians as Calvin and Theodore Beza, Calvin's successor in Geneva. "As a result of this preoccupation with the Old Law," writes a contemporary historian, "Cartwright and his disciples became convinced that they were the 'chosen people' of the New Law and therefore elected by God to build 'Jerusalem' in 'England's green and pleasant land.'"[27] This conflict of opinion became even more evident in the New England debates between Roger Williams and John Cotton. Williams denied that Canaan should be a model for political and religious life in seventeenth-century society.[28] With the end of the Israelite theocracy the judicial system under Moses served now only as a guide for civil policy. Cotton, on the other hand, insisted on carrying over ancient Israel's symbolico-legal system into the New England theocracies. English federalism had clearly taken a new direction in Calvinistic political theory.

In the midst of these struggles and confrontations the Westminster divines began the work of preparing a new confession and catechisms, destined to have wide and lasting influence. The *Confession* states that many and various judicial laws "expired together with the State of that people; not obliging any other now, further than the general equity thereof may require" (19.4). The expression "general equity" refers unambiguously to the abiding principle of natural law, that which is morally binding. The formulation of any particular civil law may vary in different nations and societies. As a whole, the judicial system under Moses is no longer binding. The principle of general equity or natural law, according to the *Confession,* entails both tables of the law. During the entire age of the Reformation the civil magistrates were expected to preserve peace within the human community and to guard and protect the Christian faith against heresy and blasphemy. Certain elements in the *Confession* indicate an orientation toward "theonomic politics." While the Chalcedon school may be at home with the teaching of the *Confession* on the duty of civil magistrates to enforce both tables of the law, it obscures or at least minimizes the confessional position that the Mosaic judicial laws serve as a guide in civil morality rather than as a norm.[29]

To summarize: In the latter half of the seventeenth century when the Puritans viewed the Mosaic civil code as normatively binding on all nations everywhere (especially England and New England), English theologians began to lose sight of the typological significance of the Old Covenant civil legislation. This new view differed considerably from early Continental Reformed theology's interpretation of the Mosaic civil order. In appealing to the Mosaic laws as the norm for public policy the Puritans gave further room for theonomic politics. Over time the Puritan civil enactments conformed more and more to the old Mosaic legislation with its accompanying sanctions, including capital punishment for heretics, adulterers and blasphemers. In so doing the Puritans obliterated the unique (typological) purpose of prescribed punishments against trangressors of God's covenant with Moses.

The results of our study in the rise and development of Calvinistic political philosophy present us with two alternative points of view regarding the nature and use of the Mosaic civil code in the formation of public policy today. Following the principal insights of the Continental Reformed tradition the civil laws of Moses serve as a useful and important guide in shaping public morality.

Whereas cultural and political circumstances change, the principle of general equity or natural law is unchanging. According to the Puritan tradition, on the other hand, the civil code of Moses is normative and therefore binding upon all nations in all times and places. It is not so much a matter of application of the Mosaic law in today's society but simply of implementing and enforcing it. In the Puritan theocracies, church and state were not coterminous – despite possible appearances to the contrary. Covenant as a civil compact and covenant as an ecclesiological bond were distinct entities in seventeenth-century Puritanism.[30] However, to the degree that the civil code of the political covenant overlapped with the civil code of the Mosaic Covenant the result was a closed, religious society. To the extent that these two codes were properly distinguished and the typological dimension of the old Mosaic Covenant preserved the outcome was an open, free society under the sovereign rule of God.

ENDNOTES

[1]The subject of God's law is given fullest treatment by Greg Bahnsen, *Theonomy and Christian Ethics* (Nutley: Presbyterian and Reformed, 1977). Meredith G. Kline presents a valuable and incisive critique of Bahnsen's work and that of the Chalcedon school as a whole in his "Comments on an Old-New Error: A Review Article," *WTJ* 41 (1978) 17-189.

[2]See, *e.g.*, Stephen E. Ozment, *The Reformation in the Cities* (New Haven: Yale University, 1975); B. Moeller, *Imperial Cities and the Reformation* (Philadelphia: Fortress, 1972).

[3]Paul Woolley writes: "The right of freedom of expression existed in a basic way nowhere in western Europe. . . . The civil magistrate everywhere assumed some power to regulate the church, the degree differing most frequently in inverse ratio to the power of the church in that particular area but, in rare instances, also because of the convictions of the ruler" ("Calvin and Toleration," in *The Heritage of John Calvin*, ed. J. H. Bratt [Grand Rapids: Eerdmans, 1973] 153).

[4]Charles S. McCoy, "The Covenant Theology of Johannes Cocceius" (Ph.D. dissertation; New Haven: Yale University, 1957) 91.

[5]See Chapter One.

[6]Franklin H. Littell, "What Calvin Learned at Strassburg," in *The Heritage of John Calvin* 78.

[7]Zacharius Ursinus was among the first to use the expression "Covenant of Nature" (*foedus naturae*) to describe the initial covenantal engagement between God and Adam at creation. This covenant rested upon man's fulfillment of the law of nature, the law or principle inherent in the moral structure of the creation order. Man's duty was to render obedience to the law of God; this was the creature's "natural" relationship to the Creator. See Zacharius Ursinus, *The Commentary of Dr Zacharias Ursinus on the Heidelberg Catechism*, tr. G. W. Williard (Grand Rapids: Eerdmans, 1954) 612ff. Wolfgang Musculus explained: "The law of nature is not called such a thing, which either besides or above that eternal law which is in God, is prescribed by our nature itself, but that which is by God himself naturally fastened and established in all men, and very agreeable unto his eternal law. . . . The law of nature is not our nature, but it is the law of God" (*Common Places of Christian Religion*, tr. J. Man [London, 1563] 30). William Ames spoke of natural law as God's "special government" of his rational creatures made in his own image and likeness. The distinctive feature of this special government of man was that it was moral (*The Marrow of Theology*, ed. J. D. Eusden [Philadelphia: Pilgrim, 1958] 1.10.1ff.). On the supposition that the concept of the *foedus naturae* led to a natural theology see August Lang, "The Reformation and Natural Law," in *Calvin and the Reformation: Four Studies*, ed. W. P. Armstrong (New York: Revell, 1909) 56-98; Otto Ritschl, *Dogmengeschichte des Protestantismus* (vol 3; Göttingen: Vandenhoeck and Ruprecht, 1926); H. E. Weber, *Reformation, Orthodozie und Rationalismus* (BFCT 2; Göttersloh: C. Berkelsmann, 1951); Mark W. Karlberg, "The Mosaic Covenant and the Concept of Works in Reformed Hermeneutics: A Historical-Critical Analysis with Particular Attention to Early Covenant Eschatology" (Th.D. dissertation; Philadelphia: Westminster Theological Seminary, 1980).

[8]See Chapters Six and Twelve.

[9]Huldreich Zwingli, *The Latin Works and the Correspondence of Huldreich Zwingli*, ed. S. M. Jackson (New York/Philadelphia, 1912-29) 3.261ff.

[10]For a recent reassessment of the Reformed doctrine of the decrees see Gordon J. Spykman, "A New Look at Election and Reprobation," in *Life Is Religion: Essays in Honor of*

H. Evan Runner, ed. H. Vander Goot (St. Catharines: Paideia, 1981). Spykman argues "that it is possible to recontextualize this question, to rearticulate our biblical-confessional framework of reference for dealing with it, and thus to restate this doctrine in such a way that, relieved of some of the dubious scholastic constructs which until now have often encumbered it, we can learn to theologize on it with renewed openness and joy as the very *cor ecclesiae*, the very heartbeat of the church" (*ibid.* 172-173). For a helpful critique of recent trends in Reformed thinking see Alvin L. Baker, *Berkouwer's Doctrine of Election: Balance or Imbalance?* (Phillipsburg: Presbyterian and Reformed, 1981).

[11]Enlightenment philosophers had "secularized" the medieval doctrine of natural law in the interests of the autonomy of the modern state. A secular view of political theory found expression in the writings of H. Grotius, T. Hobbes, J. Locke and J. J. Rousseau. These political theories arose from considerations and objectives altogether different from those of the Reformed federalists. Covenant theology and secular political theory arose from opposing philosophical and theological contexts. Consequently the origins of the modern natural-law doctrine do not lie in Calvinist theology but rather in seventeenth- and eighteenth-century moral philosophy.

[12]Heinrich Bullinger, *The Decades*, ed. T. Harding (Cambridge: Cambridge University, 1849) 1.205-206.

[13]*Ibid.* 193ff. For a better interpretation of the two tables of the law see Meredith G. Kline, *The Structure of Biblical Authority* (Grand Rapids: Eerdmans, 1972) 113-130.

[14]Bullinger, *Decades*, 3.280-282. In a recent study, *Heinrich Bullinger and the Covenant: The Other Reformed Tradition* (Athens: Ohio University, 1980), J. Wayne Baker argues that Bullinger held a unique view on the relation of church and state in the time of the early Reformation. "Although the emphasis on community and on the OT was not unique with Bullinger, the concept of magisterial discipline within the covenanted community was distinctly his. The notion of conditional covenant was the basic element of Bullinger's entire theory of Christian society. It was the Christian magistrate who enforced the conditions of the covenant in the Christian commonwealth, which meant that the civil government completely controlled discipline. Calvin and Beza, on the other hand, committed the powers of excommunication and church discipline into the hands of a consistory" (xxiii). Later Baker remarks that "the social covenant was based on the religious covenant. . . . An idea of Christian community was not in itself unusual. The climate of opinion of the late Middle Ages and the sixteenth century favored such a conception of society. It was the additional elements of covenant and magisterial sovereignty that made Bullinger's theory unusual, different from the thought of any other major reformer" (p. 166). According to Baker's interpretation, Bullinger had so closely identified Zurich with the Old Covenant people of God that he anticipated the later Puritan theocracies (see especially, pp. 105, 140, and 166).

[15]During 1531-32 Strassburg was the scene of the classic debate between Martin Bucer, representing the traditional Reformed point of view, and Pilgram Marpeck over the uses and limits of political authority. The debate ended in the expulsion of Marpeck from Strassburg by the city council in January 1532. Against the judgment of Bucer and the council, Marpeck insisted that government played no role whatever in regard to the kingdom of God on earth. Since God's kingdom is an exclusively spiritual and heavenly reality, argued Marpeck, the state could never protect the church against opposition and persecution under any situation or circumstance, let alone establish religion. See further D. J. Ziegler, "Marpeck versus Butzer: A Sixteenth-Century Debate over the Uses and Limits of Political Authority," in *Sixteenth Century Essays and Studies*, ed. C. S. Meyer (St. Louis: Foundation for Reformation Research, 1971) 95-107.

[16]E. W. Monter comments: "Calvin's Geneva was indeed a theocracy. This does not imply that she was governed by her clergy; it means rather that Geneva was in theory governed by God through a balance of spiritual and secular powers, through clergy and magistrates acting in harmony. In the sixteenth century, the intimate association of the ecclesiastical and the secular government of a community was generally assumed to be both natural and desirable" *(Calvin's Geneva* [New York: John Wiley, 1967] 144). See also David Little, *Religion, Order; and Law: A Study in Pre-Revolutionary England* (New York: Harper, 1969) 76-80; Robert M. Kingdom, "The Control of Morals in Calvin's Geneva," in *The Social History of the Reformation,* ed. L. P. Buck and J. W. Zophy (Columbus: Ohio State University, 1972).

[17]Despite the shortcomings of the Reformation age, notes Phillip Schaff, "it is nevertheless true that Calvinism, by developing the power of self-government and a manly spirit of independence which fears no man, though seated on a throne, because it fears God, the only sovereign, has been one of the chief agencies in bringing about this progress, and that civil and religious liberty triumphed first and most completely in Calvinistic countries" *(The Creeds of Christendom* [6th ed.; Grand Rapids: Baker, n.d.] 1.466). On similar lines Woolley remarks: "In great measure Calvin's desire was fulfilled. But it was fulfilled more fully and more acceptably abroad than in Geneva. The results of his work bore greater fruit in Scotland and in the Netherlands than they did in Switzerland. . . . While we cannot attempt here to prove this thesis, I am willing to say that, in my judgment, the greater fruitage of Calvin's ideas elsewhere than in Geneva is due to the fact that in other areas they were not subjected to implementation by the civil state to the same degree as was true in Geneva" (in *The Heritage of John Calvin* 156). Woolley points out that "the doctrine and ethical principles of the church were incorporated into the civil code. Some of this was against the wishes of Calvin, some of it with his thorough approval. It is here that his conception of tolerance was not adequate" (157). See further W. Stanford Reid, "Calvin and the Political Order," in *John Calvin: Contemporary Prophet,* ed. J. T. Hoogstra (Grand Bapids: Baker, 1959) 248-259.

[18]John Calvin, *Institutes of the Christian Religion,* ed. J. T. McNeill (Philadelphia: Westminster, 1960) 4.20.1.

[19]*Ibid.*

[20]*Ibid.* 4.20.3.

[21]*Ibid.* 4.20.9.

[22]Calvin remarks: "I would have preferred to pass over this matter in utter silence if I were not aware that here many dangerously go astray. For there are some who deny that a commonwealth is duly framed which neglects the political system of Moses, and is ruled by the common laws of nations. Let other men consider how perilous and seditious this notion is: it will be enough for me to have proved it false and foolish" (*ibid.* 4.20.14).

[23]*Ibid.* 4.20.16.

[24]The pedagogical use of the law, as taught by Paul (among other NT writers), has reference to the giving of the law on Mount Sinai as a specific, historical-legal arrangement regulative of the Israelite theocracy in all aspects of its life in covenant with God. This law of Moses comprises three kinds of laws (to use the traditional classification): civil, ceremonial and moral. Likewise the third use of the law (the normative or regulative) pertains to the whole law of Moses. With the inauguration of the New Covenant in Christ, covenantal law – *i.e.,* "biblical ethics" - bears only the normative function among the people of God who comprise a spiritual fellowship. The New Covenant is an exclusively spiritual administration of special grace (*cf.* 2 Cor 3:6ff.). Both the pedagogical/probationary function of the law and the civil function are no longer

regulative of the covenant order. The civil use of God's law remains as an operation of common grace in the world. See the subsequent discussion of the *Westminster Confession of Faith*, 19.4.

[25]Consult further William Haller, *The Rise of Puritanism* (Philadelphia: University of Pennsylvania, 1938), and esp. George M. Marsden, "America's 'Christian' Origins: Puritan New England as a Case Study," in *John Calvin: His Influence in the Western World,* ed. W. S. Reid (Grand Rapids: Zondervan, 1982) 244-249.

[26]See, *e.g.*, S. Bercovitch, *The American Jeremiad* (Madison: University of Wisconsin, 1978); *The American Puritan Imagination: Essays in Revaluation,* ed. S. Bercovitch (Cambridge: Cambridge University, 1974).

[27]Donald J. McGinn, *The Admonition Controversy* (New Brunswick: Rutgers University, 1949) 126-127.

[28]Irvin Polishook maintains: "In a final and sweeping attack on the theological presuppositions of his adversaries, Williams denied that the OT might serve as a pattern for a contemporary religious settlement. . . . In contrast, the OT offered the best example of the orthodoxy contemplated by the Puritans in America and in the mother country. The prescriptions of the Mosaic law provided a complete replica for the union of church and state and the punishment of religious nonconformists" *(Roger Williams, John Cotton and Religious Freedom: A Controversy in New and Old England* [Englewood Cliffs: Prentice-Hall, 1967] 32). See also S. Bercovitch, "Typology in Puritan New England: The Williams-Cotton Controversy Reassessed," *American Quarterly* 19 (1967) 166-191; D. Little, "Legislating Morality: The Role of Religion," in *Christianity and Politics: Catholic and Protestant Perspectives,* ed. C. F. Griffith (Washington: Ethics and Public Policy Center, 1981) 39-53; *cf.* L. J. Van Til's assessment of Williams' "distinctive hermeneutics" in *Liberty of Conscience: The History of a Puritan Idea* (Nutley: Craig, 1972) 61.

[29]This oversight affects James B. Jordan's reading of the sources in "Calvinism and 'The Judicial Law of Moses:' An Historical Survey," *The Journal of Christian Reconstruction,* 5 (1978-79) 17-48. In an otherwise helpful critique W. Luck is mistaken in saying that "[Bahnsen's] *Theonomy* is essentially a restatement of the Reformed position" *(JETS* 28 [1980] 76). All can agree that the Mosaic law serves as a "pattern" for public policy. But what does one mean by that term? Is the Mosaic pattern a guide or a standard? On that question the Reformed tradition was divided.

[30]Jens Møller is rightly critical of Perry Miller's approach to the Puritan literature: "English and American scholars have as a rule failed to contribute a satisfactory discussion of the idea of the covenant in Puritan theologians. One principal reason for this failure is to be found in the fact that many of these scholars are primarily interested in sociology and less in theology. Another reason stems from the tendency to isolate the Puritans in England and New England from their English background as well as from their Continental forerunners and contemporaries. Interpreters which thus tend to neglect both theology and history necessarily lead to grave misunderstandings in the presentation of Puritan covenant theology. The well-known work of Perry Miller is typical in many respects. Miller presents his interpretation of the covenant in book IV under the general heading: Sociology!" "The Beginnings of Puritan Covenant Theology," *JEH* 14 (1963) 46.

CHAPTER THREE

MOSES AND CHRIST – THE PLACE OF LAW IN SEVENTEENTH-CENTURY PURITANISM

The era of Puritanism has long been past, yet the theological and moral issues which the Puritans debated remain with us. The seventeenth and eighteenth centuries marked the period of Puritanism's religious and cultural dominance in England and America. Though clearly a demonstration of the powerful working of the Spirit of God in that period of the church's history subsequent to the formative age of the Protestant Reformation, it was not without its failures and limitations. Of no minor significance were the numerous misunderstandings concerning the doctrine of the moral law (summed up in the Decalogue) entertained by various factions within Puritanism itself. But the eventual passing of Puritanism from the scene could hardly be attributed to a lack of inner strength and vitality.[1] Its demise was more directly the result of the spread of Enlightenment thought in the second half of the eighteenth century. The challenge of modernity in society at large proved too difficult to surmount. By the nineteenth century the impact of Reformed orthodoxy in society and culture was significantly reduced. Granted the positive contributions and the enduring values of Puritanism, historical investigation requires critical, though sympathetic, assessment of the movement. As a study in the history of ideas this present essay relates Puritan theology to the broader social and political concerns of the day. In so doing, we are acknowledging the fact that Puritan theology and society are part of one seamless fabric.

Puritan doctrine was essentially Calvinistic. In the several diverse ecclesiastical traditions – anglican, presbyterian, independent, baptist, and methodist[2] – there was a shared commitment to Calvinistic soteriology, notably adherence to the doctrines of sovereign, decretive election and saving faith as God's gift of grace that is unmerited and irresistible. (The Reformed understanding of salvation is concisely summed up in the Canons of Dort, formulated in 1619.)

1. Covenant: The Cornerstone of Puritan Theology and Ethics

Once the Bible became available in the vernacular, it was the study of the Scriptures, more than any other single historical factor, which was the driving force behind the Protestant Reformation in England. Leonard J. Trinterud describes succinctly the rise of Puritanism:

> Puritanism emerged in Tudor England in the thought and work of men such as William Tyndale, John Frith, John Bale, John Hooper, John Bradford, and their associates. By these men a pattern was set which enjoyed a steady and unbroken course of development until it came to expression in the Long Parliament, the Civil Wars, the Westminster Assembly of Divines, the Commonwealth, and the Protectorate.[3]

Beginning with the two-covenant scheme of Tyndale (1484-1536), what Trinterud has correctly identified as "the basis of his entire religious outlook,"[4] the Puritan divines exploited fully the covenant idea, not only in their interpretation of the Scriptures, but also in their structuring of ecclesiastical and civil institutions. For the most part, Puritan theology was an indigenous expression of what was generic (international) Calvinism.[5] Although the theological writings of the Puritans were more polemical and issue-oriented, rather than formal and systematic as in the case of the Continental reformers, they nevertheless set forth a comprehensive exposition of covenant doctrine. And it is this doctrine of the covenant that distinguishes Reformed theology from all other theological traditions.[6]

One of the most complex topics in the whole of Christian doctrine, one particularly crucial for Reformed exegesis and theology, is the relationship between the Old and New Testaments, or to state the contrast in terms of the focus of this essay, the relationship between the law of Moses and the law of Christ. This subject deals both with the abrogation of the Mosaic law and with the restatement or renewal of the moral law by Christ. Anthony Burgess (d. 1664) remarked that he did "not find in any point of divinity learned men so confused and perplexed [as on this topic]."[7] Despite all the varieties of theological formulation held among the Puritans, however, there was underlying agreement concerning the nature and basis of salvation in Christ (specifically, the doctrine of justification by faith apart from the works of the law). The one way of salvation was applicable to the saints in all ages before and after Christ's coming. Likewise, there was unanimity concerning the binding character of the moral law for the believer (the normative or regulative use of the law). As C. F. Allison has maintained, "The question of the formal cause of justification is central to an understanding of seventeenth-century soteriology."[8]

Those united to Christ in his death and resurrection by faith are not only justified, but sanctified. Puritan authors consistently distinguish a twofold signification with God's law. John Ball (1585-1640) defines

> one as the unchangeable rule of life and manners, according to which persons in covenant ought to walk before and with the Lord, and in this it belongs to the Covenant of Grace. The other, as it is propounded in the form of a covenant, as if he must necessarily perish who neglects or breaks it in the least jot or tittle, and in this sense the Covenant of Grace and the Covenant of Works are opposite. The matter of evangelical precepts and of the moral law is the same, but the form of promulgation is not the same: the rule is one, but the Covenants differ.[9]

Similarly, Samuel Bolton (1606-1654) speaks of the believer's freedom from the moral law as a covenant

> as that from which life might be expected on the condition that due obedience was rendered. . . . The law may be considered as a rule and as a covenant. When we read that the law is still in force, it is to be understood of the law as a rule, not as a covenant. Again, when we read that the law is abrogated, and that we are freed from the law, it is to be understood of the law as a covenant, not as a rule.[10]

The believer is under the precepts of the law, but not its legal condition. That is to say, "He is not freed from the requirement of exact obedience, but from that rigour of obedience which the law required as a condition of salvation."[11] In the area of sanctification "we are freed from sin, by which I mean the guilt, the defilement and the dominion of sin."[12] This liberty in Christ does not annul the law as a rule of life, nor does it make compliance with God's law of no account. The final end of the law, states Burgess, is as the absolute rule of life (what Reformed theologians commonly call the "third use" of the law).

> The law may be considered as it is a covenant, or as it is an absolute rule, requiring conformity to it. Now it may be truly granted that the law is abolished in the former notion, though not in the latter. Only in expressing this covenant is there difference among the learned. Some make the law a Covenant of Works, and upon that ground it is abrogated. Others call it a subservient covenant to the Covenant of Grace, and make it only occasionally, as it were, introduced to put more luster and splendour upon grace. Others call it a mixed Covenant of Works and Grace, but that is hardly to be understood as possible, much less as true. I therefore think that opinion true, as shall be hereafter shown, that the law given by Moses was a Covenant of Grace, and that God did not, since man fell, ever transact with him in any other covenant, but that of grace, though indeed this Covenant of Grace did break out more clearly, in succession of ages, according to the wise dispensation of God's good pleasure. So then, the Law as a Covenant, though of grace, is abrogated because, though there is still the same essence of the former and latter covenant, yet the administration of the former is altogether antiquated.[13]

Edward Fisher (1627-1655), whose *The Marrow of Modern Divinity* written in 1645 was the center of much controversy in the first half of the eighteenth century, draws the distinction between the law of works and the law of Christ.[14] The latter pertains to the law as a perpetual rule of life for the believer. Thomas Boston (1676-1732) in his notes to the text of Fisher's *Marrow* states that "The law of works and the law of Christ are in substance but one law, even the law of the Ten Commandments - the moral law - that law which was from the beginning, continuing still the same in its own nature, but vested with different forms."[15] He emphasizes the point that the law of Christ is "not a new, proper, preceptive law, but the old, proper, preceptive law, which was from the beginning, under a new accidental form."[16] Despite the high regard that Boston has for Fisher's work, the two differ somewhat in their interpretation of the Mosaic law.[17] (This difference in our judgment is purely semantic, not substantive.) Boston views the Decalogue primarily as embodying the Covenant of Grace, whereas Fisher construes it in terms of a Covenant of Works. Yet Boston concedes that the Ten Commandments given on Mount Sinai "must come under a twofold notion or consideration, namely, as the law of Christ, and as the law of works,"[18] while Fisher makes the following qualification:

> The reason why I rather choose to call the law of the Ten Commandments the matter of the Covenant of Works, than the covenant itself, is because I conceive that the matter of it cannot properly be called the Covenant of Works, except the form be put upon it, that is to say, except the Lord require, and man undertake to yield perfect obedience thereunto, upon condition of eternal life and death.[19]

Furthermore, Fisher clarifies:

> God never made the Covenant of Works with any man since the Fall, either with expectation that he should fulfill it, or to give him life by it, for God never appoints anything to an end to which it is utterly unsuitable and improper. Now the law, as it is the Covenant of Works, is become weak and unprofitable to the purpose of salvation and, therefore, God never appointed it to man since the Fall to that end. And besides, it is manifest that the purpose of God in the covenant made with Abraham was to give life and salvation by grace and promise. Therefore, his purpose in renewing the Covenant of Works was not, neither could be, to give life and salvation by working for then there would have been contradictions in the covenants, and instability in him that made them.[20]

The decree and law of God are immutable. As a Covenant of Works the law was added because of transgression. "It was not set up as a solid rule of righteousness, as it was given to Adam in paradise, but was added. It was not set up as an entire thing by itself."[21] The Covenant of Works was not added by way of *ingrediency* as part of the Covenant of Grace "for then the same covenant should have consisted of contradictory material, [but rather] by way of *subserviency* and *attendance*, the better to advance and make effectual the Covenant of Grace, so that although the same covenant that was made with Adam was renewed on Mount Sinai, yet I say still, it was not for the same purpose."[22] In answer to the question whether the Decalogue is abolished under the Covenant of Grace, Robert Rollock (1555?-1599) replies in similar fashion:

> The moral law, as it commands works done by the strength of nature, and as it is the rule of all works of this kind, namely, of such works as are required in the Covenant of Works, that is, in respect of the first and

> proper use thereof – for it concerns properly the works of nature, which make the condition in the Covenant of Works – in this respect, I say, the moral law itself also is abolished to them which are in Christ, even in like manner as the Covenant of Works is cancelled, and of none effect against them.[23]

In terms of the second distinction drawn by Rollock the moral law continues to be the rule of covenant fellowship between God and the redeemed. Thus Boston writes:

> Wherefore I conceive the two covenants to have been both delivered on Mount Sinai to the Israelites. *First,* the Covenant of Grace with Abraham, contained in the preface, repeated and promulgated to Israel, to be believed and embraced by faith, that they might be saved; to which were annexed the Ten Commandments, given by the mediator Christ, the head of the covenant, as a rule of life to his covenant people. *Secondly,* the Covenant of Works made with Adam, contained in the same Ten Commands, delivered with thunderings and lightnings, the meaning of which was afterwards cleared by Moses, describing the righteousness of the law and sanction thereof, repeated and promulgated to the Israelites there, as the original perfect rule of righteousness, to be obeyed. . . . Thus there is no confounding of the two Covenants of Grace and Works; but the latter was added to the former as subservient to it, to turn their eyes towards the promise, or Covenant of Grace.[24]

Peter Bulkeley (1583-1659), one of the leading writers on the covenant doctrine in New England, maintains that the covenant at Sinai was not a Covenant of Works, though the law contained the sum of the Covenant of Works.

> The Law is to be considered two ways. First, absolutely, and by itself, as containing a Covenant of Works. Secondly, dependently, and with respect to the Covenant of Grace. (1) Absolutely, alone by itself, and so it was given as a covenant to *Adam* in the beginning, and so considered, it shows the way and means of life, by which we might live. (2) Respectively, as having reference to the Covenant of Grace, and so it was given to the children of *Israel* at Mount Sinai; both as antecedent and consequent thereto. As antecedent to it, to prepare them for Christ, and the Covenant of Grace; and also as subsequent to it, to teach them how to walk and please God when they were entered into a new covenant with him, and thus was it given to them.[25]

In many respects, the interpretations of Ball and Bulkeley on the Mosaic law covenant anticipate the modern view, the so-called "misinterpretation view of the law," which denies that Lev 18:5 in its original context enunciates the principle of works-inheritance (not works-salvation – the conditional element of the Mosaic covenant pertains only to *temporal* life in the ancient Israelite theocracy). In reading Lev 18:5 as the principle of inheritance-by-faith ("Grace" rather than

"Law") this theological interpretation diverged significantly from mainstream Continental Reformed thinking. (On the Continental view it was the Judaizers' misinterpretation of the law of Moses, specifically their *misapplication* of the inheritance-principle stated in Lev 18:5 that resulted in their perversion of the Mosaic Covenant into a religion of works-salvation.) Though Ball and Bulkeley adopted this new interpretation of Lev 18:5, they continued to maintain at the same time that the Mosaic Covenant (including the Ten Commandments) had the *form* of a covenant of works.

Historians of theology have held different opinions regarding which of these two views was the dominant viewpoint in Puritanism. Some identify Ball as the representative thinker on the covenant doctrine. Others point to Fisher. Regardless of how this particular question is answered, there were clearly two opposing interpretations. By the time of Roger Williams (c. 1603-1683) the traditional view of early Reformed theology, reflected in Williams' work, became the exceptional viewpoint. At the time of the writing of the *Westminster Confession of Faith* (1648), the two sides in the debate were rather evenly divided, which may then account for the wise decision of the divines to omit detailed formulations on the subject of the discontinuities between the Old and New Testaments. Instead, the *Confession* reflected the consensus of opinion held among the Westminster divines concerning the main points of covenant theology. Richard A. Muller suggests that Fisher's *Marrow* served as "a theological prelude to the issuance of the Westminster Standards."[26] If this is so, and we are inclined to agree, then mainstream Reformed thinking would have been the dominant position at this historical juncture. Certainly the doctrine of the two covenants, the Covenant of Works and the Covenant of Grace, was standard fare: it was, in the words of Michael McGiffert, "a touchstone of the Puritan mind in the making."[27]

The guiding inspiration for the development of covenant theology among both the Puritans and the Continental Reformed theologians was the apostle Paul. In his thorough study, *The Pauline Renaissance in England,* John S. Coolidge offers the following synopsis of the Puritan, biblical-covenantal interpretation of Pauline theology:

> Paul's argument from the covenant with Abraham hinges on the relationship between that and the Sinai Covenant. The first, Paul insists, does not stipulate conditions: the second he identifies altogether with the conditions it contains, usually calling it simply "the Law." The Law, he argues, cannot condition the covenant with Abraham since it was communicated, by his reckoning, 430 years later. That is to say that the covenant which constitutes the chosen people of God is not conditional upon their performance. The conditions of the Sinai Covenant were communicated, paradoxically, in order to bring the people to a recognition that their covenant with God was unconditional; for until they recognized their radical inability to fulfill God's conditions of righteousness they might imagine that they were chosen for doing so. Thus the Sinai Covenant is subordinated to the covenant with Abraham. . . . The main outline of this argument cannot be overlooked by any Christian exegete, whatever he may make of the various problems it gives rise to,

> and Luther and Calvin can hardly be said to have neglected it. They do not notice, however, or else do not care to exploit, the possibility of elucidating Paul's argument by a simple adjustment of terminology. Paul's denial that salvation comes by "the works of the Law" can be restated as a denial that it comes by the "Covenant of Works" expressed in the conditions of the Sinai Covenant. In contradistinction, the covenant with Abraham can be termed the "Covenant of Grace." Thus Paul's argument from the covenant with Abraham can be clearly stated in terms of contrasting covenants. It is this mere rephrasing of the argument which constitutes the point of departure of a distinctive Covenant or Federal Theology.[28]

Coolidge concludes: "Federal Theology works outward from Paul to a comprehensive, coherent, and cogent understanding of the Bible and thereby of all things visible and invisible. It bids fair to be the ultimate achievement of Reformation biblical theology."[29]

Much of the theological debate on both sides of the Atlantic focused on the question whether the Covenant of Grace was conditional or unconditional. (Unfortunately, a great deal of time and energy was wasted on this aspect of covenant theology. The differences here were, once again, largely semantic.) Ball's remarks are representative of the teachings of orthodox Puritanism:

> The form of this covenant stands in gracious and free promises of all good to be repaired, restored, augmented, and a restipulation of such duties as will stand with free grace and mercy. For the Covenant of Grace does not exclude all conditions, but such as will not stand with grace. . . . It is a Covenant of Grace, though it be conditional. So the pardon of sin is given of grace, and not for works, though pardon is granted only to the penitent, and faith on our part, a lively, unfeigned and working faith is required to receive the promise.[30]

The conditions of the Covenant of Grace are threefold with reference to soteric justification: repentance is precedent; faith is concomitant; and obedience is subsequent – to employ the scholastic, Aristotelian categories. (The sequence is [*theo*-]logical, not temporal.) Ball indicates that

> if by condition we understand what is required on our part, as the cause of the good promised, though only instrumental, faith or belief in the promises of free mercy is the only condition. Faith and works are opposed in the matter of justification and salvation in the covenant, not that they cannot stand together in the same subject, for they are inseparably united, but because they cannot concur or meet together in one and the same court, to the justification or absolution of man.[31]

The instrument or appropriating means of justification is faith alone, that is, faith in distinction from all of the other graces which accompany union with Christ. Although faith is inseparable from all of the other saving benefits of union with

Christ, it is faith alone which receives the righteousness of Christ in the divine act of imputation. Imputation is the legal transferral of Christ's perfect fulfillment of the law to the believer's account. And the ground or basis of the believer's righteousness and salvation is this perfect obedience of Christ. Though good works are inseparable from justifying faith, they are not accounted for (perfect) righteousness. Such is apprehended by grace through faith. But as the necessary fruit of justifying faith good works, being evidential of saving faith, sustain a confirmatory role in the final approbation of the believer at the Last Judgment. Good works "are not the cause of, but only a precedent qualification or condition to final forgiveness and eternal bliss."[32] In the words of William Ames (1576-1633):

> Faith brings forth obedience in three ways. First, it apprehends Christ who is the fountain of life and the spring of all power to do well; second, it receives and acquiesces in the arguments which God has set forth in Scripture to induce obedience, namely, promises and threatenings; third, it has the power to obtain all grace, especially that grace which occasions obedience.[33]

The reward of eternal life is not a matter of meritorious accomplishment on the part of the believer who has been renewed in the image of Christ and predestined to walk in the way of good works.

> Our observance is not the chief or meritorious cause of eternal life. For by grace we receive both the right to this life and also the life itself as a gift of God though Christ apprehended by faith. . . . Yet our obedience is in a certain way the ministering, helping, or furthering cause of possessing this life (the right to which we have already been given), and in this sense it is called the way by which we walk to heaven, Eph 2:10.[34]

In Christ our obedience "is made acceptable to God so that it is crowned with greatest reward."[35] In terms of the principles of the divine covenants (specifically, the law/gospel antithesis), Thomas Watson (c. 1620-1686) writes:

> The form of the first covenant in innocence was working: "Do this and live." Working was the ground and condition of man's justification (Gal 3:12). Not but that working is required in the Covenant of Grace, for we are bid to work out our salvation, and be rich in good works. But works in the Covenant of Grace are not required under the same notion as in the first covenant with Adam. Works are not required for the justification of our persons, but as an attestation of our love to God; not as the cause of our salvation, but as an evidence of our adoption. Works are required in the Covenant of Grace, not so much in our own strength as in the strength of another. "It is God who works in you" (Phil 2:13). As the teacher guides the child's hand, and helps him to form his letters, so that it is not so much working as the Spirit's coworking.[36]

The NT plainly teaches the normative or regulative use of God's law (also called the "third use" of the law in distinction from the "first" and "second," which are the civil and pedagogical uses of the law respectively). The moral law *in its normative usage* is the ethical standard of Christian living, as expounded in the canonical writings of the New Covenant (*i.e.*, the NT). The principle text for Bolton's treatise on this subject, *The True Bounds of Christian Freedom,* is Jn 8:36 ("If the Son therefore shall make you free, you shall be free indeed"). This text is "the main basis whereon this doctrine of Christian freedom is built."[37] Puritan theology and ethics teach that the moral life is summed up in the Decalogue. (On this point the Puritans were mistaken. Compare our discussion of the Puritan doctrine of the Christian sabbath below.) "For substance, it contains such things as are good and holy, and agreeable to the will of God, being the image of the divine will, a beam of his holiness, the sum of which is love to God and love to man."[38] It makes no difference to Bolton whether one construes this law as coming from Moses or from Christ. "Acknowledge the moral law as a rule of obedience and Christian walking, and there will be no falling out, whether you take it as promulgated by Moses, or as handed to you and renewed by Christ."[39] Of chief importance are these two points:

> (1) That the law, or the substance of it (for we speak not of the circumstances and accessories of it), remains as a rule of walking to the people of God; (2) That there was no end or use for which the law was originally given but is consistent with grace, and serviceable to the advancement of the Covenant of Grace.[40]

It follows then that "If these two propositions are made good, the doctrines of the abrogation of the law and of freedom from the law will both fall to the ground."[41] The regulative use of the law – that positive function of the law within the sphere of redemptive grace – includes conviction of sin leading to repentance.

> [The] law was given us as a glass to reveal our imperfections in duty, and for this purpose the law remains with us. Through it we perceive the imperfections of our duties, our graces, and our obedience. By this means we are kept close to Christ and kept humble. The law takes us away from reliance on ourselves and casts us upon Christ and the promises.[42]

Ames helpfully defines sanctifying grace as "the very power by which we are lifted up to accommodate our will to the will of God."[43] New obedience is implicit in the biblical idea of the New Man or the new creation as that spiritual mode of existence which is the product of union with Christ and resurrection life in the Spirit.

> The law of God might seem to be, as it were, abrogated among the faithful, since it does not have the justifying power it had in the original state of integrity nor the condemning power it had in the state of sin. But it does have the force and vigor or a directing power; and it also retains a

> certain force of condemnation, for it reproves and condemns sin in the faithful (although it cannot wholly condemn the faithful themselves because they are not under the law but under grace).[44]

2. Social and Political Ramifications of the Covenant Doctrine

Fascination with the law's tutelary (pedagogical) function in the individual's spiritual pilgrimage played a major role in the rise of Puritan casuistry, as a means of bringing order or "method" to the daily lives of the saints. Many Puritans set forth detailed portraits of the spiritual life with its conflicts with sin and worldly temptations. Alongside interest in the *visible* signs of election and one's unassailable assurance of salvation were questions relating specifically to the place of law in the conversion process and to the precise nature of the warfare between the flesh and the Spirit.[45]

Against the historical backdrop of God's covenantal transactions in the ongoing drama of redemption, Puritan exegesis of Romans 7 served as a suitable paradigm for the conversion experience. The point of transition from wrath to grace in the personal history of each believer was paradigmatically viewed in terms of the sinner's experiential encounter with the demands of the law as a Covenant of Works, leading to his/her subsequent release from bondage to the law through the regenerating and convicting work of the Holy Spirit. Rather than grasping the redemptive-historical thrust of Paul's letter to the Romans, wherein the apostle expounded with great profundity the role of the Mosaic law in the history of redemption, the Puritans interpreted Romans 7 according to a very different hermeneutic, one which centered upon the individual's experience of salvation. Consequently, this passage in Romans was used to buttress the Puritan conception of law as preparatory to grace. In the Puritan scheme of things, priority was given to the preaching of law over the preaching of grace, in order that one would first be confronted with the demands of God's law as a Covenant of Works before hearing the promises of the gospel. The apostle Paul's personal struggle with the law of God, according to the Puritans' reading of Romans 7, was thus illustrative of the pedagogical function of the law as the means of entrance into the Covenant of Grace.[46]

Muller locates the beginnings of the development of the Reformed doctrine of the spiritual warfare in the life of the believer in the Puritan exegesis of Romans 7 and Galatians 5. "Puritan casuistry arose directly out of the Reformed interpretation of the warfare of flesh and spirit in Romans 7 as a description of the regenerate."[47] From this standpoint we can better understand the significance of *The Pilgrim's Progress* by John Bunyan (1628-1688), which is the fictional account of one individual's release from bondage to law under the Covenant of Works to freedom in the Spirit under the Covenant of Grace. Bunyan's Pilgrim, weighed down by the burdens of sin and the law, ultimately finds peace of conscience and liberty of soul in the knowledge of the sinner's justification by grace alone and the personal assurance of salvation that comes from the indwelling Spirit who bears witness to and with the Word of Christ. In Muller's estimation, "Bunyan's reformulation of federalism represents a reaction against legalistic covenant theology; it is, in other words, a movement away from the center toward the antinomian side of the spectrum, which nevertheless avoids the pitfalls of true antinomianism as described by Fisher."[48]

Puritan introspection, however, produced little peace for the troubled conscience. The root of the problem was a limited and, at points, erroneous theological grasp of the teachings of Scripture, in particular the misapplication of the covenant concept in the political realm (*i.e.*, the national covenant). Several factors were at work. Preoccupation with matters relating to the *ordo salutis* doubtless contributed to the failure of the Puritans to discern the basic redemptive-historical perspective of the apostle Paul, namely, that of the *historia salutis*. Emphasis on the practical or experiential side of Christianity included the social and political dimensions of covenant theology. The ancient theocratic constitution of the nation of Israel, the civil code of Moses, became the standard or norm for public morality both in terms of the stipulations and the penal sanctions of the Mosaic law. It is precisely on this point that the Puritans misconstrued the typology of the Israelite theocracy. This was one of the unfortunate consequences of the "misinterpretation view of the Mosaic law" which was rapidly gaining popularity in Old and New England. Those who did not share this interpretation of the covenant made with Moses were oftentimes maligned. Frequent misuse of the label "Antinomian" only added further confusion to the seventeenth-century debates over the nature and role of the moral law in the Christian life. Such authors as Tobias Crisp (1600-1643) were unfairly misrepresented. Like Bunyan, Crisp was desirous of emphasizing the free and gracious nature of justification through faith apart from human works, even the best works of the faithful. There was no place for mixing law and grace. The antithesis between the principles of law and grace was properly carried over to the contrast between the Mosaic Covenant and the New Covenant.[49]

From the opening days of the Protestant Reformation in England the vision of a Christian society was particularly attractive to the reformers who believed that the English people were God's chosen instrument for the propagation and defense and preservation of the Calvinistic faith. For the most part, the sermons which were presented before the Long Parliament addressed the national crisis of the 1640s, urging that England as a nation be conformed to the will of God as revealed in the Bible. "The first premise on which the preachers rested their views of corporate piety was that God governs the destinies of individuals and nations alike."[50] The nation as well as the individual could anticipate temporal prosperity as the reward for covenant faithfulness to God. Ancient Israel provided the model for Puritan expectations: the blessings of the covenant were understood to extend to people and land. The hope of realizing this vision of a theocratic nation devoted to God and his Word was even stronger in New England where "more than ever before, the covenant community became a 'Holy nation,' a 'New Israel,' a 'remnant according to the election of grace.'"[51] No other people shared the passion of this dream for a Christian society to the same degree or intensity as the New England Puritans. Their experiments in the American colonies afforded a new opportunity to test the workings of this socio-religious ideal. Its most famous contest was the Antinomian controversy surrounding the teachings of Anne Hutchinson.[52] During the period of the New England theocracies, when attempts were made to deal with backsliders in the covenanted community, moralistic teaching (of a kind) became more pronounced. Enactment of the Halfway Covenant as a means of addressing the growing problem of moral laxity among church members created more problems than it solved.[53]

The ordinance of sabbath-observance occupied a prominent standing in the Puritan ethos. The theocratic interpretation of the Christian sabbath indicated just how divergent the Puritan understanding of the relationship between church and state was from that of the Continental reformers. Assumptions drawn from natural reason rather than from the Scriptures, specifically the biblical doctrine of the divine covenants, were formative to the Puritan view on the Christian sabbath. Typical of Puritan teaching, Ames contends:

> Natural reason dictates that some time be set apart for the worship of God, for man needs to have time for all his actions, especially his outward ones, and he cannot conveniently attend divine worship unless he cease from other works during the time. . . . Positive law decrees that his holy day should occur at least once in a week, or in the compass of seven. But this is also by unchangeable institution so that for our duty and obligation the day has the same force and reason asthose which by their nature come under moral and natural law.[54]

Continuing his defense of the Puritan understanding of sabbath-keeping, Ames remarks:

> For it is a sure rule, accepted by all the best theologians, that moral precepts were distinguished from ceremonial and judicial ones in their transmittal in that all and only moral laws were publicly proclaimed before the whole people of Israel from Mount Sinai by the voice of God himself and later written, as it were, by the finger of God himself on tablets of stone to declare their perpetual and unchangeable duration. Christ also testifies expressly that not one jot or tittle of this law should perish, Matt 5:18.[55]

The Puritan view of the Decalogue as containing perpetual and unchanging moral obligation (duty for all time and all places) is not attentive to the actual historical covenantal context of God's redemptive revelation. The widespread appeal of theocratic law as it was emerging in seventeenth-century England led the Puritans to highlight the importance of the sabbath ordinance. Indeed, observance of the Fourth Commandment became the visible sign of godly piety in Puritan society. According to John H. Primus, sabbatarianism was "the badge of Puritanism."[56] With "unprecedented rigor" Nicholas Bound (d. 1613) and many of his contemporaries urged the enforcement of the sabbath commandment, the practice of which was thought to evidence the essence of divine law.[57] "In the sabbath," Ames asserted, "there was a common and public profession of the whole of religion. This commandment closes the first table of the law and in summary contains the whole worship of God by setting a certain day for the exercise of it, Is 56:2."[58]

The issues with which the Puritans wrestled were not new. From the beginning, as P. D. L. Avis maintains, the Protestant understanding of the OT judicial laws was "an important factor in the Reformation."[59] The distinctly theocratic conception of divine law for human societies in the modern world arose out of the turbulent years of religious persecution in Old and New England. Not content with the free exercise of religion which the New England Puritans had in large measure attained, they sought to enforce the Mosaic civil code as a means of ensuring the Christian witness in community and nation. The Salem witch-trials were merely the most notorious examples of the misuse of civil authority.[60] A radically different understanding of the relationship between church and state was associated, in a singular way, with the labors of Roger Williams, whose writings embodied in its leading features the teaching of the Continental reformers.[61] As Perry Miller stated, "For the subsequent history of what became the United States, Roger Williams possesses one indubitable importance, that he stands at the beginning of it."[62]

Understanding the place of individual and corporate piety in Puritan society requires that we distinguish carefully between personal salvation based on sovereign election and national prosperity as the experience of temporal blessing from the hand of God. Concerning New England's preachers, Harry S. Stout maintains:

> As social and cultural custodians, their primary focus shifted from God's mercy to man's responsibility to honor the conditional terms of God's national covenant. Here the emotional levers were fear and the possibility of divine desertion. Unlike personal salvation, which was granted, not earned, national covenants required good works on the part of the citizens.
>
> In distinguishing the separated but overlapping covenants of grace and national peoplehood, context meant everything. As social guardians, ministers could preach a message of civic obedience and works righteousness as long as they made it plain that their message concerned corporate and temporal blessings, not eternal salvation.[63]

Efforts to build a Christian society, one in which godly piety and faith were its hallmarks, inevitably paved the way for a form of moralism, one that based temporal blessing and prosperity upon the nation's (and the individual's) obedience to God's law. As a consequence, a new kind of bondage to the law of Moses was introduced.

More seriously, the rise of moralism in Puritan theology (in distinction from political theory) jeopardized the purity of the gospel. Although it was widely understood that the believer was no longer under a Covenant of Works, either in terms of the original order of creation or in terms of the legal administration under Moses, overemphasis upon the conditionality of the Covenant of Grace all too quickly translated into a new law-covenant.[64] Some historians have alleged that the legalistic tendency in Reformed theology appeared as early as the Reformation movement itself, notably in the Tyndale-Zurich line.[65] The accuracy of this reading, however, is highly questionable. Nevertheless, the development of moralistic teachings in English Calvinism is indisputable.[66] J. Wayne Baker maintains that the Antinomians in England "emphasized free grace in reaction to an incipient trend towards works-righteousness. As the century wore on, this trend toward moralism was more fully developed."[67] The views of Richard Baxter (1615-1691) are illustrative.[68]

This account of seventeenth-century Puritanism has featured the special role that biblical law occupied in theology and society. As it turned out, the glorious age of Puritanism proved to be a mixed blessing. The Puritan Way produced a new kind of legalism. And intolerance was its final product. "Of all the functions of government," observes Stout, "none received greater attention in the 1660s than the suppression of heresy. Religious intolerance, like Congregational polity, was a badge of New England's covenant fidelity. It was essential to the preservation of the country's privileged status."[69] For the Puritans, responsible exercise of freedom in the political and civil arena demanded national compliance with the Word of God. The long shadows of the Puritan ideal for "God's America" fall across the centuries, casting their silhouette upon contemporary evangelical thinking. In the minds of many today the question lingers whether – or precisely how – Christians and nonChristians are still bound by the law of Moses. Rather than seeking to impose the spiritual and ethical commands of Scripture upon the nations of this world, are we not to view biblical law as the instrument regulative of God's *covenant* people (the community of faith)?[70]

ENDNOTES

[1]Based on his study of developments in New England, Harry S. Stout comments: "The continuity in sermon substance was the most surprising finding to emerge from my research. If there was a 'decline' and resultant 'secularization' of Puritanism, it was not evident in the regular life of the churches. The majority of inhabitants continued to go to church, and their ministers persisted in the subject matter of their sermons. No shift from piety to moralism was evident" *(The New England Soul: Preaching and Religious Culture in Colonial New England* [New York: Oxford University, 1986] 6, *cf.* 94-5). The same cannot be said of Puritanism as a whole in Old England. See later discussion of moralistic tendencies in Puritanism. Stout's work provides invaluable insight into the beginnings of Puritanism in early America.

[2]The sharp distinction that is sometimes made between "Puritanism" and "Separatism" cannot be sustained. Both were an integral part of the Puritan movement. See Timothy George, *John Robinson and the English Separatist Tradition* (Macon: Mercer University, 1982); Stephen M. Johnson, "The Soteriology of John Robinson, Pilgrim Pastor and Advocate of the Reformed Faith," *WTJ* 44 (1982) 31-57; and B. R. White, *The English Separatist Tradition: From the Marion Martyrs to the Pilgrim Fathers* (Oxford: Oxford University, 1971).

Despite many differences and conflicts within modern-day evangelicalism, the historical roots of evangelicalism extend deeply into the soil of sixteenth- and seventeenth-century Calvinistic theology. A fresh look at our common origins may help resolve some of the current debates.

[3]Leonard J. Trinterud, "The Origins of Puritanism," *CH* 20 (1951) 38.

[4]*Ibid.* 39. "Tyndale states plainly that it is *the* organizing principle for an understanding of the Scriptures" (43). *Cf.* Michael McGiffert, "William Tyndale's Conception of the Covenant," *JEH* 32 (1981) 167-84.

In his book, *The Heavenly Contract: Ideology and Organization in Pre-Revolutionary Puritanism* (Chicago: University of Chicago, 1985), David Zaret attributes "the rise of covenant theology to circumstances that lie outside the realm of divinity" (130). He argues "that the ethical core of Puritan theology was indeed influenced by socioeconomic developments in early modern capitalism" (205), but not simply as "a by-product of the socio-economic activities of the Puritan laity." Instead, Puritan theology and ethics were "mediated by the organization dynamics of a social movement" (208). Zaret's study amounts to an overstatement resulting in a thoroughgoing misrepresentation of Puritan life and thought.

[5]"In the nature of things, systematic theology is international. This was even more notably so in the sixteenth and seventeenth centuries when Protestant theologians kept rethinking and restating the ideas of the Reformation and often wrote them down in an international language, *viz.* Latin. This means that theology, whether in Cambridge or Edinburgh, Leyden or Heidelberg, was basically the same, *i.e.*, the theology of Calvin. And as Dutch theologians learned from their English-speaking colleagues, so did English theologians from the Germans. This theological relationship between Continental and English theologians can be proved from both internal and external evidence"(Jen G. Møller, "The Beginnings of Puritan Covenant Theology," *JEH* 14 [1963] 58). This opinion counters the view of M. M. Knappen who contends that Tudor Puritanism "was not an indigenous English movement, but the Anglo-Saxon branch of a Continental one, dependent on foreign theologians both for its theory and for its direction in practical matters" *(Tudor*

Puritanism: A Chapter in the History of Idealism [Chicago: University of Chicago, 1939] 4-5).

[6]See John von Rohr's concise overview of the history of covenant theology in *The Covenant of Grace in Puritan Thought* (Atlanta: Scholars, 1986) 17-33. I have reviewed this work in this collected writings.

[7]Anthony Burgess, *Vindiciae Legis* (London, 1646) 219-20. See further, Chapters One and Twelve.

[8]C. F. Allison, *The Rise of Moralism: The Proclamation of the Gospel from Hooker to Baxter* (London: SPCK, 1966) x. "The Reformed doctrine of justification *by faith alone* does not mean faith in isolation. It means that, where man's salvation is concerned, there is, negatively, no room at all for any notion of human merit, and, positively, there is only room for the merit of Christ" (Philip E. Hughes, *Theology of the English Reformers* [Grand Rapids: Eerdmans, 1965] 48).

[9]John Ball, *A Treatise of the Covenant of Grace* (London, 1645) 15.

[10]Samuel Bolton, *The True Bounds of Christian Freedom* (London: 1645; London: Banner of Truth Trust reprint, 1964) 28. Bolton's remarks refer to the pedagogical function of the law. "By 'the handwriting of ordinances,'" comments Bolton on Col 2:14, "I conceive is not meant the ceremonial law alone, but the moral law also, so far as it was against us and bound us over to the curse" (31).

There is continuity between the interpretation of the Puritan divines and that of Calvin concerning the law/gospel antithesis. "The gospel, Calvin never wearied of repeating, abrogates the rigor of the law but not the validity and claim of the law. The rigor of the law was the necessity of perfect obedience as the condition of salvation. . . . The grace of the gospel is the gift of salvation when men failed to obey the law" (John H. Leith, "Creation and Redemption: Law and Gospel in the Theology of John Calvin," in *Marburg Revisited: A Reexamination of Lutheran and Reformed Traditions,* ed. P. C. Empie and J. D. McCord (Minneapolis: Augsburg, 1966) 149). More generally, see George Marsden, "Perry Miller's Rehabilitation of the Puritans: A Critique," *CH* 39 (1970) 91-105; George Harper, "Calvin and English Calvinism to 1649: A Review Article," *CTJ* 20 (1985) 255-62; and Richard A. Muller, *Christ and the Decree: Christology and Predestination in Reformed Theology from Calvin to Perkins* (Durham: Labyrinth, 1986).

[11]Bolton, *Christian Freedom 40.*

[12]*Ibid.* 23.

[13]Burgess, *Vindiciae Legis* 205.

[14]Edward Fisher, *The Marrow of Modern Divinity,* with notes by Thomas Boston (Swengel, PA: Reiner reprint, 1978) 24. Boston's biographer writes glowingly of Fisher's *Marrow:* "To some who read these pages it may seem not a little strange that such a thesis should ever call for vindication. They must remember that they were never trained to think in terms of that noble system of covenant theology. Every theology has its point of strain. And in the covenant-system, so rich in intellectual satisfaction, one point of strain must always be the interrelations of the covenants. Was the moral law the Covenant of Works? What, then, is the standing of the moral law in the Covenant of Grace? Was the covenant between God and Christ the very same as that between God and Adam? And does the believer accept the moral law out of the hand of God the Creator or God the Redeemer? Such questions seem very far away to us. They sound unpractical. They speak a language we hardly understand. But sooner or later they must be asked and answered by every student of the covenant theology. And they were never better answered than by Fisher" (George H. Morrison, "Biographical Introduction" in Thomas Boston's *Human Nature in its Fourfold State* [London: Banner of Truth Trust reprint, 1964] 26-7).

[15]Fisher, *Marrow* 23, notes.
[16]*Ibid*
[17]G. D. Henderson regards Boston to be the most influential exponent of federal theology in Scotland ("The Idea of the Covenant in Scotland," *EvQ*, 27 [1955] 13).
[18]Fisher, *Marrow 5-7*, notes.
[19]Fisher, *Marrow* 29. Consult further, Chapter Four.
[20]Fisher, *Marrow* 62.
[21]*Ibid.* 63.
[22]*Ibid.*
[23]Robert Rollock, *A Treatise of Our Effectual Galling,* trans. Henry Holland, in *Select Works,* ed. W. M. Gunn (Edinburgh : Woodrow Society, 1849) 50.
[24]Fisher, *Marrow* 56, notes.
[25]Peter Bulkeley, *The Gospel-Covenant or the Covenant of Grace Opened* (London, 1651) 63-4. Stout describes this treatise as "the definitive work on salvation" among the New England Puritans (*New England Soul* 42).
[26]Richard A. Muller, "Covenant and Conscience in English Reformed Theology:
Three Variations on a Seventeenth Century Theme," *WTJ* 42 (1980) 311, n. 9.
[27]Michael McGiffert, "From Moses to Adam: The Making of the Covenant of Works," *The Sixteenth Century Journal* 19 (1988) 155. See also his "Grace and Works: The Rise and Division of Covenant Divinity in Elizabethan Puritanism," *HTR* 75 (1982) 464-302.
[28]John S. Collidge, *The Pauline Renaissance in England: Puritanism and the Bible* (Oxford: Oxford University, 197O) 101-2.
[29]*Ibid.* 150.
[30]Ball, *Covenant of Grace 17.*
[31]*Ibid.* 20.
[32]*Ibid.*
[33]William Ames, *The Marrow of Theology,* trans. and ed. John D. Eusden (Philadelphia: Pilgrim, 1968) 220. "The meritorious and exemplary cause of [sanctification] is the death of Christ" (p. 170). Eusden points out that "For a century and a half William Ames' *Marrow of Theology* held sway as a clear, persuasive expression of Puritan belief and practice. In England, Holland, and New England nearly all those who aspired to the Puritan way read the book" (p. 1). "In early American theological and intellectual history, William Ames was without peer" (p. 11). Ames' teacher and mentor, the famous and most illustrious William Perkins, was noted for his practical emphasis in the exposition of Puritan theology. The moral law is outlined in his work, *A Golden Chaine,* in terms of its covenantal nature and function in the life of the regenerate and the unregenerate. "After the step of repentance the conversion process reaches its climax in the grace of new obedience. The concept of new obedience was at the very heart of his piety of law and Perkins took care to define it. The first aspect of new obedience was that it was a fruit of the Holy Spirit." Perkins's description of new obedience "underscores the theme that the Christian life for Perkins is not essentially something mystical, emotional, narrowly religious and ecclesiastical, or even intellectual. The heart of the Christian life is intensely moral" (Mark R. Shaw, "Drama in the Meeting House: The Concept of Conversion in the Theology of William Perkins," *WTJ* 45 [1983] 68). See further, Richard A. Muller, "Perkins' *A Golden Chaine:* Predestinarian System or Schematized Ordo Salutis?" *The Sixteenth Century Journal* 9 (1978) 69-81; and Donald K. McKim, "William Perkins and the Theology of the Covenant" in *Studies of the Church in History: Essays Honoring Robert S. Paul on his Sixty-fifth Birthday,* ed. H. Davis; Allison Park, PA: Pickwick, 1983) 85-101.

[34]Ames, *Marrow* 223.
[35]*Ibid. Cf.*, Bolton, *Christian Freedom* 159ff.
[36]Thomas Watson, *A Body of Divinity* (London: Banner of Truth Trust reprint, 1965) 129. "One of the most significant features of the doctrines of justification associated with Reformed Orthodoxy, distinguishing them from both that of Calvin on the one hand, and those of Lutheranism on the other, is that of the covenant between God and man. This development can be traced to the Zurich reforming theology of the 1520s, but was restated in terms of a *double* covenant by Gomarus, Polanus, and Wollebius. It is this later form of the concept which would become normative within later Reformed Orthodoxy and Puritanism. So significant a role did the federal foundations of justification assume within the Reformed theological tradition that the covenant-concept was frequently defined as the "marrow *(medula)* of divinity" (Alister E. McGrath, *Justitia Dei: A History of the Christian Doctrine of Justification* [2 volumes; Cambridge: Cambridge University, 1986] 2.40-41). "One of the most important features of Puritan theologies of justification is the federal foundation upon which they are based. The concept of a covenant between God and man underlies the soteriology of the *via moderna,* the young Luther and Reformed Orthodoxy. It is the version of this federal theology initially associated with the Reformed theologian Heinrich Bullinger and subsequently with the Heidelberg theologians Zacharias Ursinus, Kaspar Olevianus and Girolamo Zanchius which appears to underlie that of Puritanism" (112-13). See further, Mark W. Karlberg, "The Mosaic Covenant and the Concept of Works in Reformed Hermeneutics" (Th.D. dissertation, Westminster Theological Seminary, 1980).
[37]Bolton, *Christian Freedom* 51.
[38]*Ibid.* 56. For a discussion of the relationship between moral law and natural law, see Ernest F. Kevan, *The Grace of Law: A Study in Puritan Theology* (Grand Rapids: Baker, 1976) 52-77.
[39]Bolton, *Christian Freedom* 57.
[40]*Ibid.* 59.
[41]*Ibid.*
[42]*Ibid.* 88. According to Boston, "The law of the Ten Commandments, being the natural law, was written on Adam's heart on his creation" (Fisher, *Marrow* 26, notes). He describes the relationship between natural law and the original Covenant of Works in this manner: "The law of the Ten Commandments given to Adam as the Covenant of Works promised eternal life upon condition of obedience and threatened eternal death in case of disobedience; and this was it that made it the Covenant of Works" (p. 113, notes).
[43]Ames, *Marrow* 220.
[44]*Ibid.* 221. "Sin or the corrupted part which remains in the sanctified is called in Scripture the *Old man, outward man, the members,* and *the body of sin.* Grace or the renewed part is called the *New man, the spirit, the mind,* and the like" (p. 171). There is, Ames observes, a continual warfare between these two parts.
[45]Concerning the relationship between justifying faith and the assurance of salvation Ames properly maintained that "Justifying faith of its own nature produces and is marked by a special, sure persuasion of the grace and mercy of God in Christ. . . . First, the feeling of persuasion is not always present. It may and often does happen either through weakness of judgment or various temptations and troubles of mind, that a person who truly believes and is by faith justified before God may for a time think that he neither believes nor is reconciled to God. Second, there are many degrees in this persuasion. Believers obviously do not have the same assurance of grace and favor of God, nor do the same ones have it at

all times. But this cannot be said of justifying faith itself, without considerable loss in the consolation and peace which Christ has left to believers" (*Marrow* 163).

According to Zaret, "Beginning in the 1590s, Puritan clerics placed the idea of a heavenly contract at the doctrinal core of their casuistries, which described in minute detail the experience of spiritual regeneration. In so doing they created a distinctively Puritan form of covenant theology, which they presented in sermons and popular treatises" (*Heavenly Contract* 141). *Cf.* John von Rohr, "Covenant and Assurance in Early English Puritanism," *CH,* 34 (1965) 195-203; and Charles Lloyd Cohen, *God's Caress: The Psychology of Puritan Religious Experience* (New York: Oxford University, 1986).

[46]For a recent covenantal-historical approach to Romans 7, see Chapter Seven.

[47]Muller, "Covenant and Conscience" 318, n. 35.

[48]*Ibid.* 320-21. "From his reading of Luther Bunyan gained a strong distaste for legalism and a profound sense of the meaning of Christian freedom" (p. 321). Muller fairly and judiciously concludes: "In moving away from the delicate theological balance achieved by Perkins, Ames, and later by Downham, the thinkers of the second half of the century did more to show the weaknesses of the system than to preserve its integrity. For if Bunyan and Baxter represent the limits to which the federal structure could be stretched, they also delineate the points beyond which Reformed theology cannot go without becoming on the one hand a metaphysical determinism and on the other a pious voluntarism. Polarization of federalism along these lines would ultimately lead to the loss of the federalist dynamic and the demise of that delicate synthesis of faith and obedience, doctrine and piety that characterized the English Reformed or Puritan covenant theology" (p. 334). *Cf.* Richard L. Greaves, "John Bunyan and Covenant Thought in the Seventeenth Century," *CH* 36 (1967) 151-69.

[49]Kevan misreads the Puritan literature on this point of doctrine. The title of his study itself, *The Grace of Law,* is misleading as a description of Puritan theology. The phrase captures only *one* aspect of the Puritan teaching on the biblical doctrine of law. His sections on "The Place of Law in the Purpose of God" and "The End of the Law" are unsatisfactory. See further, Chapter One.

[50]John F. Wilson, *Pulpit in Parliament: Puritanism during the English Civil Wars, 1640-1648* (Princeton: Princeton University, 1969) 168. "Covenant theology as it evolved over five generations of New World preaching comprised a view of history and corporate identity that could best be labeled 'providential.' In this view God entered into covenants with nations, as well as with individuals, and promised that he would uphold them by his providential might if they would acknowledge no other sovereign and observe the terms of obedience contained in his Word. Covenanted peoples like those of ancient Israel and New England were the hub around which sacred (*i.e.,* real) history revolved" (Stout, *New England Soul 7).*

[51]Norman Pettit, *The Heart Prepared: Grace and Conversion in Puritan Spiritual Life* (New Haven: Yale University, 1966) 87. *Cf.* William Haller, *The Elect Nation: The Meaning and Relevance of Foxe's Book of Martyrs* (New York: Harper & Row, 1963). "Of the two levels of typology referring to the person and work of Christ in an eternal setting and to the redemptive mission of New Israel in a temporal setting, the first was far less controversial and dominated regular preaching on OT texts. . . . For the most part, the typological meanings extracted in regular preaching were external and spiritual; more temporal and literal typological readings (for example, the promised land of Canaan as prefiguring the promised land of New England) were reserved for occasional sermons reflecting on the corporate experience of God's 'American Israel'" (Stout, *New England Soul* 45). For a recent biblical-theological exposition, see Chapter Eight.

[52]According to William K. B. Stoever, this episode was only "a minor, provincial flurry" in seventeenth-century English history. Stoever concedes, however: "It was important for the subsequent history of Massachusetts Bay because its outcome assured the ascendancy there of the strain of Puritan piety and thought represented by Winthrop, Bulkeley, and Shepard, and because it helped to stimulate further clarification of New England ecclesiology. Its historic magnitude aside, however, the New England dispute involved a major theological issue, an issue as old as Christianity and one to which Puritans were especially sensitive"(*"Faire and Easie Way to Heaven": Covenant Theology and Antinomianism in Early Massachusetts* [Middletown, CN: Wesleyan University, 1978] 184).
[53]"To ensure pure church members, congregations founded after Salem built into their period of mutual examination and confession the requirement that prospective members submit a 'relation' or 'testimony' of saving grace. Since the church covenant was nothing more than a corporate extension of each member's personal covenant of grace, it followed that membership must be limited to true believers or 'visible saints'" (Stout, *New England Soul* 18; *cf.* 58-61). Consult further, Edmund S. Morgan, *Visible Saints: The History of a Puritan Idea* (New York: New York University, 1963).
[54]Ames, *Marrow* 287. The Decalogue was commonly understood to be a restatement of natural law, discernable through human reason. It was the ethical standard for two kinds of righteousness, civil and spiritual *(cf.* Luther's doctrine of the two kingdoms). Eusden suggests that Francisco Suarez (1548-1617) exercised an important, "if not controlling, influence on Ames's theory of law" (*ibid.* 288, n. 13).
[55]*Ibid.* 291. Though his position is not persuasive on the whole, Paul K. Jewett offers much helpful background and analysis of the history and interpretation of the sabbath doctrine in *The Lord's Day: A Theological Guide to the Christian Day of Worship* (Grand Rapids: Eerdmans, 1971). See also the collection of essays in *From Sabbath to Lord's Day: A Biblical, Historical, and Theological Investigation,* ed. D. A. Carson (Grand Rapids: Zondervan, 1982); and especially the superb article by John H. Primus, "Calvin and the Puritan Sabbath: A Comparative Study," in *Exploring the Heritage of John Calvin,* ed. David E. Holwerda (Grand Rapids: Baker, 1976) 40-75.
[56]Primus, "Calvin and the Puritan Sabbath" 43.
[57]F. Ernest Stoeffler, *The Rise of Evangelical Pietism* (Leiden: E. I. Brill, 1965) 65.
[58]Ames, *Marrow* 293.
[59]P. D. L. Avis, "Moses and the Magistrate: A Study in the Rise of Protestant Legalism," *JEH* 26 (1975) 149. See Willem Blake's compelling account of Calvin on church and state in *Calvin and the Anabaptist Radicals,* trans. William J. Heymen (Grand Rapids: Eerdmans, 1981); and David Little, *Religion, Order, and Law: A Study in Pre-Revolutionary England* (New York: Harper & Row, 1969).
[60]Charles Butler has provided a helpful gauge for evaluating the New England experience. In his doctrinal dissertation Butler analyzes the various factors in Reformed covenant theology which gave rise to views of intolerance, toleration, and religious liberty in the period of 1530-1660. He argues that the Abrahamic Covenant of Grace is foundational. "If that covenant were linked to a *Corpus Christianum* National Religious Covenant the resulting system was intolerance. . . . If the Covenant of Grace were linked to the covenant of a subunity whether political or ecclesiastical, toleration resulted. . . . Religious liberty resulted when the Covenant of Grace became directly the covenant of the individual" ("Religious Liberty and Covenant Theology," [Ph.D. dissertation, Temple University, 1979] 293-94). In summation, "The Sinaitic Covenant produced intolerance when identified as a Covenant of Grace; religious liberty, when identified and rejected as a Covenant of Works (Williams, Robinson); and tolerance, when viewed as a mixed Covenant of Grace and

Covenant of Works" (p. 299). Of Greg Bahnsen's work, *Theonomy in Christian Ethics,* Butler remarks: "his own intolerance – if it does not fully merit the name of persecution – is beyond anything ever suggested by the Puritans" (p. 302). There is no simple, direct line of development from the teachings of Puritanism to that modern-day Christian Reconstructionism. Despite certain similarities there is a fundamental discontinuity between these two theological systems.

[61]Bolton taught that the judicial or civil laws were given to Israel as "a rule of common and public equity, [whereby] it distinguished them from other peoples, and it gave them a type of the government of Christ. That part of the judicial law which was typical of Christ's government has ceased, but that part which is of common and general equity remains still in force. It is a common maxim: those judgments which are common and natural are moral and perpetual" (*Christian Freedom* 56). This same viewpoint found creedal expression in the *Westminster Confession of Faith,* even though this document did contain elements of theonomic law. See further, Chapters Two and Fourteen.

[62]Perry Miller, *Roger Williams: His Contribution to American Tradition* (New York: Bobbs-Merrill, 1953) 254. Williams's arch-opponent, John Cotton, "became the symbol of the New England Way" (p. 76). *Cf.*, Edmund S. Morgan, *Roger Williams: The Church and the State* (New York: Harcourt, Brace & World, 1967).

[63]Stout, *New England Soul* 24, 27.

[64]Consult Allison, *Rise of Moralism.*

[65]Richard L. Greaves ("The Origins and Early Development of English Covenant Thought," *The Historian* [1968] 21-35) posits two strands of covenant theology: (1) the Tyndale-Zurich line which was presumably legalistic; and (2) the Calvin line which stressed promissory grace. Whereas early Puritanism followed the line of Calvin, argues Greaves, the two strands merged in later Puritanism. For similar arguments, see James B. Torrance, "Calvinism and Puritanism in England and Scotland – Some Basic Concepts in the Development of 'Federal Theology,'" in *Calvinus Reformator: His Contribution to Theology, Church and Society* (Potchefstroom: Potchefstroom University for Christian Higher Education, 1982) 264-86; and William B. Clebsch, *England's Earliest Protestants: 1520-1535* (New Haven: Yale University, 1964).

[66]"A radically significant and often unnoticed turning point for English Christianity was the watershed in the middle of the seventeenth century which separated the view of the Gospel held in the first half of the century from the view of the second half with its trend toward moralism" (Allison, *Rise of Moralism* 192).

[67]J. Wayne Baker, "*Sola Fide, Sola Gratia*: The Battle for Luther in Seventeenth-Century England," *The Sixteenth Century Journal* 16 (1985) 133. "The influence of Luther and adherence to his meaning of justification *sola fide* and *sola gratia* slowly but surely had been eroded among the English clergy in the space of one century" (*ibid.*).

[68]Baxter's views came close to those of Arminianism. *Cf.*, Richard A. Muller, "The Federal Motif in Seventeenth Century Arminian Theology," *Nederlands Archeif Voor Kerkgeschiedenis* 62 (1982) 101-22.

[69]Stout, *New England Soul* 71.

[70]See further, Chapter Fourteen.

CHAPTER FOUR

THE ORIGINAL STATE OF ADAM: TENSIONS WITHIN REFORMED THEOLOGY

Covenant theology has long been identified as the hallmark of the Reformed tradition. Recently, Jack Rogers remarked: "One doctrine which may serve to focus on the distinctively Reformed contribution to ecumenical Christianity is *covenant*. The concept of covenant sums up much of what being Reformed is all about."[1] Over against the Lutheran and Radical reformational movements of the sixteenth century the Reformed tradition developed its theological system and methodology in accordance with the biblical doctrine of the covenant. Throughout the course of history, redemptive and preredemptive, God sovereignly administered his kingdom by means of the covenants. This study of the original state of Adam considers one aspect of the doctrine of creation, namely, God's covenant with Adam, what traditionally became known as the Covenant of Works. Implicit in our treatment of the biblical doctrines of creation and covenant is adherence to the historicity of the events recorded in the first three chapters of Genesis.[2]

The purpose of this article is to analyze and evaluate Reformed interpretations of Adam's original state in creation in light of the present-day debate within Calvinism. Special attention will be given to the subject of biblical eschatology (in its widest meaning, not just end-time events) in relation to the doctrine of creation. We will argue in favor of the so-called "organic" conception of covenant, which takes into consideration the eschatological design of Adam's creation in the image of God. As type of the one to come, Adam would receive the approbation of God upon his successful completion of the probationary test. The ground for covenant blessing was faithful compliance with the legal obligations made known to Adam through natural and supernatural revelation. The reward included confirmation in original righteousness and eventual glorification (upon fulfillment of the historical mandate given to our first parents to propagate the human race and to exercise dominion over all creation).

1. Background to Reformed Thought

It had become popular among medieval scholastics to distinguish between two stages of creation corresponding to a supposedly twofold state of Adam prior to the Fall. Whether or not one assumed a temporal separation between these two stages or states of creation, what was important in the minds of the scholastics was acknowledgment of Adam's creation in a "pure" state of nature (*in puris naturalibus*), to which was added the supernatural gift of grace (the *donum superadditum*).[3] By means of God's (nonredemptive) grace Adam and all humanity could come to spiritual communion with God as their highest blessedness. The higher enjoyment (*fruitio*) of God constituted the state of grace, in distinction from the state of "pure" nature. The provision of supernatural grace itself indicated the creature's utter dependence upon God for the full blessing of life and spiritual communion with God. The beatific vision of God, *i.e.*, glorification, could not be attained by natural human strength. Oftentimes, the scholastics spoke of this subsequent state of grace in specific terms of God's covenant or pact with all humanity. The eschatological goal of creation, namely, communion and life with God in consummated glory, was to be attained in the way of covenant promise and reward. Whereas the state of nature was static, the covenant order was established by God as the means of realizing humanity's final state of glorification and beatitude.

The Thomistic dichotomy between nature and grace played a prominent role in the history of dogmatics. According to Aquinas' interpretation of 1 Cor 15:46, Adam's original state (termed "animal life") was one in which the creature did not see God in his essence. Rather, Adam was to be translated into that perfect blessedness, whereby he might behold the divine essence. Adam's true happiness would consist in the vision of God in his essential glory, and it was beyond the natural ability of the creature to arrive at that state without the additional aid of supernatural grace. "Consequently neither man nor any creature can attain final happiness through [his] natural resources."[4] Aquinas taught that the individual's own good works, called "merits," were the ground of the promised blessing. The dualism between nature (*ex puris naturalibus*) and grace (*donum superadditum*), as applied to the creation order, was carried over into the fallen state. The Fall did not rob the creature of all his/her natural ability. The fallen creature was still able to do good works, *i.e.*, perform deeds of merit; but the addition of supernatural grace became all the more necessary after the Fall. The sacraments of the Roman Church were considered to be the channel for supernatural grace.[5]

There were three critically important concepts in late medieval nominalism: the *potentia ordinata* (the ordained power of God), the *foedus* (the covenant), and the Pelagian idea of *facere quod in se est* ("doing one's very best"). In contrast to the *potentia absoluta* (the absolute power of God), by which God could do any and all things freely and without limitation, God chose to bind himself in covenant with humanity, so that by his ordained power he bestowed supernatural grace to those who did their very best. Whereas Robert Holcot was responsible for joining together the idea of the *potentia ordinata* with the doctrine of *facere quod in se est*, the widespread adoption of this teaching was to be attributed largely to two sources – the writings of Gabriel Biel, who ranks among the most important and authoritative scholastics in late medieval nominalism, and the later Christian humanist movement during the early days of the Reformation.[6] Reflecting earlier Thomistic teaching Biel conceived of the "pure" state of nature as free of the infusion of grace – prior to Adam's reception of the *donum superadditum*.

Johannes Staupitz, who had greatly influenced the young Luther, was trained in the theology of Biel. The basic structure of the covenant in Staupitz' understanding was the same as that found in nominalism generally. David Steinmetz has observed: "Adam had as a hope or promise the gift of glory (what Staupitz following Thomas Aquinas sometimes refers to as the *visio dei* and sometimes calls *fruitio,* the unhindered enjoyment and love of God as the *Summum Bonum*)."[7] However, the content of the relationship between the Creator and the creature differed significantly from earlier formulations. The new element introduced by Staupitz was the role given to Christ in the pre-Fall situation. Adam's creation in the image of God involved conformity to Jesus Christ, the source of election. Before the Fall Adam could achieve his true potential as made in God's image through the cooperative efforts of his natural powers and the grace of Christ. Likewise, after the Fall good works (nature) retained its function in conjunction with the benefits of Christ's death (grace) in the process of salvation. Staupitz failed to reach a consistent Augustinian position on the sinner's inability to do what was good in the sight of God. He still left room for human cooperation with God in salvation. On the one hand, Staupitz taught, election was not based upon any foreseen merits in the individual, and good works themselves were viewed as fruits of election. The first grace of justification (called the *gratia gratum faciens*) could not be obtained by human merit. What was necessary was a proper moral disposition for its reception. This grace was freely bestowed upon those who truly desired it (combining doctrines of the *potentia ordinata* and *facere quod in se est*). However, in Staupitz' view, this grace was owed to the elect on grounds of God's covenant obligation made in Christ (*ex debito gratia*). On the other hand, the increase of grace in the elect was a matter of the merit of one's good works.

2. Early Reformed Theology

The rise and development of covenant theology in the age of the Reformation (up to 1648) can be fully understood only against the background of medieval scholasticism as we have outlined it above. Out of this theological context John Calvin and the Protestant reformers set about to reform church dogma according to the teaching of Scripture. Calvin acknowledges the eschatological design of God's purposes in creation. Based on the apostle Paul's statements concerning creation in 1 Corinthians 15, Calvin distinguishes between the earthly life of the First Adam and the heavenly life of the Second. Through Christ's redemptive work fallen humanity is renewed according to the pattern of Christ's heavenly image: "it is a peculiar benefit conferred by Christ, that we may be renewed to a life which is *celestial,* whereas before the fall of Adam, man's life was only earthly, seeing it had no firm and settled constancy."[8] The tree of life in the garden symbolized Adam's dependence upon the goodness and beneficence of his Creator.[9] Although Calvin does not develop his thoughts beyond this, his avoidance of the scholastic dichotomy between two states of creation clearly sets his view apart from previous teaching.

Among prominent federalists of the sixteenth century who expressed views similar to Calvin were Zachary Ursinus, Casper Olevianus, and Robert Rollock.[10]

By the closing decades of the sixteenth century the creation order was expounded in explicitly covenantal terms. Although Calvin himself did not view the pre-redemptive period in terms of the covenant idea, the federalist doctrine of the Covenant of Works (or as it was sometimes called, the Covenant of Nature) was consistent with Calvin's thought. On the basis of intensive study of the Scriptures these early Reformed theologians were led to abandon the scholastic doctrine of nature and grace, and the corresponding distinction between intrinsic merit (*ex condigno*) and undeserved merit (*ex congruo*). The former meritorious works were performed out of one's own natural strength, whereas the latter were possible through God's granting of prevenient grace. According to the early Calvinists, Adam as son of God was created to enjoy life and communion with God, and he continued to live by God's sustaining love and justice. The reward of greater blessing (eternal life) for the covenant obedience of God's image-bearer would have been a matter of divine justice, even though human righteousness was not an autonomous possession or attainment. This was the Reformed "organic" conception of covenant. It stood over against scholastic notions of inherent human virtue, to which God was made a debtor on grounds of "strict justice." (Such a view made justice a standard independent of God.)

Through long years of controversy and debate Protestant dogmaticians made increasingly heavy use of scholastic distinctions and terminology. To preserve the graciousness of the first covenant with Adam most Reformed federalists employed the speculative and dualistic distinction between nature and grace. As a result, the covenant order was set over against the natural order of creation. This new development, or rather revision to an older view, appeared in the writings of Francis Junius, a highly respected Dutch scholar and professor. The covenant, according to Junius, was established with our first parents by God the Father in the love of his Son. It held out the promise of supernatural life for obedience and the curse of death and separation from God for disobedience. As a supralapsarian, Junius emphasized the sovereign, electing purpose of God in creation. Although Adam was obliged to render complete and perfect obedience to the law of God by virtue of his debt as a creature (*ex puris naturalibus*), the covenantal reward of life eternal was strictly one of grace and mercy (*ex pacto*). Prior to the Fall, argued Junius, Adam's blessedness was communicated by the three persons of the trinity, particularly by the Son, the fountain of election. The cause of life was God's sovereign grace and election. The sacrament of the tree of life symbolized supernatural life through Christ, the originator of life. Although Junius upheld the essential distinction between this original, covenantal grace of Christ and soteric grace after the Fall, his speculative view of covenant nevertheless obscured the fundamental antithesis between the order of creation (law) and the order of redemption (grace).[11]

For the first time in the history of covenant theology there appeared a significant revision of Calvinistic doctrine regarding creation and God's covenant with Adam. No longer was the covenant concept organically related to the order of creation. The result was a logical, if not temporal, abstraction of a natural order from a supernatural, covenantal order in creation. On this interpretation the covenantal order was perceived to be superimposed upon the natural. Junius' view of supernatural grace offered in the way of covenant was virtually equivalent to the scholastic notion of the *donum superadditum.* A second and more serious result of this theological deviation within Reformed thought was federalism's obscuration of the eschatological design of creation.[12] (As we will argue below the return to the biblical theme of eschatology among Reformed systematicians at the turn of the twentieth century brought about the eventual reclamation of the organic conception of the Covenant of Creation.)

The fullest exposition of the Reformed scholastic doctrine of covenant appeared in the work of Johannes Cloppenburg. Cloppenburg had undoubtedly a significant, though indirect, influence upon the framing of the theology of the covenant in the Westminster Standards. He distinguished between subjective and objective sides of Adam's creation in the image of God. The objective side involved the covenant between God and Adam; the subjective side had regard to various characteristics of the human constitution. Whereas God's revelation to Adam was both natural and supernatural, Adam's ability to know God and to trust him required the supernatural communication of grace. The covenantal relationship – *personal* communion and fellowship with God – was not natural to Adam's original state in creation, but rather rested upon a special act of condescension on God's part. Although the covenantal reward of eternal life was contingent upon Adam's compliance with the law of God, the actual granting of eternal life was itself purely a matter of God's grace. Cloppenburg made use of the distinction between reward based on "strict justice" (intrinsic merit) and reward granted in the way of the covenant. As image-bearer of God, Adam was a servant of the Creator; his elevation from the status of servanthood to sonship was contingent upon God's covenantal love and condescension.[13]

With similar precision David Dickson conceived of the covenant arrangement as an addition to the constitutive state of nature with its distinctive governing principle, the so-called law of nature (*lex naturae*). The covenantal order entered alongside, but did not supplant, natural law. The law of nature required of the creature full and perfect obedience. Prior to life in covenant with God, Adam was but an unprofitable servant of the Creator. The obedience he rendered to God was merely his due as a servant-creature. By way of the covenant Adam was to be made a "confederate friend of God." The requirements laid down in connection with the probationary test, observed Dickson, were meager in comparison with the reward of eternal life; the reward far outweighed what Adam dutifully owed his creator.[14] In the words of one of his contemporaries, Anthony Burgess, who chaired the first committee of the Westminster Assembly: "Yet, though it were a Covenant of Works, it cannot be said to be of merit. Adam, though in innocency, could not merit that happiness which God would bestow upon him."[15]

From our brief survey of representative works in sixteenth- and seventeenth-century covenant theology it is not at all surprising that the scholastic conception of covenant found its way into the *Westminster Confession of Faith and Catechisms*. The *Confession* states:

> The distance between God and the creature is so great, that although reasonable creatures do owe obedience unto him as their Creator, yet they could never have any fruition of him as their blessedness and

> reward, but by some voluntary condescension on God's part, which he bath been pleased to express by way of covenant (7.1).

The natural relationship between God and the creature, we are told, is one of law: "reasonable creatures do owe obedience unto him as their Creator." But the highest enjoyment of God – "fruition" is the scholastic term denoting the beatific vision of God (glorification) – depends upon the covenant established "by some voluntary condescension on God's part." The *Shorter Catechism* describes the covenant as a "special act of providence," suggestive of the view that posits a distinction between the natural order and the covenant order. On the one hand, the covenant with Adam is defined as a Covenant of Works.[16] On the other hand, the nature/grace dichotomy as employed by the Westminster divines in their doctrine of the covenant introduces a speculative element within the confessional formulation.

> We cannot by our best works merit pardon of sin, *or eternal life at* the hand of God, by reason of the great disproportion that is between them and the glory to come; and the infinite distance that is between us and God, whom, by them, we can neither profit, nor satisfy for the debt of our former sins, but when we have done all we can, we have done but our duty, and are unprofitable servants; and because, as they are good, they proceed from his Spirit; and as they are wrought by us, they are defiled, and mixed with so much weakness and imperfection, that they cannot endure the severity of God's judgment (16.5, *italics mine).*

With respect to the sinner and justification before God, the *Confession* is accurate in its statements. And this, to be sure, is the main emphasis in this chapter of the *Confession*. However, at the same time, the Westminster divines reiterate here a point made earlier in chapter seven cited above. Because of the "great disproportion" between the Creator and the creature, the creature cannot merit eternal life on the ground of good works. In the state of nature Adam could find favor in God's sight and enjoy temporal life as long as he remained faithful and obedient. That is to say, natural life was contingent upon good works (merit); eternal life was nonmeritorious. Yet the Westminster divines identity the covenant with Adam as a Covenant of Works. The "Covenant of Grace" terminology is an exclusively redemptive-historical category, distinguishing those divine-human covenants subsequent to the Fall. In accord with the traditional Protestant law/gospel contrast the Westminster Standards preserve the distinction between two antithetical principles of inheritance, works and faith. "The first covenant made with man was a Covenant of Works, wherein life was promised to Adam; and in him to his posterity, upon condition of perfect and personal obedience" (7.2). To be sure, competing elements within the confessional formulations introduce a measure of ambiguity and confusion within Reformed theology.[17]

3. Recent Calvinistic Formulation

Not until the latter part of the nineteenth century and on into the twentieth century was progress made in clarifying the biblical doctrine of covenant. For the most part, however, the scholastic distinction between nature and grace occupied a fixed place in Reformed thinking. According to Robert Dabney, Adam was obligated to love and obey God by virtue of creation *in puris naturalibus*. The concept of merit was applicable in describing this natural relationship between Creator and creature, a relationship defined by strict justice. It was reasonable, argued Dabney, that God honor human obedience with the reward "of that natural well-being appropriate to the creature's capacities."[18] He stated more fully:

> God's act in entering into a covenant with Adam, if it be substantiated, will be found to be one of pure grace and condescension. He might justly have held him always under his natural relationship; and Adam's obedience, however long continued, would not have brought God into his debt for the future. Thus, his holiness being mutable, his blessedness would always have hung in suspense. God, therefore, moved by pure grace, condescended to establish a covenant with his holy creature, in virtue of which a temporary obedience might be graciously accepted as a ground for God's communicating himself to him, and assuring him ever after of holiness, happiness and communion with God. Here then is the point of osculation between the Covenant of Works, and the Covenant of Grace, the Law and the Gospel. Both offer a plan of free justification, by which a righteousness should be accepted, in covenant, to acquire for the creature more than he could strictly claim of God; and thus gain him everlasting life. In the Covenant of Grace, all is "ordained in the hand of a mediator," because man's sin had else excluded him from access to God's holiness. In the Covenant of Works, no mediator was required, because man was innocent, and God's purity did not forbid him to condescend to him. But in both, there was free grace; in both a justification unto life; in both, a gracious bestowal of more than man had earned.[19]

Espousing an essentially identical point of view, James Henley Thornwell speaks of the "radical notion of justice" (*i.e.*, strict justice) as that pertains to the natural order of things, what he calls "moral government" in distinction from covenantal administration. "[Adam] can never under mere moral government be exempt from the possibility of falling. He can never be rendered absolutely and immutably safe."[20] The difference between life in the natural order and life in the covenant order is the difference between a servant and a son. "Now, in the case of the son, the ground of his expectation from God is not his own merit, but the measureless fullness of the divine benevolence. God deals with him not upon the principle of simple justice, but according to the riches of the glory of his grace."[21]

Renewed interest in biblical eschatology led Reformed dogmaticians to reassess earlier scholastic conceptions of the original state of creation. A. A. Hodge defined the natural bond between God and Adam in terms of the covenant bond.

The concept of merit pertained to the legal aspect of the covenant wherein Adam's blessing of communion and fellowship with God was contingent upon "perfect conformity to the law of absolute moral perfection."

> It was also essentially a gracious covenant, because although every creature is, as such, bound to serve the Creator to the full extent of his powers, the Creator cannot be bound as a mere matter of justice to grant the creature fellowship with himself, or to raise him to an infallible standard of moral power, or to crown him with eternal and inalienable felicity.[22]

For Hodge the Covenant of Creation was both legal and gracious. Elsewhere he spoke of the "gracious Covenant of Works," echoing the ambiguity of the Westminster Standards.[23] Regarding justification by faith, Hodge commented: "'Merit' is that which deserves on the ground of covenant promise a reward. The merit of reward is imputed to us from Christ, the merit of praiseworthiness remains his forever."[24]

Abraham Kuyper, Sr., defines Adam's creation in the image of God explicitly in terms of the covenant order established by God in creation. He suggests that the essence of the covenant relationship reflects the nature and image of the triune God. The idea of Adam being made in the image of God is to be understood covenantally. According to Romans 5, observes Kuyper, Adam was in a covenant relationship with God. This covenant arrangement indicated the eschatological goal of creation. As image of God Adam was to move from the condition of *posse non peccare et mori* (the possibility not to sin and die) to the condition of *non posse peccare et mori* (not possible to sin and die); there was to be movement from glory to higher glory. The reward of eternal life was neither *ex congruo* nor *ex condigno,* but rather *ex pacto.* Kuyper identifies his view of covenant as the "organic" conception, as opposed to the "mechanical" viewpoint. His son, Abraham Kuyper, Jr., adds that covenant life issues from the triune God and originates in the eternal counsels of the Godhead. Although affirming the gracious character of the covenant with Adam, he emphasizes the inseparability between the natural bond and the covenant bond. "Adam is called as a confederate in life and created in covenant. The covenant is given with creation, which is evident with Adam's creation in the image of God."[25]

In light of the familiar passages in 1 Corinthians 15 and Romans 5 Herman Bavinck expounds the eschatological purposes of God in creation at some length. In the beginning Adam's life was "earthly;" his hope had been set upon the attainment of "heavenly" life upon successful completion of God's will for his creation. In contrast to Junius' supralapsarianism, Bavinck interprets these Pauline passages along infralapsarian lines. The eschatological nature of God's six-day work of creation, furthermore, suggests that Adam stood not at the end, but at the beginning of the way. Covenantal blessing for obedience would first bring confirmation in righteousness, and then glorification. The reward of eternal life, both in the Covenant of Works (creation) and the Covenant of Grace (redemption), stands as "the highest ideal before man."[26]

> The Covenant of Works and the Covenant of Grace do not differ in the final goal, but only in the way which leads to that final goal. In both there is a mediator, formerly of union, now of reconciliation; in both there is a trust, formerly in God, now in God through Christ; in both there is a hope, a love, and so forth. The religion is always essentially the same; it differs only in form.[27]

The essence of the covenant is union and communion with God. The form of the covenant refers to the way or principle of inheritance, whether it be by works or by faith.

Louis Berkhof, a leading American exponent of the Dutch Reformed orthodox tradition, formulated his view of the original state of humanity in terms of the *status integritatis* (the state of integrity). Despite his use of the nature/grace dichotomy, Berkhof stressed the importance of the covenant idea in conjunction with the biblical teaching on Adam's creation in the image of God. Adam was created for "a life of communion" with God. The covenant relationship itself was related to the intertrinitarian covenant, the so-called Covenant of Redemption between the Father and the Son in eternity. "In fact, it is exactly in the trinitarian life that we find the archetype of the historical covenants, a covenant in the proper and fullest sense of the word, the parties meeting on a footing of equality, a true *suntheke*."[28] According to Berkhof, the covenant relationship as a personal bond of union and communion between God and the creature finds its supreme example in the Godhead, the very source of life and blessing.

No one has made a more lasting contribution for the Reformed understanding of eschatology than Geerhardus Vos. "Few developments in biblical studies over the past century are of such far-reaching importance as an increasing recognition of the NT writers' broadened understanding of eschatology. . . Vos was a pioneer in calling attention to this fundamental datum of New Testament teaching – what can be termed its eschatological, redemptive-historical orientation."[29] Although Vos does not free himself entirely from the speculative nature/grace dichotomy, he perceives the strength of Reformed theology to lay in its doctrine of the covenant. In his sketch of the history of the covenant formulation he notes that several Lutheran dogmaticians towards the end of the seventeenth century had taken up the idea of covenant. But, remarks Vos, "this is strange since there is no place for it in the consistent Lutheran system."[30] The reason for this, posits Vos, is that Lutheran theology has no place for eschatology in its doctrine of creation, and consequently, it does not provide a viable theological system to accommodate the covenant idea. "Because Reformed theology took hold of the Scriptures in their deepest root idea, it was in a position to work through them more fully from this central point and to let each part of their content come to its own."[31] According to Vos' assessment, it is specifically the Reformed understanding of eschatology and the divine covenants in Scripture that sets Reformed theology apart from Lutheran dogmatics. As evidence of their decidedly theocentric orientation Reformed theologians were not content to leave the covenant idea in the realm of history without tracing it back into the eternal counsels of God. Vos writes:

> it is apparent that the dogma of the Covenant of Redemption is something other than a reworking of the doctrine of election. It owes its existence not to a tendency to draw the covenant back to and take it up in the decree, but to concentrate it in the Mediator and to demonstrate the unity between the accomplishment and application of salvation in him, on the one side, and the various stages of covenant, on the other.[32]

The intertrinitarian Covenant of Redemption reveals how the economic relations between the three persons in redemption is thoroughly covenantal. "In predestination the divine persons act communally, where economically it is attributed to the Father. In the Covenant of Redemption they are related to one another judicially."[33]

4. Current Debate in Covenant Theology

Among recent detractors of traditional Reformed teaching on the Covenant of Works two proposals have appeared: (1) that we abandon altogether the federalist system of interpretation; or (2) that we undertake a thoroughgoing revision of the doctrine. Common to all these critics is denial of the validity of the Covenant of Works idea. They claim that the idea of merit does not find support in Scripture. In our view, however, it is a matter of justice for God to grant eternal life to his obedient image-bearers. Failure to recognize this element of the system of truth contained in the Scriptures leads to a defective understanding of the atonement, specifically the necessity of Christ's atoning death as means of satisfying divine justice.[34]

N. Diemer objects to the traditional doctrine of the Covenant of Works because in his opinion the concept of works or merit is speculative. In his analysis of the history and theology of the covenant Diemer locates the true Reformed understanding of covenant in its emphasis upon the sovereignty of God against all claims to inherent human worth deserving of reward. The creature can never place demands upon God. Life with God, accordingly, is a gift of pure grace; eternal life is nonmeritorious. But rather than distinguishing between speculative and biblical notions of meritorious reward, Diemer instead minimizes the Reformed consensus reflected in the adoption of the "Covenant of Works" terminology for the original arrangement between God and Adam. Diemer superficially treats this element of Reformed thought as a theological anomaly. One cannot, however, jettison the doctrine of the Covenant of Works and still espouse a truly Reformed and biblical theology.[35]

In the wake of mounting opposition to historic Reformed Christianity in modern theology Cornelius Van Til writes in defense of orthodoxy:

> Covenant theology sprang up naturally as the most consistent expression of Calvinism, in which the idea of the self-sufficient, ontological Trinity is the final reference point in all predication. It is this idea that lies at the center of covenant theology. The three persons of the Trinity have exhaustively personal relationship with one another. And the idea of exhaustive personal relationship is the idea of the covenant.[36]

And "since the internal relationship of the triune God is covenantal, God's relation to mankind is also covenantal."[37] The original state of Adam, contends Van Til, was covenantal; and the covenant itself was conditional.[38] Building on the tradition of Vos and Van Til, Meredith G. Kline adopts a covenantal formulation of Adam's creation in the image of God in his treatise on the creative and recreative work of the Spirit. "Image of God and son of God," observes Kline, "are twin concepts."[39]

> Man as created was already crowned with glory and honor, for made in the likeness of the enthroned Glory, a little lower than the angels of the divine council, man was invested with official authority to exercise dominion as priest-king in God's earthly courts. Yet, the glory of man's royal functioning would be progressive as he increasingly fulfilled his historical task of subduing the earth, his ultimate attainment of functional glory awaiting the eschatological glorification of his whole nature after the image of the radiant Glory-Spirit. Ethical glory also belonged to man as created and in this respect man would have gone from glory to glory had he not sinned, moving on from a state of simple righteousness to one of confirmed righteousness.[40]

The biblical concepts of image, glory, and sonship are covenantal and eschatological. Regarding the eschatological design of creation, Kline comments:

> It is by tracing the unfolding eschatology of Scripture that we can most deftly unravel the strands of OT religion and discover what is essential and distinctive in it. For eschatology antedates redemption. The pattern for eschatology goes back to creation. Since the creature must pattern his way after his Creator's, and since the Creator rested only after he had worked, it was a Covenant of Works which was proffered to Adam as the means by which to arrive at the consummation. In the sense that it was the door to the consummation, this original Covenant of Creation was eschatological.[41]

It is not merely the *concept* of covenant that distinguishes Reformed theology from other theological traditions, but the *content* of the doctrine. Whereas the covenant idea was commonplace in late medieval nominalism, it was the task of the Reformed theologians to invest the covenant concept with scriptural meaning. And the greatest single impetus for this was the discovery of the biblical teaching on justification by faith. The Reformed tradition distinguished itself by developing a comprehensive, biblical-theological method as means of expounding the system of doctrine contained in the Scriptures. In a word, this method was covenantal. The rise of federalism, often associated with scholastic orthodoxy, was for the most part true to the earliest expressions of Reformed thought. Though use of the scholastic and speculative dichotomy between nature and grace meant a temporary setback for Reformed theology, concern for biblical eschatology in conjunction with the Reformed exposition of the covenants of God in pre-redemptive and redemptive history led eventually to the recovery of the "organic" conception of covenant. Claimants to covenant theology of a biblical and nonspeculative variety are divided between two schools of interpretation, that of historic Reformed orthodoxy (Vos, Van Til, and Kline) and neoorthodoxy (Torrance and Berkouwer).[42] It remains for evangelicals to weigh the issues in light of the teachings of Scripture and arrive at an informed consensus within "ecumenical [orthodox] Christianity."

ENDNOTES

[1]Jack Rogers, *Presbyterian Creeds: A Guide to the Book of Confessions* (Philadelphia: Westminster, 1985) 129.

[2]For a discussion of Adam as a historical person, see J. P. Versteeg, *Is Adam a "Teaching Model" in the New Testament? An Examination of One of the Central Points in the Views of H. M. Kuitert and Others*, trans. R. B. Gaffin, Jr. (Nutley: Presbyterian and Reformed, 1978).

[3]A good overview to medieval theology is found in Reinhold Seeherg, *Textbook of the History of Doctrines*, trans. C. E. Hay (Grand Rapids: Baker, 1977).

[4]Thomas Aquinas, *Summa Theologiae*, ed. T. Gilby (New York: McGraw-Hill, n.d.) 16.131.

[5]This covenantal-sacramental aspect of ecclesiology is not peculiar to Thomas. Martin Greschat traces it back to earlier medieval Roman Catholicism, particularly with the rise of the *Genossenshaften* or *Bünde* during the eleventh and twelfth centuries ("Der Bundesgedanke in der Theologie des spaten Mittelalters," *ZKG* 81 [1970] 44-63).

[6]See the following studies by H. A. Oberman: "*Facientibus Quod in se est Deus non Denegat Grotiom:* Robert Holcot O. P. and the Beginnings of Luther's Theology," in *The Reformation in Medieval Perspective*, ed. S. E. Ozment (Chicago: Quadrangle, 1971) 119-141; "The Shape of Late Medieval Thought: The Birthpangs of the Modern Era," in *The Pursuit of Holiness in Late* Medieval and Renaissance Religion, ed. C. Trinkaus and H. A. Oberman (Leiden: Brill, 1974) 3-25; and *The Harvest of Medieval Theology: Gabriel Biel and Late Medieval Nominalism* (Revised edition; Grand Rapids: Eerdmans, 1967).

[7]David C. Steinmetz, *Misericordia Dei: The Theology of Johannes von Staupitz in its Late Medieval Setting* (Leiden: Brill, 1968) 62.

[8]John Calvin, *Commentaries on the Old Testament* (Grand Rapids: Eerdmans, n.d.), *sub.* Gen 2:7.

[9]"[God] gave the tree of life its name, not because it could confer on man that life with which he had been previously endued, but in order that it might be a symbol and memorial of the life which he received from God. . . He intended, therefore, that man, as often as he tasted the fruit of that tree, should remember whence he received his life, in order that he might acknowledge that he lives not by his own power, but by the kindness of God alone, and that life is not (as they commonly speak) an intrinsic good, but proceeds from God" (*sub.* Gen 2:9).

[10]Paul Helm, "Calvin and the Covenant: Unity and Continuity," *EvQ* 55 (1983) 65-81. With reference to this article Roger Nicole comments: "[Helm] marshalls evidence to show that certain well-formulated covenant structures can be found in Augustine, that all essential features of covenant theology, notably the Covenant of Redemption between the Father and the Son and the Covenant of Works between God and Adam, as well as the Covenant of Grace between God and the redeemed, have unmistakable roots in Calvin's theology. The later emphases, he avers, were stimulated by the need to respond to the onset of Arminianism, but the fundamental principles were in place in Calvin and a number of others well before the beginning of the seventeenth century" ("John Calvin's View of the Extent of the Atonement'" *WTJ* 47 [1985] 209; see esp. 208-210).

See also Peter A. Lillback, "Ursinus' Development of the Covenant of Creation: A Debt to Melanchthon or Calvin?' *WTJ* 43 (1981) 247-288; Lyle D. Bierma, "The Covenant Theology of Casper Olevian" (Ph.D. dissertation, Duke University, 1980). Bierma takes exception to John Murray's reading of Olevianus. However, Murray is correct in stating that Olevianus taught that in the Covenant of Works eternal life was granted to Adam on the grounds of obedience to the law of God (merit). See Bierma's discussion on pp. 176ff.

[11]Francisci Junius, *Opuscula Theologica Selecta,* ed. A. Kuyper (Amstelodami: F. Muller and J. H. Krupt, 1882), *Locus* 25, theses 1-5. Peter Y. DeJong remarks: "The most conspicuous element is the way in which [Junius] made the transition from the Covenant of Works to the Covenant of Grace depend on the already established decrees of predestination. There can be very little doubt that the supralapsarianism of Junius prevented him from developing the reason why the Covenant of Works was necessary, when the salvation of the elect was already rendered certain by the decree of God from eternity" (*The Covenant Idea in New England Theology: 1620-1847* [Grand Rapids: Eerdmans, 1945] 27).

[12]Contrast the contention of DeJong: "Although from the very beginning the Reformed theologians made constant and consistent use of the covenant idea, they were not altogether clear on two specific points. In the first place, such leaders as Bullinger and Olevianus did not clearly formulate the representative idea. Original guilt was considered transmitted to all men purely because of the natural relationship in which Adam stood to the race, thus, in much the same manner as original pollution. It was not until some time later that the idea of his legal and representative relationship to the race was stressed as distinct from the physical. In the second place, these men were not always clear in distinguishing the covenant relationship in which Adam stood to God from his relation as creature" (*ibid.* 27).

[13]Johannes T. Cloppenburg, *Exercitationes super locos communes theologicos* (Franeker, 1683*), Loci de Statu Hominis Ante Lapsum*, I, theses 1-2; *Syntagma selectarum exercitationum theologicarum* (Franekerae, 1645), Disputation I, thesis 40.

[14]David Dickson, *Therapeutica Sacra* (Second edition: Edinburgh, 1697) 105ff.

[15]Anthony Burgess, *Vindiciae Legis, Or, A Vindication of the Morall Law and* the Covenants (London, 1646) 125-126.

[16]See Chapter One, pp. 38-39.

[17]The basic structure of the Westminster Standards rests upon the proper two covenant conception (the Covenant of Works and the Covenant of Grace), rather than upon the speculative nature/grace dichotomy. Eliminating the nature/grace dualism from the confessional formulation does not jeopardize the theological system contained in the Standards. However, rejection of the two-covenant schematization results in a radical revision of Reformed theology.

[18]Robert L. Dabney, *Lectures in Systematic Theology* (Grand Rapids: Zondervan, 1972) 300.

[19]*Ibid.* 302.

[20]James Henley Thornwell, *Collected Writings* (Carlisle: The Banner of Truth Trust, 1974) 1.258. For a discussion of the natural law idea in Calvinistic jurisprudence, see Chapter Two.

[21]Thornwell, *ibid.* Regarding the natural state and the subsequent Adamic administration, John Murray remarks that the latter order or administration entails certain features lacking in the previous order of nature: "there are data which cannot be construed in terms simply of creation in the divine image and the demands of awards belonging to that relationship" (*Collected Writings* [Carlisle: The Banner of Truth Trust, 1977] 2.48). According to the principle of strict justice (natural law), "Righteousness, justification, life is an invariable combination in the government and judgment of God. There would be a relation that we may call perfect legal reciprocity. As this would be the minimum, so it would be the

maximum in terms of the relation constituted by creation in the image of God" (*ibid.*). See further Chapter One, pp. 43-46, for a critique of the views of Murray on covenant.

[22]A. A. Hodge, *Outlines of Theology* (Grand Rapids: Zondervan, 1972) 310-311.

[23]A. A. Hodge, *Evangelical Theology* (Carlisle: The Banner of Truth Trust, 1976) 163-183.

[24]Hodge, *Outlines of Theology* 501.

[25]Abraham Kuyper, Jr., *De vastigheid des Verbond* (Amsterdam: W. Kirchener, 1908) 38-39.

[26]Herman Bavinck, *Gereformeerde Dogmatiek* (Kampen: J. H. Kok, 1928) 2.526.

[27]*Ibid.* 532. See also Herman Bavinck, *Our Reasonable Faith,* trans. H. Zylstra (Grand Rapids: Baker, 1956) 271f.

[28]Louis Berkhof, *Systematic Theology* (Grand Rapids: Eerdmans, 1941) 266.

[29]Richard B. Gaffin, Jr., "Foreword" to Geerhardus Vos, *The Pauline Eschatology* (Grand Rapids: Baker, 1979).

[30]Geerhardus Vos, "The Doctrine of the Covenant in Reformed Theology," in Redemptive History and Biblical Interpretation: The Shorter Writings of *Geerhardus Vos,* ed. R. B. Gaffin, Jr. (Phillipsburg, NJ.: Presbyterian and Reformed, 1980) 241.

[31]*Ibid.* "According to the Lutherans man had already reached his destination in that God had placed him in a state of uprightness. Eternal life was already in his possession. . . . Precisely because mankind's destination had already been reached before the fall in Adam, Christ can do nothing but restore what was lost in Adam. And since the destination already realized was fully compatible with mutability and the possibility of falling, the sinner who has been brought back to his destination by Christ must necessarily have to remain at this level. Lutheran theology is, therefore, wholly consistent when it teaches an apostasy of the saints. It does not at all object to uniting the state of justification and sonship with the possibility of such an apostasy" (p. 242).

[32]*Ibid.* 251.

[33]*Ibid.* 246. Vos distinguishes between predestination (the decree or purpose of God to elect some to salvation) and the Covenant of Redemption. "In predestination there is the one, undivided, divine will. In the counsel of peace this will appears as having its own mode of existence in each person. One cannot object to this on the basis of the unity of God's being. To push unity so strongly that the persons can no longer be related to one another judicially would lead to Sabellianism and would undermine the reality of the entire economy of redemption with its person to person relationships."

[34]Consult A. A. Hodge, *The Atonement* (Grand Rapids: Baker, 1974) and Leon Morris, *The Apostolic Preaching of the Cross* (Grand Rapids: Eerdmans, 1956) for classic treatments of the Reformed position. Contrast Gustaf Aulen, *Christas Victor: An Historical Stndy of the Three Main Types of the* Atonement, trans. A. G. Hebert (New York: Macmillan, 1969). Colin E. Gunton remarks: "The dominance of Western discussion of atonement by notions of legal satisfaction has been gravely distorting. But the fundamental assertion that human ill is radical, and yet is revealed and healed by God in Christ, is not endangered by the correction of the place where stress is laid in the doctrine of the atonement (see, in particular, Aulen and Whale)" (*Yesterday and Today: A Study of Continuities in Christology* [Grand Rapids: Eerdmans, 1983] 182).

[35]N. Diemer, *Het Sheppings Verbond Met Adam (Het Verbond der Werken),* (Kampen: J. H. Kok, n.d.). W. Wilson Benton, Jr., employs unduly pejorative language in his descriptions of federal theology in "Federal Theology: Review for Revision," in *Through Christ's Word: A Festschrift for Dr. Philip E. Hughes,* ed. W. R. Godfrey and J. L. Boyd, III (Phillipsburg, NJ.: Presbyterian and Reformed, 1985) 180-204. Benton fails to convey an accu-

rate and balanced account of federalist teaching as it developed out of earlier Reformed thought. Instead, his analysis portrays a caricature of Reformed orthodoxy, typical of many recent studies in historical theology. Regrettably, the author evidences no openness to other readings of the federalist literature. More importantly, in calling for a decisive revision of such Reformed doctrines as double predestination, assurance of salvation, and the justice of God, the author ends up substituting one dogmatic "principle" for another. Benton repudiates the "system" of doctrine espoused by the Reformed federalists, and in the course of argumentation indicates his sympathy for a neoorthodox reformulation of the fundamental concept of covenant. According to Benton, the chief culprit in the rise of federalism is Ramism. For a similar argument and biased reading of the history of covenant theology, see Robert Letham, "*The Foedus Operum:* Some Factors Accounting for its Development," *The Sixteenth Century Journal* 14 (1983) 457-467.

Denial of the Reformed doctrine of the Covenant of Works leads inevitably to radical reinterpretations of other doctrinal matters such as justification by faith (apart from works of the law), the typological significance of Israel's tenure in the land of Canaan, election, and perseverance of the saints. Notable examples of this growing trend in Reformed theology are the schools of thought associated with the works of T. F. Torrance and G. C. Berkouwer.

[36]Cornelius Van Til, "Covenant Theology," in *The New Schaff-Herzog Twentieth Century Encyclopedia of Religious Knowledge,* ed. L. A. Loetscher (Grand Rapids: Baker, 1955) 1.306.

[37]*Ibid.*

[38]Cornelius Van Til, "Nature and Scripture," in *The Infallible Word: A* Symposium, ed. N. B. Stonehouse and P. Woolley (Third revised edition; Philadelphia: Presbyterian and Reformed, 1946) 267-268. Van Til presents a stimulating critique of the covenant doctrine in modern theology in his *The New Hermeneutic* (Nutley: Presbyterian and Reformed, 1974) 109-61.

Donald Macleod defends the idea of "merit" in his "Federal Theology: An Oppressive Legalism?" *The Banner of Truth* 125 (Feb.1974) 21-28.

[39]Meredith G. Kline, *Images of the Spirit* (Grand Rapids: Baker, 1980) 23.

[40]*Ibid.* 31. Likewise, the creation-sabbath motif in Scripture points to the covenantal process of work and consummation rest (110-115). See also Meredith G. Kline, "The Covenant of the Seventieth Week," in *The Law and the Prophets: Old Testament Studies Prepared in Honor of Oswald Thompson Allis,* ed. J. H. Skilton (Nutley: Presbyterian and Reformed, 1974) 452-69.

[41]Meredith G. Kline, *The Structure of Biblical Authority* (Grand Rapids: Eerdmans, 1972) 154-155; see also, Meredith G. Kline, "Of Works and Grace," *Presbyterion* 9 (1983) 85-92.

[42]*Cf.*, for example, Thomas F. Torrance, *The Mediation of Christ* (Grand Rapids: Eerdmans, 1983); G. C. Berkouwer, *Faith and Justification,* trans. L. B. Smedes (Studies in Dogmatics; Grand Rapids: Eerdmans, 1954), and, in the same series, *Divine Election,* trans. H. Bekker (Grand Rapids: Eerdmans, 1960).

CHAPTER FIVE

COVENANT THEOLOGY AND THE WESTMINSTER TRADITION (A Review Article*)

One of the aims of David Weir's study of sixteenth-century covenant theology is to provide a rationale for the transformation of early covenant theology into the scholastic form called "federal" theology that obtained confessional status in the *Westminster Confession of Faith and Catechisms* written approximately one hundred years after the beginnings of the Reformation. Comparing the *First Helvetic Confession* (1536) with the *Westminster Confession* (1646), Weir observes:

> There is a definite shift noticeable between these two confessions – two documents separated by a century of theological and ecclesiastical history. The first teaches that the Scriptures principally expound grace; the second teaches that the Scriptures principally expound duty. Even responding to God's grace is a duty of all men, according to the Westminster Standards. This shift in emphasis is largely the product of the federal theology, and its emphasis on the fundamental relationship between God and man as found in the Garden of Eden, articulated by the Covenant of Works, and characterized by Adamic duty which is binding upon Adam and all his descendants. The *First Helvetic Confession* is concerned only with the fallen world and the grace needed to correct this world, a grace revealed by Scripture. The Westminster documents are much more cosmic in character. [P. 154][1]

Westminster Theological Seminary traces its roots to the assembly at Westminster (1643-49), while bearing close ties to Scottish and Dutch Calvinism.[2] Signficantly, the seminary in recent years has produced, primarily through its graduate students, a steady stream of articles, theses, and dissertations on the history and theology of the covenants to which Weir devotes ample attention in his book. A critique of Weir's monograph, which includes the most comprehensive bibliography to date on covenant theology (prior to 1750), provides this reviewer an opportunity to interact not only with the author's research and evaluations but also with a number of other important writings, many of which have appeared in the decade following the completion of my doctoral study in 1980, relating to Weir's subject of investigation.[3] In the course of our review we will be citing extensively from the secondary literature.

The introduction, comprising the longest section of the book, sets forth a detailed overview of the early period of covenant theology as well as a survey of leading critics of the history of doctrine. In the first chapter Weir explores the sixteenth-century lexicons to determine the meaning and usage of the biblical idea of covenant. Background for the prelapsarian covenant doctrine among Reformed interpreters is provided in chap. 2. Here attention focuses upon the predestinarian views of John Calvin and Theodore Beza. The third chapter briefly treats the life and writings of Zacharias Ursinus, who, according to the author, is the originator of the federal system of theology. The subsequent development of the federal school of thought is traced in the teachings of Thomas Cartwright, Dudley Fenner, Francis Junius, and Caspar Olevianus. The concluding chapter offers a summary analysis of the author's research, followed by his valuable "Appendix: A Bibliography of the Federal Theology and the Covenant Idea before 1750." This publication is a revision of the author's 1984 doctoral dissertation completed at the Center for Theological Inquiry in Princeton, New Jersey, during his time of residency as Member of the Center (1985-87). The dissertation was previously awarded the Frank S. and Elizabeth D. Brewer Prize of the American Society of Church History and the Samuel Rutherford Distinguished Thesis Prize of the University of St. Andrews for 1984.

Frequently, Weir speaks of the far-reaching consequences of the federal system without developing his thinking to any extent. He tells us, for example, that adoption of the idea of the Covenant of Works marks "an important change in a basic presupposition of Calvinist thought, and has implications for every part of life: doctrine, preaching, the understanding of the civil and ecclesiastical realms, the perception of God, and the purpose of man's existence" (p. 3). The reader is given no clear indication how or why this is so, nor is the reader certain whether such consequences are, in the author's mind, to be welcomed. Much of Weir's analysis of federal theology is marred by a misreading of the Reformation literature. At times Weir exaggerates differences between "federal" theology of the scholastic period and early "covenant" theology. A sharp demarcation between covenant theology and federal theology, in my judgment, is highly artificial and misleading. Weir's discussion, furthermore, contains a number of imprecise restatements and summaries of Reformed theology. Most serious is the virtual neglect of the medieval background for the covenant formulations, especially the influence of late medieval nominalism. Despite these limitations and reservations, Weir's monograph is deserving of careful study and interaction.

Weir states as the central thesis of his study:

> the prelapsarian "Covenant of Works" or "Covenant of Nature" is the key identifying feature of the federal theology, a type of theology which formed, and still forms, one of the basic theological frameworks for much of Protestant theology from the seventeenth century to the present. [P. vii]
>
> Covenant theology is a theological system in which the covenant forms the basic framework and acts as the controlling idea in that theological system. Almost all Christian theologians ultimately practice some form of covenant theology, in that they must somehow distinguish themselves as Christians and not as believers under the OT dispensation. Martin

> Luther, for instance, saw this distinction in terms of Law and Gospel. John Calvin described it in terms of OT and NT. The federal theology is a specific type of covenant theology, in that the covenant holds together every detail of the theological system, and is characterized by a prelapsarian and postlapsarian covenant schema centred around the First Adam and the Second Adam, who is Jesus Christ. [P. 3]

This interpretation, as already noted, rests upon the alleged discontinuity between two kinds of theology, the covenantal and the federal, an opinion all too commonplace in recent historical scholarship. (Our discussion in the following is based on a very different conclusion regarding the relation between Reformation and post-Reformation theology.) The question of the origin of the doctrine of the prelapsarian covenant between God and Adam is of more than historical interest. The legacy of Reformed dogmatics reveals how formative the covenant idea has been for both the schematization and the explication of the doctrinal system of Reformed theology. Some have asked: Did the Reformed doctrine of the covenant with Adam at creation arise out of exegetical study of the Scriptures or out of dogmatic concerns prompted by the polemics of the Reformation age? R. Sherman Isbell suggests that the Reformed doctrine of the prelapsarsan Covenant of Works arose initially from systematic, rather than from exegetical, examination of the Bible.[4] Similarly, Weir remarks that the federal interpretation "seems to stem from systematic, dogmatic thinking, not from exegetical study of Scripture" (p. 158). He bases his conclusion on the fact that "None of the sixteenth-century commentaries on Genesis 1-3 mention the prelapsarian covenant until after 1590" (p.158). We are not to infer from this, however, that the Reformers were guilty of introducing an alien hermeneutic into their theological construct. The priority of dogmatic schematization to biblical exegesis is descriptive of the historical circumstance. There were genuine theological precursors for the doctrine of the prelapsarsan Covenant of Works. As Weir points out, Augustine was among the first in the history of Christian thought to have entertained the idea of a covenant between God and Adam prior to the Fall (p. 12). Augustine's fleeting reference to such a covenant, however, was of minor import in his theology as a whole. Much more significant was his understanding of the relationship between the Old and New Covenants in terms of the "letter"/"Spirit" contrast. The relevance of this feature in Augustine's thought will be apparent in connection with our discussion of the covenant theology of Heinrich Bullinger, a formative thinker for the later development of the doctrine of the Covenant of Works by the heirs of the Reformed theological tradition.

One of the most critical doctrines of the Protestant Reformation was justification by faith. This doctrine and the coordinate law/gospel antithesis found a central place in the Reformed exposition of the divine-human covenants in the Bible. However, the immediate stimulus for the Reformed tradition's preoccupation with the covenants in Scripture was the question of the relationship between the two Testaments – a subject urged upon the Reformers by the Anabaptists (those of the so-called "Radical Reformation").[5] The issues of infant baptism and civil magistracy sparked debates among these early disputants. In Weir's judgment, however, *the* critical topic in covenant theology was the doctrine of predestination. Although the doctrine of divine predestination, more so than the doctrine of justification by faith, rapidly became one of the hallmarks of the Reformed theological tradition, the three elements in the system of doctrine – covenant, justification, and predestination – were treated interrelatedly. There is little point in singling out one among others. Since the doctrines of divine election and justification by faith were equally applicable to God's one way of salvation in both economies, under the dispensation of the law and under the dispensation of the gospel, Reformed theologians had scriptural warrant for maintaining the unity of the two Testaments (what came to be described as the one *substance* of the covenants) over against the teachings of the Anabaptists. The essence of the gospel, according to these Reformed interpreters, is the good news of free grace – grace that is entirely unmerited, unconditioned on human initiative, and irresistible. God's distinguishing grace in redemption is sovereign and efficacious, limited in the extent of its saving benefit to fallen humanity by the sole determination and good pleasure of God's eternal counsel and will. The decree of predestination, which is twofold, manifests the supreme glory of God in the display of his great mercy and love to sinners chosen before the foundation of the world and in the display of his wrath upon the reprobate. Early Reformed exposition of the doctrine of predestination was consistent with what later became known as *double* predestination. However, emphasis on divine reprobation varied in the several formulations given by Reformed expositors. Even though the doctrine of election and reprobation would undergo further scholastic definition and refinement, it was not the invention of Beza and orthodox Reformed scholasticism.[6]

In countering the Anabaptist interpretation of church and state, Bullinger argued in favor of the continuity between the Old and New Testaments and the legitimacy of Christian magistrates to exercise spiritual discipline in the commonwealth. As heirs of medieval Christendom Bullinger and the magisterial reformers joined forces to oppose the teachings of the Anabaptists. Those of the magisterial wing of the Reformation were committed to the implementation and enforcement of Christian principles of morality, if need be by use of the sword. They believed that the Mosaic civil legislation regulative of the ancient Israelite theocracy was at the same time compatible with natural law implanted in human reason by virtue of creation in God's image.[7] Though the law of Moses was not the meritorious basis of temporal or eternal salvation, nevertheless it provided a *model* (not a norm) for civil duty. Thus, the civil code of Moses was instructive in the public ordering of life and society in every nation, especially the Christian commonwealth. This was, in traditional Protestant terminology, the "first use" of the law of God. In the second place, God's law served a pedagogical function in the history of redemption both in terms of Israel's corporate experience and the experience of the individual believer through conviction of sin leading to faith and repentance. Third, the law of God was normative for Christian living, good works being the fruit of justifying faith. Calvinism, in contrast to Lutheranism, placed a far greater emphasis upon this "third use" of the law in its theological system.[8] In light of their understanding of the OT and the gospel, the Anabaptists rejected this threefold distinction of the uses of God's law. From their viewpoint the state was fundamentally an evil institution from which Christians were called to separate.

In Bullinger's view the doctrine of soteric justification is meaningful only against the background of Adam's original purity. Life in fellowship with God was the Creator's gift to Adam and Eve. Our first parents had not lacked for any good thing: Adam was in all points "most absolutely perfect."[9] Because of Adam's transgression sin entered the human race. All humankind was accounted as unrighteous; all were guilty of breaking God's eternal law. And because of the righteous demand of the law humanity now stood under the sentence of death. Did Bullinger conceive of the special command not to eat of the tree of the knowledge of good and evil to be part of an original covenant between God and Adam, wherein Adam was promised eternal life if he proved faithful to the commandment(s) of God and eternal death if he proved unfaithful? With one possible exception (what seems to be an *allusion* to an original covenant at creation), the idea of a prelapsarian covenant is not to be found in Bullinger's writings (see discussion below). However, the underlying antithesis between the law and the gospel is crucial to Bullinger's exposition of the one and eternal covenant of grace. The historical-covenantal contrast between "letter" and "Spirit" provides ingredients for the ensuing doctrine of the two covenants, the Covenant of Works and the Covenant of Grace, that would eventually become the staple of Reformed dogmatics from the late sixteenth to the twentieth centuries.

The chief or proper use of the law, stated Bullinger, was condemnatory (the "second use" of the law).[10] The law at Sinai brought death and condemnation to Israel. In so doing God instructed his covenant people in the way of salvation through faith alone, not by meritorious observance of God's commandments (*i.e.*, by "works of the law"). The "letter" of the law had reference to the outward administration of *temporal* life in the ancient theocracy. The principle of law-inheritance was antithetical to the principle of faith, the means whereby regenerate believers partake of the spiritual essence of redemptive covenant in every age (*postlapsum*). The Sinaitic Covenant was a particular historical administration of the one and eternal Covenant of Grace. The law written upon tablets of stone revealed the universal condition of humanity outside of Christ held under bondage to sin and death. But ultimately, the law of Moses was designed to enhance God's promise of saving grace. Did this contrast or opposition between the "letter" and the "Spirit" imply a radical discontinuity between the two Testaments? Hardly so. We conclude that the implication of Bullinger's teaching on the "letter" of the law is such that the principle of law-inheritance is restricted to the legal-typological sphere of the Sinaitic Covenant, applicable to the entire Mosaic dispensation as an administration of law and condemnation (2 Cor 3:6-11). It has reference to the principle of works-inheritance as that was regulative of Israel's probationary status in the land of Canaan, the earthly type of the heavenly inheritance. The principle of law is succinctly stated in Lev 18:5 (*cf.* Gal 3:12 and elsewhere).[11]

In *De testamento seu foedere Dei unico et aeterno*[12] Bullinger speaks of a covenant reestablished by God upon tablets of stone. Is the prior covenant that which God made with Adam after the Fall (the Covenant of Grace), as Weir insists, or does Bullinger contemplate the reinstitution of a *legal* covenant, a prelapsarian Covenant of Works? It is not altogether clear what Bullinger has in view. Certainly we have here the seeds of later federal thinking. In terms of Bullinger's teaching on the "letter" and the "Spirit" as descriptions of these two Covenants of Grace, the Old and the New, we maintain that the context of the disputed passage in Bullinger's treatise (see Weir's citation and discussion on pp. 11-12) points to the legal requirement placed upon Adam in his state of innocency (during the time of probation). We are told that the covenant written on stone was temporary in duration. Like the ceremonial laws in particular, the Old Covenant in general was to pass away. The period of law was the "time of correction" (*ad tempus correctionis*), a time of "passing over without the true Spirit and without the true completed faith and thus without Christ" (*placere pronunciavit* quae *sine vero spiritu et sine vera fide perfecta adeoque sine Christo negligebat*). This Covenant of Law was established in order that God might confirm the testament of grace. The gospel (or "mystery") of Christ was signified by sacraments and visible words. Thus the covenant at Sinai, theologically conceived, possessed elements of law and gospel, whereby the covenant re-established by God was not a mere reduplication of the first covenant, the prelapsarian Covenant of Works. The temporal character of this particular covenant could hardly be attributed to the single Covenant of Grace without further elucidation. We can quite appropriately speak of an "underdeveloped notion of the prelapsarian Covenant of Works" in Bullinger's theology (to borrow Weir's phrase used in connection with his criticism of Peter Lillback's similar reading of Calvin's theology, p. 32).

Calvin builds upon Bullinger's teaching regarding the legal form of the Old Covenant. "Calvin's exposition of the promises of *foedus legis*," writes Isbell, "goes far in establishing a meaningful continuity between Calvin and the Covenant of Works theologians of the next generation."[13] And in view of Calvin's remarks in his commentary on Jeremiah, Lillback concludes:

> Calvin comes within a hair's breath of identifying the Covenant of Law with its temporary nature with the pre-Fall temporal condition of Adam. Each was built on obedience. Each was broken. Both are compared to the Covenant of Grace with the gift of the Holy Spirit and persevering grace and found wanting. Perhaps this is the first contrast of the Covenant of Works with the Covenant of Grace in the history of Reformed theology.[14]

Since he restricts covenant terminology exclusively to God's *redemptive* provision for fallen humanity, Calvin overlooks a direct connection to the creation order in his exegesis of Is 24:5 and Hos 6:7. But Michael McGiffert astutely observes: "It is essential to recognize that Calvin supposed himself to be merely defining differences within the continuous dispensation of grace, but his contrast cut too sharp and deep to be contained for long within the single-covenant plan."[15] Weir shows some ambivalence on this issue. He writes:

> While John Calvin and the earlier reformers discussed the importance of the postlapsarian Covenant of Grace, they never taught the federal theology with its prelapsarian covenant motif. Yet over eighty years after

> Calvin's death (1564) the *Westminster Confession of Faith* stated that the federal theological system was part of Reformed orthodoxy. [P. vii][16]

He admits, however, that "Before the rise of the federal theology in the late sixteenth century there were various theological conceptions of the covenant, and even some precursors to the idea of a covenant in Eden" (p. 9). And though "Calvin makes no mention in any of his works of a prelapsarian covenant with Adam" nevertheless "there is evidence that, at least to a certain degree, Calvin considered the Edenic relationship between God and Adam to be covenantal in nature" (p. 10). The remarks of Calvin in his *Institutes of the Christian Religion* (4.14.18) provide "the only evidence that I know of in Calvin's writing which points to any conception of a prelapsarian covenant in paradise" (p. 10). However, all this apparently carries little weight in Weir's mind, since he takes exception to the conclusions of Lillback and Paul Helm in their respective studies advocating continuity between Calvin's thought and that of the federalists.

It is Weir's contention that debates over the Reformed doctrine of predestination, especially the problem of the historical event of the Fall in relation to the eternal decrees of God, first prompted Ursinus to adopt the twofold doctrine of the covenants.

> The prelapsarian "Covenant of Works" motif originated between 1560 and 1590 in the Palatinate, one of the several intellectual centres of Calvinism besides Geneva. There were two stages to its development. The first stage is its proposal in 1562 by Zacharias Ursinus after a decade of controversy over the sovereignty of God and Adam's fall. While we cannot document an absolutely certain relationship between this controversy and the proposal of the prelapsarian covenant idea, we can ascribe a high degree of probability to this relationship. The controversy surrounding the Fall is the only doctrinal controversy dealing with Adam that I can find in Reformed thinking during the years preceding 1562.
>
> The second stage of the origins of the federal theology is the use of the prelapsarian covenant as a commonplace of theology between 1584 and 1590. [Pp. vii-viii]

However, in our opinion, other issues such as covenantal (or testamental) continuity/discontinuity and the antithesis between the law and the gospel (including the contrast between the "letter" and the "Spirit") played the major role in the federal interpretation of the twofold covenants, the Covenant of Works and the Covenant of Grace. Though terminology varied among the Reformed writers, the *foedus naturale* ("Covenant of Nature") was identical to the *foedus operum* ("Covenant of Works"). The latter became the more familiar nomenclature in seventeenth-century Reformed theology onwards. While differing with Weir in his analysis of Ursinus' doctrine of the *foedus naturale* it is nevertheless true that the German Reformed theologians gave distinctive emphasis to predestination (election in particular) in their covenant formulations. This, however, does not explain the origin or context of the prelapsarian covenant idea. Weir's interpretation does not do justice to the combination of factors, historical and theological, which gave rise to Ursinus' application of covenant terminology to include both redemptive and preredemptive epochs. Nor does a satisfactory explanation appear for the early date for the prelapsarian covenant in Ursinus' writings advocated by Weir and others. We cannot be certain that Ursinus arrived at his doctrine of the *foedus naturale* as early as the drafting of the *Major Catechism* in 1562, what would doubtless have been only a preliminary draft of the 1584 publication.[17] If the *foedus naturale* did appear as early as 1562, why was there such a long period of neglect (from 1562 to the late 80s or early 90s when the doctrine was received as a commonplace in Reformed dogmatics)? Why did so vital a doctrine as that of the two covenants not appear in the writing of the *Minor Catechism* and, more importantly, in the writing of the *Heidelberg Catechism*? (Ursinus and Olevianus were the primary coauthors of the *Heidelberg Catechism.*) It seems more plausible to date the origin of the *foedus naturale* somewhere in the period between 1562 and 1584, first appearing in print at the time of the publication of the *Major Catechism.* Further support for this historical reconstruction lies in the fact that the *Major Catechism* served as Ursinus' lecture notes for his theological students. We would expect to find development and refinement in his covenant formulation.

Olevianus utilized the prelapsarian covenant idea in a much more fundamental and systematic way than did Ursinus, most notably in his interpretation of the Mosaic Covenant. As Lyle Bierma points out,

> The *foedus legale* for Olevian is really no more than a postlapsarian renewal or reiteration of the *foedus creationis,* the obligation placed upon mankind at creation to conform to the righteousness and holiness of his Creator. This *pactum,* he says, was established at Mount Sinai following Israel's deliverance from Egypt and obligated the people of God to perfect obedience of the law through the exercise of their own moral powers. Those who kept the commandments were promised eternal life; those who did not stood under the wrath of God's curse.[18]

Similar teaching on the Mosaic covenant of works is found in the writings of the English federalists.[19] Clearly the idea of the prelapsarian covenant was not given serious consideration among the Reformed theologians until after 1580. Bullinger's passing allusion to the prelapsarian covenant (if such it is), what he calls "the most ancient of all covenants" made with Adam, may well have set the stage for late sixteenth-century Reformed thought and for the work of the Westminster divines in the next century.

We turn now to consider briefly several implications and ramifications (some alleged) of the federal doctrine of the Covenant of Works. According to the federal scheme, the priority of law to gospel means that there is a legal order which precedes the redemptive, and this is fully consistent with the teachings of the earliest Protestant reformers. Sinclair Ferguson contends: "A more serious challenge is posed by the question whether the order of Grace and Law is not more true to Scripture than Law (or Works) and Grace."[20] He speaks of "the apparent stringency and legality of the Covenant of Works" and views the federal conception of redemptive history as merely "the logical extension of a theological scheme."[21] But Colin Brown rightly points out that it is Karl Barth who "turns upside down the approach he inherited from his Reformed forefathers." He explains:

> Protestant theology has long been accustomed to thinking of the Christian message in terms of law and gospel. The approach goes back to the Reformers themselves who in turn had no difficulty in showing that this approach was one used by the biblical writers themselves. The law comes first to man to prepare the way for Christ. It shows him as he really is in the light of God's holy character. It convicts of guilt as a necessary first step to make a man ready for the message of grace. . . .
>
> The basic difference lies in Barth's understanding of the significance of Christ. It is summed up in the contrast between the older idea of the two covenants – the Covenant of Works and the Covenant of Grace – and Barth's idea of the single, all-embracing Covenant of Grace in Christ. However much this older idea might need restatement in modern times, this is the focal point of conflict between orthodoxy and Barthianism. (It is probably also the unconscious point of conflict between evangelicalism and a good deal of modern theology.) But if the analysis of this essay is correct, the way forward to a deeper understanding of the Christian message in the modern world lies not with Barth's teaching as it stands but with the doctrines which Barth has brought again to the forefront. It lies with the need for a deeper understanding of the covenant theology of the Bible. For in the last analysis, Barth is guilty of Brunner's charge (a charge which Brunner is himself open to) that he has erected a "Natural Theology on the basis of a statement which has a Biblical core."[22]

In Barth's view the Protestant doctrine of justification by faith and the imputation of Christ's meritorious obedience requires basic reformulation. It will not do to restrict the "merit" idea, as some have done, to Christ's satisfaction of divine law exclusively. It is utterly meaningless to speak of the merit of Christ's obedience (active and passive) without acknowledging at the same time the merit of Adam's obedience had he rendered faithfulness to God as a covenant-keeper. In that creational arrangement the eschatological reward of eternal life was contingent upon Adam's obedience.

Weir shows reservation about speaking of the eschatological design of the original covenant. He posits:

> The *foedus* made with Adam before the Fall is a covenant which deals with creation and nature. Through it, man stands before God on his own merits; coming from sixteenth-century Reformed theology that sounds heretical, but it must be borne in mind that we are not speaking here of a doctrine of grace. There is no place here for justification by grace through faith, because there is no need for justification. Man is perfect; he stands holy before a holy God. In fact, a whole array of Christian

> doctrine is not necessary at this stage for a "church" with two members. There is no sin to call a man out of, no repentance necessary, no sanctification needed, and no ecclesiology required. Depending on how you approach the paradisal state there might be room for "eschatology," in that the Edenic state might be a means to an even higher state, but that is totally within the area of speculation. [P. 62]

Here Weir's thinking is in line with Lutheran thought, not Reformed, since there is no room for eschatology in the Lutheran doctrine of creation. Contrary to Weir's charge of speculation, the Scriptures teach that the eschatological design of the Covenant of Creation defined from the very outset Adam's natural life as a creature in covenantal fellowship with his Creator. The prospect of future glorification was already registered in the institution of the sabbath as sign of the Covenant of Creation. And sabbath-rest was the eschatological goal of the entire creation. The legal basis for the grant of inheritance to Adam and his descendants, had Adam successfully completed the time of probation, would have been Adam's "one act of righteousness." Accordingly, the first covenant was one of *works.* Adam having failed in his mission, Christ, the Second Adam, submitted himself to the obligations of the Covenant of Works and secured the eternal reward on behalf of God's elect people. On the sole ground of his meritorious oblation the redeemed will, at the conclusion of history, enter into the sabbath of God, resting from their earthly labors (*cf.* Rom 5:12-21 and Heb 4:1-11). The idea of a prior state of unrelieved contingency without hope of consummate blessing in eschatological glory reintroduces into Reformed theology the speculative Thomistic dichotomy between a state of nature and a state of grace.[23]

During the period 1570-1590 English sabbatarian doctrine came to prominence, at the time the Reformed doctrine of the Covenant of Works was taking hold in the Calvinistic centers of learning. In the judgment of Derk Visser, it was the latter teaching that nurtured the former.[24] And both doctrines, he tells us, were based upon a legalistic reading of the Bible. Weir similarly maintains that "extreme sabbatarianism had its roots in the federal theology" (p. 6). Contrary to these opinions, the dominant force behind English sabbatarianism was not theological, but economic and political.[25] This is not to overlook the theological foundation on which the Puritan sabbath was said to rest. As Kenneth Parker contends, post-Reformation sabbatarianism "was [not] founded on a fundamentally different theological base than that of the medieval Church."[26] The mistake of the English sabbatarians lay in their failure to subject this older Catholic dogma to thoroughgoing revision in light of the Scriptures, especially in light of the Reformed understanding of the covenants. In his assessment of English sabbatarianism Winton Solberg remarks:

> Though basic to what occurred, Calvinism was by no means solely responsible. Had it been, similar developments should have taken place in Reformed centers on the Continent, whereas such was never the case. Holland and Switzerland imported the English doctrine but applied it less rigorously, and in France and Hungary the Reformed minorities lacked the capacity to impose the English Sunday upon their country-

> men. Not Calvinism alone, then, but Calvinism interacting with basic economic and social forces accounts for the rise of the Puritan Sabbath.[27]

Thus it is misleading to tie English sabbatarianism directly to the federal school of interpretation. The doctrine of the Covenant of Works itself is neither "legalistic" nor the cause of sabbatarian thinking. The historian must he alert to a number of factors at work here.[28]

Some critics, *e.g.*, Leonard Trinterud, have attempted to locate the origins of a moralistic theology of the covenants as early as the beginning of the Reformation in the Rhineland.[29] Weir claims that whereas Calvin and Bullinger were in fundamental disagreement concerning the doctrine of (double) predestination, the German Reformed theologians achieved a mediating position, as seen in Ursinus' doctrine of the *foedus naturale*. Bierma, among others, has effectively refuted this kind of argumentation. "What differences there were between Zurich and Geneva," he writes, "were differences of emphasis and terminology, not substance."[30] Furthermore, covenant theology did not seek to compromise the Reformed doctrine of predestination by tempering, as it were, the "harshness" of the decree of reprobation. Bierma concludes:

> At the center of Olevian's theology lies an integral relationship between covenant and predestination, a relationship in which no sharp edges are taken off the decree but in which the covenant, by its very definition as reconciliation with God through justification and sanctification, is seen as part of the unfolding of God's decree to elect, to call the elect, to justify the called, and to sanctify the just.
>
> For Olevian the Covenant of Grace in no way mollifies the double decree of election and reprobation, either by shifting attention from God's decrees to his acts in history or by shifting ultimate responsibility for one's destiny from the divine to the human partner in the covenant. If anything, Olevian tends to "dehistoricize" the covenant rather than historicize the decrees.
>
> In sum, Olevian's covenant theology was by no means incompatible with the orthodox Calvinism of the late sixteenth and early seventeenth centuries but at the same time did not share all of its scholastic features.[31]

It is clear that the predispositions and biases of the historian of doctrine (as in every other discipline) shape his or her reading of the literature of the Reformation.

One of the most important hermeneutical issues in biblical exegesis and theology is the relationship between the two Testaments. Daniel Reid, in an article appearing in the popular evangelical periodical, *Christianity Today*,[32] has outlined the revolution now taking place in contemporary theology, a revolution that seeks to dislodge the reformational understanding of justification by faith by reinterpreting the NT, especially the Pauline, polemic against first-century Judaism. Of special interest in this debate among biblical scholars of widely diverse theological persuasions (both evangelical and nonevangelical) is the affirmation or denial of the classic Protestant law-gospel antithesis. In place of the traditional view regarding the Mosaic covenant of law modern interpreters have been increasingly attracted to the so-called "misinterpretation view of the law."[33] Study of the origin and significance of the Reformed doctrine of the Covenant of Works is highly instructive in the present controversy over the law and the gospel. The doctrine of the covenants brings into clear focus the inner structure and coherence of the underlying message of salvation in Jesus Christ as that message unfolds in the course of the history of redemptive revelation. Weir's monograph directs our attention to a vital subject for such a time as this.

ENDNOTES

*David A. Weir, *The Origins of the Federal Theology in Sixteenth-Century Reformation Thought* (New York: Clarendon, 1990).

[1]See Holmes Rolston III, *John Calvin versus the Westminster Confession* (Richmond: Knox, 1972); John Leith, *Assembly at Westminster: Reformed Theology in the Making* (Richmond: Knox, 1973); and Jack Rogers, *Presbyterian Creeds: A Guide to the Book of Confessions* (Philadelphia: Westminster, 1985). Sinclair Ferguson ("The Doctrine of the Christian Life in the Teaching of Dr. John Owen [1616-1683])" [Ph. D. dissertation, University of Aberdeen, 1979] 40) remarks: "The problem of the origins of Federal Theology is an area still requiring detailed study." Since the time of this writing much has appeared along with Weir's monograph.

[2]Consult W. Robert Godfrey, "The Westminster School," in *Reformed Theology in America*, ed. David E Wells (Grand Rapids: Eerdmans, 1985) 89-101. George M. Marsden offers a provocative and generally sympathetic reading of the Old Princeton-Westminster theology in "Scotland and Philadelphia: Common Sense Philosophy from Jefferson to Westminster," *Reformed Journal* 29/3 (March 1979) 8-12. It seems, however, that Marsden does not fully understand or appreciate the apologetic thrust of Reformed dogmatics, Reformation or modern. He writes: "The Princeton-Westminster tradition itself has not been renowned for softness in approaching alternative positions" (p. 10). The views of Cornelius Van Til, as representative of the Westminster School, "include a strong dose of the heavily theological Reformational outlook of the sixteenth and seventeenth centuries. Systematic and propositional statements of truth loom large, as they have throughout this tradition" (p. 11). Marsden identifies "the spirit of uncompromising militancy" as "a hallmark of the Princeton-Westminster outlook" (*ibid.*). The fact that all Christian theologies *in the post-canonical* era "end up with some degree of synthesis with alien philosophies" (p. 10) ought not deter the biblical interpreter from contending for and defending the *fundamentals* of the faith with vigor and fervor. Nor must we overlook or minimize the vital role of the Holy Spirit in bringing to the hearts and minds of believers illumination and conviction of the truth of God's Word.

[3]Mark W. Karlberg, "The Mosaic Covenant and the Concept of Works in Reformed Hermeneutics: A Historical-Critical Analysis with Particular Attention to Early Covenant Eschatology" (Th.D. dissertation, Westminster Theological Seminary, 1980); *cf.* Chapter One.

[4]R. Sherman Isbell, "The Origin of the Concept of the Covenant of Works" (Th.M. thesis, Westminster Theological Seminary, 1976) 1.

[5]For a general introduction see George H. Williams, *The Radical Reformation* (Philadelphia: Westminster, 1962); Alvin J. Beachy, *The Concept of Grace in the Radical Reformation* (Bibliotheca humanistica & reformatorica 17; Nieuwkoop: De Graaf, 1977); and Irvin B. Horst, *The Radical Brethren: Anabaptism and the English Reformation to 1558* (Bibliotheca humanistica & reformatorica 2; Nieuwkoop: De Graff, 1972).

[6]See further, Richard A. Muller, *Christ and the Decree: Christology and Predestination in Reformed Theology from Calvin to Perkins* (SHT 2; Durham, NC: Labyrinth, 1986); Lynne C. Boughton, "Supralapsarianism and the Role of Metaphysics in Sixteenth-Century Reformed Theology," *WTJ* 48 (1986) 63-96; John S. Bray, *Theodore Beza's Doctrine of Predestination* (Nieuwkoop: De Graaf, 1975); and Robert W. A. Letham, "Theodore Beza: A Reassessment," *SJT 40* (1987) 25-40.

[7]See Chapter Two.

[8]Merwyn S. Johnson ("Calvin's Handling of the Third Use of the Law and Its Problems," in *Calviniana: Ideas and Influence of Jean Calvin,* ed. R. V Schnucker [Sixteenth Century Essays and Studies 10; Kirksville, MO: Sixteenth Century Journal Publishers, 1988] 34) observes how "Calvin's handling of the 'third use of the law' supplements and extends without denying Luther's treatment of law and gospel and thereby establishes some of the most distinctive features of Reformed theology in his train." For a critique of recent ecumenical theology and a (partial) defense of orthodox Lutheran teaching on justification, see Carl E. Braaten, *Justification: The Article by which the Church Stands or Falls* (Minneapolis: Fortress, 1990). A similar case against ecumenical theology is made by Johann Heinz in "Justification and Merit: The Interpretation and Evaluation of the Concept of Merit in Modern Catholic Theology in Relation to Luther's Doctrine of Justification," (Th.D. dissertation, Andrews University, 1981); *cf.* John Reumann in *"Righteousness" in the New Testament: Justification in the Lutheran-Roman Catholic Dialogue* (Philadelphia: Fortress, 1982).

[9]Heinrich Bullinger, *The Decades,* ed. T. Harding for the Parker Society (4 vols.; Cambridge: Cambridge University Press, 1849-52) 3.377.

[10]*Ibid.* 3.239. See also his *Compendium christianae religionis* (Zurich: Froschouer, 1569) 58.

[11]For a fuller exposition of this feature of the Mosaic Covenant, see Chapters Eight and Twelve. Concerning Augustine's teaching on "letter" and "Spirit" in light of Protestant theology, consult James S. Preus, From *Shadow to Promise: Old Testament Interpretation from Augustine to the Young Luther* (Cambridge, MA: Harvard University Press, 1969); also my dissertation, "The Mosaic Covenant and the Concept of Works" 40–45.

[12]Basel, 1537.

[13]Isbell, "Covenant of Works" 79.

[14]Peter A. Lillback, "The Binding of God: Calvin's Role in the Development of Covenant Theology" (Ph.D. dissertation, Westminster Theological Seminary, 1985) 474-75. The reference is Jer 32:40.

[15]Michael McGiffert, "Grace and Works: The Rise and Division of Covenant Divinity in Elizabethan Puritanism," *HRT* 75 (1982) 486. John Murray favored restricting the covenant concept to redemptive grace and promise, and urged, in view of his departure from traditional Reformed interpretation, a thoroughgoing reformulation and recasting of the covenant doctrine. See Chapter One, pp. 43-46. The earliest Reformed theologians, Bullinger and Calvin among them, related the covenant idea for the most part to the provisions of redemptive grace. But in the interests of systematic theology, as is evident from a study of the history of Reformed doctrine, such a restricted conceptualization could not be maintained in terms of the total witness of Scripture. We can conclude, nevertheless, that the writings of Bullinger and Calvin provide us the principal outlines of the Bible's overarching redemptive-historical, covenantal scheme, first articulated by the apostle Paul and now further elucidated and refined by the reformers. As Johnson observes, "In a real sense Calvin begins with Luther's – and Paul's – basic understanding of law and gospel as the cornerstone of his own theology" ("Calvin's Handling of the Third Use of the Law" 49).

[16]Weir further remarks: "This new scheme of biblical history has extensive implications, some of which have not been explored, and most of which came to fruition in the seventeenth century. As a consequence of this transformation of thought, there is a shift in the importance of certain *loci* of scripture. The doctrine of creation, and the relationship between Adam and Christ, took on greater importance" (p. 7). Contrary to the consensus of opinion among historians of doctrine, Ferguson posits: "Indeed the Westminster theo-

logians wrote quite self-consciously of the twofold covenant as a still undeveloped idea, speaking of 'a' Covenant of Works, and the 'commonly called' Covenant of Grace. Whatever later ages were to make of it, this is clearly the language of a document not written for the purposes of wholesale subscription" ("The Doctrine of the Christian Life" 55). He concedes, however, that "it may be possible to acknowledge the cautious expression of J. S. Coolidge [in *The Pauline Renaissance in England*] that *the substance* of the Covenant of Works 'would not appear to be in itself a substantial departure from the Bible or from Calvin'" (*ibid.* 60). B. B. Warfield correctly identifies covenant as the architectonic principle of the *Westminster Confession* (in *The Westminster Assembly and Its Work* [New York: Oxford University Press, 1931] 56-57).

[17]See Derk Visser, "The Covenant of Zacharias Ursinus," *Sixteenth Century Journal* 18 (1987) 533. Letham locates the origin of the idea of the Covenant of Works in Ursinus' conditionalism ("The *Foedus Operum:* Some Factors Accounting for its Development," *Sixteenth Century Journal* 14 (1983] 461 n. 30). Weir notes: "As the century progressed the idea of a conditional covenant became more important. Words such a 'precepts, 'law,' and 'condition' creep into the lexicons. This should be expected, for there is a definite shift in the understanding of covenant during this period" (p. 55).

[18]Lyle D. Bierma, "The Covenant Theology of Caspar Olevian" (Ph.D. dissertation, Duke University, 1980) 183. "Because God is immutably righteous and true, he accepts us into the Covenant of Grace only in such a way that the integrity of the Covenant of Nature is preserved. He does not deem us just or award us eternal life unless we conform perfectly to the standards of righteousness required in the *foedus naturale* or, failing that, unless someone else satisfies the stipulations of the law in our stead. Hence the Covenant of Grace complements the Covenant of Nature" (p. 87; *cf.* also p. 183). Weir is not persuaded that Bierma interprets this element in Olevianus' theology accurately. At this point he finds "inherent difficulties in Bierma's methodology" ("*Foedus Naturale:* The Origins of Federal Theology in Sixteenth Century Reformation Thought," [Ph. D. dissertation, University of St. Andrews, 1984] 165-66). Both Lillback and Weir share a similar understanding of the relationship between law and gospel, from which viewpoint Lillback asserts that "the Covenant of Creation [in Olevianus' thinking] is not radically opposed to the Covenant of Grace in the Christian's life. The Covenant of Creation which was the beginning of man's duty to live before God in his law is still the very 'demand' of the 'new Covenant of Grace'" ("The Binding of God" 458). Lillback derives the same teaching from his reading of Calvin. But Lillback's interpretation amounts to a misreading of Olevianus and Calvin, one which appears to obscure the biblical antithesis between law and gospel.

[19]In the opinion of McGiffert, though the English divines learned covenant theology from the Continent, "in one highly signficant respect English thought may have preceded the Continent, namely, in giving early definition to the dualistic formula that everywhere became a hallmark of covenant divinity in the seventeenth century" ("The Rise and Division of Covenant Divinity" 463-64). McGiffert suggests that the interpretation of the Mosaic Covenant held by the English divines "points toward Sinai as the birthplace of the Covenant of Works" ("From Moses to Adam: The Making of the Covenant of Works," *Sixteenth Century Journal* 19 [1988) 135). However, he believes that we lack at present "a satisfactory genealogy of the doctrine. The impression prevails that the idea appeared suddenly in Continental and British writings of the 1580s and 1590s, without fanfare or fuss, and in remarkably mature form" (*ibid.* 133). The Reformation, post-Reformation research of the last decade has, in my judgment, brought sufficient clarity to this question.

Weir misrepresents Reformed teaching when he equates the prelapsarian Covenant of Works with the Mosaic Covenant (see pp. 3-5). Here again, the decisive factor leading Weir to this conclusion is his failure to see in Scripture and in the writings of the Reformed theologians the crucial antithesis between law and gospel – the legal demand facing Adam in the first Covenant, the Covenant of Creation, and Christ's *complete* satisfaction of this demand for perfect obedience rendered on behalf of the elect.

[20]"The Doctrine of the Christian Life" 56. Ferguson refers here to the views of Holmes Rolston III. See n. 1 above and my dissertation, pp. 20-22, 213-17. For an analysis of Reformed federalism along traditional lines, see also Andrew T. B. McGowan, "Federal Theology as a Theology of Grace," *Scottish Bulletin of Evangelical Theology* 2 (1984) 41-50; B. Loonstra, "De historische wortels van de leer aangaande het verbond," *Theologia reformata* 30 (1987) 46-63; J. J. van de Schuit, *Het verbond der verloosing: antwoord op de vraag: Twee of drie verbonden?* (Kampen: Kok, 1982); Dennis A. Bratcher, "The Concepts of Conditionality and Apostasy in Relation to the Covenant," (Th.M. thesis, Westminster Theological Seminary, 1986); and especially the detailed study by C. Harinck, *De schotse verbondsleer: Van Robert Rollock tot Thomas Boston* (Utrecht: De Banier, 1986). A useful discussion on law and gospel in Luther and Calvin is found in I. John Hesselink, "Law and Gospel or Gospel and Law? Calvin's Understanding of the Relationship," in *Calviniana,* 13-32 (see above, n. 8); and "Luther and Calvin on Law and Gospel in Their Galatians Commentaries," *Reformed Review* 37 (1984) 69-82.

[21]"The Doctrine of the Christian Life" 56. We respectfully ask: Is the justice of God too demanding that God should require *legal* satisfaction from his Servant-Son for the sins of humankind in accordance with his holiness and righteousness? Whereas historical Protestantism has upheld a doctrine of merit, Ferguson implies that the idea itself might be too stringent. Daniel Fuller in his important work, *Gospel and Law: Contrast or Continuum: The Hermeneutics of Dispensationalism and Covenant Theology* (Grand Rapids: Eerdmans, 1980), is more outspoken on the matter. We maintain, however, that according to the biblical doctrine of merit the standard of righteousness applicable to the redemptive work of Christ could not have been less for Adam in his original state of integrity. God would not have withheld (eschatological) blessing from Adam had he kept covenant with his Creator-God. We differ with the judgment of Murray, who argued that Adam would only have merited life, not *eternal* life. In regard to this distinction Murray was in agreement with the views of seventeenth-century Reformed scholasticism. Fortunately, Murray's adherence to the merit concept prevented him from radically reformulating the system of doctrine as Fuller would have it.

[22]Colin Brown, *Karl Barth and the Christian Message* (Chicago: InterVarsity, 1967) 126, 139.

[23]In the judgment of Lillback, Calvin's thought achieves a "middle ground between the merit system of the medieval Schoolmen and the law/gospel hermeneutic of the Lutheran system" ("The Binding of God" 334; *cf.* pp. 328ff.). Lillback's analysis of Calvin is encumbered by the scholastic dichotomy between nature and grace that is foreign to Calvin's thinking (see further Lillback's discussion on pp. 479-82). Stephen Strehle traces the Reformed doctrine of covenant back to the Franciscan idea of *pactum,* emphasizing the volitional character of God as author of the covenant with humankind. And according to Strehle, this is consistent with the doctrine of limited atonement and supralapsarianism espoused by later Reformed scholasticism. "No merit or condition of finite man could possibly induce divine justice toward reward, apart from this antecedent commitment of God via the covenant to honor a certain performance with a specific reward" *(Calvinism, Federalism, and Scholasticsm: A Study of the Reformed Doctrine of Covenant* [Basler und

Berner Studien zur historischen und systematischen Theologie 58; New York: Lang, 1988] 2-3). This is what the medieval scholastics spoke of as congruent merit: reward from God is "fitting" for man's good endeavors. Accordingly, man's obedience is not intrinsically meritorious (here the distinction is between *meritum condigno* and *meritum congruo*). The view that covenantal blessing, which would come in the wake of successful completion of the probationary test, would not be a matter of meritorious reward deprives biblical theology of its vital juridical element. To say that the reward for Adam's obedience would have been wholly a matter of divine grace (*i.e.*, unmerited favor) suggests that God would have been equally just in withholding reward from Adam upon his successful completion of probation. God would not have been obliged to reward Adam with temporal life any more than he would have been obliged to reward him with eternal life. On this view what guarantee would Christ have in terms of the "Covenant of Redemption" (the eternal counsel of the Godhead) if the Father were not obliged to reward the Son *ex pacto* – by virtue of the eternal covenant? Some argue that only the obedience of the Son in his work of substitutionary atonement is intrinsically meritorious on behalf of God's elect. Denial of meritorious reward in the covenant between God and Adam implies that Adam's disobedience would not necessarily provoke divine judgment and condemnation. God would be free to reward blessing for disobedience and curse for obedience. (If not the former, in the minds of some Reformed thinkers, at least the latter.) Does not rejection of the doctrine of merit forbid us to speak of the justice of God as Creator-Redeemer, one attribute alongside other divine attributes such as holiness, purity, righteousness, and unchangeableness? It appears that we are then reintroduced to the medieval doctrine of a god who is inherently capricious and arbitrary in his actions and purposes, a theological dilemma resolved for the medieval schoolmen by positing a covenant wherein God arbitrarily bound himself to reward man for his best efforts. See further, Chapter Four.

[24]Visser, "The Covenant of Zacharias Ursinus" 536.

[25]*Cf.* Christopher Hill, *Society and Puritanism in Pre-Revolutionary England* (New York: Seeker and Warburg, 1964). Winton U. Solberg argues similarly: "The new doctrine was the product of forces that were transforming England at the dawn of the modern era" (*Redeem the Time: The Puritan Sabbath in Early America* [Cambridge, MA: Harvard University Press, 1977] 27).

[26]Kenneth L. Parker, *The English Sabbath: A Study of the Doctrine and Discipline from the Reformation to the Civil War* (New York: Cambridge University Press, 1988) 16.

[27]Solberg, *Redeem the Time* 27. Solberg rightly criticizes Hill for giving short shrift to the religious and moral factors in his account. "Puritanism deserves equal if not greater emphasis in accounting for the rise of Sabbatarianism" (*ibid.* 309 n. 1). He further relates sabbatarian doctrine to the development of preparationism. "The preparationists [*e.g.*, Richard Greenham and William Perkins] reduced to its essence a body of instruction on how men should act to be saved and made proper Sabbath observance a key element in that code of conduct. In sum, the Puritan doctrine of the covenant and the Puritan theology of the Sabbath were born twins" (*ibid.* 40). *Cf.* Richard L. Greaves, "The Origins of English Sabbatarian Thought," *Sixteenth Century Journal* 12 (1981) 19-34.

[28]See Chapter Three. In *Theonomy: A Reformed Critique*, ed. W. S. Barker and W. R. Godfrey (Grand Rapids: Zondervan, 1990), John Frame, Vern Poythress, and Clair Davis adopt a moderating position between modern-day theonomy and traditional covenant theology, while Sinclair Ferguson and Samuel Logan deny or substantially minimize theonomic tendencies in English Puritanism, notably in the *Westminster Confession of Faith*. The editors of this collection of essays state that the approach adopted in this faculty symposium is "from our Reformed and Presbyterian commitments to the Westmin-

ster Confessional Standards and our Calvinistic heritage as the soundest and most comprehensive understanding of biblical faith and practice. As we see it, theonomy in various ways represents a distorted view of that tradition" (p. 11). Clearly, not all the contributors adopt the same posture as that of the editors. Frame proposes that in light of the apparent impasse between these two positions we set aside systematic theology and devote our efforts to the exegesis of specific texts in Scripture. However, this proposal rests upon Frame's own perspectival methodology. Poythress, a strong advocate of multiperspectivalism, contends that the controversy among the theonomists and the covenant theologians "is not easy to resolve, because it depends partly on the hermeneutical frameworks and the sets of questions that one has when one approaches texts of the OT" (p. 103). (The same thesis is set forth in Douglas A. Oss, "The Influence of Hermeneutical Frameworks in the Theonomy Debate," *WTJ* 51 [1989] 227-58.) Perspectivalism assumes the fundamental complementarity of *apparently* contradictory or antithetical perspectives. To the contrary, I am in full agreement with the opinion of Godfrey, who writes in this volume: "The approach of theonomy is a novel one in the Reformed community and uses the Scripture in a way that is alien to Reformed Christianity" (p. 312). See further, Chapter Fourteen and my critique of perspectivalism in "On the Theological Correlation of Divine and Human Language: A Review Article," *JETS* 32 (1989) 99-105.

[29]Leonard J. Trinterud, "The Origins of Puritanism," *CH* 20 (1951) 37-57. This position has been argued more recently by J. Wayne Baker in *Heinrich Bullinger and the Covenant: The Other Reformed Tradition* (Athens, OH: University of Ohio Press, 1980).

[30]Bierma, "The Covenant Theology of Olevian" 91. See also his "The Role of Covenant Theology in Early Reformed Orthodoxy," *Sixteenth Century Journal* 21 (1990) 453-62.

[31]Bierma, "The Covenant Theology of Olevian" 117-18, 236, 239. This is in contrast to the opinion of Weir: "It is the contention of this book that the doctrine of a *foedus* with Adam developed in response to this problem as a 'milder' orthodox elaboration and explanation of the seemingly harsh decretal doctrines of Theodore Beza" (p. 63).

[32]Daniel G. Reid, "The Misunderstood Apostle," *Christianity Today* 34/10 (July 16, 1990) 25-27.

[33]For a helpful survey of current trends, see Douglas Moo, "Paul and the Law in the Last Ten Years: Article Review," *SJT* 40 (1987) 287-307. On the role of historical theology in contemporary exegesis and interpretation, see Richard A. Muller, *The Study of Theology: From Biblical Interpretation to Contemporary Formulation* (Foundations of Contemporary Interpretation 7; Grand Rapids: Zondervan, 1991).

BOOK REVIEWS

1

The Covenant of Grace in Puritan Thought by John von Rohr. Studies in Religion, American Academy of Religion, No. 45. Atlanta: Scholars Press, 1986.

This major study in Puritan covenant theology by John von Rohr, now retired from the faculty of the Pacific School of Religion, reflects the care, devotion, and thoroughness given by the author to this subject over the course of many decades. It is a work of enduring value for the study of Puritanism. Von Rohr develops the covenant idea, considered to be the heart of Puritan theology, in relation to "the broader theological context" of Puritanism in the period from 1585 to 1660. From start to finish the theology of the Puritan divines is covenantal in orientation, and decidedly Reformed in conviction.

Puritan preoccupation with the two mutual emphases of human responsibility (covenant conditionality) and divine sovereignty (covenant unconditionality), the author suggests, distinguishes the Puritan outlook within the Reformed theological tradition in general. Whereas Continental Reformed theology during this same period of time was more concerned with system-building (giving rise to the movement known as orthodox scholasticism), Puritanism was more fascinated with the spiritual pilgrimage and travail of the soul. By far the preponderance of Puritan writings were devoted to the problem of humankind's bondage to sin and God's solution through the redemptive mercies and grace of Christ. Invariably, these Puritan treatises were written explicitly in terms of the Covenant of Grace.

The tension produced by these two theological emphases in Puritanism, according to von Rohr, became more pronounced than in earlier times in the history of the Christian church. Within Puritan thinking the "theological employment of the covenant theme, especially in its central figure, the Covenant of Grace, became a means of drawing together into fruitful and structured interrelationship these conflicting perspectives on the way of salvation" (pp. 1-2). All the while the Puritan doctrine of the covenant served a distinctly *pastoral* purpose. "Thus Puritan thought faced in two directions in response to the claims of predestination and of piety, the conjunction of the two providing Puritanism with its central paradox. Although it might appear that these differences were essentially between declarations of doctrine and proddings from the pulpit, they are not to be identified simply as tensions between the theologian and the preacher. Theologians were preachers, and preachers were theologians" (p. 8). But of the two sides of the covenant the feature of human responsibility was the more prominent. One might reasonably argue that the doctrine of divine sovereignty was merely foundational for lengthy Puritan expositions on the nature, conditions, and obligations of the divine-human covenant.

To be sure, the Puritan divines under consideration were staunch defenders of God's sovereignty. For this reason, among others, Puritanism stood "firmly in the Continental Reformed tradition" (p. 2). For the most part the author correctly avoids driving too large a wedge between early Calvinism and later Reformed orthodoxy. Regarding the doctrine of reprobation, "Earlier expressions tended in general to be more restrained on this matter and later expressions more explicit" (p. 2). More important for our author, however, was the placement of the decrees in the theological system. The Puritans, following Calvin, expounded their views on the decrees in a soteriological context "rather than a metaphysically speculative one" (p. 3). In so doing, the Puritan divines adhered to Calvin's interpretation of double predestination. The doctrines of election and justification occupied an important role in the Puritan understanding of the *ordo salutis*. (Over against von Rohr's assessment of Jerome Zanchius' theology of the decrees as imbibing a different spirit from Calvin's see the balanced study by Richard A. Muller, *Christ and the Decree: Christology and Presdestination in Reformed Theology from Calvin to Perkins* [Durham: Labyrinth, 1986]. My review of this book follows below.) The decisions reached by the Synod of Dort (1618-1619) are "one part of the Puritan theological heritage" (pp. 4-5). Puritanism took every precaution to formulate its views in opposition to the teachings of the Arminians. A question arises here with regard to von Rohr's categorization of Arminianism and Antinomianism as extreme positions on the "outer edges of the Puritan movement" (p. ix). Such Antinomians as Tobias Crisp, John Saltmarsh, and John Eaton were Calvinistic in their understanding of the decrees. Their views on the nature and function of the law of God in the application of salvation, though different from mainstream Puritan thinking, were nevertheless expressive of genuine Calvinism. Clearly, the Arminians fall outside the Puritan camp. Elsewhere in his study von Rohr's evaluation of Antinomian teaching fails to do justice to the complexity of the issues being debated in the seventeenth century.

Renewed interest in the study of Puritan theology indicates "that the Puritan movement, contrary to its classic stereotype as simply a rigid dogmatism or an oppressive legalism, is more and more being seen as embodying a 'profound experientialism' and indeed as an early expression of what later came to be designated 'pietism'" (p. 5). (Here the author cites the significant works of Heinrich Heppe, F. Ernest Stoeffler, and William K. B. Stoever.) Stress upon covenant conditionality, maintains von Rohr, was not an effort to soften God's sovereign decrees. In no way did Puritan covenant theology detract from the doctrine of absolute predestination. In this regard the influential work of Perry Miller is, in von Rohr's opinion, based on a misreading of the Puritans. Specifically, von Rohr objects to "the undue stress which Miller places upon the legal character of the covenant and hence upon its use as a bargaining instrument" (p. 20). The author vigorously challenges the supposition that the Puritan idea of covenant was purely contractual in nature. Von Rohr insists: "The context for understanding the utilization of covenant conditions must also include other and more comprehensive elements in the Puritan religious consciousness" (p. 21).

As already mentioned, there are two aspects of the covenant between God and the believer. First, covenant is a mutual agreement, a bilateral relationship between two parties. The human obligations comprise the *conditional* side of the covenant. Second, the covenant is absolute, *i.e., unconditional,* with respect to the purpose or decree of God in the salvation of the elect. The term "testament" best describes the promissory nature of God's covenantal commitment. Therefore, by taking into consideration both sides of the covenant, urges von Rohr, it is inaccurate and misleading to define the covenant relationship in Puritan thought in terms of a contract or mercantile bargain. (The Puritan understanding of the bilateral covenant did not cancel out divine monergism.) As far as this study goes, "the Puritans we are examining did not take sides on this issue. They affirmed both sides. The Covenant of Grace was both conditional and absolute" (p. 17).

The Antinomians, on the other hand, objected to speaking of conditions for life in covenant-fellowship with God. To do so in their minds came perilously close to perverting the Covenant of Grace into a Covenant of Works. No doubt reflective of his low estimate of the Antinomian group von Rohr too hastily dismisses the concerns of the Antinomians as excessive and marginal in Puritanism. In my judgment, typical formulations of covenant theology by the Puritan divines all too often tended toward imbalance and confusion on the matter of covenant conditionality and unconditionality. The root of this problem was lack of theological precision in defining the nature and function of the Mosaic dispensation of the "Covenant of Grace." As long as this issue regarding the place of the Mosaic Covenant in the history of redemption remained unclear and, in most instances, ambiguous mainstream Puritan theology was open to criticism. Though there are grave weaknesses to R. T. Kendall's thesis positing a sharp discontinuity between Puritanism and Calvinism (and here I am in agreement with von Rohr's reservations concerning Kendall's work), his reading of the Puritans is at least symptomatic of deficiencies and inadequacies in Puritan covenantal formulations. The least that can be said is that Puritan voluntarism was prone to overemphasize the conditionality of the covenant at the expense of its unconditionality. Having said that, however, von Rohr is nevertheless correct in noting how "particularly grievous. . . is the work of Kendall who dismisses Puritan predestinarianism out of hand as simply an ironic, intellectual remnant in what he portrays as a Calvinist system massively corrupted by a flagrant emphasis on voluntarism" (p. 31). Von Rohr levels similar criticisms against the views of Richard Greaves and J. Wayne Baker.

Along with other students of Puritanism, like Jens Møller and Michael McGiffert, von Rohr affirms a continuity between Puritanism and Calvinism. "When McGiffert turns his attention to subsequent English developments he shares Moeller's view of the importance of Calvinist ideas for covenant thought within emerging Puritanism itself. This is reflected particularly in his probing of the question of the occasion for the origination of the idea of a Covenant of Works. . . . The biblical themes of divine law and its application could not be abandoned, but efforts for their inclusion under the one covenant describing divine-human relations could too easily lead to such infusing of it with conditionality as to degrade the very meaning of grace itself" (p. 28). Here, however, von Rohr's analysis of the Puritan idea of covenant lacks cogency and consistency. How can the Covenant of Works idea be viewed as both a positive and a negative development? Why is the idea of the Covenant of Works alone liable to misconception in late sixteenth-century Puritanism and thereafter? Von

Rohr (and others) defines the Covenant of Works in Puritan teaching as a "legal *quid pro quo* contract" (p. 28), as "a thoroughgoing contractual arrangement, a divine-human *quid pro quo*" (p. 37). Why is von Rohr less charitable in his assessment of the Covenant of Works idea than in his assessment of the Covenant of Grace in Puritan theology? Von Rohr simply does not explain. This lacuna in recent studies of Puritanism will not be overcome without a reevaluation of the meaning and significance of the doctrine of the Covenant of Works in the Reformed tradition in general.

Puritan emphasis upon human responsibility in the covenant relationship and upon the progressive unfolding of the Covenant of Grace in history did not obscure or minimize the decretive character of God's covenant purposes. In fact, precisely the opposite was the outcome in Puritan thought, specifically in its formulations of the Covenant of Redemption between the Father and the Son in eternity. "Thomas F. Torrance has alleged that the use of this concept is a sign of growing abstraction in Puritan theology, for in positing something prior to the Covenant of Grace, that theology made the distinction between God's acts beyond time and God's acts in time. If so, however, it was abstract speculation reaching concrete conclusion, for the ultimate outcome was to draw the Christ of historical revelation more directly into both the substance and the assurance of the Covenant of Grace" (pp. 43-44).

Many other important aspects of Puritan covenant theology are dealt with in this study, all serving at the same time to demonstrate the great diversity of Puritan expression. Differences arose over the role of intellect and will in the process of conversion, the relationship between saving faith and the assurance of salvation, the function of the law as preparatory for grace (another indication, in my view, of ambiguities inherent in the Puritan covenantal tradition), and the relationship between covenant and election. With regard to the last issues von Rohr observes that it was the Antinomian group which sought to define covenant along particularistic lines, thus reducing covenant to election. "This collapsing of the Covenant of Grace into the Covenant of Redemption [the covenant made between the Father and the Son on behalf of the elect] tended, however, to be more characteristic of the Antinomian wing of Puritanism where there was inclination to see as much as possible in the divine act and to keep the covenant as far away as possible from human contracting" (p. 44, *cf.* also pp. 48-89, 90-91, and 177-179). Regrettably, this proclivity to equate the sphere of covenant operation with decretive election remains rather commonplace in contemporary Reformed exposition. Finally, with reference to the so-called Weber-Tawney thesis relating Calvinism to the rise of capitalism, von Rohr denies that the Puritan understanding of the signs of election includes a correlation between spiritual blessings and material prosperity: "Such a view, however, was in no way characteristic of Calvin, nor of the Puritan divines we are examining. Though this pragmatism eventually emerged to some degree in the interpretation of providence, it is not the outlook of Puritanism in its prime" (p. 159). The brief appendix provides a generally faithful and succinct overview of Continental covenant theology.

As an analysis of mainstream Puritan doctrine von Rohr's competent study in covenant theology makes a welcome addition to the growing number of studies in

Puritanism available today. However, because the author's treatment of the material is largely descriptive, this work offers little theological advance for the Christian church's ongoing articulation of the fundamental doctrines of Scripture, in this instance the doctrine of the covenant of God.

2

Christ and the Decree: Christology and Predestination in Reformed Theology from Calvin to Perkins by Richard A. Muller. Studies in Historical Theology 2. Durham: Labyrinth, 1986.

It is rare nowadays to read a scholarly analysis of the Reformation and post-Reformation literature which renders a faithful interpretation of the theology of the reformers. Richard A. Muller's masterful study, *Christ and the Decree,* a reworking of his 1976 dissertation (Duke University), provides a welcome breath of fresh air for current studies in the history of doctrine. The author has achieved a notable contribution to the study of the doctrine of Christ in decretive theology.

Muller's treatment begins by contrasting earlier critical opinion regarding the rise of Protestant scholasticism, the theological movement that flourished in the second half of the sixteenth century into the seventeenth (and beyond). As a result of the influence of post-Kantian philosophy upon German theology, nineteenth-century theologians all too commonly imbibed a penchant for a "systematic nomism." This predisposition culminated in the familiar "central-dogma" theories to explain Protestant orthodoxy, as seen *e.g.* in the work of Alexander Schweizer. Allegedly, the scholastic method produced a speculative and rationalistic system of doctrine inimitable to biblical theology. As for the Reformed tradition in particular, the doctrine of predestination was thought to be the principal doctrine from which all else was a logical deduction. Other voices, though far fewer in number, objected to this reconstruction in the history of Reformed dogmatics. Matthias Schneckenburger discovered "a continuity throughout the Reformed systems of the sixteenth century in this conception of predestination as the result of justification, the subjective or material principle of the Reformation, seeking out its objective ground" (p. 4). What this means more precisely is the subject of Muller's treatise.

The author argues the thesis that christology was the chief interest of the early reformers and "that Protestant orthodoxy did not depart from this emphasis, that it developed a doctrinal structure more formal in definition and more scholastic in method but nevertheless concerned to maintain a doctrinal continuity with the soteriological emphasis and christological center of the theology of Calvin and his contemporaries. In this development, orthodoxy completed the transition (already evident in the work of Calvin) from piety and the preaching of reform to the system of Reformed doctrine" (p. 10). To substantiate his thesis Muller engages in a careful and detailed analysis of how certain doctrinal motifs in Calvin's teaching on christology and predestination are "echoed, elaborated, [and] developed" by the orthodox scholastics (p. 17). In short, christology (specifically the doctrine of Christ's incarnation and mediation) and predestination are "the primary *loci*" of the Reformed theological system (p. 75).

In Reformed theology's restatement of patristic christology Muller discovers the introduction of a new covenantal-historical emphasis. "Calvin's christology and, I believe, much of the Reformed christology after him is neither a traditional 'christology from above' nor a modem 'christology from below' but a christology developed out of the historical line of the covenant-promise which points, as by a soteriological necessity, to the concrete, historical person of the God-man" (p. 29). Muller thus contrasts the "a-historical and metaphysically conditioned christologies of Chalcedon and of the medieval scholastics and the pronouncedly historical and functionally oriented christology of Calvin and the Reformed tradition" (p. 33).

Beginning with a study of Calvin's thought, what occupies center stage in Reformed theology, the author finds, is not abstract speculation on divine transcendence and immutability but historical reflection on the economy of salvation. (The preoccupation, however, does not result in an abandonment of the doctrine of God "as he is in himself" [*ad intra*].) "Elements in christology and in his doctrine of predestination point, therefore, toward a systematic relationship between Christ and the decree that lies at the heart of Calvin's theology and that draws on the fundamental distinctions with which Calvin wrestled in his attempt to codify the Reformation insight" (p. 35). The work of Christ the mediator rests upon the decree, and the decree is the determination made in the eternal *pactum* between the three persons of the Godhead. Accordingly, the Son is also the author of election, not merely the means of election. Reprobation, the reverse side of election, "occurs apart from Christ and therefore apart from any mediated knowledge of God. If those men who remain in the mass of perdition inquire into themselves they can only know their own sin and infer its penalty of damnation. They cannot know of the decree of reprobation as a cause of their condition" (p. 25).

Muller states that certain theologians (*e.g.*, Bullinger, Polanus, and Perkins) refrained from viewing the Fall as decreed by God. Musculus' distinction between foreknowledge and predestination suggests to Muller that "clearly, there are things within the foreknowledge of God that God does not predestinate. We may thus understand that God foreknows evil and yet is not its cause" (p. 53). (Compare the comments in my review of Paul K. Jewett's *Election and Predestination* below.) By making room for divine "permission," Musculus demonstrates "less causal rigor than does Calvin" (p. 53). Likewise, Muller understands Bullinger to have excluded the Fall from the counsel of God and to have differed from Calvin on double predestination. (For a similar misreading, in my opinion, see Cornelius P. Venema, "Heinrich Bullinger's Correspondence on Calvin's Doctrine of Predestination, 1551-1553," *Sixteenth Century Journal* 17 [1986] 435-30.)

The mystery of divine predestination accounts, to be sure, for the complexity of theological formulation, which at times has tended to say more than is warranted from the scriptural data. Even so, Muller rightly insists: "The doctrine of predestination, then, has altered little in detail and implication and it has not become the dominant force in reformulation of other *loci*. On the other hand, the frequently neglected subject of Reformed christology has proven a fruitful area of investigation. There we encounter a considerable development of doctrinal structures, each emphasizing the way in which the divine will manifests itself in the economy of salvation or the manner in which the divine person of the mediator is revealed to us in the work of Christ" (p. 123). Again, "We may safely say that the positive doctrinal development of early orthodoxy prior to Dort – as distinct though never separate from its polemics – was not the development of a speculative doctrine of election and reprobation per se but of the elaboration of the double decree in the light of more encompassing theological, in this case, trinitarian and christological concerns" (p. 158).

Later refinements of the Reformed interpretation of the nature and extent of Christ's atonement are consistent with the teaching of Calvin and his contemporaries. Contrary to the opinion of R. T. Kendall, Muller aligns Calvin's thinking with that of the later Calvinists on the doctrine of "limited atonement" (p. 34). On this subject the author commends to the reader the work of W. Robert Godfrey.

Muller favors the idea that the merit of Christ's obedience rests upon the decree rather than being its own ground. "The merit of Christ cannot be the foundation of our salvation in and of itself; rather the foundation of salvation is the will and ordination of God according to which the mediator was constituted. The dignity and power of Christ's merit, however, rest upon the divinity of Christ's person" (p. 141). The meritorious nature of Christ's obedience, imputed to the elect through the sole instrumentality of faith (*sola fide*), underscores the sovereignty of God's grace in salvation. There is no tension or conflict here between the early Reformed understanding of the divine covenant and later federalist teaching. "Later Reformed writers were able to utilize both the monopleuric and the duopleuric definition within a single system as representative of the two poles of Christian life, salvation by grace and human responsibility" (p. 41).

The development of doctrine from the beginning of the Reformation to the period of mature scholasticism, *i.e.*, Reformed orthodoxy, did not incorporate changes or elaborations which modified the substance of Reformed teaching. The work of Calvin and his contemporaries appears "not as a finished system but as the initial, as yet incomplete, reconstruction of the theological edifice criticized, disrupted, and radically transformed by the Reformation assault upon elements in late medieval scholasticism and upon the abuses of Rome" (p. 75). Various aspects of the theological system of the late medieval period were employed in the defense of the newly articulated faith. Nevertheless, concedes Muller, the orthodox system did evince a "more speculative, logical pattern than [that found in] either Calvin or Bullinger" (p. 179). This use of logical argumentation, however, is "not to be confused with rationalism" (p. 181). In an age of intense polemical debate and controversy the increased use of scholastic distinctions and terminology were deemed necessary. "This is indeed a form of theological speculation, but it a speculation guided by the needs of piety, for the sake of the soteriological emphasis of doctrine" (p. 182).

3

Fountainhead of Federalism: Heinrich Bullinger and the Covenantal Tradition by Charles S. McCoy and J. Wayne Baker. Louisville: Westminster/John Knox, 1991.

The thesis of this book is summarized in the opening sentence: "Federal theology and political philosophy are central in the shaping of the society and the institutions of modern Western nations" (p. 7). More specifically, "Political federalism emerged alongside the theological movement. Indeed, in many federal thinkers, the theological and political are too closely intertwined to be separated and are difficult even to distinguish clearly. While political federalism did gradually take shape in ways that can be identified apart from theological federalism, the two elements are not separable until much later" (p. 44). The thesis is not new or profound, nor is it meant to be. In fact, the purpose of this book is to remind modern-day scholarship of a simple and basic fact that has largely gone unnoticed. Restated: the covenant idea which permeated sixteenth- and seventeenth-century thinking lays the foundation for modern political society in the West. (This conviction of the authors is one shared by the Center for the Study of Federalism at Temple University. The authors and I were among the participants in the workshop entitled "Covenantal Ideas in the American Political Tradition: Federal Theology – The Sixteenth- and Seventeenth-Century Crucibles," sponsored by the Center in February 1980. This study, then, grows out of this and similar interests of the authors.)

The strength of this study lies in its historical research (including the helpful bibliography) rather than in its theological analysis and interpretation. In line with this criticism, the greatest weakness of this presentation is its heavy reliance upon the prior studies of Baker, especially his interpretation of Heinrich Bullinger's covenant theology as reflective of a different school of thought within Reformed Protestantism. The reader will find here no additional support for or defense of his reading of this formative Reformation thinker. There are important theological subtleties that escape our authors' attention, resulting in a misreading of the Reformed systematicians of the Reformation and post-Reformation period.

Happily, in part two of this publication the authors provide a complete translation of Bullinger's highly influential treatise, *A Brief Exposition of the One and Eternal Testament or Covenant of God*, published in 1534. (This can be compared with Peter A. Lillback's translation of the 1537 edition appended to his 1985 Westminster doctoral dissertation, "The Binding of God: Calvin's Role in the Development of Covenant Theology.") In view of our authors' close attention to this treatise and other writings of Bullinger, it escapes this reviewer how McCoy and Baker can miss the plain, straightforward teaching of Bullinger concerning the *discontinuity* between Mosaic and New Covenants, law and gospel, as summed up in the "Covenant of Grace." (More on this below.)

As a final observation before turning to some of the particulars, this study combines, rather than integrates, two related elements in the development of Reformed federalism, the theological (chaps. 1, 2, and 4) and the political (chaps. 3 and 5). Consequently, the format in which the material is presented works somewhat against the thesis of the book and its stated objective, which is to convince the reader of the inseparability of the theological and political elements in early Reformed thought.

At the outset the authors criticize the views of one like James B. Torrance, who argues that federalism is a post-Reformation deviation from earlier Calvinism. "Whether myopia, amnesia, or inadequate scholarship," reasons the authors, "*there is no excuse* for Torrance's faulty reading of the theology of the Westminster divines" (p. 8, *emphasis mine*). On this point, McCoy and Baker rightly contend that "The federal theology did not originate among the Puritans of England" (p. 8). They are correct to view the terms "federal" and "covenantal" as "virtually interchangeable" (p. 11). This opinion underscores the real and essential continuity between Reformation and post-Reformation teaching on the covenants.

What, then, are the sources of sixteenth-century federalism?

> Impetus for the rise of explicitly federal thought in the sixteenth century came from several sources. First, the organization of the Germanic tribes that invaded and settled western Europe was covenantal or federal in structure. These social patterns were continued in the covenants that underlay feudalism, in such pacts as those represented in the defensive and commercial covenants of the Hanseatic League and in political orders like the Swiss Confederation. The most direct impact from the Middle Ages on the development of the Reformed, modern idea of federalism came from the manner in which society and the church were organized in the late Middle Ages. [Pp. 15-16]

Theologically, our authors suggest, the source of Bullinger's political covenant may lie in the writings of Irenaeus, who seems to have been the first to hint at a *conditional* covenant (p. 15).

As noted above, it is notably the contention of Baker that there are two schools within sixteenth-century Reformed theology, one represented by Bullinger and the other by Calvin. Bullinger, we are told, rejected Calvin's doctrine of the divine decrees of election *and* reprobation as well as Calvin's teaching on the discontinuity between law and gospel.

> Several scholars have attempted to show that John Calvin (1509-1564) was a covenant theologian and that he was the source of much of the later federal theology. Calvin certainly made use of the covenant idiom. Indeed, at times, he sounds much like Bullinger in his affirmation of the unity of the covenant. But Calvin, like [Johannes] Oecolampadius, distinguished between two covenants or testaments: he spoke of the spiritual covenant, or the New Testament, which was equivalent to the gospel; and he referred to the carnal covenant, or the Old Testament, by which he meant the law. [P. 23]

(The use of the adjective "carnal" on the part of our authors is most inappropriate and misleading.) Earlier we read:

> Bullinger disagreed with Luther on law and gospel: he did not agree that the law had been abolished by Christ. He did, however, believe with Luther in the election of the saints, though he could not accept Calvin's doctrine of double predestination. But Bullinger was the only one of the three who can correctly be called a covenant or federal theologian. His entire theological system was organized around the idea of a bilateral, conditional covenant, made first by God with Adam, a covenant that would endure until the end of the world. [P. 24]

We must take exception to several claims in this assessment of Bullinger. First, there was no disagreement between Bullinger and Luther on the subject of law and gospel, especially as that matter came to bear on discussions of the doctrine of justification by faith (apart from the law). Both Luther and Bullinger insisted that Christ abolished the law for all who are united to him through faith. Second, Bullinger did uphold the doctrine of the twofold decrees, although he emphazised election (almost to the exclusion of reprobation). And whereas Luther certainly cannot be classified as a covenant theologian, Calvin ranks as one of the foremost exponents of the Reformed covenantal tradition. Finally, the supposition that Bullinger held to a bilateral covenant, while Calvin espoused a unilateral covenant, rests upon a superficial reading of these two reformers. To be sure, there was something of a difference in emphasis in their respective teachings, but not in substance. The argument for two distinct schools within early Reformed Protestantism, based on whether they viewed the covenant of God as bilateral or unilateral, is greatly exaggerated. Accordingly, we cannot agree with our authors when they assert that "the differences between Bullinger and Calvin form the basis for the two alternative, though related, strands within the Reformed tradition – Federalism and Calvinism." This misreading leads them to conclude: "It has become usual among historians to reduce Reformed thought in the sixteenth and seventeenth centuries to Calvinism. This reductionism has even led many to refer to the *Westminster Confession* as a Calvinist theological statement. It is a Reformed confession, but it is most certainly much more a product of the federal tradition than of the Calvinist element" (p. 24).

On other miscellaneous matters, it is refreshing to read that Bullinger's thought, in our authors' judgment, anticipates the later Reformed teaching on the "Covenant of Works" (p. 25). When our authors consider the teachings of Johannes Veluanus and Gellius Snecanus, it is not clear whether they are viewed by McCoy and Baker as "high Calvinists," or whether they are men with some (initial) Reformed leanings who were finally attracted to the views of Cornelius Wiggertz, who is (appropriately) treated here in this same section along with Veluanus and Snecanus. It may be that the moralistic theology of Veluanus and Snecanus is more akin to our authors' own thinking. Certainly, McCoy and Baker are not sympathetic to the teachings of high Calvinism, and the three Reformation writers named here were not exponents of "pure" Calvinism.

The most important figure in the development of a Reformed political theory was Johannes Althusius, a staunch Calvinist. The substance of his teaching was a development of the earlier views of Bullinger. Specifically, as the authors summarize:

> The moral law, or the "common law," was found in the Decalogue, which informed humans about their duty to God and to their symbiotic neighbor. "Proper law" was made by the magistrate on the basis of "common law." Common law was generalized law; "proper law" made the precepts of the Decalogue specific for each commonwealth and specified the punishment for breaking this law. This allowed Althusius to distinguish between the Decalogue, which was "common law," and the Jewish judicial law, which was "proper law" and thus not germane to Christians. [Pp. 60-61]

As a concluding evaluation of Althusius our authors state:

> What is equally clear about the covenanted society and the sovereignty of the people is that both are founded upon the covenant of God that has infused moral order into creation and human nature. On a level more comprehensive than the political realm, there is a compact similar to but not identical with the divine and natural law of scholasticism. Political sovereignty, in the federal meaning of Althusius, is therefore not absolute. The covenants of humanity exist within the covenant of God. [P. 61]

With respect to the more mature formulation of the political covenant offered by Althusius we have come a great distance from the early formulations of Bullinger and Calvin. However, the political thought of Althusius now places upon us today the need for further reflection on the basic idea of covenant as both a theological and a political concept. How precisely has the covenant of God "infused moral order into creation and human nature"? Is there validity to a doctrine of natural law in modern-day jurisprudence? In pursuit of these questions we can learn from the insight of Althusius, which reminds us that political sovereignty is not absolute. Here again we are reminded of the lordship of God the Creator who governs and sustains his will in the moral and political determinations of the nations of this world.

Despite the criticisms made by this reviewer the authors have performed a valuable service in directing our attention to the subject of God's covenants as one having great significance for a proper understanding of the institution of the state, established by God and maintained by common grace. Perhaps a return to the theological writings of the great sixteenth- and seventeenth-century Calvinists will shed light on our present generation's quest for a legitimate and equitable basis for contemporary social ethics. Certainly, those (like present-day theonomists) who seek to align themselves with the Reformed theological heritage owe it to themselves to listen anew to the forebears of this formative tradition. And perhaps those of different theological conviction will, likewise, come to a new understanding of Reformed teaching, and in so doing refute the modern contention that posits a radical discontinuity between federalism and Calvinism. It is truly "myopia, amnesia, or inadequate scholarship" that would lead one to caricature the Calvinists as mere rationalistic scholastics. And the notion that federalism is something altogether different in spirit and substance from Calvinism is altogether ludicrous.

4

Calvin's Concept of the Law by I. John Hesselink. Princeton Theological Monograph Series 30. Allison Park, PA: Pickwick, 1992.

I. John Hesselink has, in the main, provided a reliable account of Calvin's teaching and a helpful guide through the maze of Calvin studies, many of which make claims too amazing to be taken seriously as credible readings of this leading Protestant reformer! Happily, the author does not hesitate to raise objections throughout his study to faulty statements made by Calvin's critics and detractors.

Calvin's Concept of the Law is a "revision, reduction, and refinement" of the author's 1961 Basel dissertation (p. ix). Unfortunately, this revision fails to interact sufficiently with studies on the subject of Calvin and the Mosaic law written after 1961, especially those of the last decade. This shortcoming contributes in a significant way to what I regard to be the major weakness in Hesselink's analysis of Calvin's thought, a weakness to be addressed later in this review. Hesselink dedicates his work "To the memory of my two Swiss mentors and friends, Karl Barth and Emil Brunner; neither of whom totally agreed with the contents of this work but both of whom were constantly supportive and encouraging" (p. v). Not surprising, then, do we find certain aspects of his interpretation of Calvin echoing the views of his mentors.

The specific focus of Hesselink's book is the so-called third use of the law, the law as normative standard in the Christian life (p. ix). In order to focus attention on this aspect of Calvin's teaching Hesselink devotes a great deal of attention to Calvin's understanding of the second use of the law, that use which brings about the conviction of sin. Some attention is also given to the law's first use, the civic function. Here Hesselink relates the moral law revealed in the Scriptures to the law of nature – the law inscribed on the hearts of all humanity, the knowledge of which has now been marred by the Fall. According to Calvin, "the Decalog is in a sense only a confirmation and clarification of the law of nature which has become obscured by sin. The law ultimately must be traced to God's orderly will in creation (p. 10). With respect to the Ten Commandments, "Even Calvin recognized that some of these commands were not absolutely unique and had parallels in other legal codes, but what gave them special significance and authority was their incorporation into God's revelation on Sinai. The determining factor is not so much their content as the context in which they were given" (*ibid.*). It is important to understand, however, that "The revealed law, the law of Moses, coincides with and confirms this law of nature, but not vice versa. We truly come to recognize the law of nature after we have been reconciled to God and illuminated by his Spirit, who writes the law (of Moses) on our hearts" (pp. 66-67). Hesselink indicates some reserve concerning Calvin's teaching on natural law, but he does not specify precisely what he has in mind.

The objection may he related to his christological reading of the Bible (*à la* Barth).

This much is clear: Calvin's treatment of the law in the *Institutes* "precludes on the one hand a legalistic understanding of the law and on the other a one-sided 'naturalistic' interpretation of the law. Positively expressed, this concentration on the law within the discussion of the work of God the Redeemer points to one of Calvin's themes, namely, that Jesus Christ is the substance and soul of the law" (p. 11). Hesselink correctly renounces a view of law in which the law stands independently alongside of God, making God subject to a legal standard outside of himself. (This view results in a false dialectic between God and law, between the freedom and the holiness of God.) Likewise, the deistic or Enlightenment doctrine of law as a "natural" and autonomous possession of the creature is rejected.

The revelation of God in the law and in the gospel is decidedly *historical.* "The form of the law is relative to time and circumstance, but the truth of the law ever remains the same. The law finds permanent expression in the Decalog, but the Decalog is only meaningful as a part of the covenant" (p. 35). This introduces us to one of the most important sections in Hesselink's study of Calvin on the Mosaic law. It is the revelation of the "Covenant of Grace" which provides the proper context for our understanding of the giving of the law on Mount Sinai.

> The law is an expression of the one will of God, which will is good and gracious as well as holy and righteous. A contrast with the Lutheran approach to the law emerges at this juncture. The law, for Calvin, is a revelation of the revealed, not the hidden, will or God. The law represents his "proper work;" it is not a "foreign work" (*opus alienum*). It comes from his right hand, not his left; it expresses the love of God, not his wrath. [P. 36]

Hesselink posits "a dualistic tendency in Luther's theology which has been taken up and developed both in Lutheran orthodoxy and by several contemporary Lutheran theologians. The antithesis between law and gospel, according to this approach, is grounded in two wills of God, two words of God, and two modes of God's activity" (pp. 36-37). Here the author fails to distinguish adequately between the teaching of Luther, on the one hand, and the teaching of one particular tradition within later Lutheranism, on the other. Hesselink's observations, furthermore, conflict with what he writes later concerning Luther (see the quotation from pp. 157-58 cited below). Although Luther's law/gospel contrast lacks the historico-covenantal context so essential to Reformed theological formulation, it is erroneous to charge traditional Lutheranism with holding to a faulty dualism in its understanding of the antithesis between law and gospel. Luther himself was entirely free of anything like the neoorthodox dialectic which now is so prominent in contemporary Lutheranism. (Neoorthodoxy has infected modern Reformed theology in other, yet analogous, ways). There is an ultimate unity between law and gospel in the divine will and in the unfolding of God's (covenantal) purposes.

Returning to the relation between law and covenant, Hesselink writes: "This distinction between the law as an integral part of the covenant and the law abstracted from the promises of the covenant is extremely important. The latter is the bare law (*nuda lex*), which, by itself, only threatens and condemns. It is the law in this restricted sense about which Paul speaks frequently in his Epistles" (p. 91). In conjunction with this,

> What is not always recognized – particularly by the critics of Calvin's view of law and gospel – is that there is not only a difference of form between the law and the gospel (or the two covenants) but also an antithesis between them in so far as the law in a narrower sense is opposed to the gospel. A case in point is Gal 3:19, where Paul sets the law given to Moses in opposition to the promise given to Abraham. In such cases Calvin does not hesitate to speak of the accusing, killing function of the law and its threats and curse. This aspect of the law in its narrower sense is taken up in Chap. 7 of Book II of the *Institutes* and is discussed even more fully in Calvin's exegetical writings on the Pauline Epistles and related texts. Here Calvin does not differ significantly from Luther, except in emphasis and discretion. Calvin often points out, for example, that when Paul and other biblical writers refer to the law in this narrow sense, that it is opposed to the gospel, it is separated from the promises of grace and is considered only from the standpoint of its "peculiar office, power and end."
>
> This law, which is the antithesis of the gospel, is not the whole law, the *tota lex*, but the bare law, the *nuda lex*. It is the law abstracted from its real setting which is the covenant. Such a law is a bare letter without the vivifying Spirit of Christ. It has nothing but rigorous demands which place all human beings under a curse and the wrath of God. The law, thus understood, can only be described as the antithesis of the gospel, for it implies a type of righteousness which is diametrically opposed to the righteousness of faith. Hence when Paul speaks of the law in passages like Rom 3:21-31 and Gal 3:10, he "rightly makes opposites of the righteousness of the law and that of the gospel." [Pp. 157-58]

It can only be stated in passing that this distinction in Calvin's formulation between the "bare law" and the "whole law" is, in my estimation, exceedingly obscure and problematic. This element of Calvin's thought requires reformulation (see below).

Hesselink contends that it is a blatant misreading of Calvin's emphasis on the unity of the law and the gospel, if that is made to obscure their difference. But he distances himself somewhat from Calvin's exegetical handling of certain texts of Scripture, *i.e.*, from exegesis "no longer tenable by contemporary canons of scholarship." Without these restraints, notes Hesselink, Calvin was led "to interpret the OT more christologically than would be possible today" (p. 182). Presumably, Hesselink is objecting to certain features of Calvin's *typological* interpretation of the OT, not to the christological focus of Calvin's biblical exegesis and interpretation, of which he speaks favorably. Hesselink thus challenges Paul Wernle's criticism of Calvin's "christianizing of the OT and its history," what Wernle labels as Calvin's "naive and unhistorical" methodology (p. 101). Hesselink responds: "Calvin, however, has proven to have a sounder approach to the OT than many of his critics of a past generation. He saw that the OT, including the law, points beyond itself. It is an eschatological book (*ibid.*).

In Hesselink's understanding of Calvin, the negative function of the law is not to be explained in terms of the law's misinterpretation or misuse. "The law as such has certain characteristics which not only differentiate it from the gospel but place it in a sense in opposition to the gospel." Our author correctly avers: "*This much is incontrovertible*" (p. 194, *italics mine*). The effort by recent critics "to blunt the sharp edge of this antithesis in their interpretations of Calvin on this question" can be traced unmistakably to Barth (p. 212 n. 187). All this is not to suggest that the subject of the relationship between the two Testaments, the Law and the Gospel, is a simple one. Indeed, the subject is exceedingly complex. In Hesselink's judgment, "the difficulty is to integrate this concept of the law with his understanding of the law as a whole" (p. 194). Hesselink notes parenthetically, "This difficulty is not peculiar to Calvin; contemporary scholars also have a hard time integrating Paul's diverse references to the law, let alone reconciling these references with the portrayal of the law in the OT" (*ibid.*). The author's solution to this problem, however, shows little improvement upon Calvin, which is to say that Hesselink's treatment does not progress much beyond the formulations of Calvin. To be sure, the Reformed tradition has wrestled long and hard with this subject. Further acquaintance with recent Reformed interpretation by our author might have opened up new insights. Hesselink's discussion provides little help regarding this crucial biblico-systematic element in the system of Reformed doctrine. In fact, Hesselink's presentation tends to further confuse the reader, rather than clarify the issues.

Far more serious is Hesselink's abandonment of Calvin on certain points of doctrine by an appeal to neoorthodox teaching. Our author does not agree with Calvin's exposition of predestination, notably the aspect of reprobation. The reason given is that Calvin "sometimes seems to speak of a God who operates apart from Jesus Christ" (p. 32). If nothing more, Hesselink's comments here are vague and ambiguous. Hesselink rejects the later Reformed doctrine of the "Covenant of Works" by superficially and erroneously equating it with legalism. At the root of Hesselink's rejection of both of these issues – Calvin's doctrine of reprobation and the federal-theological distinction between the "Covenant of Works" and the "Covenant of Grace" – is his failure to integrate fully the doctrine of the Fall into his theological system. It is Hesselink's conviction that the doctrine of sin is meaningful only in the context of God's redeeming grace in Christ. Hesselink admits that his critical interpretation of Calvin "tends to confirm Barth's contention that Jesus Christ or the Gospel are never the focal point for Calvin's doctrine of the knowledge of sin. For Calvin does not say that we are stripped of our pride, self-confidence, and self-righteousness by the preaching of the gospel, as such, nor by a confrontation with the cross of Christ. This is accomplished, according to Calvin, primarily by the law and a consciousness of God's judgment" (p. 229).

Space permits only brief comment on several other elements in the theology of Calvin relating to the Mosaic law. First, Hesselink reminds us that Calvin understands the Fourth Commandment to have been "superseded by the advent of Christ," even though the "original, universal law upon which it is founded," the Sabbath ordinance established at creation, remains perpetually valid" (p. 53). Calvin's view was distinct from the later teaching of English sabbatarianism, as reflected in the Westminster Standards. Calvin showed greater sensitivity to the historical circumstance of the Decalogue in regard to the Israelite theocracy. Second, the peculiar (typological) function of the Mosaic law dictated the "destruction [of Israel] as a nation and their dissolution as God's people" (p. 94). In this connection, Hesselink appropriately dismisses the reading of Calvin given by modern-day theonomists, *i.e.*, the advocates of Christian Reconstructionism (*cf.* pp. 269-70 n. 123). Third, Calvin stresses the vital role of the Holy Spirit to work faith and repentance in the hearts of all believers, whether before or after the advent of Christ. The regenerating work of the Spirit, requisite for the redemption of sinners, is equally applicable under both dispensations. "The fathers could neither have worshipped sincerely and with a pure conscience nor rightly obeyed God's commandments without having been 'inwardly taught by the Spirit'" (p. 184).

The investigator in the history of doctrine is required to distinguish carefully between the interpretation of the theologian under study and the historian's own interpretation of the relevance and significance of that theologian's work for contemporary formulation. In spite of reservations noted in this review, Hesselink provides a timely corrective to such recent evaluations of Calvin on the covenants as that found in Peter Lillback's "The Binding of God: Calvin's Role in the Development of Covenant Theology" (Ph.D. dissertation, Westminster Theological Seminary, 1985). For this the Reformed community owes the author a partial debt of gratitude.

5

The Federal Theology of Thomas Boston by Andrew T. B. McGowan. Rutherford Studies in Historical Theology. Edinburgh: Paternoster, 1997.

The reading of Andrew McGowen's book, what began initially as a doctoral study under Professor James Torrance, is both a delight and a disappointment. Generally speaking, the author evinces a solid grasp of the rudiments of Reformed theology, as surveyed in his treatment of the writings of the important Scottish minister and theologian Thomas Boston (1676-1732). From the standpoint of vigorous academic scholarship, however, McGowen's discussion is at times shallow. The work suffers from a lack of adequate interaction with the secondary literature on the historical development of covenant theology, particularly, interaction with the numerous critical studies which have appeared in the last two decades or so. As a popular treatment, however, McGowen's book should find a useful niche.

The "Foreward" by Sinclair Ferguson is a rather curious piece of writing. Both McGowen and Ferguson studied under James Torrance, yet they arrived at contrary assessments of federal theology. This fact is not brought out by Ferguson. Rather, one is given the impression that these two were in basic agreement. Comparison of the present study with Ferguson's doctoral dissertation proves otherwise; see his "The Doctrine of the Christian Life in the Teaching of Dr. John Owen," 2 volumes (Ph.D. thesis, University of Aberdeen, 1979). The difference between these two writers can be stated this way: whereas McGowen is highly critical of the Torrance school, Ferguson is sympathetic. The Torrance school objects vigorously to federal theology's doctrine of the twofold covenants. The chief issue in this debate is whether or not the contrast between the two covenants, the "Covenant of Works" in creation and the "Covenant of Grace" in redemption, is biblically warranted.

In the course of surveying Boston's teaching on the subject of the application of redemption (what in the science of dogmatics has been designated *ordo salutis*, the order of salvation, in distinction from *historia salutis,* the history of salvation), McGowen convincingly demonstrates that the views of Scottish divine Thomas Boston were in full accord with traditional Calvinistic teaching. After reviewing Boston's doctrine of the covenants, McGowen proceeds to a discussion of Boston's understanding of Christ's person and work. In sum: "Jesus Christ, the incarnate Son of God, entered into a covenant with God on behalf of the elect. As a public person, or federal head, he stood where Adam stood and succeeded where Adam failed. He rendered to God full and perfect obedience thus fulfilling the conditions of the Covenant of Works for all those whom he represented in the Covenant of Grace, namely, his seed, the elect. For the elect the covenant is absolute and not conditional, resulting in justification by the righteousness of Christ" (p. 15).

How, more precisely, did scholastic Reformed orthodoxy (of which Boston is representative) conceive of the relationship between the "Covenant of Works" and the "Covenant of Grace?" The answer to this question is not as simple as some might suppose. The modern interpreter must address the vexing question whether or not revived scholasticism in seventeenth Reformed Protestantism was, at all points, a help or hindrance in the theological enterprise. Specifically, was the reintroduction of scholastic distinctions and terminology justified in every instance? Problematic also was appeal to the rational "proofs" for the existence of God. Interaction with the important studies of Richard Muller, among others, would have enriched McGowen's argument.

Basic to understanding the contrasting covenants ("Works" and "Grace") is the Protestant doctrine on "Law" and "Gospel." Apart from a proper understanding and *application* of the antithetical principles of law and grace, *i.e.*, "Law and Gospel," the Protestant doctrine of justification by faith (alone) and the Reformed doctrine of the covenants are unintelligible. It was this concern that became the focal issue in the Marrow controversy. In that debate Boston and several others came to the defense of teaching found in *The Marrow of Modern Divinity*, a treatise written about a century earlier. That publication was the centerpiece in the dispute, the work which Donald Macleod correctly identified as "quintessential Federal Theology" (p. xvi). McGowen suggests that Boston "was himself one of the finest popular exponents of that theological perspective, establishing it among the common people by his influential volume, *The Fourfold State*" (p. 206). He maintains that "Boston believed that the parallel between Adam and Christ was the *key* to understanding the Christian faith" (p. 25, *emphasis mine*).

Serving as a *leitmotif* in his book, McGowen argues that the Covenant of Works "is an act of God's grace" (p. 4). He says: "It is of the utmost importance to grasp the fact that even the first covenant was an act of condescension and grace" (p. 5). "In other words," explains McGowen, "God was not obliged to give man anything, but out of the riches of his grace he entered into this covenant and promised a great and eternal benefit, upon condition of obedience. To regard the Covenant of Works, then, as a matter of putting law before grace is simply to misunderstand the nature of the covenant – at least as Boston taught it" (p. 11). This formulation of the biblical covenants, however, is subject to criticism. The modern interpreter must reckon with the fact that remnants of Roman theology, notably, distinctions that were speculative in origin, found a place in Reformed theology, beginning as early as the late sixteenth century.

Corruption had been (re)introduced into dogmatic formulation when the scholastic distinction between nature and grace was applied to the original order of creation, what the Reformed federalists identified as the first covenant (the "Covenant of Works" or the "Covenant of Nature"). It became commonplace in orthodox scholasticism to distinguish between an initial state of nature and a subsequent covenantal arrangement, one that was established by God with Adam as federal head of the human race. Another distinction which (directly or indirectly) factored into the federal interpretation of the divine covenants was that between *meritum de congruo* and *meritum de condigno*. Many of the Reformed federalists came to view the covenantal order imposed on the prior state of nature as a *gracious* arrangement, wherein Adam would merit – not in strict justice, but congruously – the reward of eternal life promised by God upon his successful completion of probation. "Thus Adam would not have been left forever in a state of subjection to the Covenant of Works," explains McGowen, "but there would have come a time when God judged that Adam had been obedient for a reasonable period" (p. 12). It was deemed fitting or "reasonable" that God would so favor Adam with everlasting life on grounds of his obedience. The dual question of the origin and validity of the scholastic dichotomy between nature and grace and the Roman conceptions of merit is not addressed by McGowen. This is a significant oversight. When our author speaks of Boston's "gracious form of federal theology" (p. 209), is he suggesting that there is a *legalistic* form of federal theology? I think not. Legalism and federal theology, he would agree, are altogether contrary systems of doctrine.

The criticisms raised in this book review are, generally speaking, applicable to Philip Ryken's related study, "Thomas Boston as Preacher of the *Fourfold State*" (D.Phil. thesis, University of Oxford, 1995). In our day, the task of separating the wheat from the chaff in post-Reformation Reformed thought is the pressing need for those engaged in the study of the history of doctrine. Scholastic federalism did have its shortcomings. But these considerations aside, *The Federal Theology of Thomas Boston* is a welcome addition to the growing corpus of historical-theological studies from an orthodox Reformed point of view. Clearly, the Barthians do not have the last word in critiquing the strengths and weaknesses of confessional Reformed orthodoxy. McGowen convincingly shows that they need to listen again to what Boston and other scholastic dogmaticians have to say. Good scholarship does not import new meaning into old words. The Rutherford House is to be commended for making McGowen's doctoral study available to the wider reading public.

6

The Extent of the Atonement: A Dilemma for Reformed Theology from Calvin to the Consensus (1536-1675) by G. Michael Thomas. Paternoster Biblical and Theological Monographs. Carlisle: Paternoster, 1997.

Consensus today among Reformed theologians is jeopardized when historians of doctrine fail to agree in their explanation of the teachings of the original shapers of the theological tradition. Michael Thomas' interpretation on the extent of the atonement must be judged erroneous by those who stand in the line of historic Reformed orthodoxy. Though comprehensive in research and helpful at times, the author fails to present an accurate account of the historical-theological period under review. Thomas argues that historic Reformed theology is inherently flawed. He proceeds to document his argument from the storehouse of theological writings, hoping to convince his readers of what he judges to be weighty differences of opinion held among leading exponents within the tradition. Thomas' Barthian convictions bear directly on his reading and analysis of Reformed theology. Among the tenets of neoorthodox historicism Thomas advocates a view of the Reformation which sees John Calvin to be at odds with later Calvinism, *i.e.*, orthodox scholasticism. The hero in Thomas' study of the period extending from Calvin to the latter part of the seventeenth century is Moïse Amyraut. The informed reader may ask: How can this be? To that question we now turn.

Not surprisingly, the chief culprit in the alleged theological deformation Thomas sees taking place in the latter part of the sixteenth century into the seventeenth is the doctrine of predestination. This doctrinal element more than any other illustrates for the Barthian school the orthodox scholastic propensity for abstract rationalization and logical deduction, hallmarks, we are told, of the theological tradition here under attack. The argument is not against theological system as such; rather, it is an argument against one particular system of doctrine, namely, that espoused by Reformed orthodoxy. (This systematization is characteristic of Protestant scholasticism as a whole). In making his case, the author attempts to offer "a more nuanced presentation of Calvin's thought on the extent of the atonement" (p. 12). And his guiding light in this forage is Karl Barth. Although it is one thing to say that Calvin did not express himself on the controverted points in the same manner or with the same degree of precision as did the later orthodox scholastics, it is another thing to say that Calvin's formulations were incompatible with those that followed. Thomas unsuccessfully sets out to restate Calvin's teaching on the question of the extent of the atonement in terms of "other, more prominent aspects of his theology" (p. 13).

With respect to Calvin and some of the subsequent figures addressed in this monograph, Thomas contends that by assessing the *effects* of God working out his salvation in the lives of believers one can properly contemplate the (prior) electing purpose of God revealed in Jesus Christ. He comments:

> It has been shown, then, that Calvin often approached election as the *ex post facto* explanation of conversion. This understanding left room for a logically prior universal promise and was capable of being combined with a doctrine of universal atonement. However, Calvin was not confined to this perspective. Although election could be presented as God's "last" act, it was also the fountain and foundation of the whole work of salvation. As such, it was the grace which constituted Christ as mediator, a synonym for the love of God. Seen as a decree to save part of humanity only, and occupying this primary position, it would seem to imply a limited scope to the whole of God's saving activity in Christ. In fact, Calvin's two ways of relating election to soteriology do not harmonize easily and ensured that an uncomfortably dual approach would emerge when he tried to define for whom Christ had died. [P. 23]

The error of the orthodox scholastics, Thomas maintains, was to dissolve the paradox by means of logical deductions respecting election and reprobation, including limiting the saving effect of Christ's atonement to the elect only. In their struggle with Calvin's "deep dualism" (p. 25), the later Calvinists ended up departing from the spirit and letter of their spiritual mentor.

It is something of a commonplace in Calvin historiography to speak of Theodore Beza as the spearhead of rationalistic scholasticism. Thomas concedes:

> It could be said that Beza aligned himself with the logical rather than the homiletic and apologetic Calvin. Whilst Beza was undoubtedly giving greater definition to Calvin's teaching, he was seeking thereby only to give it greater coherence. Calvin's apparent approval of Beza's relevant work strongly suggests that he saw his own concerns reflected there. [P. 48]

Thomas' assessment of Heinrich Bullinger's work is similarly based upon the erroneous supposition of two varieties of Reformed covenant theology, one speculative (deductionistic) and the other humanistic (biblical). Following the thesis of J. Wayne Baker, Thomas identifies Bullinger as representative of "the other Reformed tradition." Accordingly, Bullinger's teaching "constitutes a theology of history, in harmony with Bullinger's pastoral concern to avoid distressing preoccupation with the eternal decrees" (p. 74). Here, as elsewhere, the author's reading of the Reformed doctrine of the covenants obscures rather than clarifies issues.

Next, attention is given to the Heidelberg school, one of the early centers of covenant theology. Thomas writes: "A system was constructed in which God's dealings with the human race in nature and grace were radically opposed, and yet in which grace operated largely in accordance with the legal-covenantal pattern of pre-Fall nature." He further explains: "Ursinus made the conditionality of the gospel, which all Reformed theologians acknowledged to some degree, approximate to a formal legal obligation (p. 105). But Thomas concludes by falsely pitting Zacharius Ursinus' pastoral concerns against Caspar Olevianus' alleged speculative predestinarianism.

Turning to the Synod of Dort, we find that diversity of expression and occasional opposition among the Reformed delegates did not hinder genuine consensus on the main points in the theological dispute with the Arminians and Amyraudians – what Thomas would seemingly have us forget. Here several doctrinal strands converge: predestination (election and reprobation), supra- and infralapsarianism, the two contrasting covenants ("Works" and "Grace"), including the relationship between the Mosaic Covenant and the New (both under the rubric of the "Covenant of Grace"), conditionality versus nonconditionality within the covenants, the two wills of God, the free offer of the gospel (and the warrant to believe), the sufficiency versus efficiency of Christ's atoning death, and actual versus potential redemption. They are all important elements in the system of Reformed doctrine. (Superior to Thomas' assessment of the Synod of Dort is W. Robert Godfrey's study of the "tensions within international Calvinism" [Ph.D. dissertation, Stanford University, 1974]. Comparison of Godfrey and Thomas proves illuminating, especially with respect to their divergent readings on the significance of John Davenant's work prior to Dort and developments at Saumur.)

In the closing portion of our author's study attention centers on the teachings of John Cameron and Moïse Amyraut. This section (chaps. 8 through 11) constitutes the largest part of the book. Thomas argues that the distinctive teachings of these two individuals were by no means novel; they were merely a refinement and expansion of earlier themes appearing in the history of doctrine. He insists that

> although Cameron was a creative thinker, his doctrine of the extent of the atonement was not new, but rooted in an already existing Reformed tradition. Universal atonement was indeed important to Cameron and Amyraut, but they can neither be blamed nor credited with introducing it into Reformed theology. [P. 164]

Space limitations prevent us from evaluating Cameron's and Amyraut's teaching on the covenants, notably, their advocacy of a threefold classification of the covenants, rather than the traditional twofold. This much can be said: whereas the Puritan Samuel Bolton commended highly Cameron's historico-covenantal schematization, Cameron's denial of the active obedience of Christ imputed to believers in justification was deemed unorthodox. Thomas mistakenly reasons that Reformed thinkers by employing Aristotelian causality had

> viewed all historical events as means preordained by God for the accomplishment of certain ends. . . [I]nfralapsarians attempted to present

> the Fall as somehow exempt from this tight causal system, thus introducing one moment of genuine historical interaction between God and humanity. [P. 191]

This line of argument simply fails to do justice to classic Reformed theology. In the end, even Amyraut does not escape vitiating criticism. His teachings likewise are found to suffer from rationalization, thereby undermining a truly biblical theology.

> It may be granted that Amyraut came closer to a biblical approach than did his opponents in ensuring that the interaction of God with the human race in history was not lost behind a theology of comprehensive eternal decrees. However, our survey of the Saumur teaching shows that, like their opponents, Cameron and Amyraut also began with a certain concept of God, and applied it logically to the field of soteriology. . . . In fact, to the same degree to which Amyraut marks a break with the scholastic logic of the past, his preoccupation with the comprehensibility of the moral character and requirements of God seems to forshadow the rationalism of the future. [Pp. 203-204]

The remedy for all this, Thomas suggests, is found in the epochal work of Barth. The last section reads: "Reformulation: Barth on the Doctrine of Election." Thomas' study leaves us with these crucial questions: Has not God *sovereignly* decreed the eternal destinies of sinners? Has not Christ *accomplished* redemption for his own (those chosen from the foundation of the world)? And is not the work of Christ and his Spirit *unified*? Is not Christ himself, not election, the only and sufficient warrant to believe? Or does Scripture teach a potential universalism, as Thomas would have us believe? I remain convinced that Barthianism is nothing more than an ancient heresy in modern cloak, a revival of Pelagianism. Those guilty of idle speculation are not the orthodox Reformed scholastics, but the critics of consistent Calvinism.

7

Politics, Religion and the British Revolutions: The Mind of Samuel Rutherford by John Coffey. Cambridge Studies in Early Modern British History. Cambridge: Cambridge University Press, 1997.

For a superb analysis of the life and career of Samuel Rutherford (1600-61) and his impact on theology and political theory, this is the work to consult. I have reversed the order from that provided in the book title. Not only does theology have priority in Rutherford's thought – and, therefore, is the window for understanding his life and work – but the author himself has mastered his subject by virtue of his own command of theology, Reformation and modern. This book will prove invaluable for understanding this period in British ecclesiastical and political history, while at the same time providing the necessary background for understanding the American scene today. Coffey is to be commended for skillfully guiding his readers through difficult and complex issues in Calvinist political theory. He correctly sees the ambiguities and complexities in Rutherford's thinking as grounds for divergent readings of Rutherford held by contemporary Reformed theologians, both Reconstructionist and nonReconstructionist. Happily, Coffey's argument effectively calls into question the theonomist interpretation of God's law for civil rule.

After an opening introduction highlighting the contemporary relevance of Rutherford, Coffey proceeds to survey his life as scholar, Puritan pastor and theologian, political theorist, ecclesiastical statesman, and national prophet. This fascinating and absorbing study is exceedingly well written. One almost forgets just how complex the issues addressed really are. In the course of discussion Coffey helpfully identifies both strengths and weaknesses in Rutherford's work. By the end of the book the reader, hopefully, can better appreciate the daunting (if not impossible) task of constructing a Reformed/Protestant doctrine of natural law which would appeal to secular political theorists. Perhaps we theologians should be content "to render to Caesar the things that are Caesar's, and to God the things that are God's." I am not urging Christians to abdicate their participation in the public square, but rather reminding us to let the church be the church. We must not at any point or to any degree confuse the mission of the church with that of the civil magistracy. (The legitimate exercise of civil rule is itself a manifestation of God's common grace in the world.) This, it seems to me, is the lesson we must learn from the life and teachings of Rutherford.

Rutherford was a highly respected Scottish Covenanter, a delegate to the Westminster Assembly, and author of the influential treatise, *Lex, Rex* (1644), dealing with civil rule and the right of disobedience against ungodly magistrates. It is this writing which receives primary attention in Coffey's study. Although an articulate exponent of Reformed covenantal theology, Rutherford, as Coffey convincingly argues, failed to attain a correct understanding of the relationship between church and state as defined in the Bible. His conception of a religiously-based, covenantal nation and natural law theory proved ultimately irreconcilable. Coffey rightly lables *Lex, Rex* as "a deeply Thomistic book" (p. 152), one which assumes "the compatibility of natural reason's conclusions and God's revelation in Scripture" (p. 153). (See further the discussion in Chapter Two.)

It was not only Rutherford's writing of *Lex, Rex* that has shown him to be a skilled controvertialist; it was also his defense of divine-right Presbyterianism. With tireless energy Rutherford engaged in several ecclesiastical disputes. To be sure, the political and the ecclesiastical issues of his day were closely intertwined. In this study Coffey exposes "the fundamental tension in Rutherford's ecclesiastical thought between the idea of the church as a pure gathering of the godly and the idea of the church as a comprehensive national institution." He contends: "This tension can be said to parallel the tension we have seen in *Lex, Rex* between the politics of natural reason and the politics of true religion" (p. 189). Alongside his devotional and polemical writings, Rutherford was a passionate preacher, a man of intense emotion. Coffey captures well Rutherford's colorful and, at times, eccentric personality. All told, Rutherford was a remarkable and captivating figure in seventeenth-century Calvinism, a tower in the midst of storms.

The various stands of Rutherford's life can best be brought together by seeing Rutherford first and foremost as a prophet of God's covenant, one in a long line of prophets (extending back to OT times) calling wayward sinners to repentence, obedience, and devotion to God's law. Writes Coffey: "Rutherford's preaching and writing in the 1630s provides us with a classic example of 'the Scottish jeremiad tradition.' At the root of this tradition lay the assumption that a covenant existed between God and his chosen people, one which made analogies between Scotland and Israel wholly appropriate" (p. 228). Coffey concludes: "The supreme irony of Rutherford's life was that he had misread the times. He lived not at the end of history, but at the end of an era in which religion had formed a sacred canopy covering every area of life, and in which the principle of 'one realm, one religion' had been taken for granted. There lay ahead not the kingdom of God on earth but a world in which religious plurality and tolerance would gradually expand, and in which religion would eventually be pushed to the margins of political life" (p. 255). In brief, Rutherford "was trying to save a sinking ship. The fragmentation of Protestantism was too far advanced, the demands of intolerance too onerous, the attractions of pluralism too great" (*ibid.*).

If the church is to speak prophetically in our day, it is necessary that Reformed/Protestant Christians understand that, contrary to the thinking of the framers of the *Westminster Confession*, the state has not been given the task of either protecting or contending for the biblical faith. And whatever the political vicissitudes, the church alone wields the sword of the Spirit. To avoid repeating the mistakes of the past, the church must learn that her warfare is spiritual, not temporal. Anything else would be a betrayal of covenant theology, rightly interpreted. (Compare the study of Charles S. McCoy and J. Wayne Baker, *Fountainhead of Federalism: Heinrich Bullinger and the Covenantal Tradition* and my book review above.)

Coffey's study is not easy reading, but it is exceedingly worthwhile. And as one would expect from a work of this caliber, an excellent and comprehensive bibliography is appended, including among the primary sources Rutherford's many letters, sermons, and treatises.

SECTION TWO –
Biblical Theology and Exegesis

SUMMARY ARGUMENT. Recent challenges to traditional Reformed-Protestant teaching on the doctrine of justification by faith alone (*sola fide*) have called for careful exegetical and theological exposition in defense of historic orthodoxy, responding to the pressing questions of our day. What is meaning of the legal (or forensic) term "justification" in the Bible? And what is meant by the term "instrument" as applied to saving faith, the faith which justifies? The first essay in this section brings together the concerns of biblical theology and systematics. Tracing the unfolding revelation of God's justifying act in the death and resurrection of Jesus Christ through both Testaments, we find that the Mosaic Covenant occupies a central place in God's redemptive plan and purpose (as the apostle Paul, especially, makes so plain in his letters). Special attention is given to the teachings of Paul, James, and the writer to the Hebrews. Among the issues explored are the following: the principle OT texts, Lev 18:5 and Hab 2:4, the relationship between the Old and New Covenants (particularly in light of 2 Corinthians 3 and Galatians 3), and the pivotal chapter in Paul's Letter to the Romans, chap. 5. The essay concludes with a discussion of the meaning of "judgment according to works."

The second article offers a fresh, new interpretation to Romans 7, one of the most difficult Pauline texts. Foundational to this biblical exposition is the distinction between *ordo salutis*, the individual application of salvation to God's elect, and *historia salutis*, the history of redemption (*i.e.*, the unfolding of God's saving purposes in Jesus Christ from the Fall of Adam to the Consummation). The death and resurrection of Christ marks the beginning of the new aeon (inaugurated eschatology) and the birth of the New Man (the church as the body of Christ). Israel's exile depicts the death of the Old Man, her restoration to the land being anticipatory of the resurrection to life shared by all those who participate in the experience of the New Man, what in Paul's writings is a corporate image of the elect people of God. The "I" of Rom 7:7-13, it is here argued, is used by the apostle metaphorically to describe Israel's encounter with the law during the time of probation associated with the entire Mosaic epoch (when the works-inheritance principle is operative in the typological/temporal sphere associated with life in Canaan).

The relationship between Israel and the church is explored in the next chapter. The argument is made that only Reformed covenant theology, in its most consistent expression (namely, covenantal amillennialism), can do adequate justice to the biblical teaching. Typology is one, very basic element in the covenantal interpretation of the two Testaments. Crucial also in this biblical-theological formulation is the distinction between national election (pertaining only and exclusively to ancient theocratic Israel in the period from Moses to Christ) and individual election to salvation (decretive election applicable to the saints in both economies of redemption).

The subject of Paul and the (Mosaic) law, the focus of Chapter Nine, has become a battleground in contemporary NT scholarship. This brings us to the heart of the exegetical and theological dispute concerning the relationship between law and gospel (to the heart of the historic Protestant understanding of the biblical doctrine of justification by faith and the divine covenants). Once again we consider the relationship between the two Testaments and the applicability of the federal scheme which utilizes both the Covenant of Works conceptualization (in the prelapsarian and Mosaic epochs) and the Covenant of Grace conceptualization (in the redemptive epoch, which also includes the Mosaic dispensation of law). Attention is directed in this article to developments in contemporary Reformed thought, where criticism of the federal scholastic categories (*e.g.*, faith as the sole "instrument" of justification, obedience to law as the "meritorious" ground of divine blessing and favor in times of probationary testing, and the twofold covenant schematization reflecting the traditional Protestant law/gospel antithesis) has, regrettably, become all too commonplace.

In Chapter Ten we compare the replacement commentary on Romans in the *New International Commentary on the New Testament* written by Douglas Moo, a specialist on the topic of Paul and the law, with the earlier one by John Murray, long-time professor of systematics at Westminster Theological Seminary, who over his teaching career indoctrinated his students in a *revised form* of federal theology. Both authors, Moo and Murray, share a Calvinistic understanding of soteriology and, more generally, a commitment to orthodox Reformed Protestantism. This comparative study is set in the context of contemporary biblical and theological scholarship. Most notable in recent years has been the impact of "biblical theology" (as a distinct discipline in the theological curriculum) on Christian dogmatics (*i.e.* confessional orthodoxy). Crucial to Paul's exposition of the gospel revealed in Jesus Christ is the role of the Mosaic Covenant as preparatory to the new, eschatological age of the Spirit (the New Covenant). Included in his "occasional" letter to the church at Rome (which, at the same time, is thoroughly doctrinal-systematic in content) is the matter of the relationship between ethnic Israel and the people of the New Covenant (the "New Man" in Christ).

The last article in this section offers a critique of Colin Kruse's book, *Paul, the Law, and Justification*, addressing the timely issue of the relationship between (Pauline) Christianity and Judaism, a subject which increasingly bears important ecumenical overtones. As a voice for evangelical orthodoxy, Kruse upholds the traditional Protestant contrast between law and gospel in his exegetico-theological formulation. However, the weakness in his analysis of Judaism (and OT religion) lies in his faulty distinction between "nomism" and "legalism." Contrary to Kruse's argument, the teaching of Jesus and Paul on Judaism as a religion of works-salvation necessarily calls into question not only the views of such dominant spokesmen today as E. P. Sanders and James Dunn, but also those of Kruse. The Protestant reformers were correct in their insistence that OT religion and Judaism are wholly incompatible in their respective understandings of the way of salvation (God's saving action in reconciliation and justification). Lastly, attention is given to what is commonly viewed as "Lutheran" teaching on the place of the law (*i.e.* obedience to the commands of God) in the Christian life – what Kruse confusingly identifies as the "the fulfilling of the law" (Christian duty), in opposition to "the doing of the law" (legalism).

Harking back to our study of Puritanism in Section One, we do well to recall the opinion of John S. Collidge, who rightly maintained that federal theology found it biblical roots in the theology of the apostle Paul; it was that teaching which was and is formative in federalism's "comprehensive, coherent, and cogent understanding of the Bible," a formulation that in Collidge's opinion "bids fair to be the ultimate achievement of Reformation biblical theology." Contemporary exegetes and systematicians do well to appropriate anew the valid theological insights of Westminster Calvinism, insights into the Word of God which have endured the test of time.

CHAPTER SIX

JUSTIFICATION IN REDEMPTIVE HISTORY

Since the time of the Reformation, the biblical doctrine of justification by faith alone (*sola fide*) has been recognized as the fundamental and determinative doctrine of the Protestant faith. It is quite understandable, then, in light of the importance of this doctrine that much of Protestant interpretation and exposition of soteric justification would be polemical in nature. After all, Protestants believed that the church stood or fell, depending upon its adherence to or repudiation of the biblical doctrine of justification by faith. In the history of Protestant dogmatic theology, there has been the tendency so to emphasize the *sola fide* character in justification that the full relation of faith and works in forensic justification at times has been unclear or obscure. During the course of the Reformation, increasing stress upon the absolute character of faith as the sole instrument of justification was necessitated by the erroneous teaching of Roman Catholicism. As the Protestants insisted, there could he no mixture of faith and obedience in the article of justification by faith in its primary, constitutive sense. Though justifying faith inevitably produces good works, so that faith and obedience are inseparable, faith is the alone instrument of justification. The term "instrument" is a scholastic word which simply serves to identify the manner in which divine justification is received. The term, though not found in Scripture, does not import any foreign or speculative notion into the biblical teaching.

Central to the Reformers' doctrinal formulations are the teachings of the apostle Paul. Justification is apart from the works of the law. A man is justified by faith, not by works. The righteous man shall live by faith (*e.g.*, Rom 1:17; 3:19ff.; 5:1-21; Gal 3:1-18; Eph 2:8-10; and Phil 3:3ff.). But what shall we say of James, who writes: a man is justified by works, and not by faith alone (Jam 2:24)? And what of the Epistle to the Hebrews, which is an extended exposition of this same teaching found in James regarding the necessity of faith and obedience? It is frequently pointed out how Luther objected to the teachings of James and the author of Hebrews on grounds of apparent conflict with the Pauline teaching. As a consequence, Luther relegated these books (among others) to a lower status within the canon of Scripture. Regarding those passages in Hebrews which insist upon faith and obedience, Calvin Schoonhoven mistakenly suggests:

> Luther so felt the sting of these sections that he disavowed the book. Not only the dramatic pointedness bothered him, but more so what was actually said. Subsequent commentators have struggled rather much to ease the violent impact of this material. Thus it is that Luther and other commentators follow the "analogy-of-faith" hermeneutical principle, which we are convinced obstructs precise exegesis by demanding that all the biblical literature be read in the light of so-called ruling concepts derived from supposed clear statements of other Scripture. By so doing they have done great disservice to the text.[1]

The particular "ruling concept" that Schoonhoven has in mind here is the traditional law-gospel distinction.

It has become commonplace in biblical and theological interpretation to substitute the Barthian notion of "law in grace" for the traditional law versus grace distinction. Modern critics argue that biblical theology challenges the entire federalist structure of historic Reformed theology. Daniel Fuller concludes his recent study by stating: "Calvin never sensed, as biblical theology has begun to perceive, that Paul used the same term 'law' in two ways that are very opposite to each other because of the complicating factor of the power of sin."[2] Fuller's conception of "law" is entirely different from Calvin's, judged by the former's repudiation of the traditional understanding of the law/gospel distinction which is now shared by a growing number of theologians, including Schoonhoven and Geoffrey Bromiley, both of whom, like Fuller, teach at Fuller Theological Seminary, Thomas and James Torrance in Scotland, and G. C. Berkouwer and S. G. DeGraaf in The Netherlands.[3] Elsewhere, I have presented a full historical-theological analysis of the Reformed concept of "works" in the rise and development of covenant theology.[4]

This present study offers a fresh interpretation of the "apparently" contradictory teachings in the Scriptures on the role of faith and works in redemptive justification. The proper and legitimate use of the biblical-theological method of interpretation, contrary to the opinion of modern, critical exegetes, will strive to unfold and manifest the multifaceted message of redemptive revelation set forth in the Old and New Testaments. Since the beginning of Reformed theology, there has been continual development and progress in the articulation of a distinctly Reformed methodology, namely, the covenantal methodology. One of the leading modern exponents of this interpretive methodology is Geerhardus Vos, of whom Richard Gaffin, Jr. remarks:

> Writing at the height of his career, he observed that Reformed theology "has from the beginning shown itself possessed of a true historic sense in the apprehension of the progressive character of the deliverance of truth. Its doctrine of the covenants on its historical side represents the first attempt at constructing a history of revelation and may justly be considered the precursor of what is at present called Biblical Theology."[5]

It is just this concern for the *progressive* nature of biblical revelation that is requisite for an adequate interpretation of the fundamental Protestant doctrine of justification by faith. Since the Reformed biblical-theological method has matured to the point of a consciously vital and consistent approach to Scripture, we are now in a better position to appreciate the redemptive-historical character of God's revelation of justification in the way of the Covenant of Grace. Systematic theology depends upon the fruits of biblical theology. There is a mutual relationship between these two methodologies.[6] Consequently, a proper view of biblical theology will not lead to a depreciatory view of systematic theology.

Neglect of biblical theology product's an unhealthy, one-sided approach to the biblical message, which is incapable of doing justice to the various strands of redemptive revelation. Gaffin cautions:

> The tendency, in the interests of maintaining the unity and divine authorship of Scripture, to minimize or ignore the distinctiveness of each of the human writers is unfortunate not only because in its own way it suggests a conflict between divine and human elements in Scripture, but also because it bars the way to a more pointed and articulate grasp of biblical teaching. Careful attention to the writings of the various authors in all their respective individuality and particularity will only serve to disclose in all its rich diversity the organic unity of biblical revelation.[7]

The key to right understanding of the biblical teaching on justification in the Covenant of Grace is to be found in the federalist interpretation of the continuity *and* discontinuity of the Old and New Covenants. Apart from this dominant feature in the federalist interpretation of the divine covenants, one will not succeed in arriving at an accurate understanding of the role of faith and obedience in justification, as that is expounded in the epistles of Paul, James, and the writer to the Hebrews. Specifically, acknowledgment of the distinctive and characteristic law feature of the Mosaic Covenant is of paramount importance in the Pauline epistles and in Hebrews. Succinctly stated, the Mosaic administration of the Covenant of Grace incorporates the system of works-inheritance in the typical sphere of covenant life, in which physical and temporal blessings are contingent upon the obedience of the Israelite nation, as opposed to the spiritual, antitypical blessings (namely, eternal salvation) which rest exclusively upon the obedience of Christ. The spiritual blessings are an essential part of the Mosaic Covenant. The law was added to the promise given to Abraham in order that grace might abound. That is to say, the system of works-inheritance in the typical sphere serves a subservient, pedagogical function in the life of the people of God prior to the coming of Christ (Rom 5:20 and Gal 3:24-25).

With a view to the further elucidation of this teaching in the Scriptures, we proceed to a brief analysis of the OT revelation of justification in the context of the divine covenants and the ensuing demand for righteousness on the part of the recipients of grace.

1. OLD TESTAMENT - Redemption: Justification of the Godly

The history of redemption, as unfolded in the sacred writings, can be understood only in the light of Scripture's teaching on Creation and the Fall. Any attempt to minimize or obscure the historical character of the biblical account of creation and humanity's fall into sin will result in a defective view of *Heilsgeschichte*.[8] Students of theology are aware of the various and divergent interpretations of salvation-history in modern biblical and theological studies. Basic to our present interpretation of God's revelation is adherence to the historic integrity of the biblical narratives. The history of redemption is the unfolding of God's progressive revelation of himself to humankind in his saving acts of sovereign grace in Jesus Christ. It is the history of divine blessing for obedience and curse for disobedience.

The christological basis of redemption becomes increasingly clear in the ongoing administration of the single Covenant of Grace, which extends from the fall of Adam in the garden to the Consummation, the summing up of all things in heaven and earth. The love and mercy of God toward sinners is realized in and through the person and work of Jesus Christ. Our biblical-theological conception of *Heilsgeschichte* and the covenant of God differs radically from that of neoorthodoxy, particularly the views of Karl Barth. The historical nature of salvation-history is not qualitatively different from "ordinary history" (*Historie* vs. *Geschichte*). As Barth defines the divine covenant as a single Covenant of Grace in Christ, applicable to creation and redemption alike, there is no transition from wrath to grace in history, just as there is no doctrine of the Fall as a concrete, historical reality. Barth's teaching on the "Fall" stands in sharp contrast to that of Protestant orthodoxy. Barth's conception of the eternal covenant in Christ is purely speculative in origin.

Contrary to all Barthian and semi-Barthian interpretations of biblical revelation, God first declared his word of sovereign grace in Christ to Adam in the garden subsequent to Adam's transgression of the law of God. The provision of redeeming grace and love were symbolized by God's clothing of Adam and Eve (Gen 3:15,21). Upon their expulsion from the Garden of Eden, our first parents realized that protection and strength could be found only in the saving intervention of God into their personal lives.

The early chapters of Genesis set forth the history of humankind's response to God's covenant provisions. Among the covenant-keepers, Enoch is described as one who "walked with God" (Gen 5:24).[9] The expression "to walk with God" denotes covenant faithfulness and is commonly used throughout the Old and New Testament writings. Clearly, the recipients of saving grace are those who "walk with God." They are the ones who keep covenant with their God. This is strikingly evident in the life of Noah and his family. In the midst of widespread ungodliness and corruption, Noah was one who "found favor in the eyes of the Lord" (Gen 6:8). Scripture declares: "Noah was a just man and perfect in his generations, and Noah walked with God" (Gen 6:9). In the building of the ark and the gathering of the living creatures, Noah "did according to all that God commanded him" (Gen 6:22; 7:5). The godly people are those who keep covenant with God, who walk in the way of covenant obedience.

When we come to Abram's time, we reach a fuller and clearer revelation of God's Covenant of Grace. God calls Abram to leave his own country in Haran for the place of God's own choice. "So Abram departed, as the Lord had spoken unto him" (Gen 12:4). The fifteenth chapter of Genesis records for us the first divine, covenantal ratification of the promise first given to Adam and his descendants (the elect seed) after the Fall. The restoration of fellowship between God and humanity is exclusively the Lord's accomplishment. In response, Abram declares his "Amen" to God's commitment and promise.[10] (The full implications of Abram's assent of faith are drawn by the apostle Paul in Romans 4. Deeper and clearer understanding of the doctrine of justification by faith had to await the fullness of times. But in the early Genesis narrative, we are told simply that Abram took God at his word.) Abram trusts God for the future realization of the promises, which are both spiritual and physical (the latter, both typical and antitypical). The relationship between the temporal (typical) blessings and the eternal (antitypical) blessings would come into sharper focus only with the passage of time, and with the subsequent administrations of the one and eternal Covenant of Grace.[11]

Following the temporal redemption of Israel from the hands of the Egyptians, God brings his people to the wilderness of Sinai. Through the mediation of Moses, God gives his law as a covenant to the elect nation, Israel. God declares: "Now therefore, if you will obey my voice indeed, and keep my covenant, then you shall be a peculiar treasure to me above all people" (Ex 19:5). Upon hearing the law and commandments of the Lord their God, the people vow their commitment to walk in the way of the covenant with Moses. The precise nature of this covenant has been a matter of intense theological debate in recent years. Writers of both the Old and New Testament documents identify a distinctive law-principle operative in a unique and peculiar manner under the Mosaic Covenant administration. This principle comes to pointed expression in Lev 18:5. In explaining the nature and function of the law of Moses, God stipulates that his people are not to live like the Egyptians or the Canaanites, nor are they to walk in their ordinances. Rather, "You shall do my judgments, and keep my ordinances, to walk in them: I am the Lord your God. You shall therefore keep my statutes, and my judgments: which if a man practices, he shall live in them: I am the Lord (Lev 18:4-5). This principle of works is again highlighted in Ezk 20:11. It is the characteristic feature of the Mosaic Covenant. The antithetical principles of law and grace are operative within the one Mosaic administration of the Covenant of Grace. We shall consider the NT interpretation of this law-principle later in our discussion.

Among biblical exegetes who accept the historic accuracy and integrity of the scriptural accounts, there are two distinct opinions regarding the function of "law" under the Old Covenant. The first and *major* Reformed and Lutheran interpretation since the Reformation period is that the law-principle operates in close conjunction with the bestowal of temporal, earthly rewards. From this point of view, a contemporary exegete writes: "The life of the Hebrews as a nation would depend on the law, not in a totally legalistic sense, but in that the law was the basis of the covenant, and in the covenant rested their close relationship to their God." Elsewhere, this commentator remarks: "The covenant promise of the land, made first to the patriarchs, moved forward by Moses, and still to be experienced by future generations, spanned time within the framework of the purpose of God. And yet the continuity of the covenant, in its fullness, was contingent upon the obedience of the people of God."[12] According to the second Reformed viewpoint, the function of the law under Moses is explained in such a way that the law-principle operates merely in terms of general chastisement for sin. While recognizing the unique situation within the Mosaic economy (in obvious distinction from the New Covenant economy), this view contends that God had determined to discipline Israel in certain instances with immediate judgment for sin or threat of impending judgment so as to demonstrate his holiness and righteousness. Generally, divine judgment according to works, rendered in terms of Old Covenant administration, is suspended during the gospel age. In contrast to both Reformed orthodox interpretations of the Mosaic Covenant, modernists argue that these "apparent" divine judgments (which they cannot really accept according to the canons of critical reasoning) merely have been recounted in Israel's history as a witness to their socio-religious tradition. By historicizing Israel's religion, divine revelation is nothing more than human perception and response to reality as they experienced it in their cultus. We adopt the first Reformed interpretation.

Consistently, the expression "he who does the commandments shall inherit life by them" (Lev 18:5; Ezk 20:11; Lk 10:28; Rom 10:5; Gal 3:12) underscores the fact that the blessings of God are obtained on the basis of obedience (*i.e.*, the works-principle of inheritance). There is no strain of Pharisaical self-righteousness lurking in this divine mandate. The biblical principle of law observance (the works-principle of inheritance) is agreeable with law *as the eternal rule of life* (see the discussion below on Heb 3:18-4:2,6). The creature of God is by necessity bound to obey his Creator. This is his natural obligation by virtue of his creation in the image of God as one in covenant relationship with the Lord and Giver of life. "Man's whole obligation is to heed, and to the obedient Israelite was given the promise of life and rich inheritance. The fact that ultimately piety and prosperity will be united was foreshadowed in the history of the Israelite theocracy, for it symbolized the consummate kingdom of God."[13] Humanity's ability to render obedience to God since the Fall is contingent upon the gracious working of the Holy Spirit, who inscribes the law upon hearts of flesh. Those who through grace are obedient receive the favor and blessing of God. This was true of Adam, Enoch, and Noah in the days prior to the flood, and subsequently in the calling of Abraham as the father of all who believe (Gal 3:8-9; Rom 4:16). What more precisely is the meaning of the law-principle as opposite to the principle of faith within the Mosaic economy (Gal 3:11-12)? In our discussion of later biblical revelation in the NT, we will deal more fully with this question.

This much is clear: Under the Mosaic Covenant the reward of continuing temporal blessings in the land of promise is contingent upon the obedience of Israel, not upon the substitutionary obedience of another, namely, Christ. This is the principle of works-inheritance, rather than faith-inheritance. Leviticus 26 and Deuteronomy 27-28 set forth blessings and curses as the dual sanctions of the Mosaic Covenant. Blessing is the reward for covenant faithfulness, whereas curse is the just recompense for covenant faithlessness. The fact that righteousness and obedience on the part of the Israelite is possible only in terms of the immediate working of the Holy Spirit is in itself immaterial with respect to the administrative operation of the principle of law-inheritance in the symbolic-typical sphere of the Mosaic Covenant. Peter Craigie comments: "Israel, remaining faithful to the covenant God, would be renowned among other nations, not because of inherent merit, but because the covenant community would reflect the glory of the covenant God in its national life. This glory was the potential of the community of God's people but in the two chapters that follow [Deuteronomy 26], a solemn warning is issued concerning the natural disasters that would fall upon Israel in the event of unfaithfulness to the covenant God."[14] The judgment of God according to works is both individual and corporate, affecting the entire nation of Israel. An instance of individual judgment from God appears in connection with entrance into the land of promise, Canaan. For their obedience, Caleb and Joshua are granted God's favor (Num 14:20-38), whereas punishment is rendered to Moses and Aaron for transgression (Num 20:10-13).[15] Corporately, so long as Israel remained faithful to her oath of commitment, she enjoyed peace and prosperity in Canaan. When the necessary measure of corporate righteousness was lacking, God was justified in sending his people into exile (typical judgment corresponding to the land of Canaan as typical blessing).

The central motif in the collection of Psalms is observance of the commandments, wherein is blessedness for the covenant keeper. There is delight in observing God's law, just as there is reward in so doing. The Psalmist exclaims: "The Lord rewarded me according to my righteousness; according to the cleanness of my hands he has recompensed me. . . . I was also upright before him, and I kept myself from my iniquity. Therefore has the Lord recompensed me according to my righteousness, according to the cleanness of my hands in his eyesight. With the merciful you will show yourself merciful; with an upright man you will show yourself upright" (Ps 18:20, 23-25). In these so-called Psalms of confidence of the individual,[16] the individualistic motif also has corporate meaning and application. "Even in the private psalms the confidence motif has generally a collective bearing since the suppliant prays as a member of the covenant and the favor expected is for the benefit of the community."[17] The plea for vindication is a common concern in the hymns of Israelite worship (see also Ps 26:1-3; 37:28-29; 92:12-15). In terms of the peculiar, typical application of law observance in the corporate life of Israel, the vindicatory Psalms point to their ultimate fulfillment in the person and work of the Servant of the Lord, the Lord's Anointed. The reward for obedience in Israel, whether individual or corporate, typifies the redemptive work of the one man, Christ Jesus. The righteousness of godly Israel demonstrates the righteousness of God. "The Lord is our righteousness" (Jer 33:16). When the Psalmist rejoices in the Lord's salvation and deliverance from all his enemies, the song of redemption is ultimately Christ's (see, *e.g.*, Ps 18:1-3 and 28:8-9). This is the glorification in Israel of God's name and works among all the nations of the world.

In the community of God's redeemed people, there is the justification of the godly. The justified are the ones who keep covenant with their God. The prophet Habakkuk describes the godly member of Israel as the just and righteous one who obtains life through faith (Hab 2:4). We shall be observing below that this is the perspective of the writer to the Hebrews. The justification of the godly is obtained in the way of covenant faithfulness. The expression "the just shall inherit life by his faith" describes faith-inheritance (as opposed to works-inheritance).

One of the most important, and critically controversial, books in the OT is the Book of Deuteronomy. Craigie remarks: "The Book of Deuteronomy is one of the most comprehensive accounts in the OT of the covenant between God and his people. It is a book that is vital for understanding the complexities of biblical theology, for the majority of that theology is concerned with the covenant relationship between God and man."[18] Emphasis falls heavily upon the necessity for Israel to be obedient to the commandments of God in order for there to be blessing and prosperity in Canaan (Deut 4:37-40; 6:1-3).[19]

The purpose of the law of Moses is to increase transgression. The full increase of sin reaches its culmination in the period of the exile. Apart from the unique Mosaic law administration, Israel is "alive unto God" as a beneficiary of the promises given to Abraham. But when the law comes, Israel "dies," typically speaking (Rom 7:1-13).[20] Her restoration is to be accomplished by the Servant of the Covenant, Jesus Christ. In that day the Spirit will write God's law upon the hearts of his people, rather than on tables of stone (Jer 31:31ff.; 4:4; Ezk 16:59-63; cf.. Zech 8:14-17). The Lord God will vindicate the glory of his own name in the salvation of his people.

Deuteronomy prescribes that when Israel desired to have a king the one appointed should rule from the book of the law (Deut 17:18ff.). At the appointment of David, God renewed to him the oath-promise of covenant faithfulness (2 Samuel 7; 1 Chronicles 17; Ps 89:35-37). Although the Davidic Covenant is important in the ongoing revelation of the single Covenant of Grace, this covenant does not displace the definitive role of the Mosaic Covenant administration of law as a means of tutelage and bondage until the coming of Christ, who himself proclaims the acceptable day of the Lord and liberty to the captives (Is 61:1ff.). In that day, Christ terminates the law of Moses (Rom 10:4). The righteousness of God is revealed apart from the law (Rom 3:21). The full explanation of the grace of soteric justification – justification which is by faith alone, apart from the works of the law – awaits the New Covenant epoch.[21] Commenting on the idea of "truth" in the Johannine writings (including Jn 1:17) and the Epistle to the Hebrews, Vos writes that "it expresses the heavenly character of the Christian realities of revelation and redemption in which the higher world directly communicates itself, and the opposite of 'the true' is the typical, wherein the connection with the heavenly world is present only in a mediated, shadowy form."[22]

The great interpreter of the function of the Mosaic law covenant in biblical history and eschatology is the apostle Paul. As Vos observes: "The promise given to Abraham in its worldwide significance, the law as introduced by Moses in its disciplinary, convicting function, both in their relation, in case of the former positive, in case of the latter negative, to the gospel, have once for all been interpreted for us by this great philosopher of history."[23] Paul sets the history of God's covenant in the context of the familiar two-age construction, *i.e.*, the conscious awareness of the present age and the age to come. Paul's theological perspective is fundamentally eschatological. Furthermore, Paul's point of orientation is that of the history of salvation (*historia salutis*), in distinction from the application of redemption (*ordo salutis*). Consequently, Paul's discussion of justification by faith is in the first place redemptive-historical. The teaching on justification is considered in terms of the specific covenantal transactions between God and humankind, notably the Abrahamic, the Mosaic, and the New Covenants, all of which are manifestations of the one and eternal Covenant of Grace.

According to 2 Cor 3:6ff., the distinctive nature of the Mosaic Covenant is that it is a ministration of death and condemnation, in contrast to the New Covenant, which is a ministration of life and justification. The former is letter, whereas the latter is Spirit. It is commonly agreed by exegetes today that *pneuma* (Gk.) is a reference to the Holy Spirit as the One who gives life. But in what sense does the Mosaic Covenant minister death and condemnation? Under the Mosaic administration of the Covenant of Grace, God justifies the godly who walk in the way of faithful obedience to the commandments and statutes given through Moses. The OT teaching does not draw out the full implications of the manner of justification, but rather declares that the redemption of God's people is manifested in the justification of the godly as the righteous ones who inherit the promise through faith. The faith of the righteous man is demonstrated in his unreserved commitment in doing the will of God. Hab 2:4 describes the justified man. Lev 18:5 defines the characteristic law-principle of inheritance operative within the Mosaic Covenant administration, which principle is opposite to the faith-principle of inheritance. The reference to the faith of the just is to saving faith more generally defined as trust. The full unfolding of the concept of soteric, justifying faith, in the technical Pauline sense, lay beyond the OT revelation.

2. NEW TESTAMENT – Fullness of Revelation in Christ

A. Reconciliation and Justification

At the opening of his Gospel, John sharply contrasts the present revelation in Christ with the former revelation under Moses by making use of the biblical law-grace antithesis (Jn 1:17). Similarly, the apostle Paul preaches: "Be it known to you therefore, men and brethren, that through this man is preached to you the forgiveness of sins: And by him all that believe are justified from all things, from which you could not be justified by the law of Moses" (Acts 13:38-39). This is the message of reconciliation, the revelation of God which comes apart from the law, though witnessed by the law and the prophets (Rom 3:21). The discontinuity between law and grace in terms of the typical and antitypical distinction within the Mosaic Covenant is clearly brought out in the Letter to the Hebrews (8:8-13; 9:15). The characteristic operation of law under Moses is temporary, and in need of change (7:12,21-28). The termination of law includes the suspension of the Mosaic system of typology. Elsewhere, Paul tells us that the purpose of the Mosaic law is to increase transgression so that sin might abound (Rom 5:20; Gal 3:19). This is the meaning of Paul's expression "the letter kills." Although there clearly are elements of promise in and around the Mosaic Covenant, yet this covenant does not consist in promise *in its characteristic and peculiar system of typology*. (The grace-principle applies to the sacrificial cultus of the Mosaic typological system.) What distinguishes the Old Covenant from the New is the striking operation of the principle of works-inheritance in the unique, pedagogical sphere of covenant life. The apostle is able to identify the Mosaic Covenant as a covenant of law (*i.e.*, works) in opposition to grace because this particular, historical administration of the single Covenant of Grace provides a special restricted context for the works-inheritance principle. The principle of works is operative in this special sphere of typical kingdom inheritance, while at the same time the principle of sovereign grace is operative in the antitypical, spiritual sphere.

The use of the word *katargeô* in 2 Cor 3:7 has the basic meaning of "coming to an end,"[24] and refers in this context to that which is temporary and passing away. The law feature of Mosaic Covenant is of limited duration, so that the Old Covenant is passing away, while the New is eternal (*cf.*, Heb 8:13; Rom 10:4). Though the Old Covenant, along with the old age, is passing away (preparing for the semi-eschatological age of the Spirit), nevertheless the Old Covenant came in glory (2 Cor 3:9). There is both continuity and discontinuity in God's covenant dealings throughout the era of redemption (from the revelation of salvation to Adam after the Fall to the Consummation).

In a related passage, Gal 3:15-22, Paul argues that once a covenant has been made, nothing can be added to change or alter that arrangement. How much more so is this true of God's covenantal dealings with his people. However, Paul proceeds to tell us that the law *was added* (vs. 19) until the coming of Christ. The addition of the law does not alter God's previous, guaranteed commitment. The law does not annul the promise. God's grace is secure and indefectible for his elect seed (vss. 16-17). The promised inheritance is obtained by faith, through grace, and not by works. But why then the law? It served a subordinate purpose in the history of redemption. Its function was to increase sin; it was added because of transgressions. And its tutelary purpose is to lead Israel to Christ for salvation (vss. 18-19). The law, divine in origin and mediated through Moses, was given to shut Israel up under sin so that God might have mercy upon all who believe in Jesus Christ (vss. 20-22; *cf.*, Romans 2-3, 11). Consequently, the Mosaic Covenant with its distinctive law-principle did not make the promise void. The pedagogical system of typology with its operative principle of kingdom inheritance by works was subservient to the broader redemptive purpose and program.

Because of the administrative function of the works-inheritance principle in the Mosaic Covenant, a principle that was also operative in the original Covenant of Creation, Paul identifies certain legal aspects of the Mosaic Covenant with the "weak and beggarly elements" (*stoicheia*) of the world (Gal 4:3,9; *cf.*, Col 2:8,20).[25] The bondage to which Israel was subjected is part of God's consignment of all under sin and death (Gal 4:1-4; Rom 3:20; 11:32). In the case of national Israel as God's elect people, the bondage was, in the first place, typical in nature. It was the covenantal administration of death and condemnation, culminating in the exile of God's people to Babylon, the kingdom representative of this present, evil world. The term *stoicheia* refers to creation now subject to the powers and principalities of the old, corrupt age. Israel was held in bondage under the Mosaic administration (the letter of the law) until the time appointed by the Father – the glorious, eschatological age of the Spirit, the age that appears first as semi-eschatological because of its temporary overlap with the era of the present, evil world.[26] Christ's work of reconciliation brought about the defeat of the worldly principalities and powers by means of the removal of the legal charges against God's people (Col 2:2:14-15; Eph 2:15; *cf.*, the cosmic implications described in Romans 8). In principle, believers are freed from the power of sin and death, although there is still the intense struggle against sin because of their semi-eschatological existence prior to the Consummation (thus, Rom 7:14-25).

The corollary to reconciliation is the justification of God's elect, which is apart from the works of the law. "The objective reconciliation took place in the death of Christ; its subjective result is justification."[27] In justification by faith we receive the reconciliation. The underlying motif in all of Paul's discussion is the function of the Mosaic Covenant in the history of redemption. Again, the doctrine of justification is perceived by Paul from his fundamental, redemptive-historical viewpoint. In declaring the full revelation of God's justification of sinners in history, Paul considers the progressive nature of the single Covenant of Grace, specifically in relation to the covenants made with Abraham and Moses. The salvation promised to Abraham was not given through the law; its righteousness was the righteousness which is of faith. Those who seek salvation by the law make the promise of no effect, for the law (in its tutelary use) always and only works wrath. Apart from Christ, the law of God condemns the sinner (4:13ff.). The expression, "where there is no law, there is no transgression," is a redemptive-historical marker which identifies the period of the Abrahamic Covenant.[28] When the law came, Israel died, her death taking the form of exile from the typological kingdom. From the redemptive-historical point of view, Israel in accordance with the symbolic-typical picture is alive unto God under the ministration of the Abrahamic Covenant (grace), but dead through sin under the ministration of the Mosaic Covenant (law) in its special typical, earthly sphere. In these two, distinct historical-covenantal contexts, law has a twofold purpose and application. In the sphere of the grace of the Abrahamic Covenant, law has a normative or regulative function which is consistent with soteric grace. In the sphere of the Mosaic Covenant's works-principle, God's law demands compliance as the ground of inheritance, and is thus antithetical to grace. This is precisely the point of contrast Paul makes in Rom 4:14-16. The expression "adherents of the law" is used in this twofold sense, one consistent with grace, the other antithetical to grace.

The elenctic function of the Mosaic law is one with the law of the Covenant of Creation. Speaking through both covenants, the law of God serves to shut up all humankind under the curse. The principle of works-inheritance which informs both the Creation Covenant and the Mosaic Covenant *always operates in a covenantal context*, never as a "bare principle" of natural law. As a result of man's transgression of the law of God, man has become a covenant-breaker. This is the point made by the prophet Isaiah. "The earth also is defiled under the inhabitants thereof; because they have transgressed the laws, changed the ordinance, broken the everlasting covenant" (24:5). Though the prophet's immediate reference is to the Creation Covenant, which he calls the "everlasting covenant," he employs terminology from the Mosaic law administration. The law which all men have broken is the law of the Creation Covenant given by natural revelation, that is inscribed upon men's hearts (*cf.*, Rom 2:14-15). Isaiah's point is developed more fully by the apostle Paul in the opening three chapters of Romans.[29] To be under the law of condemnation, whether by virtue of the original Covenant of Creation or the law administration of the Mosaic Covenant, is to be under the "elements of the world."

According to the gospel of Jesus Christ, Paul, the apostle to the Gentiles, declares that through the redeeming work of Christ the law of Moses has been terminated. By faith we are justified, both Jew and Gentile, and freed from the bondage of the law. In the fullness of times, the revelation of justification by faith has reached its mature statement. The apex of Paul's argument in his epistle to the Romans comes in the fifth chapter, which discusses justification by faith from the standpoint of the imputation of Christ's righteousness as the ground of soteric blessing.[30] Anders Nygren writes:

> The parallelism which Paul draws between Adam and Christ has seemed so strange and unmanageable that it has made scholars the more willing to treat this section as a parenthesis. More or less consciously interpreters have acted on the assumption that something, which is so foreign to today's thought as to seem unreal, cannot have been of decisive importance to Paul either.
>
> When once one comes to realize what that means to Paul, he forthwith discovers that this passage is by no means a parenthesis or a digression in the apostle's thought. Rather do we here come to the high point of the epistle. This is the point where all the lines of his thinking converge, both those of the preceding chapters and those of the chapters that follow.[31]

The central concern of the passage is the representative headships of Adam and Christ, and more specifically the peculiar imputation of their respective acts.[32] The parallel is drawn between the imputation of Adam's sin to all those for whom Adam is the representative, on the one hand, and the imputation of Christ's obedience, the one righteous act, to all those for whom Christ is the representative, on the other. The scope of the comparison includes the entire range of history, from Creation to Consummation. Without confusing the incident of the Fall with the original creation, Paul roots all humanity in the historic occasion of the Fall. That is to say, the apostle considers all in Adam in their identification with the one sin of Adam. Paul is not teaching that sin and disobedience are coextensive with creation.[33] Though Adam was created perfect and without sin, he willingly transgressed the law of God and his disobedience was imputed to all in that all sinned in Adam's one act of transgression (*cf.*, 1 Cor 15:20-23). By Adam's demerit all humankind came under the wrath of God.[34] But by virtue of the imputation of Christ's righteousness through faith, believers are declared and constituted righteous. The verb *katastathêsontai* in Rom 5:19 cannot be translated "shall be made," but rather "shall be constituted." (Compare Paul's use of the same verb in the earlier part of the verse with reference to being constituted sinners in Adam.)

Included in the representative idea is the corporate notion of solidarity. The representative and corporate ideas are inseparably related in Paul's thought. The imputation of sin and the imputation of obedience, in the case of the two representative acts of the heads of the Covenant of Creation and the Covenant of Redemption respectively, are conceived corporately, rather than individualistically. Vs. 13 begins a parenthesis which extends to the end of vs. 17. However, Paul's reference to the Mosaic law in this parenthetical section serves an important purpose. Its importance is evidenced by the further reference to the Mosaic law in vs. 20. With reference to the period between Adam and Moses, Paul says, "sin is not imputed where there is no law" (Rom 5:13). Once again, this is a redemptive-historical way of describing the period of grace and promise (*cf.*, Rom 4:6-8, 15). It refers to that period of redemption beginning with Adam after the Fall and culminating in the covenantal ratification of God's promise made to Abraham and his seed. It is descriptive of the early history of the Covenant of Grace. However, even in this era of grace and life, death reigned over the godly line (Rom 5:14; see especially Genesis 5).[35] Paul reminds his readers that the wages of sin is death. Yet under the order of grace, God does not reckon sin unto condemnation. Under grace, there is the forgiveness of sin. According to vs. 20, the Mosaic law entered in order to increase the transgression that the offense might abound. But even so, where sin abounded grace did much more abound. Even though the Mosaic law's administration of death and condemnation served to increase the trespass, more ultimately and gloriously the purpose of the Mosaic law, in continuity with the progressive administration of the single Covenant of Grace, was to enhance the grace of God (*cf.*, Gal 3:22,24). In this climactic portion of Paul's epistle, the teaching on the doctrine of justification by faith is presented in terms of the history of redemption, and more directly in terms of the Mosaic Covenant. Under law, whether the law of creation or the law of Moses in its symbolic-typical kingdom dimension, sin is reckoned to man's account so that he stands condemned under the wrath of God. Under grace, where sin is not imputed, there is justification and life.

Apart from the law, God revealed his righteousness which is by faith in Jesus Christ to all and upon all them that believe (Rom 3:21-22). According to the teaching of Romans 5, as Vos points out, "the two transactions of reconciliation and justification are in substance identical."[36] The transition from wrath to grace in history is registered in the termination of the law administration stage of the Covenant of Grace and the establishment of the New Covenant. There is no further need for the tutelary, pedagogical function of the law of Moses. The shadow of things has given way to the fullness of revelation by way of the definitive, once-for-all accomplishment of redemption in Jesus Christ (Rom 3:21-22; 6:14; 7:6; 10:4; 11:6).

To draw out the contrast between the principles of law and grace, the apostle Paul quotes from the law of Moses its witness both to the righteousness which is of the law and to the righteousness which is of faith (Rom 10:5ff.). The principle of works-inheritance is stated in Lev 18:5 (see earlier discussion). On the one hand, the expression "the man who does the commandments shall inherit life by them" is understood to mean that God's favor (reward, justification) is obtained in the way of works, a principle antithetical to saving grace (Rom 10:5; Gal 3:12).[37] On the other hand, the expression "the just shall inherit life by his faith" in every instance is in contrast to the principle of works-inheritance. The just who obtain life by faith are those who are faithful covenant-keepers. Those who fall into this group are the beneficiaries of God's saving grace (Rom 1:17; Gal 3:11; *cf.* Heb 10:38). In the light of New Covenant revelation, the deeper meaning of the expression, "the just shall inherit life by his faith," can now be seen. The righteous man is the one who is justified by faith apart from the works of the law. His eternal inheritance is grounded exclusively upon the merits of Jesus Christ. Soteric justification in its technical sense is the imputation of the obedience of Christ to the believer. This deeper content of meaning is consistent with the earlier revelation in the OT. Lev 18:5 identifies the order of law with its principle of works-inheritance; Hab 2:4 identifies the order of grace with its underlying principle of faith-inheritance. Paul also cites Deut 30:12-14 for Moses' teaching on faith-inheritance (Rom 10:6-8).38

The administrative compatibility of these two opposing principles of inheritance within the Mosaic Covenant resides in the distinction between the two spheres of covenant life, one pedagogical (typical) and one spiritual (antitypical). At the time when the symbolic-typical system itself came to a close, Christ terminated the operation of the works-inheritance principle found within that typical sphere of Old Covenant administration. The fatal mistake of the Judaizers was that they misapplied the principle of works-inheritance, which was operative on the typical level, to the antitypical level and so sought salvation by works. They perverted the Mosaic Covenant into a religion of works-salvation. Israel followed after the law of righteousness (salvation), but did not attain unto it because they sought it as though by works (Rom 9:30-33).

The apostle Paul's great desire is that Israel might be saved. His message stresses repeatedly the sovereign nature of God's saving grace to sinners, "For whosoever shall call upon the name of the Lord shall be saved" (Rom 10:13; especially 11:1-32). Israel finds her true identity as the people of God only through Christ, by way of individual baptism into his body, the church, the new Israel (see together, Romans 6 and 11; Eph 2:1-16). In Christ God has reconciled the world unto himself. There is now no longer Jew and Gentile, but the "New Man" in Christ Jesus. In the fullness of revelation God has manifested his justification of sinners apart from the works of the law. "For what the law could not do, in that it was weak through the flesh, God sending his own Son in the likeness of sinful flesh, and for sin, condemned sin in the flesh" (Rom 8:3).

B. Eschatological Judgment and Justification

The description of the imputation of Christ's righteousness to the believer in justification does not exhaust the biblical teaching on this fundamental doctrine in the Covenant of Grace. Certainly, the primary aspect of forensic justification is constitutive. Through the imputation of the obedience of Christ, all in Christ are constituted righteous. This divine act does not take account of any inner moral transformation in the believer. Both justification with respect to the demonstrative aspect (working faith) and sanctification have in view the inner renewal. Recognition of the two, distinct and inseparable aspects of forensic, declarative justification (the constitutive and the demonstrative) is of utmost importance. To be sure, this distinction does not come as clearly into view in OT revelation, but we must appreciate the *progressive* nature of redemptive revelation. The compatibility between the Old and New Testament revelation of justification by faith in its twofold meaning (the constitutive and the demonstrative aspects) is apparent in the NT writers' use of Gen 15:6, which we shall consider in our discussion below.

Shall we say that the law of God is brought to no effect by the law of faith? In certain instances Paul responds with an unequivocal affirmative (*e.g.*, Rom 3:27-28; 4:13-15; Gal 2:16, 21). But in other places Paul answers otherwise (Rom 3:31; 6:1ff., 8:4). Here again, we must distinguish two different meanings for the word "law." In the former instances, law cannot stand with faith, whereas in the latter, compliance with the law is necessary along with saving faith. To translate this in terms of justification, in the former case we are justified by faith apart from law (the works-principle of inheritance) and in the latter case we are justified by works along with our faith, our faith being demonstrated by our works (James 2). In this latter instance, faith apart from works is a dead faith, a faith which does not justify.

Those who walk with God, who keep covenant, are declared to be *righteous.* They are justified in the sight of God. Apart from such righteousness, there is no eternal inheritance (1 Cor 6:9-11). For those who have been justified on the ground of Christ's righteousness, good works follow as the inevitable fruit of justification (Eph 2:8-10; Tit 2:11-14; 3:4-7). A criterion for consummate blessing and reward is faithful obedience to the law of God in the way of the Covenant of Grace. The final judgment of God includes both blessing and curse. The righteous saints shall receive their final approbation in accordance with their adherence to the commandments of God (2 Cor 5:9-10; *cf.*, 1 Cor 3:11-15). Justification is according to works, though not on the ground of works. The principle of divine justice and equity applies to all humankind indiscriminately (Rom 2:6-16; *cf.*, 2:29 and 3:28-30). For the righteous who keep covenant, the reward is glory, honor, immortality, and eternal life (*cf.*, also Rev 2:7: 19:7-8; 21:7-8,23-27). For those who have trampled upon the law and ordinances of God, there is indignation, wrath, tribulation, and anguish. The question as to *how* one is constituted and made righteous (*i.e.*, justified and sanctified) is not relevant to Paul's argument in Rom 2:6-16, and in other related passages.

A similar instance where law obedience is called for in regard to kingdom inheritance is Jesus' discourses with the rich young ruler (Lk 18: 18-30) and with the lawyer (Lk 10:25-37). On the one hand, Jesus affirms the principle of reward according to works, analogous to Paul's teaching in Rom 2:6-16. Furthermore, Jesus intimates the kind of righteousness which is required for life eternal in each of these two discourses. What is necessary is a radically different approach to the law of God from that of the Judaizers (*cf.*, especially Lk 19:25,29 with Matt 5:20).[39] The order of grace does not nullify the law of God, but rather establishes it. Yet, such obedience is wholly different in character from that of the self-righteous Pharisees. In these same two discourses, on the other hand, Jesus uses the law in its pedagogical, elenchtic function to convince his hearers of their guiltiness before God as sinners and to point them to the grace of forgiveness and faith-righteousness.[40]

In concluding this study of justification in redemptive history, we turn our attention to the themes of justification, covenant, and eschatology in the Epistle to the Hebrews. The proper interpretation of this book depends entirely upon our earlier discussion concerning justification in its twofold meaning. To summarize our thesis thus far: the OT teaching on justification does not bring clearly to view the idea of imputed righteousness as the sole ground of man's salvation. Saving faith is an obedient, working faith which is realized only by the power of the Spirit of God. Justification is viewed in terms of inwrought righteousness, whereby works are evidential of justifying faith. The NT teaching clarifies the constitutive and demonstrative aspects of forensic, soteric justification. The former aspect could be comprehended only in the fullness of times.

The fundamental theme which underlies the message of Hebrews is covenant continuity – the unity of the Covenant of Grace throughout redemptive history. From this perspective, the writer considers the nature of justifying faith in both covenant dispensations, the Old and the New. Recent analyses of this epistle have approached this matter of covenant continuity from a modern, critical viewpoint. The modern view repudiates the distinction between law and grace, faith and works, the distinction we have maintained in this study. According to the modern critics, there is no sense in which there is a *legitimate, divinely ordained* contrast between the covenantal administration of law and the covenantal administration of grace, either in terms of the contrasting Covenant of Creation (works) and the Covenant of Redemption (grace), or in terms of the opposing principles of law and grace within the Mosaic administration of the Covenant of Grace. In place of the traditional teaching, the critics maintain only one covenantal relationship between God and humanity from Creation to Consummation, namely, the Covenant of Grace. When we speak of law, so these critics argue, we must always speak of law in grace. From the outset of creation, God has committed himself to preserve his creative work, despite the disobedience and irresponsibility of man. (This view has little in common with the orthodox doctrine of supralapsarianism.) The neoorthodox contend that nothing can frustrate the grace of God. This promise of covenant grace is demonstrated by the sacrificial death of Christ for the sins of the world. The good news of the gospel is that God has always taken the initiative in grace to be man's blessedness. To live responsibly and authentically, man is called to a life of faith in the saving mercies of Christ. But in all of this, we must *never* speak of the (consequent) absolute necessity of the atonement, as though God the Father were somehow obliged to sacrifice his own Son in order to placate his wrath and satisfy an "abstract" demand for legal righteousness. In line with this, the critics continue to argue, we must throw out the "contractual" and "legalistic" notions of imputed righteousness as the ground and merit of justification, and faith as the alone instrumental cause of the believer's justification. A legal conception of covenant accountability jeopardizes the doctrine of sovereign grace and sacrifices the freedom and love of God. Finally, we are told that we must begin and end our theological reflection upon God and humanity from the perspective of the grace of God. All else is subordinate to God's grace.

It is our contention that this modern theological viewpoint is a clear repudiation of the historic orthodox understanding of the gospel of Christ. The modern doctrine of grace is nothing more than the agelong confusion of faith-righteousness and works-righteousness under the guise of an exclusive emphasis upon the "sovereign grace of God in Christ." And it is from this modernist position that recent challenges to the traditional interpretation of the Letter to the Hebrews have come. Based upon his study of Hebrews, Schoonhoven contends:

> There is no way that this emphasis on a necessary condition can be diminished. Though not absent from the other NT writings, it is represented so forthrightly and dramatically here that it forces a careful re-evaluation of all traditional theological categories. Indeed, salvation is by faith alone: but the very faith that saves is only such if it is or includes the obedience of faith. There is simply no way that the "analogy-of-faith" principle can modify or eradicate the conditional nature of salvation.[41]

In contrast to the traditional interpretation of Hebrews and the epistles of Paul more generally, Schoonhoven offers a novel reinterpretation of the nature of faith and works in justification according to the message of Hebrews. He draws no distinction between the constitutive and demonstrative aspects of justification. Rather, he concludes from his study:

> It is exactly in regard to this discussion of faith and obedience that the problem of an "analogy-of-faith" hermeneutic is most acute. Though Paul and the other NT writers in a different and less dramatic way say the same as the writer of Hebrews, yet somehow in many theological circles a wrong radical of revelation has achieved normative status: namely, that man is saved by faith alone and that this faith does not necessarily include "obedience."[42]

It must be pointed out here that Schoonhoven's estimate of the traditional teaching is entirely wrong in this last regard. The historic Reformed tradition maintains that faith is the alone instrument of justification (with regard to the constitutive aspect), but that such saving faith inevitably results in good works such that a man is justified by works (in terms of the demonstrative aspect). These two, distinct aspects of soteric justification are inseparable realities in the life of the believer within the Covenant of Grace. The teaching on justification in the epistles of James and the writer to the Hebrews pertains to the demonstrative function of works as evidential of saving faith.

In order to understand the message of the writer to the Hebrews, it is essential that we bring into our consideration again the biblical distinction between works-inheritance and faith-inheritance. The expression "the doers of the commandments shall inherit life by them" refers to works-inheritance, and the expression "the just shall inherit life by his faith" denotes faith-righteousness. These two expressions apply to two opposing covenantal orders, law and grace. At every point in his discussion, the writer to the Hebrews considers the covenant-keeper as one who is justified by faith. His primary concern in this letter is not the meritorious ground of justification, but rather the working nature of saving faith. His message is a summons to his readers that they respond similarly in faith and obedience. Faith is decisively eschatological, looking to the final reckoning (justification) of humankind at the day of the Lord (*e.g.*, Heb 2:1-3:

3:12-4:16; 6:1-12; 12:1-29). There is a qualitative difference between the righteousness of the believer and that of the unbeliever.

The reward of the eternal inheritance awaits those who persevere in covenant faithfulness. The reason that the Israelites of old did not enter into the rest of God is that they failed to believe and obey the God of the covenant. In this epistle, faith and obedience are *synonymous* (see especially Heb 3:18-4:2,6). The writer calls his readers to covenant faithfulness, as imitators of Jesus Christ, who himself kept covenant with his God in the face of all human opposition (3:2). Herein lies the continuity between the obedience of Israel under the Mosaic Covenant and the obedience of believers under the New. Although the principle of inheritance in the typical, earthly sphere of Old Covenant life is antithetical to the principle of inheritance in the antitypical, spiritual sphere of covenant life, nevertheless there is this *parallel*: what was required of the Israelites under the typical system of the Mosaic Covenant is identical to what is required now of believers under the New Covenant, namely, covenant faithfulness. In other words, the parallel is in terms of law as the eternal rule of life and fellowship with God, the so-called normative or regulative use of the law (*cf.*, 1 Pet 1:14-16) This same point is drawn by Paul in 1 Cor 10:6-11. The way of the covenant is the way of covenant faithfulness. We are exhorted not to be like the unfaithful and disobedient Israelites. We are to learn from their example (1 Cor 10:6,11; Heb 2:19-4:6).

The relationship of faith and works in Hebrews leads Schoonhoven to remark: "Faith cannot be separated from obedience. Obedience is included in and a part of the faith experience. Thus when the author says faith, he at the same time says obedience, for the terms are interchangeable."[43] Regrettably. this definition of faith-obedience becomes normative for Schoonhoven's interpretation of the doctrine of justification by faith (= works). The fatal mistake of Schoonhoven is that he will not grant that there are two distinct, separate functions of works in justification appropriate to the Covenant of Works and the Covenant of Grace. What is twofold in the biblical teaching is merged and confounded in the thought of Schoonhoven.

The familiar eleventh chapter of Hebrews enumerates some of the outstanding heroes of the faith. They are the just who followed the way of faith, who walked with God as covenant-keepers. The writer begins by defining faith as "the substance of things hoped for, the evidence of things not seen" (11:1). Faith is here defined in its basic covenantal and eschatological sense, applicable to both the creation covenant and the redemptive covenant. It is not faith defined in the Pauline sense as that which justifies the ungodly, in which sense faith is the receiving organ of Christ's imputed righteousness. In vs. 7 the writer describes Noah as the heir of the righteousness which is by faith, an expression equally applicable to all the others mentioned in this eleventh chapter. The expression "righteousness which is by faith" characterizes the status of the just man, the one whose covenant faithfulness meets with divine favor. It is different from the technical Pauline expression, the "righteousness which is by faith," which contrasts with the "righteousness which is by the law" (*e.g.*, Rom 10:5-6; Phil 3.9). The use of this phrase in Hebrews is appropriate to the order of grace. Even so able a Reformed exegete as Philip E. Hughes imports the Pauline meaning into the text here in Hebrews. Hughes speaks of the righteousness of faith as the righteousness of imputation.[44] Rather, this expression is to be understood as equivalent to that in Heb 10:38 which reads: "the just shall inherit life by his faith." F. F. Bruce speaks of this latter text in Hebrews as a principle *testimonium* for the doctrine of justification by faith, similar to the use of Gen 15:6 in the Epistle to the Romans and the Epistle of James (2:23).[45] The writer to the Hebrews has in view the demonstrative function of works as evidential of justifying faith.[46]

It is apparent that the writer to the Hebrews uses the concept of faith as a synonym for obedience, and thus in a general sense, rather than in the technical sense of faith as the alone instrument of constitutive justification. Faith means covenant-keeping. Vos comments, "Though not in the specific Pauline sense of justifying faith, it is saving faith no less than the faith preached by Paul."[47] Herein lies the continuity between the teaching on justification by faith in the Old and New Testaments. Implicit in the writer to the Hebrews' conception of faith is the idea of patience and perseverence in the way of the covenant. Faith apart from such well-doing is a dead faith; but covenant faithfulness receives the favor and reward of God (Heb 12:14-15; 13:7-8). "Through this whole noble description of faith rings the note of personal attachment, covenant-loyalty to God. . . . It is the responsive act on the believer's part to the act of covenant-committal on the part of God."[48] Such faith is not a matter of human resource, but solely of the sovereign grace of God in Christ (Heb 4:14-16: 10:19-25; 13:20-21).

The message of James (2:14-26) is analogous to that of the writer to the Hebrews. Whereas the apostle Paul cites Gen 15:6 as a corroboration of the doctrine of justification by faith in its primary, constitutive sense, James cites the same OT text as a corroboration of the fact that justifying faith is a faith that works. Both aspects belong to one forensic, declarative justification. James, like the writer to Hebrews, defines saving faith in the general terms of trust and commitment (1:5-6). Faith involves patience in well-doing (5:7-11), persistence in doing the will of God (1:22-25). The reward for covenant keeping is of both temporal and eternal benefit (1:12 and 5:16-18).

James and the writer to the Hebrews consider the nature and character of saving faith from the perspective of the continuity of the Old and New Covenants. The common themes in these two administrations of the single Covenant of Grace are the justification of the godly and the appeal to the criteria of works at the day of the Lord. This perspective on justifying faith differs from the emphasis of the apostle Paul. Paul considers saving faith from the perspective of the discontinuity of the covenants. The righteousness of God has been revealed from faith to faith, apart from the law. Faith, in distinction from good works, is the alone instrument of justification.

There is no contradiction between the teachings of Paul and the teachings of James and the writer to the Hebrews. The modern, critical attempt to eliminate the law-gospel distinction, and along with that the distinction between works as ground of justification and works as demonstrative of justifying faith, undermines the gospel of grace.[49] The modern interpretation misuses biblical theology by confusing the two distinct perspectives on justification held by the authors of Scripture, and in the final analysis rejects the contribution to be gained from a biblical-theological approach to the teaching of Scripture. Contrary to the opinions of Fuller and Schoonboven, they are the ones who cannot "stand up under the scrutiny of biblical theology."[50] Historic, biblical Christianity continues to stand or fall with its adherence to or denial of the doctrine of justification by faith alone. The biblical doctrine of justification takes into account the imputation of Christ's righteousness as the sole meritorious ground of salvation and works as evidential of saving faith. Shall James or the writer to the Hebrews silence the teaching of Paul on justification and the imputation of Christ's righteousness as the ground of salvation? Shall Paul silence the teaching of James and the writer to the Hebrews on the demonstrative aspect of justifying faith? Or shall we listen to what each of these writers has to say as an author of the inerrant Word of God, inspired by the Spirit himself?

ENDNOTES

[1]Calvin R. Schoonhoven, "The 'Analogy of Faith' and the Intent of Hebrews," ed., W. W. Gasque and W. S. LaSor, *Scripture, Tradition, and Interpretation: Essays Presented to Everett F. Harrison by His Students and Colleagues in Honor of His Seventy-fifth Birthday* (Grand Rapids: Eerdmans, 1978) 92-3.
[2]Daniel P. Fuller, *Gospel and Law: Contrast or Continuum? The Hermeneutics of Dispensationalism and Covenant Theology* (Grand Rapids: Eerdmans, 1980) 204.
[3]See also Geoffrey W. Bromiley, *Historical Theology: An Introduction* (Grand Rapids: Eerdmans, 1978) 305-316; Thomas F. Torrance, *The School of Faith: The Catechisms of the Reformed Church*, trans. and ed. by Torrance (New York: Harper, 1959), esp. xlix ff.; James B. Torrance, "Covenant or Contract? A Study of the Theological Background of Worship in Seventeenth-Century Scotland," *SJT* 23 (1970), 51-76; and G.C. Berkouwer, *Sin*, trans. P.C. Holtrop (Grand Rapids: Eerdmans, 1971) 187-231.
[4]Mark W. Karlberg, "The Mosaic Covenant and the Concept of Works in Reformed Hermeneutics: A Historical-Critical Analysis with Particular Attention to Early Covenant Eschatology" (Th.D. dissertation, Westminster Theological Seminary, 1980); and Chapter One.
[5]Richard B. Gaffin, Jr., "Introduction," *Redemptive History and Biblical Interpretation: The Shorter Writings of Geerhardus Vos*, ed. R. B. Gaffin, Jr. (Phillipsburg, NJ: Presbyterian and Reformed, 1980) xiii. For earlier work in biblical theology, see Robert Rainy, *Delivery and Development of Christian Doctrine,* (Edinburgh: T. & T. Clark, 1874). Consult also my dissertation, "The Mosaic Covenant and the Concept of Works in Reformed Hermeneutics," for the relation between covenant theology and biblical theology.
[6]See Gaffin's "Introduction" xvii ff. Karl Barth and neoorthodoxy in general are highly critical of systematic theology. See esp. Barth's massive work, *Church Dogmatics,* ed. G. W. Bromiley and T. F. Torrance (Edinburgh: T. & T. Clark, 1932-67).
[7]Gaffin, "Introduction" xix; *cf.* Vos, "The Idea of Biblical Theology as a Science and as a Theological Discipline," *Redemptive History* 14ff.
[8]See, *e.g.*, Cornelius Van Til, *The New Modernism: An Appraisal of the Theology of Barth and Brunner* (Philadelphia: Presbyterian and Reformed, 1947) and his *Christianity and Barthianism* (Philadelphia: Presbyterian and Reformed, 1965).
[9]Meredith G. Kline suggests that this biblical expression refers more directly to the prophet's supernatural reception of revelation through his experience of the divine council. See his *Images of the Spirit* (Grand Rapids: Baker, 1980) 57ff.
[10]Meredith G. Kline, "Abram's Amen," *WTJ* 31 (1968) 1-11.
[11]Geerhardus Vos, "Hebrews, the Epistle of the Diatheke," *Redemptive History* 227-30. "And it is important to notice how the author represents this ascent of the patriarchs' faith to the heavenly world as in no way mediated by the typical fulfillment of the promise that was to intervene between them and its final NT realization. The ascent to the heavenly country did not use as a stepping-stone the thought of the earthly Canaan; it was made directly from the vantage ground of the promises of God" (pp. 228-9).
[12]Peter C. Craigie, *The Book of Deuteronomy* (The New International Commentary on the Old Testament; Grand Rapids: Eerdmans, 1976) 129, 133. Similarly, Roland K. Harrison writes: "As long as the chosen people kept the prescribed statutes and ordinances, they could expect to live. The kind of life which the law brought would be one of divine blessing and material prosperity, consonant with the covenantal promises, but contingent always upon implicit obedience to the Will of God" *(Leviticus: An Introduction and Com-*

mentary [Tyndale Old Testament Commentaries; Downers Grove: Inter-Varsity, 1980] 185).

[13]Meredith G. Kline, *Treaty of the Great King: The Covenant Structure of Deuteronomy, Studies and Commentary* (Grand Rapids: Eerdmans, 1963) 59.

[14]Craigie, *The Book of Deuteronomy* 325.

[15]Philip E. Hughes, *A Commentary on the Epistle to the Hebrews* (Grand Rapids: Eerdmans, 1977) 153.

[16]Leopold Sabourin, *The Psalms: Their Origins and Meaning* (New enlarged and updated edition; New York: Alba House, 1974) 264ff.

[17]*Ibid.* 320. In contrast to Sabourin's position, Hermann Gunkel contends: "The current explanation of the 'I' as standing for the community is nothing more than a stubborn remnant of the allegorical interpretation of Scripture which prevailed in an earlier day" (*The Psalms: A Form-Critical Introduction*, trans. Thomas M. Homer, [Facet Books, Biblical series 19; Philadelphia: Fortress, 1967] 17).

[18]Craigie, *The Book of Deuteronomy* 73

[19]For two different interpretations of Deuteronomy, contrast Gerhard Von Rad, *Deuteronomy: A Commentary,* trans. Dorothea Barton (Philadelphia: Westminster, 1966), with Kline, *Treaty of the Great King.*

[20]See Mark W. Karlberg, "Law in Pauline Eschatology: The Historical Qualification of Justification by Faith" (Th.M. thesis, Westminster Theological Seminary, 1977), which offers an entirely new interpretation of Romans 7, along with an extensive bibliography of relevant NT literature.

[21]For a recent, alternative position on Christ's termination of the law. compare Ragnar Bring, *Christus und das Gesetz: Die Bedeutung des Gesetzes des Alten Testaments nach Paulus und sein Glauben an Christus* (Leiden: Brill, 1967).

[22]Vos, "Hebrews, the Epistle of the Diatheke," *Redemptive History* 201.

[23]Vos, "The Theology of Paul," *Redemptive History* 359.

[24]William F. Arndt and F. Wilbur Gingrich, *A Greek-English Lexicon of the New Testament and Other Early Christina Literature* (Chicago: The University of Chicago Press, 1957).

[25]*Cf.*, Andrew J. Bandstra, *The Law and the Elements of the World: An Exegetical Study in Aspects of Paul's Teaching* (Kampen: J. H. Kok, 1964).

[26]On Paul's concept of *sarx* in the context of the two-age construction, see esp. James D. G. Dunn, "Jesus – Flesh and Spirit: An Exposition of Romans 1:3-4," *JTS* 24 (1973) 40-68; and Geerhardus Vos, "The Eschatological Aspect of the Pauline Conception of the Spirit," *Biblical and Theological Studies* (New York, 1912) 209-259.

[27]Vos, "The Pauline Conception of Reconciliation," *Redemptive History* 363f.

Professor Kline first suggested to me this line of interpretation.

[28]*Cf.*, Edward J. Young, *The Book of Isaiah* (two volumes; New International Commentary on the Old Testament; Grand Rapids: Eerdmans, 1969) 156ff.

[30]Vos too takes a strong stand on the importance of the biblical concept of "merit." See his essay, "The Alleged Legalism in Paul's Doctrine of Justification," *Redemptive History* 388ff. He comments: "Paradox though it may sound, yet we believe it to he strictly true, that the motive underlying the apostle's championship of grace is at bottom identical with the motive underlying his forensic bent" (p. 396).

[31]Anders Nygren, *Commentary on Romans,* trans. C. C. Rasmussen (Philadelphia: Muhlenberg, 1949) 207, 209.

[32]For a thorough and detailed study on this matter, see John Murray, *The Imputation of Adam's Sin* (Grand Rapids: Eerdmans, 1959). A radically different interpretation is of-

fered by K. Barth in his *Christ and Adam: Man and Humanity in Romans,* trans T. A. Smail (New York, 1956).

[33]Barth writes: "And so as Adam's children and heirs, in our past as weak, sinners, godless, and enemies, we are in this provisional way still men whose nature reflects the true human nature of Christ. And so, because our nature in Adam is a provisional copy of our true nature in Christ, its formal structure can and must even in its perversion be the same" (*Christ and Adam* 47). Rudolf Bultmann contends that Barth's interpretation cannot be derived at all from the text. See his "Adam and Christ According to Romans 5," *Current Issues in New Testament Interpretation,* eds. W. Klassen and G. F. Snyder (New York, 1962) 143-165. Equally unacceptable is Herman Ridderbos' suggestion of the "supra-individual situation of sin and death represented by Adam" (*Paul: An Outline of His Theology,* trans. J. R. de Witt [Grand Rapids: Eerdmans, 1975] 99). In this connection, see especially the remarks of Gaffin in his review article "Paul as Theologian," *WTJ* 30 (1968) 213.

[34]Regarding covenant theology's doctrine of the original Covenant of Works with Adam before the Fall, Fuller states: "There the conditional promises of the Bible echo 'the Covenant of Works' into which God supposedly entered with Adam and Eve when, according to Gen 2:17, he made the enjoyment of eternal life conditional upon their refraining from eating of the tree of the knowledge of good and evil" (*Gospel and Law* ixf.). After abandoning the doctrine of the Covenant of Works, Fuller "realized that if the law is, indeed, a law of faith, enjoining only the obedience of faith and the works that proceed therefrom (1 Thess 1:3; 2 Thess 1:11), then there could no longer be any antithesis in biblical theology between the law and the gospel. I then had to accept the very drastic conclusion that the antithesis between law and gospel established by Luther, Calvin, and the covenant theologians could no longer stand up under the scrutiny of biblical theology" (p. xi).

[35]See note 28 above.

[36]Vos, "The Pauline Conception of Reconciliation," *Redemptive History* 364.

[37]*Cf.* Craigie, *The Book of Deuteronomy* 44-5, where he comments on the antithesis between law and grace. For an alternative interpretation, see C. E. B. Cranfield, "St. Paul and the Law," *SJT* 17 (1964) 43-68.

[38]Fuller notes: "It is apparent that we regard [John] Murray as wrong in thinking of 'the righteousness of the law' (Rom 10:5) as standing in contrast with the 'righteousness of faith' (Rom I0:6ff.). In drawing such a contrast, Murray reveals the deep impression that covenant theology has made on him" (*Gospel and Law* 79, note 23). Fuller goes on to argue: "Everyone would agree that 'their own righteousness' (Rom 10:3) and 'a righteousness of my own' (Phil 3:9) represent the opposite of 'the righteousness of faith' in both Phil 3:9 and Rom 10:5-8. But whereas Paul uses the word 'law' as a synonym for 'own righteousness' in Phil 3:9, the use of 'law' has no such meaning in the Rom 9:30-10:10 passage" (p. 86). "We conclude, therefore, that Paul used not only the term 'works of the law' but also, on occasion, simply the term 'law' to describe how it played a vital role in bringing sin to full fruition. There is no rule-of-thumb method for knowing when *nomos* ('law') has this meaning in Paul. Instead we allow contextual considerations such as how Gal 3:10b could argue for v. 10a, and the parallelism in Phil 3:9 between 'own righteousness' and 'law,' to conclude that Paul meant *nomos* in the bad sense in Gal 3:10a" (p. 97). Fuller's exegesis rests upon his presupposition that there is no biblical law/grace contrast.

[39]See John Murray, *Principles of Conduct: Aspects of Biblical Ethics* (Grand Rapids: Eerdmans, 1957) 151-7. "Jesus is explicit to the effect that a righteousness of a certain character is indispensable if we are to be members of the kingdom of heaven" (p. 154).

"Jesus, however, does not inform us here of the way by which we come to possess that righteousness" (p. 157). Jesus deals with the matter of kingdom righteousness, not the righteousness of imputation.

[40]*Cf.* the studies of J. A. Ziesler, *The Meaning of Righteousness in Paul: A Linguistic and Theological Enquiry* (Cambridge: University Press, 1972), and Ernst Käsemann, "God's Righteousness in Paul," *The Bultmann School of Biblical Interpretation: New Directions?* (New York: Harper and Row, 1965).

[41]Schoonhoven, "The 'Analogy of Faith'" 99.

[42]*Ibid.* 108.

[43]*Ibid.* 107. *Cf.* Fuller's similar argument, *Gospel and Law.*

[44]Hughes, *Commentary on Hebrews* 464-5.

[45]F. F. Bruce, *The Epistle to the Hebrews: The English Text with Introduction, Exposition and Notes* (The New International Commentary on the New Testament; Grand Rapids: Eerdmans, 1964) 274-5.

[46]Scripture often speaks of the believer's "righteousness of the law" in the OT sense of the justification of the godly. It is not antithetical to the order of sovereign grace (*e.g.*, Lk 1:6 and 2:5). In the period of transition from Old to New Covenant administration, Scripture identifies certain devout (just, pious) men who walk in the way of godliness and truth (Acts 2:5 and 22:12). Similarly, Paul calls himself a Pharisee, not a Sadducee, in Acts 23:6, because "a Sadducee could not become a Christian without abandoning the distinctive theological position of his party; a Pharisee could become a Christian and remain a Pharisee – in the early decades of Christianity, at least" (Bruce, *Commentary on the Book of the Acts: The English Text with Introduction, Exposition and Notes* [The New International Commentary on the New Testament; Grand Rapids: Eerdmans, 1954] 453).

[47]Vos, "Hebrews, the Epistle of the Diatheke," *Redemptive History* 228.

[48]*Ibid.* 230. "Faith in its last analysis was to the patriarchs the apprehension, the possession, the enjoyment of God Himself" (229).

[49]Fuller distinguishes between "unconditional election" and "unmeritorious conditionality" as that which is involved in both receiving and persevering in salvation (*Gospel and Law* 46, footnote). "The conclusion, then, is that instead of two sets of promises in the Bible – conditional and unconditional – there is only one kind of promise throughout Scripture, and the realization of its promises is dependent upon compliance with conditions which are well characterized as 'the obedience of faith' (Rom 1:5; 16:26)" (p. 105). Schoonhoven contends likewise: "So then, contrary to some Reformation thinking, grace or the blessing of God seems to be conditioned on obedience. And here is the nub of the problem. The Reformation and later theologians were so intent on obliterating the 'works' idea of the Roman Church that they read the texts in such a way as to conform to what they falsely regarded as a radical grace theology, a grace with no conditions attached whatever. This is a patent application of the 'analogy-of-faith' principle" ("The 'Analogy of Faith'" 94). From the perspective of "unmeritorious conditionality," Schoonhoven speaks of the threats of God as "a real and indispensable aspect of the salvation process" (p. 98).

[50]See footnote 34 above.

CHAPTER SEVEN

ISRAEL'S HISTORY PERSONIFIED: ROMANS 7:7-13 IN RELATION TO PAUL'S TEACHING ON THE "OLD MAN"

If there is any consensus among interpreters of Paul, it is that Paul's teaching on the law is highly complex. In recent years a vast amount of literature has been produced in an effort to unravel the various strands of thought in Paul's writings concerning the nature and function of the law of God. How are we to understand the positive and negative statements about the law – statements that appear to be mutually exclusive and contradictory? There are still those who join with Albert Schweitzer in speaking of the "peculiarly inconsistent attitude of the Apostle to the law."[1] Paul develops his thought regarding law and redemptive promise in terms of the great eschatological crisis associated with the coming of Jesus Christ into the world. Though correct in seeing the importance of eschatology in Paul, Schweitzer himself failed to discern the pervasively redemptive-historical orientation of the apostle concerning the end-times.

The arrival of the kingdom of God in conjunction with the earthly ministry of Jesus is the (semi-)eschatological fulfillment of the OT messianic hope.[2] There is both continuity and discontinuity between the two covenantal transactions, the Old Covenant mediated through Moses and the New Covenant mediated through Christ. Contrary to much classical Protestant interpretation, the prominent theme of justification by faith in the Epistle to the Romans, and in Paul's writings as a whole, is expounded primarily in terms of the history of redemption (*historia salutis*), rather than in terms of the application of redemption to the individual believer (*ordo salutis*). With respect to the exegesis of Romans 7, it is essential to give adequate attention to the redemptive-historical structure of Paul's theology of the law. The doctrine of Christ's reconciliation as set forth in Romans 5 through 7, as elsewhere in Paul, is inextricably bound up with the doctrine of justification by faith. But unmistakably, the emphasis of Paul is upon the former.[3]

Even a cursory reading of the Pauline letters acquaints one with the wide scope of the author's vision. The apostle does not view his own experiences in an exclusively individualistic fashion. Rather, he sees himself in solidarity with humanity, fallen and redeemed. In the opening of his Letter to the Galatians Paul places himself and his readers in the context of the world situation, what he calls "the present evil age" (1:4), and maintains that only those who are in Christ have been delivered from it. The two-age construction, the present evil age and the age to come, undergirds Paul's theology of the covenants.[4]

The character of the old age and the new age derives from the representative acts of the First and Second Adams respectively (*cf.* 1 Cor 15:22,45-9). Though redemptive eschatology as a whole is messianic, the coming of Jesus Christ into the world for salvation marks the separation between two distinctive and consecutive stages, and the beginning of the final stage. Yet even in this final stage the old age continues to overlap with the new. William Wrede observed: "The framework of the whole Pauline teaching is formed by the Jewish idea of a contrast between two worlds (aeons), one of which is present and earthly, the other future and heavenly. Here we have the foundation of the Pauline way of regarding history."[5] By virtue of his/her solidaric union with Christ in the power of his resurrection the believer experiences the realities of the new age of the Spirit, though presently only as an earnest or foretaste of the final consummation. Justification, likewise, bears the same semi-eschatological stamp – the present, definitive act of God (once-for-all) in the imputation of Christ's righteousness through the sole instrumentality of faith, and the future vindication/approbation of those who are in Christ.[6] Whatever the precise meaning of the Pauline expression "in Christ," it is clear that it cannot be defined in a purely individualistic way. Our interpretation of law and eschatology in Paul attempts to do justice to both the corporate and individual aspects of union with Christ.[7]

After stating the theme of the Epistle to the Romans in 1:16-17 the apostle proceeds to describe the universality of sin, a description of man(kind) under the law. As a result of sinful human flesh both Jew and Gentile are under the power of sin (3:9). While the Jews have the law of God revealed in the oracles of Moses (3:2), the Gentiles have the requirements of the law written in their hearts (2:15). This natural law serves a twofold purpose: (1) to define the creature's duty to love and obey the Creator; and (2) to fix in the human consciousness an awareness of the original works-inheritance arrangement established at creation. According to the apostle Paul, the entire world is now shut up under the law, held captive to the power of sin and death. This is the old age. It is the world situation as determined in Adam (*cf.* Gal 4:3-5).

Paul's message, however, is preeminently one of blessing and life. The apostle is a minister of the New Covenant, a minister of righteousness, not condemnation (*cf.* 2 Cor 3:6ff.).[8] "But now apart from the law the righteousness of God has been revealed, being witnessed by the law and the prophets, even the righteousness of God through faith in Jesus Christ to all who believe, for there is no distinction" (Rom 3:21-22). This is the new age. God's justification of sinners has now been manifested in history through the propitiatory work of Christ so that God himself might be just and the justifier of those who believe in him (3:23-26). The law of the Old Covenant, though witnessing to the gospel of sovereign grace and consistent with the promise of God (10:6-8; Gal 3:17), nevertheless gives expression to that righteousness which is not of faith (10:5; Gal 3:10-13). The purpose of the law was to shut Israel up under sin (3:19-20; 4:15; and 5:20). Yet the law's ministration of death, ordained by God, did not frustrate God's ultimate redemptive design for Israel. M. D. Hooker observes:

> Paul certainly does not deny that God's covenant with his people is effective for salvation – quite the reverse, for much of his argument is aimed at demonstrating that God's covenantal promises remain sure. Rather he is concerned to show that it is not the covenant on Mt. Sinai

> which brings salvation. Possibly this is why he does not make a great deal of use of Exodus typology. For the conversion of Gentiles has, in Paul's view, demonstrated the temporary nature of the Mosaic Law. It is the promises to Abraham which are primary in the divine scheme.[9]

The actual accomplishment of redemption in Jesus Christ is the "mystery" now made known to all nations unto the obedience of faith (16:26). Whatever the exact import of Paul's conception of the "mystery," it is a decidedly historical category. The cross and resurrection of Jesus inaugurates the messianic kingdom of the new age in the semi-eschatological age of the Spirit. The exceeding greatness of the revelation of God's saving power in raising Jesus from the dead accounts in part for the contrast between the provisional nature of the Old Covenant and the everlasting character of the New.[10] There are cosmic dimensions to Christ's reconciliation; Paul regards the believer united with Christ as a new creation (2 Cor 5:17).[11]

While it is true that the Epistle to the Romans embodies the fullest exposition of the gospel to the Gentiles, it is also true – though too often overlooked – that Paul presents the greater part of his exposition with more immediate reference to Jewish believers, those who are the spiritual as well as the natural descendants of Abraham (beginning at 2:17; note in particular 3:1,9,29, and 4:1ff.).[12] The gospel has primary reference to the Jews and secondary reference to the Gentiles who have been grafted into the olive tree (*cf.* chap. 11). Together, spiritual Jews and Gentiles comprise the "New Israel," the elect of God.

The question before the apostle in Romans 6 and 7 is: Shall we, *i.e.*, elect Israel in particular and the elect of God more generally, continue to sin, so that grace might abound? Paul answers with an emphatic No, because the elect have died to sin.[13] God's people must live in light of the reality of being united with Christ in his death and resurrection. In chaps. 6 and 7, and again in 9-11, the apostle pleads with national Israel to find her true spiritual identity as the people of God by way of individual baptism into Christ. The argument of Romans 7 flows directly out of the preceding chapter. And in chaps. 6 and 7 Paul weaves together both corporate and individual dimensions of redemption in Christ in a brilliant literary style.

Perhaps no passage in all of the apostle Paul's writings has been subjected to closer scrutiny than Rom 7:7-25. J. D. G. Dunn remarks:

> Romans 7 is one of those key passages in Paul's writings which offers us an insight into a whole dimension of Paul's thought and faith. Even more important, it is one of the few really pivotal passages in Paul's theology; by which I mean that our understanding of it will in large measure determine our understanding of Paul's theology as a whole, particularly his anthropology and soteriology.[14]

And the key to the interpretation of Romans 7 is found in Paul's use of two expressions in the sixth chapter, the "Old Man" (6:6) and "under law" (6:14). In the Old Man/New Man contrast the former is Paul's metaphor for Israel under law. Stated more precisely, the Old Man is fallen humanity represented by Israel under law, whereas the New Man is redeemed humanity. The New Man, metaphorically speaking, is the church invisible, the New Israel.[15] Against the cosmic background of the two ages, the old age and the new, the Old Man/New Man metaphors bring to view the mass of humanity under the dominion of two opposing world-orders respectively. The forensic dimension inherent in God's covenantal dealings with humanity in all ages is of paramount importance to biblical eschatology. As a result of Adam's disobedience (his failure to pass the probationary test) and on the grounds of humanity's legal relation to Adam as federal head, the human race is now under the state of fallenness, curse, and death. The old age stems from Adam; the new originates in Jesus Christ. In the course of the historical unfolding of the Covenant of Redemption (traditionally called the Covenant of Grace) the Israelite kingdom-theocracy reinstitutes a period of probation defined and regulated by the Covenant of Law given through Moses. In sum, the Old Man refers to a corporate reality, and, therefore, does not refer to the old, unregenerate nature in contrast to the new, regenerate nature of the believer.[16] And to be "under law" is to be under the dominion of sin, subject to the probationary status associated with a covenant of works-arrangement. Consequent to the broken Covenant of Works established at creation, a modified covenant of works-arrangement was reintroduced on the typological level of kingdom-inheritance at the time of Moses. It was this specific legal administration that the apostle Paul described as an administration characterized by bondage and servitude (2 Cor 3:6ff.; Gal 4:1-2).[17]

Once the cosmic-corporate point of view is established Paul proceeds to discuss the personal aspects of sin and death. Elect Israel has "died to sin" (6:2), and was "buried with [Christ] through baptism into death" (6:4). "Our Old Man," argues the apostle, "was crucified with him so that the body of sin might be rendered powerless, that we should no longer be slaves to sin" (6:6). Again, the Old Man represents more immediately Israel under law, captive to sin and death. This is the apostle Paul's way of describing metaphorically the time of Israel's exile (captivity in Babylon).[18] If we view the Old Man as an image for Israel under the administration of bondage, the death of the Old Man in Rom 6:6 symbolizes a change in God's covenantal dealings with his redeemed people. Having been baptized into Christ's death, elect Israel has been made alive in Christ. The expressions "body of sin" (6:6), "body of death" (7:24) and "body of flesh" (Col 2:11) in their separate contexts are all synonymous with the Old Man metaphor. Israel according to the flesh, the Old Man, embodies the organism of sin which is at work in humanity at large, producing fruits unto death. Similarly, the idea of "flesh," as already intimated, brings into view the organism of sin as it exercises dominion over all humanity. These three related expressions – (sinful) flesh, the Old Man, and the body of sin (or the equivalent terms) – all denote the embodiment of sin in the world of humanity. The state of being under the power or dominion of sin characterizes humanity under the old age. As a result of the Fall all flesh as an organism beyond the individual man is enmity against God. Geerhardus Vos comments:

> While the *sarx* chiefly appears as a power or principle in the subjective experience of man, yet this is by no means the only aspect under which

> Paul regards it. It is an organism, an order of things beyond the individual man, even beyond human nature. . . having [its] affiliations and ramifications in the external, physical, natural (as opposed to supernatural) constitution of things. . . . From its association with the entire present aeon, the *sarx* could derive its pervasive, comprehensive significance, in virtue of which a man can be *en sarxi* as he can be *en pneumati*; like the aeon it lends a uniform complexion to all existing things. It would also derive from this its partial coincidence with the somatic, because the whole first aeon moves on the external, provisional, physical plane. Finally it would derive from this its synonymy with evil, for according to Paul, the present aeon has become an evil aeon in its whole extent.[19]

So from this perspective, it may be granted, Israel's experience corporately is Everyman's experience individually (*cf.* Rom 3:19-21; 5:12-21).[20]

Before commenting upon the intervening verses (6:11-7:6), we will consider Rom 7:7-13, the central passage this article seeks to illuminate. In this section the apostle rehearses the history of Israel in a uniquely figurative manner. The pronoun "I" Paul employs in this unit is a personification of the Old Man in Rom 6:6. The "I" is therefore not autobiographical, but rather metaphorical. What Paul says here is illustrative of Israel as a corporate body under the covenantal administration of death and condemnation. Prior to the coming of the law, Israel was alive unto God (7:9). This is the period of the promise, the period from Abraham to Moses (*cf.* 4:13-15; 5:13,20; and Gal 3:15-25). The phrase "sin revived" (7:9) echoes the thought expressed more fully in an earlier passage in Romans (5:12-14). The purpose of the law was to reveal sin, and to slay Israel (typically) in order that in the fullness of time Israel might be resurrected in newness of life (Ezekiel 37). Once the law came, sin revived and increased, so "that through the commandment sin might become exceedingly sinful" (7:13). Formerly, under the provisions of grace (the time from Abraham to Moses) sin is not reckoned, for "where there is no law there is no sin" (4:15 and 5:13). Though the commandment was ordained unto life, Israel found it to be unto death. More ultimately, the realization of the covenant curse upon God's people was in order to demonstrate the superabounding grace of God, for through the judgment of exile the Lord preserved a remnant unto himself (Zech 13:7-9).

Sin found occasion in the commandment and beguiled Israel, and slew Israel (7:11). Paul uses the same word *exapatao* in 2 Cor 11:3 with reference to the serpent who beguiled Eve. Israel, weak in the flesh, corrupted and defiled by the organism of sin (the "body of death"), was further excited to sin by the law. Although Paul makes indirect allusion to the fall of Adam in Rom 7:7-13, the situation is not identical. Israel, unlike Adam, was under the power and dominion of sin. In vs. 12 Paul resumes the thought of vs. 7. The law is not sin, but to the contrary is holy, righteous, and good. The probationary function of the law serves God's redemptive purpose. Vs. 13 restates that purpose of the law in Israel's history.

Further support for this interpretation of the "I" in Rom 7:7-13 appears in the introductory verses (7:1-6). The illustration Paul gives is a simple one: a married woman is bound to her husband as long as he lives. But when he dies, she is free to remarry. The main point of the analogy is that as long as a man lives (the man has been indirectly identified as an Israelite in vs. 1) he is bound to the law. But when the man dies to the law he is free to belong to another, namely, Christ, in whom he has been baptized into death and raised in newness of life (*cf.* 6:3-11). Such was the experience of Israel once. When Israel was in the flesh she brought forth fruit unto death. But now by virtue of her union with Christ in his death and resurrection Israel is discharged from the law, the Old Covenant written in letters on stone, which formerly held her captive to sin, and free to serve in the newness of the Spirit (7:5-6). The reference is to spiritual Israel. This, then, is the meaning, we suggest, of the "I" in Rom 7:7-13.[21]

In Rom 6:1-10 and 7:1-13 the apostle informs us of the termination of the Mosaic Covenant as a particular historical administration of the Covenant of Redemption, an administration that was of temporary duration. The Mosaic Covenant had served a pedagogical probationary function in the history of redemption. The verb *katargeo*, which appears in Rom 7:6, is used in 2 Cor 3:7 to indicate the "coming to an end" of the old administration. Similarly, in Rom 10:4 Paul speaks of Christ as the end of the law in the sense that he marks the termination of the old covenantal order (*cf.* especially Heb 8:13).[22]

As a means of clarifying the remaining sections of Romans 6 and 7 we return briefly to the metaphor of the New Man. In Ephesians 2 Paul reminds the Gentiles of the fact that at one time they "were separate from Christ, excluded from citizenship in Israel and foreigners to the covenants of the promise, without hope and without God in the world" (vs. 12). But from the perspective of the corporate dimension of Christ's reconciliation the Gentiles now "have been brought near through the blood of Christ" (vs. 13). The purpose of Christ "was to create in himself one New Man out of the two" (vs. 15). This is the corporate aspect of cosmic reconciliation (vss. 14-18; *cf.* Col 1:15-23; 2:9-15). God's act of reconciliation includes the believer's death to sin and the breaking down of the barrier between Jew and Gentile. The expression "putting off of the body of flesh" in Col 2:11 has reference to the definitive aspect of sanctification. There are two inseparable aspects to the grace of sanctification, definitive and progressive, as there are two inseparable aspects to the grace of justification, constitutive and demonstrative.[23] The definitive aspect of sanctification involves the divine judgment rendered upon sin (*cf.* Rom 6:7) as well as deliverance from the dominion of sin for those united to Christ in his death and resurrection. It brings into view both objective and subjective elements of transforming grace. The progressive aspect of sanctification has reference to renewal in the image of Christ, who is the New Man. The New Man metaphor can also be seen to represent the corporate body of Christ, the church invisible. Paul exhorts all believers, Jew and Gentile alike, to put off the Old Man and to put on the New Man created in Christ Jesus (Eph 4:22-24; Col 3:9-11). By virtue of our heavenly session in the Spirit we are to realize both corporately and individually our life with God in Christ (Eph 1:22-23; 2:5,6). Sanctification is made effectual through the regenerating and renewing work of the Holy Spirit (Tit 3:5-7). Consequently, the New Man is the Spirit-Temple (Eph 2:21-22).[24]

We have discussed Paul's idea of the body of sin, death and flesh as a metaphor for Israel under law. The term "parts" of the body (6:13) has both corporate and individual implications. After noting Israel's union with Christ in his death and resurrection (the corporate aspect) in Rom 6:1-10, the apostle explains what this means to individual members of the body in vss. 11-13. "In the same way, count yourselves dead to sin but alive to God in Christ Jesus" (6:11). The reason for this exhortation is that a change has taken place in the divine economy of redemption. The spiritual heirs of the Abrahamic promise are no longer subject to the pedagogical system of legal righteousness (6:14). Vss. 15-23 reiterate the point Paul has been driving home to his fellow Israelites. When Israel was subject to the law, she produced fruits unto death. Now under the gracious provisions of the new and better covenant spiritual Israel is no longer in need of a tutor; the types and shadows have given way to the reality of redemption accomplished. The gospel has been clearly manifested in the fullness of times. The power of sin and the law has been broken, resulting in a veritable resurrection from the dead. "For the wages of sin is death, but the gift of God is life eternal in Christ Jesus our Lord" (6:23).

The same interweaving of corporate and individual elements found in Romans 6 repeats in the subsequent chapter. Paul changes his subject in Romans 7 from Israel personified in vss. 7-13 to the personal experiences of the apostle himself as representative of every believer in vss. 14-25. The transition is indicated in a twofold manner: (1) the abrupt change from first person singular in vss. 7-13 to first person plural in vs. 14; and (2) the change from the aorist tense in vss. 7-13 to the present tense in vss. 14-25. In this concluding section of chap. 7 Paul describes what it means to him personally to put off the Old Man and to put on the New. As one who lives in the semi-eschatological age of the Spirit, the overlapping of the old age and the new, Paul engages in an ongoing warfare between good and evil (two antithetical powers, not natures) within his own members ("parts" of the body). Victor Furnish remarks: "Man does not, precisely stated, stand 'between' the ages, but at the point where they interpenetrate."[25] The believer's entire existence is characteristically eschatological. "For Paul," writes J. D. G. Dunn, "the believer is caught between fulfillment and consummation; he lives in the overlap of the ages, where the new age of resurrection life has already begun, but the old age of existence in the flesh has not yet ended, where the final work of God has begun in him but is not yet completed (Phil 1:6)."[26]

As a new creation, Paul experiences the cosmic warfare within his own members between two antithetical powers, on the one hand the power of sin and death (the Old Man) from which he has been delivered – sin no longer has dominion over him – and on the other the power of righteousness and life (the New Man). The battle within Paul is not one between two natures; rather, it is the new nature indwelt by the Spirit fighting against the sin that yet remains. It is wrong to view the believer as having two natures simultaneously, one old and one new. The believer has but one new nature – a regenerated nature which engages in spiritual warfare against the powers of this world (Eph 6:12). The believer's victory over sin and death is obtained in the power and strength of Christ and his Spirit (Eph 6:13-18). Until the attainment of glorification (*cf.* Rom 8:18-23) two powers or principles wage war within the believer. The sum and substance of

Paul's plight is given eloquent expression in vss. 22-25a: "For I delight in the law of God according to the inner man; but I see another law in my members, waging war against the law of my mind and holding me captive to the law of sin which is in my members. What a wretched man I am! Who will deliver me from this body of death? But thanks be to God through Jesus Christ our Lord!"[27] Recognizing his responsibility for the evil he has done, Paul acknowledges his passionate displeasure and hatred for sin and his true desire to do that which is good. In the struggle to put off the Old Man, "this body of death" (the organism of sin), Christ Jesus has given the apostle Paul the victory over sin and death (8:1-17; *cf.* 1 Cor 15:56-7). And what is true for the apostle is true for every believer, Jew and Gentile alike.

In conclusion, the "I" of Rom 7:7-13 is employed metaphorically by the apostle Paul to describe Israel corporately under law, the old covenantal administration characterized by sin and death. It is not an autobiographical statement of Paul's religious experience, pre- or post-conversion. By personifying Israel's history in this manner the apostle fully identifies with those kindred people to whom belong "the adoption as sons, the glory, the covenants, the (administration of) law, the temple worship, and the promises." And of these people Paul exclaims: "Theirs are the patriarchs, and from them is the Christ according to the flesh, who is God over all, forever praised, Amen" (9:4-5; *cf.* 1:24). With great sorrow and anguish of heart Paul calls Israel to faith and repentance, the only way to the hope of glory.

ENDNOTES

[1]Alhert Schweitzer, *Paul and His Interpreters: A Critical History,* trans. W. Montgomery (London: Adam and Charles Black, 1912) 160.
[2]For an excellent introduction to the NT teaching on inaugurated eschatology, see David F. Wells, *The Person of Christ: A Biblical and Historical Analysis of the Incarnation* (Westchester: Crossway, 1984) 21-66; and Anthony A. Hoekema, *The Bible and the Future* (Grand Rapids: Eerdmans, 1979) 3-75. Consult also Hoekema's "Appendix: Recent Trends in Eschatology" 288-316.
[3]See Geerhardus Vos, "The Pauline Conception of Reconciliation," in *Redemptive History and Biblical Interpretation: The Shorter Writings of Geerhardus Vos,* ed. R. B. Gaffin, Jr. (Phillipsburg: Presbyterian and Reformed, 1980) 361-65.
[4]Geerhardus Vos observes: "What gives dogmatic coloring to his teaching is largely derived from its antithetical structure, as exhibited in the comprehensive antithesis of the First Adam and the Last Adam, sin and righteousness, the flesh and the Spirit, law and faith, and these are precisely the historic reflection of the one great transcendental antithesis between this world and the world-to-come" (*The Pauline Eschatology* [Grand Rapids: Baker, 1930] 60-61).

Our primary interest in the subject of the law of God is with what dogmaticians have traditionally called the "second use of the law." Whether or not one finds the classification of the threefold use of the law to he wholly satisfactory in systematic formulation, it does serve here to indicate that particular aspect of the biblical teaching of law to which we shall direct our attention. This study develops my earlier work, "Law in Pauline Eschatology: The Historical Qualification of Justification by Faith" (Th.M. Thesis, Westminster Theological Seminary, 1977).
[5]William Wrede, *Paul,* trans. E. Lummis (Lexington, 1962) 139-140.
[6]See my "Justification in Redemptive History," *WTJ* 43 (1981) 213-246.
[7]On the doctrine of union with Christ, *cf.* John Murray, *Redemption: Accomplished and Applied* (Grand Rapids: Eerdmans, 1955) 161-173.
[8]William L. Lane, "Covenant: The Key to Paul's Conflict with Corinth," *TynBull* 33 (1982) 3-29.
[9]Morna D. Hooker, "Paul and 'Covenantal Nomism,'" in *Paul and Paulinism: Essays in honour of C. K. Barrett,* ed. M. D. Hooker and S. G. Wilson (London: SPCK, 1982) 51-52.
[10]Geerhardus Vos, "Hebrews, the Epistle of the Diatheke," in *Redemptive History and Biblical Interpretation,* esp. 192-204.
[11]Herman Ridderbos, *Paul: An Outline of His Theology,* trans. J. R. de Witt (Grand Rapids: Eerdmans, 1975) 45, 183.
[12]The Pauline terminology, the "Israel of God," which appears only in Gal 6:16, has been variously interpreted. Some suggest that it refers only to those in the body of Christ who are of Israelite stock, that is to say, Jewish believers: *e.g.* Ernest DeWitt Burton, *A Critical and Exegetical Commentary on the Epistle to the Galatians* (Edinhurgh: T. & T. Clark, 1980) 258. On the different interpretations of this verse, see F. F. Bruce, *The Epistle to the Galations* (New International Greek Testament Commentary; Grand Rapids: Eerdmans, 1982) 273-5.
[13]Here in Romans 6 the apostle describes the proper purpose of God's redemptive covenant in terms of union with Christ. He probes more deeply into this subject in the eleventh chapter when he addresses the "mystery" of God's salvation in the last days (the purpose of God in election).

[14]J. D. G. Dunn, "Rom. 7:14-25 in the Theology of Paul," *TZ* 31(1975) 257.

[15]The expression "all Israel" in Rom 11:26 (as well as several other references to Israel in this chapter) refers to spiritual, ethnic Israel (the "Israel of God" - see n.12 above); other references are to national Israel.

[16]The translators of the RSV, the NASB and the NIV consistently mistranslate Paul's use of the term *anthrôpos*, thus obscuring the concept of the Old Man in Pauline theology.

[17]The principle of works-inheritance within the Mosaic covenant administration regulates Israel's life in the (typological) kingdom-theocracy, and does not pertain to the antitypical kingdom-realm (salvation). For a fuller treatment of the operation of the works-inheritance principle within the theocratic life of Israel, see Chapter Twelve.

[18]A proper interpretation of the system of typology associated with the old economy of redemption, the system of types and shadows, will give due consideration to the antithetical principles of law and grace. The Gospel of John and the Epistle to the Hebrews provide a particularly fruitful avenue of study into this issue. See Geerhardus Vos's comments in "Hebrews, the Epistle of the Diatheke," *Redemptive History and Biblical Interpretation* 201-204, and "'True' and 'Truth' in the Johannine Writings," *ibid.* 343-51.

[19]Geerhardus Vos, "The Eschatological Aspect of the Pauline Conception of the Spirit," in *Redemptive History and Biblical Interpretation* 123 n.55.

[20]The interpretation of Ernst Käsemann and J. D. G. Dunn, among others, misses the more fundamental redemptive-historical perspective of the apostle in Rom 6 and 7; see Ernst Käsemann, *Commentary on Romans,* trans. and ed. G. W. Bromiley (Grand Rapids: Eerdmans, 1980; and J. D. G. Dunn, "Salvation Proclaimed: Dead and Alive," *EspTim* 93 (1982) 259-64. Both identify the Old Man as Universal Man (Adam).

[21]See J. G. Strelan, "A Note on the Old Testament Background of Romans 7:7," *LTJ* 15 (1981) 23-5. "The reference to *epithymein* as the primary sinful action of Israel, comprehending in itself all other sins, suggests that in Rom 7:7-11, where *epithymein* is a key word, Paul has Israel's fall in mind as well as Adam's fall. Paul, it seems, identified Israel's experience with that Adam, and in turn he identified himself with both Adam and Israel" (24).

A. Nygren (*Commentary on Romans,* trans. C. C. Rasmussen [Philadelphia: Muhlenherg, 1949] 268) points out the striking parallelism in chapters six and seven:

Chapter 6	Chapter 7
v. 1, *he hamartia* (sin)	v. 1, *ho nomos* (the law)
v. 2, *apethanomen te hamartia* ("We died to sin")	v. 4, *ethanatothete to nomo* ("You have died to the law")
v. 4, *en kainotêti zoes peripatesomen* ("that we might walk in newness of life")	v. 6, *en kaivoteti pneumatos douleuein* ("that we serve in new life of the Spirit")
v. 7, *ho apothanon dedikaiotai apo tes hamartias* ("He who has died is free from sin	v. 6, *katergethemen apo tou nomou, apothanontes en hô kateichometh* ("we are discharged from the law, dead to that which held us captive")
v. 18, *eleutherothentes apo tes hamartias* ("having been set free from sin")	v. 3, *eleuthera apo tou nomou* ("free from the law")

[22]Compare the writer to the Hebrews' related discussion of the levitical priesthood, the order of Melchizedek versus the order of Aaron in Hebrews 7.

[23]See my "Justification in Redemptive History;" *cf.* John Murray, "Definitive Sanctification," *CTJ* 2 (1967) 5-21.
[24]Meredith G. Kline, *Images of the Spirit* (Grand Rapids: Baker, 1980) 24-6, 47-56.
[25]Victor Furnish, *Theology and Ethics in Paul* (New York: Abingdon, 1968) 134.
[26]Dunn, "Rom. 7:14-25 in the Theology of Paul" 264.
[27]The "inner man" (vs. 22) is not synonymous with the New Man, but rather signifies the deepest intention and will of the believer who has been regenerated and renewed by the Spirit of God. And it is the "law of my mind" that reflects the true, inner man in the course of his struggle with sin.

CHAPTER EIGHT

THE SIGNIFICANCE OF ISRAEL IN BIBLICAL TYPOLOGY

Recent critical studies in biblical typology have generated renewed debate among scholars of various and diverse theological traditions.[1] Leading issues pertaining to hermeneutical methodology include the relation between history and revelation on the one hand and the nature of the continuity/discontinuity between the OT and the NT on the other. The present essay focuses on the second of these two issues. The chief point of difference among evangelicals is the question of the relationship between Israel (the Old Covenant community) and the church (the New Covenant people of God).[2] Specifically, does the supplanting of the Old Covenant by the New (*cf.* the Epistle to the Hebrews) involve the dissolution of the theocratic form of the kingdom of God under Moses?

1. Israel and the Church in Covenant Perspective

Historically, dispensationalism and covenant theology have presented two alternative positions concerning the relationship between Israel and the church. Though both theological traditions have undergone significant changes in recent years – in some instances radical revision – the subject of Israel's place in redemptive history continues to be prominent in these discussions.[3] Generally speaking, both schools of interpretation recognize the importance of typology in Scripture. It is in the interest of furthering dialogue among dispensational and covenant theologians that the topic of Israel and the church is pursued here from the standpoint of biblical typology.

Of paramount importance is the matter of law and gospel (works and grace) as descriptive of the two historical administrations of the Covenant of Redemption (traditionally called the Covenant of Grace). When treating Paul's teaching on the law, a growing number of both dispensationalists and covenant theologians have adopted the so-called misinterpretation view of the Mosaic law. According to this view the Mosaic Covenant consists exclusively of a sovereign administration of grace and promise (unconditional). But the Judaizers had misinterpreted the law of Moses to teach justification (*i.e.* salvation) by works of the law. Hence the apostle Paul's negative statements concerning the law of Moses (law versus grace) are to be understood in terms of the peculiarly Judaizing point of view. Positively stated, the misinterpretation view holds that the law of Moses preaches the pure grace of Christ as the only source of life now and hereafter. The difference between the two covenants, consequently, is merely one of degree and circumstance. Under the New Covenant the gospel is proclaimed with greater fullness and clarity (along with its universal scope and application of the saving benefits of Christ's work to the elect). Contrary to this popular explanation of Paul's teaching, the apostle recognized that there was indeed a works-principle operating on the typological level of the Old Covenant and that the fatal error of the Judaizers was that they misconstrued the works-principle as though it were the basis of inheriting the antitypical reward (Rom 9:31-32).[4]

On the other side of the debate, the teaching of traditional covenant theology emphasizes the unity and continuity between the Testaments (meaning that salvation is by grace through faith in Christ in all ages subsequent to the Fall) in a way that does not obliterate the obvious discontinuity between them. The Scriptures clearly teach that there is both continuity and discontinuity between the Old and New Covenants with respect to the opposing principles of inheritance, law and grace.[5]

The principle of inheritance on the ground of works is an indispensable element in a genuinely biblical formulation of the theology of the covenants. In the case of the Old Covenant, as observed above, the works-principle operated on the typological level while the grace-principle concurrently functioned on the eternal/spiritual level. The earthly, temporal blessings were granted to God's people Israel under the conditions of the Mosaic administration. As long as Israel was faithful to the covenant with her Lord she would enjoy life and prosperity in the promised land. By reason of disobedience those temporal blessings would be forfeited by the whole house of Israel, including the remnant of grace, as actually occurred in the Babylonian exile. Hans K. LaRondelle correctly observes: "Israel would only remain God's treasured possession and holy nation if Israel would obey God and keep His covenant (Exodus 20-24). This is a clearly conditional aspect regarding Israel's future status in God's covenant."[6]

On either dispensational or covenantal interpretations one must distinguish between national, theocratic Israel (God's "elect" people) and the remnant of grace chosen according to God's sovereign purpose in election (those whom the apostle Paul calls true Jews). According to the premillennial scheme, on the one hand, a future time is posited within preconsummation history when national Israel will be restored by the Spirit of God and regathered in the land of Palestine under the theocratic rule of Christ (details vary among advocates of this position). Premillennialism suggests a twofold significance of the theocratic form of the kingdom of God under Moses: (1) prophetic (as regards the future, literal millennial reign of Christ on earth), and (2) typological (as regards the messianic, semi-eschatological realization of the promise in the age of the church). Amillennialism, on the other hand, maintains that the type (national, theocratic Israel) is comprehensively fulfilled by the antitypical reality (the kingdom that began to come in the ministry of Jesus). The decisive issue dividing these two schools of prophecy is whether national Israel in OT revelation genuinely typifies (in the true sense of the word) the messianic fulfillment, or whether national Israel possesses an independent and irrevocable status as the chosen race throughout history, despite its episodic history of divine blessing and cursing in the time prior to the establishment of the millennial kingdom. On the premillennial view, national Israel is more than a type. Does this not imply, in the final analysis, that Israel is really not a type at all? How can national Israel serve both as type (with regard to the relationship between Israel and the church and the continuity of the Testaments) and as a distinct ethnic group alongside the spiritual kingdom of Christ, the church? If one grants that national Israel in OT revelation was truly a type of the eternal kingdom of Christ, then it seems that, according to the canons of biblical typology, national Israel can no longer retain any independent status whatever.[7] For premillennialists literal fulfillment of the promise concerning the land of Palestine is essential in order to demonstrate God's supreme power and dominion over the forces of unrighteousness and wickedness in history, a prelude to the catastrophic transformation of the heavens and earth at the close of human history. Is not the Consummation, on this view, somewhat anticlimactic? Assuming that one does not accept the idea of two distinct forms of the kingdom – Israel and the church – what purpose does the restoration of national Israel serve if in fact Jesus did inaugurate the kingdom of God on earth? The NT writings clarify the spiritual meaning of Israel's election and calling, while the external shell (the shadowy and typical appearance of the kingdom) falls away. To be sure, there is still to be at the Consummation an antitypical fulfillment of the land promise, a cosmic antitype to typological Canaan-land, such as does not obtain in the present church-age stage of the New Covenant. But genuine typological interpretation rules out any additional literal fulfillment of the land-promise in a future restoration of national Israel subsequent to or alongside the messianic fulfillment, as found in certain varieties of premillennial and postmillennial schemes.[8]

2. Typology as a Legitimate Method of Interpretation

Various definitions of typology have been offered in recent studies because of differing understandings of the relation between typological interpretation and exegesis. Richard T. France correctly states:

> Typology may, indeed must, go beyond mere exegesis. But it may never introduce into the OT text a principle which was not already present and intelligible to its OT readers. Sound exegesis, and a respect for the sense of the OT text thus discovered, will prevent typology from degenerating into allegory.[9]

And David L. Baker observes: "Typology is not an exegesis or interpretation of a text but the study of relationships between events, persons and institutions recorded in biblical texts."[10] These remarks highlight the fact that typology deals with the relation between distinct yet inseparable epochs of redemptive revelation. As LaRondelle points out: "The typological approach of the NT is motivated by the idea of fulfillment in salvation history. Typology is a theology of the progression of God's acts of salvation through Jesus Christ."[11] According to E. Earle Ellis:

> For the NT writers a type has not merely the property of "typicalness" or similarity; they view Israel's history as *Heilsgeschichte*, and the significance of an OT type lies in its particular *locus* in the divine plan of redemption. When Paul speaks of the Exodus events happening *typikôs* and written "for our admonition," there can be no doubt that, in the apostle's mind, divine intent is of the essence both in their occurrence and in their inscripturation. The rationale of NT typological exegesis is not only "the continuity of God's purpose throughout the history of his covenant," but also his lordship in moulding and using history to reveal and illumine his purpose. God writes his parables in the sands of time.[12]

What is the connection between type and prophecy? The answer depends upon one's understanding of Scripture as the Word of God. In his comparison of the work of Fairbairn and von Rad on typology, John Stek favors Fairbairn's adherence to the historicity of the biblical narrative in contrast to von Rad's relativizing of biblical history. He remarks that

> a type is a historical reality which served a significant historical purpose within its own historical horizon (not merely a symbolic one), but it was also fashioned by Providence in such a way as to contribute to the larger purpose of God, namely, to reveal "in successive stages and operations the very truths and principles which were to find in the realities of the Gospel their more complete manifestation."[13]

Along similar lines Stanley N. Gundry questions neoorthodox advocates of biblical typology in particular: "Proponents of the new typology use such terms as 'analogy,' 'correspondence,' 'prefiguration,' 'pre-representation,' 'foreshadowing,' and 'corresponding reality.' But what meaning can such terms have in a system of interpretation that repudiates predictive prophecy and verbal inspiration?"[14]

The pattern for sound interpretation of the OT Scriptures was enunciated for us in the teaching of Jesus. He said that the law and the prophets witnessed concerning himself as the Messiah. Only through the eyes of faith could one grasp the true meaning of the Scriptures (Lk 24:27, 45-47). Jesus' teaching underscored the continuity and discontinuity between the old order that was in process of passing away and the new order that he was inaugurating. The NT writers, particularly Paul and the author of the Epistle to the Hebrews, further elucidated the typological significance of OT persons, events and institutions.[15] Christological interpretation of the OT, vital to Christian proclamation, was not suddenly a new way to read the OT (*cf.* 1 Pet 1:10-12). Rather, such interpretation was implicit in the sacred writings themselves. To be sure, there was greater clarity and depth of understanding with the coming of Christ. We may therefore speak of new perspectives on OT revelation. In broadest terms there is movement from promise to fulfillment, from shadow to reality. The historical, covenantal transition from old to new administrations of the kingdom of God brought about a number of changes in the life and worship of the community of faith.

The Messiah revealed himself as the New Israel. In the imagery of the vine Jesus identified his person and mission with God's purposes of old (Jn 15:1; *cf.* Ps 80:8 ff.; Is 5:1-7). And as the New Man, Jesus called all nations and peoples into his spiritual household. By his death on the cross he made satisfaction for sin, removing the curse of the law that was standing against his people (Eph 2:14-18). The apostle Paul describes the transition from Old to New Covenant in terms of the death of the Old Man – typified by Israel under the law of Moses (Rom 6:1-7:13).[16] The law as Israel's schoolmaster has terminated with the coming of Christ (10:4; Gal 3:23-4:7). In contrast to the shadowy form of OT revelation, Jesus reveals the fullness of God's self-revelation. The law came by Moses; grace and truth came in Jesus Christ (Jn 1:17; *cf.* Heb 8:13; 10:1). Geerhardus Vos remarks:

> "Truth" here [in Jn 1:17] means what it means in Hebrews; it expresses the heavenly character of the Christian realities of revelation and redemption in which the higher world directly communicates itself, and the opposite of "the true" is the typical, wherein the connection with the heavenly world is present only in a mediated, shadowy form.[17]

Israel as the Old Covenant people served a temporary purpose in God's plan of salvation. She occupied a peculiar role in redemptive history as preparation for the gospel age. The Christian church is "the true people of God, with the privileges, the responsibilities, and the destiny of Israel. . . . [It is they who] assume and carry to completion the destiny which in the OT was to be Israel's."[18] Whereas the focal point of Israelite worship was the temple, New Covenant worship is no longer localized. Consistent with the universalism of the gospel the community of believers is free to worship in the Spirit, unhindered by place and occasion (Jn 4:21-24). The temple, intended as only a temporary symbol of the dwelling of God's presence in the midst of his people, had become for unbelieving Jews something ultimate (*cf.* Jn 2:19-22; 4:1-42). What was in fact essential to spiritual communion with God was a vital hope-trust in the coming Messiah.

3. The Election and Mission of Israel

Elements of law and grace defined the peculiar nature of Israel's standing in the covenant with Moses. In the historical section of the Deuteronomic treaty Moses reminds the Israelites that their election did not rest upon their own righteousness but solely upon God's grace. In the progressively unfolding history of revelation each renewal of the covenant between God and Israel was a reaffirmation and partial fulfillment of God's promise of grace to Abraham (Gen 12:2-3; 17:3-7). One feature of the promise to Abraham involved the territorial land grant, a symbol of the heavenly inheritance bequeathed unconditionally to the elect seed of Abraham (Gen 12:1; 15:7,18-21; 17:8). The promise of a land found temporary fulfillment in the ancient Israelite theocracy. But from the standpoint of the typological works-arrangement under Moses, physical blessing in the promised land was contingent upon Israel's faithful observance of God's law. As long as the covenant with Moses was in effect Israel was obligated to keep the entire law. (Division of the Mosaic law into distinct categories – such as civil, ceremonial and moral – was unknown to the OT Israelite. Within the theocracy the law of Moses was a unified entity.[19]) The retention of the land was thus conditioned upon Israel's obedience. The principle of inheritance in the symbolic-typical sphere of covenant life was one of works, not faith.

If we are to do justice to the unity and integrity of the law of Moses we must consider the law in its proper historical setting and function as that peculiar legal instrument, instituted and ordained by God and regulative of life within the ancient theocracy. The commandments and ordinances of Moses were binding upon the people of God. A change in the priesthood and its attending regulations necessitated a change in the law (Heb 7:5,11-28). Specifically the coming of Christ in the fullness of time marked the end of the old order and the beginning of the new. The typical, earthly inheritance finds its fulfillment in Jesus Christ. The establishment of the NT church was in direct fulfillment of the promises given to Abraham, who together with all his faithful seed was looking for the heavenly inheritance (Heb 11:10,16). Calvin writes concerning the true Israelites:

> It is certain that they looked higher than that earthly land; indeed the land of Canaan was only thought of as of value for the reason that it was the type and the symbol of our spiritual inheritance. Therefore when they had obtained possession of it, they ought not to have rested, as if they had arrived at the answer to all their prayers, but rather to have thought on the spiritual meaning it contained. Those to whom David addressed the psalm enjoyed possession of the land, but they were encouraged to look for a better rest.[20]

Unlike the true and lasting inheritance, the typical kingdom-inheritance was conditioned upon Israel's obedience to the law of Moses. There is a direct correlation between the probationary status of Israel under the Mosaic administration of the Covenant of Redemption and the probationary status of Adam under the original Adamic administration of the Covenant of Creation (traditionally called the Covenant of Works).[21] In both instances the principle of kingdom-retention (or of tenure) was one of works (in contrast to faith soteriologically defined). Israel's cultic holiness, as prescribed by the legal covenant, distinguished this peculiar people from the other nations of the earth. The principle of law enunciated in Lev 18:5 operated in a manner consistent with God's saving purposes during the period from Moses to Christ and in a manner appropriate to the overall symbolic-typical picture drawn by God in the life and history of Israel.[22]

Life in the ancient theocracy is marked above all else by holiness (Ex 19:5-6; Lev 20:7). Blessing and prosperity in the land of Canaan are contingent upon obedience to the law of Moses. In keeping with the Mosaic typology a certain measure of righteousness and holiness is requisite for the well-being of God's people. "[Israel's] very existence and character as a society were to be a witness to God, a model or paradigm of his holiness expressed in the social life of a redeemed community."[23]

In contrast to this typological kingdom-administration the antitypical kingdom-inheritance was a gift of sovereign, electing grace (unconditional).[24] According to the author of the Epistle to the Hebrews, the accomplishment of redemption through Jesus' life and death was so decisive an event in history that it made necessary a new covenant. Jesus was mediator of a better covenant, one characterized by the forgiveness of sins. Commenting on Heb 7:18-19, F. F. Bruce observes:

> It was inevitable that the earlier law should be abrogated sooner or later; for all the impressive solemnity of the sacrificial ritual and the sacerdotal ministry, no real peace of conscience was procured thereby, no immediate access to God. That is not to say that faithful men and women in OT times did not enjoy peace of conscience and a sense of nearness to God; the Psalter provides evidence enough that they did. . . . The whole apparatus of worship associated with that ritual and priesthood was calculated rather to keep men at a distance from God than to bring them near. But the "hope set before us" in the gospel is better because it accomplishes this very thing which was impossible under the old ceremonial; it enables Christians to "draw nigh unto God." How it enables them to do so is explained in greater detail later on [Heb 10:19-22]; but the fact that the gospel, unlike the law, has opened up a way of free access to God is our author's ground for claiming that the gospel has achieved that perfection which the law could never bring about.[25]

Similarly in his teaching on the covenants of God in redemptive history the apostle Paul characterizes the New Covenant as a ministration of life and blessing in contrast to the Old as a ministration of death and condemnation. Repeatedly Paul asserts that the law works wrath. Although the sacrificial system of the Mosaic law made provision for atonement of sin on the typological level (to an extent appropriate to the overall symbolic-typical picture) there was no permanent and lasting satisfaction for sin. Consequently the sins of the Old Covenant people were overlooked during this period of the Mosaic economy (Heb 9:15 [8:1-10:18); Rom 3:21-26).[26] Life within the ancient theocracy was characterized by bondage and servitude. As long as the pedagogical, probationary function of the Mosaic law was in effect the people of God did not yet experience the full blessings of freedom and sonship associated with life under the New Covenant.

Another crucial distinction to be drawn is that between national election of Israel and individual election unto salvation. The latter is sure and indefectible, while the former is losable and of limited duration.[27] Whereas there is a conditional element in the covenant between God and the nation Israel, individual election is unconditional (*cf.* 1 Pet 2:4-10). Vos writes that

> the same world of heavenly spiritual realities, which has now come to light in the person and work of Christ, already existed during the course of the Old Covenant, and in a provisional typical way through revelation reflected itself in and through redemption projected itself into the religious experience of the ancient people of God, so that they in their own

> partial manner and measure had access to and communion with and enjoyment of the higher world, which has now been let down and thrown open to our full knowledge and possession.[28]

The personal assurance of salvation and the perseverance of the faithful in the way of the covenant are vital concomitants of saving grace in every age of redemptive history.

The sacrificial cultus represents the focal point of Israelite life and worship. Here the Lord God of Israel provides a remedy for the sins of his people until the time should come when true atonement for sin would be made in the offering up of God's own Son. Jesus Christ, the better sacrifice, established a new and secure way of access to God. Whereas the priestly functions were performed by the Levites according to the Mosaic legal prescriptions, these same ceremonial and theocratic practices pass away under the New Covenant (Heb 10:15-22). Symbol and type give way to reality. And once the reality has come there can be no return to the former system of types and shadows. To do so would militate against the sufficiency and finality of Christ's reconciliation and atonement. "Anyone who still holds to, or wants to restore, the shadows of the Law," Calvin remarks, "not only obscures the glory of Christ, but also deprives us of a great blessing in that he puts a barrier of space between us and God, to approach whom freedom is given us by the Gospel."[29]

Despite the shadowy and transient nature of the Old Covenant administration of the kingdom of God, his redemptive purposes were being accomplished. At every stage of the progressively unfolding Covenant of Redemption the message of God's sovereign grace in humanity's eternal salvation was revealed by prophetic word and symbolic institution (*i.e.* the typological system under Moses). The eternal, spiritual blessings were received by OT believers through faith. There was no mixture of faith and works. The principle of inheritance was faith alone (Rom 4:1-25; Gal 3:6-9). As prophet and mediator Moses interceded with God on behalf of Israel. And in the faithful exercise of his office Moses served as a preacher of gospel as well as law (Rom 10:5-8). Likewise the same Spirit who called and empowered Moses inspired the prophets to herald the New Covenant (2 Pet 1:21; *cf.* Deut 18:15-20). As God's treasured possession Israel was privileged to receive the oracles of God mediated through Moses (Rom 3:2; *cf.* Gal 3:19-20; Heb 3:1-6). And in keeping with her special calling in redemptive history Israel served as a light to the nations.[30]

The sanctions of the divine covenant were twofold: blessing for obedience, and curse for disobedience (Deuteronomy 28). The latter prophets served as agents in God's covenant lawsuit against his own rebellious people. Included in their message was the prospect of a future and glorious day when the knowledge of the Lord would cover the earth and the seas. Having endured the curse of the covenant, Israel would once again enjoy the blessing and favor of God, ultimately through the vicarious suffering of the Lord's Anointed (*cf.* Is 40:1-5). In that day the nations of the earth would come to the New Jerusalem, the heavenly city of God. The company of the faithful, the true heirs of the promise to Abraham, would find its identity in union and communion with Christ, the seed of Israel's race. In that day the typological phenomenon of the ancient Israelite theocracy would be dissolved into the antitypical reality of the church as the New Israel.[81] John the Baptist, the forerunner of the Messiah, set before the Israel of that generation the final ultimatum. The gravity of Israel's offense lay in her failure to believe Moses and the one greater than Moses (see *e.g.* Jn 6:32-33,55-58).

4. Conclusion

To appreciate the significance of Israel in the OT Scriptures one must understand the system of biblical typology associated with the Mosaic economy of redemption. The meaning of Israel's election is determined by the context of the symbolic-typological purposes of the Old Covenant in the unfolding historical drama of redemption. According to the sanctions of the covenant made between God and Israel, typological blessing was contingent upon Israel's compliance with the law of Moses. With respect to God's purpose of eternal salvation Israel's failure did not annul the promise of God. God's purposes in election stand firm in spite of the unfaithfulness of his people. The weakness of sinful human flesh was overcome by the Son of God (Rom 8:1-4). What Israel could not do, God has done in Jesus Christ. The dissolution of the temporal, earthly theocracy coincided with the New Covenant's reign of God in the hearts of his people through the Spirit. In the eschatological age of the Spirit the kingdom of God is a spiritual reality unencumbered by the shadowy, earthly forms (types) characteristic of the ancient theocracy. In the period between the advents of Christ the presence of the kingdom is in anticipation of the realization of the land-promise in the Consummation.

The destruction of the temple in 70 A.D. signals the termination of the typical-external form of the kingdom of God. The inauguration of the New Covenant with the coming of Christ results inevitably in the passing away of the old order of things. The eternal priesthood of Christ necessitates a change in the law. True spiritual worship is not bound by outward ceremonies and regulations. (This is not to deny the sacramental nature of the New Covenant signs and seals – baptism and the Lord's Supper – or to minimize, more broadly, corporate worship as a true means of grace.) As a kingdom of priests and kings the people of the New Covenant comprise a living temple of the Holy Spirit (Heb 12:18-24; Eph 2:19-22; 1 Pet 2:5; Rev 21:1-3,22).[32]

In biblical typology each type (person, event, institution) both resembles and differs from the antitype. As in the interpretation of Jesus' parables, it is necessary to discern the proper limits of types in Scripture. Otherwise typological interpretation can result in false allegorization. On the other hand, failure to recognize that the promises to Abraham were given typical prefigurement in the earthly theocracy (in conjunction with the eternal redemptive realities enjoyed by the spiritual seed of Abraham throughout the period of the Mosaic economy) represents a major oversight in biblical interpretation. National Israel as such does not retain its covenant identity in the new, eschatological age of the Spirit.[33] Israel's future is shaped by the great event at Pentecost: the outpouring of the Spirit upon the church and the present ingathering of the nations. As elect Israelites are provoked to jealousy, the remnant of grace is perpetuated in Israel until the full number of the elect of God (both Jews and Gentiles) is attained

(Rom 9-11; Rev 22:14,17-19). In these last days the gospel goes out to all peoples, calling sinners to faith and repentance. The writer to the Hebrews exhorts both Jew and Gentile alike: “Since the promise of entering his rest still stands, let us be careful that none of you be found to have fallen short of it” (Heb 4:1).

ENDNOTES

[1]See especially the articles by Walter Eichrodt, Gerhard von Rad and H. W. Wolff in *Essays on Old Testament Hermeneutics,* ed. C. Westermaun (Richmond: John Knox, 1968); *cf.* also G. W. H. Lampe and K. J. Woollcombe, *Essays on Typology* (SBT; Naperville: Allenson, 1957); Lampe, "Typological Exegesis," *Theology,* 50 (1953) 201-208.
[2]*Cf.* most recently David L. Turner, "The Continuity of Scripture and Eschatology: Key Hermeneutical Issues," *GTJ* 6 (1985) 275-287.
[3]See Chapter Twelve. In modifying and clarifying earlier dispensational teachings present-day dispensationalism approximates the classic premillennial interpretation.
[4]I have treated the exegetical and theological inadequacies of the misinterpretation view in Chapter Six; see also Chapter One.
[5]In the Chapters referred to in the previous note I have attempted to go beyond the ambiguities of earlier Reformed statements. The reader should consult these studies for fuller treatment of this subject than can be provided here.
[6]Hans K. LaRondelle, *The Israel of God in Prophecy: Principles of Prophetic Interpretation* (Berrien Springs: Andrews University, 1983) 83.
[7]On the other side of the argument Turner writes: "Genuine typology and analogy between OT and NT should not he viewed as destructive to the literal fulfillment of the OT promises to Israel, but rather an indication of a greater continuity between Israel and the church than dispensationalists have often been willing to admit" ("Continuity" 282). The both/and position of Turner cannot be maintained by the analogy-of-Scripture principle in a consistent biblical-theological exegesis of the text of Scripture. Consult further Geerhardus Vos, *The Kingdom of God and the Church* (Nutley: Presbyterian and Reformed, 1972).
[8]In an attempt to break from traditional patterns of interpretation among pre-, post- and amillennialists, Willem VanGemeren explores new avenues of approach to the agelong question of Israel's place in redemptive history. See his two-part series, "Israel as the Hermeneutical Crux in the Interpretation of Prophecy," in *WTJ* 45 (1983) 132-144; *WTJ* 46 (1984) 254-297. In addition to my critique of the first of these two articles in "Discontinuities" 16 ff., objection must be raised to VanGemeren's reading of the history of Reformed eschatology in his second installment. What consensus does he have in mind when he states that "there is no clearly-defined position on Israel in Calvin's writings" (p. 254)? Did Calvin need the impetus of Jewish nationalism to arrive at a position on the Jews? Certainly Calvin has not given the last word on this subject among Reformed interpreters. There is still room for greater clarity that comes with the ongoing theological reflection of the church. But Calvin has reached a mature understanding of the relation between Israel and the church. The cause for VanGemeren's reassessment of eschatological options among Reformed theologians is his reservation concerning typological interpretation of Scripture as commonly expounded (pp. 282-284). It is just at this point, however, that he is no longer faithful to the views of Calvin (contrary to his own claims). The balance of his second article, by far the lengthiest section, is taken up with the development of VanGemeren's view of eschatology. Arising out of his objection to the typological interpretation of Scripture as formulated by amillennialists, VanGemeren entertains an erroneous conception of the relation between exegesis and biblical theology. He favors a literalistic "historico-grammatical interpretation of the text" (p. 272). He supports his views by misleading citations from Calvin's commentaries. In place of the promise/fulfillment pattern of interpreting the relation between the Testaments VanGemeren proposes the idea of promise/confirmation (pp. 280 ff.). Despite his distaste

for systematization, one wonders just how different crucial aspects of VanGemeren's views are from certain varieties of present-day dispensationalism. There appears to be mutual sympathy for a both/and approach to the subject of Israel and the church (see n. 6 above). A similar, though favorable, evaluation of VanGemeren's position is made by Turner, "Continuity" 282 n. 24. It would be helpful if VanGemeren and other evangelicals interacted more extensively and critically with some of the recent literature of contemporary theologians such as Hendrikus Berkhof and A. A. Van Ruler. The following is a representative sampling of current thinking: "Many theologians are used to defining the church in a more or less thoughtless way as 'the New Israel.' They believe that in the NT the church is the more spiritualized heir of a nation called Israel, which was in a former stage the shape of God's people in the world. Nowhere in the NT, however, is Israel considered as the first stage of the 'salvation rocket,' thrown off at the right moment after having served its turn. . . . We believe that in one way or another we have to consider them as the other half of God's people" (Hendrikus Berkhof, "Israel as a Theological Problem in the Christian Church," *JES* 6 [1969] 335). Van Ruler urges us to recognize "that there is a special place for the people of Israel in God's plan for the world. If we relate the OT exclusively to Christ and find the people of Israel only in the body of Christ, we cannot integrate the Jews, the synagogue, and the State of Israel into our systematic theology" (*The Christian Church and the Old Testament* [Grand Rapids: Eerdmans, 1971] 35). He concludes with the question: "Does everything, not only Israel, but history and creation, exist for the sake of the church? Or is the church only one among many forms of the kingdom of God?" (98).

[9]Richard T. France, *Jesus and the Old Testament* (London: Tyndale, 1971) 41.

[10]David L. Baker, "Typology and the Christian Use of the Old Testament," *SJT* 29 (1976) 41 (*italics mine*). "The biblical text has only one meaning, its literal meaning, and this is to be found by means of grammatical-historical study."

[11]LaRondelle, *Israel* 44. A good example of typological interpretation of Scripture is found in LaRondelle's essay, "The Biblical Concept of Armageddon," *JETS* 28 (1985) 21-31. "The nature of John's use of typology in the Apocalypse can be characterized as the consummation of the NT christological and ecclesiological applications" (p. 27).

[12]E. Earle Ellis, *Paul's Use of the Old Testament* (Grand Rapids: Baker, 1957) 127-128.

[13]John Stek, "Biblical Typology Yesterday and Today," *CTJ* 5 (1970) 139. Mistakenly, Stek detects a kind of dispensationalism in Fairbairn's work, in which "a dispensation of merely earthly symbols [is] followed by a dispensation of spiritual realities" (p. 159). See especially his critique of Fairbairn on pp. 140-141.

[14]Stanley N. Gundry, "Typology as a Means of Interpretation: Past and Present," *JETS* 12 (1969) 240.

[15]Leondard Goppelt, *Typos* (Grand Rapids: Eerdmans, 1982); C. H. Dodd, *According to the Scriptures* (New York: Scribner's, 1958). Herman Ridderbos comments: "The nature of that which has taken place in Christ is rightly known only from prophecy, just as, on the other hand, it becomes clear in the light of the fulfilling action of God how much the OT is the book of Christ (2 Cor. 3:14; 1 Cor. 10:4; Gal. 3:16). For this reason one of the leading motifs of Paul's preaching is that his gospel is according to the Scriptures (Rom 1:17; 3:28; *cf.* Rom 4; Gal 1:6ff.; 4:21ff.; 1 Cor 10:1-10; Rom 15:4; 1 Cor 9:10; 2 Tim 3:16, *et al.*)" (*Paul: An Outline of His Theology* [Grand Rapids: Eerdmans, 1975] 51).

[16]See Chapter Seven.

[17]Geerhardus Vos, *Redemptive History and Biblical Interpretation: The Shorter Writings of Geerhardus Vos*, ed. R. B. Gaffin, Jr (Phillipsburg: Presbyterian and Reformed, 1980) 201.

[18]France, *Jesus* 61,65. "The implication is that the Jewish nation has no longer a place as the special people of God; that place has been taken by the Christian community, and in them God's purposes for Israel are to be fulfilled" (p. 67).
[19]Concerning the law as a temporary provision within the administration of God's kingdom F. F. Bruce remarks: "If we like, we may say that Paul has the moral law mainly in mind [in Gal 3:24-25], whereas the author of Hebrews is concerned more with the ceremonial law – although the distinction between the moral and ceremonial law is drawn by Christian theologians, not by those who accepted the whole law as the will of God, nor yet by the NT writers" (*The Epistle to the Hebrews* [NICNT; Grand Rapids: Eerdmans, 1964] 145). "This does not mean that the distinction is not a valid one," states Bruce, "but it does not come to the fore in either OT or NT" (*ibid.* n. 48). See also the remarks of D. A. Carson, "Jesus and the Sabbath in the Four Gospels," in *From Sabbath to Lord's Day*, ed. D. A. Carson (Grand Rapids: Zondervan, 1982) 68, 91 n. 74.
[20]John Calvin, *The Epistle of Paul the Apostle to the Hebrews and the First and Second Epistles of St. Peter* (Grand Rapids: Eerdmans, 1963) 48.
[21]See further Chapter Four.
[22]"The two Covenants [the Abrahamic and the Mosaic] also provide the structural framework upon which the Exodus typology is built. The Abrahamic Covenant stands in continuity with the 'New Covenant' (*kaine diatheke*); the *palaia diatheke* of Sinai stands in contrast. The events of the Exodus, the 'redemption' under the 'Old Covenant,' provide a pattern of 'types, foreshadowing the redemption in Christ'" (Ellis, *Paul's Use* 130-131). "Some elements in Pauline typology are obscure, and it is sometimes difficult to determine whether a 'type' or merely an illustration is in mind. Some OT references which are probably no more than analogies or application of principles may conform to a typological frame of reference. NT typology did not involve merely a catalogue of 'types'; it penetrated into the spirit of NT exegesis in all its forms. In the Pauline writings two basic typological patterns appear – Adamic or creation typology and covenant typology. Each is related to a particular aspect of God's redemptive purpose in Christ, and, over all, they unite to form one interrelated whole" (p. 134). *Cf.* Grant E. Osborne, "Type, Typology," in *Evangelical Dictionary of Theology*, ed. W. A. Elwell (Grand Rapids: Baker, 1984) 1117-1119.
[23]Christopher J. H. Wright, *An Eye for an Eye* (Downers Grove: InterVarsity, 1988) 48. Wright offers here a very helpful introduction to the question of OT ethics and its application to issues of personal and social morality in contemporary society. *Cf.* also Chapter Two.
[24]The original bestowal of the typological kingdom (as distinguished from its retention) was an act of grace, even though not an election to permanent kingdom possession.
[25]Bruce, *Hebrews* 148-149.
[26]Early Reformed federalists sometimes distinguished between the forgiveness of sins of God's people under the New Covenant (*aphesis*) and the passing over of sins under the Old Covenant (*paresis*).
[27]*Cf.* recent criticisms of traditional Reformed teaching on the doctrine of election in Harry Boer, *The Doctrine of Reprobation in the Christian Reformed Church* (Grand Rapids: Eerdmans, 1983); Neal Punt, *Unconditional Good News: Toward an Understanding of Biblical Universalism* (Grand Rapids: Eerdmans, 1980). For a defense of the traditional formulations see Fred Klooster, "Harry Boer's Battle Against Reprobation: A Review Article," *CTJ* 19 (1984) 50-68.
[28]Vos, *Redemptive History* 199.

[29]Calvin, *Hebrews* 100. "The shadows flea away at the sight of the substance. Therefore our first concern must always be to teach that Christ is the end of the Law" (p. 49).
[30]From the modern ecumenical point of view T. F. Torrance writes: "If we are to understand and interpret divine revelation in the specific spatio-temporal forms which it assumed in and through Israel, we cannot detach the OT Scriptures from the land any more than from the people of Israel. The people of the book and the people of the land belong inseparably together, for they have been forged together by the way that God himself has taken in the actualisation and the dynamic course of his covenant partnership with Israel. What happens when the inner constitutive connections between people, land and revelation are severed, can be seen from what happened to Judaism when the Jews themselves suffered radical detachment from the spatio-temporal milieu of God's self-revelation. Judaism tended to become an abstract ethical religion, largely bereft of its all-important priestly and redemptive tradition and characterized by a serious loss of relevance in space and time" (*The Mediation of Christ* [Grand Rapids: Eerdmans, 1983] 25-26). "Thus in all our relations with the Jew, we must learn to appreciate that he is what he is for our sake, and that it is through what he has done, even in the rejection of Christ, that reconciliation has come upon us Gentiles also. But this means that we may look upon the Jew only in the light of Jesus, the Jew in whom the Son of God became man, and who in gathering up in himself the whole movement of God's reconciling love in and through Israel, gave himself in atoning sacrifice for us and all men. Our indebtedness to the Jew and our faith in Jesus Christ are inextricably woven together in the fulfilled mediation of reconciliation" (pp. 44-45). "God has been making it clear to us in our day, as perhaps never before since the first century, that Israel retains in the purpose of God's grace an essential role in the mediation of reconciliation, and that the Christian church will not be able to fulfill its own mission in proclaiming that God was in Christ reconciling the world to himself, except in so far as it is incorporated with Israel in the one mission of God's love for all his creatures. That is what the fullness of the mediation of reconciliation in Jesus Christ means" (pp. 55-56). For a critique of the similar views of Paul van Buren, see Chapter Thirteen.
[31]"In the application of *testimonia* from the OT, it is a fundamental postulate that the church is the true, and ultimate, people of God, the heir of the divinely-guided history of Israel, which emerged out of the crisis in which God visited his people in judgment and redemption" (Dodd, *According* 111). The "mystery" revealed in the NT age, contrary to the teaching of dispensationalism, is not the church. The mystery is God-come-in-the-flesh, crucified and risen. It is the actual historical accomplishment of redemption through Christ's atoning death. From the standpoint of God's everlasting decree, Christ was slain before the foundation of the world. Now, in the fullness of time, God's salvation has effected a new age, such that if anyone be in Christ he/she is a new creation (2 Cor 5:17). *Cf.* Ridderbos, *Paul* 44-49.
[32]Upon receiving the revelation of Jesus Christ on the island of Patmos the apostle John views himself to be already in the kingdom of God (Rev 1:6, 9). The kingdom is a present spiritual reality, not futuristic (as some dispensationalists maintain). As far as Christ's spiritual kingdom is concerned, the barrier between Jew and Greek has been broken down once for all. There are no ethnic distinctions in the present age, nor will there be in the age to come.
[33]Comparison of VanGemeren's review of LaRondelle's *The Israel of God in Prophecy* (*WTJ* 47 [1985] 110-118) and that of Anthony A. Hoekema (*CTJ* 20 [1985] 110-112) is illuminating. Unfortunately, Reformed theology in recent years has not come any closer to reaching a consensus on even basic issues in the doctrine of eschatology. Biblical theology, consistently set forth, is synonymous with covenant theology, as evidenced both by the

historical development of the discipline and by the writings of such exponents of covenant theology as Geerhardus Vos, Meredith G. Kline and Hoekema. In addition to works cited earlier see Vos, *Biblical Theology* (Grand Rapids: Eerdmans, 1948); Kline, *Images of the Spirit* (Grand Rapids: Baker, 1980); "Kingdom Prologue" (2 volumes; privately published, 1981, 1988); and Hoekema, *The Bible and the Future* (Grand Rapids: Eerdmans, 1979). Among the various schools of prophetic interpretation within the Reformed tradition only amillennialism is fully compatible with covenant theology – specifically, covenant typology.

CHAPTER NINE

THE SEARCH FOR AN EVANGELICAL CONSENSUS ON PAUL AND THE LAW

From the perspective of evangelical Protestantism historically defined, one would have thought that in our day the doctrine of justification by faith alone would remain one of the central tenets of the faith, a doctrinal element foundational to the one gospel of Jesus Christ faithfully proclaimed in every age and every culture. Presumably a Protestant of the reputedly evangelical variety would have regarded this doctrine as a theological nonnegotiable. Regrettably, such is not the case in contemporary Protestantism. The doctrine that once distinguished Protestantism from Roman Catholicism has begun to fade into the background. The sharp line of demarcation between Scriptural fidelity and apostasy – respecting that which historic Protestantism considered to be the doctrine upon which the church stood or fell – has virtually been obliterated. The document "Evangelicals and Catholics Together" has signaled an ominous future for American Christianity. Of this, however, we can be certain: Biblical Christianity – present and future – will not be party to what, in any fair and balanced analysis, amounts to a betrayal of the gospel of salvation by grace through faith alone. Evangelical Protestants continue to pray for Rome's repudiation of those teachings that are contrary to the teachings of Scripture. They also hope that Protestants who have strayed from Reformation teaching will yet reclaim these vital truths.[1]

My concern in this paper is not, in the first place, with this unsettling development among Protestants and Catholics but with the doctrinal error found today within the Reformed camp in particular. This is to show that the threat of theological deviancy is not isolated to any one peculiar corner on the ecclesiastical map. The problem is all about us. Perhaps it is merely indicative of the age in which we live, an age characterized by individualism and by that unrelenting drive toward relativism, the gradual undermining of truth and authority. The great creeds and confessions of Protestant orthodoxy no longer carry the weight and respect they once did. More often than not they are viewed as relics of the past, as historic curiosities. Unchecked, the contemporary disregard for historic Christian dogma will only lead to the further erosion of evangelical witness in our generation.

Although the contemporary theological landscape is rocky, the prospects for evangelical consensus on Paul and the law remain encouraging (at least with respect to the essentials of the Christian faith). This study is the culmination of two earlier unpublished papers of mine.[2] Some of the material in them appears in what follows. Curiously, Craig Blomberg comments (prior to the publication of Frank Thielman's study):

> The work on Paul and the law which encourages me the most, however, is T. R. Schreiner's quite recent monograph [*The Law and Its Fulfillment*]. Here I think we come closest to preserving the valid insights of both Luther and Calvin, preserving the unity of Torah and the salvation-historical shift of the ages which permeates Paul's thought, while nevertheless incorporating the equally valid insights of the new perspective on Paul.[8]

The works of Thomas Schreiner and Thielman are strikingly similar, although the latter, in my judgment, is a slight advance upon the former.

Paul's understanding of God's purpose in placing ancient, theocratic Israel under the law of Moses has a direct bearing upon the doctrine of justification by faith. (One has only to read Paul's letters to the Romans and the Galatians to confirm this basic but often overlooked ingredient.) What precisely is the nature of the Mosaic law, and what is the relationship between the Old and New Covenants? These theological questions bring into view a wide range of hermeneutical issues, more than I can adequately address in this paper. My own theological persuasion is that of Reformed, amillennial covenant theology. Typology is but one somewhat obscure feature of that system of doctrine set forth in the Westminster standards. This confessional formulation, written at the close of the Reformation era, I enthusiastically adopt – with some minor revision – as the teaching of Scripture.

The key to the current doctrinal dispute concerning the nature of the Mosaic law and the relationship between the covenants is the biblical teaching concerning God's covenant with Adam at creation, what Reformed theologians commonly call the Covenant of Works. The opposition between the law and the gospel, whether in the writings of Paul or Protestant orthodoxy, pertains to the two antithetical principles of inheritance, one of works and one of faith. The Judaizers (and later the Roman Church) turned biblical religion into a religion of works-salvation. The ideas of works-righteousness and works-salvation are entirely distinct from each other. Reformed orthodoxy teaches that the principle of works – "this do and you shall live" (Lev 18:5) – is contrary to the principle of faith. Reformed interpreters have differed, however, in their understanding of the nature and operation of this works-principle within the Mosaic administration of the single Covenant of Grace spanning the entire period of redemptive history from the Fall to the Consummation. Whatever the differences between the OT and NT, there is nevertheless an underlying unity in God's saving purposes for Israel and the church. God has not abandoned his promises to the patriarchs Abraham, Isaac and Jacob. The ingathering of the Gentile nations in the latter days will, by electing grace, provoke many Jews to saving faith. In such manner all (elect) Israel will be saved. The true Israel of God includes both believing Jews and Gentiles. Election is not based in any way upon national privilege or human merit but solely upon God's sovereign good pleasure and foreordination. Parenthetically, Reformed biblical Christianity offers no credence to the two-covenants theory favored by modern-day ecumenists. According to the Scriptures, OT religion is one in substance with that of the NT. There is no other name under heaven whereby one must be saved from the wrath and condemnation that is coming.[4]

The apostle Paul identifies the Mosaic law as "letter" in contrast to the New Covenant, which is "Spirit" (2 Cor 3:6; Rom 7:6; *cf.* Jer 31:31-34; Ezk 36:24-27; 37:14). The former is an administration of death and condemnation, not life and righteousness. Does this Pauline comparison imply that the Holy Spirit as the agent of regeneration is active only in the new, eschatological age? Or does it merely bring into view differing degrees of enablement so that under the New Covenant the Spirit of Christ manifests a fuller outpouring of redemptive grace?[5] Is Paul's negative reading of the Mosaic dispensation to be explained along the lines suggested by Patrick Fairbairn and John Murray – namely, in terms of Jewish misinterpretation of the law of God? Or is the period from Moses to Christ to be properly viewed as a parenthesis in redemptive history, a period of discontinuity, a period in which the temporal blessings were administered to theocratic Israel on grounds of legal obedience? These are important questions confronting us in our study of Paul and the law.

1. Moses and Christ Revisited (Law versus Gospel)

Even a casual reader of the Bible will be struck by the differing emphases found in the OT on the one hand and the NT on the other. Although the message of God's saving grace is apparent throughout the OT, nevertheless during the Mosaic epoch of redemptive revelation the accent falls undeniably upon judgment and curse for covenant transgression. The drama of redemption portrayed in ancient Israelite history has been enacted in order to demonstrate humankind's need for God's mercy and forgiveness. Israel's plight is everyone's plight. This theme of the universality of sin is developed at great length in Paul's letter to the Romans.

So striking is the contrast between the two covenants – the covenant made at Sinai and the New Covenant in Christ's blood – that Paul, as we have already observed, describes the former as a ministration of death and condemnation and the latter as a ministration of Spirit and life. In a very crucial sense the law of Moses is deemed to be contrary to the law of Christ. Most interpreters concede that Paul, as well as other NT authors, employs the term "law" (*nomos*) in different senses. It is necessary, accordingly, that our biblical and systematic theologies take full account of this datum. That there is little hope for consensus among contemporary biblical interpreters of diverse theological persuasion regarding the larger issues on Paul and the law should neither surprise nor discourage us. Our immediate concern is with evangelical scholarship. Disappointingly, the stunning impact of E. P. Sanders' rereading of the Bible (through the spectacles of Palestinian Judaism) seems to have left an indelible mark. Quoting again from Blomberg:

> Although seventeen years have elapsed since Sanders' groundbreaking work, there is no end in sight of studies on Paul and the law. The amount of confusion that still exists on the topic and the foundational nature of the theological issues at stake surely justify continuing attention, not least on the part of Evangelicals. More so than in many areas of biblical research, the field seems to be dominated by major protagonists repeatedly reworking much of the same material, and each proposing credible but one-sided theses. What is needed is a synthesis of the work done that avoids numerous false dichotomies.[6]

This strategy proposed by Blomberg will not work. What is needed is not a synthesis but a thoroughgoing critique of the various proposals, especially the biblico-theological and dogmatic presuppositions at work in each of the interpretations. Only then will headway be made through this present morass.

To be sure, as Richard Gaffin observes, the question of Paul on the law has become "the 'storm centre' of scholarly controversy."[7] Unfortunately Gaffin's adherence to the neoorthodox interpretation of the covenants has led him away from historic Reformed teaching, which he regards to be misguided with respect to Paul and the law. (Others who follow this now-dominant school of thought within Reformed circles include such names as Willem VanGemeren and Sinclair Ferguson.) Obsession with the Protestant law/gospel antithesis, contends Gaffin, has prevented Reformed theology from rightly interpreting Paul. It has prevented Paul from speaking on his own terms. Gaffin speaks of the "distorted conception of Paul [that] results, in part, from failing to recognise [Paul's] positive use and application of the law."[8] In terms of classic formulation Gaffin denies the "second use of the law" in the application of redemption, affirming only the vivifying or normative (*i.e.* "third") use of the law in the life of believers in every age of redemptive history. Like many modern interpreters, Gaffin maintains that the law principle enunciated in Lev 18:5 in its original OT context is identical with the faith principle.[9] It is not surprising, then, to hear it said that the biblical expressions "justification by faith" and "justification by works" are interchangeable. Based on the alleged synonymity of faith and works, no difference is found between Paul and James in their formulations on justification.

This popular nuancing of the debate leads me to wonder whether Gaffin (and modern scholarship in general) agrees with J. Christiaan Beker's contention that the apostle Paul is first and foremost a hermeneutic theologian rather than a systematic theologian.[10] The shift in contemporary theology away from traditional dogmatics to semantics and lexicography does not bode well for biblical studies at the present time. It may well be that evangelicals, by and large, are in need of reassessing the role of creedal orthodoxy in the interpretive enterprise.[11]

The Reformed tradition has always stressed the normative or regulative use of the law in the life of the Christian, but never at the expense of the pedagogical or elenctic. So important was the latter that evangelical theology at the time of the Protestant Reformation emphasized over and over again the opposition of law to gospel. Both Lutheranism and Calvinism held tenaciously to this theological distinction. Nowadays we are told (in the words of Ferguson): "A more serious challenge is posed by the question whether the order of Grace and Law is not more true to Scripture than Law (or Works) and Grace."[12] Ferguson further speaks of "the apparent stringency and legality of the Covenant of Works." He portrays the Reformed (*i.e.* federal) conception of redemptive history as merely "the logical extension of a theological scheme."[13] Here lies the difference between orthodox and neoorthodox formulation.

In Rom 10:5-13 Paul sets Moses' teaching against Christ's. In terms of their proper offices, Moses preached the law and Christ the gospel. These are not two contrary ways of salvation. Rather, they are two contrary means to the attainment of divine blessing and reward. These contrary means were ordained by God. Under the Sinaitic arrangement obedience to the law (*i.e.* works) was the means of inheriting temporal reward: prosperity in the land of Canaan. Justifying faith was and is the means of inheriting the antitypical, spiritual reward (fellowship with God through divine reconciliation). Accordingly the Mosaic law served a subordinate role in the history of redemption. This, I submit, is the only consistent and viable explanation of the legal contrast between the Old and New Covenants.[14]

More important, however, than a solution to the problem of the relationship between the OT and the NT is the doctrine of Christ's substitutionary atonement. The Reformed tradition arose in the midst of intense polemical debate. Reformed leaders set their teachings over against those of the Anabaptists, the so-called Radical reformers. Preeminent in these disputes were the biblical doctrines of justification, sovereign election, and the covenants, especially the sacrament of baptism. Early in the development of Reformed theology the federal representative headship of the First and Second Adams was emphasized. Romans 5 was (and remains) a pivotal text in the Reformed arsenal. The basis of spiritual life and blessing in the Covenant of Grace is Christ's satisfaction of the legal demands of the original covenant with Adam. Succinctly stated, where Adam failed, Christ succeeded.

In distinction from Lutheran dogmatics an additional theological element had been introduced into the Reformed system of doctrine at the beginning of the latter half of the sixteenth century – namely, the doctrine of the Covenant of Works. From that time onward this element was regarded by the Reformed orthodox as crucial to the system of doctrine. The Westminster standards teach that in the first covenant between God and Adam (the Covenant of Works) the reward of confirmed life and communion with God would have been granted on condition of Adam's perfect and personal obedience to the law of God.[15] According to Reformed federalism, Christ's earning of eternal life necessarily entailed legal and vicarious satisfaction of God's law. As Second Adam, Christ obtained for the elect what the First Adam failed to obtain – namely, the reward of life everlasting on grounds of perfect, personal righteousness. Both the active and passive obedience of Christ were requisite in achieving the salvation of those for whom Christ died. To be sure, God was not obliged to deal with humankind on the basis of federal imputation any more than he was obliged to create the world and all that is in it. The covenant (and federal) relationship itself was a manifestation of the Father's love to Adam, son of God, made in his own image.

Protestant orthodoxy teaches that justification is by faith alone. Faith is the sole instrument that appropriates Christ's righteousness. Good works are evidential of genuine, saving faith. In truth, justifying faith cannot stand apart from good works. But it is faith alone – faith apart from all other saving graces – that receives the perfect righteousness of Christ, the meritorious ground of our salvation. In an attempt to reformulate the classic Reformed doctrine of justification by faith and the covenants Norman Shepherd and Gaffin have maintained that good works are not merely evidential of justifying faith. Nonmeritorious works, they contend, bear an analogous role to faith in the procurement of divine justification. Accordingly faith is not the "alone" instrument of justification. In the Shepherd-Gaffin position faith does not justify apart from good works, which is to say that believers are justified by faith and (nonmeritorious) works. In an essay soon to be published Gaffin argues that initial justification is contingent upon final justification (or judgment according to works).[16] These two are one. According to Gaffin's interpretation of "single justification by faith," the "already" of justification is not made complete until the eschaton. The Protestant reformers, Gaffin argues, have failed to do justice to the eschatological – the already/not-yet – structure of biblical revelation. He states that "the integral tie between that future acquittal and present justification needs to be made clear: as a single justification by faith, the one is the consummation of the other." This statement of the doctrine is both unclear and misleading. How can the "already" (the fixed, once-for-all) aspect of justification await future completion? The implication by Gaffin is that faith must persevere in order for genuine faith to justify. But such a formulation is flatly contradictory. In the same paper Gaffin contends that the life of the justified is not "storm-free." There is a real possibility of apostasy even among the elect. The warnings in Scripture against covenant-breaking suggest to Gaffin that even the elect are capable of apostatizing from the faith and falling from grace.[17] Parenthetically, this position sees an analogous situation with respect to national Israel under the old economy. The distinction between individual election unto salvation and ancient Israel's national election is lost.[18]

To the contrary, Reformed theology insists that the elect in all ages cannot lose their justification. God will preserve his work of grace, enabling the saints to persevere in all faith and obedience. He will guard them against ultimate harm, so that on the day of judgment they stand victorious in their Savior. According to historic Protestant theology, the evidential working of faith through love in no way adds to definitive, once-for-all justification. The believer is constituted righteous through faith on the grounds of Christ's meritorious obedience. Good works are demonstrative of justifying faith. For the believer, judgment according to works issues in the acquittal of the righteous through faith (on the sole basis of Christ's righteousness) and in the approbation/vindication of the saints for their good works: works done in righteousness.[19]

The root of the Shepherd-Gaffin error is denial of the traditional Reformed doctrine of the Covenant of Works. Shepherd and Gaffin contend that the reward of communion with God (including life eternal) under the first covenant between God and Adam would have been purely a matter of gratuitous promise (or divine beneficence), not Adam's meritorious accomplishment of a divinely appointed task (what Paul in Rom 5:18 identifies as the "one act of righteousness"). There is, they insist, no earning of reward on the part of the creature, whether in the Covenant of Works or the Covenant of Grace. In this neoorthodox formulation there is no antithesis between law and grace, law and gospel. Just as blessing is conditioned upon obedience in the first covenant, in the same way (according to this position) blessing is conditioned upon obedience in the Covenant of Grace. Having jettisoned the law/gospel contrast, these revisionists assure us that the works done by the righteous (those who are in a right relationship with God) are nonmeritorious, whether under the first Covenant of Creation or the subsequent Covenant of Redemption.[20]

This anti-Reformational understanding of law and gospel leads one like Gaffin to a very different conception of Christ's active obedience. Although he applies the concept of merit to the righteousness of Christ imputed to all who have been justified through faith, he denies that the parallel drawn by Paul between the First and Second Adams must necessarily include the positive side - the prospect of meritorious accomplishment on the part of Adam. In Gaffin's view the merit of Christ's righteousness is merely set over against Adam's demerit which has accrued as a result of the Fall. And whereas Adam was never in a position to earn anything from God, Gaffin contends, what Adam did merit through his breaking of the covenant was eternal death for all humanity. According to this view, Christ's reconciling work, which brings about the believer's union with Christ through the Spirit, places the believer in the same position as Adam (before the Fall), obligating him/her to perpetual (though non-meritorious) obedience to the law of God. Such teaching undermines the doctrine of Christ's substitutionary satisfaction of the law of God.[21]

Fortunately all has not been lost in the contemporary polemical cross fires. The classic Protestant law/gospel distinction still plays a formative role in evangelical theology.[22] Additionally, important elements of Reformed federalism – notably the feature of continuity throughout the period of the Covenant of Grace (both the Mosaic and new dispensations) – have gradually been assimilated into the system of evangelical doctrine. The recent rapprochement between covenant theology and modern dispensationalism is in part illustrative. But nagging differences still remain between these longstanding disputants, and new points of contention have arisen within the respective camps.

2. The Drama of Redemption Unfolded

There is no question that the popularity of the so-called misinterpretation view of the Mosaic law has helped bring about a degree of consolidation within evangelical thinking. That is not to say that any like consensus of opinion has been reached on the complex question regarding the nature and purpose of the Mosaic law in the progressive unfolding of redemptive history. But with all the significant changes that have taken place thus far in dispensationalism in particular, attention has focused once again on the Reformation theme of law and gospel. Current preoccupation with the history of salvation among evangelicals – the category of *historia salutis* in distinction from *ordo salutis* – has occasioned a fresh look at traditional Protestant formulation on Paul and the law. In this setting the work of Schreiner and Thielman should command our full attention.[23]

It is gratifying to read that after extended theological and exegetical study Schreiner remains convinced that "the reformers understood Paul better than those who are espousing new approaches."[24] The central message is this, explains Schreiner: "No one can be justified by the works of the law, for no one keeps perfectly the law's demands."[25] This is the (unfulfilled) legal requirement of the covenant between God and humankind, the duty of the creature to the Creator. It is one aspect of the natural (*i.e.* covenantal) bond between the Father and the son. It distinguishes the first relationship established in creation from subsequent reconciliation between the Redeemer and the redeemed, those formerly estranged from God. Happily, Schreiner is not a blind disciple of Daniel Fuller. He takes exception to Fuller's understanding of the Pauline expression "the works of the law." Schreiner rightly insists that a contrast, not a continuum, between the law and the gospel is contemplated by the apostle. This insight of Schreiner, however, needs to be applied even more consistently than he presently allows.

On the one hand, writes Schreiner, "Paul contrasts faith and works fundamentally, not just as two periods of salvation history."[26] The Mosaic Covenant is to be regarded as an "interim covenant" spanning the epoch wherein "the law functioned apart from the Spirit."[27] Schreiner adds: "The statement that Christ is 'the end of the law' in Rom 10:4 seems to harmonize with the idea that the Mosaic Covenant was not intended to be in force forever."[28] Unfortunately Schreiner does not free himself from the dispensational error of denying the essential role of the Holy Spirit in regenerating, sanctifying and justifying OT believers. Some lingering dispensational distinctives militate against proper understanding of the essential (or substantive) continuity between the OT and the NT.

A pivotal element in Schreiner's argument is his contention that corporate Israel stands condemned under the law of Moses because she has not kept the law perfectly. To say this, however, Schreiner must acknowledge that ancient Israel was in some sense under a covenant of works. But this he is unwilling to do. He favors Moisés Silva's exegesis of Gal 3:12. This proposal is nothing other than a variation on the misinterpretation view of the law, the view that Schreiner himself aims to refute in his work.[29] The Schreiner-Silva reading still obscures the covenantal contrast drawn by Paul between the principle of faith and the principle of works, between the Abrahamic promise and the Mosaic law. In the words of Timothy George: "It is either law or promise, works or faith, grace or merit."[30] That contrast must refer to the covenants themselves. Schreiner readily admits that Paul entertains the proper use of the law, not its misuse. The law was designed to work death and condemnation for those under its dominion. Summarily, Schreiner's failure is twofold: (1) his refusal to grant the operation of the principle of works within the restricted symbolico-typological sphere of the Mosaic economy, and (2) his failure to discern the fundamental disparity between the views of Fuller and Murray on Paul and the law (whatever other similarities there are).[31]

Thielman's contextual analysis of Paul on the law and his thematic presentation reflect the author's own systematic proclivity – that is, his contextual approach to Paul, though helpful, does not stand as a corrective to alternative approaches. (And this is the reason why Thielman's work and Schreiner's complement one another so well.) What is distinctive in Thielman's analysis is his employment of the concept of paradox to describe Paul's teaching on the law.

What appears to be old and ready to pass away at the dawning of the new, eschatological age of the Spirit, Thielman argues, may not actually be so. Although the Mosaic Covenant had indeed been abolished upon the establishment of the covenant in Christ Jesus, "certain commandments within the law are still valid."[32] And although the New Covenant signals the breakdown of the ethnic barrier between Jew and Gentile, nevertheless the restored people, the church, resembles Israel of old. "It stands in continuity with ancient Israel and can be described in terms formerly applied to Israel, but it is itself a new entity."[33] The most puzzling feature of the relationship between the OT and the NT, Thielman admits, is the discontinuity. The solution, he suggests, is to be found in the NT reinterpretation of the Mosaic law. "The law of Moses still contains for believers the word of God, but it is interpreted in light of the eschatologically significant events that brought the new people of God into existence."[34] What has changed is "the outward boundary markers . . . [not] the general pattern of God's dealings with his people."[35] Thielman further observes that the letter/Spirit contrast is neither a contrast between two ways of interpreting the OT and NT, nor between Jewish misuse and proper use of the law, nor between two ways of ethical service. It is a contrast between two distinctive eras, "the first dominated by the law and its condemnation and the second dominated by the Spirit and righteousness."[36] In my judgment the same criticisms leveled against Schreiner's interpretation above are equally applicable to Thielman's. Thielman and Schreiner go so far in their argument but no farther. It is like baking a cake and leaving out the leaven. It falls flat.

The basic question is this: What does the law require? Does the law demand something less than full and perfect obedience? At one point in his argumentation Thielman speaks of "the provisional and ultimately inadequate righteousness that was available on the basis of the Mosaic law [which] has been replaced by 'the righteousness that comes from God by faith.'"[37] This idea of provisional righteousness based on observance of the law of Moses is in need of further explication or even reformulation. The Scriptures clearly teach that under the Mosaic law the bondservant was obligated to keep the law in its entirety. What was appropriate in former times under Moses is now no longer appropriate. Since the coming of Christ, reversion to the law of Moses and its demand for works-righteousness as grounds for temporal blessing in the land of Canaan would obscure, if not undermine, the surpassing glory of Christ's atoning work – specifically, his procurement of our eternal salvation – which theocratic Israel experienced only in type and shadow. (Of course the elect within Israel were true heirs of eternal life through faith in the Messiah who was yet to come.) Reverting to the old law would once again place God's people under a yoke of bondage. But Christ freed his covenant people from the servitude of the old law-administration. A change in status – from childhood to sonship – has taken place in history for the people of God. In the unfolding of redemptive history it was God's design that the Mosaic law should work death and condemnation in Israel (symbolized by her exile in Babylon).[38] The law served a pedagogical, tutelary purpose in the history of redemption. Nothing hypothetical or improper here. The goal of the law was not to produce false confidence in the flesh nor to elicit some kind of provisional, less-than-perfect righteousness in the lives of the godly saints but rather to consign all (Jew and Gentile) under sin and death, to point sinners to Christ for eternal salvation, and thus to magnify the grace of God. That was the lesson to be drawn from Israel's history, a history illustrative of divine blessing for obedience and curse for disobedience. The way of wisdom begins with the fear of the Lord and the keeping of his commandments. The reward for covenant fidelity awaits the consummate return of Christ (see *e.g.* Prov 12:28; 13:23).

Both Thielman and Schreiner perpetuate the error of traditional Protestant interpretation when they suggest that God offered Israel salvation hypothetically on grounds of works-righteousness. According to Thielman, Rom 2:5-16 and the book of Deuteronomy as a whole posit hypothetical salvation by works:

> Paul argues only for the possibility that keeping the law could lead to eternal life, glory, honor and peace (vv. 7,10), not that any one actually achieves these ends by doing so. . . . He is saying nothing other than what Deuteronomy says when it claims that God will grant life to his people if they obey the law (Deut 28:1-14) but then goes on to predict that Israel will instead disobey and receive the covenant's curses (28:15-68; 30:22-29). The possibility of life is extended to the people of Israel if they should keep the law, but, Deuteronomy affirms, they will disobey the law and choose death rather than life (30:15-20).[39]

Over against this reading it is my contention that Israel's retention of the land was contingent upon her own compliance with the law of Moses. The grounds for the temporal reward was legal obedience.[40] To paraphrase Scripture: "Do this and you, ancient Israel, will live and prosper in the land I have given you. Otherwise, I, the Lord your God, will bring a curse on the land." In the period from Moses to Christ theocratic Israel was placed on probation, subject to the stipulations and sanctions of the covenant established at Sinai.[41]

3. Concluding Remarks (An Apologetic Appeal)

As we draw this study to a conclusion, a brief word about the typological significance of the land of Canaan in biblical times is in order. To be sure, our understanding of this issue plays a decisive role in biblical hermeneutics. No system of theology – no theological interpretation of the Bible – can avoid the subject. And of course one's position on this matter bears directly upon the millennial question. In this century the biblical theology of Geerhardus Vos has shown convincingly the centrality of eschatology, the doctrine of last things, within the pages of the OT and NT. Reformed covenant theology, more generally speaking, has viewed typology as an essential ingredient in the christological interpretation of the Scriptures. The pattern of teaching is already found in the teachings of Jesus and in the apostolic writings. It is left to subsequent Christian interpretation to extend the typological reading to all of redemptive revelation, not just those persons, events and institutions explicitly identified in the NT. The Law, the Prophets and the Writings all speak of Christ, his person and work. Both biblical symbolism and prophetic idealism – that is, the premessianic vision of the future age entertained by the OT prophets – require us to view the land of Canaan as a temporary sign depicting the eternal kingdom, the promised land, which has already begun to manifest itself in this present, preconsummation epoch of inaugurated eschatology.[42] (Thus, *e.g.*, the temple of God is now the post-Pentecost, Spirit-filled people of God.) The crucial questions that remain unanswered in modern-day dispensationalism are these: What is the relationship between the purported, future millennial reign of Christ in Palestine and the everlasting kingdom? What is the proper understanding of the original promise to Abraham regarding the land as an eternal possession? Are believing Jews to be granted special status among the one people of God in the eternal state? These questions have largely been skirted in the current debate.[43]

I began this three-part study of Paul and the law asking the question: Is it naive optimism to hope that the Christian church today can fully recover the evangelical doctrine of law and gospel, that which was part of the Protestant theological consensus at the time of the Reformation? To be sure, the future of evangelicalism remains uncertain. James Montgomery Boice has rightly observed: "The evangelical church is in a perilous condition, even to the point of abandoning the gospel which brought it into being."[44] In the opinion of Charles Spurgeon, "he who understands the covenant has reached the very core and marrow of the Gospel."[45] On the one hand, historic Reformed theology has something important to say in current discussions. On the other, many modern-day exponents (or, rather, detractors) of Reformed theology have much to rediscover in the orthodox Protestant heritage. As we prepare to enter the twenty-first century we stand at a critical threshold, a watershed in the history of the church. As I see it, one of the tasks of the Evangelical Theological Society is to clarify issues relating to what is, after all, the heart of the gospel: justification by faith alone.

ENDNOTES

[1]Compare Carl F. H. Henry, "Trouble at the Peak: Emerging Leadership Challenges Plague Evangelicalism," *World* (August 12/19, 1995) 25; "Breaking Ranks: Evangelicals and Catholics Divided: Is ECT to Blame?" *World* (August 26/September 2, 1995) 25; "Justification: A Doctrine in Crisis," *JETS* 88 (1995) 57-65. See also R. C. Sproul, *Faith Alone: The Evangelical Doctrine of Justification* (Grand Rapids: Baker, 1995); N. L. Geisler and R. E. MacKenzie, *Roman Catholics and Evangelicals: Agreements and Differences* (Grand Rapids: Baker, 1995) 491-502.
[2]Mark W. Karlberg, "Israel under a Covenant of Works: An Evaluation of Thomas R. Schreiner's *The Law and Its Fulfillment*" (paper read at the Eastern regional meeting of the Evangelical Theological Society in Philadephia, PA, March 4, 1994); and "Israel under Probation: An Evaluation of Frank Thielman's *Paul and the Law,"* (paper read at the Eastern regional meeting of the Evangelical Theological Society in Valley Forge, PA, April 4, 1995).
[3]Craig L. Blomberg, "Critical Issues in New Testament Studies for Evangelicals Today," *A Pathway into the Holy Scripture,* ed. P. E. Satterthwaite and D. F. Wright (Grand Rapids: Eerdmans, 1994) 58-59.
[4]See further David E. Holwerda, *Jesus and Israel: One Covenant or Two?* (Grand Rapids: Eerdmans, 1995).
[5]Willem VanGemeren explains the essence of the New Covenant in terms of "God's deeper commitment to the new community." He believes that the postexilic community already enjoyed some realization of these promises [prophesied by Jeremiah]" ("A Response," in *Dispensationalism, Israel and the Church: The Search for Definition,* ed. C. A. Blaising and D. L. Bock [Grand Rapids: Zondervan, 1992] 338).
[6]Blomberg, "Critical" 57.
[7]Richard B. Gaffin, Jr., "Justification in Luke-Acts," *Right with God: Justification in the Bible and the World,* ed. D. A. Carson (Grand Rapids: Baker, 1992) 122. Timothy George describes justification by faith as "the theological lodestar in Paul's body of divinity" (*Galatians* [Nashville: Broadman & Holman, 1994] 181 n. 154).
[8]Gaffin, "Justification" 122; see further "Pentecost: Before and After," *Kerux* 10/2 (September 1995) 3-24.
[9]This position is ably refuted by M. C. Kauk, "Paul's Use of the Old Testament in Romans 10:6-8" (Ph.D. dissertation, Westminster Theological Seminary, 1994). Robert L. Saucy argues unsuccessfully that under the New Covenant the Holy Spirit brings an increase of sanctifying grace that was not present under the Old: "Surely some added measure of enabling grace is included in the New Covenant that was absent under the old economy" (*The Case for Progressive Dispensationalism: The Interface Between Dispensational and Non-Dispensational Theology* [Grand Rapids: Zondervan, 1998] 17). In a footnote he adds: "If the concept of a law-demand without complete enablement for fulfillment constitutes a form of the Covenant of Works, then it is difficult to deny some aspect of this covenant from under the Mosaic economy" (p. 17 n. 11). Later he speaks of the "conditional Sinaitic covenant" in contrast to the "unconditional new Covenant of Grace" (p. 226 n. 11).
[10]J. Christiaan Beker, "The Faithfulness of God and the Priority of Israel in Paul's Letter to the Romans," *HTR* 79 (1986) 10. In *Paul the Apostle: The Triumph of God in Life and Thought* (Philadelphia: Fortress, 1980) Beker declares: "Paul's hermeneutic is characterized by the deliberate use of a 'mixed language' that ultimately defies logical precision (p. 286).

[11]See Chapter Sixteen.
[12]Sinclair Ferguson, "The Doctrine of the Christian Life in the Teaching of Dr. John Owen," (Ph.D. dissertation, University of Aberdeen, 1979) 56.
[13]*Ibid.* Ferguson works out the implications of this understanding of law in grace (or grace in law) in "Reformed Theology: Reformed Life-Style: I," *Banner of Truth* (October 1994) 22-28. J. B. Torrance, under whom Ferguson studied, insists: "Law is the gift of grace, spells out the obligation of grace and leads to grace – its fulfilment in Christ. That is the inner meaning of the Torah. That is true not only in the life of Israel, but in Creation" ("Strengths and Weaknesses of the Westminster Theology," *The Westminster Confession in the Church Today*, ed. A. I. Heron [Edinburgh: Saint Andrew, 1982] 49). Contrast the interpretation of Reformed covenant theology offered by C. Graafland, *Van Calvijn tot Comrie: Oorsprong en ontwikkeling van de leer van het verbond in het Gereformeerd Protestantisme* (Zoetermeer: Uitgeverij, 1992-), and D. N. J. Poole, *Stages of Religious Faith in the Classical Reformation Tradition: The Covenant Approach to the* Ordo Salutis (Lewiston: Mellon, 1995), with that found in C. Harinck, *De Schotse Verbondsleer Van Robert Rollock tot Thomas Boston* (Utrecht: De Banier, 1986), and Mark W. Karlberg, "The Mosaic Covenant and the Concept of Works in Reformed Hermeneutics" (Th.D. dissertation, Westminster Theological Seminary, 1980).
[14]This view is set forth in the *New Geneva Study Bible*, gen. ed. R. C. Sproul (Nashville: Thomas Nelson, 1995). The Mosaic Covenant reinstitutes in modified fashion the Covenant of Works. "The Old Covenant calls for a heart religion, but it failed through human weakness and became obsolete after its fulfillment at Calvary (Rom 8:3; Heb 7:12; 8:13)" (introduction to Deuteronomy, 240). The legal principle enunciated in Lev 18:5 remains operative under the covenant with David. "There was a conditional element in the Davidic Covenant. His physical descendants would only rule successfully in Jerusalem if they were obedient to the covenant" (note on Ps 132:12). "The Mosaic Covenant offered life for obedience (Lev. 18:5; Rom. 10:5). Israel's failure to merit life in the land testifies to the universal need for a Substitute through whom the righteous requirements of the law might be fully met on behalf of those who could not meet these terms on their own (Rom. 8:3,4)" (note on Neh 9:29). In "Kingdom Promises as Spiritual" (*Continuity and Discontinuity: Perspective on the Relationship Between the Old and New Testaments,* ed. J. S. Feinberg [Westchester: Crossway, 1988] 269) B. K. Waltke writes: "As Abraham was the father of 'true Israel' (his physical seed that believed in Christ), Moses was the founder of national Israel (Abraham's natural and spiritual seed as administered under the law). God's soteriological kingdom, originally founded on the principle of promise-faith, now became united in a kingdom with the contrary principle of law- inheritance. . . . Both the New and Old Covenants were righteous and promised life; but whereas the former was unconditional, because it depended solely on God's sovereign grace, the latter was conditional, because it depended on fallen man to keep it (Gal 3:10-14; Rom 10:5-13)."
[15]Geerhardus Vos states: "The tree [of the knowledge of good and evil] was associated with the higher, the unchangeable, the eternal life to be secured by obedience throughout his probation" (*Biblical Theology: Old and New Testaments* [Grand Rapids: Eerdmans, 1948] 28). Orthodox Reformed scholasticism introduced the notion of dispropostionality into their formulation of the Covenant of Works. Positing an infinite disproportion between the meager obedience required of Adam under the probationary covenant and the reward of confirmed life and communion with God, the federalists maintained that the reward – eternal life (in distinction from that life with God that the creature already enjoyed by virtue of creation) – was more than Adam could justly earn on the basis of his own works. Gaffin further reasons that since the creature of the dust is, in his view, in-

capable of meriting anything at all from the hand of God, the federalists were wrong to set law against promise (grace). Obedience as the legal grounds of blessing in the original covenant with Adam is thereby denied. For further analysis see Chapter Four.

[16]Richard B. Gaffin, Jr., "The Vitality of Reformed Dogmatics" (unpublishsd paper). Intimations of Gaffin's reformulation are found in his earlier essay, "The Holy Spirit and Eschatology," in *'N Woord op sy tyd: 'N Teologiese Feesbundel aangebied aan Professor Johan Heyns Ter Herdenking van sy Sestigste Vergaarsday,* ed. C. J. Wethmar and C. J. A. Vos (Pretoria; NG Kerkboekhandel, 1988) 43-52. Contemporary dogmatics, Gaffin insists, must complete what was left unfinished by the Protestant reformers: "An important and fruitful challenge for the teaching ministry of the church is to clarify further the nature of justification within the already/not-yet structure of NT eschatology, at the same time ensuring that commensurate attention is given to the eschatological nature of sanctification and the present work of the Holy Spirit" (p. 49). The unfortunate legacy of the Reformation, contends Gaffin, was the "tendency, at least in practice, to separate or even polarize justification and sanctification" (p. 48).

[17]Compare N. Shepherd, "Perseverance: The Gift (I)," *The Outlook* 42 (February 1992) 10-11; "The Need to Persevere (II)," *The Outlook* 42 (March 1992) 20-21.

[18]Responding to modern-day dispensationalism's openness and receptivity to the teachings of Reformed covenant theology, John H. Walton unpersuasively sets forth "a new proposal regarding covenant" (*Covenant: God's Purpose, God's Plan* [Grand Rapids: Zondervan, 1994] 24). "In the Mosaic phase the key point of election is that Israel is chosen to be the people of God. I have defined and interpreted this phrase in a revelatory sense. With the New Covenant, the new elect body is identified as all who respond in faith to the salvation offered through Christ. This is a soteriological definition" (p. 123). According to Walton, the church does not replace Israel: "Rather a new group is taking shape and, though it uses the same label to indicate a special relationship with God that Israel had, the relationship is on quite a different basis. Therefore this is not one people replacing another, it is one definition of people of God replacing another" (p. 125). Equally unsatisfactory is W. H. Glenny's argument that "the church represents a pattern and thus is a fulfillment of the promises made to Israel. . . . Peter uses Israel's historical situation as the people of God as a pattern of his recipients' relationship with God; he is not saying that the church is a new Israel replacing the nation" ("The Israelite Imagery of 1 Peter 2," *Dispensationalism, Israel and the Church* 183). Glenny reiterates: "Peter's argument does not suggest or necessitate that his recipients replace Israel in God's program. Peter's point is that their relationship with Christ represents a continuation of the pattern God established in his election of Israel to be his people. So if God's election of Israel in the OT was somehow annulled and therefore not an eternal election, it would destroy the argument of 2:4-10 as well as that of the whole epistle (*cf.* 1:1,2,5)" (p. 185).

[19]See further Chapter Six. R. C. Sproul ("Justification by Faith Alone: The Forensic Nature of Justification, " *Justification by Faith Alone: Affirming the Doctrine by which the Church and the Individual Stands or Falls,* ed. D. Kistler (Morgan: Soli Deo Gloria, 1995] 23-52) arrives at a formulation similar to mine. To accommodate the total biblical witness concerning the believer's state of justification, Sproul speaks of "the complex of justification," comprising justification in the "narrow sense" and the "wider sense" (p. 44).

[20]The impact of this doctrinal error is clearly evident in the recent Protestant/Roman-Catholic discussions. In *Protestants and Catholics: Do They Now Agree?* (Eugene: Harvest House, 1995) John Ankerberg and J. Weldon conclude their critique by noting: "A final illustration should reveal the seriousness of this issue. Yet another story of conversion to Rome is found in the person of Scott Hahn, author of *Rome, Sweet Home*" (p. 207).

The teaching of Shepherd helped cement Hahn in his theological convictions regarding the role of faith and works in justification. (Compare Hahn's own account in S. Hahn and K. Hahn, *Rome, Sweet Home: Our Journey to Catholicism* [San Francisco: Iguatius, 1993) 31,129-130.) For further reading on this matter see Kim Riddlebarger, "No Place Like Rome? Why Are Evangelicals Joining the Catholic Church," *Roman Catholicism: Evangelical Protestants Analyze What Divides and Unites Us,* ed. J. Armstrong (Chicago: Moody, 1994) 221-243; A. Sandlin, "Deviations from Historic Solafideism in the Reformed Community," *Chalcedon Report* (February 1995) 18-27.

[21]Contrast David B. McWilliams' analysis, "The Covenant Theology of the 'Westminster Confession of Faith' and Recent Criticism," *WTJ* 53 (1991) 109-124, with mine in Chapter Five and that of Ronald S. Ward, "Recent Criticisms of the Westminster Confession of Faith," *Proceedings of the International Conference of Reformed Churches* (Alberta: Inheritance, 1993) 184-202.

[22]See the important study by Stephen Westerholm, *Israel's Law and the Church's Faith: Paul and His Recent Interpreters* (Grand Rapids: Eerdmans, 1988), as well as the thoughtful reviews by Andrew J. Bandstra ("Paul and the Law: Some Recent Developments and an Extraordinary Book," *CTJ* 25 [1990] 249-261) and Moisés Silva (*WTJ* 51 [1989] 174-177). *Cf.* my review of *The Law, the Gospel, and the Modern Christian: Five Views,* ed. W. G. Strickland (Grand Rapids: Zondervan, 1993) included here in this volume.

[23]Gaffin, following the lead of G. C. Berkouwer and Herman Ridderbos, attempts to overturn traditional Reformed interpretation of the Mosaic Covenant. In "Pentecost" he substitutes the indicative/imperative construct for the traditional law/gospel antithesis. From the standpoint of the history of redemption (*historia salutis*) Gaffin argues that the law of Moses – summed up in the Decalogue or more succinctly in the imperative "do this and live" (Lev 15:5) – sets forth God's naked command, the fulfillment of which awaits the New Covenant era when spiritual union with the risen and exalted Christ is effectuated. In the eschatological age, Christ becomes "life-giving Spirit" (1 Cor 15:45). Under law the present imperative stands apart from the future indicative. G. Zimmermann argues conversely: "Erst wenn, mit anderen Worten, die Zehn Gebote nicht als objektiver Imperativ, sondern als subjektiver Indikativ, nicht als aüssere Hindernis und aüssere Begrenzung, sondern als innerer Motor and innerer Impuls verstanden werden, konnen sie ausgeführt und vergegenwärtigt werden" ("Gottesbund und Gesetz in der Westminster Confession," *ZKG,* 106 [1995] 191). Gaffin's interpretation is marred by glaring contradiction and misapplication of the indicative/imperative construct.

[24]Thomas R. Schreiner, *The Law and Its Fulfillment: A Pauline Theology of Law* (Grand Rapids: Baker, 1993) 11. Consult David L. Puckett, *John Calvin's Exegesis of the Old Testament* (Louisville: Westminster/John Knox, 1995); and Westerbolm, *Israel's Law.*

[25]Schreiner, *Law* 15.

[26]*Ibid.* 101. See also Thomas R. Schreiner, "Works of the Law," *Dictionary of Paul and His Letters,* ed. G. F. Hawthorne and R. P. Martin (Downers Grove: InterVarsity, 1993) 975-979.

[27]Schreiner, *Law* 124.

[28]*Ibid.* 184.

[29]Moisés Silva has in recent years moved away somewhat from his earlier formulation. In "The New Testament Use of the Old Testament: Text Form and Authority" (*Scripture and Truth,* ed. D. A. Carson and J. D. Woodbridge [Grand Rapids: Baker, 1992] 147-165) Silva adopted Ridderbos' interpretation of Paul on the law, wherein "Paul's hostile tone when speaking of the law should be understood in light of the synagogue's handling of the

law. . . . Consider Gal 3:11-12, where Paul apparently opposes Hab 2:4 to Lev 18:5, as though the OT taught two mutually exclusive approaches to salvation. One of the many attempts to solve the problem is to suggest that Lev 18:5 was something like the Judaizers' motto, so that Paul's use of that passage would have been understood by his readers as a reference to the Judaizing point of view. Even if we disagree with this particular interpretation of Galatians 3, is there a principial reason to set aside such an approach" (p. 159)? Silva now adopts John Murray's interpretation of Lev 18:5, arguing that the law functions as a bare principle." However inadequate exegetically, at least this reading preserves the crucial theological distinction between the law and the gospel.

[30]George, *Galatians* 252.

[31]Appreciation is acknowledged for the personal correspondence with Schreiner in the summer of 1994. Concerning the teaching of Fuller, consult further the timely essay by Meredith G. Kline, "Covenant Theology Under Attack," *New Horizons* 15/2 (February 1994) 3-5; "Of Works and Grace," *Presbyterion* 9 (1983) 85-92. This entire issue of *Presbyterion* is devoted to the subject of justification and includes a response by Fuller.

[32]Frank Thielman, *Paul and the Law: A Contextual Approach* (Downers Grove: Inter-Varsity, 1994) 237.

[33]*Ibid.* 89.

[34]*Ibid.* 103.

[35]*Ibid.* 106. The influence of J. D. G. Dunn's interpretation is apparent here.

[37]*Ibid.* 268 n. 38. Elsewhere Thielman writes: "The change of covenants was necessary because no individual could keep the stipulations of the Old Covenant, a fact which Israel had demonstrated at the national level. The change was also necessary because after the covenant was broken, Israel used the Law to erect barriers between itself and the Gentile world" ("Law," *Dictionary of Paul* 541-542).

[37]Thielman, *Paul* 155. He speaks of this righteousness of faith as an "alien righteousness" (p. 273 n. 19), a righteousness imputed to the believer. He reasons: "This righteousness implied that the 'righteousness that comes by the law' was provisional and proleptic" (p. 285 n. 39).

[38]The analogy between Israel and Adam is given rhetorical effect in Romans 7. The similar exegetical treatments of this highly-contested passage by Douglas Moo and myself are discussed in Donald B. Garlington, "Romans 7:14-25 and the Creation Theology of Paul," *TrinJ* 11NS (1990) 197-235, and In-Gyu Hong, *The Law in Galatians* (JSNTSup 81; Sheffield: Sheffield Academic, 1993) 153 n. 2.

[39]Thielman, *Paul* 172-173. Protestant interpreters have applied the hypothetical offer of salvation on grounds of works in a variety of ways. Geerhardus Vos, for example, maintained that God had "held up before us constantly the ideal of eternal life to be obtained by keeping the law, a lost ideal though it be. . . . When the work of the Spirit by means of the law and the gospel leads to true conversion, in this conversion the longing for this lost ideal of the covenant appears as an essential part. From the above we can also explain why the older theologians did not always clearly distinguish between the Covenant of Works and the Sinaitic Covenant. At Sinai it was not the 'bare' law that was given, but a reflection of the Covenant of Works revived, as it were, in the interests of the Covenant of Grace continued at Sinai" ("The Doctrine of the Covenant in Reformed Theology," *Redemptive History and Biblical Interpretation: The Shorter Writings of Geerhardus Vos*, ed. R. B. Gaffin, Jr. [Phillipsburg: Presbyterian and Reformed, 1980] 254-255). Moo takes exception to Glenn N. Davies' suggestion (*Faith and Obedience in Romans: A Study in Romans 1-4* [JSNTSup 39; Sheffield: Sheffield Academic, 1990]) that Rom 2:6 ff. is dealing with pre-Christian Jews and Gentiles (Douglas Moo, "Romans 2: Saved Apart

from the Gospel?," *Through No Fault of Their Own? The Fate of Those Who Have Never Heard,* ed. W. V. Crockett and J. G. Sigountos [Grand Rapids: Baker, 1991] 137-145).

[40]William J. Dumbrell explains: "We have noted how the possession of the land was regarded in the OT as the spiritual index of Israel's political health. The ultimate blessing for Israel had been conceived of in terms of a good national life in the promised land, the enjoyment of the divine presence associated with it, and the material blessings which the land offered. . . . Covenant obedience, Israel knew, would result in the retention of the land, covenant disobedience in the temporary withdrawal of its gifts and in its final loss" (*Covenant and Creation: A Theology of the Old Testament Covenants* [Grand Rapids: Baker, 1984] 165). The Sinaitic Covenant, like the original Edenic Covenant, was "irretrievably breached" (p. 120). Unlike the unconditional covenant (traditionally called the Covenant of Grace) established on the merits of Christ's substitutionary obedience and for the sake of God's elect, these two covenants made blessing contingent upon obedience (p. 155). Craig G. Bartholomew interacts with this work and other recent studies in "Covenant and Creation: Covenant Overload or Covenantal Deconstruction," *CTJ* 80(1995) 11-83.

[41]Kenneth L. Barker expounds his theology of the covenants in "The Scope and Center of Old and New Testament Theology and Hope" (*Dispensationalism, Israel and the Church* 298-828). He summarily dismisses covenant theology's typological interpretation of the OT and NT, agreeing with Willem VanGemeren's analysis that Mark W. Karlberg has made an attempt at defining 'legitimate discontinuities,' but fails to be convincing because of his [?] prior understanding of typology" (p. 298 n. 4). In seeking a moderating position between dispensational and covenantal interpretations Barker favors a contrast of promise and fulfillment as opposed to shadow and reality. Precisely here Barker destroys any genuine typology in Scripture, leaving him at best with only a vague redemptive-historical analogy. He cannot do justice to the discontinuity between Old and New Covenants because he refuses to acknowledge a legal – that is, conditional – element in the Sinaitic arrangement. Approaching this subject from a position different from Barker's, Saucy misreads my view when he has me saying that "Israel's blessing and prosperity in the land were *always* related to the conditional Mosaic Covenant" (*Case* 226 n. 11; *italics mine*). Though characterized by its law-inheritance principle, the principle operative in the typological sphere of the ancient Israelite theocracy, the Mosaic Covenant is itself a renewal of the promise announced to Abraham and, before that, to our first parents after their fall into sin (all of which is subsumed under the overarching Covenant of Grace). Initially the land grant is God's unconditional gift of sovereign grace and promise, as is Israel's restoration to the land after the Babylonian exile, preparatory to and anticipatory of the new and better covenant. (A typological reading of the prophecy of Isaiah, however, would view Israel's exile – seventy years of captivity – as payment for her sin, as satisfaction of the curse sanction of the Mosaic Covenant.) Ultimate fulfillment of the land promise is the everlasting kingdom of Christ, of which earthly Canaan was a symbol and type. Saucy views Israel's restoration as God's gracious response to her repentance so that the restoration promise is no longer tied to the conditional Sinaitic Covenant, but it is now related to the unconditional new Covenant of Grace" (*ibid.*). According to my reading, OT history demonstrates that Israel could not obtain (or retain) God's temporal blessing in the land on grounds of her obedience to the law of Moses. When Israel corporately or individually was blessed for her works-obedience, she as the servant-son of God was representative of the greater Servant-Son who was yet to come. In such instances Israel was a type of Christ. (The interplay of the corporate and individual is particularly apparent throughout the book of Psalms.)

[42]In defense of the doctrine of the future millennial reign of Christ on earth, Saucy contends: "The divine plan for the restoration of all things according to the prophets, therefore, involved two stages. One stage included a kingdom characterized by an internal spiritual salvation and the glorious reign of the Messiah over all his enemies – for the first time in human history, a rule over the whole earth by man as a representative of God's will. A certain regeneration of nature will also take place. But sin, although unable to contest the powerful rule of the Messiah, will still be present. Only after this temporary period, with the final elimination of evil from the heavens and earth and the making of all things new, will the restoration be complete" (*Case* 240-241).
[43]Waltke prognosticates on the future of dispensationalism in the wake of the changes that have been sweeping across evangelicalism, foreseeing the complete demise of dispensationalism as a school of interpretation. Lamenting the opinion expressed by Waltke, Charles Ryrie in his revised and expanded work, *Dispensationalism* (Chicago: Moody, 1995), attempts to revive classical dispensational teaching. From the standpoint of the history of interpretation, Waltke has rightly identified dispensationalism as an "aberration in Christian theology" (cited in Ryrie, *Dispensationalism* 15). In *Dispensationalism, Israel and the Church* note especially the exchange between Waltke ("A Response" 347-859), Barker ("Scope and Center" 888-394) and the editors ("Assessment and Dialogue" 377-394, esp. 389-390).
[44]Cited on the jacket cover of Sproul, *Faith Alone.*
[45]Cited in Peter E. Golding, "The Development of the Covenant: An Introductory Study in Biblical Theology'," *Reformed Theological Journal* 9 (1993) 60.

[This paper was first read at the 47th annual meeting of the Evangelical Theological Society in Philadelphia, Pennsylvania on November 18, 1995.]

CHAPTER TEN

PAUL'S LETTER TO THE ROMANS IN THE *NEW INTERNATIONAL COMMENTARY ON THE NEW TESTAMENT* AND IN CONTEMPORARY REFORMED THOUGHT

Almost forty years have elapsed since the publication of the first volume of John Murray's two-volume commentary on Romans in the *New International Commentary on the New Testament.* (The second part appeared in 1965, the first in 1959.) Douglas Moo's 1996 contribution to this commentary series marks a significant development in twentieth-century evangelical theology. According to Gordon Fee, current general editor of the *NICNT,* Moo was chosen to replace the older work for the reason that his theological sympathies lay in the direction of Murray's interpretation of the great apostle Paul. Thus, in the estimation of the editor Moo's theology falls squarely within the Reformed camp. Moo, however, identifies himself as a "modified Lutheran."[1] Does this in any way indicate on the part of Fee a misreading or misunderstanding of these two highly influential and respected authors? Not at all. In my judgment, the modified Lutheranism of Moo is very close to (traditional) Reformed teaching. More strikingly, with respect to the doctrine of the covenants – notably, interpretation of the relationship between the Mosaic and New Covenants – Moo's position is closer to that of mainstream historic Reformed doctrine than is Murray's.

This important development in the history of the William B. Eerdman's commentary series provides a fitting occasion to compare and analyze the work of Murray and Moo in the context of contemporary Reformed thought. The literature on Romans (and the theology of Paul generally) is voluminous. The purpose of this article is to focus more narrowly on *Reformed* theological interpretation. Needless to say, Reformed exegesis and theology has profited from dialogue within the larger evangelical community of scholars. Hopefully, our present discussion will provoke thoughtful interaction from this wider arena. Just possibly greater doctrinal consensus among evangelicals may yet be achieved as the Christian church moves into the twenty-first century.

The strength of both commentaries lies in *theological exegesis.* In the preface to the second volume of Murray on Romans the then current general editor, F. F. Bruce, praised Murray's work as that "of a fellow-Scot who worthily maintains the noble tradition of theological exegesis which has for long been one of the glories of our native land."[2] Indeed, readers of Murray's commentary are treated to some of the best of the Scottish Reformed heritage. And Moo enriches that particular expression of Christian theology by engaging extensively not only with

Murray but other theologians across the wide spectrum of current evangelical thought. Too often emphasis on language and semantics has inhibited *doctrinal* exposition. Some of the recent commentaries simply sell theology short; others advocate theological eclecticism to one degree or another. Thankfully, neither Murray nor Moo shows any sympathy for such a methodology.[3]

1. Orientation to Paul's Letter to the Romans

The commentaries of Murray and Moo on Romans are representative of the contemporary school of salvation-historical (or redemptive-historical) interpretation of the Scriptures, Old and New Testaments. This approach is by no means original with developments in twentieth-century biblical studies. Actually, this methodology is rooted in the Reformed theological tradition. It is implicit, if not always explicit, in the rise and development of *covenant theology*. Curiously, Moo has shown reluctance over the years to speak of himself as a covenant theologian, yet clearly the doctrine of the covenants plays a formative role in his understanding of the Bible. (For Moo the problem may simply be one of nomenclature.) Both take into consideration the distinction between the "already" and the "not yet," as well as the distinction between the old and new aeons. There are those benefits of Christ's saving work *already* experienced and those *not yet* experienced by the believer in this present (semi-eschatological) age of the Spirit; the old age/new age contrast arises from the epochal event of Christ's death and resurrection in the fullness of time. So significant is Christ's reconciling work that an entirely *new* age has been inaugurated. The Christian life is lived out in the tension between that which is passing away and that which has dawned with the arrival of the kingdom of God. The contrast between the ages is essentially in the nature of things old and new, not mere chronological sequence. (Abraham, Moo reminds us, existentially participated in the realities of the life to come, *i.e.* the new age, wherein righteousness and peace reign.) Simply stated, Moo argues, the old age/new age contrast is a "conceptual tool;"[4] it is the "most basic theological conception in Paul."[5]

Murray develops his exposition of Romans in terms of the underlying redemptive-historical contrast between OT promise and NT fulfilment.[6] As we shall see, one of the central issues confronting the reader of this letter of the apostle Paul is the relation between Israel and the NT church. The transition from Old to New Covenants coincides with the arrival of the kingdom of Christ and the overlap of the old and new aeons. The first advent marks the great divide in cosmic history. In the words of N. T. Wright, Christ is the "climax of the covenant."[7] The fulfillment of the ages arrives with the appearance of Jesus Christ. He is Immanuel, God with us. The future regeneration and renewal of heaven and earth is inextricably tied to Christ's personal glorification. By virtue of his resurrection from the dead Christ is declared to be Son of God *in power*; he has been elevated to the state of exaltation in glory. Both Murray and Moo follow the interpretation of Geerhardus Vos on this crucial Pauline text, Rom 1:3,4. Murray speaks of this transition in the life of Jesus as that which results in Christ's "pneumatic endowment," and thus stands in contrast to his pre-resurrection state (*cf.* 1 Cor 15:45; 2 Cor 3:17). The assumption of human flesh marks Christ's entrance into the initial state of humiliation. The term "flesh" itself covers a spectrum of meaning in Pauline theology, its basic meaning denoting *preconsummate* human weakness (see 1 Cor 15:44-49).[8] Herein the First and Second Adams shared an identical humanity, free from sin and its consequences. (Of course, the First Adam fell from that original state of moral rectitude.) The "natural body" possessed by Adam in creation was not yet the consummate, eschatologico-pneumatic body of future Sabbath bliss promised to Adam upon successful conclusion of his probation. Humankind would have entered God's Sabbath-rest after its historical development and fulfillment of the cultural mandate (spanning the period between Creation and Consummation). As Second Adam, Christ earns universal dominion and lordship after his historical fulfillment of that covenant established between the Father and Son in eternity. Murray rightly notes that this lordship of Christ "did not belong to Christ by native right as the Son of God; it had to be secured. It is the lordship of redemptive relationship and such did not inhere in the sovereignty that belongs to him in virtue of his creatorhood. It is achieved by mediatorial accomplishment and is the reward of his humiliation."[9]

Though crucial to Paul's explication of the gospel now made known in these last days, the doctrine of justification by faith alone is nevertheless subordinate to Paul's teaching on the great eschatological event of God's sending of his Son in fulfillment of the ancient promise to Abraham (and prior to him, to Adam in the Garden subsequent to the Fall).[10] The prominence that Paul gives to the doctrine of justification by faith is but one aspect, however foundational, of his elucidation of the gospel. In the judgment of Moo, "If, then, justification by faith is not the center of Romans or of Paul's thought in the logical sense, in another sense it expresses a central, driving force in Paul's thought." Moo concludes: "In this respect, the reformers were not far wrong in giving to justification by faith the attention they did."[11] Both the Lutheran and the Reformed traditions acknowledge the vital role this doctrine plays in Pauline theology and in the NT generally. Modern-day revisionists erroneously contend, however, that the reformers introduced a speculative, rationalistic element into Protestant theology by placing the "Law" against the "Gospel." Yet, apart from this theological law/gospel contrast the *sola fide* doctrine crumbles to the ground. Historic Protestant interpretation placed great emphasis upon the *sola fide* character of the biblical teaching on salvation. A subtle, but nonetheless radical, shift has gradually been surfacing in (quasi-) evangelical and Reformed thinking over the course of the last several decades, notably during the period between the time of the publication of Murray's commentary on Romans and that of Moo's. Attention is now drawn to Paul's expression "the obedience of faith" in Rom 1:5 as the key to the apostle's understanding of the Christian life. The new perspective calls into question the traditional Protestant doctrine of justification by faith (*sola fide*).[12]

The determining factor in resolving the contemporary riddle – the answer having been given by the Protestant reformers almost five centuries ago – is the Pauline understanding of the righteousness of God. Contemporary evangelical and Reformed theology is in dire need of reclaiming the teaching of its Protestant forebears. The righteousness of God which is unto salvation (*i.e.* justification) is an alien righteousness, the righteousness of Christ imputed to all who believe. (As the reformers correctly maintained, faith is the alone instrument that receives the righteousness of Christ.) The foundation of the Christian life is God's justifying act in raising Christ from the dead. By union with Christ in his death and resurrection (through the sole instrumentality of justifying faith) all of the saving benefits of salvation are bestowed upon the elect. And union with Christ is attained by means of the effectual working of the Spirit of Christ. This is the central thrust of Paul's teaching in Romans 1-8.

2. The Pauline *Ordo Salutis*

From the above discussion it should be clear that the theological categories of *historia salutis* (the accomplishment of salvation, the fulfillment of the ancient promise in the fullness of time) and *ordo salutis* (the application of salvation to the elect before and after Christ) are mutually interpretive of God's redemption. These two aspects of God's saving work are not two perspectives on a single event complex, the Christ event They are two distinct, though inseparable, components of Christ's salvation. The Spirit efficaciously applies only that which Christ has actually earned on the basis of his meritorious obedience. With respect to the accomplishment and application of salvation, the work of Christ and the Spirit are considered as one in the economy of redemption (see, *e.g.*, 1 Cor 15:45 and 2 Cor 3:17). Effectual union with Christ in his death and resurrection ties together the individual believer's experiential appropriation of the benefits of salvation to the historic actualization of God's promise in the reconciling and atoning work of Christ (Romans 6). The various benefits accruing to the elect of God are the complete possession of every believer. Those effectually called are justified and adopted, sanctified and preserved, regenerated and glorified. Each of the benefits of union with Christ belongs to all the saints. Whatever the logical and temporal relation between them, they are inseparably bound together as a manifold package (*cf.* Rom 8:29,30). Believers do not enjoy one benefit to the exclusion of any of the others, though some are received only in anticipation of the Eschaton. Thus, bodily resurrection, judgment according to works (*i.e.* final approbation, wherein good works are evidential of true, saving faith [*cf.* Rom 2:5-11 and 2 Cor 5:10]), and glorification await the end times.[13] Needless to say, we cannot contemplate the benefits of union with Christ without reference to Christ's submission to and fulfillment of the covenant of works previously established with his Father in eternity, oftentimes called the Covenant of Redemption (see footnote 9 above). The proper purpose of the Covenant of Grace is the salvation of the elect, those for whom Christ died. *Ordo salutis* and *historia salutis* are aspectivally related.

Returning to Rom 1:16,17, we consider again the foundational act of God in declaring sinners righteous in his sight on grounds of the (active and passive) obedience of Christ. The way of salvation is that of faith, not works. "The power of God unto salvation of which the gospel is the embodiment," writes Murray, "is not unconditionally and universally operative unto salvation. It is of this we are advised in the words 'to every one that believeth.' This informs us that salvation is not accomplished irrespective of faith."[14] It is the peculiar nature of saving faith to receive and rest upon Christ for salvation. Though there is "the priority of effectual calling and of regeneration in the *ordo salutis*," Murray adds, it is faith which is the alone instrumental cause of justification. "It is preeminently in connection with justification that the accent falls upon faith."[15] What is required for our salvation is the righteousness of God, a righteousness that "meets all the demands of [God's] justice and therefore avails before God."[16] The Protestant reformers were unanimous in their belief that works of any kind find no place in the article of justification (*i.e.* the justification of sinners).[17] "Grace through faith" stands in contrast to "reward according to merit."[18] What Murray calls the "all-important aspect" of Rom 9:15 is the distinction between God's mercy and justice. "Justice presupposes rightful claims, and mercy can be operative only where no claim of justice exists. . . . Back of this thesis is the polemic of the apostle in the earlier part of the epistle for the principle of grace."[19] The point here is this: the principle of work-inheritance (law) and the principle of faith-inheritance (grace) are radically antithetical. There can be no mixture of the two with respect to the means to salvation.

3. The Contrasting Covenants: Mosaic and New

This section brings us to the focal issue in this comparative critique of Murray and Moo on Romans. We begin by taking note that the apostle Paul's argument in the letter to the Romans is advanced specifically in terms of Gentile-Jewish relations. Although the Roman church was comprised primarily of Gentile Christians, Paul addresses both Gentiles and Jews. And with respect to Jewry itself Paul has in view not only converts to Christianity but also those outside the faith, notably those of the party of the Pharisees. Paul speaks to those who know the law, those to whom belong the adoption as sons, the divine glory, the covenants, the law, the temple worship, and the promises (Rom 9:4). Many of those numbered among Israel have the form of godliness, but not the reality. The problem of Israelite unbelief is the focus of chaps. 9-11. But before reviewing that section of the letter, we turn our attention to Paul's understanding of the purpose of the Mosaic law.

Murray's interpretation of Paul on the law is in several respects unrepresentative of Reformed federal theology. Over the course of Murray's teaching career, he was intent on "recasting" the covenant concept. In particular, the Reformed scholastic doctrine of the Covenant of Works came under close scrutiny, only to be cast aside as unhelpful and misleading. *According to Murray's definition of the term, covenant is a sovereign administration of (redemptive) grace and promise.* By definition, the original Adamic administration (including the elements of probation and representative headship) could not be viewed by Murray as a *covenantal* disposition of God's original plan and purpose for humankind made in his own image. The natural state of Adam, the creational order of moral government, was one of law; the principle of government was that of "perfect legal reciprocity."[20] So long as Adam rendered obedience to natural law, the law of creation (*i.e.* the moral law of God), God was obliged, according to the dictates of his own justice to reward Adam with life and blessing. In the words of the *Westminster Confession of Faith* life with God was contingent upon "perfect and personal obedience."[21] Eternal life proffered to Adam would have been bestowed upon Adam and the entire human race at the conclusion of his successful probation (the immediate reward would have been *confirmation in righteousness*). Eternal life was not something Adam as a creature could merit by his own obedience (works). Here Murray employs the Thomistic distinction between nature and grace, what was later carried over into Reformed scholastic theology as the dichotomy between the natural bond and the covenantal bond. According to scholastic federalism, the covenant arrangement was *superimposed* upon the natural order of law. Unlike Murray, however, the federalists maintained that this covenant was one of works. Because it was still necessary for Adam to render full and perfect obedience (even though the gift of eternal life was more than Adam could have properly earned for himself and his posterity), the federal theologians called the covenant at creation the "Covenant of Works." (All subsequent covenants between God and man in the course of biblical history fall under the rubric of the "Covenant of Grace.")

From Murray's point of view, the concept of the covenant was antithetical to the notion of law as a system of merit. Accordingly, covenant and law were *by Murray's definition* contrary means of justification. Murray's doctrine of the covenants marks a significant (but not radical) departure from the teachings of historic Reformed theology. It would be wrong to view Murray's position as a return to the teaching of John Calvin. It is true, the earliest exponents of Reformed theology, Calvin included, restricted the term covenant to the era of redemption. Yet at the same time these first-generation reformers acknowledged the operation of a works-principle in the Mosaic economy. It would only be a matter of time before the (logical) demands of dogmatic formulation – including, notably, exegesis of Romans 5 (the parallel between the First and Second Adams) – would yield the twofold doctrine of the covenants, the "Covenant of Works" and the "Covenant of Grace," highlighting the covenantal structure of history before and after the Fall. This doctrine became – and remained – a vital element in the newly emerging *Reformed system of doctrine*. (Of course, there never has been a straight line of development in the history of Christian doctrine. There are instances of doctrinal deformation – even in the Reformed tradition! Such is evident, for example, in the federalists' adoption of the Thomistic nature/grace dichotomy.) Among today's revisionists, the notion of a Covenant of Works itself is deemed speculative in origin. *But Murray's objections to the Reformed doctrine of the Covenant of Works are based on altogether different considerations from those offered by present-day revisionists. Simply put, Murray's theology falls within the pale of Protestant, Reformed orthodoxy because of his adherence to the classic law/gospel antithesis.*[22]

A second instance where Murray parted company with (mainstream) historic Reformed theology was in his articulation of what is now popularly known as the misinterpretation view of the Mosaic law. Such a view reflects a faulty and contradictory interpretation of the covenants. Fortunately, Moo's replacement volume in the *NICNT* series guides the reader back on track. Here is sound exegesis on the controverted issues respecting Paul and the law. Before summarizing Moo's position, however, we consider the problems inherent in the misinterpretation view.

The difficulty for Murray, as representative of this dominant view in contemporary biblical studies, is apparent in his tortuous handling of Lev 18:5. From the standpoint of his definition of covenant the Mosaic administration of the single Covenant of Grace stretching over the course of redemptive history is exclusively one of grace and promise, with no element of works. Contrary to the consensus of traditional Protestant theology, both Lutheran and Reformed, Murray maintains that there are no contrasting principles operating in the administration of the Mosaic Covenant. It is a covenant of pure grace. According to Murray, the principle of law enunciated in Lev 18:5 is the principle of *law in grace*, or *grace in law* (equivalent to that which is known in Reformed theology as the "third use of the law"). The principle "do this and live" is the principle of faith. This is how the OT citation is to be read in its original context, says Murray. How Paul can cite the Leviticus passage in support of antithetic principles of inheritance (law versus grace) is admittedly problematic. Murray resorts to speaking of "law as law" or "law in general" (the bare principle of the law, *i.e.* the law of nature underlying the original order of creation), not the law of Moses. From the standpoint of what law can and cannot do, the claims of justice require payment of what is justly earned on the basis of merit or demerit. Where there is (perfect) obedience there is life and blessing. Where there is transgression, death and condemnation ensue. That is the inextricable operation of divine law. When Paul asserts that those who are united to Christ as members of the New Man are no longer under law, but under grace (Rom. 6:14), Murray construes Paul to be speaking of law as law, law as commandment. Murray insists that Paul is not contrasting an earlier *legal* dispensation under Moses to a *gracious* dispensation in the present age. The letter/Spirit contrast cannot, in Murray's thinking, be descriptive of two sequential administrations of the "Covenant of Grace," the Mosaic and the New. Commenting on Rom 7:6, Murray explains: "'the oldness of the letter' refers to the law, and the law is called the letter because it was written. . . . It is law simply as written that is characterized as oldness and the oldness consists in the law."[23] He adds: "believers no longer serve in the servitude which law [law as law – not the Mosaic Covenant] ministers but in the newness of the liberty of which the Holy Spirit is the author."[24] Thus the contrast is between an *external writing of the law* (which is spiritual deadness) and an *internal writing of the law* (which is spiritual life).

This interpretation led Murray to conclude that Christ is the end of the law (Rom 10:4) in the sense that in Christ one no longer has need of seeking justification by means of the works of the law. Christ is the end of the law *to every one who believes.* Murray noted: "The foregoing observation regarding the force of the apostle's statement bears also upon an erroneous interpretation of this verse, enunciated by several commentators to the effect that the Mosaic law had propounded law as the means of procuring righteousness."[25] Murray clarified his objection when he denied that "in the [Israelite] theocracy works of law had been represented as the basis of salvation and that now by virtue of Christ's death this method had been displaced by the righteousness of faith."[26] On this latter point we have no quarrel with Murray. However, there were two insurmountable obstacles which stood in the way of Murray's reading of Scripture on these controverted points. First, there was his underlying antipathy for the notion of merit in connection with the Mosaic administration of the Covenant of Grace. (Covenant and merit were incongruous in his thinking.) This, in the second place, prevented him from seeing that the works-merit principle was operative *in the typological level of the Mosaic dispensation of grace.* (Although covenant theologians from the earliest days of the Reformation recognized a works-principle operative in the Mosaic Covenant, they generally failed to restrict its applicability to the temporal, typical sphere of the Israelite theocracy, in distinction from the eternal, antitypical sphere of heavenly salvation. There have been, nevertheless, notable exceptions here and there in the history of Reformed theology.) Present-day revisionists, unlike Murray, have gone one step further; they deny that the merit concept has any applicability to the (natural) relationship between God and Adam at creation. In their interpretation of the original "Covenant of Life" it is the grace of God, not law (*i.e.* merit), which is the basis of the promised reward. The inheritance held out to Adam, they contend, is obtained by sovereign (nonredemptive) grace, not works (law).

A former exponent of Murray's position on Paul and the law, Moisés Silva, has now joined the ranks of the revisionists by jettisoning the traditional law/gospel contrast altogether. This translates into a radically new understanding of the biblical covenants and of justification by faith (and good works). Silva acknowledges: "of all the themes touched on by Paul – indeed, of all the topics covered in NT theology – none has created more controversy than the apostle's view of the Mosaic law."[27] He observes that "Paul's specific statements about the law cannot be appreciated if they are treated in isolation from his more comprehensive views."[28] In the context of Galatians – and here the exegetical problem is the same as in Romans 10 – Silva begins by asking the question: does Paul's polemic with the Jews have a direct bearing on the apostle's citation of Lev 18:5? Might the apostle Paul possibly be employing the Judaistic (mis)interpretation of the Mosaic law for rhetorical effect? Silva says of Herman Ridderbos' solution that it is "too simple and appears contrived."[29] But, he urges, we are not to conclude that Paul had in mind the Mosaic law "pure and simple." That would lead to the error "common in the Lutheran tradition and in other circles (such as dispensationalism) that stress the discontinuity between law and gospel."[30] Silva's criticism also extends to exponents of Reformed theology (he names Meredith Kline as one example). It is "a middle way" that Silva champions in his most recent theological work, *Explorations in Exegetical Method: Galatians as a Test Case*. The contrast between law and promise, he theorizes, has respect to "instruments or sources of inheritance, life, and righteousness."[31] Where, if any place, does this principle of law actually pertain? If not in the Mosaic, does it function in the pre-Fall Adamic arrangement? Silva, the revisionist, presupposes that all covenants in Scripture are *gracious* dispositions on God's part (there is no place for human merit in the Creator/creature relationship). The key to Paul's theology of the law is his eschatology. From this vantage point, argues Silva, "the mode of existence based on the works of the law is eschatologically obsolete," thus implying that there was a time "before faith came" (Gal 3:23) when the principle of inheritance by law was in effect.[32] It eludes me how the criticism Silva levels against the traditional interpretation of Galatians does not also apply to his. In my judgment, Silva's proposed "middle way" leads to a dead end.

The dilemma Silva has created for himself causes him to reformulate the traditional interpretation of Hab 2:4. Here "we are faced with a major exegetical and theological problem."[33] The solution, Silva proposes, is found in the recognition that "for Habakkuk there was no such dichotomy between faith and faithfulness [= obedience] as we often assume."[34] Protestant orthodoxy, in Silva's judgment, misconstrued Paul's teaching on the law. (Lutheranism is thought to be the chief culprit.) The traditional Protestant distinction between faith and works, he suggests, is too sharp.

We turn to Moo, whom we regard to be a reliable and faithful interpreter of Paul on the law. Moo finds Paul's remarks in Rom 9:30-33 to be particularly relevant. (To be sure, one's theology of the law will have a direct bearing on the exegesis of this Pauline text.[35]) Moo contends that "this paragraph bears an importance out of proportion to its length."[36] He correctly relates the "law of righteousness" in Rom 9:31 to the "righteousness based on the law" in Rom 10:5. "Israel," explains Moo, "has failed to achieve a law that could confer righteousness because she could not produce those works that would be necessary to meet the law's demands and so secure the righteousness it promises."[37] This reading is not far removed from that of T. David Gordon, a reading which Moo finds "intriguing."[38] Both maintain that Israel was not to be faulted for identifying a works-principle in the Mosaic Covenant. No, her fatal error was in regarding that principle as the means of salvation. The difference between Gordon and Moo is that the latter concludes that the principle of law in the postlapsarian epoch is merely hypothetical, whereas the former rightly sees this principle as regulative of Israel's *temporal life* in Canaan.

Precisely how does Moo view the Mosaic Covenant, in contrast to the New? Or to pose the question in Moo's own words: "to what degree and in what sense does Paul regard the law as a means of justification?"[39] Moo answers:

> The view that God gave the law to Israel as a means of justification [= salvation] is now generally discredited, and rightly so. The OT presents the law as a means of regulating the covenant relationship that had already been established through God's grace. But, granted that the law was not given for the purpose of securing one's relationship before God [*i.e.* salvation], it may still be questioned whether it sets forth in theory a means of justification. We would argue that it does.[40]

If, following the interpretation of Moo, we were to construe the principle of law in the Mosaic Covenant as theoretical or hypothetical, how can we at the same time deny that "God gave the law to Israel as a means of justification?" This view, commonly held by Reformed covenant theologians, is inherently contradictory.[41] Earlier in his commentary on Rom 3:27-31 Moo recognized that in contrasting *torah,* the Mosaic Covenant, to the Abrahamic promise the apostle Paul is setting the principle of works over against the principle of faith. That is to say, Paul's negative assessment of the law is not directed merely to "law as law," or "law in general," as Murray posited, but to the Mosaic law in particular. "Rather than being entirely metaphorical, then, Paul's use of *nomos* embodies a 'play on words,' in which the characteristic demand of the Mosaic Covenant – works – is contrasted with the basic demand of the New Covenant (and of the OT, broadly understood; *cf.* chap. 4) – faith."[42] The reference of the term *nomos* is twofold: the law of nature established in the creation order and subsequently republished in the law of Moses. Moo rightly objects to Murray's exclusion of the latter from Paul's radical critique of the law.

Difficulties in Moo's position appear, however, in his exegesis of passages like Rom 5:13 ("where there is no law, there is no transgression," *cf.* Rom 4:15). What the apostle is saying here is that the declaration of the forgiveness of sins respecting those who are the recipients of God's love and mercy results in release from the legal demand of the *covenant of works,* the termination of *probation under law* (what was applicable to Adam at creation and to Israel under Moses – see especially Rom 7:7-13.)[43] The period from Moses to Christ is a parenthesis in the history of redemption.[44] The law was added to the promise; it served a tutelary function. The Mosaic administration of the Covenant of Grace was characterized by the peculiar works-principle regulative of Israel's *temporal* inheritance. (Salvation is always and only by grace through faith.)

The letter/Spirit contrast is the contrast between two administrations of the Covenant of Grace, one characterized by the external writing of the law on tablets of stone (the Mosaic Covenant) and another by the internal writing of the law on the fleshly tablets of the heart (the New Covenant). The former works condemnation and death (the letter kills); the latter righteousness and life (the Spirit makes alive).[45] The purpose of the Mosaic Covenant was to slay Israel, and in so doing convict her of sin and point her to Christ, the only one who could satisfy the righteous demands of God's law. It was not a misinterpretation of the law of Moses that slew Israel; it was Israel's failure to keep the covenant God made with her at Sinai. It was on the basis of Israel's own law-keeping, not that of another, that Israel was judged. Her covenant transgression was the grounds for condemnation. From the standpoint of biblical typology Israel's captivity in Babylon – what was just payment for her disobedience (according to the terms of the covenant established with Israel at Sinai) – symbolized the Hell-punishment which the Servant would suffer for his people. In so doing, the Son of God tasted the cup of God's wrath.

4. Romans 7: A Case Study

Doubtless the most notoriously difficult chapter in the NT is Romans 7. Satisfactory exegesis of this section in Paul's argument will necessarily have to accord with Paul's theology as a whole. Specifically, what is the nature of the regenerative work of God in the life of the believer? What is his/her relation to the law of God? How are we to understand the Christian's ongoing struggle with sin? And with respect to the elenctic function of the law of God what does it mean to be delivered from sin's dominion, such that we are no longer under law, but under grace?

Here Paul probes more fully into the subject of sanctification previously introduced in chap. 6 and concluded in chap. 8. He begins his discussion of the role of the law with an illustration from marriage (vss. 1-6). As long as the law is in effect – as long as one's spouse is living – the marriage partner is bound to fulfill his/her covenantal obligations. Death of the one party results in the severance of the covenantal (marriage) bond. The previous state of "bondage" gives way to liberty. The marriage analogy serves to illustrate Israel's place in the history of redemption. Paul's perspective here belongs to *historia salutis*. As long as the law of Moses is in effect (in the period from Sinai to Calvary), God's people are governed by the principle of temporal inheritance by works (law functioning here as a covenant of works) The dual sanctions of the covenant, blessing or curse (prosperity or hardship) in the land of promise, are associated with the Mosaic administration of redemptive covenant. Now that Christ has come the law as a covenant of works (operative in the restricted sphere of temporal life in Canaan) has been abrogated (Rom 10:4). Such was the tutelary purpose of the law for Israel under age (*cf.* Gal 3:6-4:7).

The subject of vss. 7-13 is particularly enigmatic. Murray entitles this section "Transitional Experience." In his opinion these verses are descriptive of the apostle's "pre-regenerate experience," wherein the unconverted Paul has been "aroused from his spiritual torpor and awakened to a sense of sin."[46] Saul has not yet been delivered from sin's dominion; he is still under the law. In this preparatory state he has not experienced the regenerating and quickening power of the Spirit of God. According to Murray's reading, vss. 14-25 describe Paul's battle with sin as a Christian. (This is indicated by the change in tense, from aorist to present.) How well does Murray's conception of a "transitional" state of preparation accord with the NT teaching on union with Christ, especially justification and sanctification? It is quite apparent that Murray's exegesis of these difficult verses of Paul introduces an erroneous conception of *preparation* into the conversion process, something that is out of accord with Reformed (and Pauline) soteriology. The solution lies elsewhere.

Moo regards Romans 7 as the climax of Paul's negative critique of the Mosaic law.[47] (For this reason this passage deserves our close attention.) Being much more sensitive to the redemptive-historical orientation of the apostle Paul than was Murray in his commentary, Moo looks to Paul's earlier remarks in this letter concerning the place of the law in the history of salvation. From the standpoint of the history of the covenants, the law served a temporary purpose; it served to exacerbate Israel's spiritual plight. Moo suggests that the *egô* of vss. 7-13 "is not Israel, but *egô* is Paul in solidarity with Israel."[48] Moo explains: "In the years before Sinai sin was 'dead' to Israel."[49] During this time Israel was alive, which is to say, she was "existing." The law enters Israel's experience in order to convict her of sin, to place Israel, together with all people, under the curse of the law. Moo understands the principle of law enunciated in Lev 18:5 to have reference to a purely *hypothetical* situation of salvation obtained on the basis of perfect obedience (*if* that were possible).[50]

What is most notable in Moo's approach to Romans 7 is the prominence given to Pauline perspective on *historia salutis*. Former preoccupation with *ordo salutis* prevented exegetes from rightly interpreting this text. Such was the case in Murray's commentary. The difficulties for the interpreter, however, do not end here. Equally problematic are the closing verses of the chapter. Is Paul in vss. 14-25 describing the Christian's struggle with sin? Murray, following the Augustinian tradition, answers in the affirmative. Moo is persuaded otherwise; he believes that Paul is analyzing the life of the unregenerate person. The central issue in these verses still remains the relation between the law, *i.e.* the commandments of

God, and life in the Spirit. We will return subsequently to this matter when we consider the Christian's experience with the law of God in this present (semi-)eschatological age, the age characterized by the overlap of old and new aeons. But first, Paul's teaching on the place of Israel in the plan of God.

5. Israel and the New Covenant

Whether or not the apex of the apostle's theological argument is found here in Romans 9-11 (or earlier in chap. 5), this section of the letter is pivotal to the whole of the argument. Setting aside the doctrine of double predestination, election and reprobation, concerning which both Murray and Moo concur in their interpretation of Paul, the chief issue in this section is twofold: (1) the nature of ancient Israel's election, and (2) the meaning of the term "fulness" in chap. 11.

Murray's interpretation on covenant and election is in need of reformulation. Although Murray distinguishes between decretive election, *i.e.* individual election unto salvation, and Israel's national election, he maintains that both are based on sovereign grace. To be sure, ancient Israel's election was not based on her own righteousness or merit (see Deut 9:1-6). It was an expression of God's own sovereign good pleasure and purpose. The national election of Israel was a sovereign act and it was an act of grace – *if* we are referring to the original choice of Israel in distinction from the continuing bestowal of the typological kingdom blessings. (The "common grace" covenant established by God with all creation after the Noahic flood was a sovereign administration of *nonredemptive* grace.) In order to avoid ambiguity in our theological formulation on covenant and election, however, it is necessary that the phrase "sovereign grace" be reserved for God's redemptive provision, Christ being the surety of salvation for the elect (consistent with Calvinistic soteriology). In light of Murray's imprecision it is not surprising to find in his theology of the covenant(s) a virtual equation between covenant and election.[51] Closer to the biblical conception is the distinction found in traditional covenant theology between covenant in the broader and narrower senses. And better still is Kline's formulation in *By Oath Consigned*, wherein he speaks of the "proper purpose" of redemptive covenant as the salvation of the elect.[52] Kline rightly resists the temptation to reduce redemptive covenant to election.

The point of all this is that God's "proper purpose" in covenanting with Israel at Mount Sinai was her salvation. But God's saving purpose pertained only to the true Israel of God. Not all the sons and daughters of Israel are true Israel. There is a distinction between the natural seed and the elect seed, between Abraham's children, Ishmael and Isaac, and his grandchildren, Jacob and Esau. There was and remains a remnant according to grace throughout the ages. As Murray observes, the promises of God, properly speaking, pertain to the remnant, not the mass of Israel. (We further add: the Pauline conception of the "fullness of Israel" is decidedly eschatological, not strictly numerical or quantitative.[53])

The question remains: how are we to understand the relationship between ancient, theocratic Israel and the New Covenant people of God? Does ethnic Israel retain a special place in the history of redemption? What does Paul mean when he says that "all Israel" will be saved in the latter days (Rom 11:26)? Both Murray's and Moo's answer to these questions could be strengthened by fuller and clearer discussion of the nature of the Mosaic theocracy.[54] Firstly, the theocratic kingdom of Israel has been supplanted by the New Covenant community, ordered according to principles laid down in the NT canon. Ethnic Israel is no longer the holy nation. The symbolico-typological dimension of the Mosaic economy has given way to the realities of the Spirit-born people of God, the pentecostal church of Christ. Now we worship in Spirit and truth, rather than in shadow and type (Jn 4:23,24). Spiritual worship is eschatological at its core.[55] Secondly, the concept of the remnant according to grace has relevance to the entire period of the church down to the close of the age. Then the church will attain to the fullness of Christ, its head. The apostle speaks both of the "fullness" of the Gentiles and the "fullness" of Israel. This Pauline conception, what is part of the mystery revealed in the present time, applies equally to (converted) Jews and Gentiles; it brings into view the total number of the elect of God, not, as Moo conjectures, "the corporate entity of the nation of Israel as it exists at a particular point in time."[56] The fullness of "Israel" comprises the salvation of elect Jews and Gentiles, the true Israel of God (Gal 6:16). That Paul is entertaining the idea of a massive conversion of Jews and Gentiles at the end of the age is unlikely. What is certain, ethnic Israel retains no special status in the period between the two advents of Christ (nor in the eternal kingdom). In Christ there is no distinction between Jew and Gentile. Moo is mistaken in thinking that in Romans 11 Paul "needed to remind Gentile Christians of the continuing significance of Israel's [national] election."[57] The revelation of the "mystery" is made known in Christ, the fulfillment of the ancient covenant promises (Rom 11:25; 16:25-27), the one who has torn down once for all the dividing wall (Eph 2:14).

6. Eschatological Life: The Tension and the Resolution

In the case study presented by the apostle in Romans 7 we observed that the author weaved together two distinct aspects, that of *historia salutis* and *ordo salutis*. Moo understands the "I" of vss. 7-13 as a personification of Israel's experience under the gospel (the promise given to Abraham) and under the law (the covenant mediated through Moses).[58] The remaining verses of the chapter rehearse Paul's own experience with the law. At this point Murray's interpretation of Rom 7:1-25 is to be preferred over Moo's. The closing portion of the seventh chapter is best understood as a description of the regenerate's experience of the law of God, one which comports well with what Paul stated earlier in Romans 6 in connection with the believer's experiential union with Christ. One of the practical benefits of that union is deliverance from the dominion of sin. The sin that yet remains in the believer's members is still the source of spiritual conflict. This remaining sin is identified as the "law of sin," and its effect is altogether different from the dominion of sin which formerly held sway over the unregenerate life. The warfare is real and intense, yet the believer's union with Christ has broken the sinner's bondage to sin and death. The deliverance is "already" experienced, but "not yet" perfected in sanctification. Although the believer has been definitively sanctified by virtue of union with Christ – and continues to be made more and more holy through the renewing and cleansing work of the Spirit of God (the progressive aspect of sanctification) – that perfection in holiness awaits our translation into heaven (the intermediate state) or, more appropriately, future glorification.[59] For the present time the Christian is weighed down by this "body of death," and in the intermediate state, being "naked," he/she longs to be clothed with the heavenly dwelling (2 Cor 5:1-5). Despite differences in the interpretation of this passage in Romans, both Murray and Moo fundamentally share a Reformed soteriological understanding of Pauline theology.

Gleaning from both Murray and Moo, we propose the following summary of Paul's teaching on sanctification: the Christian possesses a new, regenerate nature, not two warring natures (the old and the new). Christians, whose spiritual experience is characterized by the tension between the two ages, notably, the tension between what has already been realized by the Spirit of Christ and what awaits future consummation, presently wrestle with the lingering effects of the old age, the "law of sin." The definitive breach with sin means that believers are no longer identified with the Old Man (Adam), but rather with the New Man (Christ Jesus). The fulfillment of the covenant made with Abraham, Moses, and David is, according to Paul's teaching, threefold in signification: (1) cosmic, the antithesis between old and new aeons; (2) corporate, the antithesis between the Old Man and the New Man; and (3) individual, the antithesis between flesh and Spirit. (There is some degree of overlap between these contrasting pairs. For example, the flesh/Spirit antithesis has cosmic and corporate implications as well.) There is, likewise, the interplay between the "indicative" and the "imperative." The Pauline parenesis is based on the reality of that which belongs to every believer by virtue of his/her union with Christ. Christians are exhorted to obey the commandments of God because they have been empowered by the Spirit to fulfill the righteous demands of the law (see, *e.g.* Rom 8:1-11 and chaps. 12-16).

Much remains to be discussed in Paul's grandest letter of all, the Letter to the Romans. The present focus on Paul's theology of the law has enabled us to compare (in limited space) these worthy commentaries of Murray and Moo. Clearly, we are indebted to both of them for their meticulous work and studied opinions. The selection of Moo to replace Murray in the *NICNT* series provides the reader exposure to some of the best thinking in contemporary Reformed scholarship. Evangelical theology in its most consistent expression is Reformed theology. And it is the nature of this theology to be reformed and ever reforming according to the teaching of Scripture. The *solas* of the Protestant Reformation - notably the formal principle, Scripture alone, and the material principle, (justification by) faith alone - remain as vital to the formulation of biblical theology today as in the past. God's salvation is the manifestation of his sovereign grace and mercy in Christ Jesus (Rom 3:21-26). Paul's letter to the Roman Christians sets forth for us the apostle's fullest theological explication of this saving action of God. The Reformed tradition's slogan *sola Deo gloria* might well serve as a succinct summary of Paul's words of doxology in Rom 11:33-36 and 16:25-27, a spontaneous response of faith which looks to Christ, the hope of glory.

ENDNOTES

[1]See the important discussion in *The Law, the Gospel, and the Modern Christian: Five Views*, ed. W. G. Strickland (Grand Rapids, 1993), reviewed by the present writer elsewhere in this volume.
[2]Murray 2.vii.
[3]Consult Donald A. Carson's helpful essay, "Unity and Diversity in the New Testament: The Possibility of Systematic Theology," in *Scripture and Truth,* ed. D. A. Carson and J. D. Woodbridge (Grand Rapids: Zondervan, 1983); also Robert L Thomas, "Current Hermeneutical Trends: Toward Explanation or Obfuscation?" *JETS* 39 (1996) 241-256.
[4]Moo 27.
[5]*Ibid.* 221.
[6]Murray 1:4. Murray contrasts Israel under age in the period of the Old Covenant with her "mature, full-fledged sonship" under the New Covenant. "The adoption of the Old," says Murray, "was propaedeutic" (2:5).
[7]N. T. Wright, *The Climax of the Covenant: Christ and the Law in Pauline Theology* (Edinburgh, 1991; Minneapolis, 1993). See Moo's review in *JETS* 39 (1996) 663-664.
[8]Moo correctly observes: "'Flesh' (*sarx*) is a key Pauline theological term. It refers essentially to human existence, with emphasis on the transitory, weak, frail nature of that existence" (Moo 47).
[9]Murray 2.182. Murray is reticent to employ the covenant concept to the pact made between the Father and the Son in eternity. The reason is threefold: (1) the term "covenant" in the Bible first appears in Gen 6 (the postlapsarian era); (2) the incongruity drawn by Murray between covenant (as a *gracious* disposition) and the principle of "merit" (what Murray explains as the principle of "perfect legal reciprocity"); and (3) Murray's peculiar distinction between man-righteousness and God-righteousness (only the latter, argues Murray, can be the basis of man's reception of eternal life). Compare further my doctoral study, "The Mosaic Covenant and the Concept of Works in Reformed Hermeneutics" (Th.D. dissertation, Westminster Theological Seminary, 1980) 242-249. See also note 16 below.
[10]F. F. Bruce maintains that Paul "writes this greatest polemic in the exposition and defense of the gospel of grace" (Murray l:xiii).
[11]Moo 90. The question of the "center" of Paul's theology (or the Bible more generally) oftentimes carries more weight than is warranted. There is a richness and diversity in the canonical writings that makes difficult any attempt to reduce the message of Scripture to one central thought or idea.
[12]See, *e.g.*, Don B. Garlington, *Faith, Obedience and Perseverance* (*Wissenchaftliche Untersuchungen zum Neuen Testament,* 79; Tubingen, 1994) and my review of this study included in this collected writings.
[13]On the subject of justification and (future) judgment according to works, see Chapter Six.
[14]*Ibid.* 1.27.
[15]*Ibid.* 1.27, n.21.
[15]*Ibid.* 1.31. Murray adds: "Man-righteousness, even though perfect and measuring up to all the demands of God's perfection, would never be adequate to the situation created by our sins. . . . Nothing serves to point up the effectiveness, completeness, and irrevocableness of the justification which it is the apostle's purpose to establish and vindicate than this datum set forth at the outset – the righteousness which is unto justification is one characterized by the perfection belonging to all that God is and does. It is a "God-

righteousness.'" The justification of sinners is, as Murray notes, "complete and irreversible" (1.274).

His identification of the righteousness given to sinners justified by grace as a God-level righteousness is tantamount to blurring the Creator/creature distinction. (According to Murray, even the reward of eternal life that would have been granted to Adam after successful completion of probation would have been based upon God's own faithfulness to his word of promise, eternal life being grounded upon a God-righteousness). Murray's formulation confounds the ontologic and the juridical categories; it also falls to do justice to the biblical teaching that Christ as the Second Adam accomplished our *full* salvation, having obtained for the elect both the forgiveness of sins and life everlasting on grounds of his perfect obedience.

[17]"When Paul says 'without the law' the absoluteness of this negation must not be toned down. He means this without any reservation or equivocation in reference to the justifying righteousness which is the theme of this part of the epistle. . . . To equivocate here is to distort what could not be more plainly and consistently stated" (*ibid.* 1.109). Murray later explains: "In the sustained argument of the preceding verses [Rom 3:27ff.] the negation of works of law as having any instrumentality or efficiency in justification has in view works performed in obedience to divine commandment and therefore the law contemplated is the law of commandment from whatever aspect it may be regarded. What is in view is law as commanding to compliance and performance. And the insistence of the apostle is that any works in performance of any such commandment are of no avail in justification" (1.126).

[18]*Ibid.* 1:135.

[19]*Ibid.* 2.26.

[20]Compare Murray's discussion in "Appendix B" (2.249-251) with his essay "The Adamic Administration," *Collected Writings of John Murray* (4 volumes; Edinburgh: The Banner of Truth Trust, 1977-1982) 2.47-59. Geerhardus Vos articulates clearly the classic Protestant understanding, stating that "the right of God to curse in case of transgression of the law is, from Paul's point of view, after all but the reverse side of his prerogative to bless and reward with the gift of eternal life where the law is obeyed" ("The Alleged Legalism in Paul's Doctrine of Justification," *Redemptive History and Biblical Interpretation: The Shorter Writings of Geerhardus Vos,* ed. R. B. Gaffin, Jr. [Phillipsburg, 1980], 389). Vos speaks of the "twofold function of rewarding obedience and punishing disobedience, as a supreme and inalienable attribute of the divine nature, something which God cannot deny without denying himself" (p. 392).

As an exponent of the revisionist school, Robert Letham undermines the parallel drawn by the apostle Paul in Romans 5 between the obedience of the two Adams. He asserts: "In divine justice, the link between sin and punishment is vital" (*The Word of Christ* [Contours of Christian Theology; Downers Grove, 1993], 126). Missing here is the vital link between obedience and reward. The same view is argued by David McWilliams in "The Covenant Theology of the 'Westminster Confession of Faith' and Recent Criticism," *WTJ* 53 (1991) 109-24.

[21]*The Confession of Faith* (Inverness, 1976) 42. Herman Bavinck notes that power was granted to Adam in the beginning "to keep the law and earn eternal life" (*The Last Things: Hope for this World and the Next,* ed. J. Bolt and trans. J. Vriend [Grand Rapids: Baker, 1996] 66).

[22]For a concise summary of the biblical teaching on justification see J. I. Packer, "Justification," *New Bible Dictionary* (third edition; Downers Grove: InterVarsity, 1996), 636-640; consult further, P. T. O'Brien, "Justification in Paul and Some Crucial Issues of the Last Two Decades," *Right with God: Justification in the Bible and the World*, ed. D. A.

Carson (Grand Rapids: Baker, 1992) 69-95. For analysis of the diversity of Reformed thought, see Chapters One and Four.
[23]Murray 1.246. Murray's exegesis and interpretation are anticipated in Patrick Fairbairn, *The Revelation of Law in Scripture* (Phillipsburg: Presbyterian and Reformed, 1996 [original 1869], see esp. 445-446.
[24]*Ibid.* 1.247.
[25]*Ibid.* 2.50. Murray is unclear as to when and under what conditions justification by works prevailed. Is he thinking of the pre- or postlapsarian epochs? If the latter, it would be of necessity only *hypothetical.* (We contest the notion of a hypothetical principle of works-salvation as much as we contest the early dispensational teaching that God tested Israel in the time of the Old Covenant by offering salvation on the basis of Israel's own obedience. After Adam's fall into sin, the way to [eternal] life is impossible for humankind on grounds of works-righteousness. The original Covenant of Works has forever been broken, thus necessitating the God-man to do for sinners what they can not do for themselves. Jesus' conversation with the rich young ruler only serves to highlight the folly and frustration of contemplating or attempting the impossible.)
[26]*Ibid.* 2.51.
[27]Moisés Silva, *Explorations in Exegetical Method: Galatians as a Test Case* (Grand Rapids: Baker, 1996) 159. Silva considers Thomas R. Schreiner and Frank Thielman to be defenders of "a well-nuanced traditional view" (p. 159, n.2). Compare my critique of these works in Chapter Nine.
[28]*Ibid.* 169. Silva adds: "The *place* of the Mosaic law in that history [*i.e.* the history of redemption] therefore becomes the fundamental problem before us. Or to put it more provocatively, we cannot possibly grasp Paul's teaching about the law unless we understand his eschatology."
[29]*Ibid.* 193.
[30]*Ibid.* 190.
[31]*Ibid.* 193.
[32]*Ibid.* 176, *original italicized.*
[33]*Ibid.* 166.
[34]*Ibid.* 167.
[35]No responsible exegete can avoid the need for theological coherence (the systematic or dogmatic impulse). Presuppositionalism is operative at every level of the exegetico-theological enterprise. The real question is: which presuppositions are consistent and true to the teaching of Scripture. Ultimately, Scripture is its own interpreter; there is a circular relationship between theology (including biblical presuppositionalism) and exegesis.
[36]Moo 620.
[37]*Ibid.* 627, *italics his.*
[38]*Ibid.* 626, n.41. See T. David Gordon, "Why Israel did not Obtain Torah-Righteousness: A Translation Note on Rom 9:32," *WTJ* 54 (1992) 163-166.
[39]Moo 155.
[40]*Ibid.*
[41]Moo maintains that Rom 2:7-13 and 7:10 suggest such a view. "This issue," he notes, "is related in traditional Reformed theology to the debate over the existence and nature of the 'Covenant of Works' and the place of the Mosaic law within that covenant" (p. 156). Moo refers here to R. T. Beckwith's "hypothetical Covenant of Works" (p. 155, n.74).
[42]*Ibid.* 249-250.
[43]Compare Meredith G. Kline, "Gospel until the Law: Rom 5:1-14 and the Old Covenant," *JETS* 34 (1991) 433-446.

[44]Bavinck speaks of the Mosaic epoch as an "intermezzo" (*The Last Things* 97). Willem VanGemeren objects to this interpretation; see his *The Progress of Redemption: The Story of Salvation from Creation to the New Jerusalem* (Grand Rapids: Zondervan, 1988) 489, n.14. VanGemeren's biblical-theological exposition, however, falters on a lack of understanding of the history of Reformed doctrine. That which VanGemeren criticizes, namely, the idea of the works-principle operative in the Mosaic Covenant, is standard fare in mainstream Reformed thought, not the anomaly he imagines.
[45]Moo 421. Moo's theology of the Mosaic Covenant fares better than that of Murray or Silva, both in terms of Moo's straightforward exegesis of Lev 18:5cited in Paul's letters and in Moo's identification of the Mosaic Covenant as (formally) one of works (law), not faith (gospel). As noted, in his most recent writing Silva rejects the classic ("Lutheran") law/gospel antithesis.
[46]Murray 1.255.
[47]Moo 423.
[48]*Ibid.* 431.
[49]*Ibid.* 437.
[50]*Ibid.* 439.
[51]Moo properly distinguishes between "a general election of Israel as a nation" and "a specific election to salvation of individual Israelites, and others (p. 675, n.20). Murray adds a further note of clarification regarding his understanding: "It is worthy of note that although Paul distinguishes between Israel and Israel, seed and seed, children and children (*cf.* 9:6-13) he does not make this discrimination in terms of covenant so as to distinguish between those who are in the covenant in a broader sense and those who are actual partakers of its grace" (2.100, n.47).
[52]Meredith G. Kline, *By Oath Consigned: A Reinterpretation of the Covenant Signs of Circumcision and Baptism* (Grand Rapids: Eerdmans, 1968) 34. For a summary analysis of the teaching of early covenant theology, see Lyle D. Bierma, *German Calvinism in the Confessional Age: The Covenant Theology of Caspar Olevianus* (Grand Rapids: Baker, 1996), esp. 48-49.
[53]Compare Herman Ribberbos' discussion of "fullness" in *Paul: An Outline of His Theology,* trans. J. R. de Witt (Grand Rapids: Eerdmans, 1975) 354-361.
[54]Justifiably, Moo finds no evidence in Romans 11 for "a restoration of the land as integral to the eschatological rejuvenation of Israel," contrary to the opinion of Walter C. Kaiser and others (p. 724, n.59). On the broader issues relating to Israel and the church see the following studies: *Continuity and Discontinuity: Perspectives on the Relationship Between the Old and New Testaments,* ed. J. S. Feinberg (Westchester: Crossway, 1988); *Dispensationalism and the Church: The Search for Definition,* ed. C. A. Blaising and D. L Bock (Grand Rapids: Zondervan, 1992); David E. Holwerda, *Jesus and Israel: One Covenant or Two?* (Grand Rapids: Eerdmans, 1995); and my treatment of the subject in Chapter Fifteen.
[55]See especially Geerhardus Vos, "The Eschatological Aspect of the Pauline Conception of the Spirit," *Redemptive History* 125; and his *The Pauline Eschatology* (Grand Rapids: Eerdmans, 1979).
[56]Moo 723. Paul's argument turns full circle. Earlier in chap. 9 the apostle distinguished between Israel according to the flesh and true Israel (the elect seed comprising faithful Jews and Gentiles).
[57]Moo 739.

[58]Compare Mark W. Karlberg, "Law in Pauline Eschatology: The Historical Qualification of Justification by Faith" (Th.M. thesis, Westminster Theological Seminary, 1977), and my revision of that thesis here in Chapter Seven.
[59]See esp. John Murray, "The Agency in Definitive Sanctification," *Collected Writings* 2.285-2

CHAPTER ELEVEN

PAUL, THE OLD TESTAMENT, AND JUDAISM (A Review Article*)

Discussions on the topic of Paul and the Mosaic law continue to occupy some of the best minds in contemporary theology. The complexity of the issues involved and the importance of the subject for a biblical theology of the Old and New Testaments and for Christian dogmatics account for current preoccupation with this topic. In the interests of contributing further to ongoing dialogue, interaction with Colin G. Kruse's recent study, *Paul, the Law, and Justification*, is, I believe, timely and constructive. Kruse begins by surveying briefly recent trends in NT scholarship. The limited space afforded to this overview, however, may account for the author's at times less than accurate summary of the various positions. As regards Kruse's position, special mention should be made of the views of Frank Thielman and Thomas Schreiner: somewhat surprising, however, is the omission of Douglas Moo's work in this opening survey.

From the standpoint of historical theology, Kruse's interpretation is characteristically Lutheran, rather than Reformed. The following essay will indicate reasons for this classification, as well as address the central exegetico-theological issue in the current debate. The pressing question is whether or not the Protestant reformers of the sixteenth and seventeenth centuries understood correctly the foundational doctrine of justification by grace through faith. Respecting the broader theological issues at stake, the modern-day controversy brings to the fore the agelong problem concerning the relationship between the Old and New Covenants, including the question of the relationship between ancient, theocratic Israel's compliance with the stipulations of the law of Moses and God's bestowal of temporal rewards and punishments. Is the classic Protestant antithesis between law and gospel valid? According to James D. G. Dunn, one of the most influential critics of the traditional view, the Pauline expression "works of the law" has exclusive reference to the ethnic "boundary markers" of theocratic Israel, namely, the ceremonial laws. While Kruse is correct in opposing this line of interpretation, he does not succeed in producing a consistent and thoroughgoing critique.[1]

A focal issue in Kruse's interpretation of the Mosaic law is Paul's teaching on OT religion seen in the light of Christ's coming. Like Thielman's *Paul and the Law*, this study offers a contextual analysis of Paul's letters, starting with the Letter to the Galatians, the benchmark for Paul's theology of the law.[2] Basic to his interpretation of Paul, Kruse rightly contends that Paul's negative assessments of the Mosaic law are not merely aimed at Judaistic misunderstanding of the law. "The works of the law," writes Kruse, "are the carrying out of all those things which the law requires."[3] Unfortunately, however, Kruse misreads Judaism itself. "To say that Paul regarded the works of the law as good works done to amass merit," notes Kruse, "is to have him misrepresent Judaism, for in principle Judaism was not a religion in which the law was observed for this reason, but simply because it was required under the terms of the Mosaic Covenant."[4] This reading of Judaism conflicts with the portrait given in the NT; across its pages we find Judaism's soteriology to be fundamentally at odds with the teachings of Christ.

Kruse concedes that his own view is not without problems. "To escape the horns of this dilemma," he writes, "it is probably best to say that Paul's argument was not with Judaism in principle, and certainly not with the religion of the OT, but with those who, by the demands they were placing upon his Galatian converts, were insisting that salvation did depend upon the observance of certain demands of the law."[5] As regards the doctrine of salvation, the NT lays out the clear-cut, irreconcilable differences between the teaching of Judaism and the OT. To be sure, first-century Judaism contains a diverse body of beliefs. Nevertheless, a common thread runs through Judaism as a whole. The major cleavage between Judaism and OT religion lies in their respective doctrines of sin and the law of God.[6] Though the central theme in the opening chapters of Romans, Paul's teaching on the universal plight of humankind is prominent throughout his writings. All humankind is guilty of transgression of God's law. The law at Sinai, stipulating obedience *as the meritorious grounds of temporal blessing* (see Lev 18:5 and its NT citations), reinstitutes the original law of creation in a manner appropriate to the Mosaic dispensation of the economy of redemption.[7] In the Israelite theocracy the reward for obedience is life and prosperity in the land of Canaan. Under the Sinaitic Covenant the principle of works-inheritance operative in the restricted sphere of temporal life in the promised land, was uniquely adapted to the historico-covenantal context of theocratic Israel. The works-inheritance principle, functioning within the broader economy of redemption, served God's sovereign, electing purpose in salvation. Temporal blessing(s), appropriate to the typological setting of Israel's life in Canaan, was contingent upon Israel's satisfaction of the legal demand of the Mosaic law, which obligation appeared as a reinstatement of the original demand placed upon the First Adam at creation. Herein lies the significance of the law's pedagogical, tutelary function (*cf.* Galatians 3 and 4).[8] Accordingly, the reintroduction of the "Covenant of Works" was modified in postlapsarian, redemptive history. The covenant of law under Moses was, after all, a renewal of the single "Covenant of Grace" spanning the entire age from the Fall to the Consummation. Salvation is only by grace through faith, and rests exclusively upon the merits of Christ's substitutionary obedience, not human works. With respect to faith and works (grace and law), there is no mixing or mingling of the two.[9]

Contrary to the teaching of Judaism, both Jew and Gentile stand guilty before God. The law works wrath and those under the law, whether the law of Moses or the law of creation, are under the curse of God for transgression (*cf.* Hos 6:7 and

Is 24:5).[10] The fatal error of the Judaizers lay in their misunderstanding and misuse of the Mosaic law; the Jews thought that salvation could be obtained on the basis of works-righteousness. (Obedience to the law was thus mistakenly viewed as the meritorious grounds of salvation, *i.e.*, life everlasting.) Unlike OT religion, Judaism not only minimized the power of sin, it also assumed a natural ability on the part of sinners to covenant with God (to enter into and/or maintain the covenant relationship). It effectively obscured the need for vicarious atonement, that which was to be accomplished by the coming messianic Servant of the Lord, indeed by the One who had come, fulfilling the promise of God to Abraham. A true Jew, Paul taught, was one who believed and practiced the teachings of OT religion.[11] On the road to Damascus Paul experienced the regenerating and renewing work of the Spirit necessary for divine reconciliation. Having been converted and received into membership within the Israel of God, the apostle renounced Judaism for Christianity, the full-flowering of OT religion (Gal 6:16; *cf.* Phil 3:3-11 and Rom 2:25-29).

Speaking of the believers whom Paul confronted in Galatia, Kruse remarks: "They must recognize that just as they began their new life as believers with the Spirit (and independently of the works of the law), so they must seek its completion in the same way. The question implies of course, that the nomistic thrust of the Judaizers' teaching was erroneous."[12] Kruse adds that "both the legalistic and nomistic implications of the Judaizers' teaching were wrong. The works of the law make possible neither the initial experience of the Spirit nor his ongoing activity among believers; believing what was heard is all that is needed."[13] The problem with this interpretation is twofold: first, in this monograph Kruse's definition of legalism and nomism is ambiguous and ill-defined; second, his understanding of the place of obedience under the New Covenant is misformulated. What, according to our author, constitutes nomism and what constitutes legalism? In raising this issue we are addressing the question regarding the chief (and peculiar) function of the Mosaic law in the history of redemption. What does the law require? Why does Paul set faith over against works precisely in regards to the two contrasting covenants, the Mosaic and the New? Why does he place the principle of works (Lev 18:5) in opposition to the principle of faith (Hab 2:4)? And why does Paul state that the (Mosaic) law is "not of faith" (Gal 3:12)? What did he mean when he said that the law was *added* to the promise? The only satisfactory explanation, we contend, is found in the apostle Paul's *typological* interpretation of Israelite history. (The ancient, theocratic kingdom of Israel was finally abolished at the time of the destruction of Jerusalem in 70 A.D.). The apostle recognized a *legal* principle at work on the symbolico-typical level of physical life in Canaan: temporal blessing and prosperity were contingent upon Israel's own obedience, not upon the substitutionary obedience of the Lord's Anointed. Herein lies the grounds for the contrasting principles of inheritance, faith and works (grace and law).[14]

Kruse confusingly describes the Mosaic Covenant as nomistic, not legalistic. Under the former dispensation, the dispensation of law, we are told, Israelite believers were obliged to keep the commandments in order to enjoy God's blessing(s). While not the meritorious ground of reward, obedience to the Mosaic law was nevertheless required. What was requisite of Israel as a nation and as individual members is no longer requisite of Gentiles in this present dispensation, the new age inaugurated by Christ. Kruse explains:

> In the case of the Gentile believers in particular, Paul insists that they must be free from the law as a regulatory norm, *i.e.* they were not to become covenantal nomists, people justified by grace through faith but then required to live under the law. Jewish believers might live like nomists if they wished, because they were used to living under the law and for them it meant no change in lifestyle, it entailed no extra conditions for justification apart from faith in Jesus Christ. But in the case of the Gentiles it would mean a change in lifestyle; it would involve extra conditions for justification. So then, what was covenantal nomism for the Jewish believers became legalism when applied to the Gentiles.[15]

Despite disagreement with Dunn's position, Kruse ends up holding a similar reading on Paul. He cannot consistently uphold the classic Protestant law/gospel antithesis. The difference between Old and New Covenants is reduced to that between what is merely external ("letter") and what is internal ("Spirit"): the Old is characterized by outward, ceremonial observance of the Mosaic law, what Kruse views simply as a matter of "lifestyle." Kruse counters Reformed teaching on the "third use" of the law, namely, the regulative or normative use of the law in the life of the Christian. But contrary to Kruse and Lutheran interpreters, obedience to the commandments of God is required of believers in both dispensations of the "Covenant of Grace," Old and New. *Obedience to God's law, however, functions in different ways with respect to the particular covenantal arrangement established by God, whether legal or gracious.* While Israel's obedience to the whole law of God (civil, moral, ceremonial) was never the meritorious grounds of salvation, it was the basis of temporal prosperity in Canaan. On the spiritual level, God's sanctifying work of grace made obedience the necessary outworking of true, saving faith. (There is no difference in this respect between OT and NT saints.[16]) Kruse's view of covenantal nomism cannot make sense of the radical Pauline contrast between two principles of inheritance (law versus gospel). "Seeing that neither the traditional Reformation view nor Dunn's view is without problems," Kruse concludes, "a third option was seen to be preferable. The works of the law are best understood as the fulfillment of all that the law requires, not in any sense of amassing merit before God, but simply because that was what was required under the terms of the Mosaic covenant."[17] He then offers the following as an explanation:

> What [Paul] warns [the Galatian believers] against is probably not a "bad" legalism which requires the doing of good works to *amass merit* (it is questionable whether first century Jews themselves operated in this way). Rather, he warns them against what might be called a "good" legalism which involves doing the works of the law, simply because this is what the law itself demands, and believing that this will bring justification. Even this so-called "good" legalism must be avoided because "all who rely on the works of the law are under a curse."[18]

The line drawn by Kruse between nomism and legalism becomes exceedingly thin. Paul the apostle, on the other hand, speaks of the Old Covenant unequivocally as a ministration of death and condemnation, a legal dispensation which gave the appearance of jeopardizing God's promise to Abraham.[19] Since the arrival of Jesus the Messiah, whom N. T. Wright identifies as "the climax of the covenant," no longer is it a question of Gentiles being assimilated into the old, national covenant.[20] In short, the Israelite theocracy had come to an end. God's saving act in Christ does not bring about a mere change in lifestyle, but marks a decisive transition in the history of redemption. Under the the new and better covenant the operation of the works-principle had been *abrogated* and the shadowy form of the Old Covenant, including the symbolico-typical aspect of Israel's life in earthly Canaan, had given way to the realities of the new, eschatological age of the Spirit (*cf.* Jn 4:24).[21] Kruse's nomistic reading of the law obscures the fact that the curse of the Mosaic law had been laid upon the entire house of Israel, comprising both the elect and the nonelect. Kruse mistakenly reasons that "When [Paul] says that those who are of the law are under a curse, he is not necessarily overlooking the fact that the law makes provision for repentance and forgiveness for those who trust in the covenant grace of God. What it is saying is that those who trust, not in that covenant grace, but in their fulfillment of the law's demands, will come under the curse of that law."[22]

Contrary to Kruse's interpretation, all Israel was made subject to God's wrath and indignation for covenant unfaithfulness: according to the terms of God's covenant with Israel, exile in a foreign land was just payment for the sin of disobedience. Those who were once "my people" became "not my people" (Hosea 1-2). The Mosaic administration thus served its tutelary function in convicting Israel of transgression; her bondage to sin and death was typified in the Babylonian exile. Although not consistently applied, Kruse does acknowledge that "the law operates on the principle of performance, calling for obedience to its requirements, and promising life to those who do obey. This is not the principle of faith which calls people to trust in God's promise of justification, even when they find themselves under the curse of the law for having failed to do what it demands."[23] At this point in his argument Kruse incorporates the traditional Protestant law/gospel contrast. The law's function is "to keep [Israel] from moral danger until Christ should appear." He explains: "Thus, in Galatians, Paul portrays a custodial and disciplinarian role for the law. It kept people from danger until the coming of faith. It could not itself provide people who were under the power of sin with a means of justification. But its role was positive in the sense that it was intended to keep people from danger until the coming of Christ and faith in him."[24] The function of the Mosaic law was chiefly negative, though ultimately serving the purpose of God's sovereign, electing grace. (The Mosaic Covenant was, assuredly, an administration of the Covenant of Grace.) At an earlier point in his work Kruse stated that with the coming of Christ "believing Gentiles have become, and continue to be, true children of Abraham without the necessity of law observance. Both the legalistic and the nomistic implications of the Judaizers' demands are to be rejected."[25] Viewed as a whole, Kruse's interpretation does not make for a clear, coherent analysis of Paul on the law.

Kruse concludes his discussion of Galatians by reflecting upon the role of obedience in the Christian life. In Lutheran fashion, Kruse defines New Covenant obedience in terms of Christian love, maintaining that "Paul is defining love in terms of the law, not reinstating the Mosaic law as a regulatory norm, every part of which believers must obey."[26] He draws a distinction between "fulfilling the law" and "doing the law," insisting that Paul is "*describing*, not prescribing, Christian behaviour." Reformed theology, on the other hand, upholds the regulative use of the law, seeing that the NT does prescribe a code of ethics which is normative for Christian living. The difference here between Lutheran and Reformed interpretation is more than semantics. Decisive in answering this question concerning law-keeping is the proper understanding of the *covenantal context* in which that code of ethics functions, whether under law or under grace.[27] Kruse is wrong when he asserts that "the law was not reintroduced as a set of demands to be observed as a regulatory norm," serving under the New Covenant dispensation only as "a paradigm for Christian behaviour." Kruse concedes: "while the demands of the Mosaic law were not binding upon believers, the commands of Christ were."[28] Is not this at odds with his contention that the law of God is not binding upon the people of God as a *regulatory norm*? We maintain that if the commands of Christ are binding, then they are normative for Christian conduct.[29] Kruse properly distinguishes sanctification from justification, while acknowledging the vital relationship between the two. Nevertheless, Kruse fails to incorporate the biblical idea of divine imputation. In his exposition of Romans 5, where one expects to find mention of this essential act of God constituting sinners righteous on grounds of the meritorious obedience of Christ, there is silence.[30] Kruse does recognize that Christ's obedience sustains a unique relationship to God's justifying act acquitting transgressors of sin's guilt, but he is of the opinion that Scripture does not provide an explanation how this is so. Accordingly, Reformed theology – in Kruse's judgment – says more than is warranted.[31]

As in many recent studies on Paul and the law, Kruse makes no reference to the covenant made between God and Adam in creation, what Reformed dogmaticians from the late sixteenth century up to the present have identified as the "Covenant of Works." Are we to construe this silence as repudiation of that doctrine of Scripture which has exercised so pivotal a role in Reformed systematics?[32] However that question is answered, Kruse's neglect accounts for his misreading of the apostle Paul, notably, Paul's sustained argument in Romans 5 through 7. The "likeness to Adam's transgression" (5:14), we contend, has reference to probationary testing under a covenant-of-works arrangement, that which was applicable to Adam, Christ, and Israel of old. As representative (federal) heads of the covenants in creation and in redemption respectively, the First and Second Adam while under probation were subject to the legal requirement of perfect obedience.[33] As argued above, Israel's probation under the terms of the Mosaic Covenant bears both similarity and dissimilarity to the probation-testing of the two Adams.

Within twentieth-century evangelical scholarship the verdict is not yet in concerning the question of the relationship between the biblical covenants, including interpretation of the administration of law in the creational order (the Covenant of Creation) and the Mosaic epoch of redemption (the Covenant of Redemption).

But the battle lines in this modern-day controversy have now been clearly drawn. Students eager to make their way through very difficult terrane in contemporary theology and exegesis will not find a steady guide in Kruse. In the judgment of this reviewer, Kruse's critique of the current literature and his analysis of Paul on the Mosaic law suggest that ongoing discussion and debate remain the order of the day. Openness to another interpretive approach – one firmly rooted in the biblical and Reformed theology of the Protestant Reformation – stands as the only hope for a satisfactory resolution of present differences among evangelicals on issues of fundamental import, issues concerning the faithful articulation the one, true gospel of Jesus Christ.

ENDNOTES

*Colin G. Kruse, *Paul, the Law, and Justification* (Peabody: Hendrickson, 1996).
[1]See James D. G. Dunn, "Paul and Justification by Faith," in *The Road from Damascus: The Impact of Paul's Conversion on His Life, Thought and Ministry* (Grand Rapids: Eerdmans, 1997) 85-101. Consult also the collection of essays in *Paul and the Mosaic Law: The Third Durham-Tübingen Research Symposium on Earliest Christianity and Judaism,* ed. J. D. G. Dunn (Tübingen: J. C. B. Mohr [Paul Siebeck], 1996).
[2]The remainder of the book canvases the other Pauline letters, highlighting and reinforcing the argument laid out in the chapter on Galatians. Focus shifts from interpretation to application, *viz.*, consideration of the manner in which the apostle Paul is understood to apply the Mosaic law as a paradigm, not regulatory norm, for Christian living. Compare the discussion in Frank Thielman's *Paul and the Law: A Contextual Approach* (Downers Grove, InterVarsity, 1994), esp. 214-237.

Among the newest studies in Galatians, the argument of Ben Witherington III in *Grace in Galatia: A Commentary on Paul's Letter to the Galatians* (Grand Rapids: Eerdmans, 1998) moves in the right direction. The same cannot be said for Bruce W. Longenecker in *The Truimph of Abraham's God: The Transformation of Identity in Galatians* (Nashville, Abingdon, 1998).
[3]*Paul* 69. So also Douglas Moo, "'Law,' 'Works of the Law,' and Legalism in Paul," *WTJ* 45 (1983) 73-100; *The Epistle to the Romans* (New International Commentary on the New Testament; Grand Rapids: Eerdmans, 1996) and Thomas Schreiner, *The Law and Its Fulfillment: A Pauline Theology of Law* (Grand Rapids: Baker, 1993); *Romans* (Baker Exegetical Commentary on the New Testament; Grand Rapids: Baker, 1998).
[4]*Paul* 69.
[5]*Ibid.*
[6]*Cf.* the remarks by Schreiner in *Romans* 164, 184.
[7]Kruse explains: "In the original context Lev 18:5 constitutes a promise of continued enjoyment of physical life within the promised land to an obedient Israel. Paul picks up the quotation, not to deny that the law could deliver what it promised, but to show that it operates on the principle of performance, unlike the promise which operates on the principle of faith. Paul does not deny that the law could deliver what it promised, but rather that the law, operating on the principle of performance, could not bring life and justification to those who broke it" (*Paul* 289). *Cf.* In-Gyu Hong, "Does Paul Misrepresent the Jewish Law? Law and Covenant in Gal. 3:1-14," *Nov Test* 36 (1994) 164-182.
[8]Kruse rightly maintains that *telos* in Rom 10:4 "is best construed as 'termination.' Thus in Romans Paul alludes to the time when the law was introduced, and to the time when its role as both an (ineffective) means for righteousness and a regulatory norm for believers came to an end" (*Paul* 243). Schreiner's exegesis of this text (*Romans* 544-48) is not persuasive.
[9]Moisés Silva, *Explorations in Exegetical Method: Galatians as a Test Case* (Grand Rapids: Baker, 1996), adopts the view of Don B. Garlington and Richard Gaffin, Jr. on justifying grace as including faith and good works. Departing from traditional Protestant interpretation, these authors understand faith and (nonmeritorious) works to be the means of appropriating divine justification. Although the main thrust of his argument favors traditional Protestant teaching, Schreiner attempts to accommodate the new – and contrary – viewpoint (*á la* Silva). He asserts that whereas entrance into the covenant is by faith, not works, the covenant is maintained by (nonmeritorious) works. He goes so far as to say that the *already/not-yet* structure of covenantal eschatology lends credence to the view that

good works do play an instrumental role in procuring the believer's justification before God. "These two ideas," writes Schreiner, "are not contradictory. Believers are already justified, because the eschaton has penetrated the present age. But in another sense justification will be completed only on the day of redemption (*cf.* Gal 5:5)" (*Romans* 290, n.15; see also his comments on pp.75, 144-45). For further analysis of recent exegetico-theological trends, see Chapters Nine and Ten; and my review of Garlington's *Faith, Obedience and Perseverance* in included in this collected writings. Judith M. Gundry-Volf offers a similar critique of Garlington and analysis of the theological issues in her review of Garlington, *EvQ* 69 (1997) 82-84, and in *Paul and Perseverance: Staying in and Falling Away* (Tübingen: J. C. B. Mohr [Paul Siebeck], 1990).

[10]Were righteousness based on the law attainable (after Adam's fall into sin) the work of Christ would have been in vain.

[11]F. F. Bruce (in "Christ Our Righteousness," *Jesus: Past Present and Future: The Work of Christ* [Downers Grove, InterVarsity, 1979] 51-52) describes the unconverted Paul as "a more dyed-in-the-wool Jew than any of the original apostles of Jesus." He adds: "His religion was based on the works of the law, not on the work of Christ." A fair reading of the Scriptures must conclude that Judaism was/is a departure from OT religion. Contrast, *e.g.*, the humble piety of Mary and Elizabeth with that of self-righteous Saul in Lk 1:6 and Phil 3:4-9. Jesus' earthly ministry to the lost house of Israel is set against the backdrop of Jewish hostility to his ministry and message, based on their misinterpretation of the OT scriptures. They did not understand the gospel of justification, nor did they know the power of God in salvation. With reference to Rom 9:30-33, Kruse wrongly concludes: "To say that the Jews pursued the law for righteousness is not to say that first-century Judaism was *in principle* a religion in which acceptance before God depended upon amassing merit by keeping the law. Rather, we should think of first century Judaism as a covenantal and nomistic religion, within which the nomistic obligations of the covenant were sometimes over-emphasized at the expense of God's saving grace. And what was essentially a nomistic religion often degenerated, in practice, into a legalistic one" (*Paul* 225; see note 21 below). Schreiner speaks of this text as a "battleground in scholarship given the recent debate on Paul's view of the law" (*Romans* 539). Though Kruse is correct in challenging Schreiner's exegesis, his critique falls short. On the issue of supersessionism, see David E. Holwerda, *Jesus and Israel: One Covenant or Two?* (Grand Rapids: Eerdmans, 1995), and the critique of this book by Meredith G. Kline in *JETS* 40 (1997) 485-487.

[12]*Paul* 75.

[13]*Ibid.* 76.

[14]Bruce comments: "Anyone who – in theory, at least – gained life through keeping the law gained it as the reward which his achievement had earned. It was a matter of work and merit. But anyone who had failed to keep the law – and that meant everyone – could make no claim to such a reward. The law which pronounced blessing and life on those who obeyed it pronounced cursing and death on those who disobeyed it. If those who disobeyed it were nevertheless admitted to blessing and life, it could not be on the score of merit, but on the ground of God's grace" ("Christ our Righteousness" 54-55). With reference to Heb 12:1-3 Geerhardus Vos comments: "The manner in which patience becomes subservient to the attainment of the prize can be variously conceived of." In the case of Jesus, Vos continues, "there was a direct meritorious connection. What he endured in the race of his earthly life became the legal ground on which God based the bestowal upon him of all the glory and blessedness of his exalted state" ("Running the Race," *Grace and Glory: Sermons Preached in the Chapel of Princeton Theological Seminary* [Edinburgh: Banner of Truth Trust, 1994] 135).

On the application of the merit concept to the legal covenant at Sinai, see the discussion in Schreiner, "Appendix: Mark Karlberg's View of the Mosaic Law," in *The Law and its Fulfillment* 247-52. Oddly, Schreiner enthusiastically commends Scott J. Hafemann, who in a recent study labors to dissolve the theological law/gospel contrast (see Schreiner's review of *Paul, Moses, and the History of Israel: The Letter/Spirit Contrast and the Argument from Scripture in 2 Corinthians 3* in *JETS* 41 [1998] 493-96). For one who seeks to defend the vital law/gospel construct, Schreiner has yet to carry through consistently the implications of the antithesis for Paul's understanding of the Mosaic law. For further detailed discussion see my three-part study, "Israel Under a Covenant of Works: An Evaluation of Thomas R. Schreiner's *The Law and its Fulfillment*," paper read at the Eastern regional meeting of the Evangelical Theological Society in Philadelphia, PA (March 4, 1994); "Israel Under Probation: An Evaluation of Frank Thielman's *Paul and the Law*," read at the Eastern regional meeting of the Society in Valley Forge, PA (April 4, 1995); and "The Search for an Evangelical Consensus on Paul and the Law," read at the national meeting of the Society in Philadelphia, PA (November 18, 1995), published in *JETS* and included in this collected writings as Chapter Nine. See note 9 above.

[15]*Paul* 111,12.

[16]See Chapter Six.

[17]*Ibid.* 79.

[18]*Ibid.* 80.

[19]Kruse correctly asserts: "The ministry of the Old Covenant was one of the law, the ministry of the New Covenant was one of the gospel" (*Paul* 153). See note 22 below.

[20]N. T. Wright, *Climax of the Covenant: Christ and the Law in Pauline Theology* (Minneapolis: Fortress, 1991). Wright's writings, prolific and stimulating though they be, fail to offer the solution to the modern-day question regarding Paul's view of the law.

[21]Law-keeping was the means of retaining the temporal inheritance. It is this feature of OT religion, namely, Israel's governance under the Mosaic law, which justifies the description "covenantal nomism." Apart from this understanding of the terminology, all other interpretations of Paul and the law end up mired in confusion and contradiction. (Kruse here expresses indebtedness to Richard Longenecker for his distinction between legalism and nomism [*Paul* 69, n.38].) Mark A. Seifrid rightly observes: "Sanders' 'covenantal nomism' is at root quite similar to the medieval understanding of *facienti quod in se est Deus non denegat gratiam*, particularly in the *via moderna*" ("Blind Alleys in the Controversy over the Paul of History," *TynBull* 45 [1994] 92.

Unity and coherence of thought are requisite in biblico-systematic theology. Colin Gunton astutely remarks: "Being systematic in theology involves, first, responsibility for the overall consistency of what one says. The systematic [and biblical] theologian must be aware of the relation to each other of different parts of the content of a theology" ("Historical and Systematic Theology," in *The Cambridge Companion to Christian Doctrine*, ed. C. E. Gunton (Cambridge: Cambridge University Press, 1997] 12).

[22]*Paul* 83. Comparison here with the views of Schreiner are instructive. A major plank in his argument is that "the law itself provides [the individual] no ability to keep it" (*Romans* 109). Accordingly, the Mosaic Covenant only works condemnation, not salvation. No sinner is able to meet the requirement of perfection obedience. Yet, as Schreiner reminds us, elect Israelites (*i.e.*, the righteous remnant) were saved under the Old Covenant. The letter/Spirit contrast, he reasons, is to be explained in terms of the history of redemption – the old economy being characterized by the "externality of the law" and "the inadequacy of the law alone" – the law functioning apart from the Spirit of regeneration (*ibid.* 142). The New Covenant, argues Schreiner, is superior to the Old because of the gift of the Holy

Spirit which accompanies the former. The question then arises: what does this say about the righteous remnant saved by grace through faith (of whom Schreiner spoke earlier)? Were they not also saved by the personal, regenerating work of the Spirit of God? (Schreiner has shown himself to be a promoter and defender of Calvinist soteriology; see his *Romans* and the collection of essays in *The Grace of God, the Bondage of the Will* (Volume 1, Biblical and Practical Perspectives on Calvinism, ed. T. R. Schreiner and B. A. Ware; Grand Rapids: Baker, 1995).

[23]*Paul* 84. Comparing the typology of the Old and New Testaments, Bruce observes: "The Israelites' experiences had been on the earthly level, whereas those of the early Christians were on the spiritual level; but the former served as a kind of allegory in advance for the latter" ("Before the Incarnation," in *Jesus: Past, Present and Future* 99). Regarding the antithetical principles of law and grace, Bruce explains: "By contrast with the New Covenant and its life-giving message, the law is described in terms of 'the Old Covenant.' The law did indeed hold out life to those who kept it – 'Do this and you shall live' – but it pronounced a curse on those who broke it; and since the lawbreakers were always more numerous than the law-keepers, the general tendency of the Old Covenant was death. The gospel, however presents the way of life; through it the law-breaker who repents of his law-breaking finds forgiveness and justification by grace. Paul rejoices to be the administrator of a covenant which is life-giving and not death-dealing, a covenant which, far from imposing a yoke of bondage, conveys that freedom which rules wherever the Spirit of the Lord is, and he sees the gospel invested with a greater glory than attended the administration of the law" (*The New Testament Development of Old Testament Themes* [Grand Rapids: Eerdmans, 1968] 55).

[24]*Paul* 109.

[25]*Ibid.* 100.

[26]*Ibid.* 103,4.

[27]On the one side of the current debate, we find Silva parting company with his former teacher, John Murray, regarding what the law can and cannot do. Silva is now eager to cast aside traditional Reformed, Protestant teaching regarding the law/gospel antithesis as seen in his most recent study, *Explorations*. On the other side of the debate, Kruse commends the view of Morna D. Hooker, who argues "that the law was temporary in so far as its offer of life to those who fulfill its demands has been superseded with the coming of Christ. The law is abiding, however, in so far as it is a witness to Christ" (*Paul* 154, n.8). For more on the law/gospel debate, consult the provocative study by Lutheran scholar Stephen Westerholm, *Israel's Law and The Church's Faith: Paul and His Recent Interpreters* (Grand Rapids: Eerdmans, 1988).

[28]*Paul* 119, 140

[29]Kruse contends that "it is easier to say what *ennomos Christou* does not mean than to determine what it does mean." In this study his argument has been that "to live *ennomos Christou* involved at least the obligation to keep the commands of Christ and to live by the law of love (in the power of the Spirit), and that it probably also involved living for the Christ who died for us" (*Paul* 147). Later Kruse writes: "While Paul insists that believers are free from the law, and that they must maintain that freedom if they want to live holy lives that bear fruit for God, he argues, paradoxically, that the law nevertheless finds fulfillment in the lives of believers" (*ibid.* 285).

Agreeably, the application of the OT judicial laws in today's social and political context must be in accordance with the principle of "general equity." Kruse refers the reader to the work of Christopher J. H. Wright (*ibid.* 119, n.7). For a historical-theological overview of this facet of Protestant theology, see Chapters Two and Three.

[30]Here Schreiner's exegesis fares better (*Romans* 267-93).
[31]Kruse reasons: "Justification comes through Christ's blood (Rom 5:9), and Christ's act of obedience (primarily his death) effects justification for all those who believe (Rom 5:12-21)" (*Paul* 281). Compare the similar argument of Richard B. Gaffin, Jr., in "Justification in Luke-Acts," *Right with God: Justification in the Bible and the World,* ed. D. A. Carson (Grand Rapids: Paternoster, 1992) 106-125. Gaffin elucidates Christ's reconciling and justifying work exclusively in terms of his passive obedience. For further discussion of trends in contemporary theology, see Philip Eveson, *The Great Exchange: Justification by Faith Alone in the Light of Recent Thought* (Kent: Day One, 1996).
[32]See Chapter One.
[33]*Cf.* the argument presented in Chapters Six and Seven.

BOOK REVIEWS

1

Typos: The Typological Interpretation of the Old Testament in the New by Leonhard Goppelt. Translated by Donald H. Madvig. Grand Rapids: Eerdmans, 1982.

This publication makes available in English translation Goppelt's 1939 doctoral study with the addition of a journal article that appeared in 1964. The fact that an older work is reappearing in translation is indicative of the continued importance of this study for biblical hermeneutics. Though somewhat dated (and here the reader should consult the informative "Foreword" by E. Earle Ellis), Goppelt's presentation has much to offer by way of challenging present-day hermeneutical methods of radical historicism and existentialism.

According to Goppelt "a genuine Christian typology" (p. 64), which is nothing other than legitimate and proper exegesis of the Scriptures, elucidates the place of Jesus in the history of redemption, more specifically in terms of the new age of the Eschaton. Such exegesis is oriented to a distinctively redemptive-historical point of view. As instructed by the Lord himself the NT writers interpreted the person and work of Jesus in light of his typological fulfillment of the OT Scriptures (pp. 87-95). Goppelt creates the impression, however, that typological interpretation alone provides the solution to the perennial question of the relationship between the OT and the NT. Rather, typological exegesis must be seen as one aspect, however prominent, of biblical hermeneutics.

In a refreshing manner Goppelt highlights the fact that "the new creation is not a repetition of the first, nor is it simply a reversal of the Fall; it is a perfect, *i.e.*, a typological, renewing of creation" (pp. 134-135). It is from this decisively eschatological perspective that the author's cautionary word against an unwarranted (but all too prevalent) moralizing of OT persons and events takes on added significance. Commenting on 1 Pet 3:5-6 he says, "What is being emphasized is not moral conduct per se, but a trait that is fitting for the faith of a people 'who put their hope in God'. . . . Their ethical behavior is not in itself exemplary for the church, but it is exemplary as a characteristic that is appropriate for the faith that God's people have; it is an essential element in their relationship to God" (pp. 157-158). In his covenantal relationship with his people, "God dealt in a typical way (*typikôs*) with Israel in the wilderness, in a manner that is a pattern for his dealing with the church in the last days. The fortunes of Israel are types (*typoi*) of the experiences of the church (1 Cor 10:6,11; *cf.* Rom 5:14)" (pp. 4-5). Recognition of God's dealing with Israel as a pattern for and example to the New Covenant people of God underscores the importance of careful study of the OT

Scriptures. Spiritual growth and maturity of believers as the body of Christ depend on diligent study of the whole Word of God.

> The results of typological exegesis are primarily statements about NT salvation, not statements about the OT. . . . Typology also gives certainty and clarity concerning Christ's destiny and the corresponding destiny of his church. The Son of Man must suffer, die and rise again. It is no strange thing which happens to the church and its servants when persecution from without and various temptations from within oppress them. Typology removes the redemptive history of the NT from simple fortuitous factuality and places it under God's eternal redemptive decree. This does not lead to complacency but to obedience. . . . Typology not only brings the assurance of salvation, but it always provides a rationale for its warnings against contempt for this salvation. It clarifies the nature of salvation and justifies the warning against its misuse. The typological relationship to the punishment of Israel under divine forbearance (*anochê*) indicates that contempt and misuse will result in the eternal loss of the true salvation. [Pp. 200-201]

Although Goppelt speaks of the peculiar redemptive-historical function of the law of Moses as "a negative preparation for the gospel," this crucial aspect of the discontinuity between the Old and New Covenants remains undeveloped in his thought. What Goppelt identifies as a works principle of inheritance under the Mosaic Covenant is not consistently worked out in his interpretation of the gracious nature of all God's redemptive covenants. Goppelt remarks: "When Paul speaks of the 'law,' which was added later (Gal 3:18f.), he is not thinking only of the revelation of God's commands, but also of the status of this law according to the Sinaitic order: its fulfillment is a requirement for existence before God" (p. 138 n. 36). As it is, Goppelt's treatment of "law" within the biblical system of typology is inadequate at this point.

In general, Goppelt achieves his stated purpose of allowing the Scriptures to speak for themselves on the matter of the relation between the two Testaments. The author states by way of conclusion: "Our study of OT typology in the NT has introduced us to a comprehensive and profound view of redemptive history. This is not a modern or more sophisticated justification of the NT use of Scripture that is based on a more recent view of history; it is a point of view that is integral to the NT itself" (p. 198).

The strength of this study lies in the author's ability to canvass a vast amount of biblical material clearly and concisely. His argument for the major place of OT typology in the NT is at once compelling and convincing. The controversial issue of the relation between the Testaments has occupied a prominent position in the history of biblical interpretation. Although Goppelt's work does not attempt to place the hermeneutical discussion in the context of historical theology in any comprehensive way, the author's purpose of simply considering the NT writer's use of the OT as the way to resolve the ongoing debate suggests a degree of insensitivity to the complexities arising in the history of doctrinal formulation. But more important than his failure to grapple with problems relating to the development of doctrine, Goppelt fails to do justice to the creative role of the Holy Spirit as both the primary author and the interpreter of Scripture.

The author's underlying (neoorthodox) premise is that the biblical writings, the OT and NT canonical documents, comprise the community of faith's apprehension of God's redemptive-historical revelation In Christ. Goppelt presupposes that the biblical writers have produced a collection of writings that are historically and critically fallible. Consequently Goppelt's discussion of biblical typology as a redemptive-historical category is weighed down by the dialectical tension between history and theology.

The nature of OT prophecy is treated in an entirely unsatisfactory manner. What exactly is OT prophecy according to Goppelt? The answer is found in his proposed understanding of covenant typology. "This typology is not to be distinguished from prophecy; rather, it is a principle that forms and uphold it" (p. 228). Here lies the fundamental error in Goppelt's argumentation. First, just the reverse of what Goppelt maintains is valid. It is the prophetic character of God's revelation that forms and upholds the typological system of redemptive covenant. Second, Goppelt's definition of covenant typology is relational and anthropocentric rather than truly redemptive-historical and theocentric. He writes:

> Typology is not a hermeneutical method with specific rules of interpretation. It is a spiritual approach that looks forward to the consummation of salvation and recognizes the individual types of that consummation in redemptive history. . . . The discovery of individual typological relationships is governed by the following principles (unconsciously, of course, and simply as a consequence of the nature of the subject matter): Persons, events, and institutions are interpreted only insofar as they express some aspect of man's relationship to God. Consequently, typology does not deal with inherent or external features in the events and accounts in the OT. Because Christ alone is the fulfillment of this relationship to God, another principle is always added that arises from the subject matter. This principle specifies that all typology proceeds through Christ and exists in him. From these two principles it follows as a matter of course that the antitypes, like the types, are not merely inherent or external features, but are the important elements in the perfect relationship between God and man. [P. 202]

This brings us to the more immediate problem of the relation between history and theology. According to Goppelt, the biblical writers engage in redactional activity for typological (*i.e.*, theological) purposes:

> A type has validity also for us if a historical event in the Exodus or in the wilderness wandering that was governed by a revelatory word made a life from God possible for Israel, and if contempt for this experience resulted in judgment. The validity is not diminished even if many details in the description of the wilderness wandering are a reflection of subsequent divine revelations to Israel. If it is true, as we have indicated, that the OT type has not been molded by the church's experience of

> redemption, then that experience only confirms the significance of the type. Accordingly, the validity of a typology does not depend on the historicity of individual scenes, but on the truth and reality of God's revelation of himself in history and on a standard for the historical phenomena that can only be developed from the subject matter. In principle, typology is not dependent on a greater amount of historicity than any other biblical revelation, as long as one maintains that true typology represents an important element in God's relationship to man. [Pp. 232-233]

Goppelt suggests that the typological basis of Jesus' resurrection and ascension is theological, not historical. It is an article of faith (p. 82). Similarly the question of the historicity of Adam, as another example, is a matter of speculation. Assuredly the apostle Paul's interest is "genuine typology," which is apparent only through the eyes of faith. The eschatological presence of God in history is a spiritual reality, an experience not subject to historical and scientific verification (see 134ff.).

Goppelt's hermeneutical principle, the typological principle, comes into sharper focus when he discusses the creative role of the biblical authors in their use of typology. According to Matthew's understanding of Ps 22 in Matt 28:10, Goppelt asks:

> Did the evangelists interpret these statements about the righteous sufferer that are taken from the Psalms as direct prophecies or in some typological way? We cannot ask them this pointed question. Their only concern is that these statements from the Psalms were fulfilled in Jesus' experience; they are not interested in what the poet had in mind originally. The way in which the OT passages are introduced suggests that theirs is a typological approach which looks for similarity in essentials, not simply for the fulfillment of external features. There are no explicit statements that prophecy has been fulfilled, such as we might have expected, especially from Matthew; the passages are simply alluded to. The distress of the saint that is portrayed by the psalmist is fulfilled in Jesus. [P. 103; *cf.* pp. 122-123]

The "essential" ingredient in covenant typology, according to Goppelt, is relational and existential. It pertains to man's encounter with God. The peculiar, typological interpretation of the OT in the NT differs from our way of thinking and "our standards of logic" (p. 162). Jesus himself employed the typological method of OT interpretation, which grew out of the tradition of the Israelite community of faith and contemporary Judaism (p. 79). Here Goppelt implicitly obscures the scriptural teaching concerning the ontological oneness of the Father and the Son. He perceives Jesus' messianic consciousness to be something learned exclusively through the OT tradition of faith in the God of promise. Furthermore the place that Goppelt gives to the canonical writers as bearers of redemptive revelation has the effect of relegating Jesus' unique role as the messianic fulfillment and interpreter of the OT Scriptures to one of secondary and derivative status:

> Jesus and the evangelists found a scriptural basis for their conviction that the Messiah had to be rejected by his people and had to pass through suffering and death on his way to glory. From our study thus far it would be natural to suppose that with the aid of typology they found this basis in an idea that occurs throughout the OT, the idea of the prophet, king, and as the whole passion narrative indicates, righteous man. In the pursuit of his calling he suffers, dies, and rises again for God's sake. [P. 95]

Thus "Jesus faced death consciously and deliberately as being the destiny of the Messiah that had been ordained by God's redemptive decree and would, therefore, issue in victory" (p. 102).

In the course of his development of a typological understanding of the relation between OT and NT Goppelt treats the theme of eschatology by reference to promise and fulfillment, covenant continuity and discontinuity, and what Ellis describes as "historical correspondence and escalation" (p. x). As already indicated, the cogency of Goppelt's redemptive-historical construction of biblical typology founders on his uncritical adoption of a neoorthodox conception of history and theology. The solution to the problem of the relation between the Mosaic Covenant and the New Covenant depends on recognition of and submission to the self-interpreting character of the Scriptures as the infallible and inerrant Word of God. Only on such a basis is the exegete and theologian critically responsible in his hermeneutical task. Although Goppelt's study may raise more questions than it finally answers, its chief contribution will be to encourage us to return to the NT writings themselves for understanding the relation between the two Testaments, and in so doing come to acknowledge the biblical hermeneutic of the self-interpreting Christ speaking through the Scriptures of the Old and New Covenants.

2

Faith, Obedience and Perseverance: Aspects of Paul's Letter to the Romans by Don B. Garlington. Wissenschaftliche Untersuchungen zum Neuen Testament 79. Tübingen: J. C. B. Mohr (Paul Siebeck), 1994.

Burgeoning study on Paul and the law shows no signs of abating, due largely to the failure to reach a consensus of opinion among contemporary scholars. In *Faith, Obedience and Perseverance* Don Garlington demonstrates a solid command of the literature, while offering a stimulating and provocative (at times too provocative!) discussion of a number of key exegetical and theological issues. This study comprises an extensive revision of several previously published articles as well as the addition of its closing chapter. The author's indebtedness to the work of J. D. G. Dunn and E. P. Sanders is apparent throughout.

Chaps. 1 and 2 contrast what the apostle Paul calls "the obedience of faith" (*hupakoe pisteos* Rom 1:5; 16:26) with the disobedience of Israel mentioned in 2:22, and denoted as Israel's "sacrilege." Chaps. 3 and 4 relate the obedience of faith to the doing of the law (2:13) and to the obedience of Christ (5:1-21). The description of the obedience of faith as "life between two worlds" (7:13-25) concludes the exegetical portion of the study. The final chapter, entitled "Reflections," draws the implications of Garlington's analysis for contemporary systematic theology. Like many other recent studies, this one calls for a revision of traditional Protestant teaching, most notably the doctrine of justification and sanctification, which comprises the central issue in this book.

The author contends that "only 'the doers of the law' will be 'justified' in eschatological judgment" (p. 1). The precise nuance given to this assertion is that eschatological judgment (that is, final justification) is *contingent* upon faith working through love (*cf.* Gal 5:6): it is faith and (non-meritorious) works that procure the believer's salvation from the coming wrath of God. Throughout his presentation, Garlington is emphatic that this work of grace – the believer's faith and good works – is the outworking of *Christ's* life in the believer by means of the internal operation of the Holy Spirit. (This viewpoint is compared favorably to that of Scot McKnight in his treatment of perseverance in the Letter to the Hebrews [p. 3].) Garlington concedes that some of his argument is controversial.

> Among the most hotly debatable issues, which have been placed on the agenda of Protestant/Roman Catholic dialogue from the Reformation onward, are two: (1) a future (eschatological) dimension of justification which takes into account "works;" (2) the relation of "justification" and "sanctification" as the two, in Reformed theology particularly, have been subsumed under an *ordo salutis*. In both cases, it has appeared to me that adjustments to the customary Protestant/Reformed scheme are in order. [P. 4]

The main plank in Garlington's thesis is Paul's "intentionally ambiguous" (p. 144) use of the phrase, "the obedience of faith." After surveying the grammatical options, Garlington opts for the adjectival genitive. In the words of Hans-Werner Bartsch: "Faith and obedience are one action. Faith has to be proven by obedience" (p. 18). Actually, two ideas are present: (1) the synonymity of faith and obedience; and (2) the evidential outworking of faith in good works. None of this, writes Garlington, is meant to obscure the *sola fide* character of justification as heralded by the Protestant Reformation (and the Counter-Reformation!).

> While Paul is adamant that it is faith alone which justifies here and now, he is equally insistent that it is the "doers of the Law," Rom 2:13, who will be justified in eschatological judgment. As [Charles] Cosgrove rightly stresses, justification, not simply judgment, belongs not only at the beginning of life in Christ but also at its final consummation: there are, in fact, two moments of justification. . . . [And] it is none other than "faith's obedience" which bridges the gap between these seemingly polar opposites. [P. 44]

Good works are "the outgrowth of 'the obedience of faith,' which alone satisfies the demands of the law" (p. 65). This is a rather curious (and troubling) assertion. It raises the all-important question: How are we to understand the demand(s) of the law? Is it perfect obedience or something less, namely, what Garlington and others have called "covenantal nomism?" Contra the position of Moisés Silva, Douglas Moo, and others (this reviewer included), Garlington insists: "Even a foundation text like Lev 18:5 does not have in view sinless perfection, but perseverance within the standards of the covenant [*i.e.*, covenantal nomism]" (p. 141; *cf.* p. 147, n. 15). Garlington maintains that this demand of the law is (equally?) applicable to the pre-Fall situation. He states: "'the doers of the law' to be justified in eschatological judgment (2:13) are defined not in terms of allegiance to the Torah but of Adam's original mandate to pursue glory, honor, and immortality (2:7)" (p. 114). Garlington elucidates Paul's teaching in terms of "creation theology," not in terms of the (Reformed) biblical-covenantal distinction between law and gospel. At the opening of his study Garlington noted:

> In Romans Paul takes creation (rather than the Torah) as his point of theological departure. For him creation sets the outermost limits of biblical religion. Not least, this ideology of creation bears on his conception of "righteousness," which as argued effectively by [Ernst] Käsemann, is God's commitment to his creation. [P. 2, n. 2]

Nowhere in his treatment of Paul on the law does Garlington espouse the Protestant doctrine of the imputation of Christ's righteousness as (meritorious) ground of salvation. Rather, the author commends the argument of J. Christiaan Beker. He explains:

> Once grace in Paul has been loosed from its privatistic Western moorings, says Beker, and placed in its original apocalyptic setting, it is seen to refer to both a cosmic power and to the domain of our life in Christ. Hence, Beker is correct that the historic debate concerning *gratia imputata* versus *gratia infusa* by passes Paul's basic intent. [P. 76, n. 13]

Garlington argues that in Christ the believer is "made" righteous rather than "constituted" righteous. (Criticism is also raised against the traditional Reformed doctrine of the imputation of Adam's sin. The best that can be said, Garlington posits, is that in Adam we enter the world devoid of the Spirit of God.) It is the infusion of grace, faith's obedience, or what is described as God's work of "rightwising," the impartation of Christ's righteousness, that is in view here. The indwelling, empowering Spirit of God sets the believer free from the curse of Adam's sin and places him/her on the new path of righteousness.

We come now to Garlington's interpretation of the New Covenant and the inauguration of the (semi-)eschatological age of the Spirit. Both the corporate and individual aspects of Christ's saving work are implicit in Paul's teaching on union with Christ.

> It is the Christian's union with Christ and the gift of his Spirit (Rom 8:9; 2 Cor 1:22; 5:5; Eph 1:14, etc.) which are the fountainhead of the obedience of faith: it is *in Christ* that one becomes a doer of the law, not in the sense of sinless perfection but of one's commitment to God's (new) covenant, which *kurios* is Christ. . . "Doing the law," in Rom 2:13, is no different in kind than the OT's classic statement of "covenantal nomism," Lev 18:5: one continues to live within the covenant relationship by compliance with its terms, *i.e.*, perseverance. [P. 70]

This doing of the law is not "'works-righteousness' or unaided human achievement; it is rather, 'the obedience of faith,' *i.e.*, continuance in the Creator/creature relationship as articulated by Paul's christological gospel" (p. 71). With the establishment of the covenant in Christ believers are free to serve in the newness of the Spirit, not in the oldness of the letter (p. 73). What this means is that the people of God are no longer shackled by the Torah, no longer subject to ethnic and ritual distinctions. Paul's reference to "the works of the law" has these "boundary markers" in mind. Garlington faults the Protestant reformers for misconstruing Paul's teaching on justification, not only by imposing the concept of human "merit" upon the law's demands, but also by failing to come to grips with the "already/not yet" structure of Pauline eschatology. In Christ the believer has become a new creation. The leading feature of the new life in Christ is persevering obedience (p. 77).

According to Garlington, Israel failed to comprehend the temporal nature of the Torah, whose purpose was to serve as Israel's tutor until the arrival of the Messiah in the fullness of time.

> The disobedience of the Palestinian Jews, in this light, is precisely the opposite of "the obedience of faith". . . . Israel, in Paul's estimation, though able to fulfill the law on the "nationalistic" level, could not do so on the more profound level demanded by "the obedience of faith." [P. 30]

The sacrilege committed by Israel consisted in the elevation of the Torah to eternal status. Israel's idolatrous practice climaxed in her rejection of Jesus and his gospel. Israel gloried in her own righteousness, "a righteousness peculiar to itself (= national righteousness) as defined by the Sinai covenant ([Rom] 10:3), rather than submit to the righteousness of God in Christ, who is the *telos* of the law (10:4)" (p. 62). Thus, Israel, like humanity in general, evinced her solidarity with sinful Adam. Her disobedience was "the by product of the apostasy bequeathed by Adam whose hallmark is the absence of the Spirit. . . . We might say that whereas the First Adam forfeited the Spirit, the Last Adam, in his role as life-giver, restores the Spirit (1 Cor 15:45)" (p. 86).

Remaining space permits only brief comment regarding Garlington's exegesis of Romans 7 (including his understanding of theocratic Israel's role in redemptive history) and his criticism of the traditional *ordo salutis*. In his exegesis of Romans 7 (as well as Romans 5), Garlington's "creation typology" hinders a satisfactory reading of Paul on the law. The root of this misreading is the author's rejection of the classic Protestant law/gospel contrast (*cf.* his exegesis of Lev 18:5). It is the principle of works-inheritance, antithetical to that of faith-inheritance, which is regulative of Israel's tenure in Canaan. The "letter" of the law is descriptive of this peculiar operation of the law principle within the temporal sphere. Equally unsatisfactory is Garlington's interpretation of the Pauline flesh/Spirit contrast. Contrary to Garlington's argument, the apostle Paul does not contemplate the believer's existence in this overlap of the ages to be simultaneously flesh and Spirit. With Paul's experience illustrative of all believers, the conflict between flesh and Spirit is the conflict between two competing *principles,* sin and obedience, not two states or natures. (This is not to deny that the term "flesh" bears a spectrum of meaning in Paul.) Garlington acknowledges that the believer has become a new creation, wherein the old has passed away. Through union with Christ, he/she has died to sin, having crucified the flesh and its passions. The spiritual warfare, therefore, does not entail "the antithesis of the two creations" (p. 143).

Following the views of G. C. Berkouwer and, more recently, Richard Gaffin, Garlington substitutes "the way of salvation" for the traditional *ordo salutis.* The latter is thought to be "devoid of the exclusively eschatological air which pervades the entire Pauline eschatology" (p. 158). The new viewpoint, however, ends up blurring the crucial distinction between justification and sanctification. The impetus for this reformulation is twofold: (1) Berkouwer's correlation between faith and good works; and (2) contemporary reinterpretation of Paul's theology of the law. Whereas Garlington speaks of "the dynamic of justification" (p. 156), Gaffin, arguing from the standpoint of the eschatological already/not yet and the "single act" of God in the application of redemption (*i.e.,* union with Christ), maintains that justification is realized only in the mode of perseverance (p. 158). Both of these formulations accent the contingent nature of justifying faith working through love. Cornelius Van Til rightly views this new sysnthesis as a synthesis between the teachings of historic Reformed theology and that of neoorthodoxy. (Compare also Philip Eveson's searching critique in "Interpreting Justification Today," *Foundations: A Journal of Evangelical Theology* 27 [1991] 12-18). Clearly we have not read the last word on Paul and the law in this present-day debate. In the meantime, perhaps Garlington and others will pause to reevaluate their work in the light of the orthodox Protestant/Reformed doctrine of justification by faith apart from the works of the law.

SECTION THREE – Systematic Theology

SUMMARY ARGUMENT. The opening essay in this section was my reply in the pages of the *Journal of the Evangelical Theological Society* to the invitation of Kenneth Barker, a spokesman for modern dispensationalism, for an amillennial covenant theologian to address the subject of the discontinuities between the two Testaments. (Barker in his article presented the case against false dichotomies between the Testaments. His presentation highlights changes that have been taking place in recent years in the dispensationalist school.) The design of this exchange, as conceived by Barker, was to identify what has oftentimes been viewed as the weak points in each of these two (opposing) schools of biblical interpretation. What appears to have prompted Barker to engage in this dialogue is his realization of the growing rapprochement between modern-day dispensationalism, known as *progressive dispensationalism*, and (modified) covenant theology. Hermeneutics is the discipline that brings together *all* facets of theological reflection (biblical-exegetical, historical, and systematic) to bear in the interpretation of Scripture. The focal issues in this exchange are these: the law/gospel contrast, the question of the future of ethnic Israel in the plan of God, and biblical typology. A catalyst in much of the contemporary debate is Daniel Fuller's study, *Gospel and Law: Contrast or Continuum? The Hermeneutics of Dispensationalism and Covenant Theology.*

Orthodox Christianity has always had to battle error, not only from outside the institutional walls of the church, but also from within. The Arian controversy was one of the greatest threats in the early period of the church's history. In modern times assaults from Protestant liberalism make itself felt even within evangelicalism, the most notable example being that of Barthianism, a system of doctrine which oftentimes gives the *appearance* of orthodoxy (it frequently employs traditional theological language and categories). Theology can be deceptive. The teaching career of Paul van Buren gives us a picture of the ease with which a theologian can move from one heterodox system of thought to another, all the while never grasping the biblical hermeneutic of the Protestant Reformation, the principle of *sola scriptura.* The work featured in this review article (Chapter Thirteen) employs modern language analysis in the context of the secularization of Protestantism in the latter half of the twentieth century, secularism being the product of autonomous human speculation left to its own powers of reason. Curiously, van Buren's study, *A Christian Theology of the People Israel,* must rework the basic issues confronting Protestant interpreters of the Bible since the time of the Reformation, namely, the relationship between law and gospel, Israel and the church, promise and fulfillment (or, in van Buren's schematization, promise and confirmation). These are determinative issues in any theology, and van Buren's analysis is highly instructive on this account. God has truly acted in history: he has made himself known in the person and work of Jesus Christ. The history of humankind can only be rightly interpreted in the light of God's self-revelation. This essay, then, is an exercise in Christian apologetics, that indispensable component of the church's witness and mission in the world (*viz.*, the propagation and defense of the one true faith).

The third essay in this section compares the teachings of historic Reformed covenant theology with that of modern-day theonomy, also known as Christian Reconstructionism (or dominion theology). The focal issue in this debate is the application of the civil code of Moses in society. Christian Reconstructionism is a return, in part, to the Puritan ideal of a godly commonwealth which bases its civil morality upon the principles of biblical Christianity (implementing and enforcing the stipulations and sanctions of the Mosaic civil laws). Theonomy builds upon the postmillennial expectation of Christianity's global conquest prior to the return of Christ and the establishment of the eternal kingdom in the New Heavens and the New Earth. The featured work of this review article, Gary North's *Dominion and Common Grace,* attempts to expose the error in the Reformed amillennial interpretation as represented principally in the writings of theologian and apologist Cornelius Van Til, late professor at Westminster Seminary and leading Reformed apologist of the twentieth century.[1] One of the main issues in this dispute is the question whether common grace increases (Van Til) or decreases (North) over the course of postlapsarian history. In my judgment, neither disputant scores on this point, for common grace neither increases nor decreases, but rather remains *constant* throughout history. Also at issue is the question of the relationship between the kingdom-building activity of the people of God, the church of Christ, and cultural development and advance (what in NT times is the question of the nature and mission of the church [*cf.* the Great Commission] and the cultural mandate as reissued after humankind's fall into sin). Complicating matters in this debate are the conflicting teachings found in the *Westminster Confession of Faith.*

Much has been written in the last several years regarding developments taking place both in modern-day dispensationalism and Reformed theology. The last chapter in this section, a review article of the collection of essays entitled *Continuity and Discontinuity: Perspectives on the Relationship Between the Old and New Testaments,* interacts with the first (and, in my judgment, the best) of these recent exchanges. Particular attention is given to the similarities and the differences between dispensational (*i.e.* "literal") hermeneutics and the interpretive method of Reformed covenant theology – with a view to changes that have occurred in both schools of thought. The critical issue that still divides dispensational and nondispensational theologians concerns the role of ethnic Israel in redemptive history, including the question of Israel's place in the final Eschaton. (More broadly conceived, it is the hermeneutical issue of the kingdom of God as a present and future reality.) What is the meaning and significance of the promise first given to Abraham, the father of all believers, regarding the land of Palestine? In terms of the Mosaic economy of redemption how is Israel's "election" to be understood? Is spiritual Israel distinct from the church (under both economies of redemption, the new and the old)? And what is the role of the Holy Spirit in the salvation of sinners under both Testaments? These continue to be the pressing topics of discussion in the ongoing dialogue.

NOTE

For a defense of Van Tilian apologetics in light of the challenge of (multi)perspectivalism, one current variety of theological relativism and eclecticism, see Mark W. Karlberg, "On the Theological Correlation of Divine and Human Language: A Review Article," *JETS* 32 (1989) 99-105; and "John Frame and the Recasting of Van Tilian Apologetics: A Review Article," *Mid-America Journal of Theology* 9 (1993) 279-296. Frame attempts (unsuccessfully) to answer his critics in his rejoinder to my criticism of his work in the same issue of the *Mid-America Journal.*

CHAPTER TWELVE

LEGITIMATE DISCONTINUITIES BETWEEN THE TESTAMENTS [*Hermeneutics*]

Kenneth Barker in "False Dichotomies Between the Testaments," a stimulating and informative article published in *JETS* 25 (1982) 3-16, invites an amillennial covenant theologian to address in reciprocal fashion the topic of legitimate discontinuities between the OT and NT or, more properly, between the Mosaic Covenant and the New Covenant in Christ.

Federal theology has been known for its emphasis on the unity and continuity of the two covenants. Critics frequently charge covenant theology with minimizing meaningful discussion of legitimate discontinuities between the Covenant of Law mediated through Moses and the New Covenant administration of grace established by Jesus Christ (Jn 1:17). Charles Ryrie asserts: "Covenant theology can only emphasize the unity, and in so doing overemphasizes it until it becomes the sole governing category of interpretation."[1] Dispensationalism has rightly insisted on the importance of the law-gospel distinction in a comparison of the Old and New Covenants. This distinction, deeply rooted in Protestant theology since the beginning of the Reformation, highlights the antithesis between the blessing of God received on the ground of law-keeping (merit) and blessing received on the basis of Christ's atonement for sin (redemptive grace). (The latter way of divine blessing rests on the merit of Christ, the ground of soteric justification and life.) Had Adam before the Fall remained faithful to the covenant with his God, he would have merited eternal life for himself and all his posterity. With the entrance of sin into the world, the reconciliation between God and the sinner has been secured through the redemptive work of Christ. As an aspect of the atonement, Christ satisfies divine justice by rendering full and perfect obedience to the law of God and, so doing, fulfills the covenantal-legal obligations. A parallel obtains here between the First and Second Adams as representative heads under two distinct covenants (commonly called the Covenant of Works and the Covenant of Grace). There is a similar parallel between the first covenant with Adam at creation and the later giving of the law at Mount Sinai. A principle of works-inheritance operative in the original covenant with Adam is reestablished in the Mosaic Covenant, although this principle is restricted in its field of operation. Different explanations for the apparently contradictory data in Scripture descriptive of the Mosaic Covenant have led to two distinct schools of interpretation within evangelicalism – namely, dispensationalism and covenant theology. Fortunately, the current theological scene evidences remarkable change, particularly a growing rapprochement between modern dispensationalism and covenant theology. In the course of this paper I will indicate some of the reasons for this trend.

Assessing the writings of Lewis Chafer, Charles Ryrie, John Calvin and Charles Hodge (to name only a few representative theologians from both schools) and taking into account the way readers have interpreted their writings, one must admit to a measure of ambiguity in their formulations. As I have stated elsewhere with respect to federalism:

> Quite clearly, Reformed theology is in need of clarification here. With good reason Daniel Fuller has remarked: "It is extremely difficult to grasp covenant theology's explanations of how a line of thought, which has the structure of the covenant of works, nevertheless functions as part of the covenant of grace."[2]

On the other side Robert Saucy acknowledges:

> The focus on distinctive expressions of the will of God for human life on earth has led to many accusations that dispensationalism teaches more than one way of salvation. In response, most dispensationalists will acknowledge a lack of clarity and even exaggeration in some statements made by early advocates of this system. But outside of the difficulty that many have had to elucidate clearly the distinction of life for the believer living under the Mosaic law and the believer under the New Covenant, a certain allowance must be granted in consideration of the reactive nature of some of early dispensationalism.[3]

The obvious reason for much of the confusion is the exceeding complexity of the issues involved. Jonathan Edwards once observed: "There is perhaps no part of divinity attended with so much intricacy, and wherein orthodox divines do so much differ as stating the precise agreement and difference between the two dispensations of Moses and Christ."[4]

After studying the history and development of federal theology and evaluating the two rival Calvinist interpretations of the Mosaic Covenant, I can understand the polemical nature of the vigorous ongoing debate among evangelicals today pertaining to the traditional law-gospel distinction between the two covenants.[5] But I would hope that evangelicals are in unanimous agreement with the opinion of Walter Kaiser: "The classic theme of all truly evangelical theology is the problem of law and grace."[6] Martin Luther and the reformers in general spoke of justification by faith alone as the crucial doctrine of the standing or falling church. In many ways the most significant current treatment of this subject is that of Daniel Fuller, entitled *Gospel and Law: Contrast or Continuum? The Hermeneutics of Dispensationalism and Covenant Theology*. Serious criticism has been raised against Fuller's historical and theological analysis. Anthony Hoekema, for example, has difficulty with Fuller's reading of Calvin and subsequent covenant theology.

> Implicit in the title of the book is the thought that covenant theology posits a contrast rather than a continuum between law and gospel. . . . Law and gospel are sometimes seen as antithetical by Calvin and the covenant theologians. Apparently, however, according to Fuller, the only relationship seen between law and gospel by Calvin and the covenant theologians is that of antithesis. But this understanding is hardly correct.[7]

More important than Fuller's overstatement, in my judgment, is his basic misunderstanding of the Calvinist teaching concerning the legitimate discontinuity between the law and the gospel.

Although the following formulation is not original with him, John Calvin states that "the covenant made with all the patriarchs is so much like ours in substance and reality that the two are actually one and the same. Yet they differ in mode of administration."[8] In sharing the same substance and reality, there is genuine continuity between the two administrations of God's redemptive program – that is, as pertains to the essence of the Mosaic order or economy, eternal salvation is by grace through faith in Jesus Christ. Works, though necessary as evidence of justifying faith, do not merit justification or sanctification.[9] The purpose of this paper is to indicate how the Old and New Covenants differ in "mode of administration."

In the *Institutes* Calvin discusses at length a fivefold dissimilarity between the OT and NT. First, the spiritual blessings of the Mosaic Covenant (or the Mosaic economy more broadly) are typified by temporal conditions and regulations. Second, truth is communicated in the Mosaic economy by numerous symbols and ceremonies typifying Christ. Third, whereas the OT is literal (of the "letter"), the NT is spiritual (of the "Spirit"). Fourth, there is bondage under the old order, freedom under the new. (This fourth aspect involves the antithetical yet administratively compatible principles of law and grace operative within the covenant under Moses. This feature is described more fully in Calvin's commentaries.)[10] Fifth, covenant administration is restricted to one nation under the old economy, whereas it extends to all nations under the new. These five differences, Calvin explains, stem from the freedom and sovereignty of God in ordering the affairs of his people.[11]

Although Calvin is best known for distinguishing the two covenants along the lines of promise and fulfillment, shadow and reality, he also identifies the peculiar nature of the Mosaic Covenant in terms of its legal administration. The typological kingdom inheritance is granted to Israel on the grounds of her compliance with the law of Moses. This inheritance principle is that of works, not faith (Gal 3:10 ff.).[12] While the principle of works is distinctive of the Mosaic Covenant, the ultimate and more important principle informing the old economy as a whole (of which the Mosaic Covenant is a part) is, to be sure, redemptive grace. The law of Moses occupies a subservient function in the historical and progressive revelation of the Covenant of Redemption (of "Covenant of Grace"). Reformed theology has rightly stressed the essential continuity between the OT and NT. The law that was added 430 years after the promise to Abraham was limited in duration, serving a pedagogical role in the life of the old covenant people of God.

Richard Longenecker notes the many indications in the writings of the apostle Paul where he "did distinguish between the two purposes of the law in the OT."[13] First, there is the law as regulative of life with God (the normative use of the law). Second, there is the law as "contractual obligation," the law as "the Covenant of Works." According to Longenecker we are now discharged from the contractual obligation of the law that held Israel captive. Parenthetically, it is preferable to speak here of the "probationary" use of the law rather than the "nomistic" or "contractual." The term "contractual" in particular is unsuitable and even misleading. Stephen Westerholm makes the following observation:

> Paul means seriously that those who lived under the law were obligated to fulfill the "letter." He is of course adamant in his denial that such fulfillment could only be achieved if those who were under its yoke were in fact obligated to observe all of its terms. This is certainly suggested by his references to the (now obsolete) obedience to the "letter"; it is confirmed by such texts as Gal 3:10 and 5:3. The "letter" could not save, but was to be observed; now, when salvation through faith has been revealed, the Christian is no longer obligated to observe the "letter."[14]

What must be acknowledged, Westerholm insists, is the antithesis between "two different ways of rendering service" to the covenant Lord. As the Epistle to the Hebrews clearly points out, the old economy placed believers under a form of bondage and servitude. In keeping with the typology of the Mosaic arrangement this period of time under the law was probationary in nature, as was the original Covenant of Works with Adam at the beginning. In contrast to the bondage of the "letter" (whereby the earthly inheritance was to be obtained in the way of works) the "something better" of Heb 11:40 is the semi-eschatological enjoyment of life and salvation under the New Covenant inaugurated through the atoning work of Christ, the Second Adam, who fulfilled the conditions of the Covenant of Works on our behalf.

Is the theological concept of the law-gospel antithesis itself biblically valid? A growing number of critics both within and without the Reformed tradition have so emphasized the continuity between law and gospel, Old and New Covenants, that any suggestion of antithesis is opposed altogether. Perhaps we can best understand the dimensions of this controversy by reviewing the major premise of Fuller's study. Basic to problems inherent to dispensationalism and covenant theology, argues Fuller, is the illegitimate use of the law-gospel contrast. The idea that Adam prior to the Fall could have merited blessing from God in the way of confirmation in righteousness and ultimate glorification Fuller finds repugnant. Such a misconception of biblical teaching, Fuller contends, distorts the message of sovereign grace. But to the contrary it is Fuller's view that jeopardizes the biblical doctrine of Christ's atonement for sin, propitiation of God's holy wrath, and satisfaction of God's justice. Fuller's theology involves a clear repudiation of the meritorious nature of the Second Adam's obedience, which the apostle Paul speaks of as the "one act of righteousness" imputed through faith for our justification (Rom 5: 18).[15]

What have been other reactions to Fuller's thesis? Norman Geisler regards it to be "of the greatest doctrinal consequence."[16] In the judgment of Meredith Kline,

> Fuller's failing is not simply a flaw in his biblical theological reconstruction of one redemptive economy but an error of massive proportions in his systematic theology, involving the totality of God's covenant administration of his kingdom.[17]

Similarly, Douglas Moo observes that

> the general tenor of the book does suggest a melding of promise and law as theological categories and OT and NT as temporal categories to an extent that meaningful distinctions cease to exist. But the wiping out of these distinctions, to this extent, entails a radical revision of large segments of traditional theology – a revision which can hardly be justified biblically.[18]

Particularly troublesome is Fuller's exegetical handling of Gal 3:10. According to the popular "misinterpretation view of the law" many exegetes, like Fuller, assume that the apostle Paul's quotation of Lev 18:5 is part of an *ad hominem* argument against Judaizers. "You who know the law," says Paul in effect, "must keep the law in its entirety if you wish to merit eternal life." The apostle, we are told, lifts the statement of Lev 18:5 out of its proper OT context of faith and grace. For the sake of argument, the apostle sets the law of Moses thus misconstrued over against the gospel. Proponents of this viewpoint are correct to insist that the law as ordained by God through Moses has nothing to do with salvation by works (for eternal life is the gift of sovereign, redemptive grace), but they are wrong to deny the subordinate operation of a principle of works inheritance on the typological level. Further, theologians sympathetic with this newer exegesis of Lev 18:5 have either wrongly attempted to read their view back into the thought of Calvin (and perhaps some of the later covenant theologians) or have forthrightly indicated their departure from Calvin on this point. Moo points out how Fuller's exegesis undermines the doctrine of the substitutionary character of Christ's atonement. F. F. Bruce, in challenging the exegesis of Ragnar Bring, sees "an even greater strain involved in D. P. Fuller's interpretation."[19]

An exposition of the biblical teaching on the atonement must give adequate consideration to the place of the law of God in relation to Christ's procurement of redemption. Jesus Christ, in submission to the will of his Father and as representative head of elect humanity, fulfilled the legal demand of the everlasting covenant (see Is 24:5; Romans 3-5). The First Adam having defaulted on his representative task, the Second Adam merited the eternal reward on behalf of God's elect. Through his obedience, both active and passive, Christ made complete satisfaction of the justice of God the Father and at the same time secured the heavenly inheritance (1 Cor 15:22,45-49). They who are in Christ have not only been restored to fellowship and communion with God but have also been made heirs of the heavenly kingdom (Eph 1:3-14). The atoning sacrifice of Jesus Christ demonstrates the supreme love, mercy and grace of God to sinners (Rom 3:24-26; 5:6-11). With regard to these fundamental aspects of the biblical revelation concerning redemption in Christ, the concept of law (merit) is essential to the proclamation of the gospel.

Granting the fact that God's covenant mediated through Moses was restricted to one nation, how are we to construe the nature of Israel's calling as the Old Covenant people of God? What degree of continuity or discontinuity is there between Israel and the church? On this subject important differences remain between dispensationalism and covenant theology.[20] Reformed federalism recognizes that the national, theocratic standing of Israel has relevance as long as the Old Covenant is in force. Once that covenant has been replaced by the new and better covenant in Christ there can be no return to the outmoded, theocratic administration of law (included here is what the early Protestant reformers spoke of as the civil and ceremonial law). With the passing of the Old and the establishment of the New in the fullness of time, there is now no longer Jew or Greek, spiritually speaking. Such a historical-covenantal transition by no means seeks to eradicate natural ethnic, social and cultural distinctions or obscure the fact that the NT church originates in the faith of the patriarchs (Romans 9-11). Unless it can be shown otherwise from the Scriptures, the expectation of a future return of national Israel to Palestine in fulfillment of OT prophecy involving a reestablishment of the old Mosaic order is unwarranted.

Alongside dispensationalism and traditional covenant theology, a third position is emerging in biblical and theological studies. J. A. Ziesler, for example, suggests that Israel retains for all time a special status regardless of her rejection of the Messiah. "At present, therefore, they are not true Israel, nor exactly non-Israel. They have tendered their resignation as Israel, all unwittingly. This resignation lies on the table and will not finally be accepted." In Ziesler's view the apostle Paul "expresses the hope that at the End all Israel will be gathered in without saying that they will become Christian."[21] Historic Reformed theology, on the other hand, maintains that the national election of Israel had served a symbolic and typological purpose in redemptive history. The later drama of redemption was foreshadowed in Israel's exodus from Egypt. In the fullness of time the greater exodus of God's people hitherto held captive to Satan was accomplished through the sacrifice of Jesus Christ, the true passover Lamb and faithful Servant of the Lord.

Some Reformed interpreters have modified this third position along more conservative lines. For present purposes I will identify this particular view as the "new Dutch interpretation."[22] Representative of this newer Reformed thinking, Willem VanGemeren in a review article urges "a positive confession pertaining to Israel."[23] He argues for a distinct place for national Israel in the historical plan and purpose of God. "The fulfillment of the prophetic word takes place between the first and the second comings of Jesus Christ."[24] As concerns Israel's hope, VanGemeren places the focus of attention on the present era in which we live rather than on a future period of time as is done, for example, by premillennialists. Details of Israel's eschatological hope, he argues, can only be discerned in the actual outworkings of history. God has not given us information regarding the when and how of this promise. "The fulfillment is a hope, and hope is no longer hope when we know in detail how everything fits together. An exclusion of Israel from this hope is presumptuous, because it assumes to know exactly what God's plan for Israel is."[25]

The "new Dutch interpretation" entails a markedly different, and in some cases radical, approach to the OT Scriptures. Quoting C. Graafland, whose book VanGemeren reviews: "The character of the promise of salvation has meaning in understanding the OT, when it pertains to the future expectation of and for Israel."[26] This view maintains that even as NT believers we understand the OT aright when we consider it in terms of Israel, not the church. Consequently, this approach insists that covenant hermeneutics is not adequate for the task. A different theological method is needed to open the meaning of the OT. In calling for special recognition of the state of Israel as the chosen people of God, these interpreters offer a corrective to what they judge to be traditional covenant theology's disregard for the unconditional promise God made to Israel. Repeating the charge made long ago by dispensationalists, spokesmen for this new Reformed view find covenant theology guilty of "spiritualizing." VanGemeren "rejects an eschatological hope which spiritualizes OT promises and transfers them to the spiritual Israel, the church."[27] His theological preference is for a kind of "tension" and "openness" rather than a historical dogmatizing and historical closure, which he perceives as an all-too-prevalent inclination among Reformed systematicians. VanGemeren points out the difference between the views of William Brakel and Calvin on the nature of God's promissory word to Israel regarding the land of Canaan. According to Brake], notes VanGemeren,

> the church could not he identified with the New Israel. . . . Brakel expected *all* twelve tribes to repent and express faith in Jesus as the Messiah. He also held that the Jews would be privileged to return to their land. The promise of the land is not just a type of the eternal rest or of heaven, rather it is part and parcel with the Covenant of Grace which God made to and affirmed with Israel. Brakel kept Israel and church together. There is *one* covenant, one covenant people, one salvation, and one Savior.[28]

VanGemeren commends Graafland's study "for reintroducing hope [*i.e.*, the hope of Israel] as a vital aspect of faith. The hope of the church focuses on a full appreciation of God's promises, and this includes a hope that God's promises to Israel will be realized, while at the same time the manner of the fulfillment remains hidden from us."[29]

Those who share some of VanGemeren's concerns and outlook, both millinarians and nonmillenarians, anticipate a literal fulfillment of the earthly promises in history prior to the consummation of history. One decisive difference between modern dispensationalism and the "new Dutch interpretation" is the former's projection of the final, climactic fulfillment of God's promises to Israel into the millennium, the literal thousand-year reign of Christ preceding the end of history.[30] Amillennial covenant theology affirms the messianic fulfillment of the OT promises in the "millennium," the semi-eschatological period of time extending from the first to the second coming of Christ. According to amillennialism, the present age of the NT church is a first phase of the kingdom of God (= kingdom of heaven) inaugurated and established by Christ himself in actual fulfillment of the promise given to Abraham, Moses and David. The present kingdom manifestation prior to the consummation of God's covenant promises in the eternal kingdom (Acts 3:21) is already an age of realized eschatology. The consummating work of God results in the establishment of the everlasting kingdom, wherein the external, physical dimension comes finally into its own. (The present distinction between church and kingdom of God will no longer be applicable.) With respect to the ancient Israelite theocracy, the typical, earthly prefiguration finds ultimate fulfillment in the New Heavens and the New Earth. It is possible for an amillennial covenant theologian to speak of a future kingdom fulfillment in addition to the present messianic fulfillment of the OT promises. That future kingdom fulfillment would then simply be the consummation of the present kingdom reality. (This idea is conveyed in the eschatological terminology of the "already" and the "not yet.") As a supernatural inbreaking of God into history, the consummation brings about the glorious eternal state.[31]

Whereas traditional covenant theology regards the earthly promises associated with the Mosaic economy to be symbolic and typical (and thus fulfilled by Christ in two phases: first, in the new, semi-eschatological age of the Spirit, and second, in the New Heavens and the New Earth yet to come), dispensationalism goes beyond this position by retaining an additional, literal fulfillment in Palestine during the millennium. The dispensational interpretation of the millennium raises the following important questions: (1) Does not the glorious age of the church seemingly fade in comparison with the glory of the earthly, thousand-year, theocratic rule of Christ in Palestine? (2) Is national Israel or the true, spiritual Israel (the church) the immediate object of God's saving activity revealed in the incarnation, life and death of Jesus Christ, in the Father's raising of his Son in the power of the Spirit, and in the subsequent outpouring of the Spirit upon the church? (3) Does not the idea of a distinct (future) messianic-kingdom climax prior to the eternal state undermine the sufficiency and finality of the reconciling work of Christ (Eph 2:11-22)? Resolution of lingering differences of interpretation among evangelicals depends, to a large extent, on a proper assessment of the nature and function of OT typology.[32]

Holding to the unconditional promise of Israel's eternal inheritance of the land of Palestine, dispensationalists are apparently satisfied in thinking that a future millennial kingdom-theocracy does full justice to their reading of OT prophecy. It seems to me that dispensationalism ultimately ends up in a kind of "spiritualizing" (if I may use that unfortunate expression). If it is true that there are not two distinct and eternal destinies for separate peoples of God (Israel and the church), as acknowledged by many present-day dispensationalists, then what purpose does the thousand-year, theocratic rule of the state of Israel serve other than to satisfy a literal reading of certain elements in Revelation 20? As suggested earlier, the key to the hermeneutical impasse (between modern dispensationalism, traditional covenant theology and the "new Dutch interpretation") is the proper understanding of the system of typology in Scripture. 0. T. Allis' classic critique of early dispensationalism is still quite useful in understanding modern dispensationalism. "The primary aim [of the book] has been to show that dispensationalism has its source in a faulty and unscriptural literalism which, in the important field of prophecy, ignores the typical and preparatory character of the OT dispensation."[33] Agreeing with a point made by Herman Bavinck, Allis sees Israel, not the church, as the divine parenthesis in history. Similarly, Kline regards the Israelite theocracy as "the provisional prefiguration of the eternal kingdom of the New Covenant."[34] It appears to me that the subject of biblical typology will move to the forefront of discussion in years ahead. This prospect offers hope of further fruitful lines of discussion as together we explore the richness of God's Word. Tremendous progress has been made among evangelicals in recent decades. May the Lord grant us continued growth and mutual understanding.

Whatever our millennial position, for the sake of Christ's church and the cause of evangelicalism we need to cooperate more effectively in the proclamation and defense of the gospel of Christ in our day. Allis wisely observed: "Whether there is to be such a millennium is a question which must be decided in the light of Scripture. It does not seem to involve any issue sufficiently serious to warrant its being a divisive factor among those that are of the household of faith."[35] But it is vital to the gospel that in any discussion of legitimate discontinuities between the OT and NT we adhere to the biblical-theological distinction between law (works) and gospel (grace). And in this connection it is of critical importance that dispensationalism and covenant theology recognize and expound more clearly the subservient, probationary function of the law of Moses as regulative of Israel's enjoyment of the land under the temporary conditions of that particular historical administration of the Covenant of Redemption.

ENDNOTES

[1]Charles C. Ryrie, *Dispensationalism Today* (Chicago: Moody, 1965) 35.
[2]See Chapter One, p. 38.
[3]Robert Saucy, "Contemporary Dispensational Thought," *TSF Bulletin* (March-April 1984) 10. A sampling of some of the objectionable statements in the original *Scofield Reference Bible* include: "The Christian is not under the conditional Mosaic covenant of works, the law, but under the unconditional New Covenant of grace" (p. 95 n. 1). "As a dispensation, grace begins with the death and resurrection of Christ (Rom 3:24-26; 4:24,25). The point of testing is no longer legal obedience as the condition of salvation, but acceptance or rejection of Christ, with good works as a fruit of salvation" (p. 1115 n. 1). In light of such statements as these, O. T. Allis' criticism is valid: "The fundamental error in the attitude toward the Sinaitic Covenant which is shown in the *Scofield Bible* lies in the failure to distinguish between the law as Covenant of Works and the law as a ministration or dispensation of the Covenant of Grace, in other words in the failure to recognize that the Sinaltic Covenant belongs to the Covenant of Grace" ("Modern Dispensationalism and the Law of God," *EvQ* 8 [1936] 280). This present paper attempts to clarify further the point made by Allis.
[4]Cited in Daniel P. Fuller, *Gospel and Law: Contrast or Continuum? The Hermeneutics of Dispensationalism and Covenant Theology* (Grand Rapids: Eerdmans, 1980) 5-6.
[5]See my work, "The Mosaic Covenant and the Concept of works in Reformed Hermeneutics: A Historical-Critical Analysis with Particular Attention to Early Covenant Eschatology" (Th.D. dissertation, Westminster Theological Seminary, 1980).
[6]Walter C. Kaiser, Jr., "Leviticus 18:5 and Paul: 'Do This and You Shall Live (Eternally?),'" *JETS* 14 (1971) 19. John Murray comments: "No subject is more intimately bound up with the nature of the gospel than that of law and grace. In the degree to which error is entertained at this point, in the same degree is our conception of the gospel perverted" (*Principles of Conduct* [Grand Rapids: Eerdmans, 1957] 181). In defining the biblical idea of "law" Murray writes: "Law not only enunciates justice; it guards justice. It ensures that where there is righteousness to the full extent of its demand there will be the corresponding justification and life. Only when there is deviation from its demands does any adverse judgment proceed from the law" (*ibid.* 184).
[7]Anthony A. Hoekema, review of Fuller, *Calvin Theological Journal* 17 (1982) 111-112. Similarly Douglas J. Moo questions "whether Fuller has really understood the positions he criticizes or allowed sufficiently for the nuances of various approaches" (review of Fuller, *TrinJ* 3 NS 3 [1982] 101). I agree with Moo's judgment that while Fuller's analysis of dispensationalism is helpful at points, "I am not sure he has always represented the position accurately" (*ibid.* 100).
[8]John Calvin, *Institutes of the Christian Religion,* ed. J. T. McNeill (Philadelphia: Westminster, 1960) 2.10.2
[9]For further discussion of the doctrine of justification from a biblical-theological perspective see Chapter Six.
[10]Andrew J. Bandstra notes that the law-gospel antithesis is clearly presented by Calvin in his commentaries but that in the *Institutes* the law-gospel contrast tends to dissolve into a series of "differences." Consequently, if one restricts himself to the *Institutes* alone the idea of antithesis would not clearly emerge. "Thus Calvin himself may have to shoulder some of the blame for the fact that his views on law and gospel have often been only partially presented. . . . On the other hand, the *Institutes*, no matter how important, do not represent Calvin's total view. Calvin the exegete is as important as Calvin the theologian.

Surely the commentary materials need to be taken seriously in attempting to assess the whole of Calvin's view on the law-gospel motif. When this is done, it is clear that the antithesis of law and gospel, properly defined, is a necessary and important part of his total perspective" ("Law and Gospel in Calvin and in Paul," in *Exploring the Heritage of John Calvin,* ed. D. E. Holwerda [Grand Rapids: Baker, 1976] 38).

[11]Compare the similar treatment of this subject in other representative works in the Reformed tradition: Girolamo Zanchi, *Operum Theologicorum* (n.p., 1618), 8.796ff.; Peter Martyr, *The Common Places* (London, 1583) 582ff.; Zacharias Ursinus, *The Commentary of Dr. Zacharias Ursinus on the Heidelberg Catechism* (Grand Rapids: Eerdmans, 1954) 99ff.; Johann H. Alstedius, *Theologia scholastica didactica* (Hanoviae, 1618) 785ff. One of the thorny issues in comparing the two Testaments is the question concerning the role of the Holy Spirit in each economy of redemption. Ryrie comments: "It is true that there was a sharp contrast between the enablement under the law and the work of the Holy Spirit today (Jn 14:17), but it is not accurate to say there was no enablement under the law. The Spirit indwelt many (Dn 4:8; 1 Pet 1:11) and came upon many others for special power (Jdg 3:10; 1 Sam 10:9-10; Ex 28:3), but there was no guarantee that he would permanently or universally indwell God's people as he does today" (*Dispensationalism Today* 120). Compare B. B. Warfield's treatment of this subject in "The Spirit of God in the Old Testament" in *Biblical and Theological Studies,* ed. S. G. Craig (Philadelphia: Presbyterian and Reformed, 1968) 127-156.

[12]For a survey of the historical development of this Calvinist doctrine see Chapter One.

[13]Richard N. Longenecker, *Paul: Apostle of Liberty* (New York: Harper, 1964) 145; see also "The Pedagogical Nature of the Law in Galatians 3:19-4:7," *JETS* 25 (1952) 53-61.

[14]Stephen Westerholm, "Letter and Spirit: The Foundation of Pauline Ethics," *NTS* 30 (1984) 240. Westerholm concludes his study: "It would, I suggest, be difficult to find a better starting-point for a study of Pauline ethics than the letter-spirit antithesis. But it is essential that we understand the antithesis as Paul himself intended it, marking not two ways of reading the scriptures, but the ways of service enjoined under the old dispensation and the new" (p. 246). The idea of bondage associated with the Mosaic law – that is, the peculiar covenantal arrangement under Moses – is meaningful only in conjunction with the administrative principle of works-inheritance (enunciated in Lev 18:5), which is operative in the restricted symbolic-typical sphere of life in the covenant of God. The bondage is best defined in terms of the setting forth of the whole law of Moses, not just the civil and ceremonial. During the period of the law God's people were held captive to sin (this being the elenchtic function of the law – see Rom 7:1-13), subject to guardianship until the coming of Christ and bound to the law of Moses, which was regulative of Israel's tenure in the land of promise. The nature of the bondage under the Old Covenant is treated more fully in Chapter Six.

[15]Many striking parallels have been drawn between Fuller's interpretation and that of Norman Shepherd; see W. Robert Godfrey, "Back to Basics: A Response to the Robertson-Fuller Dialogue," *Presbyterion* 9 (1988) 80-84; Meredith G. Kline, "Of works and Grace," *Presbyterion* 9 (1983) 85-92.

[16]Norman L. Geisler, review of Fuller, *Bsac* 138 (1981) 278.

[17]Kline, "Of works and Grace" 87.

[18]Moo, review of Fuller, 102-103. Moo concludes: "It has by now become clear that, however attractive and stimulating the thesis of *Gospel and Law* may be, it suffers from some serious flaws. While any treatment of a topic so large and complex is bound to have weaknesses, I feel that the weaknesses in this case are serious enough to render the thesis unacceptable" (p. 103).

[19]F. F. Bruce, *The Epistle to the Galatians* (Grand Rapids: Eerdmans, 1982) 158.
[20]Saucy comments: "In particular it is the distinction between Israel and the church which all recognize as the essential mark of dispensationalism. . . . Although all dispensationalists maintain a distinction between Israel and the church, there are significant differences as to the extent of their separation in the purposes and programs of God. These differences focus on the relationship of the present church age with the messianic promises of the OT" ("Contemporary Dispensational Thought" 10).
[21]J. A. Ziesler, *Pauline Christianity* (New York: Oxford University, 1983) 66,67.
[22]This nomenclature serves to indicate the dominant influence of certain leading Dutch theologians in some circles of present-day Calvinism.
[23]Willem A. VanGemeren, "Israel as the Hermeneutical Crux in the Interpretation of Prophecy," a review article of C. Graafland's *Het Vaste Verbond. Israel en het Oude Testament bij Calvijn en het Gereformeerd Protestantisme, WTJ* 45 (1983) 143. Graafland's study is marred by an uncritical dependence on the earlier work of H. H. Wolf, *Die Einheit des Bundes. Das Verhältnis von Altem und Neuem Testament bet Calvin* (Neukirchen: Neukirchen Kreis Moors, 1958).
[24]*Ibid.* 144.
[25]*Ibid.*
[26]*Ibid.* Compare A. A. van Ruler's attempt to find many forms of the kingdom of God, Israel and the church being only two of such forms (*The Christian Church and the Old Testament* [Grand Rapids: Eerdmans, 1971]). Hendrikus Berkhof argues that "the millennial kingdom, also called the kingdom of peace, or the intermediate kingdom because it falls between our dispensation and the consummation. . . will take place in our space and time; a recovered Israel will he the center of it" (*Christ the Meaning of History* [London: SCM, 1966] 153). Both the "millennium" and the "consummation" are symbolic terms in the thinking of Berkhof. "Because sin and death still reign, a brief but fierce setback [prior to the "consummation"] is unavoidable. But this represents the transition to the union of heaven and earth, which is reflected in the kingdom of peace by the abolition of their boundaries" (p. 168). In a later section Berkhof clarifies his meaning: "Talk about history is talk about consummation" (p. 180). "The consummation as the glorification of existence will not mean that we are taken out of time and delivered from time, but that time as the form of our glorified existence will also be fulfilled and glorified. . . . We cannot discuss the consummation as though it were merely the end of history. For the consummation also takes place within the bounds of time" (p. 188). Berkhof's neoorthodox views are given systematic treatment in his *Christian Faith: An Introduction to the Study of the Faith* (Grand Rapids: Eerdmans, 1979). See the helpful critique of this important work in Martin H. Woudstra, "The Old Testament in Biblical Theology and Dogmatics," *CTJ* 18 (1988) 47-60.
[27]VanGemeren, "Israel as the Hermeneutical Crux" 143.
[28]*Ibid.* 142-143. To be sure, VanGemeren is emphatic that Israel's election to salvation is made efficacious through the personal operation of the Holy Spirit in the heart of the true Jew (p. 142).
[29]*Ibid.* 143. At the conclusion of his review article VanGemeren remarks: "A positive confessional statement regarding Israel would affect the manner in which the church proclaims the OT as Scripture. The promise of the OT gives a new dimension to the faith of the church. The inclusion of Israel in the confessions would prevent the immediate application of OT texts to the NT church" (p. 143). Compare the similar concern for this matter in Paul M. van Buren, *A Christian Theology of the People Israel: Part II. A Theology of the Jewish-Christian Reality* (New York: Seabury, 1983). This is the second of a

multiple-volume study in systematics written from a thoroughly neoorthodox perspective. It is indicative of widespread trends in ecumenical religious studies.

[30]Ryrie remarks: "Concerning the goal of history, dispensationalists find it in the establishment of the millennial kingdom on earth, while the covenant theologian regards it as the eternal state" (*Dispensationalism Today* 17). Later he notes: "The entire program culminates not in eternity but in history, in the millennial kingdom of the Lord Christ. This millennial culmination is the climax of history and the great goal of God's program for the ages" (p. 104). Historic premillennialists rest their case almost exclusively on their interpretation of Rev 20:1-6. George E. Ladd maintains: "Premillennialism is the doctrine stating that after the Second Coming of Christ, he will reign for a thousand years in the new heavens and the new earth of the Age to Come. This is the natural reading of Rev 20:1-6" (*The Meaning of the Millennium: Four Views*, ed. R. G. Clouse (Downers Grove: InterVarsity, 1977] 17). For a more thorough discussion see Ladd's *Crucial Questions About the Kingdom of God* (Grand Rapids: Eerdmans, 1952).

[31]Herman Hoyt insists that although the NT applies OT prophecies to the NT church "it does not do so in the sense of identifying the church as spiritual Israel. It makes such application merely for the purpose of explaining something that is true of both" (*The Meaning of the Millennium* 43). Ladd, a former dispensationalist, understands dispensationalism to teach that "the millennium is not a stage in the redemptive work of Christ but the fulfillment of the theocratic promises to Israel" (*The New Bible Dictionary*, ed. J. D. Douglas [Grand Rapids: Eerdmans, 1962] 390). Kenneth Barker distinguishes between preliminary fulfillment in the NT period or in the continuing church age and final, complete fulfillment in the millennium ("False Dichotomies Between the Testaments"). The relationship between this final fulfillment in the earthly millennium and the eternal state is unclear. On the supposition of the reestablishment of the Israelite theocracy in the millennium, Louis Berkhof correctly insists: "The theocratic nation itself was merely a type, a shadow of the spiritual realities of a better day, and therefore destined to vanish as soon as the antitype made its appearance. The restoration of the ancient theocracy in the future would simply mean the recurrence of the type – to what purpose? – and not at all the establishment of the Kingdom. It should be borne in mind that the beginnings of the Kingdom of God existed long before the theocracy was established, and continued to develop, and even after it lost its national existence. And the founding of the Kingdom in the new dispensation was in no way dependent on the fortunes of the Jewish nation" (*The Kingdom of God: The Development of the Idea of the Kingdom, Especially Since the Eighteenth Century* [Grand Rapids: Eerdmans, 1951] 170-171).

[32]See, *e.g.*, Leonhard Goppelt, *Typos: The Typological Interpretation of the Old Testament in the* New (Grand Rapids: Eerdmans, 1982); Richard M. Davidson, *Typological Structures in the Old and New Testaments* (Berrien Springs: Andrews University, 1981). I have included my review of Goppelt's book here in this collected writings. Roger Nicole's summarization and evaluation of the teaching of Patrick Fairbairn on biblical typology is especially useful. Nicole contends: "It is high time that in the midst of controversies in which all kinds of accusations are levelled against the use of the OT by NT authors the painstaking work of Patrick Fairbairn and his monumental scholarship be once again taken into consideration" ("Patrick Fairbairn and Biblical Hermeneutics as Related to the Quotations of the Old Testament in the New," in *Hermeneutics, Inerrancy, and the Bible*, ed. E. D. Radmacher and R. D. Preus [Grand Rapids: Zondervan, 1984] 774). Helpful also are the response papers of Ronald F. Youngblood and S. Lewis Johnson in the same volume.

[33]O. T. Allis, *Prophecy and the Church* (Grand Rapids: Baker, 1969) 256. For a more recent discussion of this subject see the excellent and thorough study by Anthony A. Hoekema, *The Bible and the Future* (Grand Rapids: Eerdmans, 1979).
[34]Meredith G. Kline, "Genesis," in *The New Bible Commentary: Revised,* ed. D. Guthrie and J. A. Motyer (Grand Rapids: Eerdmans, 1970) 80.
[35]Allis, *Prophecy and the Church* 261.

CHAPTER THIRTEEN

ISRAEL AS LIGHT TO THE NATIONS (A Review Article*) [*Apologetics*]

For those interested in the relationship between the OT and NT, Paul van Buren in the second volume of his projected four-volume systematic theology takes a new look at an old issue in the history of doctrine. As an ardent spokesman for ecumenical pluralism van Buren seeks to (re)construct Jewish-Christian relations on the foundation of an enlightened understanding of the nature of human experience and religious language. The religion department of Temple University, of which van Buren was a senior member, has been a leading voice in promoting interfaith dialogue. (The *Journal of Ecumenical Studies* is published by the University.) Although evangelical theology and modern theology are worlds apart, much may be gained through serious interaction with the various forms of modern thought. Radical theologians like van Buren can be of service in provoking today's evangelicals to fresh consideration of traditionally-held Christian doctrines and in providing a meaningful context in which they can articulate and reaffirm the biblical basis for those historic doctrines of the faith.

Van Buren's study of historical theology began with his doctoral work under Karl Barth on the topic of Calvin's christology.[1] From a Barthian perspective on the "biblical testimony to God's self-revelation in Jesus Christ" van Buren set out by means of linguistic analysis to elucidate the meaning of the Christian message for secular man in a subsequent, controversial book.[2] At this stage in van Buren's theological quest an attempt was made to isolate the existential meaning of "God-language" in ancient thought. Critical of the Bultmannian school, van Buren urged a thorough revision of our understanding of the function and meaning of religious language itself.

> The theological "left" has urged us to think through Christian faith in the light of the critique of modern thought. Again. "Amen" – but we would take this demand seriously. It will not do simply to translate the difficult word "God" into some highly or subtly qualified phrase such as our "ultimate concern," or worse, "transcendent reality," or even, "the ground and end of all things." These expressions are masquerading as empirical name tags, and they are used as though they referred to something, but they lead us right back into the problem of ancient thought, or they put us in the worse situation of speaking a meaningless language. Light can be thrown on the assertions of ancient thought, however, and

> help can be found in finding a way to speak which is honest and loyal to the way we think today, by a careful analysis of the function of the words and statements of Christian faith. We may learn what sort they are, and their meaning, which is their use, will become clear. In this way, we more than meet the concerns of Bultmann and Ogden, even if we do so in a way quite different from that which they suggest, and with rather different results.[3]

The idea of a transcendent God, argued van Buren, is untenable in the modern scientific age. In common with the "death-of-God" theologians of the 1960s van Buren rejected the orthodox conception of God as eternal, impassible, transcendent Being. Indications of this thinking were already apparent in his doctoral study.

In the prolegomena to his recent study in systematics[4] van Buren remarks that "God-talk" is something we learn from our parents. It is the expression of an otherwise common human experience. The language of faith in the Jewish-Christian traditions is expressive of human experience within a particular linguistic community.[5] The task of Jewish and Christian theologians is to call us to our common "walk in the Way." Van Buren admits to having been mistaken in his earlier attempt in *The Secular Meaning of the Gospel* to secularize this way of faith.[6] He has now come to realize that "we have been called into a Way that is not that of the world."[7] Once hesitant to attempt a definition of "God," van Buren freely acknowledges that "the One whom we worship and dare to call our Father, the only God we know, is the Lord, the God of Israel, who by his Spirit through his Son has drawn us Gentiles into his Way."[8] Yet, remarks van Buren,

> there are indeed problems in how we speak of God, but they are the result neither of attempting to put our creaturely language to a task for which it is not suited, nor of the inconsistency of such talk with the premise of secularity. The problems which we need to take seriously are those which have to do with the coherence of our talk of God with the Way he has given us to walk, that is, with our own premises. These problems of coherence can be considered by reflecting on how we speak of God's person and presence, his power and freedom and his love and suffering.[9]

In short, confesses van Buren, "God is a person."[10]

With this new apprehension of "God" van Buren describes the nature of Israel's testimony to God in the present sequel to *Discerning the Way*. Israel's story is a "narrative metaphysics."[11] "Since Israel's affirmation of God as Creator and the world as God's creation is, logically, a metaphysical one, it cannot be either in agreement or in disagreement with the natural sciences, for science, when it is true to itself, is not a metaphysical enterprise."[12] Metaphysical language, the language of faith, reflects human experience; it is a linguistic phenomenon.[13] Faith affirms "the incarnate, temporal involvement of God in Creation, in his election of Israel, and in his call to both Israel and the church to work and pray that his reign of righteousness come and his will of justice and love be done on earth."[14] Central to Israel's faith and the church's is the covenant of God with Israel.[15] Van Buren's theology of the covenant, as he himself notes repeatedly in his writings, bears no affinity to that of classical Reformed theology, which position he finds abhorrent.[16] The law-gospel dichotomy in Protestant theology, postulates van Buren, reflects an outmoded world-view founded upon the Roman legal tradition.[17] Here is the nub of the current debate in biblical and theological studies concerning the relationship between the Testaments. In the following quotation van Buren assesses the significance and dimensions of the controversy:

> In recent years, there have also appeared some Christians who, having learned something about Judaism and its teachings, and having assumed that Paul knew at least as much about it as they did, have also begun to reject the church's traditional picture of Paul and this traditional other "gospel." Some have, but certainly not the majority. The church is presently engaged in a debate, conducted largely among biblical scholars and generally ignored by most of the church, as to which is the real Paul. Much is at stake in this debate, including ecclesiastical traditions, beloved teachers, and esteemed fathers. Indeed, the debate is ultimately about which is the real gospel![18]

In van Buren's interpretation of "covenant" in the Scriptures - that is, the OT writings in distinction from the NT writings, which van Buren labels "the Apostolic Writings" – the event of God's self-revelation to his people at Sinai defines Israel's existence and purpose in history. Beyond its formative significance for the people Israel, "covenant" serves as a useful paradigm for understanding the historical role and mission of Jesus of Nazareth.[19]

> Jesus stood before and in the midst of his people as God's model of "being Israel." By no means does he stand there in order to draw his fellow Jews away from being Jewish for the sake of some "goyish" enterprise called Christianity. On the contrary, Jesus' call to his people in his lifetime and to this day is rather that they be Jews as he was a Jew, that they be *God's* Jews.[20]

In the apostle Paul's teaching on unity "in Christ," observes van Buren, we discover

> the heart of the mystery of Israel and of Jesus' role as Israel-for-the-Gentiles. God set Jesus in the world to be there for all the others by making him to be Israel in exemplary fashion. Jesus could be for all the others because Israel was and had always been for all the others. Abraham had been called for the sake of the world. Now in Jesus this calling of Israel had been put into effect for all the Gentiles.[21]

As van Buren makes clear at the outset of his study, the mission of the church "would serve, and therefore never seek to hinder Israel's own mission. Its mission to the Jewish people, therefore, would be to help Israel to be itself and carry out its role in God's plan for the redemption of creation."[22]

What, then, is the relationship between Israel and the church? Traditionally that relationship has been defined in terms of "promise and fulfillment." This terminology, suggests van Buren, is at best inadequate and at worst distorted in its theological grasp of the true relationship between the Testaments.

> As a confirmation of the Scriptures [the OT writings], the Apostolic Writings testify to Jesus Christ as God's Yes to all his promises. To confirm a promise, however, is not the same as to fulfill it. God's promises to Israel include, for example, possession of the land. In Jesus Christ, if we are to believe the apostle Paul, God said Yes also to that promise. The church of Jesus Christ, therefore, cannot coherently do other than confirm and support the promise of the Land to the Jewish people. It cannot twist this promise to the Jews into a spiritualized promise to the church, for to do so would be to witness to Jesus Christ as God's No to this particular and by no means peripheral promise of his. Coherence requires that the church be at the least much more cautious with its use of the word "fulfillment" than it has been in the past. Instead of struggling with weaker expressions, such as "partial fulfillment," or "fulfillment in principle," the church will be better served if a Christian theology of Israel proposes a better model. We therefore propose and will use an alternative model: that of promise and confirmation. We do so because it seems to us to be clear that God's church cannot be itself without confirming his choice of, covenant with, and promises to his people Israel.[23]

Classical Protestant theology, argues van Buren, has erroneously maintained a mere typological meaning for the land of Canaan. That viewpoint, along with its theological system of interpretation, is totally misguided. To be sure, the connection between Israel and the land is elusive. "The ambiguity of Israel's present life in the land raises the question whether it was ever otherwise, and therefore whether God's revelation has not always shared in this ambiguity."[24] Consistent with van Buren's Barthian persuasion of earlier years he writes: "The reality and therefore the ambiguity of landed life is the only context which God has chosen for his revelation to his people Israel. We are forced to conclude, therefore, that God has chosen ambiguity for all of his revelation."[25] Such is the dialectic between the sovereignty of God and human responsibility, or what van Buren prefers to speak of as the freedom of God and the freedom of God's people. This ambiguity pertaining to Israel and the land, however does not negate Israel's right and claim to Palestine. The election of Israel is bound up with God's promise of the land. Israel's tenure in the land throughout history rests ultimately upon the inscrutable and incomprehensible will of God. "Reversing eighteen centuries of its teaching, the church is now asserting officially [?] that if Israel was once elected, its election endures. God's covenant with Israel, it is being argued, is eternal, for this is surely the message of Israel's (and the church's!) Scriptures."[26]

According to van Buren, Israel is a nation, not a religion.[27] As a people of the land, Israel is unique – unlike all the other nations.[28] To her belong the covenant, the promises, the Scriptures. But God's revelation to his elect people does not end with the canonical Scriptures.[29]

> In acknowledging Israel's Scriptures as its Canon, however, the church failed to consider the implications of the fact that Israel, without respect to the church, continued to read, preserve, interpret, and live from those Scriptures. . . . For the church, [its failure] produced ears deaf to the witness of God's people and a consequent misunderstanding of God's Torah, leading to a theological misconstruction of "Law" and "Gospel," a polarity of the church's invention.[30]

God continues to speak to his people Israel. Of at least equal significance to the Exodus event for the modern Jew are the revelatory events ("Event") of the Holocaust and the establishment of the state of Israel.[31]

Van Buren takes exception to Barth's understanding of the criterion of theology; "Because we see the commission of Israel and the church more broadly than Barth, we cannot so narrowly conceive the Bible itself as the Word of God, but must see it also as Torah, as instruction, as pointers to the Way into which God has called Israel and the church to walk with him through history."[32] For this reason van Buren develops his theology of the Jewish-Christian reality around the concept of the Way. Just how clear and decisive is van Buren's criterion for theology?

> The honest answer is that ours is not as clear as Barth's. We cannot honestly point to the Bible and say, there is our norm. Our norm includes and is even centered on the Bible, but it is the Bible as it has been carried and interpreted, not only by the church, but also by the Jewish people. . . .
>
> Our intent is to discern the finger and voice of the Lord God of Israel in the postbiblical history of both Israel and the church, as well as in the Scriptures and the Apostolic Writings.[33]

From this theological position, how are we to understand the church's confession of the triune God, one God in three persons? In light of his objections to Barth's view, notes van Buren,

> we conclude that we were not wrong in developing the Prolegomenon to our *Theology of the Jewish-Christian Reality* around the concept of the Way, rather than that of the Word of God, or revelation, and that we had no alternative but to develop the doctrine of the Trinity within it as a testimony to the action of the God of Israel, and therefore to the God who acted so to call the Gentiles into his service, alongside Israel, by his Spirit, through Jesus Christ. The result may be called a historical-functional doctrine of the Trinity, not constructed out of a strained analy-

> sis of a theological concept, but as testimony to the conviction that God was truly himself in doing this strange new thing of producing, alongside his people Israel, also his Gentile church.[34]

Similarly van Buren replaces the orthodox conception of the "divinity of Christ" with a vague notion of Jesus as "Son of God" – that is, Son of "Israel's God."[35] In the work under review the author thus resumes his case for a thoroughgoing revision of orthodox christology along neoBarthian lines, as suggested in *Christ in Our Place*, being more explicit now on his views regarding the Trinity. The catholic, orthodox interpretation of God and Christ are relegated to the world of ancient thought that no longer speaks the language of modern faith.

Just how far afield van Buren's work in theology is should be apparent to the readers of the *Journal of the Evangelical Theological Society*. Fundamentally, van Buren's view of "revelation" makes havoc of Christian theology. Working from an immanentistic conception of God, van Buren identifies human experience as the source of theology rather than the transcendent God speaking in the Scriptures, OT and NT, as taught by orthodox Christianity. However, van Buren's "language-game," if one will pardon this popular expression for the serious discipline of knowing God (theology), is regrettably not wholly foreign to certain formulations of contemporary evangelical and Reformed theology. Traditional views regarding the abiding validity of the law-gospel contrast, the person and work of Christ, and the normativity and infallibility of the canonical Scriptures – to name but a few of the issues raised in van Buren's systematics – are all being challenged in one form or another by some who number themselves among the evangelicals. Several recent, "evangelical" reinterpretations of doctrine betray presuppositions inimical to a genuinely biblical theology. Even on an issue such as the relation between Jews and the land many evangelical, Reformed and modern interpreters are finding that they share much in common.[36] Perhaps closer, critical discussion of modern theology by evangelicals would bring about both clarification and rethinking of these basic theological issues.

The prospects of van Buren's exposition of a Christian theology of the people Israel extend beyond the particularism of the Jewish-Christian tradition (if we are to accent the continuity between Israel and the church). As an aspect of the current, wider context of American theology,[37] van Buren says: "One of the more difficult challenges which they [Christians and Jews] will do well to face together is that of their understanding of the way in which the God of Abraham, Isaac, and Jacob has been and is at work in the People of the Book (Islam), and in the peoples of many books (Hindus and Buddhists, and others)."[38] An underlying premise in van Buren's work is acceptance of the diverse, pluriform character of truth. Conflicts between competing religious systems can be resolved by way of theological contextualization. And the hinge that opens the door to ecumenical dialogue is the modern understanding of the language of faith obtained through linguistic analysis. Before taking up the questions of other religions in a final volume of his systematics, van Buren will turn his attention once more to the matter of christology in the third volume. In the meantime the thrust of van Buren's theology of the people of Israel is to encourage the Jew to affirm his "spiritual" (that is, national) identity for the sake of the world's redemption.

"Jewish faithfulness to Torah involves a rejection of traditional Christianity and of the church's understanding of Paul's gospel."[39] The author leaves us to ponder anew the question of the church's traditional understanding of the Jewish people. "The church today has to decide now whether the covenant between God and Israel, which Paul believed to be irrevocable in his day, is still in force."[40] In the last analysis, van Buren's work raises the question concerning the particularity of the Christian faith and in so doing calls for a response from those committed to the defense of historic, orthodox doctrine.

ENDNOTES

*Paul N. van Buren, *A Christian Theology of the People Israel: Part II. A Theology of the Jewish-Christian Reality* (New York: Seabury, 1983).
[1]Paul N. van Buren, *Christ in Our Place: The Substitutionary Character of Calvin's Doctrine of Reconciliation* (Grand Rapids: Eerdmans, 1957).
[2]Paul N. van Buren, *The Secular Meaning of the Gospel: Based on an Analysis of Its Language* (New York: Macmillan, 1963).
[3]*Ibid.* 170.
[4]Paul M. van Buren, *Discerning the Way: A Theology of the Jewish-Christian Reality* (New York: Seabury, 1980).
[5]*Ibid.* 30.
[6]*Ibid.* 58.
[7]*Ibid.* 59.
[8]*Ibid.* 86.
[9]*Ibid.* 102.
[10]*Ibid.* 111.
[11]*A Christian Theology of the People Israel* 50.
[12]*Ibid.* 52.
[13]See further Paul M. van Buren, *The Edges of Language: An Essay in the Logic of a Religion* (New York: Macmillan, 1972).
[14]*A Christian Theology of the People Israel* 268.
[15]*Cf.* also *Secular* 45.
[16]*A Christian Theology of the People Israel* 76-77; see also *Discerning* 20-21 and *Secular* 46 n.26.
[17]*A Christian Theology of the People Israel* 210. Contrast the reviewer's analysis of covenant theology in Chapter One of this collected writings.
[18]*A Christian Theology of the People Israel* 281.
[19]*Secular* 50-51.
[20]*A Christian Theology of the People Israel* 258, *italics his.*
[21]*Ibid.* 260.
[22]*Ibid.* 42.
[23]*Ibid.* 30.
[24]*Ibid.* 187.
[25]*Ibid.* 188.
[26]*Ibid.* 22.
[27]*Ibid.* 31.
[28]*Ibid.* 124.
[29]*Ibid.* 9. See also *Discerning* 161, 176.
[30]*Ibid.* 26.
[31]*Discerning* 176.
[32]*A Christian Theology of the People Israel* 8.
[33]*Ibid.* 8-9.
[34]*Ibid.* 8.
[35]*Ibid.* 261.
[36]See my comments on this matter in Chapter Twelve.
[37]Paul van Buren, *The Burden of Freedom: Americans and the God of Israel* (New York: Seabury, 1976) 1ff.
[38]*A Christian Theology of the People Israel* 262-263.

[39]*Ibid*. 268.
[40]*Ibid*. 283.

CHAPTER FOURTEEN

COVENANT AND COMMON GRACE (A Review Article*) [*Theonomy, or the Doctrine of Divine Providence*]

Gaining considerable notoriety in American evangelicalism in the last quarter of the twentieth century, the movement known as Theonomy or Christian Reconstruction has as its aim the reconstruction of American society along the lines of the ancient covenant between God and the nation of Israel. Christian Reconstructionists seek to reinstitute the civil code of Moses as the standard for social morality in America, and they view this as a return to the principles and standards of our original founders. Though there is a historical precedent for theonomic social ethics, it is clear that the teachings of the Christian Reconstructionist movement are a departure from Calvinist theology.[1]

For purposes of this present discussion we shall refer to this theological movement in terms of its characteristic teaching, that which is determinative of its system of doctrine, namely, dominion theology. We begin with a brief outline of this theology as developed in Gary North's *Dominion and Common Grace*, and then proceed to a critical analysis of his position. Of fundamental import in North's study is the restructuring of the history of God's covenantal dealings with humanity in creation and redemption. Rejecting the traditional doctrine of the Covenant of Works, North regards the original Covenant of Creation as remaining in effect after the Fall. This covenant between God and all humankind, which North calls the dominion covenant, continues to shape the course of civilization. All biblical law is a republishing of the law of the creation covenant: obedience brings blessings, while disobedience brings curses.

According to North, there is a progressive manifestation of God's kingdom seen in the emergence of Christian dominion over all the earth, so that "the civilization of the world will gradually reflect God's biblically revealed law-order."[2] Repeatedly, North stresses that this global extension of biblical law necessitates only an external compliance on the part of the nations' citizens. "People at that last day need only be externally obedient to the terms of the covenant, meaning biblical law. This book attempts to explain how this externally faithful living might operate."[3] To achieve this goal North argues for a particular version of the common grace doctrine, one which, North admits, differs from traditional Reformed thinking.

The author addresses the question of how God regards the good that is done by individuals in society – specifically, what is God's attitude towards those who render mere external compliance to biblical law? Does he show any favor to the reprobate in history? North considers Herman Hoeksema to be the guiding light in his interpretation of history, indeed as "perhaps the most brilliant systematic theologian in America in this century."[4] Hoeksema and those who followed him were convinced that, contrary to the decision of the [Christian Reformed Church], there is no such thing as common grace.[5] That is to say, the "gifts" enjoyed by the reprobate in history do not indicate an attitude of favor by God upon them. Contrary to the teachings of historic Reformed theology, there is no common grace in the sense of divine favor upon the reprobate. What Hoeksema has called mere "gifts" of God to the unregenerate, North calls common grace. There is no substantive difference, however, in these two viewpoints. Both deny that God shows favor to the unregenerate. They affirm that God's attitude to the reprobate throughout history and eternity is one of perfect hatred. Being holy God cannot look upon the wicked with favor, even though he does bestow good gifts (or "favors") upon the ungodly. Instead, the wrath of God abides upon them ever and exclusively.

> God does not favor the unregenerate at any time after the rebellion of man. Man is totally depraved, and there is nothing in him deserving praise or favor, nor does God look favorably on him. God grants the unregenerate man favors (not favor) in order to heap coals of fire on his head (if he is not part of the elect) or else to call him to repentance (which God's special grace accomplishes). Thus, God is hostile to the ethical rebel throughout history and eternity. God hates unregenerate men with a perfect hatred from beginning to end, for they are totally depraved from beginning to end.[6]

The thrust of North's argument is that the doctrine of common grace finds consistent expression only in terms of theonomic postmillennialism.[7] Common grace, the author asserts, is about eschatology. By indicating inadequacies in Cornelius Van Til's interpretation of common grace North hopes to demonstrate that the root of the problem lies in Van Til's amillennial eschatology. Rather than teaching that common grace decreases over time, as Van Til has done, North contends that common grace increases throughout the course of history, keeping pace with the (assumed) actualizing of Christian dominion prior to Christ's return in judgment. Common grace is "future grace;" it is "later grace."[8] As special grace increases over time in the postmillennial scheme of things, so does common grace. "This is the essence of common grace: it increases for generations, and then it is removed overnight."[9] In the teaching of Jesus in Matt 15:21-28 North interprets the bread on the table to refer to special grace for the elect of God and the crumbs which fall on the floor to refer to common grace for the reprobate. What this means concretely is that "As the world gets richer and more peaceful, the 'dogs' benefit."[10] Dominion theology, as developed in the writings of North, propounds a specific theory of economics.[11] With the increase of spiritual blessing (special grace) throughout the world there is a corresponding increase of material prosperity (common grace), which is received and enjoyed by the elect and the reprobate in different ways. In the theonomic postmillennial vision, as Christians become culturally dominant the blessings of common grace produce lasting victory for the elect and temporary enjoyment for the reprobate prior to their complete destruction at the close of history. At the height of cultural dominance by Christians comes the final rebellion by the unregenerate, at which time "God will intervene at the end of time to save his *briefly threatened* church."[12] Incidentally, though North takes Van Til the amillennialist to task for his defective view on common grace, he overlooks the fact that Hoeksema, whose teaching on common grace is comparable to his own, is also an amillennialist. Apparently a doctrine of common grace that denies divine favor to the reprobate and postmillennialism are not as inseparable as North contends.

Although North's work has major theological flaws, it does address several extremely important issues that need to be dealt with in systematic fashion. Indeed, the main contribution of this study is the plea for *systematic* coherence in the exposition of the doctrines of the Reformed faith, a trait that has largely fallen by the wayside of late. Accepting this challenge we will evaluate dominion theology in terms of the Reformed system of covenant theology.

According to traditional covenant theology every person since the Fall is a covenant-breaker. Fallen humanity stands *outside* the covenant of God. The atonement of Christ, though limited in its saving benefits to the elect, makes possible the establishment of a special covenant community, which in the course of redemptive history includes both elect and some nonelect. The proper purpose of redemptive covenant is spiritual union and communion with Christ. Since Christ died for his own, the saving benefits of his death are efficacious to the elect alone. The atonement of Christ, accordingly, is particular and definite. That is to say, in terms of the saving efficacy of the cross the extent of the atonement is limited, not universal. However, a concomitant of this program of redemption is common grace, which provides temporal, not eternal, benefits for all humankind indiscriminately. The operation of common grace in the world extends from the Fall to the Return of Christ. Common grace is neither "earlier grace" (*à la* Van Til) nor "later grace" (*à la* North). John Murray correctly defines common grace as "every favor of whatever kind or degree, falling short of salvation, which this undeserving and sin-cursed world enjoys at the hand of God."[13]

Outside the redemptive covenant community of Israel, to which the law of Moses was given, that law serves with respect to the formation of the laws of the common grace state only as a guide. Ultimately, it is God in his providence who establishes and upholds nations and societies both in terms of the adoption and the practice of civil mores. To be sure, Reformed theology opposes any and all forms of autonomous natural theology, including natural law. Morality is established directly by God through supernatural or special revelation in the theocracy and in the nontheocratic community of faith. Civil morality in a religiously diverse and pluralistic society is determined by the consent of the people, all of them recipients of natural or general revelation. Just as every individual knows the true God, though not savingly, each person has the things of the law written upon his/her heart (Rom 1:18-2:16).

Of course, both the formation and the implementation of public policy fall under the sovereign rule and providential guidance of God. When God withholds his goodness and (common) grace, when he leaves a people to their own evil devices, that nation falls into gross idolatry and wickedness, impugning the law of God written upon the human heart while suppressing the truth of the knowledge of God. There is common grace and there is common wrath: history is a process of ebb and flow. Civil righteousness serves a limited, though essential, function in the divine ordering and preservation of society. It is in this political and social setting that the church ministers the gospel of Christ to all the world. To quote again from Murray: "Civil government as such is not a redemptive ordinance. But it provides, and is intended to provide, that outward peace and order within which the ordinances of redemption may work to the accomplishment of God's saving purposes."[14]

The Reformed doctrine of natural law, contrary to North's reading, stands over against modern theories of secular jurisprudence arising out of the Enlightenment. It is true that Van Til brought further clarification in Reformed thinking. North correctly notes that "Van Til destroyed any remaining hope in natural law or a common-ground philosophy. He took the insights of Abraham Kuyper and Herman Bavinck and extended these insights to their biblical and logical conclusion: *the impossibility of any natural law common ground link between covenant-keepers and covenant-breakers*."[15] Since it is inconceivable to North that the state might proceed legitimately in the exercise of moral discipline on some basis other than biblical laws, particularlv the Mosaic legislation, he and the Christian Reconstructionists call for the enforcement of these laws by the state. Not even Van Til, states North, was perceptive enough to see this point and to carry through the logic of his own teaching. "Van Til never adopted biblical law as an alternative to the natural law systems that he so thoroughly destroyed. This always hampered the development of his own philosophy, for the older Reformed view of the moral law was based squarely on the natural-law concepts Van Til had destroyed. He was unwilling to challenge the older Reformed creeds on this point."[16]

It is commendable that North openly acknowledges his several differences with the formulations in the Westminster Standards (though misinterpreting early Reformed teaching on natural law in the process). The deficiencies, he remarks, "have made creedal revisions mandatory. . . , leading to more biblically precise definitions of such seventeenth-century concepts as 'general equity,' 'moral law,' and 'the Covenant of Works.'"[17] These observations point to fundamental theological differences – differences which indicate a decisive and radical departure from covenant theology on the part of North. Adopting the biblical and confessional idea of "general equity" Van Til, unlike North, construed Israel's civil law to be a model, rather than a norm, for the laws of other nations.[18] More importantly, Van Til's adherence to the Reformed doctrine of the Covenant of Works, as well as his understanding of the Mosaic Covenant and its accompanying system of typology, prevented him from obscuring the crucial differences between the Old and New Covenants, between the ancient Israelite theocracy and nontheocratic church or state institutions.[19]

The underlying difference between the views of North and Van Til on the subject of civil morality and common grace is their opposing conceptions of covenantal law. North bases civil morality on Israelite law in the OT, whereas Van Til, while determining the functions of the civil government from the biblical revelation concerning the state, sees civil morality as dependent on the testimony of natural law implanted by God upon the human heart. Natural law, according to Van Til as representative of covenant theology, is one of the benefits of common grace in the fallen world. It is perhaps failure on the part of theonomists to give credence to the biblical doctrine of divine sovereignty and providence in sociopolitical affairs that inhibits a proper reading of natural law doctrine. Fear that Christians will suffer defeat and loss when left to the will of a nonChristian society prompts the theonomists' desire to reconstruct public policy in terms of the Mosaic laws for theocratic Israel. But the scriptural teaching that we are to render to Caesar the things that belong to Caesar and to God the things that belong to God clearly contradicts the theonomist teaching which sees the state as itself embodying the laws and powers of the kingdom of God.[20]

North's break with the fundamental distinctions made in the traditional system of covenant theology, *e.g.*, between works and grace, common and holy, is evident in his insistence that although the unregenerate are covenant-breakers "All men are under the terms of the dominion covenant (Gen 1:27, 28)."[21] All humankind is bound to this continuing creational covenant by virtue of the original ordinances as republished in the Mosaic laws. In keeping with this, the special holy covenant of God with Israel, detailed in full in the Deuteronomic treaty of the Great King, is secularized by North into God's covenant with every nation.[22] As a result, he crusades for a theocratic ordering of all societies and nations according to the requirements of the laws of biblical covenant, and thus theonomically conceived.

Moreover, on the basis of North's postmillennial interpretation of the prophetic promises of the covenant, he expects the objectives of this crusade to be attained. North believes that "Authority is steadily captured by Christians because of their greater covenantal faithfulness, better judgment, and greater reliability."[23] He anticipates that "Christians will some day possess cultural, economic, and political power through their adherence to biblical law. Therefore, in order to compete with the righteous, unregenerate men will have to imitate special covenantal faithfulness by adhering to the external demands of God's covenants."[24] As we observed earlier, North assumes that covenant obedience results in material prosperity. As there is progress in the development of doctrine, so also is there "a parallel growth in wealth, knowledge, and culture."[25] These visible blessings "are to serve as *confirmations of the covenant*. God therefore gives men health and wealth 'that he may establish his covenant.'"[26] (The author calls this bond "God's social covenant.")[27] In North's interpretation of history, "It was the Reformation, and especially the Puritan vision, which brought the idea of progress to the west. The Puritans believed that there is a relationship between covenantal obedience and cultural advance. This optimistic outlook was secularized by seventeenth-century Enlightenment thinkers."[28]

It is apparent that dominion theology fails to distinguish properly between redemptive covenant (traditionally called the Covenant of Grace) and the cultural mandate in its radically modified postlapsarian form. Contrary to the teachings of Scripture that cultural development has been assigned, under a separate Covenant of Common Grace, to humankind in general, North maintains that it belongs to the sphere of the holy covenant that administers the eternal kingdom. He views cultural achievement as a benefit of Christ's atonement, as a temporary blessing of the covenant for the unregenerate, as something which they help bring to fruition.

North and many Reformed theologians today err in thinking that human culture, being a fruit of the kingdom covenant, will continue on in glorified form into eternity. To the contrary, the blessings of common grace endure only to the close of history. At Christ's return, preconsummation culture will have served its historical function and will no longer be relevant to the new order. It will be replaced by the introduction of a new Glorification-culture, the New Heavens and New Earth, produced by the supernatural intervention of God. No human labor, redeemed or unredeemed, is capable of contributing to the realization of this climactic event of redemptive history. God will dwell in the midst of his people: he alone will glorify himself in the works of his hands. As a result of the Fall cultural activity (outside special limited, theocratic situations, especially Israel) is no longer holy kingdom-of-God activity. It is common, not holy. (Of course, all human thought and endeavor has a religious character.) Presently, human culture serves the limited role of providing temporal support for the growth and development of the human race, as well as satisfying the aesthetic and creative aspirations of humankind made in the image of God. To the praise of God's glory, metaculture far surpasses all expressions of earthly culture.[29]

As indicated previously, the biblical distinction between law and gospel, works and faith, is not consistently sustained by North, and in terms of the covenant structure of biblical revelation it is obliterated altogether. The result is that North levels all covenants by continuing the dominion covenant on into the postlapsarian world. In so doing, he not only blurs the works-grace distinction, but he also obscures the distinction between the holy and the common. The Genesis 9 common grace covenant, in particular, does not come into focus. Accordingly, North maintains that the principle of judicial retribution – blessing for obedience and curse for disobedience – operates *uniformly* throughout all ages, both temporal (the preredemptive and redemptive periods) and eternal. Although reward is always based upon human works of obedience, argues North, all reward to creatures is nonmeritorious. In acknowledging the grace of salvation North is correct to reject human merit in regard to the believer's inheritance in Christ. The central meaning of the word "grace" in the Bible, North points out, is saving grace in Christ. "Grace is not strictly unmerited, for Christ merits every gift, but in terms of the merit of creation – merit deserved by a creature because of its mere creaturehood – there is none. In short, when we speak of any aspect of the creation, other than the incarnate Jesus Christ, grace is defined as an *unmerited gift*."[30] Surely the Creator is not obligated to reward the creature by virtue of any inherent right in the creature (*i.e.*, "because of its mere creaturehood"). Yet, contrary to North's teaching, God by his covenant with Adam in creation obligates himself to bless Adam for his faithful obedience to the covenant. What Adam loses by demerit, Christ merits for us. The principle of works-inheritance (merit) in the covenant with Adam also informs the covenant between the Father and the Son on behalf of the elect. Blurring of the law-gospel antithesis can further be seen in North's adoption of the idea that future rewards and punishments are based upon the good deeds of the regenerate and the unregenerate. North insists that "God's blessings must always be seen in terms of God's general covenant with mankind, and this covenant always involves biblical law."[31] Though there are a number of similarities between the views of North and Hoeksema on the doctrine of the covenant, Hoeksema rightly denies this idea of rewards based on works, *i.e.*, gradations in heaven and hell, "because it would evidently explain the reward of grace apart from the death and obedience of Christ. And this is impossible. All that we ever have and ever will have in eternal glory certainly flows from the sacrifice of Christ as its meritorious cause."[32] All the faithful saints will receive eternal life as their crown of victory.

Perhaps the single, most important element in dominion theology is postmillennial eschatology. In answer to the amillennialists North says "we must deal with the question of the historical development of the wheat and tares. We must see that this process of time leads to Christian victory in the *pre-consummation* New Heavens and New Earth (Is 65:17-20)."[33] The idea of the preconsummation New Heavens and New Earth occupies a critical place in theonomic postmillennialism. It rests in large measure upon a certain reading of Is 65:20. "There is no verse in the Bible," writes North, "more devastating to amillennial eschatology. Amillennialists must allegorize it away, or better yet, ignore it."[34] Postmillennial interpretations oftentimes overlook the OT prophetic perspective on the advent(s) of Christ as a single event-complex. More to the point, although there are OT prophecies in which the semi-eschatological nature of the new age is suggested, *i.e.*, a time in which God's people are still living within the provisional world-order, North's mishandling of Is 65:20 is due to a failure to see that biblical prophecy (OT and NT) uses the ideal typological situation to depict the eternal kingdom.

What bothers North most about amillennial eschatology is its refusal to grant the Christian church a place of dominance in culture and society prior to the final rebellion by the wicked. Dominion theology sees the conquest of the world by the church of Christ as the time in which the blessings of material prosperity – the visible manifestation of the church's victory in history – are temporarily enjoyed by the reprobate, but only as a prelude to their ultimate destruction. Emerging acutely in this postmillennialist reconstruction is the problem with North's concept of common grace as operative throughout history. "Common grace is therefore a form of long-term (eternal) curse to the rebellious, and a long-term (eternal) blessing to the righteous."[35] Accordingly, there is nothing at all really common among the regenerate and the unregenerate in history. In the judgment of theonomists the idea of commonness promotes a "common-ground philosophy," an area or sphere of human existence that is religiously neutral. Dominion theology misconstrues the nature and significance of the cultural mandate in the post-Fall situation, resulting in a misinterpretation of common grace in relation to redemptive covenant.

Despite North's own classification of theonomy as "a type of covenant theology,"[36] it is evident that the tenets of dominion theology lie so far outside the bounds of traditional covenant theology that it must be regarded as an aberration from covenant theology. These two are opposing systems of doctrine. North betrays this when he dubs as "antinomian" all those (like Jonathan Edwards[37]) who do not adopt the theonomist position.

It is an irony of English Reformed theology that elements of both theonomic law and covenant theology found their way into the formulations of the Westminster Standards. There is urgent and pressing need to resolve the several tensions found in the confessional statements, especially if the Reformed churches today are to achieve greater purity in doctrine, peace, and discipline among the fellowship. Neither side in the debate over theonomic polity can claim confessional support on all points. Despite certain ambiguities and misconceptions in the Westminster Standards, the system of doctrine is unambiguously antitheonomic. Even if the time is not ripe for revision and clarification of the Westminster Standards, however desirable for the strength and vitality of Reformed Christianity, perhaps reconsideration of the nature and role of confessional subscription will temporarily help alleviate present tensions.[38]

The dilemma can best be illustrated by reference to the doctrine of the sabbath. The *Westminster Confession* (19.5 and 21.1,7,8) contains elements of a theonomic interpretation of biblical law which are at variance with the teaching of Scripture. (Other elements of theonomic law were removed earlier in the American revision of the *Confession*.) Although the sabbath ordinance is a binding obligation upon the people of God in all ages, the manner of observance changes over the course of covenant history, most notably between the Mosaic and New Covenants. Contrary to the teaching of the *Confession*, the sabbath as sign of God's covenant is not binding upon nonbelievers, simply because they are not recipients of the covenant-sign. Furthermore, the sabbath institution under the present nontheocratic administration of the covenant, *i.e.*, the New Covenant order, pertains exclusively to cultic, not cultural, activity. The idea of cessation from worldly labors, though applicable to sabbath observance under the pre-Fall creation arrangement and the Mosaic order (the original creation-theocracy was reinstituted with certain modifications under Moses as a typological picture of things to come), does not pertain to the Christian sabbath. It is, rather, the corporate worship of God's people on the first day of the week that is required under the New Covenant. The puritan doctrine, as stated in the Westminster Standards, is theocratic in its understanding.

Contemporary issues of debate in Reformed theology help to isolate and crystallize different points of view, which in turn necessitate doctrinal, *i.e.*, confessional, clarification or revision in the ongoing history of doctrinal development. Will we assume the responsibility laid before us to defend the faith once-for-all delivered to the saints? The particular issue raised in North's book is whether or not the Reformed churches will repudiate the historic, orthodox doctrine of the covenants and cease to be a Reformed confessional body.

ENDNOTES

*Gary North, *Dominion and Common Grace: The Biblical Basis of Progress* (Tyler, Texas: Institute for Christian Economics, 1987).
[1]See Chapter Two; and L. John van Til, "The Reconstructionist Movement: In the Calvinist Tradition?" *Pro Rege* 14 (1986) 19-28.
[2]*Dominion and Common Grace* xv.
[3]*Ibid.*
[4]*Ibid.* 6.
[5]*Ibid.*
[6]*Ibid.* 93. A concern shared by North and Van Til is the phenomenon of historical differentiation, the experience of genuine movement of individuals from wrath to grace in history. If Satan is a finished product in history, wonders North, why are not reprobate men also finished products? "Satan has been given time, knowledge, power, and all the other gifts given to man. So wherein lies the fundamental difference? Why aren't unmerited gifts from God to Satan proof of God's favor to Satan, if God's gifts of unmerited gifts to unregenerate men *are* proof of his common favor" (p. 42)? Like Hoeksema, North's extreme supralapsarian position on the decrees of God results in a defective view of common grace and history.
[7]North sees himself as clarifying and/or correcting the views of other theonomists, *e.g.*, Greg Bahnsen and Rousas J. Rushdoony (whom he regards as "the most wide-ranging and influential Reformed scholar of the second half of the twentieth century" [*ibid.* 89 n. 5) on the doctrine of common grace. Despite minor differences, they are all committed to postmillennialism of the theonomic variety. In North's judgment, the postmillennial position of Jonathan Edwards was wholly inadequate. He writes: "The great defect with the postmillennial revival inaugurated by Jonathan Edwards and his followers in the mid-eighteenth century was their neglect of biblical law. They expected to see the blessings of God come as a result of merely soteriological preaching. . . . There is nothing on the law of God or culture" (p. 175). He concludes: "Those who preach postmillennial victory apart from adherence to the law are simply pietists in disguise, and postmillennial pietism has always fallen into emotionalism, morbid introspection, and cultural defeat. Jonathan Edwards is the classic example. He was not the last Puritan; he was the *destroyer* of the remnant of Puritanism" (p. 179).
[8]*Ibid.* 91,92.
[9]*Ibid.* 83.
[10]*Ibid.* 92.
[11]See Gary North, *An Introduction to Christian Economics* (Tyler, Texas: Institute for Christian Economics, 1973), and his *The Sinai Strategy: Economics and the Ten Commandments* (Tyler, Texas: Institute for Christian Economics, 1986).
[12]North, *Dominion and Common Grace*, 108. "History will end because the Christians will have come so close to self-consistent living that rebels cannot stand to live close to them. So God will at last separate the wheat from the tares. This is the central theme of this book" (pp. 33-34).
[13]John Murray, "Common Grace," *WTJ* 5 (1942) 4. (*The original is all italicized.*) This essay is also found in his *Collected Writings* (vol.2; Edinburgh: Banner of Truth Trust, 1977).
[14]*Ibid.* 21.
[15]North, *Dominion and Common Grace* 115.
[16]*Ibid.*

[17]*Ibid.*
[18]North remarks that "theonomists have indeed abandoned Calvin's sixteenth-century understanding of natural law. Van Til has left them no choice. He destroyed the intellectual case for natural law" (p. 121). Contrast James B. Jordan, "Calvinism and 'The Judicial Law of Moses:' An Historical Survey," *The Journal of Christian Reconstruction* 5 (1978-79) 17-48, and my argument presented in Chapter Two.
[19]North comments: "If they [the Hebrews] were faithful, God said, they would not suffer the burdens of sickness, and no one and no animal would suffer miscarriages (Ex 23:24-26). Special grace leads to a commitment to the law; the commitment to God's law permits God to reduce the common curse element of nature's law, leaving proportionately more common grace – the reign of beneficient common law. The curse of nature can therefore be steadily reduced, but only if men conform themselves to revealed law or to the work of the law in their hearts. One important visible blessing then comes in the form of a more productive, less scarcity-dominated nature" (p. 99). Contrast Cornelius Van Til's understanding of the rigors of the law of Moses within the Israelite theocracy in *Christian Theistic Ethics* (In Defense of the Faith 3; published syllabus, 1974) 92-105.
[20]Legitimate civil legislation does not create conflict with biblical ethics. When conflict does arise, it is the result of the state's misuse or usurpation of power and authority, or failure to honor natural revelation. Under such circumstances Christians have the duty to obey God rather than the state.
[21]North, *Dominion and Common Grace* 78.
[22]See the perceptive remarks of Meredith G. Kline in "Comments on an Old-New Error: A Review Article," *WTJ* 41 (1978) 172-89, esp. 178. This article remains the finest critique of theonomy from the perspective of covenant theology.
[23]North, *Dominion and Common Grace* 78.
[24]*Ibid.* 97-98. "Progress culturally, economically, and politically is intimately linked to the extension and application of biblical law. The blessings promised in Romans, chap. eleven, concerning the effects of the promised conversion of Israel (not necessarily the state of Israel) to the gospel, will be in part the product of biblical law. But those blessings do not necessarily include universal regeneration. The blessings only require the extension of Christian culture. For the long-term progress of culture, of course, this increase of common grace (or reduction of the common curse) must be reinforced (rejuvenated and renewed) by special grace-conversions" (pp. 175-76). Earlier in the book North reasons that "We get richer, wiser, and culturally dominant when we are faithful to God's law (Deut 28:1-14); our opponents get poorer, more foolish, and culturally irrelevant when they violate the terms of the covenant (Deut 29:15-68)" (p. 70).
[25]*Ibid.* 101.
[26]*Ibid.* 11.
[27]*Ibid.* 212.
[28]*Ibid.* 113. Compare my review of John von Rohr's *The Covenant of Grace in Puritan Thought* included here in this collected writings.
[29]See Meredith C. Kline, *Kingdom Prologue* (3 vols., privately published, 1985-86).
[30]North, *Dominion and Common Grace* 4. North interprets 1 Tim 4:10 to mean that "Christ died for all men, giving unmerited gifts to all men in time and on earth. Some people go to eternal destruction, and others are resurrected to live with Christ eternally. But all men have at least the unmerited gift of life, at least for a time. There are therefore two kinds of salvation: special (eternal) and temporal (earthly)" (p. 5).

According to Hoeksema, all that Adam could have expected on the basis of his obedience to God's covenant at creation was earthly life. Subsequent to the Fall, Christ merits both earthly and eternal life, the latter not being something that Adam could have merited even if he remained faithful to God. Hoeksema asks: "If eternal life and glory could have been attained in the first man, Adam, would God have chosen the long and deep way through the death of His Son? He would not. And the fact is that it was quite impossible for Adam to attain to the heavenly level of immortal life. Immortality and heavenly glory are in Christ Jesus alone. And outside of the Son of God come into the flesh they were never attainable" (*Reformed Dogmatics* [Grand Rapids: Reformed Free Publishing Association, 1966] 220). For a historical-theological analysis and critique of this and similar views, see Chapter Four.

[31]North, *Dominion and Common Grace* 25-26.

[32]Hoeksema, *Reformed Dogmatics* 516.

[33]North, *Dominion and Common Grace* 68. Hoeksema remarks: "Scripture certainly does not sustain the notion that in the end all the world will accept Christ, that righteousness and peace will reign supreme, and that the church will experience a period of great prosperity, antecedent to the coming of the Lord. The very opposite is true. . . . Besides, the idea that the present age will gradually develop into the age of the kingdom of glory is also anti-Scriptural" (*Reformed Dogmatics* 817).

[34]North, *Dominion and Common Grace* 79. North distorts and misrepresents the teachings of amillennialism by stating that "The church fails in its mission to evangelize the world, disciple the nations, and subdue the earth to the glory of God" (*ibid.* 123). He regards R. B. Kuiper's amillennial conception of history to be "essentially Barthian" (p. 125). Kuiper's statements on the victorious hope of the church can only be interpreted, says North, in terms of a "hidden history," *i.e.*, the Barthian idea of *Geschichte.*

[35]*Ibid.* 25. "Law does not save men's soul, but *partial obedience to it does save their bodies and their culture*" (p. 173).

[36]*Ibid.* 121.

[37]*Ibid.* 141. See note 4 above.

[38]American Presbyterians in the tradition of historic Reformed theology have been divided almost from the beginning between those who understand subscription to the Westminster Standards to mean agreement with the system of doctrine contained therein, which is something less than affirming agreement with the confessional formulations in their entirety, and those who adopt the Standards *in toto,* without any deviation or modification whatsoever. The fact that the *Westminster Confession of Faith* has previously undergone revision indicates that Reformed Christians have recognized the subordinate and provisional character of the creeds and confessions of the church to the teachings of Scripture.

CHAPTER FIFTEEN

ISRAEL AND THE ESCHATON (A Review Article*) [*Eschatology*]

The evangelical community is indebted to John Feinberg, the editor of the S. Lewis Johnson *Festschrift*, for this exceptional contribution to the ongoing dialogue between dispensational and covenantal theologians. The collection of essays is well organized, and the individual contributors are to be commended, on the whole, for their courteous and irenic presentation of opposing points of view. The subject of this volume is exceedingly complex. It is particularly encouraging to find many of the contributors anticipating and answering problems raised by others within this study. There is ample justification for Feinberg's closing observation that "members of both sides in this discussion are listening seriously to what scholars on the other side of the issue are saying."[1]

In terms of the substance of discussson among our theological disputants three major, interrelated issues occupy our attention in this review article: soteriology (including christology, pneumatology, and ecclesiology), typology, and eschatology.[2] For the purposes of this review we define soteriology as the study of the way in which believers under the Old and New Covenants appropriate the saving benefits of God's redemption. Typology, as a division of hermeneutics, is the study of the christological relationship between the Old and New Testaments (the study of the biblico-theological correspondence between OT events, persons, and institutions and the person and work of Jesus Christ as revealed in the pages of the NT). Typological interpretation is synonymous with messianic interpretation of the Bible. The crucial issue in eschatology dividing evangelicals into two schools of interpretation, *viz.*, dispensationalism and covenant theology, is whether or not Israel is an entity ("organism") distinct from the church. Then the question is: Does ethnic Israel have a special, distinctive future kingdom experience?

The theme of the book, stated in its title, is one which addresses a subject of fundamental importance. "The first question in the interpretation of Scripture for the Christian after acknowledging the Lordship of Jesus Christ," writes Rodney Petersen, "is how to relate the Hebrew Scriptures to the 'New' Testament."[3] Douglas Moo correctly states that "Few issues are of greater significance to biblical theology and, ultimately, to systematic theology as the relation between the Testaments."[4] More than once in this volume the suggestion is made that evangelical interpreters of the Bible fall along a continuum from extreme emphasis upon the discontinuities between the Testaments to extreme emphasis upon the continuities between them. However, the differences between these two schools of thought, as evidenced in this collection of essays, are not readily explained in terms of a continuum. Some rather surprising conclusions are reached by writers from both theological camps on a variety of issues relating to testamental continuity/discontinuity. The developing rapprochement between dispensationalism and covenant theology in the last quarter of the twentieth century has been a mixed blessing for biblical (evangelical) theology. Some recent claimants to covenant theology have departed significantly from historic Reformed doctrine. The recent popularity of the "misinterpretation view of the Mosaic law" among many dispensational and covenantal theologians (see later discussion) has been a major factor in bringing both sides together on a number of issues, exegetical and theological.

After an opening essay (Part I) that provides limited historical perspective on the theological understanding of the relationship between the two Testaments among writers in the ancient church down to the present, the editor arranges the remaining essays in six pairs, each pair addressing one aspect of the overall theme from both the covenantal and dispensational points of view (in that order): in Part II, the theological systems of covenant theology and dispensationalism (Willem VanGemeren and John S. Feinberg); in Part III, the corresponding principles of hermeneutics underlying these two systems of thought (0. Palmer Robertson and Paul D. Feinberg); in Part IV the question of the method or way of salvation in Old and New Testaments (Fred H. Klooster and Allen P Ross); in Part V, the place of the Mosaic law in the history of redemption (Knox Chamblin and Douglas J. Moo); in Part VI, the issue relating to the people (or peoples) of God and the election of Israel (Marten H. Woudstra and Robert L. Saucy); and in Part VII, the nature of the kingdom promises and the manner of their fulfillment in history and in the consummation (Bruce K. Waltke and Walter C. Kaiser, Jr.). The volume concludes with a brief epilogue by the editor and personal tributes to S. Lewis Johnson by John A. Sproule and C. Samuel Storms.

The weakest section of the book is Part III, "Hermeneutics and the Testaments." Disappointingly, Palmer Robertson misses the opportunity to delineate the method of covenantal hermeneutics, specifically the biblico-theological or redemptive-historical method associated with Reformed theology. (Instead he offers an exegesis and interpretation of Am 9:11-15 as a case study.) More seriously, Paul Feinberg's essay mistakenly pits historical-grammatical interpretation against typological interpretation.[5] His particular variety of "literal" interpretation (what may well represent mainstream dispensational thinking) reflects a fundamental misunderstanding of historical-grammatical exegesis. Happily, the articles by Knox Chamblin and Douglas Moo (Part V, "The Law and the Testaments") for the most part complement one another rather than present sharply differing theological interpretations. Moo's essay is particularly helpful and insightful. The title of Bruce Waltke's article, "Kingdom Promises as Spiritual," unfortunately obscures from view the consummate realization of the ancient promises in the everlasting kingdom as that aspect of biblical eschatology is developed by Waltke (*à la* Geerhardus Vos).

Turning now to the substance of the work we focus our attention upon the two essays in Part II, "Theological Systems and the Testaments," written by Willem VanGemeren and John Feinberg. For economy of space and argument remarks on other essays in this collection will be integrated into the critique of VanGemeren and Feinberg. (Each of the other articles merits closer attention than we can provide in this review article.)

The greatest disappointment in the book is the selection of VanGemeren for the exposition of the Reformed covenantal system (and this should be of special concern to the readers of *The Westminster Theological Journal*). VanGemeren regrettably does not represent Reformed teaching on the covenant doctrine. Instead he has become a leading critic of its historical development. His sketch of the rise and development of Reformed federalism rests largely upon an uncritical acceptance of T. F. Torrance's reading and critique.[6] Unfortunately, VanGemeren's views do reflect much of the mood of contemporary evangelical thinking.

VanGemeren claims that the covenant idea in Reformed theology "has undergone philosophical developments beyond recognition" resulting in the "setback of Reformed doctrine."[7] The origins of the corruption of early Reformed covenantal theology (what others have called "pure Calvinism") lie in seventeenth-century Reformed scholasticism. Here "a significant crystallization and ossification of Calvin's thought" took place.[8] The culprits in this alleged corruption were "the federal theologians [who] operated with a mistaken concept of covenant and abstracted the covenant motif increasingly more from the Bible."[9] The abstract, scholastic notion of covenant "became an overarching principle by which to explain election and predestination."[10] The climax of Reformed scholasticism, contends VanGemeren, appears in the writings of Gisbertus Voetius (1588-1676) and Francis Turretin (1623-1687). These two men provided "the essential framework of Reformed Theology for several centuries."[11] What impact did their work have on Reformed theology for succeeding generations? "[Voetius'] insistence on Federalism affected the understanding and interpretation of the Bible, because the Bible became practically a handmaiden to theology, a resource book, and a manual of proof-texts."[12] That is to say, Voetius' work was, in VanGemeren's estimation, characterized by theological sterility. VanGemeren's criticism of Turretin is even more strident. "From the contractual concept Turretin developed a rational framework for the salvation of man."[13] VanGemeren suggests that "Turretin's approach to Covenant Theology may well have prepared the way for dead orthodoxy, the failure to capture the minds of men in the period of the Enlightenment, and also of the New England theology."[14] VanGemeren adopts the critical jargon typical of recent studies in Calvin's theology from a Barthian or neoorthodox perspective without penetrating the heart of the theological dispute.

VanGemeren attributes the reclamation of Calvin's historically conditioned concept of the divine covenants in large part to the teaching of Westminster Seminary.

> The stress on static, unchangeable "truth" and the insensitivity of the Princeton theology to adjust to the new issues and to the "historical conditioning" of Scripture put Princeton in a dangerous position. By the end of the nineteenth century changes were forthcoming. The changes were twofold and were continued at Westminster Theological Seminary. First, the appointment of Geerhardus Vos (1862-1949) to the newly-created Chair of Biblical Theology (1893). Second, a new openness to the diversity in Reformed Theology, as evidenced by the links between the Dutch theologians Kuyper and Bavinck with Princeton Seminary.[15]

We are not challenging the importance and far-reaching significance of these two changes but VanGemeren's reading of them. Furthermore, VanGemeren's analysis of the Westminster school fails to discern the perhaps subtle, but nevertheless real, differences between Vos and John Murray on the doctrine of the covenants.[16] What must be pointed out as underlying VanGemeren's critique of traditional Reformed systematics, especially its formulations on the covenants, is his own peculiar variety of theological eclecticism. He prefers to speak of "tension" and "openness" in theological interpretation.[17] Such an approach then allows room for Israel in the unfolding of God's plan for the ages, as he sees it. Rejecting a-, pre-, and postmillennialism, VanGemeren anticipates new revelation from God in history. The theologian, notes VanGemeren, plays a special role in this process. "Theology does not have the key to unlock eternity, but provides a way of *dialogue* with God."[18] More importantly,

> Dialogue also involves Israel. I have asked and am still asking that the exegetical case of Israel in the plan of God be reopened. Eschatological perspectives have at times resolved the tension between time and eternity, this world and the world to come, Israel and the nations. If we were to permit the witness of the old to have a bearing on the new and to leave "problematic" texts as witnesses to our humanness, the biblical structures of thought would continually cultivate a sense of awe and wonder at the wisdom of God. So Torrance observes: "This dialogue of God with Israel leads throughout the whole history of that people to its fulfillment in Christ who, as the Word of God made flesh, is both the embodiment of God's Word to man, and the embodiment of man's obedient Word to God." Hermeneutic openness to Israel is a concrete expression of openness to the Word of God and to the eschatological events.[19]

Feinberg identifies six distinctives of dispensationalism. First, there is the dispensationalist's recognition of the multiple senses of various expressions and terms in the Bible, *e.g.*, "Israel" and the "seed of Abraham." Either of these two examples refers to the physical descendants of Israel or to the spiritual (elect) seed, *i.e.*, true Israel (those who in the words of the apostle Paul are "true Jews"). But nondispensationalists also acknowledge this point. We must look then to the remaining five for clarification of this first dispensational distinctive. The second is dispensationalism's use of "literal" hermeneutics in contrast to typological interpretation as advocated by covenant theologians. Third, with a view to dispensationalism's literal hermeneutic, the unconditional promises made to Abraham require that at some point in history both the spiritual and material blessings find simultaneous fulfillment. Additional data from Scripture indicate to the dispensational reader that the time of this fulfillment is the return of Christ to set up the millennial kingdom on earth. Fourth, dispensationalism insists upon a distinctive future for ethnic Israel. In distinction from postmillennialism, dispensationalists teach that Israel's future blessings include a return to Palestine, a restoration of the Davidic throne on which Christ will physically reign over the nations for a literal one-thousand-year period. In distinction from historic premillennialism, they teach the rapture of the church out of the world at some point during the beginning of the millennial age (the precise time varies according to different schools within dispensationalism), the resurrection of believing Jews who died in OT history to reign with Christ on earth, and, most importantly, the rebuilding of the temple and the reinstitution of the sacrificial system. (Not all dispensationalists grant this last feature, but a consistent use of literal hermeneutics requires it.) Fifth, the church as the NT organism is distinct from Israel. (This does not necessarily imply two peoples of God. The distinction between Israel and the church in the dispensational system, however, does require the rapture of the church during the beginning stage of the millennium.) Sixth and lastly, dispensationalism is characterized by a specific philosophy of history. Feinberg contends that history for the dispensationalist is not merely salvation history, but kingdom history. By that he means that the unconditional promises to Abraham are both spiritual and material and they must find their simultaneous fulfillment in history. (Amillennialism as the most consistent expression of Reformed covenantal theology maintains that the fulfillment of the Abrahamic promises awaits the *Consummation*, the present age of the Spirit being semi-eschatological.) In summary, writes Feinberg: "I think the debate stems from three fundamental issues, *viz.*, the relation of the progress of revelation to the priority of one Testament over the other, the understanding and implications of NT use of the OT; and the understanding and implications of typology."[20] Feinberg approvingly cites George E. Ladd:

> Here is the basic watershed between a dispensational and a nondispensational theology. Dispensationalism forms its eschatology by a literal interpretation of the OT and then fits the NT into it. A nondispensational eschatology forms its theology from the explicit teaching of the NT.[21]

The crucial issue for the dispensationalist in the interpretation of biblical prophecy is the following: "While a prophecy given unconditionally to Israel has a fulfillment for the church if the NT *applies* it to the church, it must also be fulfilled to Israel. Progress of revelation cannot cancel unconditional promises."[22] The fundamental problem with the premillennial scheme is that it misplaces the ("literal") fulfillment of the unconditional promises to Abraham in the period of an earthly millennium, rather than in the eternal state. Dispensational premillennialism is characteristically more concerned in its doctrine of end-times with the alleged millennial reign of Christ on earth than with the everlasting reign of Christ with all the saints in the New Heavens and New Earth. Progress in the dialogue between dispensational and covenantal theologians could be made if the former were to give adequate attention to the final state of affairs, especially the place of ethnic Israel in the *consummate* kingdom. In the dispensational scheme of things what precise significance does the restoration of Israel in Palestine during the physical, one-thousand-year reign of Christ have for the final eschaton? Does not the apostle Paul maintain that there is no distinction between Jew and Gentile in the present age of the church and in the age to come? How do dispensationalists like Feinberg relate the everlasting kingdom of Christ to God's original promise to Abraham concerning the land as an everlasting possession?

Feinberg argues that "Double fulfillment, then, is necessitated by the NT's application of the passage to the church and by maintaining the integrity of the OT's meaning, especially in view of the unconditional nature of the promises to Israel."[23] Dispensational hermeneutics frequently distinguishes between meaning and application of the OT text. Bruce Waltke argues against this false bifurcation of the text. The meaning of the biblical text is one. As Waltke explains, "the canonical process approach combines further revelation with the sharpening focus of history itself and disallows the possibility of reinterpretation."[24] When Jesus interprets the OT concerning himself, he is not "applying" the OT text in a new and different way. He is conveying the true meaning of the OT (in the Johannine sense of the word "true"). The establishment of the NT church is neither a parenthesis in God's dealings with Israel nor an "application" of the Abrahamic promise. It is the *semi*-eschatological realization of the ancient promises: the final eschatological fulfillment awaits the Consummation. Waltke writes: "As the heavenly original ('truth') breaks into history, the antitype supersedes the type."[25] According to covenantal amillennialism,

> The typological approach of the NT is grounded in an understanding that the new age in Christ fulfills the salvation toward which the old is reaching. Retrogression from the surpassing antitype to the shadows at the end of history would have God walk backward and would draw an abhorrent veil over the glory of Christ and his church now revealed.[26]

The distinction between semi-eschatological fulfillment and final, consummate fulfillment in (amillennial) covenant theology is altogether different from dispensationalism's concept of "double fulfillment."[27] Parenthetically, would the consummation phase of the kingdom of God be viewed in dispensationalism as a "triple" fulfillment of the Abrahamic promise?

Dispensationalists adopt typological interpretation in order to make room for semi-eschatology in their system. But typological interpretation is viewed by them as NT *application* of the OT, not the literal fulfillment of the OT in its OT meaning. Feinberg writes:

> Nondispensational systems stress that the type is shadow and the antitype is reality; therefore, the meaning of the antitype supersedes and cancels the meaning of the type in its own context. Dispensationalists do

> not think types necessarily are shadows, and they demand that both type and antitype be given their due meanings in their own contexts while maintaining a typological relation to one another.
>
> NT reinterpretations of OT passages are neither explicit nor implicit cancellations of the meaning of the OT. Likewise, NT antitypes neither explicitly nor implicitly cancel the meaning of OT types. Thinking they do misunderstands typology.[28]

Why, we ask, do Feinberg and many modern-day dispensationalists reason this way? It follows from their *prior* commitment to literal hermeneutics as the "natural" way of interpreting the Bible. On the one hand, covenant theology is guided by the principle of *sola Scriptura*. The Scriptures are self-interpreting: this is what is meant by the Reformational principle of the analogy of Scripture. Taking their cue from the NT's use of the OT, covenant theologians formulate their theological method in terms of the biblical pattern of promise and fulfillment. On the other hand, the dispensational hermeneutic, it seems to me, imposes an *a priori* definition of "literalness" upon the meaning and interpretation of Scripture. (See especially the contribution of Paul Feinberg for the argument of such a literal approach. Curiously, VanGemeren accuses amillennial covenant theology of imposing a method of interpretation upon the Bible.[29] It is not surprising then that we find him advocating the hermeneutical approach of Walter Kaiser.) If literal interpretation is the leading distinctive (or one of the leading distinctives) of dispensational theology, how can dispensationalism as a system of interpretation truly accommodate biblical typology? To C. I. Scofield's credit, his doctrine of the church as a parenthesis is at least consistent with the dispensational hermeneutic. Contrary to the attempts made by premillennialists, especially those of dispensational persuasion, the argument for a twofold fulfillment – one typological (in the establishment of the NT church) and one literal (in the return of Israel to Palestine and reconstitution as a nation) – lacks convincing biblical support.[30]

This brings us to the issue of the Palestinian land-grant. How exactly are we to understand the promise of God to Abraham concerning the geophysical land of Canaan, especially as that relates to the ancient Israelite theocracy? It would appear that the failure to recognize the operation of the works-inheritance principle under the Mosaic administration of the redemptive covenant only aggravates the problem of how to explain Israel's exile in Babylon in relation to the curse sanction of the Mosaic law covenant. By adopting the "misinterpretation view of the law," which contends that the Mosaic Covenant was exclusively an administration of grace and promise devoid of any conditional element, many recent interpreters have rejected the traditional exegesis of Lev 18:5, seeing the principle of law here as an expression of grace (rather than seeing law and grace as antithetical principles of inheritance).[31] With reference to the Pauline teaching, Moo rightly argues:

> Paul certainly does criticize "legalism" at times; but he uses phrases like seeking justification "on the basis of" (*ek*) the law (*cf.* Rom 10:5; Phil

> 3:9) or through "works of the law" (Gal 2:16, etc.) to designate it. In other words, it is not the word *nomos* itself that denotes "legalism" in Paul, but various phrases in which the law (as God gave it) is falsely understood as the basis for salvation. In the context of Romans 6-7, the "legalistic" meaning is particularly inappropriate.[32]

Both VanGemeren and Allen Ross fail to understand how the antithetical principles of law and grace can function simultaneously within the Mosaic Covenant. In response to their objections to my view it is to be underscored that the principle of law (works) operates exclusively on the temporal, earthly level of the Israelite kingdom-theocracy, not on the eternal, heavenly level. Nor is there any optional "either/or" reading of the principles informing these two distinct levels of kingdom-inheritance, one typical and the other antitypical. Most importantly, these contrasting principles of inheritance do not imply competing methods of salvation.[33]

In terms of biblical typology the land of Canaan in OT history prefigures the whole world as Israel's everlasting inheritance – Israel representing the full number of elect among Jews and Gentiles. The dispensational belief in Israel's future return to Palestine for the reestablishment of the kingdom-theocracy not only preempts the need for the consummate realization of the promise to Abraham, but it requires the reinstitution of the Mosaic Covenant, whole or in part, which is in direct conflict with the teachings of the NT, particularly the teachings of the apostle Paul and the writer to the Hebrews. John Feinberg concedes that "the Mosaic Code has ended. . . [We] are not under the Mosaic Law and thus, are are not required to live in a theocracy."[34] But in the dispensational system how do the two kingdoms, the ancient Israelite kingdom and the future millennial kingdom featuring a revived Israel, differ as institutions of theocratic law? Dispensational premillennialism teaches that Jesus Christ, the messianic king, will reign over the nations from Jerusalem. Will he restore the Mosaic civil code? Or does the Sermon on the Mount substitute for the law of Moses in the millennial kingdom?

Feinberg contends that "the total complex of promises (spiritual and material). . . has never been realized conjointly in the history of this nation [Israel]."[35] In the judgment of Robert Saucy, Israel's destiny is "to be the agent of establishing God's kingdom in the world. . . . It is obvious from history that Israel has not to this point accomplished this mission."[36] From one standpoint Feinberg and Saucy overlook the significance of Israel's golden age under Solomon (*cf.* especially the books of Chronicles). The ideal theocratic picture arising from this period under Solomon (or even, for the sake of argument, the future millennial kingdom) would only be a *foreshadowing* of the everlasting kingdom. Israel in the days of Solomon was typological of the eternal, antitypical kingdom.

Feinberg rightly argues that "only Dispensationalism clearly sees a distinctive future for ethnic Israel as a nation."[37] But he erroneously maintains that "a distinctive future [for ethnic Israel] is a logical outgrowth of God's election of Israel."[38] Likewise, Saucy posits, "any interpretation which suggests that the promises to the nation of Israel have been assigned to the church because of the failure of that nation raises the question of the security involved in all of God's elective purposes."[39] Such an argument ignores the crucial biblical distinction between national election (pertaining only to Israel in the OT period) and individual election to salvation. G. C. Berkouwer, whom Feinberg cites in support of his position, rejects this fundamental distinction. Berkouwer asks:

> Can a past that has been qualified by election ever come to naught? Can "election of God" as we usually understand it ever be changed into "rejection"? Can the church inherit the place of the chosen people of Israel, so that election passes over to the church? Do we not usually consider God's election as something irrevocable, definitive, and all-powerful; and is it consequently meaningless to assume that the election of Israel could be negated by human reaction, even unbelief?[40]

How do Feinberg and Saucy explain the fact that at one time Israel is Ammi ("my people") and at another time, Lo-Ammi ("not my people" [Hosea 1])? Granted, the purpose of God's election of Israel to bring salvation to all the nations cannot be frustrated by Israel's sins. And in addition, God by his sovereign grace will preserve a faithful remnant in Israel and among the nations throughout the course of world history. The irrevocability of God's calling assures the ultimate realization of his saving purposes.[41] If one denies the conditional aspect of the Mosaic Covenant (as we have defined it above), and if the earthly promises to the nation of Israel are understood to be unconditional (as are the heavenly promises), how can disobedient Israel experience the temporal wrath of God, *i.e.*, the curse sanctions of the covenant? And if Israel's election is election to salvation, whereby God's election of Israel cannot be vitiated by Israel's unbelief, how can disobedient Jews experience the eternal wrath of God? Feinberg reasons inconsistently that "not every last Jew ethnically speaking, will receive the benefits of those promises. Individual blessing under the promises is always conditioned upon obedience to the God who made the covenant."[42] Does not this qualification amount to an acknowledgement of the biblical distinction between national and decretive election (the latter being election to salvation)?[43]

Dispensationalism teaches that the church as a NT organism is wholly distinct from Israel (*i.e.*., the organism comprising believing Jews under the Old Covenant and in the future millennial kingdom).[44] Consequently, asserts Feinberg, "the church did not exist in any form in the OT."[45] Representative of the teaching of modern-day dispensationalism, Saucy remarks: "The earlier dispensational teaching that divided the people of God into an earthly and heavenly people (*i.e.*, the church and Israel), with fundamentally no continuity in the plan of God on the historical plane, must be rejected as well."[46] He concludes that

> In the final sense it is perhaps best to say that "the people of God" is one people, since all will be related to him through the same covenant salvation. But the affirmation of this fundamental unity in a relation to God through Christ does not eliminate the distinctiveness of Israel as a special nation called of God for a unique ministry in the world as a nation among nations.[47]

(Our chief dispute with Saucy is over the dispensational understanding of the restoration of Israel in the future, earthly millennium.) Feinberg points out that "In the OT and NT eras, people are always saved by grace through faith in the truth God has revealed; but being saved is not the only defining characteristic of the church."[48]

This introduces us to the most important issue in the present theological debate. Both dispensational and covenantal theologians agree that the NT church begins at Pentecost. "The church, with Christ as its head and duly appointed officers representing Christ," writes Fred Klooster, "is the unique NT institution of Christ related to both the covenant and the kingdom. . . . It is Christ's special kingdom instrument fitted to the post-Pentecost situation."[49] Something truly new and glorious occurs when the Spirit of God is poured out upon all peoples. This outpouring of the Spirit, however, does not imply that the Spirit now permanently indwells believers for the first time in redemptive history, as is suggested by several dispensational writers in this volume. Nor does this redemptive-historical event imply that saving faith now includes union with God our savior, as though spiritual union and communion with God in Christ were an exclusively New Covenant reality.[50]

Although the content and knowledge of the person and work of Christ is significantly fuller and clearer in NT revelation, the content of saving faith in all ages is nothing other than Jesus Christ. Aspects of the person and work of the Messiah who was to come were revealed in the pages of the OT, especially in the various types and shadows of the better things to come. This anticipatory revelation, however shadowy, provided adequate knowledge of God's Son, even though fuller and clearer revelation unfolds only in the day of his appearance. Surely OT believers trusted that God would one day provide the final sacrifice for sins, and their hope rested in this one whom they saw through the eyes of faith (*i.e.*, through the Spirit's illumination). Ross acknowledges that with respect to the OT sacrifices, "God chose to legislate a detailed sacrificial system for Israel that would point to Christ *typologically*. Only when the antitype was revealed was a full understanding of the type available."[51] The same, however, must be said in regard to all other types in Scripture. By substituting the word "typically" for the word "literally" in Ross' statement, would not Ross agree that "the person and work of Jesus Christ was [typically] revealed to OT believers as the content of saving faith"?[52] Along with Ross we deplore a hermeneutical method which ignores or minimizes the shadowy-typical form of OT revelation or that seeks "to read the full revelation of the antitype back into the type."[53] But it is evident that Ross himself minimizes the adequacy and sufficiency of typological revelation in the OT as regards Jesus Christ as the sole content of saving faith throughout all the ages. Does not Hebrews 11 indicate that those who followed in the steps of Abraham, the father of all the faithful, looked by faith to the *heavenly* inheritance? They looked beyond the type to the antitype and, like Isaiah, they rejoiced to see the day of Christ's appearing. Abraham's faith in God included faith in God as savior, the one who would make atonement for sin (Genesis 12-15, 22; *cf.* the earliest announcement of God's redemptive provision in Gen 3:15).[54] Martin Woudstra is right in observing that

> In spite of the relatively greater emphasis within the OT and the Mosaic economy upon the physical benefits of the covenant – such as land possession, abundance of crops, outward peace, and safety enjoyed under the vine and fig tree – these outward benefits do not form the true heart and core of Israel's relationship with its covenant God.[55]

As the sixth and final characteristic of dispensationalism, Feinberg distinguishes between what he regards to be covenant theology's truncated view of God's saving work in history, what he calls "salvation history," and dispensationalism's comprehensive view of God's work, identified as "kingdom history."[56] Salvation history, so it appears to Feinberg, relates merely to the soteriological and spiritual aspects of God's redemption, whereas kingdom history includes the material aspect as well. (This is a common misunderstanding among critics of covenantal amillennialism.) "In a real sense," writes Feinberg, "this is a critical watershed for continuity and discontinuity systems."[57] While the evangelistic mission of the church (what Feinberg calls the "spiritual aspect" of God's kingdom activity) is distinct from the present cultural task of the state, only in the millennial kingdom, the dispensationalist argues, will the spiritual and material aspects of God's kingdom be brought together by means of the reinstitution of the final, earthly theocracy. This feature of dispensationalism harks back to the third and fourth distinctives as outlined by Feinberg (see the critique given above).

The basic issue dividing dispensational teaching from the teaching of covenant theology is the meaning and significance of Israel's election in OT times. Judging from the contributions made by the dispensational writers in this collection of essays it appears that the problem of the method of salvation in the OT (especially the role of the Holy Spirit) has not been entirely resolved. Hopefully, our review article will contribute to the ongoing dialogue. Remaining differences among dispenstionalists (especially those like Feinberg who have Calvinistic leanings) and covenant theologians can be overcome as we continue to wrestle through the complex subject of the relationship between the Testaments. May God grant that agreement between these two theological traditions be based upon the truths of God's Word.

ENDNOTES

Continuity and Discontinuity: Perspectives on the Relationship Between the Old and New Testaments. Essays in Honor of S. Lewis Johnson, Jr., ed. J. S. Feinberg (Westchester, IL: Crossway, 1988).

[1]John S. Feinherg, "Epilogue" 309.

[2]John Feinberg remarks: "The keys to determining whether or not one is a dispensationalist rest in hermeneutical, ecclesiological, and eschatological issues, not soteriology. Obviously, the distinction between Israel and the church is of crucial import for both eschatology and ecclesiology. I do not, however, see any soteriological position that is inherent to and thus necessitated by dispensationalism" ("Salvation in the Old Testament," in *Tradition and Testament: Essays in Honor of Charles Lee Feinberg*, ed. J. S. and P D. Feinberg [Chicago: Moody, 1981] 48). See our discussion below of the dispensational understanding of the indwelling of the Spirit.

[3]Rodney Petersen, "Continuity and Discontinuity: The Debate Throughout Church History" 17.

[4]Douglas J. Moo, "The Law of Moses or the Law of Christ" 203.

[5]Paul D. Feinberg suggests that "types and analogies are not prohibited by so-called literal interpretation or what I prefer to call historical-grammatical hermeneutics. These are appropriate forms of communication within such hermeneutics. They will require special rules of interpretation, but they are not instances of spiritualizing. Historical-grammatical interpretation allows for *symbols, types* and *analogies*. What will be required is argumentation that any specific item is a symbol, a type, or an analogy. All of this is quite a different matter from advocating typological or analogical henmeneutical principles in interpreting the OT. This comes close to spiritualizing the OT" ("Hermeneutics of Discontinuity" 123).

[6]Willem VanGemeren, "Systems of Continuity" 37-62; "The Spirit of Restoration," *WTJ* 50 (1988) 81-102; and *The Progress of Redemption: The Story of Salvation from Creation to the New Jerusalem* (Grand Rapids: Zondervan, 1988). In these writings VanGemeren has expressed indebtedness to and appreciation for the work of Torrance.

[7]"Systems of Continuity" 37.

[8]*Ibid.* 42.

[9]*Ibid.*

[10]*Ibid.* 43.

[11]*Ibid.* 45.

[12]*Ibid.*

[13]*Ibid.* 46.

[14]*Ibid.*

[15]*Ibid.* 47.

[16]See Chapter One, pp. 43-46.

[17]"Systems of Continuity" 52ff. See my remarks on VanGemeren in Chapter Twelve, pp. 278-281, and in Chapter Eight, pp.203-204, n.8.

[18]"Systems of Continuity" 60.

[19]*Ibid.* 61. "We stand in the presence of God with awe, as he is sovereign and free. In his sovereignty and freedom he has revealed aspects of his eternal plan in *time*, in the *language* of man, and in *metaphors*. Therefore, it is impossible to bind God to any eschatological (millennial) system" (p. 62).

[21]John S. Feinberg, "Systems of Discontinuity" 75.

[22]*Ibid.* This is a surprising admission on Feinberg's part.

[22]*Ibid.* 76. Paul Feinberg comments: "Moreover, while historical-grammatical interpretation allows for symbols, types and analogies, I see no evidence that Israel is a symbol for the church, Palestine for the new Jerusalem, *et al.* If that is the case, then I do not see how the requirements of historical-grammatical interpretation have been met by those who would change or reinterpret the OT predictions" ("Hermeneutics of Discontinuity" 124).
[23]"Systems of Discontinuity" 77.
[24]Waltke, "Kingdom Premises as Spiritual" 284.
[25]*Ibid.* 276.
[26]*Ibid.* 279. See the development of these ideas in Chapter Eight. Marten H. Woudstra comments: "While it is granted that the prophecies concerning Israel's future are largely couched in language that suggests an earthly realization of salvation, it should be remembered that the prophets, in order to be understood by the people of their own time, would naturally embody their thoughts and revelations in such language" ("Israel and the Church: A Case for Continuity" 232). From a similar perspective, Moo observes how "Matthew presents a theology of salvation history which pictures the *entire* OT as anticipating and looking forward to Jesus" ("The Law of Moses or the Law of Christ" 205, *emphasis added*).
[27]Paul Feinberg argues that "the OT economy must not be forced upon the New. . . . On the other hand, it is equally as grievous an error to impose the NT on the Old, as though there was some need to 'christianize' it" ("Henmeneutics of Discontinuity" 127). Was Jesus guilty of 'christianizing' the OT (*cf.* Lk 24:27)?
[28]"Systems of Discontinuity" 78-79.
[29]Willem A. VanGemeren, "Israel as the Hermeneutical Crux in the Interpretation of Prophecy," *WTJ* 45 (1983) 132-44 and *WTJ* 46 (1984) 254-97. Compare Feinberg's citation of Ladd above (p. 313).
[30]*Cf.* Chapter Eight, pp. 193-195, esp. 203, n.7.
[31]See Chapter Six. For a helpful introduction and analysis of the current literature, see Stephen Westerholm, *Israel's Law and the Church's Faith: Paul and His Recent Interpreters* (Grand Rapids: Eerdmans, 1988).
[32]"The Law of Moses or the Law of Christ" 210-11.
[33]Accordingly, the exile of Israel to Babylon and the final dissolution of the Israelite theocracy in 70 A.D. were the divine judgments for Israel's transgression of the covenant made with Moses, specifically the infliction of the curse sanction of the law. The temporary restoration of Israel after the seventy-year exile was itself a matter of divine grace – a renewal of God's promise to Abraham. It was preparatory for the coming of the Messiah and the establishment of the new and better covenant. The ultimate fulfillment of the land-grant is the consummate kingdom of God, the New Heavens and New Earth. The church in the semi-eschatological age of the Spirit is described in the Letter to the Hebrews as a people of the wilderness, strangers in this world having no place to call their own.

Earlier in the history of redemption, God's granting of Canaan to Abraham and his (physical) seed was not conditioned upon human obedience (works). It was a matter of sovereign grace and promise, not human merit (law). (We are not addressing here the matter of the typological kingdom-grant. On this feature see Meredith G. Kline, *Kingdom Prologue* [vol.3; privately published, 1986] 55-59.) In the course of the historical administration of God's redemptive covenant, however, a new and antithetical element enters into the covenant between God and Israel. Israel's retention of the land is, for typological purposes, contingent upon Israel's compliance with the law of Moses. As we have argued more fully elsewhere, the principle operative on the temporal, typological level of the Mosaic theocracy is that of works, not faith (Lev 18:5). See further Chapter Eight.

[34]"Systems of Discontinuity" 77. Moo's essay offers a very helpful and succinct analysis of the NT teaching. "The OT law is not to be abandoned. Indeed, it must continue to be taught (Matt 5:19) – but interpreted and applied in light of its fulfillment by Christ. In other words, it stands no longer as the ultimate standard of conduct for God's people, but must always be viewed through the lenses of Jesus' ministry and teaching" ("The Law of Moses or the Law of Christ" 206). According to Rom 10:4, "Christ being the *telos* of the law means that he is the point of culmination for the Mosaic Law. He is its 'goal,' in the sense that the law has always anticipated and looked forward to Christ. But he is also its 'end' in that his fulfillment of the law brings to an end that period of time when it was a key element in the plan of God" (p. 207). Responding to scholarly debate over the exegesis of Rom 10:4, Moo correctly observes: "Elements of both 'end' and 'goal,' along with nuances from other English words, are involved. This does not mean that we are accepting a 'double meaning' for *telos*, as Badenas seems to think is the case if such a meaning is adopted" (*ibid.*). Moo points out that the apostle Paul's teaching on the law in Rom 10:4 is in line with the teaching of Jesus in Matt 5:17. Moo refers to the work of NT scholar Herman Ridderbos, who "offers a long and penetrating discussion of this matter, concluding that there is no doubt that '. . . the category of the law has not been abrogated with Christ's advent, but rather has been maintained and interpreted in its radical sense ("fulfilled"; Matt 5:17); on the other hand, that the church no longer has to do with the law in any other way than in Christ and thus is *ennomos Christou*'" (p. 217).

[35]"Systems of Discontinuity" 80.

[36]Saucy, "Israel and the Church: A Case for Discontinuity" 256.

[37]"Systems of Discontinuity" 83.

[38]*Ibid.*

[39]"Israel and the Church: A Case for Discontinuity" 259.

[40]Cited in "Systems of Discontinuity" 83. *Cf.* Alvin L. Baker, *Berkouwer's Doctrine of Election: Balance or Imbalance* (Phillipsburg, NJ: Presbyterian and Reformed, 1981); and Cornelius Van Til, "The *Umkehr* at Amsterdam," in *The Law and the Prophets: Old Testament Studies Prepared in Honor of Oswald Thompson Allis*, ed. J. H. Skilton (Nutley, NJ: Presbyterian and Reformed, 1974) 35-53.

[41]On the indiscriminating use of Jewish writers by modern-day ecumenists (and a number of evangelicals) in support of their interpretation of Israel as the chosen people of God, see the comments of Waltke ("Kingdom Promises as Spiritual" 264) and myself in Chapter Thirteen.

[42]"Systems of Discontinuity" 79.

[43]In the exegesis of Romans 11 it is important to bear in mind this distinction between national and decretive election. Waltke maintains: "The cultivated olive tree, however, in this text represents not national Israel but God's mediatorial kingdom, for branches live in this tree by faith, and dead branches are broken off for unbelief according to the sovereign grace and power of God" ("Kingdom Promises as Spiritual" 274). Woudstra comments: "The saving of 'all Israel' [Rom 11:26] is still going on, for the fullness of the Gentiles is also still being brought in. But at all events some of the Jews who are now hardened in part will be grafted into the one olive tree. They will not form a separate program or a separate entity next to the church" ("Israel and the Church: A Case for Continuity" 237).

[44]According to dispensational premillennialism, OT Jewish believers will experience the first resurrection at the beginning of the millennial age. NT Jewish believers who are living at the time of Christ's return – those who have been united to Christ and are members

of his mystical body – will be raptured out with the church, since they are part of the NT organism.
[45]"Systems of Discontinuity" 83.
[46]"Israel and the Church: A Case for Discontinuity" 239-40.
[47]*Ibid.* 241.
[48]"Systems of Discontinuity" 83-84.
[49]Fred H. Klooster, "The Biblical Method of Salvation: A Case for Continuity" 159.
[50]To be sure, union with the resurrected Christ is a New Covenant experience, one which adds depth and intimacy to life in covenant with God. Apart from the internal working of God's Spirit in the believer's heart under the Old and New Testaments, however, there can be no true faith. OT revelation of the Spirit of God features the Spirit's ministry of equipping various individuals in Israel for theocratic service. The explicit revelation of the Spirit's universal indwelling of believers (what is requisite at all times for saving faith) awaits Christ's accomplishment of redemption. The NT writers expound the interrelationship between Christ's accomplishment of redemption and the Spirit's application of redemption. In the economy of salvation the work of Christ and his Spirit are one: Christ is life-giving Spirit (1 Cor 15:45; 2 Cor 3:17-18). Just as Christ's satisfaction for sin is applicable to believers prior to his first advent, so also is the ministry of the Spirit who applies the benefits of Christ's death and resurrection to the elect of God. Contrary to John Feinberg's contention, the dispensational teaching that the Spirit indwells only NT believers, not OT believers, is at variance with the doctrine of Calvinism. Departing from the dispensational norm, Saucy cautions: "Rather than in spiritual realities related to New Covenant soteriology, the distinction between the church and Israel is to be found in Israel's identity as a nation" ("Israel and the Church: A Case for Discontinuity" 251). *Cf.* Benjamin B. Warfield, "The Spirit of God in the Old Testament," in *Biblical and Theological Studies* (Philadelphia: Presbyterian and Reformed, 1968) 127-56.
[51]Allen P Ross, "The Biblical Method of Salvation: A Case for Discontinuity" 171.
[52]*Ibid.* 170.
[53]*Ibid.* 172.
[54]See Klooster's analysis in "The Biblical Method of Salvation: A Case for Continuity" 135-37.
[55]"Israel and the Church: A Case for Continuity" 227.
[56]Note how Klooster describes his position as "Kingdom-Covenant Theology." His views on the kingdom of God convey a distinctively Dutch Reformed understanding of the relationship between Christianity and culture. He writes: "The realm of Christ's kingdom is present in Christian families, Christian schools, the church, and wherever life is lived in obedience to the king, wherever Christians 'seek first his kingdom and his righteousness' (Matt 6:33). All of life, the whole of society, social, economic, political, must be claimed and redeemed in the name of Christ the King" ("The Biblical Method of Salvation: A Case for Continuity" 159). For an alternative interpretation see my discussion in Chapter Fourteen.
[57]"Systems of Discontinuity" 85.

BOOK REVIEWS

1

Election and Predestination by Paul K. Jewett. Foreword by Vernon Grounds. Grand Rapids: Eerdmans [Exeter: Paternoster] 1985.

Here is a highly commendable treatment of an exceedingly difficult and controversial subject in the history of Christian doctrine. Paul K. Jewett's study is well balanced and irenic in spirit, a special credit to the author writing on such a hotly debated issue. Perhaps these qualities are to be attributed in part to the multidenominational setting of Fuller Seminary described by Professor Jewett in his "Preface." Fortunately, a much larger audience can now learn from the years of study and teaching which have gone into the writing of this book.

The author begins by presenting a brief historical overview of the doctrine of election, indicating at the outset his own commitment to the Augustinian-Reformed view. He concludes the opening section by commenting upon the place (*locus*) of the doctrine of election in systematics. While acknowledging differences held by such theologians as Calvin and Beza, Jewett rightly calls into question the currently popular notion that posits a sharp discontinuity between the thought of Calvin and the later Calvinists. Jewett remarks: "For all the difference of emphasis, there is a fundamental continuity between the thought of the reformers and their Calvinistic successors in the matter of predestination" (p. 23). (On this matter, see especially the recent and perceptive critique of R. T. Kendall's work by George W. Harper in "Calvin and English Calvinism to 1649: A Review Article," *CTJ* 20 [1985] 255-62.)

From the historical background Jewett proceeds to discuss the biblical basis for decretal theology. The author is clearly just as much at home in the biblical material as he is in the history of doctrine. True to the spirit of the Reformed tradition, Jewett's treatment of the "harshness" of the doctrine of double predestination (as some would describe it) is tempered by his exposition of the doctrine of God's covenants in Scripture. In the course of his biblical-theological formulation of the doctrine of election Jewett asserts: "God's covenant love was first manifested in his choice of Israel. The root of the biblical doctrine of election is the concept that Israel, as God's chosen people, is the object of his unmerited love. . . . If *covenant* is the central word in Israel's vocabulary, it is hardly too much to say that *election* is the word that gives the covenant its distinctive meaning" (p. 30). In the closing paragraph we shall return to comment upon Jewett's understanding of the nature of ancient Israel's election. But at this point it is important to note that Jewett properly identifies the continuity between the people of God under the Old Covenant and the people of God under the New in terms of the doctrine of the Remnant. "The Remnant comprises the true people of God, who are the descendants of Abraham regardless of their natural pedigree, because of their faithfulness to the covenant. In turn, the doctrine of the Remnant becomes the basis of the NT supposition that the elect community is made up of those who walk in the steps of Abraham's faith, whether they be Jews or Gentiles. Hence, the conclusion of the writers of the NT that those who embrace the covenant as newly mediated in Christ are God's chosen people is quite in keeping with the theology of the OT" (p. 32).

After considering the corporate implications of Israel's election, Jewett addresses the subject of individual election to salvation by interacting with Karl Barth's interpretation of Jesus Christ as the Elect and the Reprobate Man standing in for all humanity. Not unexpectedly from one committed to the Reformed orthodox understanding of election and reprobation, Jewett engages in a substantive and searching critique of Barth's unscriptural views. In the course of his analysis Jewett correctly argues that "to solve the problem of double predestination as Barth does is to take more than a furtive glance in the direction of universalism" (p. 51).

One of the strongest sections in Jewett's study is his judicious handling and assessment of the debate between supralapsarianism and infralapsarianism. The former position contemplates the individual's ultimate destiny from the standpoint of eternity (*sub specie aeternitatis*), whereas the latter so emphasizes the historical outworking of God's decrees in creation, the Fall, and redemption as to retain this same sequence in the logical ordering of the decrees as well. Thus, the infralapsarians teach the following logical ordering of the decrees: creation, fall, and election/reprobation. The supralapsarians maintain otherwise: election/reprobation, creation, and fall. In this controversy "we are speaking not of a temporal but of a logical order. We are concerned with the question of the divine purpose as such, not the carrying out of that purpose in time. Obviously God could neither save the elect nor condemn the reprobate before their creation and fall into sin, any more than he could raise Jesus from the dead before he was crucified" (pp. 84-85).

Despite the impressive strengths of supralapsarianism, Jewett judges this view to be "intolerable for its ethical implications" (p. 90). This leads Jewett to wonder: "Is it not possible that both views, each in its own way, is incompatible with Scripture?" (p. 91; *cf.*, however, pp. 91-97). The opposite conclusion is reached by Cornelius Van Til in *The Theology of James Daane* (Philadelphia: Presbyterian and Reformed, 1959). Van Til believes that both views find support in the Scriptures. Furthermore, it is his contention that neither view by itself is free from abstract speculation. In this reviewer's opinion, however, both Jewett and Van Til arrive at the same place: here we are faced with the mystery of God's sovereign purpose in creation and redemption, specifically, in the mystery of the Fall. Jewett observes: "The doctrine of the Fall confronts us with further mystery: on the one hand it is an act of rebellion against the will of God, but on the other it is not outside the will of God. But can we bring these two affirmations together logically? Can we – should we – seek to *explain* this paradox" (p. 92, *emphasis mine*)? Though theologians often speak of God's permission with respect to the Fall, this is not to imply that the Reformed are hesitant to regard the Fall as actually decreed. God's decrees are not the cause of particular acts or events. Thus, for example. God's decree to elect sinners to salvation is not the cause of salvation. (Among the causes of salvation, the Reformed systematicians [Calvin included] speak of the efficacious cause as the love of God the Father and the meritorious cause as the obedience of Jesus Christ.) The decree pertaining to the Fall does not suggest in any way that God is the author of sin. Furthermore. God does not elect and reprobate in the same manner (*in eodem modo*). There is what Jewett calls an "asymmetry" in the doctrine of double predestination (p. 93). The bottom line is: "While there is unconditional election, there is no unconditional reprobation" (p. 94), though I would hasten to add that in the act of preterition (the divine passing by those who are not the objects of God's distinguishing love and mercy) the feature of unconditionality does apply.

Much more can be said of a positive nature concerning this book. The reviewer, however, is obliged to draw attention to one, rather troublesome weakness in an otherwise valuable and competent study. Jewett's treatment or the nature of Israel's (corporate) election and her future as the people of God is problematic, both in terms or the teaching or Scripture itself and in terms of his evaluation of Protestant polemics in the age of the Reformation. Presumably, Jewett is responding to allegations made against traditional Protestant teaching without having fully entered into the critical debate in contemporary theology concerning Israel and the church. (For further analysis and critique of recent trends, see my treatment here in Chapter Thirteen.) Except for this one area of reservation, Jewett's work deserves widespread reading and interaction from those of Arminian persuasion. Or perhaps the eloquence of Jewett's argument will give him the last word on the subject! In any case, the author has rendered the Christian church a genuine service in affirming anew the sovereign grace of God in humanity's salvation and Jesus Christ as the world's only Savior.

2

Created in God's Image by Anthony A. Hoekema. Grand Rapids: Eerdmans, 1986.

From the pen of the well-known and highly respected Reformed theologian, Anthony A. Hoekema, the late professor of theology at Calvin Seminary, comes a second major study in the field of systematics (dogmatics). Like his previous volume on eschatology, *The Bible and the Future* (Grand Rapids: Eerdmans, 1979), this present work on theological anthropology is written for the informed lay reader as well as the beginning seminarian. For this reason alone, Hoekema has performed an important service for the Reformed churches in the ongoing edification of God's people. At a number of points the author introduces material which reflects current biblical-theological scholarship. Some of his proposed modifications of traditional formulations are constructive, others not so.

Hoekema begins in chaps. 1-2 with a brief discussion of the importance of the doctrine of man in the contemporary scene, setting the Christian view over against a variety of nonChristian anthropologies, both ancient and modern. What is man? According to our author, he is best described as a "created person." "In sum, the human being is both a creature and a person; he or she is a *created person.* This, now, is the central mystery of man: how can man be both a creature and a person at the same time? To be a creature, as we have seen, means absolute dependence on God; to be a person means relative independence" (p. 6). Though critical of certain speculative dichotomies found in traditional formulations of the doctrine of man, Hoekema succumbs to the same error by defining man as both creature *and* person, resulting in a problematic treatment of human dependency and independency (pp. 6-7). All that need be said is that Adam was created a living person, a creature of God. What distinguishes man the creature from all other creatures is that he is at the same time a person.

Close to one half of the book deals with the formative role of the image concept, an emphasis indicated by the title of the book. The author treats this topic under three divisions: biblical, historical, and theological (chaps. 3-5). The discussion of man's self-image in chap. 6 appears somewhat out of place in a dogmatic presentation such as this. Chaps. 7-10 deal with the doctrine of sin: its origin, spread, nature, and restraint.

Before analysing Hoekema's views on man as image-bearer we will consider other matters in his study. It is refreshing to note the emphasis placed upon the historicity of Adam (pp. 112-17). Earlier, Hoekema objected to Barth's interpretation: "It is hard to know what Barth means here by 'the Fall,' but it is clear that he would not allow for any fellowship between God and man in a state of integrity" (p. 51). With regard to original sin the author correctly argues that all who are in Adam (the total number of humankind) are guilty of breaking God's law. "Guilt is the state of deserving condemnation or of being liable to punishment because the law has been violated" (p. 148). However, Hoekema's understanding of humanity's relationship to the one sin of Adam does not do full justice to the teaching of Scripture. In striving to find a middle position between realism and direct imputation the author relinquishes ties to the consistent view of direct imputation (pp. 163-65). Hoekema speaks of the concept of imputation as "an inference from the scriptural data" (p. 165). We would add that direct imputation is a *necessary* inference from the biblical data. (Compare John Murray, *The Imputation of Adam's Sin* [Grand Rapids: Eerdmans, 1959] 71-95, esp. 56-88.)

As to the question of those who die in infancy, Hoekema's views are not those of Herman Bavinck. Hoekema contends: "To be sure, all infants are under the condemnation of Adam's sin as soon as they are born. But the Bible clearly teaches that God will judge everyone according to his or her works. And those who die in infancy are incapable of doing any works, whether good or bad" (p. 165). This view appears to be something less than consistent Calvinism. Is not the basis of salvation the sovereign, electing purpose of God in Christ, rather than any consideration of human performance either in the case of adults or infants?

Hoekema's comments on the Ten Commandments and natural law evince an older view that has rightly received criticism today (p. 170). Over against the position of Hoekema, it has been argued, the Scriptures teach that the Decalogue is a code of morality reflecting the perfect ethical standards that a holy God requires of his creatures at all times and in all places, but applies such moral principles in a particular historical and covenantal context. As such, it is not an unqualified "reduplication" of natural law which is eternal and unchanging. (For example, the *Mosaic* ordinance of Sabbath-observance is no longer binding upon the New Covenant people of God.)

Lastly in this section on hamartiology Hoekema's discussion of gradations of sin would be clearer and more profitable if such distinctions were understood to be meaningful only in the historical context, not the final judgment – thinking here particularly of the problematic Reformed doctrine of future rewards (gains and losses) for the faithful saints based upon their good works. More to the point, will there be degrees of punishment corresponding to degrees of reward in the final state? Do we have a biblical basis for suggesting that it is better for one to be a "good heathen" rather than a perverse apostate as concerns the ultimate destiny of man? In the case of God's elect, what does it mean to speak of "nonmeritorious" reward *based on good works*? (*Cf.* Hoekema, *The Bible and the Future* 262-64.)

Chap. 11 discusses the "whole man," man as a psychosomatic unity. In rejecting the speculative views of trichotomy and dichotomy the author properly stresses the idea of wholeness. Instead of distinguishing two or three parts in man's composition, Hoekema posits two *aspects* of man, the bodily and the spiritual. Hopefully, this material will stimulate students of the Bible to reassess earlier thinking. At the same time further help might have been offered by the author in developing his interpretation of man as a psychosomatic unity by applying this concept to the related issue regarding the nature and constitution of man in the dispute between creationism and traducianism.

The final chapter returns to the problem of human freedom, the topic with which the book opens. Neither here nor anywhere else in this study does the author treat the doctrine of double predestination. Perhaps this indicates a reserve which might otherwise have exposed deeper problems in Hoekema's decretive theology – a softening of the decrees concerning sin, and more specifically the decree of reprobation. A full-orbed doctrine of human freedom must be formulated in accordance with Scripture's teaching on the sovereignty of God, including election and reprobation.

The remainder of this review critiques Hoekema's interpretation of man as image-bearer of God. The most obvious omission is any reference to or interaction with the views of Meredith G. Kline in his *Images of the Spirit* (Grand Rapids: Baker, 1980), though it is listed in the bibliography. At a number of points in his argumentation Hoekema arrives at conclusions that do not rest upon convincing exegesis. A careful study and analysis of Kline's work might have led Hoekema to make a more convincing case for his own views.

As formative as the image concept is in this book one searches in vain for a concise definition of the image. Instead we find a long list of features and characteristics of man, the more important being man's exercise of dominion over God's creation, the male-female relation (partnership and companionship), and man's structure and function. The essence of the image is defined as love for God and man. The image concept is broadened out so extensively that it fails to convey the biblical usage. (This has been one of the weaknesses of the traditional formulations which distinguish between broader and narrower aspects of the image.) Then too, Hoekema erroneously contends that man as created person relates to God covenantally only in the context of redemption. According to Hoekema, only as redeemed sinner is man both image-bearer *and* covenant servant. Such a view as the one espoused by the author posits a defective interpretation of man's original state in creation. By adopting Murray's construction of Adam's state in creation (the so-called Adamic Administration) as opposed to a covenantal understanding of the relationship between God and Adam at the inception of creation (the so-called "organic" view of the covenant held by such exponents as Abraham Kuyper, Herman Bavinck, and Geerhardus Vos) Hoekema revives the nature-grace dualism of earlier times. (See further my analysis in Chapter Four.) Unsuspectingly, Hoekema himself falls prey to speculative dichotomizing. We observed this earlier in connection with the author's dichotomy between man as creature (determinism) and man as person (indeterminism). Additionally, Hoekema's discussion perpetuates the traditional problematics over the issue whether the Covenant of Grace is conditional or unconditional.

More seriously, Hoekema's current thinking on the doctrine of the covenant leads him away from historic Reformed teaching by rejecting the doctrine of the Covenant of Creation (*i.e.*, the "Covenant of Works"). Departing from the position he held in his doctoral study, "Herman Bavinck's Doctrine of the Covenant" (Th.D. dissertation, Princeton Theological Seminary, 1953), Hoekema no longer finds this view compatible with Scripture. Here again, one might expect to read weightier arguments pro and con than what Hoekema provides. He concedes: "Bavinck considers the doctrine of the Covenant of Works so important that he states more than once that the Covenant of Works and the Covenant of Grace stand or fall together" (p. 118). How can a doctrine once regarded by the author himself to be essential to biblical faith be so quickly jettisoned? In the judgment of Hoekema is Bavinck now guilty of perverting biblical truth?

The dilemma that Hoekema creates for himself in denying the principle of works-inheritance (merit) requires him to find some other means of explaining the function of the promises and threats within the Covenant of Grace (pp. 10,180). His view implies that the curses associated with the Mosaic Covenant are not peculiar to that ancient people, but rather are normative in the Covenant of Grace in all ages.

The element of creation-eschatology that Hoekema recognizes comes into its own only within a covenantal interpretation of Adam's creation in the image of God. (Compare similar criticisms on this point and others raised by Howard Griffith in his review article of Hoekema's *The Bible and the Future* in *WTJ* 49 [1987] 387-396.) In his objection to a covenantal understanding of God's work in creation the author would, presumably, hold to some form of the doctrine of "moral government" taught by such representatives as Robert Dabney and James Thornwell.

Hoekema proposes as another feature of man's sanctification the development of a distinctively Christian culture (pp. 94-95, 201-2). He suggests that "the best contributions of each nation will enrich life on the new earth, and that whatever potentialities and gifts have been of value in this present life will somehow, in some way, be retained and enriched in the life to come. This implies that there will be continuity as well as discontinuity between the present life and the life to come, and that therefore our cultural, scientific, educational, and political endeavors today help to prepare for a fuller and richer life on the new earth" (pp. 94-95). It is not so certain, however, that this vision reflects the teaching of Scripture. Does not the radical and supernatural inbreaking of the Consummation necessitate the destruction of man's cultural achievements (despite the fact that these cultural and technological pursuits are legitimate and necessary activities in the present course of history – activities deriving from the obligation placed upon the human race at creation [the cultural mandate], and made possible after the Fall through God's operation of common grace)? How can we explain the fact that God has providentially entrusted the ungodly line with cultural development and advancement, whereas the godly line has been entrusted with the far more glorious ministry of reconciliation through the preaching of the gospel of salvation (*cf.* Gen 4:17-22; 2 Cor 5:18-19)? Are we justified in thinking that the works of the unrighteous will follow after them in the eternal kingdom while they themselves burn in hell-fire? In comparison, are the few and feeble (cultural) offerings of the saints to be transformed in the heavenly kingdom – a kingdom not made by human hands? Rather than speculate upon the enduring value of culture (which, as I read Scripture, will pass away), ought we not to glory in God alone?

Although we have drawn attention to a number of differences with our author, some more serious than others, this book is a worthy addition to everyone's library. Not all of the objections and criticisms raised in this review will find ready acceptance among exponents of Reformed theology today. The issues, however, will continue to arouse debate and encourage all of us to a more faithful reading of the Scriptures themselves, freed from historical and philosophical biases which so frequently beset theologians, even some of the best among us.

3

The Law, the Gospel, and the Modern Christian: Five Views, edited by Wayne G. Strickland. Grand Rapids: Zondervan, 1993.

This timely volume takes up one of the most important doctrines of the Christian faith, that of justification by faith as it relates to sanctification. Critical to the subject is the relationship between the Mosaic Covenant (the Law) and the New Covenant (the Gospel). One would have hoped to find a consensus among evangelicals on so cardinal a doctrine, but such a consensus does not exist. After two millennia of church history the controversy rages on.

Editor Strickland identifies his own contribution as the dispensational position and labels the others as follows: nontheonomic Reformed (Willem A. VanGemeren), theonomic Reformed (Greg L. Bahnsen), unlabeled (Walter C. Kaiser, Jr.), and modified Lutheran (Douglas Moo). Two points of dissent with respect to the editor's labels: (1) VanGemeren's position differs from traditional Reformed covenant theology; (2) the distinctive tenets of theonomy are incompatible with Reformed thought. The teachings of Christian Reconstructionism and historic

Reformed theology reflect two very different systems of interpretation; see my analysis in Chapters Two and Fourteen.

The issues arising out of the volume are many and exceedingly complex. I will focus chief attention on VanGemeren's essay, "The Law is the Perfection of Righteousness in Jesus Christ," and responses to it. VanGemeren begins by acknowledging "that the system of doctrine as set forth in the *Westminster Confession* and *Catechisms* is taught in the Scriptures" (p. 14). The *Confession* knows of only two basic covenantal structures: the Covenant of Works and the Covenant of Grace" (p. 15). The substance of VanGemeren's argument here and elsewhere in his published writings, however, undermines that Reformed teaching. By applying the concept of "grace" to the preredemptive covenant with Adam, VanGemeren obscures the classic Protestant law/gospel antithesis. This results in a great deal of theological confusion. Included in his six major stages of redemptive history is the period of creation (p. 17). More expressly, states VanGemeren, the covenant with creation "may be defined *as a sovereign administration of grace*" (p. 17 n. 13, *italics his*; *cf.* pp. 46-47). Accordingly "the Mosaic Covenant is a development of God's covenant with creation (*i.e.* a sovereign administration of grace) and with Abraham (*i.e.* a sovereign administration of grace and promise)" (p. 28). Elsewhere VanGemeren expresses his indebtedness to the teaching of Norman Shepherd and Richard Gaffin for his theological understanding. The new, revisionist interpretation reflected here, however, marks a radical departure from historic Reformed theology. The new view stands in closer affinity to that of Daniel Fuller; see further Chapters One and Five of this collected writings.

Why, then, is the former administration of the Covenant of Grace identified in Scripture as "Law" rather than "promise"? According to VanGemeren the reason is to be found in the curse sanctions for covenant transgression. The threats "open up a function of the Law that is antithetical to the Gospel" (p. 29). Kaiser, whose general position is similar to VanGemeren's, castigates VanGemeren for theological inconsistency here, especially for his reticence to decide the issue between John Murray and Meredith G. Kline as regards the discontinuity between the Mosaic Covenant and the New Covenant. Whereas Murray propounds the misinterpretation view of the law, denying the operation of a works-inheritance principle in the Mosaic Covenant, Kline maintains that just such a works principle is regulative of Israel's enjoyment of temporal blessings in the land of Canaan. Accordingly the unresolved tension in VanGemeren's formulation, notes Kaiser, "sounds like saying everybody on this issue must be right. But how can that be, given such contradictory conclusions?" (p. 74). Kaiser himself, however, fails to grasp the issues in this exegetico-theological dispute. This much is clear: The element of discontinuity – specifically, the law/gospel contrast – remains an enigma in the Kaiser/VanGemeren interpretation.

Perhaps the most important biblical text in the debate concerning law and gospel is Lev 18:5. According to VanGemeren and a host of modern interpreters, the law principle enunciated here sums up the ethical requirements for growth in sanctification. Thus VanGemeren contends: "Set within its context, Lev 18:5 is the essence of the Gospel" (p. 282). (VanGemeren substitutes Calvin's third or normative use of the law for the second use.) In an attempt to do justice to the

Pauline contrast between the law and the promise, between the Mosaic Covenant and the Abrahamic, VanGemeren cites with approval Moisés Silva's nuancing of Gal 3:21, "the crux of Paul's interpretation of the law" (p. 42). According to Silva, the law preaches "Do this and live" but cannot in and of itself confer life. Essentially Silva's position is a reworking of the misinterpretation view of the Mosaic law espoused by Murray (*cf.* p. 37 n. 42). Contrary to this teaching, however, the Mosaic law, although it was not given as a means of salvation, was the means whereby Israel would enjoy temporal life in the theocracy. The legal principle grounds the inheritance on works, not faith; see further Chapter Eight.

Failure on the part of our several disputants to distinguish clearly between the law as works-principle of inheritance and the law as rule of life (or standard of conduct) contributes to further theological confusion. Strickland, for example, in "The Inauguration of the Law of Christ with the Gospel of Christ" contrasts the external writing of the law on tablets of stone under the Old Covenant with the internal writing of the law on the tablets of the heart through the indwelling of the Spirit of God under the New Covenant. As part of the newness of the New Covenant, the law of Christ "is no mere rephrasing of the Mosaic law, for it consists not of a concrete corpus or demands, but rather of basic principles, for each believer is promised permanent indwelling by the Holy Spirit. Since the Holy Spirit ministers in the life of the NT believer on behalf of Jesus Christ, there is no need for any lengthy, detailed, codified, external means of restraint as in the Mosaic law" (p. 277). Dispensationalism denies the essential role of the Holy Spirit in working faith and obedience in the regenerate hearts of OT believers. The same dispensational contrast appears in Moo's essay, "The Law of Christ as the Fulfillment of the Law of Moses."

How does the "law of Christ" relate to the law of nature? Moo posits: "We can confidently expect that everything within the Mosaic law that reflected God's 'eternal moral will' for his people is caught up into and repeated in the 'law of Christ'" (p. 370). Similarly, comments Strickland, "the nature of the law has not changed, so its revelatory purpose transcends the Mosaic economy and remains valid in the church dispensation" (p. 278). Bahnsen in his contribution to the dialogue, "The Theonomic Reformed Approach to Law and Gospel," likewise relates the moral law in OT and NT to natural law. However, he gives the discussion his own theonomic stamp. Specifically, "the moral laws of God were never restricted in their validity to the Jewish nation. . . . God did not have a double standard of morality, one for Israel and one for the Gentiles" (p. 110). It is the responsibility of every civil magistrate, Christian and non-Christian, "to enforce [the] civil provisions in the moral law of God, and only those provisions" (p. 128). Distrust for civil ministers who base their beliefs "upon the ruinous sands of other opinions [than those laid down in the Bible]" drives Bahnsen to his peculiar theonomic interpretation of natural law (p. 116). He acknowledges the operation of common grace in the civil domain but does not do justice to this reality because "the content and benefit of special revelation exceeds that of natural revelation" (p. 116 n. 13). As Moo correctly observes: "The claim of theonomists to have found an assured alternative to the dangers of subjectivism in ethical interpretation [in public policy-making] is illusory" (p. 166).

Space permits only brief comment on the remaining nondescript essay by Kaiser, "The Law as God's Gracious Guidance for the Promotion of Holiness." Kaiser's major concern – a legitimate one, to be sure – is to guard against any suggestion that the law was given to Israel or to any sinner as means of salvation, even hypothetically. With characteristic vigor Kaiser embraces the misinterpretation view of the Mosaic law. But, as Moo rightly insists, "this whole approach to Paul's teaching on the law must be rejected" (p. 332). A misreading of alternative views contributes in large measure to Kaiser's failure to comprehend not only the biblical data but the issues as they are currently being debated.

A theology of the covenants is no longer the exclusive domain of the Reformed tradition, as was the case in the Reformation period of the church. It is fast becoming a staple of evangelical theology. The crucial issue in the present-day dispute is one that lies below the surface of the exchange of evangelical opinion found in this book. That issue is whether the theological concept of "merit" has a vital place in biblical theology (especially in the case of the two Adams). In terms of the historical development of doctrine, the debate in our day sets the teaching of historic Reformed orthodoxy over against that of neoorthodoxy. Nothing less than the forensic basis of soteric justification is at stake. Is the obedience of Christ (both his active and passive obedience) the exclusive meritorious grounds of our justification and reception of the heavenly inheritance? It is a (the) major failing of the volume under review that it does not address that key question. Abandoning the shattered arguments left in the aftermath of the skirmish between our five contestants, the field is open for a fresh appreciation of classic covenant theology as still providing the right answer.

4

The Holy Spirit by Sinclair B. Ferguson. Contours of Christian Theology. Gerald Bray, general editor. Downers Grove, IL: InterVarsity, 1996.

In many respects this study incorporates much that is standard fare in Reformed dogmatics, while at the same time staking out a number of highly significant departures from that tradition. Overall, Ferguson's recasting of Reformed theology follows closely on the heels of his senior faculty colleague, Richard B. Gaffin, Jr., to whom frequent reference is made. Ferguson's discussion, like Gaffin's, is not always clear, nor convincing. But the present work does serve to introduce the reader to changes in the contours of contemporary theology. Whether all facets of this theological exposition can be deemed "Christian" (*i.e.*., evangelical and Reformed) is the pressing question. Viewed in the best light, this work, like other volumes in the series, aims to combine the rich insights of biblical theology with traditional (Reformed) dogmatics. In the hands of the present writer, however, the final product is a modification – at times *radical* modification – of the system of doctrine. Chiefly, there is the shift of emphasis from the traditional *ordo salutis* – the temporal and logical ordering of the various benefits of Christ's atoning work in the application of redemption by the Holy Spirit, who is the Spirit of Christ – to the doctrine of union with Christ as that is articulated in these pages. Before looking at this material, some comments about the work as a whole are necessary by way of review.

Ferguson begins by considering the basic meaning of "Spirit" (Heb. *ruach,* Gk. *pneuma).* He rightly concludes that "*ruach* denotes more than simply the energy of God; it describes God extending himself in active engagement with his creation in a personal way" (p. 18). The Spirit's work encompasses both creation and redemption. (The closing chapter is entitled "The Cosmic Spirit," underscoring the comprehensive role of the Spirit of Christ in the renewal of the heavens and the earth.) The "Let us make" in Gen 1:26 is construed as a reference to the trinity, however indirect and obscure. (The full-bodied teaching on the triunity of the Godhead awaits the NT.) Though referring the reader to the insightful study of Meredith Kline, *Images of the Spirit,* Ferguson ends up misinterpreting this OT text. Particularly helpful is Ferguson's treatment of the following subjects: the gift/gifts of the Spirit, the *filioque* clause in the Nicene Creed, and the real presence of Christ in the sacrament of the eucharist. Prominent throughout the book is an exposition of covenant theology, at least a variety that is rapidly becoming dominant in contemporary theology. Most startling of all is Ferguson's scant treatment of the doctrine of justification, that which occupies a major section in standard texts in pneumatology, for example, the studies of John Owen and Abraham Kuyper which are commended by Ferguson. The reason for this neglect becomes apparent when the attentive reader captures the new direction taken by the author (see below).

Generally speaking, Ferguson's covenant theology embodies some of the distinctive elements found in dispensational theology. Early on, Ferguson speaks confusedly of regeneration (*i.e.* the new birth) as a peculiarly NT experience, whereas "new life" in the old economy was anticipatory of the new (pp. 25-26). Twice in this book the author deals with the experience of David who, in the author's opinion, feared losing his salvation after committing grievous sin. The *permanent* indwelling of the Spirit is understood here as strictly a New Covenant experience. "In the Old Covenant, God was immanent among his people through the Spirit; the consummation of this immanence is found in Christ, and one who is anointed with the Spirit's presence and power; the consequence of his work is the giving of the Spirit to indwell believers" (p. 176). The implication is that salvation (at least in the OT) is *losable.* According to Ferguson, only under the New Covenant is the intimacy of one's saving relationship with God experienced by all, and not just some (p. 30).

From the author's point of view, the covenant between God and humankind is a dynamic encounter reflecting the historical ambiguities of human experience in this present world-age. Ferguson's formulation of the "tension" between covenant and election stands in contrast to the proper balance struck by Reformed orthodoxy. The same problem resurfaces in Ferguson's exposition of the doctrine of union with Christ. According to Ferguson, it is union with Christ that is "the dominant motif and architectonic principle of the order of salvation" (p. 100). Is this statement intended to complement B. B. Warfield's contention that the biblical doctrine of the covenants was the architectonic principle of the Reformed system of doctrine (as reflected, for example, in the *Westminster Confession of Faith*)? What precisely does Ferguson have in mind? After all, Reformed dogmaticians have always – since the time of John Calvin and Caspar Olevianus – emphasized the importance of the biblical teaching on union with Christ. What is new in the present discussion is the inordinate stress given to the *eschatological tension* between the "already" and "not yet" of the Christian's life in the Spirit.

The recent approach in biblical-theological studies is to accent "the vital eschatological dimension (and tension) which features so largely in NT thought" (p. 102). According to this school of thought, the older dogmatic model (which posits a "chain" linking various benefits in logical, if not temporal sequence) obscures the already/not yet tension, specifically, how "each blessing is capable of it's own distinctive consummation" (p. 102). Ferguson's model, which is by no means original with him, *relativizes* the definitive aspect of soteric justification, despite efforts to affirm the decisive, once-for-all act of God reckoning sinner's righteous in his sight by means of the imputation of Christ's righteousness. In precisely what sense does justification (as one of many benefits of Christ's death and resurrection) *await* future consummation? Clearly, Ferguson is saying something different from traditional Reformed theology.

The crux of the new theology lies in its repudiation of the classic Protestant law/gospel distinction. There is no place in Ferguson's theology of the covenants for this antithetical contrast with reference to the history of God's covenant dealings with humankind. Ferguson knows of only one *covenant of grace* in creation and redemption *(à la* the Torrance school). Rather the relationship is always one of complementarity; it is law *in* grace, or grace *in* law. Thus, reasons the author, the end of the law spoken of in Rom 10:4 is the believer's *sanctification* (p. 144). With respect to godliness the indicative and imperative of biblical religion operate within the context of the single covenant of grace, before and after the Fall. Law becomes a dead letter only when it is divorced from the indicatives of grace. As a corollary, Ferguson recognizes only the fulfillment of the moral law for the believer, not its abrogation, a point of contention in the history of evangelical and Reformed theology. (Compare further my discussion in Chapter Nine, pp. 211-215.)

Over and against the modern view, Reformed orthodoxy has always maintained the clear distinction between justification and sanctification in the *ordo salutis* (as well as all the other benefits accruing to the elect of God). No ambiguity or fuzziness here. Unlike Ferguson and the new school, historic Reformed theology held unanimously to the twofold doctrine of the covenants – the Covenant of Works and the Covenant of Grace – the very doctrine that Warfield (and others like Geerhardus Vos) hailed as the distinguishing achievement of Reformed thought. This doctrine, however, has largely been abandoned in contemporary Reformed theology, of which Ferguson's ruminations are a part. What we find here is an attempt to place side by side two disparate and irreconcilable theologies. It has the effect of cloaking Gaffin's interpretation to appear as something other than it really is – an adaptation of neoorthodox teaching. On virtually all points in dispute, the theology of Ferguson and Gaffin is at sharp variance with that of John Murray, their predecessor in the systematics department. The reader is advised to peruse *The Holy Spirit* with caution and discernment, making careful comparison with the teaching of Scripture itself and that of historic Reformed orthodoxy.

EPILOGUE

These writings in Reformed covenant theology have indicated something of the strengths and the weaknesses of Westminster Calvinism. They serve to remind the reader that even the greatest of the Reformation creeds cannot be placed on a par with Scripture, which is uniquely authoritative for faith and practice. Unlike the sacred writings, the creedal documents are fallible, and therefore subject to change and revision. True to her maxim, Calvinistic churches are reformed and ever reforming according to the teachings of the Bible. One of the most pressing needs in the church today is a modern (Reformed) statement of faith, something that does not yet appear on the horizon. (Is this indicative of the disunity and division among the churches of our day?[1]) Assuredly, the theological task is not yet completed. The subject of the first of two essays in this closing section of our studies in covenant theology is that of doctrinal development in the history of the Christian church. Although the *Westminster Confession of Faith* stands as the most eloquent summary of Reformed theology at the close of the age of the Reformation, it does not suspend the church's ongoing task in the restatement and reformulation of Christian doctrine.

"Doctrinal Development in Scripture and Tradition" is written against the background of present-day ecumenism and contextualization, two trends which characterize much of the theological reflection which has taken place in the twentieth century. Some Protestant theologians have called for a thoroughgoing *revision* of Christian doctrine, one that gives adequate weight and attention to modern concerns. It is the opinion of this writer that Scripture alone contains the "deposit of truth"; what we find in the history of Christian theology (dogmatics) is the elucidation of biblical truth in the context of polemical debate, all of which reflects the church's gradual *apprehension* of biblical truth over time. The locus of authority, however, resides not in Christian tradition, but in Scripture alone. (It is essential to distinguish between the "system of doctrine" contained in the creedal statements of the church, on the one hand, and nonessential elements, on the other.) The opening essay in this Epilogue, then, is a (critical) defense of confessional Protestant-Reformed orthodoxy. (The introduction of two essays in the Epilogue is intended to draw attention to the most important and constructive issues still needing to be addressed by contemporary evangelical-Reformed theologians.)

The final entry highlights the singular contributions of OT scholar and theologian Meredith G. Kline to Reformed systematics. Kline stands as a contemporary exponent of Vossian biblical theology. Geerhardus Vos (1862-1947) has been regarded as the pioneer of (revived) biblical theology in twentieth-century Reformed orthodoxy. Regrettably, neither the works of Vos nor Kline are widely known or studied. This entry is taken from the long-delayed *Festschrift* entitled *Creator, Redeemer, and Consummator: Essays in Biblical Theology Presented to Meredith G. Kline* (eds. J. Muether and H. Griffith). It was written primarily "as an introduction to the writings of Kline in the broader context of current theological discussion." It is the view of Kline and myself that – to quote I. John Hesselink – "Reformed theology is covenant theology." Covenant theology itself gives rise to the complementary disciplines of "biblical theology" and "systematics" in the modern theological curriculum. Featured in my discussion is a summary of the leading insights of Professor Kline, insights into the meaning of the biblical text that are invaluable for the contemporary restatement and reformulation of Reformed systematic theology.[2]

Hopefully this republication of my writings will contribute to ongoing discussion and debate. More especially, it is hoped that it will arouse interest in the theological labors of Geerhardus Vos and Meredith Kline. May the attainment of this goal thus advance further the cause of Reformed federalism at the opening of this new millennium in the history of Christianity.

NOTES

[1]See my discussion in "Current Theological Trends in Reformed Seminaries: The Dilemma in Ministerial Education," paper read at the Eastern regional meeting of the Evangelical Theological Society in Lancaster, PA (April 3, 1998); available through the Society.

[2]As one example, so basic a dogmatico-theological concept as "grace" is itself in need of reformulation, as Kline convincingly argues. Deep-seated within the systems of Catholic and Protestant-Reformed scholasticism, both medieval and modern, is the Thomistic nature/grace dichotomy (discussed in Chapter Four and elsewhere in this collection of writings). This speculative distinction between a natural and a supernatural order – the latter involving the bestowal of divine "grace" – surfaces, *e.g.*, in twentieth-century Reformed thought in the work of Geerhardus Vos and John Murray, both of whom exercised a formative influence in shaping what would become the Westminster school of theology. (As suggested by several of the preceding essays in this volume, it is necessary to distinguish between "Old Westminster" and "New Westminster.")

Standing as background to Westminster Seminary's controversy over justification and the divine covenants, a controversy yet to be resolved in the seminary community (East and West), is the Reformed scholastic doctrine of a "*gracious* Covenant of Works" (the precise terminology used here is that of Old Princeton theologian A. A. Hodge), the covenant established by God with Adam in the original creation epoch, *i.e.*, before Adam's fall into sin. Among modern-day disputants favoring such a construction, the following six reasons – all variations on a common theme – are advanced: (1) to guard the sovereignty of God in the covenant relationship; (2) to underscore the infinite distance between the Creator and the creature; (3) to counter the suggestion that God is made a debtor to man, except by way of voluntary condescension on God's part in covenanting with Adam (see the *Westminster Confession of Faith* 7:1); (4) to refute an abstract notion of "merit," wherein man's obedience to God is thought to have an *intrinsic* value obligating God to reward man for that which, in the first place, is merely man's duty to God (this is meant to oppose the erroneous notion of law as a standard of justice apart from God, an independent standard to which God himself is subject); (5) to deny that man's best work is able to merit God's favor and blessing (the Southern Presbyterian Robert Dabney believed that God was free to destroy Adam, creature of the dust, even if he did render full and perfect obedience); and lastly, (6) to uphold the idea that *eternal life* promised to Adam in the Garden is purely and exclusively a *gift* of God's undeserved grace and mercy to creatures of the dust.

The watershed at Westminster Seminary had been the doctrine of justification and the covenants of God (including the doctrine of divine election). Central to this theological dispute – its first phase extending from the mid 1970s to the early 1980s – were the teachings of Norman Shepherd, Murray's successor in the department of systematic theology. (Shepherd's dismissal from the seminary faculty marks the close of this opening period of debate.) Whereas Murray distinguished between an order of nature characterized by the works-inheritance principle (*viz.*, the principle of "perfect legal reciprocity") and a subsequent order of grace (which Murray preferably called "the Adamic administration"), Shepherd rightly understood that the covenant relationship between God and Adam applied at the very outset of Adam's creation in the image of God, and therefore was not an arrangement or relational bond superimposed upon an alleged prior state of nature (resulting in a nature/covenant dichotomy). At the same time, Shepherd made a *radical* departure from Murray's interpretation and that of historic Reformed federalism by jettisoning the works-inheritance principle altogether. There was no place for "merit" in this new theology. But contrary to Shepherd and those in his camp, the merit concept, rightly defined, is not only theologically justified, but essential within the system of Reformed doctrine. Repudiation of the idea of merit in connection with either the First or the Second Adams jeopardizes the gospel of grace, resulting in another gospel, which is no gospel at all. (Elimination of the nature/grace dichotomy from Reformed federalism, on the other hand, does not substantially alter the system of doctrine.) What distinguishes Shepherd's theology from that of Murray is the former's *anti-juridical* stance, that which is reflected in much of contemporary theology, notably since the time of Karl Barth.

As a counter-argument to the above, I offer the following points which also are six in number: (1) the biblical concept of divine grace contemplates human *demerit*, resulting from Adam's transgression, the breaking of the Covenant of Works; (2) the obedience of Christ imputed to believers (through the sole instrumentality of faith apart form the works of the law) satisfies both the penal *and* legal obligations of the first covenant; (3) the righteousness, holiness, and truth of God ensure that God will not recompense evil for good (God cannot deny himself); (4) neither the doctrine of God's sovereignty nor the Creator/creature distinction precludes God's reward of blessing to man in creation for righteousness "performed in the strength of nature," *i.e.*, for righteousness based on law-keeping; (5) Adam's sonship, enjoyed at the very outset of his creation in the image of God, does not preclude the meritorious obtainment of divine blessing, any more than the Second Adam's relationship with his heavenly Father precludes his meritorious obtainment of the kingdom promised the Son in the covenant made in eternity (the dichotomy between servant and son, corresponding to the nature/grace dichotomy, is here rejected); and finally, (6) the Scriptures, Old and New Testaments, testify singularly to the *contrasting* principles of inheritance, *i.e.*, law and gospel (= grace), works and faith. The erroneous notion of a "*gracious* Covenant of Works" in federal Reformed scholasticism does not dissolve this more basic contrast between the law and the gospel. Historic Reformed orthodoxy upholds tenaciously the doctrine of the vicarious, substitutionary atonement of Christ, wherein Christ's active and passive obedience is regarded to be the *exclusive, meritorious ground of life and salvation for God's elect.*

CHAPTER SIXTEEN

DOCTRINAL DEVELOPMENT IN SCRIPTURE AND TRADITION: A REFORMED ASSESSMENT OF THE CHURCH'S THEOLOGICAL TASK

1. Introduction: The Problem of Development

In response to modern-day pluralism in the church and in society, contemporary systematicians in increasing numbers are calling for a redefinition of the normative status of theological tradition. Recent ecumenical dialogue has prompted even some evangelicals to reassess the traditional claim regarding the uniqueness of the Christian message of salvation in Jesus Christ, the only Savior of the world.[1] Hendrikus Berkhof, a leading voice in neoorthodoxy, urges the Christian dogmatician to "listen to the testimonies of world religions with a receptive mind" in the hope of gaining deeper insight into the gospel of Christ.[2] The Christian message, declares Berkhof, is but one particular witness to the revelation of God known universally among all peoples.

Less radical but no less startling, is the proposition now espoused by many evangelicals that all theological discourse is relative, or *contextual,* in nature. In their joint publication, *What Christians Believe*, Alan Johnson and Robert Webber exclaim: "Happily the way of doing theology in evangelical circles has undergone a significant revolution in recent years. . . . The revolution of which we speak is this: *Evangelicals are in the process of shifting away from a rigid theological system of thought toward a recognition that all theological systems reflect the particular cultural grid in which they were originally written.* This newer approach to theology has been called a contextualized theology"[3] It entails, as Stanley Grenz indicates, "an implicit rejection of the older evangelical conception of theology as the construction of truth on the basis of the Bible alone."[4] This theological innovation Grenz regards as nothing other than the long overdue revision of the Reformation heritage. No longer are the Scriptures to be regarded as the sole *theological* norm. This group of evangelical scholars, in the estimation of Johnson and Webber, denounces that view of theology that sees in it "a system of divinely revealed truth. Instead we see theology as a discipline that reflects on the truth. We do not thereby repudiate theological systems. Rather, we put them into their proper setting."[5] Contextual theology emphasizes the *provisional, non-binding* character of all doctrinal statements. The theological normativity of traditional Protestant dogmatics has now given way to culturally conditioned statements of faith that are the product of "human effort not to be confused with 'the changeless, absolute truth that remains in the mind of God' and is 'beyond our reach.'"[6] According to these contextualists, the church's comprehension of the Word of God is merely a fallible, human approximation of divine truth.[7] In our day the idea that Scripture does not contain a system of doctrine is similarly becoming a theological commonplace. Such philosophico-theological predispositions have important implications for confessional theology.[8]

Indeed, contextualization stands as a watershed for the church's contemporary witness to the gospel. Alert to present dangers in mainline Presbyterianism, John Leith perceptively and engagingly addresses this modern crisis of faith in his book, *The Reformed Imperative: What the Church Has to Say That No One Else Can Say*.[9] Leith points out how modern society's emphasis upon individual rights, as defined by secular humanism, has only served to undermine authority, both civil and ecclesiastical. He reminds us that faithful proclamation of the gospel, even in the presence of radical secularism, is not only integral to the church's calling but is the only means of challenging the pagan philosophies of our age. It is upon Christ and his Word that the Christian church stands. And it is through the sanctifying Spirit of God that the church is nurtured and sustained. The proclamation or restatement of the faith reflects in large measure the church's understanding of her theological task from the standpoint of the historical development of Christian doctrine.

How are we to view the formation of doctrine over the course of church history? Since the beginning of her tradition, the Reformed church has formulated her dogma by taking into account two factors: first, the progressive unfolding of doctrine within the biblical canon of the Old and New Testament; and second, the historical context of doctrinal development since the time of the early church onward. Contemporary Reformed scholarship, however, has not given sufficient attention to the matter of the relationship between the development of doctrine in Scripture and the development of doctrine in tradition. Such neglect has contributed, in part, to widespread ambivalence regarding the discipline of systematics itself and to a growing doctrinal malaise in modern-day evangelicalism. In this essay I will offer a response to theological pluralism and contextualism (both evangelical and nonevangelical varieties) from the perspective of a Reformed understanding of doctrinal development. By bringing the reformational hermeneutic of the *analogia scriptura* to bear on this subject, we can better grasp the church's ongoing theological task in reformulating the "faith once-for-all delivered to the saints" (Jude 3).

Tracing the historical course of redemptive revelation is the domain of biblical theology, while the reformulation of biblical truth for the church in the present is the task of systematics. Systematic theology, in the proper sense of the term, is to be distinguished from doctrinal or dogmatic theology. As described by Richard Muller, systematics

> must consider all of the constructive topics in theology – dogmatics, apologetics, philosophical theology, philosophy and phenomenology of

> religion, ethics – and draw them out in the light of the materials provided in the historical analyses of biblical study and church history.[10]

Though the term is oftentimes used synonymously with systematics, doctrinal theology focuses specifically upon the restatement of biblical truth in the ongoing life and witness of the church and is, therefore, *confessional, i.e.*, "dogmatic," in nature. The function of ecclesiastical dogma is to propagate and preserve the truth of Christian doctrine in light of a particular theological tradition, be it Reformed, Lutheran, or Arminian. It is the role of systematics to bring together, by way of biblico-philosophical and historico-cultural analysis, the fruits of each of the separate disciplines within the theological encyclopedia: exegetical theology, biblical theology, dogmatic theology, and historical theology.

In the past it was commonplace to speak of systematics as the "queen of the sciences," the crown jewel of the theological enterprise. The medieval theoreticians were not entirely wrong in their estimation. Although systematic formulation rests upon the labors of the other sciences, in a real and fundamental way, it also informs the other disciplines in their work. There is both a circularity and a (theo-)logical priority in the study of the Scriptures. Given the truth-claims of biblical revelation, Christian dogma follows as a logical consequence of the scientific discipline of theology.

> Doctrinal theology, given its dogmatic character, cannot arise prior to biblical and historical theology and cannot impose itself as a methodological rule on biblical or historical study: it is a result, not premise of the other disciplines. Nonetheless, this regulatory function does stand in a fundamental relationship to the other primary theological disciplines.[11]

The "pure" development of Christian doctrine transcends particular theological traditions, even though confessional theologians contend that their own tradition, among the traditions, offers the most faithful and consistent expression of biblical truth. Genuine, *i.e.*, true, development of doctrine leads the church universal into a fuller, clearer comprehension of God's revelation, not merely to a relative, provisional approximation of it.[12] To be sure, the church's understanding of the faith is never a wholly pure development but rather a mixture of truth and error.

A major theological concern before the church today, as in the past, is the matter of biblical authority. Historic Protestantism insists on the uniqueness of Scripture over against ecclesiastical tradition. Mistakenly, Leith suggests that the locus of authority rests in the Christian community. Since Protestants have no infallible teaching office, reasons Leith, the test of the validity of their witness lies in "the approval of the people of God, the priesthood of believers, over a period of time."[13] Thus, ecclesiastical judgment can only be relative, not definitive and precise. But, in contrast contrast to this opinion, Reformed orthodoxy regards the sovereign, providential working of the Spirit as the effectual cause of the church's proclamation of the gospel. It is the Spirit of God who preserves, in varying degrees, the faithful witness of the church throughout the generations. One of the hallmarks of the Reformed tradition is the acknowledgement that the church is ever to be reformed and reforming according to the Word of God. The exposition, defense, and preservation of the truth is the fruit of God's own working by his Word and Spirit in the long centuries of the church's history. The crucial point is simply this: True doctrine is not defined by consensus of opinion; it is defined by Scripture alone. The Scots Confession (chap. 18) states it this way:

> The interpretation of Scripture, we confess, does not belong to any private or public person, not yet to any Kirk for preeminence or precedence, personal or local, which it has above others, but pertains to the Spirit of God by whom the Scriptures were written. When controversy arises about the right understanding of any passage or sentence of Scripture, or for the reformation of any abuse within the Kirk of God, we ought not so much to ask what men have said or done before us, as what the Holy Spirit uniformly speaks within the body of the Scriptures and what Christ Jesus himself did and commanded.[14]

The theological task of the church in every period of her history prior to the Consummation is to proclaim, defend, and preserve the truth(s) of Scripture, *i.e.*, to hold forth the unchanging Word of God in changing times and in varied circumstances, historical and cultural. Development of doctrine in the history of the Christian church reflects the scriptural pattern of progression. As the Scriptures reveal the gradual unfolding of redemptive revelation over the course of biblical history, so also the history of doctrine manifests the church's growing understanding and apprehension of God's Word. In the remainder of this essay I shall provide a summary of the nineteenth-century Reformed historian of doctrine Robert Rainy's discussion of progressive revelation in Scripture (section 2), and then consider his idea of the development of doctrine in the Christian tradition as illustrative of nineteenth-century thought (section 3). In section 4 I will compare nineteenth-century and twentieth-century Reformed teaching on the subject of doctrinal development, with particular attention given to a critique of the views of contemporary historian of doctrine, Peter Toon. His views are representative of evangelical theories of contextualization. The conclusion of the essay (section 5) identifies several issues I regard as critical in the current debate.

2. Biblical Revelation as Historically Unfolding

The origin of the discipline of biblical theology as a distinct science within the theological encyclopedia is frequently attributed to the work of Johann Gabler, especially his *Oratio de justo discrimine theologiae biblicae et theologiae dogmaticae* (1787). In point of fact, the biblical-theological method is rooted in the Reformed covenantal tradition that gave initial attention to the relationship between the Testaments, specifically the unity and continuity of biblical revelation. The discipline or science of biblical theology, as distinct from dogmatics, did not appear in Reformed orthodoxy, however, until the early twentieth century in the work of Geerhardus Vos.[15]

Prior to explicit formulation of the biblical-theological method in Reformed orthodoxy, John Henry Cardinal Newman's study on the historical development of doctrine set the stage for the work of the Reformed historian of doctrine, Robert Rainy. In his *Delivery and Development of Christian Doctrine*[16] Rainy directed attention to the subject of the interrelationship between biblical theology and dogmatics. He began by treating the development of doctrine in Scripture – in both Old and New Covenant epochs – and concluded with a discussion of the development of doctrine in the history of the Christian church.

According to Rainy's interpretation of the biblical doctrine of creation, man was constituted a historical being. Development in knowledge and understanding was consistent with man's creaturely finitude. Humankind would encounter successive, new revelation from God, and would adapt to changes in environment brought about through the pursuit of cultural fulfillment and global dominion. This "historical method" is proper to humankind, not merely as sinful but as image-bearer of the Creator (pp. 327-28). Complete and perfect understanding of God, the world, and humanity develops over time, and in direct dependence upon God's self-disclosure. The event of the Fall, and the introduction of common grace/common wrath in the historical order of things, made the learning process more difficult and more arduous. Most important, humankind's ethical and religious rebellion against the Creator in the period subsequent to the Fall prohibits its attainment of the eschatological goal established in creation. The obstacle brought about by sin could be overcome only by way of supernatural, redemptive intervention on the part of the Creator-Redeemer. Such gracious provision has been granted by the Father in the eternal covenant with his Son.[17]

The administration of the kingdom of Christ varies in accordance with the several historical-covenantal transactions spanning the so-called "Covenant of Grace," the period from the Fall to the Consummation. In the history of redemption both continuity and discontinuity are descriptive of the several covenantal administrations of the kingdom of God. In accordance with classical Reformed teaching, Rainy finds in the Mosaic law "a character so unique, and in some respects so difficult to trace out" (p. 55) that one might overlook the unity of God's redemptive plan. The radical antithesis between the law (the covenant with Moses) and the promise of God (the covenant with Abraham) – what Protestant theologians traditionally distinguish as the law and the gospel – does not erase the underlying continuity of the redemptive covenants. This much is clear: The elenchtic purpose of the covenant of law pertains to "the discipline and the exercise of OT believers" (p. 55). That is to say, the legal principle operative within the Mosaic administration serves a pedagogical, tutelary function in the Israelite theocracy.[18] Despite variations in the interpretation of the Mosaic Covenant, theologians of the Reformed tradition, like Rainy, affirm the unity and continuity of old and new dispensations, notably in the "suggestions, embodiments, shadows, figures of the way of salvation by Jesus Christ, the crucified" (p. 56). The redemptive, eschatological blessing of eternal life is secured by the merits of Christ's righteousness alone. But in accordance with the peculiar role of the Mosaic law, bestowal of the *temporal* blessings of the covenant was grounded upon Israel's compliance with the law and commandments of God.

The works-principle of inheritance (operating on the *typological* level of the Israelite theocracy) is the distinguishing feature of the Mosaic Covenant and accounts for the biblical contrast between the law and the gospel.[19] The covenant God made with Israel bore "stringent conditions"; it was established as a temporary dispensation having "a disciplinary and administrative purpose, as shadow of things not yet seen" (p. 57). In laying the foundation for the New, the Old Covenant anticipates the messianic kingdom of Christ. The Mosaic Covenant "supplies the historical antecedents"; it provides "the historical propaedeutic" for the new order of things (p. 69). This historical unfolding of redemptive revelation in OT history is carried over into the New Covenant dispensation. "If it be true that the OT is essentially historical, its lessons rising out of transactions and events, the same is equally true of the NT" (p. 80). Succinctly stated: "The foundation of the Scripture method is historical" (p. 129). The development of doctrine in the Old and New Testaments is part of the progressive unfolding of redemptive revelation (p. 175).

It is the task of biblical theology to delineate the historical, "organic" character of revelation in Scripture. The Reformed tradition has developed this aspect explicitly in terms of the "Covenant of Grace" – a biblico-theological concept emphasizing historical continuity, but not, however, to the exclusion of historical discontinuity and diversity in God's covenantal administrations of his kingdom on earth. The divine-human covenants, sovereignly initiated and established by God, order the life of the community of faith over the course of redemptive history from the Fall to the Consummation. The premessianic administrations of the kingdom culminate in the establishment of the new and better covenant in the blood of Jesus Christ. With the New Covenant comes the full and perfect revelation of God's saving acts, including the manifestation of the church as the body of Christ, the New Man. The teaching of the NT amplifies and clarifies the revelation of grace contained in the OT Scriptures. Although the accomplishment of redemption takes place in the death of Christ, wherein the Old Covenant was preparatory for the New, the application of redemption is the same. The saving benefits of Christ's substitutionary atonement, however, are more fully explicated in NT revelation.[20] Reformed theology, especially in its typological interpretation of the OT, adheres to the Augustinian dictum that the NT reveals what the OT conceals.

3. Early Directions in Historical Theology

According to Rainy, the idea of doctrinal development in the period since the close of the NT canon met resistance among orthodox theologians of his day, largely because of arguments advanced by the rationalists and Romanists, most notably the theory set forth by Newman. Rainy maintains:

> The old Protestant position in the polemic against Rome was not friendly to a theory of development. Not only was the original or primitive teaching of the Scriptures asserted as the proper test or standard; but it appeared suitable to assume and assert a corresponding original faith in the

> church, which had been corrupted by Antichrist, but to which the Reformation had brought the church back. [Pp. 178-79]

Study of the development of Christian doctrine begins from "the measure of understanding which the church had of the revelation at the time when apostolic guidance ended" (p. 179). Here Rainy draws a connection between the completed revelation of God in the inscripturated Word and the early church's apprehension of the Word. There is similarity and dissimilarity. Regarding the latter, "The difference between the completed revelation and the church's apprehension of it was as great as that between the brightness of the sun and the reflection of it in some imperfectly-polished surface, that gives it back again really, constantly, but with a diminished, imperfect, wavering lustre" (pp. 184-85). The starting-point for the history of the teachings of the Christian church is not apostolic teaching as such, but rather "the initial attainments of the church under that teaching" (p. 195). In the words of Leith:

> The development of Christian doctrine requires time. The comprehensive statements of Christian faith that were produced by the Protestant reformers of the sixteenth century simply could not have been produced in the early church. The Christian community had not had time to think through the meaning of the Christian faith, to develop adequate concepts, or to put individual doctrines together in some consistent statement.[21]

Foundational principles for the theological interpretation of Scripture were laid in the early church. But from the outset the church was confronted by approaches to biblical interpretation that were alien and even hostile to the Bible itself.[22] Such approaches either directly or indirectly undermined Scripture's own witness. The hermeneutical problem came into sharp focus during the medieval period.[23] Alongside the rising sacramentalism and hierarchicalism of the Roman church, including abuse of the powers and offices of the institutional church, came rapid and widespread corruption of doctrine. It was the Reformation that marked a decisive return to Scripture as the unique and authoritative source of Christian doctrine and life by means of the recovery of the hermeneutical principle that Scripture is its own best interpreter (*sola scriptura*).

As a spokesman for nineteenth-century Protestant liberalism, Adolf Harnack called for a return to the simple gospel, to what he called the "essence of Christianity."[24] But contrary to Harnack's historical reconstruction, it was the Protestant Reformation, not rationalistic nineteenth-century German theology, which restored the biblical foundations of Christianity. As Rainy earlier observed, the period of the Reformation was the period of great doctrinal development, not merely in clearing away the corruptions introduced by Romanism but also in making genuine progress in the church's understanding of the Scriptures. "Such development," wrote Rainy, "was not to consist merely in deductive inference from principles established by Scripture." Rather, the church's deepening understanding of the divine revelation "consists in a more full, exact, and detailed acquaintance with the teaching of Scripture, embodied in the form of doctrine" (p. 223).

One of the tasks of historians of doctrine is to trace out what contemporary theologian Peter Toon has (disparagingly) called "the homogeneous evolution of dogma" in Protestant orthodoxy.[25] The nineteenth-century Reformed theologian, William Cunningham, described the task of historical theology in the following terms:

> The most valuable object that the student of historical and polemic theology can aim at is to endeavor to trace, by a survey of controversial discussions, how far God's completed revelation of his will was rightly used by the church for guiding to a correct knowledge and application of divine truth, and how far it was misapplied and perverted.[26]

A century later, M. Eugene Osterhaven added the note: "There is more to defining doctrine than clarifying and unfolding anew the same articles of faith. Development also takes place in the sense of new insights, deeper understanding, and clearer perception of the teachings of Scripture."[27] What we find through an investigation of the history of doctrine is genuine development and progress in the church's understanding of divine revelation. This doctrinal development, however, does not add to the deposit of truth contained in the Scriptures (2 Tim 1:13-14). "Christian doctrine arises from the interaction of the Christian community of faith with Scripture, and it is limited to what is explicitly given in Scripture or derived from it by good and necessary inference."[28] As the *Westminster Confession of Faith* (1:6) states: "The whole counsel of God concerning all things necessary for His own glory, man's salvation, faith and life, is either expressly set down in Scripture, or by good and necessary consequence may be deduced from Scripture: unto which nothing at any time is to be added, whether by new revelations of the Spirit, or traditions of men."[29] *Accordingly, post-canonical Christian theology contributes nothing new by way of doctrinal teaching to that which is given in biblical revelation. Rather the role of Christian theology is to explicate the "system" of truth contained in the Scriptures.*

Catholic theologians – those contemporary with Rainy – insisted that the errors that arose during the course of the history of the Christian church never affected the Roman communion in her *official* teaching. The apostolic faith, according to Rome, had been maintained in pure and uncorrupted form by the teaching magisterium of the church. The Protestant reformers, however, readily acknowledged a mixture of truth and error in the teachings of the church. They rightly maintained that the church's dogma had to be judged continually in the light of Scripture. It was necessary that the teachings of the church conform to biblical revelation, not to churchly creeds, councils, or tradition. Thus accordingly, Scripture alone was regarded as the final standard for faith and practice. Cunningham explained:

> The character and doctrine of the visible church, or of any of its branches at any particular period, is a matter of fact, to be ascertained by the application of the ordinary principles and materials of historical evi-

> dence; and when the character and doctrine of any church or individual has been ascertained in the ordinary way, by appropriate means and evidence applicable to matter of fact, they should be judged of, or estimated, by the standard of the Word of God.[30]

Historical theologians of the nineteenth century, like Rainy, recognized genuine development in the church's understanding of the Scriptures. Such development, however, did not take place apart from the admixture of doctrinal error. Only by means of the Spirit's vital work in illuminating the hearts and minds of believers could truth be rightly distinguished from error. Of equal importance was the recognition that interpretation of Scripture was not dependent upon ecclesiastical tradition. Contrary to the teachings of Rome, it was not a matter of Scripture and tradition. The authority of Scripture was considered to be self-authenticating, an authority inherent in Scripture, not imposed by the people of God.

The testimony of church history, including the great Christian creeds and confessions, was to be received in accordance with Scripture's own witness to the truth of God, not on the basis of theological consensus. Over the course of church history, doctrinal development did not result in the addition of truth to what was already contained in the Scriptures. The modern idea that Christian doctrine is historically and culturally conditioned was never even as much as intimated by nineteenth-century orthodox Protestants. Rather, dogmatic theology was understood to give expression to the system of doctrine contained in Scripture itself. The task of Christian theology was to clarify and elucidate further the truths of the Bible, truths that had been made known by God for the sake of humanity's salvation.

4. New Directions in Contemporary Theology

Whereas in nineteenth-century Reformed thought a high doctrine of Scripture was held to be crucial for a proper understanding of the nature and task of Christian theology, such was not the case in the century that followed. The rise of modern biblical criticism and, more important, direct assaults upon scriptural authority and infallibility introduced radically new ideas and perspectives into theological discourse.

In view of the lack of consensus among evangelicals in our day, Peter Toon is reluctant to adopt the Reformed orthodox doctrine of Scripture.[31] He argues that the theological methodology associated with orthodox scholasticism had introduced a speculative, rationalistic element into Reformed teaching (especially in its doctrine of biblical inspiration). In contrasting Cunningham and Rainy, Toon describes the former as "the solid, scholastic High Calvinist of the early Victorian era" and the latter as "the cultured, moderate Calvinist of the later Victorian era" (pp. 31, 33). And whereas the former conveys, in Toon's judgment, a "rather simple explanation" of divine revelation, the latter resists the tendency toward dogmatism. In this connection Toon expresses reservations regarding the orthodox scholastics' view of dogmatic theology as comprising "mere summaries or compendia of Scripture teaching" (p. 78). These criticisms prompt Toon to remark: "If we merely reproduce the statements of the past in the present, then we are in danger of teaching misleading doctrine" (p. 82). Agreeably, doctrinal development in the Christian tradition is "not an organic, regular growth but rather a complex one" (p. 106). And as Leith observes, "no theology is ever the theology or the final statement of Christian faith. God's Word is final, but the human apprehensions of that Word are never complete or wholly accurate."[32] Scripture, however, is the primary norm in theological interpretation. The authority of churchly doctrine rests upon Scripture alone; it is, accordingly, derivative in nature.

In our judgment, Toon is mistaken when he argues that "whatever development of doctrine exists within the Bible, such as, from the Old to the New Testament and from the Gospels to the Epistles, it has no *direct* bearing on the development of doctrine in the historical church after the days of the apostles" (p. 106). The development of doctrine in Christian tradition does bear an *analogy* to the development of doctrine in Scripture. The self-same Spirit who formerly inspired the biblical authors now actively preserves the church as the pillar and foundation of the truth (I Tim 3:15). An analogy can be drawn between God's unfolding revelation throughout the course of redemptive history and the development of doctrine in the history of the church since the closing of the canon of Scripture. There is both unity and diversity in theological expression in Scripture and in Christian tradition. On the one hand, the seed of divine truth opens up in its fullness with Christ's coming into the world. On the other hand, the church's understanding of the inscripturated Word develops gradually over time – to be sure, with a mixture of truth and error.

Diversity of theological viewpoint, as well as doctrinal conflict spanning the history of Christian interpretation, has led many in our own day to more radical assessments of all religious truth-claims. Both pluralism and relativism employ a syncretistic approach to truth. Problematic also is the (multi)perspectival method advanced by John Frame and Vern Poythress.[33] Here one finds an evangelical variation on Hegel's theory of development – development of doctrine forged through the fires of intense polemical debate. Perspectivalism's golden mean is the theological synthesis of thesis and antithesis. In view of both the contextual nature of Christian interpretation and the contrariety of theological perspectives, Frame and Poythress have begun to move in the direction of theological relativism. Apparently contradictory interpretations of the Bible, whether ancient or modern, are explained by Frame and Poythress in terms of what they see as the inherent ambiguity and vagueness of biblical language itself. These architects of multiperspectivalism repeatedly caution theologians against the temptation to reformulate biblical doctrine with a degree of theological precision not warranted by the text of Scripture.[34]

Two other factors bear upon our subject of doctrinal development and exposition. First, the modern idea of a hermeneutical *circle* points to the importance of interdisciplinary study within the theological discipline viewed as a whole. Whereas biblical theology as a distinctive discipline points "directly toward the history of Christian doctrine, with which it shares its historical-doctrinal method and outlook,"[35] the interrelationship between biblical theology and systematics is clearly evident with respect to the Reformed exposition of the divine-human covenants. And covenant theology, needless to say, occupies a formative place in the Reformed system of doctrine. (Reformed theology, in point of fact, can be said to be synonymous with covenant theology.[36]) Hendrikus Berkhof, who is representative of present-day historical criticism, objects to orthodox scholasticism's use of Scripture citation, whereby the biblical text is (allegedly) prevented from speaking for itself. What we discover, suggests Berkhof, is a use of proof-texting that merely serves as a foil for preconceived ideas.[37] To the contrary, a fair and accurate reading of the literature indicates that the scholastic federalists, as well as the orthodox Protestants in general, were in fact drawing upon a rich and, to be sure, diversified exegetico-theological tradition. As systematicians, the primary task of the Protestant scholastics did not consist in the presentation of detailed exegesis but in the exposition of the system of doctrine that was itself the fruit of biblical exegesis. "To accuse the result of proof-texting is to ignore division of labor and to fail to respect careful distinction of topic – this latter being a characteristic of orthodoxy."[38]

Second, the language of the church's creeds and confessions, as well as the technical vocabulary used by the systematicians, does not *necessarily* introduce alien or speculative elements into ecclesiastical dogma. As Toon himself recognizes, there is no inherent problem in the use of creedal terminology, as distinct from the language employed by the biblical writers themselves. Theological vocabulary is valid and necessary for the theological task (p. 107). "Theological language," as Muller reminds us, "is not a special, exalted language delivered by God and preserved somehow from involvement in the world. Theological language is ordinary language, and it follows the rules of ordinary language. Theology can be intelligible only when it speaks the linguistic coin of the realm."[39]

5. Conclusion

Contemporary theology of the evangelical and nonevangelical varieties has issued a call for the reformulation of traditional Christian dogma explicitly in terms of the changing historical contexts out of which all doctrinal statements arise. In the final analysis, it seems to this writer, the critical issue raised by theological contextualism is twofold: (1) the nature of biblical authority, including the Reformation principle of *sola scriptura*; and (2) the role of confessional theology in the propagation and defense of the gospel. One of the leading evangelical representatives of the new theological direction is the historical theologian Peter Toon. Our study of doctrinal development, however, has led us to raise the question whether Toon's understanding of ecclesiastical dogma does not effectively undermine the normative status of the great creeds of the church as a rule of faith, a secondary norm alongside Scripture, the primary rule. Contrary to the views of earlier Reformed theologians, notably that of Robert Rainy, it is Toon's contention that the creedal statements of the West are not necessary tools in the ongoing articulation of Christian doctrine. The creeds that came out of the Protestant Reformation, Toon posits, are essentially historic documents, statements of faith bound by a particular time and circumstance, and therefore of limited value in the ongoing work of the church. But over against this view of Toon it is essential to recognize the transcultural value of Reformed orthodoxy. To be sure, dogmatic theology – no less than any other branch of the theological discipline – bears the traits of the particular historical context in which it is framed, including certain linguistic, philosophical, and sociological peculiarities, among others. Nevertheless, it is the duty of Christian theology to transcend the cultural and historical relativities in the restatement of biblical truth and in the application of God's eternal unchanging Word in the present setting of the church's life and witness.

Accordingly, we take exception to Grenz's plea – cited at the beginning of this essay – for a "rejection of the older evangelical conception of theology as the construction of truth on the basis of the Bible alone."[40] Although the historical spectacles through which Christians view the Scriptures may at times obscure biblical teaching, exegetes and dogmaticians are to be guided always by the hermeneutical principle that Scripture is its own best interpreter. Scripture is not merely the first among many norms regulative of the Christian tradition. It is the norm that singularly defines biblical faith, the norm that governs all other norms in the theological enterprise. In the Protestant and Reformed tradition, historically speaking, the canon of the Old and New Testament constitutes the final authority. Recognition of the centrality of Scripture in the interpretive process leads inevitably to critical reflection on the secondary, derivative authority of dogmatic formulation. To the degree that the creeds of the church faithfully represent the teachings of Scripture, to that degree they are always and everywhere binding upon believers. Though fallible, human documents, the confessional standards are, nonetheless, instruments used by God in the maintenance and propagation of the truth through the many centuries of the church's history and are, therefore, not to be viewed as merely provisional statements of faith bound to a former place and time.

ENDNOTES

[1]See, *e.g.*, Clark Pinnock, *A Wideness in God's Mercy: The Finality of Jesus Christ in a World of Religions* (Grand Rapids: Zondervan, 1992). Contrast Alister E. McGrath, "The Challenge of Pluralism for the Contemporary Christian Church," *JETS* 35 (1992) 361-73; and "The Church's Response to Pluralism," *JETS* 35 (1992) 487-501.

[2]Hendrikus Berkhof, *Introduction to the Study of Dogmatics*, trans. J. Vriend (Grand Rapids: Eerdmans, 1985) 49.

[3]Alan F. Johnson and Robert E. Webber, *What Christians Believe: A Biblical and Historical Summary* (Grand Rapids: Zondervan, 1989) ix-x, *their emphasis*.

[4]Stanley J. Grenz, *Revisioning Evangelical Theology: A Fresh Agenda for the Twenty-first Century* (Downers Grove, IL: InterVarsity, 1993) 89-90. For an alternative position, see John Jefferson Davis, *Foundations of Evangelical Theology* (Grand Rapids: Baker, 1984).

[5]Johnson and Webber, *What Christians Believe* x.

[6]Carl F. H. Henry, "The Cultural Relativizing of Revelation," review of *Christianity in Culture*, by Charles H. Kraft, *TrinJ* 1 NS (1980) 153-64. On the broader issue of religious pluralism, consult David F. Wells, *No Place for Truth: Or Whatever Happened to Evangelical Theology?* (Grand Rapids: Eerdmans, 1993) 264.

[7]See Harvie M. Conn, *Eternal Word and Changing Worlds: Theology, Anthropology, and Mission in Triologue* (Grand Rapids: Zondervan, 1984).

[8]The place of presuppositionalism in theological argument is discussed by Cornelius Van Til in *A Christian Theory of Knowledge* (Grand Rapids: Baker, 1969); and *The New Hermeneutic* (Nutley, NJ: Presbyterian and Reformed, 1974). Consult also Richard A. Muller's insightful analysis of this element in theological prolegomena, *Post-Reformation Reformed Dogmatics* (vol. 1, Prolegomena to Theology; Grand Rapids: Baker, 1987), as well as his analysis of the relationship between Scripture and tradition in *Post-Reformation Reformed Dogmatics* (vol.2, Holy Scripture: The Cognitive Foundation of Theology; Grand Rapids: Baker, 1993).

[9]John Leith, *The Reformed Imperative: What the Church Has to Say That No One Else Can Say* (Philadelphia: Westminster, 1988). This book and its sequel, *From Generation to Generation: The Renewal of the Church According to Its Own Theology and Practice* (Louisville: Westminster/John Knox, 1990), reiterate and develop ideas expressed in Leith's earlier study, *Introduction to the Reformed Tradition: A Way of Being the Christian Community* (Atlanta: John Knox, 1978). These otherwise illuminating analyses of the teachings of the Reformed tradition are marred by the author's failure to discern the essential incompatibility between the teachings of Karl Barth and that of historic Reformed orthodoxy. Leith mistakenly portrays Barth as a faithful interpreter of John Calvin, though he does admit that there has been "the temptation in Christian theology, since the advent of critical historical studies, to minimize historical knowledge," adding that "This was especially true of such modern theologians as Rudolf Bultmann and even of Barth and Brunner" (*Basic Christian Doctrine* [Louisville: Westminster/John Knox, 1993] 126). See the helpful critiques of neourthodoxy given by Cornelius Van Til, *The New Modernism: An Appraisal of the Theology of Barth and Brunner* (Philadelphia: Presbyterian and Reformed, 1946); *Christianity and Barthianism* (Philadelphia: Presbyterian and Reformed, 1965); and Richard A. Muller, "The Place and Importance of Karl Barth in the Twentieth Century," *WTJ* 50 (1988) 127-56; "Karl Barth and the Path of Theology into the Twentieth Century: Historical Observations," *WTJ* 51 (1989) 25-50.

[10]Richard A. Muller, *The Study of Theology: From Biblical Interpretation to Contemporary Formulation* (Foundations of Contemporary Interpretation, vol 7; Grand Rapids: Zondervan, 1991) 126-27. See also Muller, "The Role of Church History in the Study of Systematic Theology," in *Doing Theology in Today's World,* ed. Thomas MeComiskey and John Woodbridge (Grand Rapids: Zondervan, 1990); and Grant R. Osborne, *The Hermeneutical Spiral: A Comprehensive Introduction to Biblical Interpretation* (Downers Grove, IL: InterVarsity, 1991) 263-317.
[11]Muller, *Study of Theology* 129.
[12]Compare the views of Van Til on the doctrine of the knowledge of God in *A Christian Theory of Knowledge.*
[13]*The Reformed Imperative* 31.
[14]*The Constitution of the Presbyterian Church (U.S.A.),* Part I: The Book of Confessions (Louisville: The Office of the General Assembly, 1991) 3.18.
[14]For Vos's place in the history of Reformed thought see Roger Nicole, "The Relationship between Biblical Theology and Systematic Theology," in *Evangelical Roots: A Tribute to Wilbur Smith* (New York: Thomas Nelson, 1978) 185-94; Richard Lints, "Two Theologies or One? Warfield and Vos on the Nature of Theology," *WTJ* 54 (1992) 235-53; and *The Fabric of Theology: A Prolegomenon to Evangelical Theology* (Grand Rapids: Eerdmans, 1993).
[16]Robert Rainy, *Delivery and Development of Christian Doctrine* (Edinburgh: T. & T. Clark, 1874). Page references that follow in the text are to this work.
[17]Leith's use of the term gracious with reference to the order of creation introduces a degree of theological confusion in the doctrine of Christ's reconciling and atoning work. See Chapter Four.
[18]J. Gresham Machen, *What is Faith?* (1925 reprint, Carlisle, PA: Banner of Truth Trust, 1991) 183-218. Compare his study on Paul's letter to the Galatians, *Machen's Notes on Galatians,* ed. John H. Skilton (Philadelphia: Presbyterian and Reformed, 1972) 178-81; and his *The Christian View of Man* (London: Banner of Truth Trust, 1937) 149-60. At issue in the present-day theological dispute is the Reformed doctrine of the Covenant of Works. See Richard Lints, "The Progressive Covenant from Machen to Murray" (paper read at the 45th annual meeting of the Evangelical Theological Society, Washington, D.C., November 18-20, 1993); and Chapter One of this collected writings.
[19]For a biblical-theological exposition of this theme, see my treatment in Chapter Eight; and Peter E. Golding, "The Development of the Covenant: An Introductory Study in Biblical Theology," *Reformed Theological Journal* 9 (1993) 46-61. Compare Thomas Schreiner's recent exegetical-theological study of Paul on the law, *The Law and Its Fulfillment: A Pauline Theology of Law* (Grand Rapids: Baker, 1993).
[20]Compare F. F. Bruce, *The New Testament Development of Old Testament Themes* (Grand Rapids: Eerdmans, 1968) 51-67. In this connection, see especially the pioneering work of Geerhardus Vos, *Biblical Theology: Old and New Testaments* (Grand Rapids: Eerdmans, 1948).
[21]Leith, *An Introduction to the Reformed Tradition* 110.
[23]See, *e.g*., the works of J. N. D. Kelly, *Early Christian Doctrines* (2d ed.; New York: Harper and Row, 1960); Frederic W. Farrer, *History of Interpretation* (1886; reprint, Grand Rapids: Baker, 1961); and Reinhold Seeberg, *The History of Doctrines* (Grand Rapids: Baker, 1977, reprint).
[23]Consult Muller, *Post-Reformation Reformed Dogmatics*, vol.2.
[24]Adolf von Harnack, *What Is Christianity?,* trans. T. B. Saunders (New York: G. P. Putman, 1902).

[25]Peter Toon, *The Development of Doctrine in the Church* (Grand Rapids: Eerdmans, 1979) 81. Jan Walgrave maintains: "The history of dogma is an inherent part of the systematic treatment of dogma itself" (*Unfolding Revelation: The Nature of Doctrinal Development* [Philadelphia: Westminster, 1971] 4).
[26]William Cunningham, *Historical Theology: A Review of the Principal Doctrinal Discussions in the Christian Church Since the Apostolic Age* (vol.1; 1860; reprint, London: Banner of Truth Trust, 1969) 7. Compare Rainy, *Delivery and Development* 225-26. Martin I. Klauber ("Francis Turretin on Biblical Accommodation: Loyal Calvinist or Reformed Scholastic?" *WTJ* 55 [1993] 80) points out: "In order to protect the Protestant concept of *sola Scriptura*, Turretin argued that the fundamental articles of the faith, those that are necessary for salvation, are clearly revealed throughout Scripture. Granted, the NT is clearer, but the substance of doctrine is communicated throughout the Bible."
[27]M. Eugene Osterhaven, *The Faith of the Church: A Reformed Perspective on Its Historical Development* (Grand Rapids: Eerdmans, 1982) 18.
[28]*Ibid.* 19.
[29]*The Constitution of the Presbyterian Church (U.S.A.)* 6.006; also, *The Confession of Faith* (The Publications Committee of the Free Presbyterian Church of Scotland, 1976) 22.
[30]Cunningham, *Historical Theology* 1.36.
[31]Toon, *The Development of Doctrine in the Church* 87. Page references that follow in the text are to this work. The literature on the Protestant doctrine of Scripture is extensive. See, *e.g.*, the collection of essays in *Inerrancy,* ed. Norman L. Geisler (Grand Rapids: Zondervan, 1979); contrast Donald K. McKim, *The Bible in Theology and Preaching*, rev. ed. (Nashville: Abingdon, 1993). McKim offers a concise summary of various, divergent theological positions, along with helpful bibliographical references.
[32]Leith, *An Introduction to the Reformed Tradition* 90.
[33]See especially, John M. Frame, *The Doctrine of the Knowledge of God* (A Theology of Lordship: A Series; Phillipsburg, NJ: Presbyterian and Reformed, 1987); and Vern S. Poythress, *Symphonic Theology: The Validity of Multiple Perspectives in Theology* (Grand Rapids: Zondervan, 1987).
[34]Additional critique is found in Mark W. Karlberg, "On the Theological Correlation of Divine and Human Language: A Review Article," *JETS* 32 (1989) 99-105. Consult also the panel discussion of perspectivalism and related issues under the topic, "Developments in Reformed Theology in the Twentieth Century," held at the 45th annual meeting of the Evangelical Theological Society, especially the response papers by W. Robert Godfrey and Cornelis P. Venema (see note 18 above).
[35]Muller, *The Study of Theology* 94-95.
[36]Richard Muller, for example, speaks of the "architectonic potential of the doctrine" in his discussion of covenant theology in *Post-Reformation Reformed Dogmatics* 2.118. Regrettably, Toon rejects federalism as a mere human "invention" (*The Development of Doctrine in the Church* 118).
[37]Berkhof, *Introduction to the Study of Dogmatics* 34. Compare my review of this work in *WTJ* 48 (1986) 385-88.
[38]Muller, *Post-Reformation Reformed Dogmatics* 2.526-27.
[39]Muller, *The Study of Theology* 209.
[40]See note 4.

CHAPTER SEVENTEEN

REFORMED THEOLOGY AS THE THEOLOGY OF THE COVENANTS: THE CONTRIBUTIONS OF MEREDITH G. KLINE TO REFORMED SYSTEMATICS

It is with a deep sense of personal admiration and esteem for Professor Kline that I address the topic of the significance of his work for contemporary Reformed theology. Kline's thought has played an infuential role in the shaping of my understanding of the Scriptures, especially the biblical-theological interpretation of God's covenants.[1] May this tribute to my very dear friend and mentor give expression to my indebtedness to him, while helping in some small measure to rekindle in the Reformed churches a renewed awareness and appreciation for the doctrine of the covenants and to emphasize the importance of this teaching for the presentation and defense of the gospel in our day.

In many respects this essay serves as an introduction to the writings of Kline in the broader context of current theological discussion. As a largely descriptive analysis of Kline's work our present treatment will necessarily be selective and brief, addressing what I consider to be among Kline's most formative insights into contemporary reformulation of Reformed doctrine. Adoption of Kline's interpretations leads inevitably to a number of significant modifications of traditional dogmatic exposition. And the fact that his work itself bears a decisively *theological* orientation greatly facilitates the writing of this article.

The theme on which many of Kline's writings have centered is the covenantal nature of divine revelation, both special and general. In his most recent study, *Kingdom Prologue*, Kline acknowledges that the covenant theme offers but one perspective on scriptural revelation.

> To select a theme for the role of organizing a biblical theological survey does not necessarily imply that one judges that theme to be the most important or fundamental or sublime of all biblical themes. Nor does it necessarily imply that one thinks that theme best expresses the uniqueness of biblical religion. The situation is not that there is only one appropriate controlling perspective for an overall biblical theology so that it becomes necessary to determine which biblical theme is most central or vital or distinctive. There is room and even need for a variety of biblical theologies pursuing various perspectives. This is not to consent with those who

> believe the Bible contains various conflicting theologies that make it impossible to speak of a single "biblical" theology. It is rather to recognize the variegated fullness of the biblical faith and to acknowledge that the adequate exposition of it all requires a variety of biblical theological treatments, each making a contribution complementary to the others.[2]

These remarks, however, do not overlook the importance given to the doctrine of the covenants in the history of the Reformed tradition, nor do they minimize the hermeneutical and methodological significance of covenant theology for the Reformed biblico-systematic exposition of divine truth. Elsewhere Kline affirms: "It would be difficult to select a subject of more basic import for the study of biblical theology and hermeneutics than the nature and structure of the divine covenants."[3]

Several dogmaticians and historians of doctrine have made similar observations. I. John Hesselink contends that "Reformed theology is covenant theology."[4] And B. B. Warfield speaks of the covenant teaching as the "architectonic principle" of the *Westminster Confession of Faith* (one of the definitive creedal statements of the Reformed faith), and as "the most commodious mode of presenting the *corpus* of Reformed doctrine."[5] In view of the modifications and clarifications of the covenant doctrine introduced in the history of dogmatics, Kline's recent formulations are not only provocative, but they are crucial to contemporary theological debate.[6] Before considering the specific contributions of Kline to Reformed systematics, it will be instructive to take note of three distinctive aspects of his hermeneutical approach to biblical and theological interpretation.

Kline's work builds upon the thinking of three giants in the Reformed tradition – John Calvin, Geerhardus Vos, and Cornelius Van Til. His skillful employment of extra-biblical material for the interpretation of Scripture, notably the ancient Near Eastern treaty documents, and his keen perception of the compatibility between general and special revelation (*i.e.*, nature and Scripture) reflect something of Kline's debt to Van Til. Both of these theologians have emphasized the covenantal nature of all God's revelation and in so doing have demonstrated the fruitful interaction of general and special revelation. A covenantal understanding of God's disclosures in nature and Scripture is an indispensable element in theistic presuppositionalism as advocated by Van Til.[7] Examples in Kline's writings of this distinctively Reformed understanding of general and special revelation include his interpretation of the Genesis accounts of creation (including the matter of the relationship between Scripture and modern science[8]), comparisons between circumcision and baptism in the biblical covenants and the oath rituals of the ancient Near East, and the formal analogies between biblical canon and the international suzerainty treaties. Each of these will be dealt with in the discussion below.

Secondly, Kline's extensive use of biblical theology distinguishes him as the leading contemporary exponent of the tradition of Vos. Historically speaking, the rise and development of covenant theology have close ties to the discipline of biblical theology.[9] Nowhere is this more evident than in the exposition of the theology of the covenants. Kline writes;

> It is difficult at best to distinguish between the functions of biblical theology and systematic theology in the treatment of the divine covenants. To analyze these covenants is to trace the history of revelation and divine-human relationship, which is precisely the domain of biblical theology. Certainly, too, biblical theology involves the systematization of the covenantal data under relatively broad historical epochs.[10]

What Kline says here equally pertains to the history of the origins of these two theological methods.

This brings us more directly, in the third place, to the role of systematics in Kline's theological presentations. The unifying of certain biblical covenants, observes Kline, has scriptural precedent. In Ps 105:9-10, for example, there is "a virtual identifying of God's separate covenantal transactions with Abraham, Isaac, and Jacob."[11] So also, the various covenants enacted by Moses are viewed together as the "first" covenant in contrast to the "new" or "second" covenant (Heb 8: 6-8). Kline cautions: "Surely it does not become systematic theology to unravel what has been thus synthesized to a degree even in the Scriptures. Systematic theology ought rather to weave together the related biblical strands yet more systematically."[12]

Perhaps the single, most notable feature of Kline's systematic conception of biblical truth is his vigorous defense of amillennial eschatology, an insight shared by Vos and Van Til.[13] Kline rightly insists that "The amillennial position is the only interpretation of eschatology that is systematically compatible with Reformed theology."[14] But this Reformed conviction is by no means of recent vintage. Perhaps rarely admitted or acknowledged is the fact that Calvin held to the view of eschatology later known as amillennialism.[15] Vos, the premier biblical theologian and systematician in the first half of the twentieth century, set forth the teaching of the apostle Paul under the rubric of eschatology, thereby understanding the apostle to have systematically treated the revelation of God in redemptive history in terms of the eschatological design of creation and subsequently of recreation, thus acknowledging the legitimacy of a systematic presentation of divine revelation, *i.e.*, the *system* of doctrine contained in the Scriptures.[16] At one and the same time Vos emphasized the continuity and discontinuity of God's kingdom program as it has progressively unfolded in redemptive history. Kline, more than any other single individual, has developed and refined the amillennial interpretation of the two testaments. Covenant theology is biblical theology eschatologically informed, that is to say, Reformed theology of the Vossian variety.

These three aspects of Kline's hermeneutical method – Van Tilian presuppositionalism, Vossian biblical theology, and Calvinian eschatology – are distinctively covenantal. Kline jocundly describes his brand of theology as "the Van Tilian Reformed, Covenantal, garden variety of Christian[ity]."[17] Such a vigorously presuppositional and consistently covenantal-theological method enhances a thoroughgoing biblical, nonspeculative, exposition of the teaching of Scripture. The efforts of modern Reformed theologians like Vos, Van Til, and Kline have sharpened and deepened our understanding of the Scripture principle, the principle of the self-attesting Christ speaking through the Scriptures of the Old and New Testaments.[18]

In what follows our discussion will proceed according to the traditional order of dogmatics – revelation and Scripture, God and humanity, and church and eschatology. Comparisons between various portions of the OT Scriptures, particularly the Decalogue and the Book of Deuteronomy, and the ancient international treaties have shed considerable light upon the nature and meaning of biblical canonicity. Before the discovery of these ancient Near Eastern treaty documents, orthodox dogmatics was deprived of a genuinely covenantal and authentically historical conception of canon. Kline remarks how

> concrete historical analysis has tended to yield to formulation of scriptural authority in the dogmatic categories of the Bible's own objective self-authentication as Word of God and the Holy Spirit's internal testimony to the Word, and the relation of these to individual faith and the church's sealing attestation to the Word. But the more precise delineation of biblical canonicity requires that it be perceived as fully as possible in its specific historical character.[19]

The arguments advanced by Kline regarding the covenantal nature of biblical authority and canonicity, including reclamation of a historically authentic conception of canon, call for an additional clarification and refinement in traditional interpretations regarding the origin and formal structure of biblical revelation. Kline's description of Scripture as a divine house-building not only captures the rich imagery of Scripture itself but more importantly for our consideration here it underscores the peculiarly covenantal-historical process superintended by God through special providence in the very formation of the Scriptures.

Implicit in this canonical understanding of the Old and New Testaments is the distinction between "life norms" and "faith norms," a distinction essential for a proper formulation of biblical ethics as taught in the two successive testaments. The church's Scriptures, comprising the Old and New Testaments, contain two distinct canons. The form of government appointed in the Old Covenant is not the community polity for the church of the New Covenant, its ritual legislation is not a directory for the church's cultic practice, nor can the program of conquest it prescribes be equated with the evangelistic mission of the church in this world. A distinction thus arises for the Christian church between canon and Scripture.[20]

Understanding the covenantal structure of the two canons helps us to perceive the underlying unity of the message of redemption set forth in the Bible and the diversity of composition of the sacred writings. All of Scripture, as Kline persuasively argues, is covenantal. The idea of a *covenantal Bible* is pregnant with meaning.

> To arrive at a covenantal identification of the various parts of the OT, an identification suggested by their covenantalized provenance and supported by formal correspondences to the ancient covenants, is not to claim that all the literary forms of the OT derived from the treaty form nor even that particular features common to, say, OT prophetic or

> wisdom literature and the treaties were peculiar to the treaties outside the Scriptures or had their ultimate source in them. . . . The primary purpose for which the various types of literature were utilized in the OT was to serve as instruments of the covenantal administration of God's lordship over Israel. And we would maintain that thereby and in that sense a covenantal character was imparted to the entire OT which comprised these several literary forms.[21]

Traditional covenant terminology likewise undergoes refinement in Kline's presentations, notably in his magnum opus, *Kingdom Prologue*. Here Kline offers the following scheme for the divine covenants.[22] The major divisions of the administration of God's kingdom are twofold: the Covenant of Creation and the Covenant of Redemption. Within the Covenant of Creation (traditionally called the Covenant of Works) there is the Covenant with Adam and the subsequent Covenant of Confirmation. Had Adam been faithful to the Lord God and had he successfully completed the probationary test, he would have been confirmed in true righteousness and holiness and would have been granted the promised reward of eternal life, though its full realization would have had to await the consummation of history – the fulfillment of the historical task given to Adam and the human race in the cultural mandate.[23]

For there to be divine blessing and favor for humankind after Adam's fall into sin it was necessary that there be another covenant, the Covenant of Redemption (traditionally called the Covenant of Grace). Here again, Kline distinguishes between two separate covenants; first, the Covenant with Christ in eternity (the Counsel of Peace or the Covenant of Redemption in the older terminology[24]) and, second, the Covenant of Conferment. These terminological modifications help clarify a number of important distinctions that need to be drawn among the various divine covenants, preredemptive and redemptive. The kingdom of God, its inauguration and its historical development, is the eschatological realization, wherein each of the several covenants points to the final consummation of God's creative and recreative purposes. Covenant history and eschatology are mutually interpretive of one another.

> Essentially the same eschatological goal that is offered in the Covenant of Conferment secured through the Second Adam was already envisaged for the Covenant of Confirmation that would have followed a successful probation of the First Adam. In both cases the blessing sanctions of the covenant consisted in a consummation of the kingdom of God.[25]

Kline's exposition of covenant theology suggests that an appropriate place to begin a biblical-theological formulation of the doctrine of God is Jn 4:24, where we read of Jesus instructing the Samaritan woman in the true nature of God and in the worship of God. "God is Spirit, and they who worship him must worship in Spirit and truth" (*cf.* Jn 6:63). The eschatological contrast is between the provisional Aaronic institution of Israelite worship and true ("abiding") worship in the Spirit (*cf.* Jn 15:4,26 and 14:15-17): the contrast is between old and new economies of redemption, between types and shadows on the one hand and truth (in the

Johannine sense) and reality on the other. The restoration of man's communion with God is explained in terms of the substance and reality of the New Covenant, namely, Jesus the Christ (*cf.* Lk 24:13-47). Jesus portrays this ("Spiritual") blessing of redemption as the satisfying of man's thirst with the water of life flowing from him who is life-giving Spirit (*cf.* Jn 7:37-39; 1 Cor 15:45; and 2 Cor 3:18).[26]

The trinitarian character of divine revelation appears from the very beginning of God's self-disclosure to Adam. "God the Logos as well as God the Spirit was revealed in the theophanic Glory in Eden."[27] In the gospel accounts the unique identification of God's only Son occurs at the time of special, theophanic manifestation of the Spirit (*e.g.*, at the baptism and transfiguration of Jesus). On these occasions, and others, Jesus displays the very Glory that he shared with the Father since before the worlds were made. The Glory-theophany is a trinitarian revelation of the Lord of the covenant. Man's creation and renewal in the image of the Spirit is a creaturely participation in the divine nature (*cf.* Jn 17:20-24; 2 Pet 1:3-4; and Heb 1:3; 2:10). The building of the true and living temple of God is a manifestation of the Spirit who is the Lord. The redemptive refashioning of humankind into the image of Christ entails both objective and subjective aspects.[28]

The revelation of God's covenant to our first parents came by way of general and special revelation. All God's works are covenantal: all creation witnesses to the covenantal Word and works of the sovereign Lord. Alongside natural revelation is the special, theophanic revelation of the Glory-Spirit. Kline's study, *Images of the Spirit*, presents a brilliant and illuminating exposition of man's creation in the image of God. By identifying the Glory-Spirit as the divine paradigm Kline has not only called into question traditional formulations of the image concept, but he has also provided a convincing analysis of the offices originally occupied by man as image of God in the covenant of Creation.

According to Kline, the image consists in the dual offices of priesthood and kingship. Differing with traditional views, Kline understands the prophetic office to belong to the postlapsarian era: it is redemptive in nature. Prophecy itself, however, is an element of the original Covenant of Creation, in which the righteous judgment of God determines the future course of God's kingdom rule over humanity and all creation. In terms of the official responsibilities originally given to Adam and humankind there is a priority of priesthood to kingship. "Priesthood's primacy is not just a matter of historical priorities but of the teleological subordination of the kingly occupation to priestly-cultic objectives."[29] The redemptive recreation of man in the image of God is further developed in terms of the priestly and prophetic *models.* As Kline argues, the prophetic experience itself is "an instance of creation in the image of God," and as such "sheds light on the nature of the prophetic office" (see further discussion below).[30] Kline's treatment of the prophetic material reflects a thoroughgoing eschatological understanding, one that is straightforwardly amillennial. This is crucial to his interpretation of the ministry of the Spirit in the Mosaic epoch of redemptive revelation.

The revelation given through Moses is the Speech-Act of God, the divinely inspired interpretation of God's wondrous works. Moses presents the program of redemption in terms of the replication of the Glory-Spirit on both macrocosmic and microcosmic levels. The glory of the Lord is revealed in the heavens and in the earthly (tabernacle-)temple, itself a replica of the heavenly Glory-temple. Likewise, the glory of the Lord is reflected in the priestly garments and the articles of the tabernacle. In the prelapsarian era the cultural labors of humankind would also have carried the divine signature, the mirror-image of the Glory-Spirit. "Human culture was a creaturely replication of the glory of God as revealed in the theophanic Glory itself, the Archetype of both cosmos and man."[31] The rich typological symbolism of Old Testament revelation is creatively explored by Kline in *Images of the Spirit.* Some ask, however, how far one can take this symbolism without falling into allegorization.[32] The answer is found in a proper reading of the system of typology in Scripture as a feature of the progressive revelation of God in redemptive history, particularly in the consideration of the OT as the preparation for the coming of Christ. Kline's emphasis upon the historical character of biblical symbolism insures the validity of his approach to the subject of biblical typology. To be sure, typology is a vital aspect of biblical theology.

The opening chapters of the Book of Genesis, what is part of the historical prologue to God's covenant with Israel, set forth an account of the creation of the heavens and the earth. Kline makes a distinction in the biblical literature between extended allegory and straightforward historical record, whether prose or poetry, which employs figures of speech. Genesis 1-3 falls into the latter category, *i.e.*, historical record. The brevity of the first eleven chapters as a whole is "explained by the particular purpose and nature of the Scriptures."[33] Concerning the importance of literary analysis for the exegesis of Scripture, Kline wisely suggests: "It would perhaps alert us to this requirement if we labeled our exegetical approach more comprehensively as literary-historical instead of grammatico-historical."[34]

In contrast to the views of Kline, Howard Van Till distinguishes between the story of origins (Genesis 1-2) and the subsequent record of primeval history (Genesis 3-11) as two distinct literary genres. (Other portions of OT literature, observes Van Till, also fall into the category of "primeval history."[35] Van Till brings to his reading of these early chapters of Genesis the modern scientific view of history and uniformity in nature. The creation of the earth and cosmos takes place over a protracted period of time, determined solely by the findings of the natural sciences (*e.g.*, astronomy and geology). These scientific studies confirm, in Van Till's judgment, the doctrine of uniformity. The whole creation is "formed according to a single set of coherently related patterns for material behavior."[36] But what about the occurrence of miracles and special providence in Van Till's view of cosmic history? With respect to the Genesis record of creation how does Van Till's view allow for the unique origination of man (as well as the variety of plants and animals, each created "according to its kind")?[37] Van Till's adherence to the modern scientific view of "coherence, continuity, and authenticity" hinders the clear and unambiguous reading of the biblical text.

Kline, on the other hand, interprets "the seven solar days of Genesis 1 [as] a pictorial form, a figurative chronological framework sabbatical in pattern, in which the data of the creation process are arranged – and that, topically." Unlike Van Till's view, Kline's interpretation allows for the *legitimate* input of the natural sciences. As such, Kline's exegesis of Genesis 1 is "adjustable to any chronological disclosures of geology, whether as to the duration or sequence of the creation process."[38]

The entrance of death into the world of humanity, contends Kline, serves no other necessary historical function than as part of the common curse. The general resurrection of the godly and ungodly at the Day of the Lord coincides with the eternal state of humankind, either in glory or in wrath. But as the wages of sin in this present world course, bodily death merely signifies the spiritual estrangement between God and humanity brought about through Adam's one act of transgression. The explanation for human guilt and depravity is given in the federal understanding of sin as taught in Romans 5.[39] Kline further observes that "the disembodied state we commonly call death was not contemplated in what was threatened in the curse sanction of Genesis 2:17."[40] Rather, what was in view was the eternal separation from God, the everlasting displeasure of God upon the covenant-breaker. This understanding of death in the world of humanity may have a direct bearing upon recent discussions concerning the constitutional nature of man as comprising body and soul (over against the teaching of dichotomy and trichotomy). The older views contemplate a partitive, rather than a unitary, conception of man. But Kline's interpretation adds weight to the argument that dissolution of the physical body in death does not imply that man in his essence is spirit (or soul). Rather, man in his wholeness (body and soul) is the image of God. Traditional formulations which mistakenly define the image in terms of broader and narrower aspects of man's moral-spiritual nature obscure the biblical data which Kline's view has recaptured.[41]

One of the most important and critical elements in Kline's formulation of the divine covenants - one that is highly contested in contemporary theology – is his vigorous defense and employment of the traditional Protestant law-gospel contrast. Kline is one of the few remaining advocates of the Reformed orthodox doctrine of the covenants, specifically the doctrine of the Covenant of Works.[42] Throughout the history of Reformed theology, federalism has had both its ardent defenders and outspoken critics. But it is here that historic Reformed theology faces its greatest challenge today – a challenge necessitating renewed articulation and defense of the gospel of sovereign grace.[43]

Kline makes extensive use of the contrasting principles of inheritance, *viz.*, that of works and faith. The principle that informs the Covenant of Creation and the Covenant with Christ (among other covenants in the history of redemption) is one of works. The way of eschatological blessing in the covenant of God is the way of perfect obedience to God's law. And though the covenant relationship is never a *quid pro quo* contract, Kline rightly maintains that "We are obliged by the biblical facts to define works and justice in such a way that we can apply both the legal-commercial and family-paternal models to explicate the same covenants."[44] Repudiation of the Covenant of Works idea leads inevitably to a radical reconstruction of the Reformed system of doctrine along Barthian lines.

Essential to a proper understanding of the Mosaic economy and its accompanying typological system is the recognition of the works-inheritance principle operating on the symbolico-typical level of God's kingdom administration.[45] The covenant established by God with Israel at Sinai involves "Two levels of fulfillment of the promises of the Abrahamic Covenant."[46] This twofold realization of the covenant promises brings to our consideration the typological relationship between the Testaments.

> The Bible, as Old and New Testaments, was designed to provide constitutions for these Old and New Covenants, and in these covenants, the conferral of the kingdom-grant promised in God's covenant with Christ takes place, in typological symbol under the Old and in consummate reality under the New.[47]

The promise to Abraham concerning the land of Canaan functioned on two distinct levels. Ultimately, the promise of the land had reference to eternal inheritance, the new heavens and the new earth. In the Book of Hebrews we learn that Abraham looked for a city not made by human hands, the heavenly city of God which comes down from above. But on the secondary level, the promise to Abraham involved the actual grant of the land of Palestine. The provisional fulfillment of the promise to Abraham thus found realization at the time of Joshua's conquest of the land. But this event itself anticipated the consummate fulfillment of the Abrahamic promises in the eternal state.[48] Retention of the land was a matter of compliance with God's law (the principle of works-inheritance [merit]). During the first phase of the messianic fulfillment – what Vos has called the semi-eschatological age of the Spirit – the physical feature of the land-promise is held in abeyance. The church's present experience is comparable to that of the patriarchs. The people of the New Covenant are likewise without a physical land and home to call their own.[49] There are many complex issues in theological interpretation. But unquestionably, one of the most difficult is the subject of the relationship between the Testaments, *viz.*, the relationship between the Old (Mosaic) and the New Covenants. Otto Weber has remarked: "Dogmatics finds itself here at the most sensitive point in its relationship to exegesis. . . . Of all the questions which concern both exegesis and dogmatics equally, the relationship of the two halves of the Bible appears as a particularly complicated one."[50] Kline summarizes his thinking on the Mosaic Covenant:

> What we have found then is that once the typological kingdom was inaugurated under the Mosaic Covenant, Israel's retention of it was governed by a principle of works applied on a national scale. The standard of judgment in this national probation was one of typological legibility, that is, the message must remain reasonably readable that enjoyment of the felicity of God's holy kingdom goes hand in hand with righteousness. Without holiness we do not see God. But if the ground of Israel's tenure in Canaan was their covenant obedience, their election to receive the typological kingdom in the first place was emphatically not based on any merit of theirs (*cf.* Deut 9:5,6). Their original reception of this kingdom, as well as their restoration to it after the loss of their national election in Babylonian exile, are repeatedly attributed to God's remembrance of his promissory commitments of grace to Abraham, Isaac, and Jacob (Ex 2:24; 3:6ff; 6:2ff, 32:13; Deut 9:27; 10:15; Lev 26:42).[51]

Though important qualifications must be made in comparing the various covenants, *e.g.*, the Covenant of Creation and the Covenant with Christ, as well as the prediluvian covenant with Noah and the Sinaitic covenant, all of these covenants named here share in common the Covenant of Works classification. Unlike the first two mentioned, which are pure forms of the Covenant of Works, the latter two are suited to the conditions of their redemptive-historical situation. The works-principle in these latter two covenants function on the typological level of kingdom administration. As Kline observes, "the Old Covenant with Israel, though it was something more, was also a re-enactment (with necessary adjustments) of mankind's primal probation – and fall."[52]

In a stimulating review article Karl Cooper compares Kline's interpretation of the Mosaic Covenant with E. P. Sanders' analysis of covenantal nomism in Palestinian Judaism, and in so doing finds corroboration for Kline's position. Cooper notes, however, that there is one important difference between the two interpretations. Kline, unlike Sanders, restricts the principle of retribution (what Kline calls the principle of works-inheritance) to the typical, temporary sphere of life in the Israelite theocracy. Cooper then proceeds to compare the views of Kline and Sanders on the Mosaic Covenant with the system of soteriology found in late medieval nominalism. All three, argues Cooper, interpret the covenantal reward of divine favor as that which is based on obedience, though "not according to strict justice, but according to justice tempered with mercy."[53] The parallel between Jewish nomism and medieval nominalism is particularly striking: "Both Palestinian Judaism and medieval nominalism grounded *ultimate* salvation on imperfect obedience brought as an appeal to God's mercy in the context of a gracious covenant relationship."[54]

Cooper's comparison between the views of Sanders and Kline on the matter of the structure of the covenant, it must be stressed, is purely *formal*, not substantive. Furthermore, a second crucial difference needs to be drawn between these two interpretations of the Mosaic Covenant. Unlike Sanders, Kline regards the Mosaic legal covenant to be *a revelation of the Covenant of Redemption*. This places the discussion of law covenant in an entirely different (theological) setting. From this point of view all similarities made between the views of Kline and Sanders are merely formal. In light of the fact that the Mosaic Covenant is part of the progressive, ongoing revelation of the Covenant of Redemption, the sovereign purpose of God in the salvation of the elect insures the administrative compatibility of the two contrasting principles of law and grace operating on separate levels, one typological and the other eternal. Apart from this wider (and more important) redemptive-historical context the peculiar function of the law of Moses cannot be interpreted correctly. In fact, such was the error of the Judaizers who mistakenly applied the works-principle operating in the typical sphere to the eternal sphere of salvation where it did not apply (Rom 9:32). In the final place, Palestinian Judaism failed to discern the *messianic*, typological dimension of the OT revelation (see *e.g.*, Jn 5:39). This oversight, then, constitutes a major flaw in Sanders' analysis of the Mosaic Covenant.

Denial of the principle of works (merit) militates against the idea of probation – the denial that Adam or Christ had a definite task to perform in order to receive the Father's grant of the eternal kingdom (Col 1:15-20; *cf.* 1 Cor 15:22-

28). Having rejected the biblical idea of merit, modern theologians are obligated to reinterpret the doctrine of Christ's atonement. The reconciliation of the sinner to God achieved by Christ must be construed as the mere restoration of the believer to the original standing of Adam before the Fall. Hence, on this view the believer is once more placed in the way of covenant obedience: fellowship and life with God is maintained in the way of (nonmeritorious) law-keeping. According to this conception, the nature of the obligation to obedience in the original state of creation and in the covenant between the Father and the Son in eternity (the Counsel of Peace) is nonmeritorious in both cases. Consequently, the imputation of Christ's righteousness in soteric justification is not understood in legal terms as though the obedience of Christ, according to traditional Protestant orthodoxy, were the (meritorious) "ground" of the believer's right-standing before God. Christ's substitutionary atonement, we are now being told, merely satisfies the demerit of Adam's transgression, without altering in any way the underlying legal (nonmeritorious) demand of the covenant. If the integrity of the gospel is to be preserved, this unorthodox notion of the relationship between law and grace must be rejected.[55]

Kline correctly insists that the biblical idea of merit refers to "benefits granted as a matter of justice."[56] Agreeably, Adam's achievement would not have been an "autonomous accomplishment." In late sixteenth- and seventeenth-century Reformed scholasticism, attempts were made to resolve the apparent tension between divine benevolence and meritorious reward by appeal to the medieval, scholastic distinction between two states of creation, the natural and the covenantal. Reformed orthodoxy thus revived the speculative, nonbiblical dichotomy between nature and grace. Modern theologians, understandably critical of this theological construction, have unfortunately abandoned the concept of merit altogether. But ironically, these recent formulations of the divine-human covenant have not broken free of speculative thinking. For with regard to the original state of creation the notion of divine grace as applied to the covenant relationship has effectively nullified the legal demand of God's covenant with Adam. Kline rightly contends that "There is absolutely no warrant for introducing the idea of grace into the theological analysis of such an achievement of justification and thereby clouding and indeed contradicting its meritorious character and the works-justice nature of this covenant."[57] There is no legitimacy in distinguishing between a state of nature and a state of grace in the pre-Fall situation, in which the covenant arrangement is viewed as being superimposed upon the natural order. (The ramifications of this speculative element in Reformed theology are apparent in current debates concerning the relationship between law and gospel.[58])

Developing further the biblical-theological interpretation of the antithetical principles of law and grace within the Mosaic dispensation, Kline relates the formation of the prophetic literature directly to the peculiar legal aspect of the Mosaic Covenant as we have described it above. The prophets served as agents of God's lawsuit against a wicked and rebellious nation. The specific role of the prophets was to carry out on behalf of the Great King the curse sanction of the covenant against the transgressors. We noted earlier that Kline traces the beginnings and essence of prophecy to the blessing and curse sanctions of God's original covenant with Adam. The law administration of the Mosaic Covenant thus reintroduces the conditional feature of probation into the theocratic experience of Israel as a nation: probation and a covenant of works arrangement are coextensive. "Banishment from Canaan came as the final result of a protracted legal process which God instituted against Israel, a covenant lawsuit he conducted through his servants the prophets."[59]

The covenantal mission of the prophets involved "a constructive shaping of the kingdom-house of God." The experience of the prophets who were "caught up in the Spirit" corresponds to

> the royal functioning aspect of the *imago Dei* as it was bestowed on man at the beginning. The investment of prophet with heavenly authority to shape the historical course of the kingdom of God in the midst of the kingdoms on earth in the name of the royal Lord of the council was a renewal of the original assignment to man as a God-like dominion over the world, adapted now, of course, to the redemptive situation. It was an act of recreation in the glory-image of God.[60]

As servants of the covenant the prophets enforced the sanctions of the covenant mediated through Moses. The eschatological thrust of the prophetic word pointed to the coming judgment of God. The typical judgments, whether in blessing or curse, were an anticipation of the final judgment. These judgments are viewed by Kline as the intrusion of the heavenly principles and powers of the eschaton.[61] The predictive element is part of the composition of the prophetic message.[62] Yet none of the OT prophets were like Moses, for he alone spoke to God "face to face" (Deut 34:10). He stood in a unique relationship to the Spirit of prophecy. These and other considerations warrant the characterization of Moses as "the paradigm prophet of the Old Covenant"[63] and the Glory-Spirit as "the original true prophet"[64] who first announced to Adam the dual sanctions of the Covenant of Creation.

In the first covenant, as in all later redemptive covenants, the sabbath was the sign of God's consummation rest held out to the faithful covenant-keeper. The sabbatical structuring of man's days testifies to this creation ordinance.[65] As sign of covenantal promise and eschatological blessing, the sabbath ordinance in the postlapsarian era had relevance to the redemptive community exclusively. It was a sign of special, not common, grace. However, under the Mosaic arrangement the sabbath institution assumed a peculiar typological cast, reflecting the theocratic order of things in the original creation, in which priesthood and kingship alike were holy activities. The Israelite theocracy comprised a holy nation, a kingdom of priests and kings. Here again, cultic and cultural activities were holy, not common. Consequently, the Sabbath as sign and seal of redemptive covenant was affixed to both the cultic and cultural dimensions of Israelite theocratic life. Kline remarks that "though the cultic and the cultural-political are distinguishable dimensions of human functioning, they are integrated into an institutional unity by the theocratic principle of the covenant kingdom."[66] Under the New Covenant, in contrast to the Old, cultural activity is no longer holy, but common. Appropriately, the sign of the covenant in the new order is restricted to the holy realm of kingdom life, namely, the cultic sphere. Observance of the sabbath under the Old and New Covenants, therefore, reflects both the continuity and the discontinuity of God's administration of his kingdom in this world before and after the coming of Christ.

Circumcision and baptism, the sacramental signs of redemptive covenant, bear the same eschatological stamp as does the sabbath-sign. Comparisons with the ancient Near Eastern oaths and trial ordeals give further indication that the import of the biblical oath-signs is juridical. The covenantal pledges of allegiance involve the submission of the party undertaking the oath to the dual sanctions of the covenant-treaty. But the core significance of this oath-taking is an identification with the covenant curse. Safe passage through the ancient ordeal (by trial or by pledge) was a ritual passage through death to life. In redemptive covenant, the way of eschatological blessing is the way of death – the way of vicarious, substitutionary atonement provided by the Lord's true servant, the Christ of the covenant. In the judgment of John H. Stek, Kline's discussions on the oath-signs present

> one of the most significant contributions to a theology of baptism to appear in many a year. Such is the force of the evidence here adduced, and so broad the implications of the conclusions for covenant theology in general, that this study will undoubtedly be at the center of discussion for some time to come.[67]

Analogous to the ancient oath-practices is the operation of the family or household authority principle of the administration of redemptive covenant. For the children of believing parents, notes Kline, "It is not a matter of promise but of the parental authority principle."[68] Failure to distinguish between election, the proper purpose of redemptive covenant, and the administrative principle of the covenant (*viz*., parental authority) creates an unresolvable theological problem.

> Unfortunately, Covenant Theology has exhibited a strong bent towards such a reduction of covenant to election. To do so is to substitute a logical abstraction for the historical reality and to shunt systematic theology from its peculiar end of synthetic summation. The covenantal data of historical exegesis which the dogmatic theologian has failed to do justice to in his definition will eventually have to be dealt with somehow or other, but the treatment of them will be problematic and awkward. In fact, it will be impossible to incorporate elements like correlative promise-threat or actual divine vengeance against the disobedient as covenantal elements.[69]

Much more remains to be explored in the thought of Kline than space here permits. Our discussion of the contributions of Kline as an OT scholar and theologian to contemporary Reformed systematics has centered largely upon the doctrine of the divine covenants, resulting in a comprehensive reformulation of the biblical teaching from a distinctively Reformed biblical-theological (and amillennial) perspective. The vitality and freshness of Kline's theological constructions are due to his acute exegetical and systematic skills in expounding the truth of Scripture. His presentations are an eloquent and persuasive argument for the validity and usefulness of a *covenantal* interpretation of the Bible. Though Reformed theology is more than the exposition of the covenants, it is certainly no less: for this reason we maintain that Reformed theology is the theology of the covenants. The prospects for future systematic reflection on the truths of Scripture are bright indeed. The Reformed church today owes a great debt to Professor Kline for his teaching and insights, gifts of God's grace to all the church. To God be the glory.

ENDNOTES

[1]See Mark W. Karlberg, "The Mosaic Covenant and the Concept of Works in Reformed Hermeneutics: A Historical-Critical Analysis with Particular Attention to Early Covenant Eschatology," (Th.D. dissertation, Westminster Theological Seminary, 1980). *Cf.* Chapter One of this collected writings.

[2]Meredith G. Kline, *Kingdom Prologue* (S. Hamilton: Privately printed, 1985, 1986) 1.1. Anticipating later comments on the relationship between biblical theology and systematics in this article, it must be pointed out here that the method of perspectivalism as advocated by John Frame and Vern Poythress undermines the discipline of systematics. See my review of John Frame's *The Doctrine of the Knowledge of God* in "On the Theological Correlation of Divine and Human Language," *JETS* 32 (1989) 99-105.

[3]Meredith G. Kline, Review of Thomas E. McComiskey, *The Covenants of Promise* in *JETS* 30 (1987) 77.

[4]I. John Hesselink, *On Being Reformed* (Ann Arbor: Servant Books, 1983) 57.

[5]B. B. Warfield, *The Westminster Assembly and Its Work* (New York: Oxford, 1931) 56-57.

[6]For evaluation of current trends in evangelical and Reformed thinking, see Kenneth Barker, "False Dichotomies Between the Testaments," *JETS* 25 (1982) 3-16 and my response article found above (Chapter Twelve).

[7]Cornelius Van Til writes: "God's revelation in nature, together with God's revelation in Scripture, form God's one grand scheme of covenant revelation of himself to man. The two forms of revelation must therefore be seen as presupposing and supplementing one another. They are aspects of one general philosophy of history. Revelation in nature and revelation in Scripture are mutually meaningless without one another and mutually fruitful when taken together" ("Nature and Scripture," in *The Infallible Word: A Symposium*, ed. Paul Woolley (3d ed.; Phillipsburg, N.J.: Presbyterian and Reformed, 1967) 267, 269). See also his *A Christian Theory of Knowledge* (Grand Rapids: Baker, 1969) 25-27.

[8]See Meredith G. Kline, Review of Bernard Ramm, *The Christian View of Science and Scripture*, in *WTJ* 18 (1955-1956) 49-55.

[9]Roger Nicole, "The Relationship Between Biblical Theology and Systematic Theology," in *Evangelical Roots: A Tribute to Wilbur Smith,* ed. K. Kantzer (New York: Thomas Nelson, 1978) 185-94. *Cf.* Geerhardus Vos, "The Idea of Biblical Theology as a Science and as a Theological Discipline," and "The Doctrine of the Covenant in Reformed Theology," in *Redemptive History and Biblical Interpretation: The Shorter Writings of Geerhardus Vos*, ed. R. B. Gaffin, Jr. (Phillipsburg, N.J.: Presbyterian and Reformed, 1980) 3-24, 234-67.

[10]Meredith G. Kline, *By Oath Consigned: A Reinterpretation of the Covenant Signs of Circumcision and Baptism* (Grand Rapids: Eerdmans, 1968) 26 n. 1.

[11]Kline, *Kingdom Prologue* 1:5.

[12]Kline, *By Oath Consigned* 29.

[13]See my review of Gary North, *Dominion and Common Grace* in Chapter Fourteen.

[14]Meredith G. Kline, "Comments On an Old-New Error: A Review Article," *WTJ* 41 (1978) 185.

[15]See David E. Holwerda, "Eschatology and History: A Look at Calvin's Eschatological Vision," in *Exploring the Heritage of John Calvin,* ed. D. F. Holwerda (Grand Rapids: Baker, 1976) 127-39; and Anthony A. Hoekema, *The Bible and the Future* (Grand Rapids: Eerdmans, 1979) 297-301.

[16]Geerhardus Vos, *The Pauline Eschatology*, (Grand Rapids: Baker, 1979).

[17]Meredith G. Kline, "The First Resurrection: A Reaffirmation," *WTJ* 39 (1976) 115.
[18]The work of G. C. Berkouwer is noteworthy here by way of contrast. Berkouwer has devoted a lifetime to searching for a theological hermeneutic that is true to the Reformation principle of Scripture and free of all philosophical speculation. J. C. de Moor has provided an exhaustive evaluation of Berkouwer's method in *Towards a Biblically Theo-Logical Method: A Structural Analysis and a Further Elaboration of Dr. G. C. Berkouwer's Hermeneutic-Dogmatic Method* (Kampen: Kok, 1980). An appropriately critical assessment of Berkouwer is found in Carl W. Bogue, "Berkouwer: The Evolution of a Twentieth Century Theologian," *The Journal of Christian Reconstruction* 7 (1980) 135-74.

Formally speaking, Hendrikus Berkhof's *Christian Faith: An Introduction to the Study of the Faith*, trans. Sierd Woudstra (Grand Rapids: Eerdmans, 1979) serves as a model for dogmatics incorporating biblical theology into the structure and content of dogmatics. Among the traditional *loci* Berkhof devotes a chapter to "Israel." See the constructive and insightful essay by Marten H. Woudstra, "The Old Testament in Biblical Theology and Dogmatics," *CTJ* 16 (1983) 47-60.
[19]Meredith G. Kline, "The Correlation of the Concepts of Canon and Covenant," in *New Perspectives on the Old Testament*, ed. J. B. Payne (Waco, Tex.: Word, 1970) 266. "Pre-occupation with the critique of aberrant current reconstructions has forestalled the orthodox elaboration of a genuinely biblico-historical version of the formation of the OT canon" (p. 265).

Elsewhere Kline writes: "For those who do not perceive that Deuteronomy as a whole exhibits the treaty pattern, one fact demands more serious attention than it has hitherto received. Such treaties were sealed legal witnesses not subject to scribal revision. When changes in the covenant arrangement were required, that was accomplished by preparing a new treaty, not by fictionally projecting the modified situation with its new terms within a bygone historical framework" (*The Structure of Biblical Authority* [Grand Rapids: Eerdmans, 1972] 14). See also Roger Beckwith, *The Old Testament Canon of the New Testament Church and its Background in Early Judaism,* (Grand Rapids: Eerdmans, 1985) 56.

The thesis of R. E. Clements in "Covenant and Canon in the Old Testament" in *Creation, Christ and Culture: Studies in Honour of T. F Torrance* (Edinburgh: T. &. T. Clark, 1976) is "that it is the process of the formation of the OT scriptures into a sacred canon which has done most to relate them to a concept of covenant, and that it is the Sinai-Horeb Covenant which is consistently the point to which this reference is made. Canonization has evidently been a process in which the key concept of covenant has played a decisive role" (p. 4).
[20]Kline, *The Structure of Biblical Authority* 99. See Kline, "The Correlation of the Concepts of Canon and Covenant" 274-75.

The opinion of John Frame argued at length in his unpublished paper "Thoughts on Theonomy" that the views of Meredith G. Kline and Greg Bahnsen differ only in emphasis is completely indefensible. For a thoroughgoing critique of theonomic law, see Kline's "Comments on an Old-New Error." For a historical case against the theonomic argument, see my analysis in Chapter Two; and L. John Van Til, "The Reconstructionist Movement: In the Calvinist Tradition?" *Pro Rege* 14 (1986) 19-28.
[21]Kline, "The Correlation of the Concepts of Canon and Covenant" 271. *Cf. The Structure of Biblical Authority* 47.
[22]Kline, *Kingdom Prologue* 2.1.
[23]*Ibid.* 1.74.

[24]For a recent discussion of the Reformed doctrine of the Covenant of Redemption, see J. J. van de Schuit, *Het Verbond der Verlossing: Antwoord op de vraag: Twee od drie verbonden?* (Kampen: Kok, 1982).
[25]Kline, *Kingdom Prologue* 1.74.
[26]For an alternative, but unsatistactory, treatment, see F. F. Bruce, "Christ and the Spirit in Paul," *BJRL* 59 (1976-1977) 259-85, as well as his "Paul and the Law of Moses," *BJRL* 57 (1974-1975) 259-79; and J. D. G. Dunn, "2 Cor 3: 17 – 'The Lord is the Spirit'," *JTS* 21 (1970) 309-20.
[27]Kline, *Kingdom Prologue* 2.7.
[28]See Chapters Six and Seven.
[29]Kline, *Kingdom Prologue* 1.68.
[30]Meredith G. Kline, *Images of the Spirit* (Grand Rapids: Baker, 1980), 57. "In the original sinless situation," notes Kline, "there would have been no mediatorial priesthood" (*Kingdom Prologue* 1.58).
[31]Kline, *Kingdom Prologue* 1.61; see also 1.77.
[32]*E.g.*, see the comments of Alex T. M. Cheung in "The Priest As the Redeemed Man: A Biblical-Theological Study. of the Priesthood," *JETS* 29 (1986) 268.
[33]Kline, *Kingdom Prologue* 1.9. "The Old and New Testaments are designed to serve as constitutions respectively for the kingdom of Israel and for the church of the New Covenant. And, of course, the Bible's concentration on the climactic advent of Christ and the Israelite epoch of revelation immediately preparatory to its also reflects the supreme significance of this focal period of history with its decisive redemptive events" (*ibid.*). *Cf.* Walter C. Kaiser, Jr., "The Literary Form of Genesis 1-11," in *New Perspectives on the Old Testament* 48-65; and Bruce K. Waltke, "Oral Tradition," in *A Tribute to Gleason Archer*, ed. W. C. Kaiser, Jr. and R. F. Youngblood (Chicago: Moody, 1986) 17-34.
[34]Kline, Review of Bernard Ramm, 54.
[35]Primeval history comprises stories which "are true in the sense that they illustrate and convey truths about the identity of God, humanity, nature, and their relationships to one another. It is the purpose of primeval history to answer precisely these questions, and by faith we believe that the scriptural answers are true. The truth of a concrete story in ancient Hebrew literature does not necessarily lie in its specific details but rather in the eternal verities it illustrates" (Howard J. Van Till, *The Fourth Day: What the Bible and the Heavens Are Telling Us about the Creation* [Grand Rapids: Eerdmans, 1986] 82-83).
[36]*Ibid.* 254.
[37]Contrast the essay by B. B. Warfield, "Calvin's Doctrine of Creation," *PTR* 13 (1915) 190-255 with the article bearing the same title written by John Murray in *WTJ* 17 (1954-1955) 21-43. The latter provides a more convincing reading of Calvin. See also, John Murray, "The Origin of Man," in *The Law and the Prophets: Old Testament Studies in Honor of Oswald Thompson Allis*, ed. J. H. Skilton (Nutley, N.J.: Presbyterian and Reformed, 1974) 147-57.

Note the recent study by Davis A. Young, "Scripture in the Hands of Geologists," *WTJ* 49 (1987) 1-34, 257-304, including his review of Alan Hayward's *Creation and Evolution: The Facts and the Fallacies*, 454-458. Young's approach and argument is similar to H. Van Till's. In contrast to their views Hayward adopts the position that the successive acts of creation extend over a long period of time, in which the supernatural (miraculous) intervention of God marked the entire period of creation, not just the origination of Adam and Eve. Neither Young nor Van Till espouses the historicity or miraculous origin of Adam and Eve.

[38]Kline, Review of Bernard Ramm, 53-54. See further, Henri Blocher, *In the Beginning: The Opening Chapters of Genesis*, trans. D. G. Preston (Downers Grove: InterVarsity Press, 1984).

Representative of the modern viewpoint is Bernard W. Anderson: "More and more we are coming to realize that the word creation belongs to a language which has a vocabulary and syntax of its own, a theological language whose affirmations should not be confused with statements made in the context of scientific language" (*Creation versus Chaos* [New York: Association, 1967] 81). In a similar vein, G. B. Caird writes: "myth and eschatology are used in the Old and New Testaments as metaphor systems for the theological interpretation of historical events" (*The Language and Imagery of the Bible* (London: Duckworth, 1980) 219.

[39]"There is a general persuasion abroad that Genesis 3 is without influence on theological developments in the rest of the OT. And when Genesis 3 is thus regarded as an isolated, unfruitful phenomenon, Paul's federal-covenantal reconstruction in Romans 5 is left without a supportive canonical linkage" (Meredith G. Kline, "Death, Leviathan, and the Martyrs," in *A Tribute to Gleason Archer*, 234-35). See also Kline's discussion of the phenomenon of death in the original creation order in *Kingdom Prologue* 1.40-44.

[40]Kline, *Kingdom Prologue* 1.78.

[41]The narrower aspect of the image pertains to the true knowledge, righteousness, and holiness which was lost in the Fall. The broader aspect refers to the remaining spiritual-moral attributes of human nature which remain after the Fall, though marred by sin and depravity. For a critical analysis of traditional formulations of the doctrine of the image of God consult G. C. Berkouwer, *Man: The Image of God*, trans. D. W. Jellema (Grand Rapids: Eerdmans, 1962). He observes: "Scripture's emphasis on the whole man as the image of God has triumphed time and time again over all objections and opposing principles. Scripture never makes a distinction between man's spiritual and bodily attributes in order to limit the image of God to the spiritual, as furnishing the only possible analogy between man and God" (p. 77). However, Berkouwer's reconceptualization of the *imago Dei* offers little improvement upon the older views, due in large measure to his semi-Barthian reading of Scripture.

Fallen man remains the image-bearer of God in terms of his kingly office, though, as Kline points out, man in the lake of fire no longer bears the image of God since the historical office of kingship ceases for the reprobate.

[42]Kline, *Kingdom Prologue* 1.83-90.

[43]Hesselink asserts: "For in federal theology used in the technical sense, it is taught that in the Bible there are two major covenants which God made with man: a Covenant of Works made with Adam and a Covenant of Grace in Jesus Christ. According to this approach, since Adam failed to keep the agreement which God made with him at creation, it was necessary for God to enter into a second agreement with Christ on behalf of the elect. Amazingly, this unbiblical notion became the organizing principle of later Reformed and Puritan theologies" (*On Being Reformed* 59). In a footnote he further remarks that "Until fairly recently this view was accepted by conservative Reformed theologians (*e.g.* Louis Berkhof) but is now being repudiated by most Reformed theologians" (p. 149 n. 13). He substantiates this claim by reference to the work of John Murray. See Chapter One, pp. 43-46.

[44]Kline, *Kingdom Prologue* 1.85. See Kline, *By Oath Consigned* 37.

[45]"This works principle is elaborately expounded in the Book of Deuteronomy, the treaty record of the subsequent renewal of the Sinaitic Covenant, just before Israel entered the land" (Kline, *Kingdom Prologue* 1.91). See also, Meredith 0. Kline, *Treaty of the Great*

King: The Covenant Structure of Deuteronomy, Studies and Commentary (Grand Rapids: Eerdmans, 1963).

[46]Kline, *Kingdom Prologue* 2.4.

[47]*Ibid.*, also 2.7. See my review of Leonard Goppelt's *Typos: The Typological Interpretation of the Old Testament in the New* (included in this collection of writings) and Chapter Eight.

[48]Kline, Review of McComiskey, 79. The problem concerning the relationship between Israel and the land, in the judgment of John Goldingay, "comes when a non-literal approach such as typology becomes the chief key to interpreting the OT. We are then not actually interpreting the OT. We are not listening to what God was actually saying to his people before Christ. We have silenced the OT's own word" ("The Jews, the Land, and the Kingdom," *Anvil* 4 [1987] 17). This view entails a rejection of the covenantal hermeneutic of the Reformed theological tradition. As Robert Badenas reminds us, "Calvin weaves closely together the pedagogical use of the law with the typological system of the Old Testament, so that the gospel points out with the finger what the law foreshadowed under types" (*Christ the End of the Law* [Journal for the Study of the New Testament Supplement Series 10; Sheffield: Journal for the Study of the Old Testament, 1985] 178 n. 157). A representative misreading of Calvin is C. Graafland, *Het Vaste Verbond: Israel en Het Oude Testament Bij Calvijn en Bei Gereformeerd Protestantisme* (Amsterdam: Uitgeverij ton Bolland, 1978), a study which follows along the neoorthodox lines of H. Berkhof, G. C. Berkouwer, H. H. Wolf, and A. A. van Ruler. See note 47 above; also *cf.* Charles H. Talbert, "Paul on the Covenant," *Review and Expositor* 84 (1987) 229-313; and Mary Ann Getty, "Paul on the Covenants and the Future of Israel," *Biblical Theology Bulletin* 17 (1987) 92-99.

[49]Kline, *Kingdom Prologue* 3.68.

[50]Otto Weber, *Foundations of Dogmatics*, trans. and annotated by D. L. Guder (2 vols.; Grand Rapids: Eerdmans, 1981, 1983) 1.287.

[51]Kline, *Kingdom Prologue* 3.56-57. "Recognition of the exceptional intrusive character of things holy within the common world is of vital importance in biblical hermeneutics, particularly in the interpretation of OT legislation and prophecy. When interpreting laws, we must constantly reckon with the possibility that a particular stipulation of the Old Covenant was shaped to a greater or lesser degree by the unique intrusive nature of the holy-kingdom order which was regulated by that covenant. Since the intruded holiness of the heavenly kingdom extended to the Israelite theocratic structure as a whole, to its cultural as well as cultic dimensions, we always have the responsibility, whether dealing with laws of cultic ceremony or laws of community life, to distinguish which features of Israelite law were peculiarly theocratic and which are still normative in our present non-theocratic situation" (*ibid.* 2.19).

[52]*Ibid.* 1.85. "The Sinaitic Covenant as reviewed in Deuteronomy was a law arrangement in the sense that it entailed a principle of works which stood in contrast to the promise-faith principle (Gal 3:12,18). The continuance of corporate Israel as the kingdom-possessing covenant community – the continuance of the Sinaitic Covenant as such – was made dependent on Israel's covenant keeping. This interpretation of the law character of the Mosaic Covenant encounters resistance on all sides. Yet, unless one recognizes that such a law principle was operative, regulating the enforcement of the sanctions of the Old Covenant, he will find the history and fate of corporate Israel quite inexplicable. Only under the government of such a law principle could the exile-rejection of Israel have transpired. God's covenant as a total arrangement cannot in this manner be broken where (as in the New Covenant, in continuance and fulfillment of the Lord's never-annulled

commitment to Abraham) the promise-faith principle is the controlling factor (Jer 31:3 1ff)" (Meredith G. Kline, Review of Peter C. Craigie's *The Book of Deuteronomy* in *CTJ* 13 (1978) 69-70.
[53]Karl T. Cooper, "Paul and Rabbinic Soteriology: A Review Article," *WTJ* 44 (1982) 127.
[54]*Ibid.* 129.
[55]For a recent dogmatic treatment of the concepts of merit and the covenant of works as legitimate and necessary theological concepts, see Johan A. Heyns, *Dogmatiek* (Pretoria. N. G. Kerkboekhandel, 1978), hoofstuk 9, "Die Verbond" 200-228.
[56]Kline, *Kingdom Prologue* 1.83.
[57]*Ibid.* 1.85.
[58]See my discussion in Chapter Four.
[59]Kline, *Kingdom Prologue* 1.91. William L. Lane writes: "The dynamics of the administration of the covenant illumine the distinctive character of the ministry of the prophets as servants of the covenant. But reflection upon the covenant and its administration is not limited to the documents of the OT" ("Covenant The Key to Paul's Conflict with Corinth," *TynBull* 33 (1982) 6.
[60]Kline, *Images of the Spirit* 59.
[61]Kline, *The Structure of Biblical Authority* 154-71.
[62]Contrast the opinion of Brevard S. Childs: "To speak of 'prediction' and 'supernatural' has shifted the mode of thought and discourse far away from the true biblical witness. Indeed the prophets spoke of the future, but the future as the arena in which God exercised his kingship in bringing life out of death and forgiveness in spite of rebellion. The OT prophets were not soothsayers, but proclaimers of the will of God who both kills and brings to life. To identify this understanding of prophecy with prediction is to lose its real theological content and to fall into an error just as grievous as that of modern critical rationalism" (*Old Testament Theology in a Canonical Context* [Philadelphia: Fortress, 1986] 132).
[63]Kline, *Kingdom Prologue* 3.86.
[64]*Ibid.* 1.101.
[65]*Ibid.* 1.61. *Cf.* Meredith G. Kline, "The Covenant of the Seventieth Week," in *The Law and the Prophets* 460-61.

Kline's interpretation of the Spirit-Parousia and the advent of the Day of the Lord suggests to me that the phrase "in the Spirit" in Rev 1:10 is epexegetical for "in the Day of the Lord," and therefore not a reference to the Lord's day being the first day of the week.
[66]Kline, *Kingdom Prologue* 1.52. "Glorification, by which man enters this Sabbath realm of glory, is as much a supernatural act of God as the original act of man's creation" (*ibid.* 1.76).
[67]John H. Stek, "A New Theology of Baptism?" *CTJ* 1 (1966) 73.
[68]Kline, *Kingdom Prologue* 3.84. See also, Kline, *By Oath Consigned* 90, including footnote 12. David H. Chilton remarks: "Meredith Kline has cogently argued that the notion of covenant itself does not simply involve promise, but rather responsibility. As Dr. Kline examined the meaning of the covenantal sign of circumcision and baptism, he realized that they pointed to 'the potential of both curse and blessing'" ("Infant Baptism and Covenantal Responsibility," *The Journal of Christian Reconstruction* 4 (1977-1978) 83).
[69]Kline, *By Oath Consigned* 34. Indicative of an extreme supralapsarian construction of the doctrine of electing grace, the correlation of covenant and election has led in some cases to the rejection of the theological distinction between the visible (institutional) church and the invisible church, the full number of the elect as it is known in the mind of God. See, *e.g.*, John Murray, *Christian Baptism* (Grand Rapids: Baker, 1962) 34-47; and

Johan A. Heyns, *The Church*, trans. D. Roy Briggs (Pretoria: N. G. Kerkboekhandel, 1980) 180-187. (The latter study is, for the most part, an exceptionally fine exposition of the doctrine of the church.)

SELECTED BIBLIOGRAPHY ON COVENANT THEOLOGY

A. Primary Readings in Sixteenth- and Seventeenth-Century Sources

Alstedius, Johann Heinrich. *Theologia Scholastica Didactica.* Hanoviae, 1618.

Ames, William. *The Marrow of Theology.* Trans. and ed. J. D. Eusden. Philadelphia: Pilgrim, 1968.

Ball, John. *A Treatise of the Covenant of Grace.* London: Miller, 1645.

Bolton, Samuel. *The True Bounds of Christian Freedom.* London: The Banner of Truth Trust, 1964. [Based on the 1645 edition]

Bulkeley, Peter. *The Gospel-Covenant or the Covenant of Grace Opened.* London, 1651.

Bullinger, Henry. *Compendium Christianae Religionis.* Zurich: Froschouser, 1569.

_____. *De Testamento seu Foedere Dei Unico et Aeterno. Commentarii H. Bullingeri in omnes Apostolicus Epistolas.* Basel, 1537.

_____. *The Decades.* Ed. T. Harding for the Parker Society. Trans. H. I. 5 volumes in 4. Cambridge: University Press, 1849.

Burgess, Anthony. *Vindiciae Legis, Or, A Vindication of the Morall Law and the Covenants.* London, 1646.

Calvin, John. *Institutes of the Christian Religion.* Ed. J. T. McNeill. Trans. F. L. Battles. Library of Christian Classics 20-21. Philadelphia: Westminster, 1960.

_____. *Commentaries on the New Testament.* Eds. D. W. Torrance and T. F. Torrance. 14 volumes. Grand Rapids: Eerdmans, 1972.

_____. *Commentaries on the Old Testament.* 30 volumes. Grand Rapids, Eerdmans, n.d. [Reprint of Edinburgh edition]

Cloppenburg, Johannes T. *Exercitationes super locus Communes Theologicos.* Franeker, 1653.

_____. *Grangraena Theologiae Anabaptisticae.* Franekerae, 1645.

_____. *Syntagma Selectarum Exercitationum Theologicarum.* Franekerae, 1645.

_____. *Theologica Opera Omnia.* 2 volumes. Amstelodami, 1684.

Cocceius, Johannes. *Summa Doctrinae de Foedere et Testamento Dei* in *Opera.* Tom VI. Amsterdam, 1673.

Crisp, Tobias. *Christ Alone Exalted* in *Complete Works of Tobias Crisp.* Ed. J. Gill. Volume 2. London: Bennett, 1832.

Dickson, David. *Therapeutica Sacra.* Edinburgh, 1697. [Second edition]

Fisher, Edward. *The Marrow of Modern Divinity.* With notes by T. Boston. Philadelphia: Presbyterian Board of Publication, n.d.

Junius, Francisci. *Opuscula Theologica Selecta.* Ed. A. Kuyper. Amstelodami: Muller and Krupt, 1882.

Musculus, Wolfgang. *Common Places of Christian Religion.* Trans. J. Man. London, 1563.

Olevianus, Gasper. *An Exposition of the Symbole of the Apostles.* Trans. J. Fielde. London, 1581.

_____. *De Substantia Foederis Gratuiti inter Deum et Electos.* Geneva: Eustathium Vignon, 1585.

Perkins, William. *A Golden Chaine* in *The Works of W. Perkins.* Volume 1. London: Legatt, 1612.

Preston, John. *The New Covenant, or the Saints Portion.* London: Bourne, 1639.

Rollock, Robert. *A Treatise of Our Effectual Calling,* in *Select Works.* Ed. W. M. Gunn. Volume 1. Edinburgh: Woodrow Society, 1849.

Sibbes, Richard. *The Excellency of the Gospel above the Law* in *The Complete Works of Richard Sibbes.* Ed. A. B. Grosart. Volume 4. Edinburgh, 1668.

Tyndale, William. *Doctrinal Treatises and Introductions to Different Portions of the Holy Scriptures.* Ed. H. Walter for the Parker Society. Cambridge: University Press, 1848.

_____. *The Works of the English Reformers: William Tyndale and John Frith.* Ed. T. Russell. London, 1831.

Ursinus, Zacharias. *Opera Theologica.* Heidelberg, 1612.

_____. *The Commentary of Dr. Zacharias Ursinus on the Heidelberg Catechism.* Trans. G. W. Williard. Grand Rapids: Eerdmans, 1954.

_____. *The Summe of Christian Religion.* Trans. D. H. Parry. London, 1633.

Ussher, James. *A Body of Divinity: Or, the Sum and Substance of Christian Religion.* London, 1702. [Eighth edition]

Voetius, Gisbert. *Selectarum Disputationum Fasciculus.* Ed. A. Kuyper. Amstelodami: Wormser, 1887.

Wollebius, Johannes. *Compendium of Christian Theology* in *Reformed Dogmatics: J. Wollebius, G. Voetius and F. Turretin.* Trans. and ed. J. W. Beardslee, III. A Library of Protestant Thought. New York: Oxford University Press, 1965.

Zanchius, Girolamo. *Operum Theologicorum.* 3 volumes. N.p., 1618.

Zwingli, Huldreich. *The Latin Works and the Correspondence of Huldreich Zwingli.* Ed. S. M. Jackson. 3 volumes. Philadelphia, 1922.

_____. *Sämtliche Werke.* Ed. E. Egli and G. Finsler. 14 volumes. Berlin: Schwetschke, 1905-59.

B. Dogmatics and the History of Doctrine

Allis, Oswald T. "The Covenant of Works" in *Basic Christian Doctrines.* Ed. C. F. H. Henry. Twin Brook Series. Grand Rapids: Baker, 1962. 96-102.

Althaus, Paul. *Die Prinzipien der deutschen reformierten Dogmatik im Zeitalter der aristotelischen Scholastik.* Leipzig: Deichtertsche, 1914.

Armstrong, Brian G. *Calvinism and the Amyraut Heresy: Protestant Scholasticism and Humanism in Seventeenth-Century France.* Madison: University of Wisconsin Press, 1969.

Aulén, Gustaf. *Christus Victor: An Historical Study of the Three Main Types of the Atonement.* Trans. A. G. Hebert. New York: Macmillan, 1969.

Avis, P. D. L. "Moses and the Magistrate: A Study in the Rise of Protestant Legalism." *Journal of Ecclesiastical History* 26 (1975) 149-172.

Baker, Alvin L. *Berkouwer's Doctrine of Election: Balance or Imbalance?* Phillipsburg, NJ: Presbyterian and Reformed, 1981.

Bahnsen, Greg L. *Theonomy in Christian Ethics.* Nutley: Presbyterian and Reformed, 1977.

Baker, J. Wayne. *Heinrich Bullinger and the Covenant: The Other Reformed Tradition.* Athens: Ohio University Press, 1980.

Bandstra, Andrew J. "Law and Gospel in Calvin and in Paul" in *Exploring the Heritage of John Calvin.* Ed. D. E. Holwerda. Grand Rapids: Baker, 1976. 11-39.

Barker, William S. and W. Robert Godfrey, eds. *Theonomy: A Reformed Critique.* Grand Rapids: Zondervan, 1990.

Bavinck, Herman. *Gereformeerde Dogmatiek.* 4 volumes. Kampen: Kok, 1928.

_____. *Our Reasonable Faith.* Trans. H. Zylstra. Twin Brook Series. Grand Rapids: Baker, 1956.

_____. *The Last Things: Hope for this World and the Next.* Ed. J. Bolt and trans. J. Vriend. Grand Rapids: Baker, 1996.

Benton, W. Wilson, Jr. "Federal Theology: Review for Revision" in *Through Christ's Word: A Festschrift for Dr. Philip E. Hughes.* Ed. W. R. Godfrey and J. L. Boyd, III. Phillipsburg: Presbyterian and Reformed, 1985. 180-204.

Berkhof, Hendrikus. *The Christian Faith: An Introduction to the Study of the Faith.* Trans. S. Woudstra. Grand Rapids: Eerdmans, 1979.

_____. *Introduction to the Study of Dogmatics.* Trans. J. Vriend. Grand Rapids: Eerdmans, 1985.

Berkhof, Louis. *Systematic Theology.* Grand Rapids: Eerdmans, 1941. [Fourth edition]

Berkouwer, G. C. *Divine Election.* Trans. H. Bekker. Studies in Dogmatics. Grand Rapids: Eerdmans, 1960.

_____. *Faith and Justification.* Trans. L. B. Smedes. Studies in Dogmatics. Grand Rapids: Eerdmans, 1954.

_____. *Sin.* Trans. P. C. Holtrop. Studies in Dogmatics. Grand Rapids: Eerdmans, 1971.

Bierma, Lyle D. *German Calvinism in the Confessional Age: The Covenant Theology of Caspar Olevianus.* Grand Rapids: Baker, 1996.

_____. "The Covenant Theology of Caspar Olevian." Ph.D. dissertation, Duke University, 1980.

_____. "The Role of Covenant in Early Reformed Orthodoxy." *Sixteenth Century Journal* 21 (1990) 453-462.

Bogue, Carl W. "Berkouwer: The Evolution of a Twentieth Century Theologian." *The Journal of Christian Reconstruction* 7 (1980) 135-174.

Bratcher, Dennis A. "The Concepts of Conditionality and Apostasy in Relation to the Covenant." Th.M. thesis, Westminster Theological Seminary, 1986.

Brown, W. Adams. "Covenant Theology" in *Encyclopedia of Religion and Ethics.* Ed. J. Hastings. Volume 4. New York: Scribner, 1912. 216-224.

Butler, Charles. "Religious Liberty and Covenant Theology." Ph.D. dissertation, Temple University, 1979.

Coffey, John. "How Should Evangelicals Think About Politics? Roger Williams and the Case for Principled Pulralism." *The Evangelical Quarterly* 69 1997) 39-62.

_____. *Politics, Religion and the British Revolutions: The Mind of Samuel Rutherford.* Cambridge Studies in Early Modern British History. Cambridge: Cambridge University Press, 1997.

Conn, Harvie M. *Eternal Word and Changing Worlds: Theology, Anthropology, and Mission in Trialogue.* Grand Rapids: Zondervan, 1984.

Cottrell, Jack Warren. "Covenant and Baptism in the Theology of H. Zwingli." Th.D. dissertation, Princeton Theological Seminary, 1971.

Cunningham, William. *Historical Theology: A Review of the Principal Doctrinal Discussion in the Christian Church Since the Apostolic Age.* 2 volumes. London: The Banner of Truth Trust, 1969.

_____. *The Reformers and the Theology of the Reformation.* Student's Reformed Theological Library. London: The Banner of Truth Trust, 1967.

Dabney, Robert L. *Lectures in Systematic Theology.* Grand Rapids: Zondervan, 1972.

Davis, John Jefferson. *Foundations of Evangelical Theology.* Grand Rapids: Baker, 1984.

De Moor, J. C. *Towards a Biblically Theo-Logical Method: A Structural Analysis and a Further Elaboration of Dr. G. C. Berkouwer's Hermeneutic-Dogmatic Method.* Kampen: Kok, 1980.

DeJong, Peter Y. *The Covenant Idea in New England Theology: 1620-1847.* Grand Rapids: Eerdmans, 1945.

Diemer, N. *Het Scheppings Verbond Met Adam (Het Verbond der Werken).* Kampen: Kok, n.d.

Diestel, Ludwig. "Studien zur Föderaltheologie." *Jahrbücher für deutsche Theologie* 10 (1865) 209-276.

Duncan, J. Ligon. "A Response to Recent Objections to Covenant Theology." Paper read at the annual meeting of the Evangelical Theological Society (Danvers, MA, November 17-19, 1999).

Elazar, Daniel J. and John Kincaid, eds. *The Covenant Connection: From Federal Theology to Modern Federalism.* New York: Lexington, 2000.

Emerson, Everett H. "Calvin and Covenant Theology." *Church History* 25 (1956) 136-144.

Eveson, Philip. *The Great Exchange: Justification by Faith Alone in the Light of Recent Thought.* Kent: Day One, 1996.

Ferguson, Sinclair B. "The Doctrine of the Christian Life in the Teaching of Dr. John Owen [1616-1683]." Ph.D. dissertation, University of Aberdeen, 1979.

_____. "Reformed Theology: Reformed Life-Style: I." *The Banner of Truth* (October 1994) 22-28.

_____. "The Teaching of the Confession" in *The Westminster Confession in the Church Today: Papers Prepared for the Church of Scotland Panel on Doctrine.* Ed. A. I. C. Heron. Edinburgh: Saint Andrews, 1982. 28-39.

Geisler, Norman L. and Ralph E. MacKenzie. *Roman Catholics and Evangelicals: Agreements and Differences.* Grand Rapids: Baker, 1995.

Godfrey, W. Robert. "Back to Basics: A Response to the Robertson-Fuller Dialogue." *Presbyterion* 9 (1983) 80-84.

_____. "Tensions Within International Calvinism: The Debate on the Atonement at the Synod of Dort, 1618-1619." Ph.D. dissertation, Stanford University, 1974.

_____. "The Westminster School" in *Reformed Theology in America.* Ed. D. F. Wells. Grand Rapids: Eerdmans, 1985. 89-101.

Graafland, C. *Calvijn tot Comrie: Oorsprong en ontwikkeling van de leer van het verbond in het Reformeerd Protestantisme.* Zoeterneer: Uitgeverij, 1992.

_____. *Het Vaste Verbond: Israel en het Oude Testament bij Calvijn en het Gereformeerd Protestantisme.* Amsterdam: Uitgeverij ton Bolland, 1978.

Greaves, Richard L. "John Knox and the Covenant Tradition." *Journal of Ecclesiastical History* 24 (1973) 23-32.

_____. "The Origins and Early Development of English Covenant Thought." *The Historian* 31 (1968) 21-35.

_____. "The Origins of English Sabbatarian Thought." *Sixteenth Century Journal* 12 (1981) 19-34.

Grenz, Stanley J. *Revisioning Evangelical Theology: A Fresh Agenda for the Twenty-first Century.* Downers Grove: InterVarsity, 1993.

Greschat, Martin. "Der Bundesgedanke in der Theologie des später Mittelalters." *Zeitschrift für Kirkengeschichte* 81 (1970) 44-63.

Gründler, Otto. "Thomism and Calvinism in the Theology of Girolamo Zanchi 1516-1590)." Th.D. dissertation, Princeton Theological Seminary, 1961.

Hagen, Kenneth. "From Testament to Covenant in the Early Sixteenth Century." *Sixteenth Century Journal* 3 (1972) 1-24.

Hägglund, Bengt. *The Background of Luther's Doctrine of Justification in Late Medieval Theology.* Facet Books: Historical Series. Philadelphia: Fortress, 1971.

Hall, Basil. "Calvin Against the Calvinists" in *John Calvin: A Collection of Distinguished Essays.* Ed. G. E. Duffield. Grand Rapids: Eerdmans, 1966. 19-37.

Harinck, C. *De schotse verbondsleer: Van Robert Rollock tot Thomas Boston.* Utrecht: De Banier, 1986.

Harper, George W. "Calvin and English Calvinism to 1649: A Review Article." *Calvin Theological Journal* 20 (1985) 255-262.

Heinz, Johann. "Justification and Merit: The Interpretation and Evaluation of the Concept of Merit in Modern Catholic Theology in Relation to Luther's Doctrine of Justification." Th.D. dissertation, Andrews University, 1981.

Helm, Paul. "Calvin and the Covenant: Unity and Continuity." *The Evangelical Quarterly* 55 (1983) 65-81.

Henderson, G. D. "The Idea of the Covenant in Scotland." *The Evangelical Quarterly* 27 (1955) 2-14.

Henry, Carl F. H. "The Cultural Relativizing of Revelation." *Trinity Journal* 1 NS (1980) 153-164.

Heppe, Heinrich. *Dogmatik des deutschen Protestantismus im sechzehnten Jahrhundert.* 3 band. Gotha, 1857.

_____. *Geschichte des Pietismus und der Mystik in der Reformierten Kirche, Namentlich der Niederlands.* Leiden: Brill, 1879.

Heron, Alasdair I. C., ed. *The Westminster Confession in the Church Today: Papers Prepared for the Church of Scotland Panel on Doctrine.* Edinburgh: Saint Andrews, 1982.

Hesselink, I. John. *Calvin's Concept of Law.* Princeton Theological Monograph Series 30. Allison Park, PA: Pickwick, 1992.

_____. "Law and Gospel or Gospel and Law? Calvin's Understanding of the Relationship" in *Calviniana: Ideas and Influence of Jean Calvin.* Ed. R. V. Schnucker. Sixteenth Century Essays and Studies 10. Kirksville, MO: Sixteenth Century Journal Publishers, 1988. 13-32.

_____. "Luther and Calvin on Law and Gospel in Their Galatians Commentaries." *Reformed Review* 37 (1984) 69-82.

Heyns, Johan A. *Dogmatiek.* Pretoria: N. G. Kerkboekhandel, 1978.

_____. *The Church.* Trans. D. R. Briggs. Pretoria: N. G. Kerkboekhandel, 1980.

Hodge, A. A. *Evangelical Theology.* Carlisle: The Banner of Truth Trust, 1976.

_____. *Outlines of Theology.* Grand Rapids: Zondervan, 1972. [Edition of 1879]

_____. *The Atonement.* Grand Rapids: Baker, 1974.

Hodge, Charles. *Systematic Theology.* 3 volumes. Grand Rapids: Eerdmans, 1973.

Hoekema, Anthony A. "Covenant of Grace in Calvin's Teaching." *Calvin Theological Journal* 2 (1967) 133-161.

_____. *Created in God's Image.* Grand Rapids: Eerdmans, 1986.

_____. *The Bible and the Future.* Grand Rapids: Eerdmans, 1979.

Holifield, E. Brooks. *The Covenant Sealed: The Development of Puritan Sacramental Theology in Old and New England, 1570-1720.* New Haven: Yale University Press, 1974.

Holverda, David E. "Eschatology and History: A Look at Calvin's Eschatological Vision" in *Exploring the Heritage of John Calvin.* Ed. D. E. Holverda. Grand Rapids, Baker, 1976.

Isbell, R. Sherman. "The Origin of the Concept of the Covenant of Works." Th.M. thesis, Westminster Theological Seminary, 1976.

Jewett, Paul K. *Election and Predestination.* Grand Rapids: Eerdmans, 1985.

Jeon, Jeong Koo. *Covenant Theology: John Murray's and Meredith G. Kline's Response to the Historical Development of Federal Theology in Reformed Thought.* Lanham: University Press of America, 1999.

Johnson, Alan F. and Robert E. Webber. *What Christians Believe: A Biblical and Historical Summary.* Grand Rapids: Zondervan, 1989.

Johnson, Merwyn S. "Calvin's Handling of the Third Use of the Law and its Problems" in *Calviniana: Ideas and Influence of Jean Calvin.* Ed. R. V. Schnucker. Sixteenth Century Essays and Studies 10. Kirksville, MO: Sixteenth Century Journal Publishers, 1988. 33-50.

Jordan, James B. "Calvinism and "The Judicial Law of Moses': An Historical Survey." *The Journal of Christian Reconstruction* 5 (1978-1979) 17-48.

Karlberg, Mark W. "Covenant and Common Grace: A Review Article." *The Westminster Theological Journal* 50 (1988) 323-337.

_____. "Covenant Theology and the Westminster Tradition: A Review Article." *The Westminster Theological Journal* 54 (1992) 135-152.

_____. "Doctrinal Development in Scripture and Tradition: A Reformed Assessment of the Church's Theological Task." *Calvin Theological Journal* 30 (1995) 401-418.

_____. "Israel and the Eschaton: A Review Article." *The Westminster Theological Journal* 52 (1990) 117-130.

_____. "Israel as Light to the Nations: A Review Article." *Journal of the Evangelical Theological Society* 28 (1985) 201-211.

_____. *John Piper on the Christian Life: An Examination of His Controversial View of "Faith Alone" in* Future Grace. Great Bromley: CRN [Christian Research Network], 1999.

_____. "Moses and Christ: The Place of Law in Seventeenth-Century Puritanism." *Trinity Journal* 10 NS (1989) 11-32.

_____. "Reformation Politics: The Relevance of Old Testament Ethics in Calvinist Political Theory." *Journal of the Evangelical Theological Society* 29 (1986) 179-191.

_____. "Reformed Interpretation of the Mosaic Covenant." *The Westminster Theological Journal* 43 (1980) 1-57.

_____. "The Original State of Adam: Tensions in Reformed Theology." *The Evangelical Quarterly* 59 (1987) 291-309.

Kevin, Ernest K. *The Grace of Law: A Study in Puritan Theology.* Twin Brook Series. Grand Rapids: Baker, 1976.

Klassen, William. *Covenant and Community: The Life, Writings and Hermeneutics of Pilgram Marpeck.* Grand Rapids: Eerdmans, 1968.

Kline, Meredith G. "Comments on an Old-New Error: A Review Article." *The Westminster Theological Journal* 41 (1978) 172-189.

_____. "Covenant Theology Under Attack." *New Horizons* 15 (February 1994) 3-5.

_____. "Of Works and Grace." *Presbyterion* 9 (1983) 85-92.

Kuyper, Abraham, Jr. *De Vastigheid des Verbonds.* Amsterdam: Kirchener, 1908.

Kuyper, Abraham, Sr. *De Leer der Verbonden.* Kampen: Kok, 1909.

_____. *Dictaten.* Volume 4. Grand Rapids: Hulst, 1910.

Leith, John H. "Creation and Redemption: Law and Gospel in the Theology of John Calvin" in *Marburg Revisited: A Reexamination of Lutheran and Reformed Traditions.* Eds. P. C. Empie and J. D. McCord. Minneapolis: Augsburg, 1966. 141-151.

_____. *Assembly at Westminster: Reformed Theology in the Making.* Richmond: Knox, 1972.

Letham, Robert. "The *Foedus Operum:* Some Factors Accounting for its Development." *Sixteenth Century Journal* 14 (1983) 457-467.

Lillback, Peter A. "The Binding of God: Calvin's Role in the Development of Covenant Theology." Ph.D. dissertation, Westminster Theological Seminary, 1985.

_____. "Ursinus' Development of the Covenant of Creation: A Debt to Melanchthon or Calvin? *The Westminster Theological Journal* 43 (1981) 247-288.

Lints, Richard. *The Fabric of Theology: A Prolegomenon to Evangelical Theology.* Grand Rapids: Eerdmans, 1993.

Loonstra, B. "De historische wortels van de leer aangaande het verbond." *Theologia reformata* 30 (1987) 46-63.

Lyall, Francis. "Of Metaphors and Analogies: Legal Language and Covenant Theology." *The Scottish Journal of Theology* 32 (1979) 1-18.

MacLeod, Donald. "Covenant Theology" in *Dictionary of Scottish Church History and Theology.* Eds. N. M. de S. Cameron, D. F. Wright, D. C. Lackman, and D. E. Meeks. Downers Grove: InterVarsity, 1993. 214-218.

_____. "Federal Theology: An Oppressive Legalism?" *The Banner of Truth* 125 (February 1974) 21-28.

Marsden, George M. "Perry Miller's Rehabilitation of the Puritans: A Critique." *Church History* 39 (1970) 91-105.

McCoy, Charles S. "Johannes Cocceius: Federal Theologian." *The Scottish Journal of Theology* 16 (1963) 352-370.

_____. "The Covenant Theology of Johannes Cocceius." Ph.D. dissertation, Yale University, 1957).

McCoy, Charles S. and J. Wayne Baker. *Fountainhead of Federalism: Heinrich Bullinger and the Covenantal Tradition.* Louisville: Westminster/John Knox, 1991.

McGiffert, Michael. "From Moses to Adam: The Making of the Covenant of Works." *The Sixteenth Century Journal* 19 (1988) 131-155.

_____. "Grace and Works: The Rise and Division of Covenant Divinity in Elizabethan Puritanism." *Harvard Theological Review* 75 (1982) 464-502.

_____. "William Tyndale's Conception of the Covenant." *Journal of Ecclesiastical History* 32 (1981) 167-184.

McGowen, Andrew T. B. "Federal Theology as a Theology of Grace." *Scottish Bulletin of Evangelical Theology* 2 (1984) 41-50.

_____. *The Federal Theology of Thomas Boston.* Rutherford Studies in Historical Theology. Edinburgh: Paternoster, 1997.

McKim, Donald K. "William Perkins and the Theology of the Covenant" in *Studies of the Church in History: Essays honoring Robert S. Paul on his Sixty-fifth Birthday*. Ed. H. Davies. Allison Park, PA: Pickwick, 1983.

McLelland, Joseph C. "Covenant Theology: A Re-evaluation." *Canadian Journal of Theology* 3 (1957) 182-188.

McWilliams, David B. "The Covenant Theology of the 'Westminster Confession of Faith' and Recent Criticism." *The Westminster Theological Journal* 53 (1991) 109-124.

Møller, Jens. "The Beginnings of Puritan Covenant Theology." *Journal of Ecclesiastical History* 14 (1963) 46-67.

Morgan, Edmund S. *Visible Saints: The History of a Puritan Idea.* New York: New York University, 1963.

Muller, Richard A. *Christ and the Decree: Christology and Predestination in Reformed Theology from Calvin to Perkins.* Studies in Historical Theology 2. Durham: Labyrinth, 1986.

_____. "Covenant and Conscience in English Reformed Theology: Three Variations on a Seventeenth Century Theme." *The Westminster Theological Journal* 42 (1980) 308-334.

_____. "Karl Barth and the Path of Theology into the Twentieth Century: Historical Observations." *The Westminster Theological Journal* 51 (1989) 25-50.

_____. "Perkins' *A Golden Chaine:* Predestinarian System or Schematized *Ordo Salutis.*" *The Sixteenth Century Journal* 9 (1978) 69-81.

_____. *Post-Reformation Reformed Dogmatics.* 2 volumes. Grand Rapids: Baker, 1987, 1993.

_____. "The Place and Importance of Karl Barth in the Twentieth Century." *The Westminster Theological Journal* 50 (1988) 127-156.

_____. "The Federal Motif in Seventeenth Century Arminian Theology." *Nederlands Archeif Voor Kerkgeschiedenis* 62 (1982) 101-122.

_____. *The Study of Theology: From Biblical Interpretation to Contemporary Formulation.* Foundations of Contemporary Interpretation 7. Grand Rapids, Zondervan, 1991.

Murray, John. *Collected Writings.* 4 volumes. Carlisle: The Banner of Truth Trust, 1976-1982.

_____. "Covenant Theology" in *The Encyclopedia of Christianity*. Marshallton: National Foundation for Christian Education, 1972. 199-216.

_____. *Principles of Conduct: Aspects of Biblical Ethics*. Grand Rapids: Eerdmans, 1957.

_____. *Redemption: Accomplished and Applied*. Grand Rapids Eerdmans, 1957.

_____. *The Imputation of Adam's Sin*. Grand Rapids: Eerdmans, 1959.

_____. *The Covenant of Grace: A Biblico-Theological Study*. London: Tyndale, 1954.

_____. "The Theology of the Westminster Confession of Faith" in *Scripture and Confession: A Book About Confessions Old and New*. Ed. J. H. Skilton. Nutley: Presbyterian and Reformed, 1973. 125-148.

Nicole, Roger. "John Calvin's View of the Extent of the Atonement." *The Westminster Theological Journal* 47 (1985) 197-225.

North, Gary. *Dominion and Common Grace: The Biblical Basis of Progress*. Tyler: Institute for Christian Economics, 1987.

Oberman, Heiko A. *"Facientibus Quod in se est Deus non Denegat Gratiam:* Robert Holcot O. P. and the Beginnings of Luther's Theology" in *The Reformation in Medieval Perspective*. Ed. S. E. Ozment. Chicago: Quadrangle Books, 1971). 119-141.

_____. *Forerunners of the Reformation: The Shape of Late Medieval Thought Illustrated by Key Documents*. Hew York: Holt Rinhart and Winston, 1966.

_____. *The Harvest of Medieval Theology: Gabriel Biel and Late Medieval Nominalism*. Grand Rapids: Eerdmans, 1967.

_____. "The Shape of Late Medieval Thought: The Birthpangs of the Modern Era" in *The Pursuit of Holiness in Late Medieval and Renaissance Religion*. Ed. C. Trinkaus and H. A. Oberman. Studies in Medieval and Reformation Thought. Leiden: Brill, 1974. 3-25.

Oss, Douglas A. "The Influence of Hermeneutical Frameworks in the Theonomy Debate." *The Westminster Theological Journal* 51 (1989) 227-258.

Osterhaven, M. Eugene. *The Faith of the Church: A Reformed Perspective on its Historical Development*. Grand Rapids: Eerdmans, 1982.

Parker, Kenneth L. *The English Sabbath: A Study of the Doctrine and Discipline from the Reformation to the Civil War*. New York: Cambridge University Press, 1988.

Poole, David N. J. *Stages of Religious Faith in the Classical Reformation Tradition: The Covenant Approach to the* Ordo Salutis. Lewiston: Mellon, 1995.

Primus, John H. "Calvin and the Puritan Sabbath: A Comparative Study" in *Exploring the Heritage of John Calvin.* Ed. D. E. Holwerda. Grand Rapids, Baker, 1976. 40-75.

Puckett, David L. *John Calvin's Exegesis of the Old Testament.* Columbia Series in Reformed Theology. Louisville: Westminster/John Knox, 1995.

Rainy, Robert. *Delivery and Development of Christian Doctrine.* Edinburgh: Clark, 1874.

Raitt, Jill. *The Eucharistic Theology of Theodore Beza: Development of the Reformed Doctrine.* American Academy of Religion Studies in Religion 4. Atlanta: Scholars Press, 1972.

Reymond, Robert L. *A New Systematic Theology of the Christian Faith.* Nashville: Nelson, 1998.

Riddlebarger, Kim. "No Place Like Rome? Why are Evangelicals Joining the Catholic Church" in *Roman Catholicism: Evangelical Protestants Analyze What Divides and Unites Us.* Ed. J. Armstrong. Chicago: Moody, 1994. 221-243.

Ritschl, Otto. *Dogmengeschichte des Protestantismus.* Volume 3. Göttingen: Vandenhoeck and Ruprecht, 1926.

Robertson, O. Palmer. *The Current Justification Controversy.* St. Louis, 1983.

Rogers, Jack. *Presbyterian Creeds: A Guide to the Book of Confessions.* Philadelphia: Westminster, 1985.

Rolston, Holmes, III. *John Calvin Versus The Westminster Confession.* Richmond, Knox, 1972.

_____. "Responsible Man in Reformed Theology: Calvin Versus the *Westminster Confession.*" *The Scottish Journal of Theology* 23 (1970) 129-156.

Sandlin, A. "Deviations from Historic Solafideism in the Reformed Community." *Chalcedon Report* (February 1995) 18-27.

Schrenk, Gottlob. *Gottesreich und Bund im Aelteren Protestantismus Vornehmlich bei Johannes Cocceius.* Darmstadt: Wissenschaftliche Buchgesellschaft, 1967.

Seeberg, Reinhold. *Textbook of the History of Doctrines.* Trans. C. E. Hay. Grand Rapids: Baker, 1977.

Shepherd, Norman. *The Call of Grace: How the Covenant Illuminates Salvation and Evangelism.* Phillipsburg: Presbyterian and Reformed, 2000.

Solberg, Winton U. *Redeem the Time: The Puritan Sabbath in Early America.* Cambridge, MA: Harvard University Press, 1977.

Steinmetz, David C. Misericordia Dei: *The Theology of Johannes von Staupitz in its Late Medieval Setting.* Leiden: Brill, 1968.

_____. *Reformers in the Wings.* Philadelphia: Fortress, 1971.

Stoeffler, F. Ernest. *The Rise of Evangelical Pietism.* Leiden: E. J. Brill, 1965.

Stoever, William K. B. *'A Faire and Easie Way to Heaven': Covenant Theology and Antinomianism in Early Massachusetts.* Middletown: Wesleyan University, 1978.

Strehle, Stephen. *Calvinism, Federalism, and Scholasticism: A Study of the Reformed Doctrine of Covenant.* Basler und Berner Studien zur historischen und systematischen Theologie 58. New York: Lang, 1988.

Thomas, G. Michael. *The Extent of the Atonement: A Dilemma for Reformed Theology from Calvin to the Consensus (1536-1675).* Paternoster Biblical and Theological Monographs. Carlisle: Paternoster, 1997.

Thornwell, James Henley. *Collected Writings.* Carlisle: The Banner of Truth Trust, 1974.

Toon, Peter. *The Development of Doctrine in the Church.* Grand Rapids: Eerdmans, 1979.

Torrance, James B. "Calvinism and Puritanism in England and Scotland – Some Basic Concepts in the Development of 'Federal Theology'" in *Calvinus Reformator: His Contribution to Theology, Church and Society.* Potchefstroom: Potchefstroom University for Christian Higher Education, 1982. 264-286.

_____. "Covenant or Contract? A Study of the Theological Background of Worship in Seventeen-Century Scotland." *The Scottish Journal of Theology* 23 (1970) 51-76.

_____. "The Strengths and Weaknesses of the Westminster Theology" in *The Westminster Confession in the Church Today.* Ed. A. I. Heron. Edinburgh: Saint Andrew, 1982. 40-53.

Torrance, Thomas F. *The School of Faith: The Catechisms of the Reformed Church.* Trans. and with an introduction by T. F. Torrance. New York: Harper, 1959.

Trinterud, Leonard J. "The Origins of Puritanism." *Church History* 20 (1951) 37-57.

Visser, Dirk. "The Covenant of Zacharias Ursinus." *Sixteenth Century Journal* 18 (1987) 531-544.

Van Buren, Paul M. *A Christian Theology of the People Israel: Part II, A Theology of the Jewish-Christian Reality.* New York: Seabury, 1983.

Van de Schuit, J. J. *Het Verbond der Verloosing: Antwoord op de Vraag: Twee of Drie Verbonded?* Kampen: Kok, 1982.

Van Til, Cornelius. *Christianity and Barthianism.* Philadelphia: Presbyterian and Reformed, 1965.

_____. "Covenant Theology" in *The New Schaff-Herzog Twentieth Century Encyclopedia of Religious Knowledge.* Ed. L. A. Loetscher. Grand Rapids: Baker, 1955. 306.

_____. *The New Hermeneutic.* Nutley: Presbyterian and Reformed, 1974.

_____. *The New Modernism: An Appraisal of the Theology of Barth and Brunner.* Philadelphia: Presbyterian and Reformed, 1947.

_____. *The Sovereignty of Grace: An Appraisal of G. C. Berkouwer's View of Dordt.* Philadelphia: Presbyterian and Reformed, 1969.

_____. *The Theology of James Daane.* Philadelphia: Presbyterian and Reformed, 1959.

_____. "The *Umkehr* at Amsterdam" in *The Law and the Prophets: Old Testament Studies Prepared in Honor of Oswald Thompson Allis.* Ed. J. H. Skilton. Nutley: Presbyterian and Reformed, 1974. 35-53.

Van Til, L. John. "The Reconstructionist Movement: In the Calvinist Tradition? *Pro Rege* 14 (1986) 19-28.

Van Zandt, A. B. "The Doctrine of the Covenants Considered as the Central Principle of Theology." *The Presbyterian Review* 3 (1883) 28-39.

Venema, Cornelis P. "Recent Criticisms of the 'Covenant of Works' in the Westminster Confession of Faith." *Mid-America Journal of Theology* 9 (1993) 165-198.

Von Rohr, John. *The Covenant of Grace in Puritan Thought.* Studies in Religion: American Academy of Religion 45. Atlanta: Scholars, 1986.

Vos, Geerhardus. "The Doctrine of the Covenant in Reformed Theology" in *Redemptive History and Biblical Interpretation: The Shorter Writings of Geerhardus Vos.* Ed. R. B. Gaffin, Jr. Phillipsburg: Presbyterian and Reformed, 1980. 234-267.

Walgrave, Jan. *Unfolding Revelation: The Nature of Doctrinal Development.* Philadelphia: Westminster, 1971.

Ward, R. S. "Recent Criticisms of the Westminster Confession of Faith" in *Proceedings of the International Conference of Reformed Churches.* Alberta: Inheritance, 1993.

Warfield. Benjamin B. *The Westminster Assembly and its Work.* New York: Oxford University Press, 1931.

Weber, Hans Emil. *Reformation, Orthodoxie und Rationalismus.* Beiträge zur Förderung Christlicher Theologie. 3 volumes in 2. Gütersloh: Bertelsmann, 1937-51.

Weber, Otto. *Foundations of Dogmatics.* Trans. and annotated by D. L. Guder. 2 volumes. Grand Rapids: Eerdmans, 1981, 1983.

Wells, David F. *No Place for Truth: Or Whatever Happened to Evangelical Theology?* Grand Rapids: Eerdmans, 1984.

Weir, David A. *The Origins of the Federal Theology in Sixteenth-Century Reformation Thought.* New York: Clarendon, 1990.

Westminster Theological Seminary. "Reason and Specifications Supporting the Action of the Board of Trustees in Removing Professor Shepherd Approved by the Executive Committee of the Board." Philadelphia (February 26, 1982).

_____. "Westminster Statement on Justification." Philadelphia (May 27, 1980).

Wolf, H. H. *Die Einheit des Bundes: Das Verhältnis von Altem und Neuem Testament bei Calvin.* Beiträge zur Geschichte und Lehre der Reformierten Kirche 10. Neukirchen: Moers, 1958.

Zimmerman, G. "Gottesbund und Gesetz in der Westminster Confession." *Zeitschrift für Kirkengeschichte* 106 (1995) 179-199.

C. Biblical Theology

Badenas, Robert. *Christ, the End of the Law. Romans 10:4 in Pauline Perspective*. Journal for the Study of the New Testament Supplement Series 10. Sheffield: JSOT Press, 1985.

Baker, David L. "Typology and the Christian Use of the Old Testament." *The Scottish Journal of Theology* 29 (1976) 137-157.

Bandstra, Andrew J. "Paul and the Law: Some Recent Developments and an Extraordinary Book." *Calvin Theological Journal* 25 (1990) 249-261.

_____. *The Law and the Elements of the World: An Exegetical Study in Aspects of Paul's Teaching*. Kampen: Kok, 1964.

Barker, Kenneth. "False Dichotomies Between the Testaments." *Journal of the Evangelical Theological Society* 25 (1982) 3-16.

Barth, Karl. *Christ and Adam: Man and Humanity in Romans 5*. Trans. T. A. Smail. New York, 1956.

Bartholomew, Craig G. "Covenant and Creation: Covenant Overload or Covenantal Deconstruction?" *Calvin Theological Journal* 30 (1995) 11-33.

Becker, J. Christiaan. *Paul the Apostle: The Triumph of God in Life and Thought*. Philadelphia: Fortress, 1980.

_____. "The Faithfulness of God and the Priority of Israel in Paul's Letter to the Romans." *Harvard Theological Review* 79 (1986) 10-16.

Berkhof, Hendrikus. "Israel as a Theological Problem in the Christian Church." *Journal of Ecumenical Studies* 6 (1969) 329-347.

Blaising, Craig A. and David L. Bock, eds. *Dispensationalism, Israel and the Church: The Search for Definition*. Grand Rapids: Zondervan, 1992.

Bloomberg, Craig L. "Critical Issues in New Testament Studies for Evangelicals Today" in *A Pathway into the Holy Scripture*. Ed. P. E. Satterthwaite and D. F. Wright. Grand Rapids: Eerdmans, 1994. 51-79.

Bring, Ragnar. *Christus und das Gesetz: Die Bedeutung des Gesetzes des Alten Testaments nach Paulus und sein Glauben an Christus*. Leiden: Brill, 1967.

Bruce, F. F. *Commentary on the Book of the Acts*. The New International Commentary on the New Testament. Grand Rapids: Eerdmans, 1954.

_____. *The Epistle to the Galatians.* The New International Greek Testament Commentary. Grand Rapids: Eerdmans, 1982.

_____. *The Epistle to the Hebrews.* The New International Commentary on the New Testament. Grand Rapids: Eerdmans, 1964.

Burton, Ernest DeWitt. *A Critical and Exegetical Commentary on the Epistle ot the Galatians.* International Critical Commentary. Edinburgh: Clark, 1921.

Carson, D. A., ed. *From Sabbath to Lord's Day.* Grand Rapids: Zondervan, 1982.

Carson, D. A., ed. *Right With God: Justification in the Bible and the World.* Theological Commission of the World Evangelical Fellowship. Grand Rapids: Baker, 1992.

Cosgrove, Charles H. "The Mosaic Law Preaches Faith: Study in Galatians 3." *The Westminster Theological Journal* 41 (1978) 146-164.

Craigie, Peter C. *The Book of Deuteronomy.* The New International Commentary on the Old Testament. Grand Rapids: Eerdmans, 1976.

Cranfield, C. E. B. "St. Paul and the Law." *The Scottish Journal of Theology* 17 (1964) 43-68.

Davidson, Richard M. *Typological Structures in the Old and New Testaments.* Berrien Springs: Andrews University Press, 1981.

Davies, Glenn N. *Faith and Obedience in Romans: A Study in Romans 1-4.* Journal for the Study of the New Testament Supplement 39. Sheffield: Sheffield Academic, 1990.

Dodd, C. H. *According to the Scripture.* New York: Scribner, 1953.

Dumbrell, William J. *Covenant and Creation: A Theology of the Old Testament Covenants.* Grand Rapids: Baker, 1984.

Dunn, James D. G. "Jesus – Flesh and Spirit: An Exposition of Romans 1-3." *Journal of Theological Studies* 24 (1973) 40-68.

_____. "Paul and Justification by Faith" in *The Road from Damascus: The Impact of Paul's Conversion on His Life, Thought, and Ministry.* Ed. R. N. Longenecker. Grand Rapids: Eerdmans, 1997. 85-101.

_____. "Rom 7:14-25 in the Theology of Paul." *Theologische Zeitschrift* 31 (1975) 257.

_____. "Salvation Proclaimed: Romans 6:1-11: Dead and Alive." *Expository Times* 93 (1982) 259-264.

Dunn, James D. G., ed. *Paul and the Mosaic Law: The Third Durham-Tübingen Research Symposium on earliest Christianity and Judaism.* Tübingen: Mohr, 1996.

Ellis, E. E. *Paul's Use of the Old Testament.* Grand Rapids: Baker, 1957.

Fairbairn, Patrick. *The Revelation of Law in Scripture.* Phillipsburg: Presbyterian and Reformed, 1996. [Original, 1869]

Feinberg, John S., ed. *Continuity and Discontinuity: Perspectives on the Relationship Between the Old and New Testaments: Essays in Honor of S. Lewis Johnson, Jr.* Westchester: Crossway, 1988.

France, Richard T. *Jesus and the Old Testament.* London: Tyndale, 1971.

Fuller, Daniel P. *Gospel and Law: Contrast or Continuum? The Hermeneutics of Dispensationalism and Covenant Theology.* Grand Rapids: Eerdmans, 1980.

_____. "Paul and 'The Works of the Law'." *The Westminster Theological Journal* 38 (1975) 28-42.

Furnish, Victor. *Theology and Ethics in Paul.* New York: Abingdon, 1968.

Gaffin, Richard B., Jr. "Systematic Theology and Biblical Theology." *The Westminster Theological Journal* 38 (1976) 281-299.

_____. "The Holy Spirit and Eschatology" in *'N Woord op sy tyd: 'N Teologiese Feesbundel aangebied aan Professor Johan Heyns ter Herdenking van sy Sestigste Vergaarsday.* Ed. C. J. Wethmar and C. J. A. Vos. Pretoria: NG Kerkboekhandel, 1988. 43-52.

_____. "Paul as Theologian: A Review Article." *The Westminster Theological Journal* 30 (1968) 213.

_____. "Pentecost: Before and After." *Kerux* 10 (1995) 3-24.

_____. "The Vitality of Reformed Dogmatics" in *The Vitality of Reformed Theology.* Proceedings of the International Theological Congress, June 20-24, 1994 (Noordwijkerhout, the Netherlands). Eds. J. M. Batteau, J. W. Maris, and K. Veling. Kampen: Kok, 1994. 16-50.

Garlington, Don B. *Faith, Obedience and Perseverance: Aspects of Paul's Letter to the Romans.* Wissenschaftliche Untersuchungen zum Neuen Testament 79. Tübingen: Mohr, 1994.

_____. "Romans 7:14-25 and the Creation Theology of Paul." *Trinity Journal* 11 NS (1990) 197-235.

Golding, Peter E. "The Development of the Covenant: An Introductory Study in Biblical Theology." *Reformed Theological Journal* 9 (1993) 46-61.

Goppelt, Leonhard. *Typos: The Typological Interpretation of the Old Testament in the New.* Grand Rapids: Eerdmans, 1982.

Gundry, Stanley N. "Typology as a Means of Interpretation: Past and Present." *Journal of the Evangelical Theological Society* 12 (1969) 233-240.

Gundry-Volf, M. *Paul and Perseverance: Staying In and Falling Away.* Tübingen Mohr, 1990.

Hafemann, Scott J. *Paul, Moses, and the History of Israel: The Letter/Spirit Contrast and the Argument from Scripture in 2 Corinthians 3.* Wissenschaftliche Untersuchungen zum Neuen Testament 81. Tübingen: Mohr, 1995.

Harrison, Roland K. *Leviticus: An Introduction and Commentary.* Tyndale Old Testament Commentaries. Downers Grove: InterVarsity, 1980.

Holwerda, David E. *Jesus and Israel: One Covenant or Two?* Grand Rapids: Eerdmans, 1995.

Hong, In-Gyu. "Does Paul Misrepresent the Jewish Law? Law and Covenant n Gal 3:1-14." *Novum Testamentum* 36 (1994) 164-182.

_____. *The Law in Galatians.* Journal for the Study of the New Testament Supplement 81. Sheffield: Sheffield Academic, 1993.

Hooker, Morna D. "Paul and 'Covenantal Nomism'" in *Paul and Paulinism: Essays in Honour of C. K. Barrett.* Ed. M. D. Hooker and S. G. Wilson. London: SPCK, 1982. 47-56.

Hughes, Philip E. *A Commentary on the Epistle to the Hebrews.* Grand Rapids: Eerdmans, 1977.

Kaiser, Walter C., Jr. "Leviticus 18:5 and Paul: 'Do This and You Shall Live' (Eternally?." *Journal of the Evangelical Theological Society* 14 (1971) 19-28.

Karlberg, Mark W. "Israel's History Personified: Romans 7:7-13 in Relation to Paul's Teaching on the 'Old Man'." *Trinity Journal* 7 NS (1986) 65-74.

_____. "Justification in Redemptive History." *The Westminster Theological Journal* 43 (1981) 213-246.

_____. "Legitimate Discontinuities Between the Testaments." *Journal of the Evangelical Theological Society* 28 (1985) 9-20.

_____. "Paul, the Old Testament, and Judaism: A Review Article." *Foundations: A Journal of Evangelical Theology* 43 (1999) 36-44.

_____. "Paul's Letter to the Romans in the *New International Commentary on the New Testament* and in Contemporary Reformed Thought." *The Evangelical Quarterly* 71 (1999) 3-24.

_____. "The Search for an Evangelical Consensus on Paul and the Law." *Journal of the Evangelical Theological Society* 40 (1997) 563-579.

_____. "The Significance of Israel in Biblical Typology." *Journal of the Evangelical Theological Society* 31 (1988) 257-269.

Käsemann, Ernst. "God's Righteousness in Paul" in *The Bultmann School of Interpretation: New Directions?* New York: Harper and Row, 1965. 100-110.

_____. *Commentary on Romans.* Trans. and ed. G. W. Bromiley. Grand Rapids: Eerdmans, 1980.

Kauk, Marvin C. "Paul's Use of the Old Testament in Romans 10:6-8." Ph.D. dissertation, Westminster Theological Seminary, 1994.

Kline, Meredith G. *By Oath Consigned: A Reinterpretation of the Covenant Signs of Circumcision and Baptism.* Grand Rapids: Eerdmans, 1968.

_____. *Glory in Our Midst.* Eugene,OR: Wipf and Stock, 2000.

_____. "Gospel until the Law: Romans 5:13-14 and the Old Covenant." *Journal of the Evangelical Theological Society* 34 (1991) 433-446.

_____. *Images of the Spirit.* Grand Rapids: Baker, 1980.

_____. *Kingdom Prologue.* 3 volumes. South Hamilton: privately published, 1985, 1986.

_____. *The Structure of Biblical Authority.* Grand Rapids: Eerdmans, 1972.

_____. *Treaty of the Great King: The Covenant Structure of Deuteronomy. Studies and Commentary.* Grand Rapids: Eerdmans, 1963.

Kruse, Colin G. *Paul, the Law, and Justification.* Peabody: Hendrickson, 1996.

Kümmel, W. G. *Römer 7 und das Bild des Menschen in Neuen Testament: Zwei Studien.* Munich: Kaiser, 1974.

Lampe, G. W. H. "Typological Exegesis." *Theology* 56 (1953) 201-208.

Lampe, G. W. H. and K. J. Woollcombe. *Essays on Typology.* Studies in Biblical Theology. Naperville: Allenson, 1957.

Lane, William L. "Covenant: The Key to Paul's Conflict with Corinth." *Tyndale Bulletin* 33 (1982) 3-29.

LaRondelle, Hans K. *The Israel of God in Prophecy: Principles of Prophetic Interpretation.* Berrien Springs: Andrews University Press, 1983.

Longenecker, Richard N. "The Pedagogical Nature of the Law in Galatians 3:19-4:7." *Journal of the Evangelical Theological Society* 25 (1982) 53-61.

Moo, Douglas. "Israel and Paul in Romans 7:7-12." *New Testament Studies* 32 1986) 122-135.

_____. "Paul and the Law in the Last Ten Years: Article Review." *The Scottish Journal of Theology* 40 (1987) 287-307.

_____. *The Epistle to the Romans.* The New International Commentary on the New Testament. Grand Rapids: Eerdmans, 1996.

Murray, John. *The Epistle to the Romans.* The New International Commentary on the New Testament. 2 volumes in 1. Grand Rapids, Eerdmans, 1968.

Nicole, Roger. "Patrick Fairbairn and Biblical Hermeneutics as Related to the Quotations of the Old Testament in the New" in *Hermeneutics, Inerrancy, and the Bible.* Ed. E. D. Radmacher and R. D. Preus. Grand Rapids: Zondervan, 1984. 765-776.

_____. "The Relationship Between Biblical Theology and Systematic Theology" in *Evangelical Roots: A Tribute to Wilbur Smith.* Ed. K. Kantzer. New York: Nelson, 1978. 185-194.

Nygren Anders. *Commentary on Romans.* Trans. C. C. Rasmussen. Philadelphia: Muhlenberg Press, 1949.

Osborne, Grant. "Type, typology" in *Evangelical Dictionary of Theology.* Ed. W. A. Elwell. Grand Rapids: Baker, 1984. 1117-1119.

Ridderbos, Herman. *Paul: An Outline of His Theology.* Trans. J. R. de Witt. Grand Rapids: Eerdmans, 1975.

Sabourin, Leopold. *The Psalms: Their Origin and Meaning.* New York: Alba House, 1974. [New enlarged, updated edition]

Sanders, E. P. *Paul and Palestinian Judaism: A Comparison of Patterns of Religion*. London: SCM, 1977.

Saucy, Robert L. *The Case for Progressive Dispensationalism: The Interface Between Dispensational and Non-Dispensational Theology.* Grand Rapids: Zondervan, 1993.

Schoonhoven, Calvin R. "The 'Analogy of Faith' and the Intent of Hebrews" in *Scripture, Tradition, and Interpretation: Essays Presented to Everett F. Harrison by His Students and Colleagues in Honor of His Seventy-fifth Birthday.* Ed. W. W. Gasque and W. LaSor. Grand Rapids: Eerdmans, 1978. 92-110.

Schreiner, Thomas R. *Romans.* Baker Exegetical Commentary on the New Testament. Grand Rapids: Baker, 1998.

_____. *The Law and Its Fulfillment: A Pauline Theology of Law.* Grand Rapids: Baker, 1993.

_____. "Works of the Law" in *Dictionary of Paul and His Letters.* Ed. G. F. Hawthorne and R. P. Martin. Downers Grove: InterVarsity, 1993. 975-979.

Schweitzer, Albert. *Paul and His Interpreters: A Critical History.* Trans. W. Montgomery. London: Black, 1912.

Shepherd, Norman. "Perseverance: The Gift (I)." *The Outlook* 42 (February 1992) 10-11.

_____. "The Need to Persevere (II)." *The Outlook* 42 (March 19992) 20-21.

Silva, Moisés. *Explorations in Exegetical Method: Galatians as a Test Case.* Grand Rapids: Baker, 1996.

Stek, John. "Biblical Typology Yesterday and Today." *Calvin Theological Journal* 5 (1970) 133-162.

Strelan, J. D. "A Note on the Old Testament Background of Romans 7:7." *Lutheran Theological Journal* 15 (1981) 23-25.

Strickland, Wayne G., ed. *The Law, the Gospel, and the Modern Christian: Five Views.* Grand Rapids: Zondervan, 1993.

Thielman, Frank. "Law" in *Dictionary of Paul and His Letters.* Ed. G. F. Hawthorne and R. P. Martin. Downers Grove: InterVarsity, 1993.

_____. *Paul and the Law: A Contextual Approach.* Downers Grove: InterVarsity, 1994.

Turner, David L. "The Continuity of Scripture and Eschatology: Key Hermeneutical Issues." *Grace Theological Journal* 6 (1985) 275-287.

VanGemeren, Willem A. "Israel as the Hermeneutical Crux in the Interpretation of Prophecy." In Two-parts. *The Westminster Theological Journal* 45 (1983) 132-144, 46 (1984) 254-297.

_____. *The Progress of Redemption: The Story of Salvation from creation to the New Jerusalem.* Grand Rapids: Zondervan, 1988.

Van Ruler, A. A. *The Christian Church and the Old Testament.* Grand Rapids: Eerdmans, 1971.

Vos, Geerhardus. *Biblical Theology: Old and New Testaments.* Grand Rapids: Eerdmans, 1948.

_____. *The Pauline Eschatology.* Grand Rapids: Baker, 1979.

_____. *Redemptive History and Biblical Interpretation: The Shorter Writings of Geerhardus Vos.* Ed. R. B. Gaffin, Jr. Phillipsburg: Presbyterian and Reformed, 1980.

Walton, John. *Covenant: God's Purpose, God's Plan.* Grand Rapids: Zondervan, 1994.

Westermann, C., ed. *Essays on Old Testament Hermeneutics.* Richmond: Knox, 1963.

Westerholm, Stephen. *Israel's Law and the Church's Faith: Paul and His Recent Interpreters.* Grand Rapids: Eerdmans, 1988.

Woudstra, Martin. "The Old Testament in Biblical Theology and Dogmatics." *Calvin Theological Journal* 16 (1983) 47-60.

Wrede, William. *Paul.* Trans. E. Lummis. Lexington, 1962.

Wright, Christopher J. H. *An Eye for an Eye: The Place of Old Testament Ethics Today.* Downers Grove: InterVarsity, 1983.

Wright, N. T. *The Climax of the Covenant: Christ and the Law in Pauline Theology.* Minneapolis, 1993.

Young, Edward J. *The Book of Isaiah.* New International Commentary on the Old Testament. 3 volumes. Grand Rapids: Eerdmans, 1965-1972

Ziesler, J. A. *The Meaning of Righteousness in Paul: A Linguistic and Theological Enquiry.* Cambridge: University Press, 1972.

Ziesler, J. A. *The Meaning of Righteousness in Paul: A Linguistic and Theological Enquiry*. Cambridge: University Press, 1972.

SCRIPTURE INDEX

Amos

Habakkuk

Zechariah

Matthew

Luke

John

Acts

Romans

1 Corinthians

2 Corinthians

Galatians

Ephesians

Philippians

Colossians

1 Thessalonians

2 Thessalonians

1 Timothy

2 Timothy

Titus

Hebrews

James

1 Peter

2 Peter

Jude

Revelation

NAME INDEX